Ingolf Hel...
Leiptiger S...
08371 flauchau
Tel.: 03763 / 3479

Understanding GPS

Principles and Applications

For a complete listing of the *Artech House Mobile Communications Library,* turn to the back of this book.

Understanding GPS

Principles and Applications

Elliott D. Kaplan
Editor

Artech House
Boston • London

Library of Congress Cataloging-in-Publication Data
Kaplan, Elliott D.
    Understanding GPS: principles and applications / Elliott D. Kaplan.
        p.   cm.
    Includes bibliographical references and index.
    ISBN 0-89006-793-7 (alk. paper)
    1. Global Positioning System.   I. Title
G109.5.K36   1996
623.89'3—dc20   95-49984
                                                                     CIP

British Library Cataloguing in Publication Data
Kaplan, Elliott D.
    Understanding GPS: principles and applications
    1. Global positioning system   2. Artificial satellites in navigation
    I. Title
    629' .045

ISBN 0-89006-793-7

Cover design by Cheryl J. Cook.
Cover image courtesy of Lockheed Martin Corporation.

© 1996 ARTECH HOUSE, INC.
685 Canton Street
Norwood, MA 02062

International Standard Book Number: 0-89006-793-7
Library of Congress Catalog Card Number: 95-49984

10 9 8 7 6

To my wife Andrea and children Aaron, Benjamin, and Carrie, who unselfishly supported me throughout the entire endeavor. They make it all worthwhile.

▼▼▼

CONTENTS

▼▼▼

PREFACE

This book is an outgrowth of a GPS course presented by several colleagues and myself that was developed for the Boston chapter of the IEEE in November 1993. Sometime during the length of the course, I was contacted by Artech House and asked if I and the other lecturers would be interested in "putting the vugraphs to words."

I wanted to form a multidisciplinary team of individuals whose expertise in relevant areas would provide a thorough treatment of key GPS aspects. My motivation for compiling this work was that a GPS book that addressed the needs of the engineering/scientific community did not exist. Information was available in the form of technical papers or texts specializing in survey applications; however, there was no single text available that provided the reader with a complete systems engineering treatment of the subject matter. In this edition, I have attempted to provide the necessary material to ensure a broad but comprehensive treatment of GPS. In addition to GPS, the Russian GLONASS system and forthcoming INMARSAT overlay are also covered.

The book has been structured such that a reader with a general science background can learn the basics of GPS and how it works within the first few chapters, whereas, the reader with a stronger engineering/scientific background will be able to delve deeper and benefit from the more in-depth technical material. I believe it is this "ramp up" of mathematical/technical complexity along with the treatment of key topics that will allow this publication to serve as a student text as well as a reference source.

While the book has generally been written for the engineering/scientific community, one full chapter is devoted to GPS markets and applications. This latter material is intended for sales and marketing personnel to forecast the multibillion dollar market associated with satellite navigation based products and services.

Chapter 1 serves as an introduction to the text while Chapter 2 presents the fundamentals of position, velocity, and time determination using GPS. A description of GPS system architecture is presented in Chapter 3. Chapters 4, 5, and 6 address satellite signal generation, receiver signal acquisition and tracking, and receiver operation in the presence of RF interference, respectively. Standalone GPS performance is covered in Chapter 7 while differential techniques are addressed in Chapter 8. In Chapter 9, the integration of GPS and other sensors is discussed. The Russian GLONASS system is described in Chapter 10. The INMARSAT geostationary overlay is discussed in Chapter 11. Chapter 12 focuses on GPS markets and applications.

As mentioned above, this text was compiled by individuals with expertise in the various aspects of GPS. Unlike other books where the authors may have collaborated to form a particular chapter, that was not the case in this writing (with one exception). Each author either wrote an entire chapter, a specific section, or multiple sections. This made my job as editor somewhat more difficult, but I believe that this has resulted in a significant contribution to the engineering/scientific community. Although at times the experience was quite trying, it was generally a pleasure working with such a high caliber of individuals. Each author illuminated each topic with his or her expertise. Mike Pavloff generated the section on fundamentals of satellite orbits; Joe Leva wrote sections addressing user velocity determination and position error analyses as well as the appendix on least squares; Larry Wiederholt generated the sections on GPS system architecture; Phil Ward authored the chapters on satellite signal generation, signal acquisition and tracking, and receiver operation in an interference environment; Maarten Uijt de Haag provided text on pseudorange measurement errors; and Karen Van Dyke addressed standalone availability and integrity. Local and wide area code-based differential GPS (DGPS) techniques were covered by Ron Cosentino, while Dave Diggle addressed local area DGPS carrier phase measurements. GPS/inertial integration was written by Mike Foss, with Jeff Geier providing sections on multisensor integration for automotive applications. GLONASS was covered by Richard Clark, Scott Feairheller, and Jay Purvis. Jim Nagle and Ron Cosentino wrote the INMARSAT chapter. Markets and applications were put forth by Scott Lewis. In addition to coordinating the effort and editing the text, I was responsible for authoring the introductory chapter. I also wrote sections pertaining to user position and time determination as well as user receiving equipment. In closing, the opinions presented here are those of the authors and do not reflect the views of the MITRE Corporation.

Elliott D. Kaplan
Andover, MA
February 1996

▼▼▼

ACKNOWLEDGMENTS

Much appreciation is extended to the numerous technical reviewers and administrative support personnel listed below whose comments and suggestions greatly contributed to the success of this effort. Our apologies are extended to anyone whom we may have inadvertently missed.

Geoffery "Phil" Barnes
Cheryl Batherwich
Michael Braasch
Grover Brown
Rob Conley
Peter Daly
John Dobyne
Virginia Fitzgerald
Ron Hatch
Barry Irwin
Rudy Kalafus
Steve Malys
Sean McKenna

Pratap Misra
Albert Paradis
Bob Pizzano
George Providakes
Marc Richard
Angelo Rossi
Chris Shank
Peter Smyton
Richard St. Jean
John Studenny
Paul Turney
Brian White

CHAPTER 1

▼▼▼

INTRODUCTION

Elliott D. Kaplan
The MITRE Corporation

1.1 INTRODUCTION

Navigation is defined as the science of getting a craft or person from one place to another. Each one of us conducts some form of navigation in our daily lives. Driving to work or walking to a store requires that we employ fundamental navigation skills. For most of us, these skills require utilizing our eyes, common sense, and landmarks. However, in some cases where a more accurate knowledge of either our position, intended course, and/or transit time to a desired destination is required, navigation aids other than landmarks are used. These may be in the form of a simple clock to determine the velocity over a known distance or the odometer in our car to keep track of the distance traveled. Some other navigation aids are more complex and transmit electronic signals. These are referred to as radionavigation aids.

Signals from one or more radionavigation aids enable a person (herein referred to as the user) to compute their position. (Some radionavigation aids provide the capability for velocity determination and time dissemination as well.) It is important to note that it is the user's radionavigation receiver that processes these signals and computes the position fix. The receiver performs the necessary computations (e.g., range, bearing, estimated time of arrival) for the user to navigate to a desired location. In some applications, the receiver may only process the received signals with the navigation computations performed by a separate processor.

Various types of radionavigation aids exist, and for the purposes of this text they can be categorized as either ground-based or space-based. For the most part, the accuracy of ground-based radionavigation aids is proportional to their operating frequency. Highly accurate systems generally transmit at relatively short wavelengths and the user must remain within line-of-sight, whereas systems broadcasting at lower frequencies (longer wavelengths) are not limited to line-of-sight but are less accurate.

Early developed spaced-based systems (namely the United States (U.S.) Navy Navigation Satellite System—referred to as Transit—and the Russian Tsikada system) provide a two dimensional high-accuracy positioning service. However, the frequency of obtaining a position fix varies with latitude. Theoretically, a Transit user at the equator could obtain a position fix on the average of once every 110 minutes; whereas, at 80° latitude the fix rate would improve to an average of once every 30 minutes [1]. Limitations applicable to both systems are that each position fix requires approximately 10 to 15 minutes of receiver processing and an estimate of the user's position. These attributes were suitable for shipboard navigation because of the low velocities, but not for aircraft and high-dynamic users [2]. It was these shortcomings that led to the development of both the U.S. Global Positioning System (GPS) and the Russian Global Navigation Satellite System (GLONASS).

1.2 CONDENSED GPS PROGRAM HISTORY

In the early 1960s, several U.S. government organizations including the military, the National Aeronautics and Space Administration (NASA), and the Department of Transportation (DOT) were interested in developing satellite systems for position determination. The optimum system was viewed as having the following attributes: global coverage, continuous/all weather operation, ability to serve high-dynamic platforms, and high accuracy. When Transit became operational in 1964, it was widely accepted for use on low dynamic platforms. However, due to its inherent limitations (cited in the preceding paragraphs), the Navy sought to enhance Transit or develop another satellite navigation system with the desired capabilities mentioned above. Several variants of the original Transit system were proposed by its developers at the Johns Hopkins University Applied Physics Laboratory. Concurrently, the Naval Research Laboratory (NRL) was conducting experiments with highly stable space-based clocks to achieve precise time transfer. This program was denoted as Timation. Modifications were made to Timation satellites to provide a ranging capability for two-dimensional position determination. Timation employed a side-tone modulation for satellite-to-user ranging [3–5].

At the same time as the Transit enhancements were being considered and the Timation efforts were underway, the Air Force conceptualized a satellite positioning system denoted as System 621B. It was envisioned that System 621B satellites would be in elliptical orbits at inclination angles of 0°, 30°, and 60°. Numerous variations of the number of satellites (15 to 20) and their orbital configurations were examined.

The use of pseudorandom noise (PRN) modulation for ranging with digital signals was proposed. System 621B was to provide three-dimensional coverage and continuous worldwide service. The concept and operational techniques were verified at Holloman AFB and White Sands Missile Range using an inverted range in which pseudolites (i.e., ground-based satellites) transmitted satellite signals for aircraft positioning [3–5]. Furthermore, the Army at Ft. Mommouth, NJ, was investigating many candidate techniques including ranging, angle determination, and the use of Doppler measurements. The results of the Army investigations recommended that ranging using PRN modulation (i.e., pseudoranging) was the desired approach [5].

In 1969, the Office of the Secretary of Defense (OSD) established the Defense Navigation Satellite System (DNSS) program to consolidate the independent development efforts of each military service to form a single joint-use system. The OSD also established the Navigation Satellite Executive Steering Group, which was charged with determining the viability of a DNSS and planning its development. From this effort, the system concept for NAVSTAR GPS was formed. The NAVSTAR GPS program was developed by the GPS Joint Program Office (JPO) [5]. At the time of this writing, the GPS JPO continues to oversee the development and production of new satellites, ground control equipment, and military user receivers. Also, the system is generally referred to as simply "GPS."

1.3 GPS OVERVIEW

Presently, GPS is fully operational and meets the criteria established in the 1960s for an optimum positioning system. The system provides accurate, continuous, worldwide, three-dimensional position and velocity information to users with the appropriate receiving equipment. GPS also disseminates a form of Coordinated Universal Time (UTC). The satellite constellation consists of 24 satellites arranged in 6 orbital planes with 4 satellites per plane. A worldwide ground control/monitoring network monitors the health and status of the satellites. This network also uploads navigation and other data to the satellites. GPS can provide service to an unlimited number of users since the user receivers operate passively (i.e., receive only). The system utilizes the concept of one-way time of arrival (TOA) ranging. Satellite transmissions are referenced to highly accurate atomic frequency standards onboard the satellites, which are in synchronism with an internal GPS *system time* base. The satellites broadcast ranging codes and navigation data on two frequencies using a technique called code division multiple access (CDMA); that is, there are only two frequencies in use by the system, called L1 (1575.42 MHz) and L2 (1227.6 MHz). Each satellite transmits on these frequencies, but with different ranging codes than those employed by other satellites. These codes were selected because they have low cross-correlation properties with respect to one another. (Satellite signal characteristics are discussed in Chapter 4.) The navigation data provides the means for the receiver to determine the location of the satellite at the time of signal transmission, whereas the ranging code enables the user's receiver to determine the transit (i.e., propagation) time of the signal and thereby determine the satellite-to-user range. This technique requires that the user receiver also contain a clock. Utilizing this technique to measure the receiver's three-dimensional location requires that TOA ranging measurements be made to four satellites. If the receiver clock was synchronized with the satellite clocks, only three range measurements would be required. However, a crystal clock is usually employed in navigation receivers to minimize the cost, complexity, and size of the receiver. Thus, four measurements are required to determine user latitude, longitude, height, and receiver clock offset from internal system time. If either system time or altitude is accurately known, less than four satellites are required. Chapter 2 provides elaboration on TOA ranging as well as user position, velocity, and time (PVT) determination.

GPS provides two services: the Standard Positioning Service (SPS) and the Precise Positioning Service (PPS). The SPS is designated for the civil community, whereas the PPS is slated for U.S. authorized military and select government agency users. Access to the GPS PPS is controlled through cryptography. Descriptions of these services are presented in the following sections.

1.3.1 Precise Positioning Service

The PPS is specified to provide a predictable accuracy of at least 22m (2 drms, 95%) in the horizontal plane and 27.7m (95%) in the vertical plane. The distance root mean square (or drms) is a common measure used in navigation. Twice the drms value, or 2 drms, is the radius of a circle that contains at least 95% of all possible fixes that can be obtained with a system (in this case, the PPS) at any one place. The PPS provides a UTC time transfer accuracy within 200 nsec (95%) referenced to the time kept at the U.S. Naval Observatory and is denoted as UTC(USNO) [1]. Velocity measurement accuracy is specified as 0.2 m/sec (95%) [4].

As stated above, the PPS is primarily intended for military and select government agency users. Civilian use is permitted but only upon special U.S. Department of Defense (DOD) approval. Access to the aforementioned PPS position accuracies is controlled through two cryptographic features denoted as Antispoofing (AS) and Selective Availability (SA). AS is a mechanism intended to defeat deception jamming. Deception jamming is a technique in which an adversary would replicate one or more of the satellite ranging codes, navigation data signal(s), and carrier frequency Doppler effects with the intent of deceiving a victim receiver. Further, under current DOD policy, SA is implemented to deny full system accuracy to SPS users. SA "dithers" the satellite's clock, thereby corrupting TOA measurement accuracy. Further, SA induces errors into the broadcast navigation data parameters [6]. PPS users remove SA effects through cryptography [4].

The PPS reached full operational capability (FOC) in spring 1995, when the entire 24 production satellite constellation was in place and extensive testing of the ground control segment and its interactions with the constellation was completed.

1.3.2 Standard Positioning Service

The SPS is available to all users worldwide. There are no restrictions on SPS usage. This service provides predictable accuracies of 100m (2 drms, 95%) in the horizontal plane and 156m (95%) in the vertical plane. UTC(USNO) time dissemination accuracy is within 340 nsec (95%) [1]. Reference [1] stipulates that the accuracy of this service is established by both the U.S. DOD and DOT based on U.S. security interests. SA is usually a prime error source in a SPS-derived position fix. However, techniques to mitigate its effects are described in Chapter 8.

SPS initial operating capability (IOC) was attained in December 1993, when a combination of 24 prototype and production satellites were available and position determination/timing services complied with the associated specified predictable accuracies.

1.4 GLOBAL NAVIGATION SATELLITE SYSTEM (GLONASS)

GLONASS is a Russian space-based radionavigation system that provides the capability for three-dimensional position and velocity determination as well as time dissemination on a worldwide basis. In many respects, GLONASS is quite similar to GPS. The system consists of a 24 satellite constellation, a ground monitoring network, and various types of user equipment. The constellation consists of 3 orbital planes with 8 satellites per plane. The ground network consists of a number of satellite monitoring and data uploading facilities located throughout Russia. There are several manufacturers of user receiving equipment within Russia as well as throughout the world. Some manufacturers build combined GPS/GLONASS receivers.

GLONASS is operated by Russia's Ministry of Defense. Like GPS, the program was instituted in the mid-1970s with military design goals. However, in a similar manner to GPS, the number of civil applications quickly became apparent and the system is now truly dual-use. PVT determination is performed using PRN ranging signals. However, the satellite transmissions differ from GPS. GLONASS employs frequency division multiple access (FDMA), in which each satellite transmits on a different frequency. This technique allows the same ranging codes to be broadcast from each satellite.

GLONASS provides separate civil and military services. The specified positioning accuracies of the civil service are 100m (2 drms, 95%) in the horizontal plane and 150m (95%) in the vertical. Civil velocity accuracy is specified at 0.15 m/sec (95%) [7]. At the time of this writing, GLONASS has not employed an SA feature and actual measured civil accuracies are 26m (2 drms, 95 %) in the horizontal plane and 45m (95 %) in the vertical. Velocity measurements are on the order of 0.03 to 0.05 m/sec [7, 8]. Observations by the University of Leeds and 3S Corporation indicate that the military service yields accuracies comparable to the GPS PPS. Although the military service was not encrypted at the time of this writing, Russia states that it is solely for military use [7, 9]. The time dissemination capability is within 5 msec of UTC (Soviet Union) [7].

1.5 AUGMENTATIONS

Augmentations are available to enhance standalone GPS or GLONASS performance. In fact, the systems can be used jointly to enhance navigation service. Further, user equipment can be configured to make use of inertial sensors for added robustness in the presence of jamming or to aid in vehicle navigation when the satellite signals are blocked in "urban canyons" (i.e., tall city buildings). (See Chapter 9 for more detail.)

Some applications, such as precision farming, oil exploration and open pit mining, require far more accuracy than standalone GPS or GLONASS accuracies. These applications utilize techniques that dramatically improve standalone system accuracy performance, referred to as differential GPS or differential GLONASS. Accuracy is improved by removing the correlated (i.e., common) errors between two or more receivers performing range measurements to the same satellites. One receiver is called the reference receiver and is surveyed in; that is, its geographic location is precisely-known. One method of achieving common error removal is to take the difference between the reference receiver's surveyed position and it's electronically derived position at a discrete time point. This difference represents the error at the measurement time and is denoted as the differential correction. This correction may be broadcast via data link to the user receiving equipment such that the user receiver can remove the error from its solution. Alternatively, in non-real-time applications, the differential corrections can be stored along with the user's position data and applied after the data collection period. This non-real-time technique is typically used in surveying.

If the reference station is within line-of-sight of the user, the technique is usually referred to as local area differential. However, as the distance increases between the user and reference station, some ranging errors become decorrelated. This problem can be overcome by installing a network of reference stations throughout a large geographic area (i.e., country, continent) and broadcasting the differential corrections via geostationary satellite. The reference stations relay their collected data to one or more central processing stations where differential corrections are formed and satellite signal integrity is checked. The central processing stations send the corrections and integrity data to a satellite Earth station for uplink to the geostationary satellite. This technique is referred to as wide area differential. (Code- and carrier-based differential techniques are covered in Chapter 8.)

1.5.1 INMARSAT Civil Navigation Satellite Overlay

The INMARSAT overlay is an implementation of a wide area differential service. INMARSAT is an international consortium providing mobile services on a global basis and was comprised of 76 signatory countries in January 1995. In 1996, INMARSAT plans to launch 4 geostationary satellites that will provide complete coverage of the entire globe from ±70° in latitude. However, it must be noted that the data broadcast by the satellite is applicable to users in regions that have a corresponding ground station network. The ground station network would be operated by the service provider (e.g., civil aviation administration (CAA)); whereas, INMARSAT is responsible for the space segment. The uplink Earth stations are operated by the respective INMARSAT signatory affiliate (e.g., COMSAT in the U.S.).

The overlay message format has provisions for GPS and GLONASS differential corrections and integrity data. In addition to providing this data, the satellites will transmit a ranging code similar to those broadcast by the GPS satellites. Therefore, INMARSAT-3 satellites can also be used as ranging sources. Unlike GPS and GLONASS satellites, which have their own navigation payloads, INMARSAT-3 satellites contain navigation repeaters that rebroadcast the uplinked signals to users. Although the accuracy associated with the overlay is a function of numerous factors including the ground network architecture, expected accuracies for the U.S. Federal Aviation Administration (FAA) Wide Area Augmentation System (WAAS) are on the order of 7.6m (2 drms, 95%) in the horizontal plane and 7.6m (95%) in the vertical plane. (The WAAS is described in Chapters 7 and 11.)

1.6 APPLICATIONS

As mentioned above, both GLONASS and GPS have evolved from dedicated military systems to true dual-use. Satellite navigation technology is being utilized in numerous civil and military applications that range from leisure hiking to spacecraft guidance. Numerous disciplines including all sectors of transportation have been affected. Users are no longer restricted to specific routes due to accuracy and/or coverage limitations of ground-based navigation aids. As long as a user is in line-of-sight to the satellites, accurate navigation is obtainable. To illustrate the diverse use of satellite navigation technology, several examples of current and projected applications are presented below. Further discussion on applications and market projections is contained in Chapter 12.

1.6.1 Aviation

The aviation community has propelled the use of a global navigation satellite system (GNSS) and various augmentations to provide guidance for the en route through precision approach phases of flight. (The International Civil Aviation Organization [ICAO] defines a system that contains at least one or more satellite navigation systems as a GNSS.) The continuous global coverage capability of GNSS permits aircraft to fly directly from one location to another provided factors such as obstacle clearance and required procedures are adhered to. Incorporation of a data link with a GNSS receiver enables the transmission of aircraft location to other aircraft and/or to air traffic control (ATC). This function, called automatic dependent surveillance (ADS), is in use in some Pacific Ocean regions as an outgrowth of ICAO Future Air Navigation Systems (FANS) Working Group activities. Key benefits are ATC monitoring for collision avoidance and optimized routing to reduce travel time and, consequently, fuel consumption. ADS techniques are also being applied to airport surface surveillance of both aircraft and ground support vehicles.

1.6.2 Spacecraft Guidance

Since 1992, a GPS receiver has been employed on the TOPEX/POSEIDON satellite which is being used to study ocean circulation [10]. This is a joint NASA and CNES (French Space Agency) project. GPS has been used on several NASA Space Shuttle flights. In 1998, the Space Shuttle is expected to utilize GPS for guidance in all phases of operation (e.g., ground launch, on-orbit, and re-entry and landing.) The International Space Station (ISS) will employ GNSS to support control functions, data collection activities, and navigation. Furthermore, GPS is planned to be used on NASA "small" satellite programs such as Lewis and Clark [1].

1.6.3 Maritime

GNSS has been embraced by both the commercial and recreational maritime communities. Navigation is enhanced on all bodies of waters; from oceanic travel to riverways, especially in inclement weather. Several nations are developing local area differential GPS networks to increase system accuracy for harbor, harbor approach and river usage. The Commonwealth of Independent States is considering the implementation of a local area differential GLONASS network [7]. Wide area differential GPS has been utilized by the offshore oil exploration community for several years.

One area in which differential GNSS will play a larger role is in vessel traffic services (VTSs). The combination of a datalink and differential GNSS receiver permits broadcast of the vessel's position to a control center. VTSs are used for collision avoidance and to expedite the flow of traffic during periods of restricted visibility and ice cover [1]. VTSs can be used in conjunction with the electronic chart display information system (ECDIS). ECDIS displays a vessel's position in relation to charted objects, navigation aids, land as well as unseen hazards.

1.6.4 Land

The surveying community has relied on differential GPS to achieve measurement accuracies in the millimeter range. Similar techniques are in use within the railroad community to obtain train location with respect to an adjacent set of tracks. GPS is a key component in intelligent transportation systems (ITS). In terms of vehicle applications, GNSS will be used for route guidance, tracking, and emergency messaging. Integrating a GNSS receiver with a street database, digital moving map display, and processor will allow the driver to obtain directions and/or the shortest most efficient route. Combining a cellular phone or data link function with this system will enable vehicle tracking (i.e., form of ADS) and/or emergency messaging. A vehicle's position can be automatically reported to a control center for fleet management. The activation of a "panic" button by the driver broadcasts an emergency message, vehicle characteristics, and vehicle location to law enforcement authorities for assistance. (ITS automotive applications are covered in Chapter 9.)

1.7 ORGANIZATION OF THE TEXT

This book is structured to first familiarize the reader with the fundamentals of PVT determination using GPS. Once this groundwork has been established, a description of the GPS system architecture is presented. Next, the discussion focuses on satellite signal characteristics and their generation. Received signal acquisition and tracking as well as range and velocity measurement processes are then examined. Signal acquisition and tracking is also analyzed in the presence of interference. GPS performance (accuracy, availability, and integrity) is then assessed. A discussion of GPS differential techniques follows. Sensor aiding techniques including ITS automotive applications are presented. These topics are followed by comprehensive treatment of both GLONASS and the INMARSAT overlay. Finally, information on GPS applications and their corresponding market projections is presented. Highlights of each chapter are summarized below.

Chapter 2 provides the fundamentals of user PVT determination. Beginning with the concept of TOA ranging, the chapter develops the principles for obtaining three-dimensional user position and velocity as well as UTC(USNO) from GPS.

Included in this chapter are primers on GPS reference coordinate systems, Earth models, and satellite orbits.

In Chapter 3, the GPS system architecture is presented. This includes descriptions of the space, operational control (i.e., worldwide ground control/monitoring network) and user (equipment) segments. Particulars of the constellation are described. Satellite types and corresponding attributes are provided. One will note the increase in satellite functionality as satellite technology matures. Of considerable interest are interactions between the operational control segment (OCS) and the satellites. Most users are unaware of the "around the clock" satellite tracking and data uploading processes performed by the OCS worldwide network to provide the user with optimum service. An overview of user receiving equipment is presented as well as related selection criteria. This criteria is relevant to both civil and military users.

Chapter 4 describes the GPS satellite signals and their generation. In this chapter, we examine the properties of the GPS satellite signals including frequency assignment, modulation format, and PRN code generation. This discussion is accompanied by a description of received signal power levels as well as their associated autocorrelation and cross-correlation characteristics.

Receiver signal acquisition and tracking is presented in Chapter 5. A portion of this material is new to the GPS user community. This is the first time that such an elaborate description of GPS signal acquisition and tracking has been presented in a single document. Extensive details of the various topics that must be addressed when designing or analyzing a GPS receiver are offered. Signal acquisition and tracking strategies are examined, including those required for high-dynamic stress environments. The processes of obtaining pseudorange, delta range, and integrated Doppler measurements are described. These parameters are the key observables in range and velocity measurements.

In Chapter 6, the effects of intentional (i.e., jamming) and nonintentional (e.g., television signal harmonics) interference on receiver signal acquisition and tracking are analyzed. Interference mitigation techniques including adaptive antennas, carrier loop aiding, and front-end filtering are discussed. The effect of RF interference on the receiver analog-to-digital (A/D) conversion process is also examined. It is shown that a precorrelation A/D converter can easily be "captured" by a continuous wave (CW) interferer, which disables the receiver at lower than predicted interference levels. Adaptive nonlinear A/D conversion is proposed to mitigate this effect.

GPS performance in terms of accuracy, availability and integrity is examined in Chapter 7. It is shown how the computed user position error results from range measurement errors and user/satellite relative geometry. These range measurement errors are attributed to factors such as propagation delay of the satellite signals from the ionosphere and troposphere, relativistic effects, SA, and receiver noise. These and other range measurement errors are elaborated upon. A mix of conventional GPS theory and some interesting extensions are presented. The traditional dilution of precision (DOP) parameters are defined. The DOP parameters are user/satellite geometry factors that relate parameters of the user position and time errors to those of the range measurement errors. It is shown how DOP parameters and range measurement errors can be combined to estimate distribution characteristics of the user's vertical and horizontal position estimates. Both the standard theory and an interesting extension that includes a probabilistic treatment of DOP are discussed. In the standard treatment, the user/satellite geometry is considered fixed. This is appropriate for estimating accuracy characteristics at a fixed location over a short time interval. In the probabilistic treatment, the user's location and/or the time of observation is considered to vary over a range of values. The question posed is to determine the accuracy of the position estimate for a user picked at random from a range of locations and from a range of times. Methods are presented for combining distributions of DOP and UERE to determine the distribution of the location accuracy that can be obtained. This type of analysis is relevant to understanding the composite accuracy provided by a GPS service over a geographical area and/or over a designated time interval.

The examination of GPS performance is continued with a discussion of the availability of GPS as a navigation service. Service availability translates to having the appropriate satellite geometry for the specific application. Via the use of computer simulation results, global GPS service availability is shown for a full constellation and for a constellation with up to three failed satellites. Integrity is also examined. In this context, integrity is the ability of the system to provide a warning when it should not be used for navigation. Integrity is an important parameter since each satellite illuminates approximately one-third of the Earth. System integrity can be enhanced by a receiver satellite consistency check algorithm or via an external source such as the INMARSAT overlay. The consistency check algorithm is referred to as receiver autonomous integrity monitoring (RAIM).

Differential GPS (herein referred to as DGPS) accuracy enhancements are discussed in Chapter 8. These techniques make use of the satellite broadcast pseudorandom code and/or carrier frequency measurements. Local area DGPS is first covered and an accuracy comparison is made to standalone GPS. This is followed by a description of error removal techniques. As mentioned above, real-time DGPS techniques require a datalink between the reference receiver and the user receiver(s). Generally, a standard message format is used. A message format was defined by the Radio Technical Commission for Maritime services (RTCM) and is in widespread use. Elaboration on RTCM message types is provided. Following this, an examination of the common (i.e., correlated) satellite viewing errors is presented. As the users increase their separation from the reference station, some errors become uncorrelated, thus the errors are not entirely removed when the differential correction is applied. This problem is avoided with the use of multiple reference stations to formulate a wide area DGPS (WADGPS) network. Extensive treatment of WADGPS is provided.

Chapter 8 also covers DGPS using interferometry. This technique is occasionally referred to as "carrier-phase tracking." Extremely high accuracies (20 cm in dynamic applications and millimeter level for static applications) can routinely be achieved by processing the received satellite signal Doppler frequencies. This frequency information is integrated to form phase measurements, which are processed to achieve the aforementioned accuracies. One key problem associated with this technique is cycle ambiguity resolution. A technique is presented that resolves this problem.

In some applications, GPS is not robust enough to provide continuous user PVT. Receiver operation will most likely be degraded in an "urban canyon" where satellite signals are blocked by tall buildings or when intentional/nonintentional interference is encountered. Hence, other sensors are required to augment the user receiver. This subject area is discussed in Chapter 9. The integration of GPS and inertial sensor technology is first treated. This is usually accomplished with a Kalman filter. A description of Kalman filtering is presented, followed by various descriptions of GPS/inertial navigation system (INS) integrated architectures. An example is provided to illustrate the processing of GPS and INS measurements in a tightly coupled configuration.

Chapter 9 also covers ITS automotive applications. The integration of a GPS receiver, a digital map display, a street database, and a driver interface unit to provide route guidance is discussed. Furthermore, incorporation of a data link enables vehicle tracking and/or emergency messaging. As stated above, the line-of-sight from the vehicle's antenna to the satellite may be blocked by obstructions such as tall buildings and tunnels. In order to maintain accurate guidance through these outages, external sensors are used. These may be in the form of transmission or wheel sensors to measure the number of wheel revolutions or low-cost accelerometers and/or gyros to provide position and velocity information. Equipment integration and system modeling is addressed. The chapter closes with an example of vehicle tracking system integration including test results obtained in Buenos Aires, San Francisco, and Tokyo.

The Russian GLONASS system is described in Chapter 10. An overview of the program is first presented, accompanied with significant historical facts. The constellation and associated orbital plane characteristics are then discussed. This is followed by a description of existing spacecraft design and the ground control/monitoring network. User equipment is then discussed. The current trend is to produce receivers that utilize both GPS and GLONASS systems. The GLONASS coordinate system, Earth model, and time reference are also presented. These are different than those utilized by GPS. GLONASS satellite signal characteristics are discussed. System performance in terms of accuracy and availability is covered. Elaboration is provided on intended GLONASS developments that will improve all system segments. Differential services are also being planned.

Chapter 11 discusses the INMARSAT overlay and its corresponding accuracy, availability, and integrity enhancements to both GPS and GLONASS. The overlay will benefit the aviation industry by providing en route through landing guidance.

Additionally, the overlay will enable decreased spacing between aircraft, which translates into increased traffic flow. Land-based, maritime, and space-based users will also gain from this service. A technical description of the INMARSAT-3 satellite is presented as well as the planned constellation. These satellites are expected to be launched in 1996. Extensive elaboration is provided on the INMARSAT message structure to be used for the FAA WAAS. The chapter closes with a discussion of the development of a proposed civil satellite constellation.

Chapter 12 is dedicated to GPS markets and applications. As mentioned earlier, GPS has been widely accepted in all sectors of transportation. In terms of marine applications, there are approximately 50 million vessels worldwide, with about 18 million boats in North America alone. This represents a large potential market for GPS. Furthermore, the planned removal of ground-based aviation navigation aids within the U.S. starting in the 2000 timeframe [1] will force the aviation community to rely almost strictly on GPS and approved augmentations such as inertial guidance. It has been predicted that the worldwide air traffic management market may be as large as 200 billion dollars in the 10-year period from 1994 to 2004. Due to its vast size, the land vehicle market appears to be the most promising. There are over 420 million cars and 130 million trucks in the world, with more than 150 million and 40 million North American portions. Integration of the technology described in Chapter 9 is viable for a portion of these vehicles. Chapter 12 also covers surveying, geographical information systems (GIS), mapping applications, and their associated markets. Similar projections are made for military and space applications. A list of major receiver manufacturers and their products types is also provided.

References

[1] Department of Defense/Department of Transportation, *1994 Federal Radionavigation Plan*, Springfield, VA, National Technical Information Service, May 1995.
[2] Parkinson, B., "A History of Satellite Navigation," *NAVIGATION: Journal of Navigation*, Vol. 42, No. 1, Spring 1995, pp. 109–164.
[3] GPS Joint Program Office, *NAVSTAR GPS User Equipment Introduction*, Public Release Version, Feb. 1991.
[4] NAVSTAR GPS Joint Program Office (JPO), *GPS NAVSTAR User's Overview*, YEE-82-009D, GPS JPO, March 1991.
[5] McDonald, K., "Navigation Satellite Systems—A Perspective," *Proc. 1st Int. Symposium Real Time Differential Applications of the Global Positioning System*, Vol. 1, Braunschweig, Federal Republic of Germany, 1991, pp. 20–35.
[6] Doucet, K., and Y. Georgiadou, "The Issue of Selective Availability," *GPS World Magazine*, Sept./Oct. 1990, pp. 53–56.
[7] ANSER, Russia's Global Navigation Satellite System, Contract Number F33657-90-D-0096, Arlington, Virginia, May 1994.
[8] Misra, P., "Integrated Use of GPS and GLONASS in Civil Aviation," *MIT Lincoln Laboratory Journal*, Vol. 6, No. 2, Summer/Fall 1993.
[9] Beser, J., and J. Danaher, "The 3S Navigation R-100 Family of Integrated GPS/GLONASS Receivers:

Description and Performance Results," *Proc. of the US Institute of Navigation National Technical Meeting*, Jan. 20–22, 1993, pp. 25–46.

[10] Seeber, G., *Satellite Geodessy: Foundations, Methods, and Applications*, New York, NY: Walter De Gruyter, 1993.

CHAPTER 2
▼▼▼

FUNDAMENTALS OF SATELLITE NAVIGATION

E. D. Kaplan and J. L. Leva
The MITRE Corporation

M. S. Pavloff
Hughes Space and Communications Company

2.1 CONCEPT OF RANGING USING TIME-OF-ARRIVAL MEASUREMENTS

GPS utilizes the concept of time-of-arrival (TOA) ranging to determine user position. This concept entails measuring the time it takes for a signal transmitted by an emitter (e.g., foghorn, radiobeacon, satellite) at a known location to reach a user receiver. This time interval, referred to as the signal propagation time, is then multiplied by the speed of the signal (e.g., speed of sound, speed of light) to obtain the emitter-to-receiver distance. By measuring the propagation time of signals broadcast from multiple emitters (i.e., navigation aids) at known locations, the receiver can determine its position. An example of two-dimensional positioning is provided below.

2.1.1 Two-Dimensional Position Determination

Consider the case of a mariner at sea determining his or her vessel's position from a foghorn. (This introductory example was originally presented in [1] and is contained herein because it provides an excellent overview of TOA position determination concepts.) Assume that the vessel is equipped with an accurate clock and the mariner has an approximate knowledge of the vessel's position. Also, assume that the foghorn whistle is sounded precisely on the minute mark and that the vessel's clock is synchronized to the foghorn clock. The mariner notes the elapsed time from the minute mark until the foghorn whistle is heard. The foghorn whistle propagation time is the time it took for the foghorn whistle to leave the foghorn and travel to the mariner's ear. This propagation time multiplied by the speed of sound (approximately 335 m/sec) is the distance from the foghorn to the mariner. If the foghorn signal took 5 sec to reach the mariner's ear, then the distance to the foghorn is 1,675m. Let this distance be denoted as $R1$. Thus, with only one measurement, the mariner knows that the vessel is somewhere on a circle with radius $R1$ centered about the foghorn, which is denoted as Foghorn 1 in Figure 2.1.

Hypothetically, if the mariner simultaneously measured the range from a second foghorn in the same way, the vessel would be at range $R1$ from Foghorn 1 and range $R2$ from Foghorn 2, as shown in Figure 2.2. It is assumed that the foghorn transmissions are synchronized to a common time base and the mariner has knowledge of both foghorn whistle transmission times. Therefore, the vessel relative to the foghorns is at one of the intersections of the range circles. Since it was assumed that the mariner has approximate knowledge of the vessel's position, the unlikely fix can be discarded. Resolving the ambiguity can also be achieved by making a range measurement to a third foghorn, as shown in Figure 2.3.

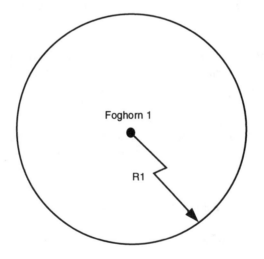

Figure 2.1 Range determination from a single source. (*After:* [1].)

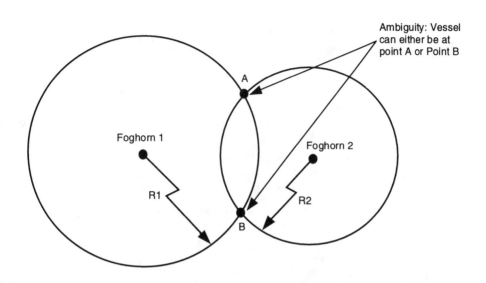

Figure 2.2 Ambiguity resulting from measurements to two sources. (*After*: [1].)

2.1.1.1 Common Clock Offset and Compensation

The above development assumed that the vessel's clock was precisely synchronized with the foghorn time base. However, this might not be the case. Let us presume that the vessel's clock is advanced with respect to the foghorn time base by 1 sec. That is, the vessel's clock believes the minute mark is occurring 1 sec earlier. The propagation intervals measured by the mariner will be larger by 1 sec due to the offset. The timing offsets are the same for each measurement (i.e., the offsets are common) because the same incorrect time base is being used for each measurement. The timing offset equates to a range error of 335m and is denoted as ϵ in Figure 2.4. The separation of intersections C, D, and E from the true vessel position, A, is a function of the vessel's clock offset. If the offset could be removed or compensated for, the range circles would then intersect at point A.

2.1.1.2 Effect of Independent Measurement Errors on Position Certainty

If this hypothetical scenario were realized, the TOA measurements would not be perfect due to errors from atmospheric effects, foghorn clock offset from the foghorn time base, and interfering sounds. Unlike the vessel's clock offset condition cited above, these errors would be generally independent and not common to all measurements. They would affect each measurement in a unique manner and result in

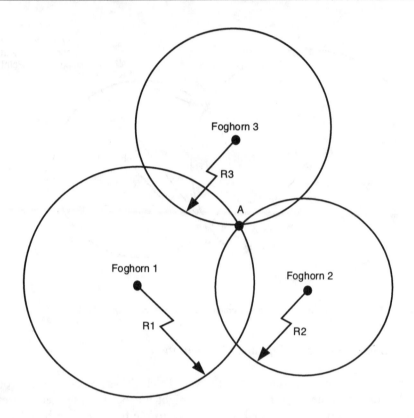

Figure 2.3 Position ambiguity removal by additional measurement. (*After:* [1].)

inaccurate distance computations. Figure 2.5 shows the effect of independent errors (i.e., ϵ_1, ϵ_2, and ϵ_3) on position determination assuming foghorn timebase/mariner clock synchronization. Instead of the three range circles intersecting at a single point, the vessel location is somewhere within the triangular error space.

2.1.2 Principle of Position Determination via Satellite-Generated Ranging Signals

GPS employs TOA ranging for user position determination. By making TOA measurements to multiple satellites, three-dimensional positioning is achieved. We will observe that this technique is analogous to the preceding foghorn example; however, satellite ranging signals travel at the speed of light, which is approximately 3×10^8 m/sec. It is assumed that the satellite ephemerides are accurate (i.e., the satellite locations are precisely known).

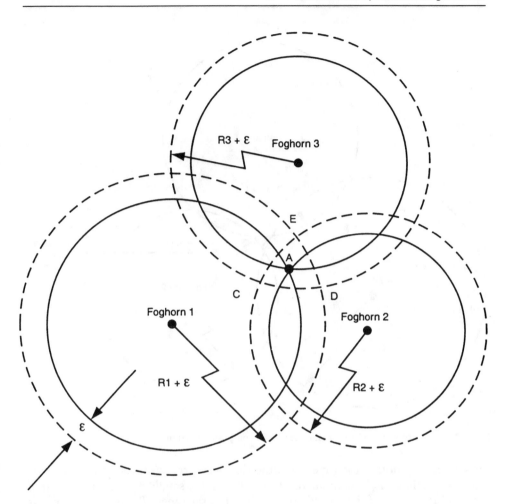

Figure 2.4 Effect of receiver clock offset on TOA measurements. (*After*: [1].)

2.1.2.1 Three-Dimensional Position Location via Intersection of Multiple Spheres

Assume that there is a single satellite transmitting a ranging signal. A clock onboard the satellite controls the timing of the ranging signal broadcast. This clock and others onboard each of the satellites within the constellation are effectively synchronized to an internal system time scale denoted as GPS system time (herein referred to as system time). The user's receiver also contains a clock that (for the moment) we assume to be synchronized to system time. Timing information is embedded within the satellite ranging signal that enables the receiver to calculate when the signal left

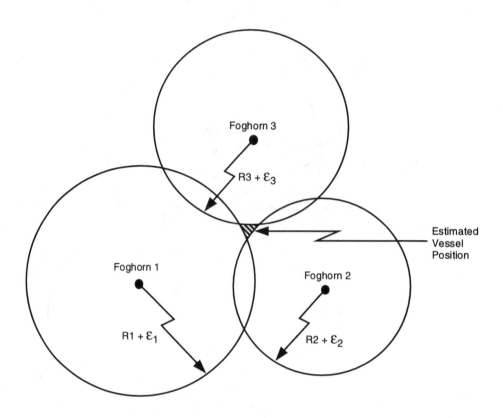

Figure 2.5 Effect of independent measurement errors on position certainty.

the satellite. By noting the time when the signal was received, the satellite-to-user propagation time can be computed. The product of the satellite-to-user propagation time and the speed of light yields the satellite-to-user range, R. As a result of this measurement process, the user would be located somewhere on the surface of a sphere centered about the satellite as shown in Figure 2.6(a). If a measurement was simultaneously made using the ranging signal of a second satellite, the user would also be located on the surface of a second sphere that is concentric about the second satellite. Thus, the user would then be somewhere on the surface of both spheres, which could be either on the perimeter of the shaded circle in Figure 2.6(b) that denotes the plane of intersection of these spheres or at a single point tangent to both spheres (i.e., where the spheres just touch). This latter case could only occur if the user was collinear with the satellites, which is not the typical case. The plane of intersection is perpendicular to a line connecting the satellites, as shown in Figure 2.6(c).

Repeating the measurement process using a third satellite collocates the user on the perimeter of the circle and the surface of the third sphere. This third sphere

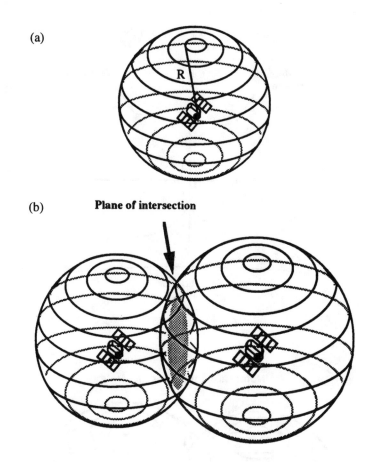

(a)

(b)   **Plane of intersection**

Figure 2.6 (a) User located on surface of sphere; (b) user located on perimeter of shaded circle (*source*: [2], reprinted with permission); (c) plane of intersection; (d) user located at one of two points on shaded circle (*source*: [2], reprinted with permission); (e) user located at one of two points on circle perimeter.

intersects the shaded circle perimeter at two points; however, only one of the points is the correct user position, as shown in Figure 2.6(d). A view of the intersection is shown in Figure 2.6(e). It can be observed that the candidate locations are mirror images of one another with respect to the plane of the satellites. For a user on the Earth's surface, it is apparent that the lower point will be the true position. However, users that are above the Earth's surface may employ measurements from satellites at negative elevation angles. This complicates the determination of an unambiguous solution. Airborne/spaceborne receiver solutions may be above or below the plane

(c)

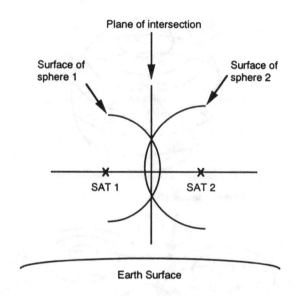

Plane of intersection

Surface of
sphere 1

Surface of
sphere 2

SAT 1

SAT 2

Earth Surface

(d)

Note: Circle tilted for illustration

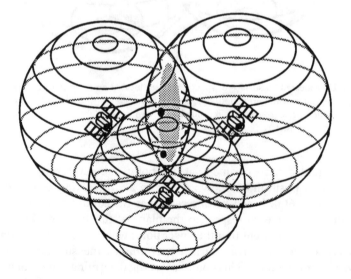

Figure 2.6 (continued)

(e)

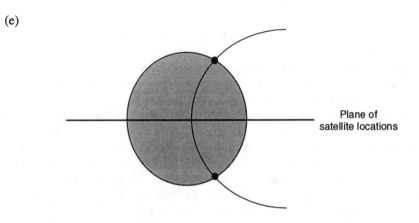

Plane of
satellite locations

Figure 2.6 (continued)

containing the satellites, and it may not be clear which point to select unless the user has ancillary information.

2.2 REFERENCE COORDINATE SYSTEMS

To formulate the mathematics of the satellite navigation problem, it is necessary to choose a reference coordinate system in which the states of both the satellite and the receiver can be represented. In this formulation, it is typical to describe satellite and receiver states in terms of position and velocity vectors measured in a Cartesian coordinate system. There are a number of commonly used Cartesian coordinate systems, including inertial and rotating systems. In this section, an overview is provided of the coordinate systems used for GPS.

2.2.1 Earth-Centered Inertial (ECI) Coordinate System

For the purposes of measuring and determining the orbits of the GPS satellites, it is convenient to use an Earth-centered inertial (ECI) coordinate system, in which the origin is at the center of mass of the Earth. An ECI system is inertial in the sense that the equations of motion of an Earth-orbiting satellite can be modeled as if the ECI system were unaccelerated. In other words, a GPS satellite obeys Newton's laws of motion and gravitation in an ECI coordinate system. In typical ECI coordinate systems, the xy-plane is taken to coincide with the Earth's equatorial plane, the $+x$-axis is permanently fixed in a particular direction relative to the celestial sphere, the $+z$-axis is taken normal to the xy-plane in the direction of the north pole, and the $+y$-axis is chosen so as to form a right-handed coordinate system. Determination and propagation of the GPS satellite orbits are carried out in an ECI coordinate system.

One subtlety in the definition of an ECI coordinate system arises due to irregularities in the Earth's motion. The Earth's shape is oblate, and due largely to the gravitational pull of the Sun and the Moon on the Earth's equatorial bulge, the equatorial plane moves with respect to the celestial sphere. Because the *x*-axis is defined relative to the celestial sphere and the *z*-axis is defined relative to the equatorial plane, the irregularities in the Earth's motion would cause the ECI frame as defined above not to be truly inertial. The solution to this problem is to define the orientation of the axes *at a particular instant in time*, or epoch. The GPS ECI coordinate system uses the orientation of the equatorial plane at 1200 hr UTC(USNO) on January 1, 2000, as its basis. The +*x*-axis is taken to point from the center of mass of the Earth to the direction of vernal equinox, and the *y*- and *z*-axes are defined as described above, all at the aforementioned epoch. Since the orientation of the axes remains fixed, the ECI coordinate system defined in this way can be considered inertial for GPS purposes.

2.2.2 Earth-Centered Earth-Fixed (ECEF) Coordinate System

For the purpose of computing the position of a GPS receiver, it is more convenient to use a coordinate system that rotates with the Earth, known as an Earth-centered Earth-fixed (ECEF) system. In such a coordinate system, it is easier to compute the latitude, longitude, and height parameters that the receiver displays. As with the ECI coordinate system, the ECEF coordinate system used for GPS has its *xy*-plane coincident with the Earth's equatorial plane. However, in the ECEF system, the +*x*-axis points in the direction of 0° longitude, and the +*y*-axis points in the direction of 90° E longitude. The *x*- and *y*-axes therefore rotate with the Earth and no longer describe fixed directions in inertial space. In this ECEF system, the *z*-axis is chosen to be normal to the equatorial plane in the direction of the geographical north pole (i.e., where the lines of longitude meet in the northern hemisphere), thereby completing the right-handed coordinate system.

Before computing the position of the GPS receiver, it is necessary to transform the satellite ephemeris information from the ECI to the ECEF coordinate system. Such transformations are accomplished by the application of rotation matrices to the satellite position and velocity vectors in the ECI coordinate system, as described, for example, in [3]. For the purposes of this text in describing the solution to the GPS navigation problem, it is assumed that the satellite position and velocity vectors are already available in the ECEF system. Thus, we proceed to formulate the GPS navigation problem in the ECEF system without discussing the details of the orbit determination or the transformation to the ECEF system.

As a result of the GPS navigation computation process, the Cartesian coordinates (x_u, y_u, z_u) of the user's receiver are computed in the ECEF system, as described in Section 2.4.2. It is typical to transform these Cartesian coordinates to latitude, longitude, and height of the receiver. In order to carry out this transformation, it is necessary to have a physical model describing the Earth.

2.2.3 World Geodetic System (WGS-84)

The standard physical model of the Earth used for GPS applications is the DOD's World Geodetic System 1984 (WGS-84) [4]. One part of WGS-84 is a detailed model of the Earth's gravitational irregularities. Such information is necessary to derive accurate satellite ephemeris information; however, we are concerned here with estimating the latitude, longitude, and height of a GPS receiver. For this purpose, WGS-84 provides an ellipsoidal model of the Earth's shape, as shown in Figure 2.7. In this model, cross-sections of the Earth parallel to the equatorial plane are circular. The equatorial cross-section of the Earth has radius 6,378.137 km, which is the mean equatorial radius of the Earth. In the WGS-84 Earth model, cross-sections of the Earth normal to the equatorial plane are ellipsoidal. In an ellipsoidal cross-section containing the z-axis, the major axis coincides with the equatorial diameter of the Earth. Therefore, the semimajor axis, a, has the same value as the mean equatorial radius given above. The minor axis of the ellipsoidal cross-section shown in Figure 2.7 corresponds to the polar diameter of the Earth, and the semiminor axis, b, in WGS-84 is taken to be 6,356.7523142 km. Thus, the eccentricity of the Earth ellipsoid, e, and the flattening, f, can be determined by

$$e = \sqrt{1 - \frac{b^2}{a^2}}$$

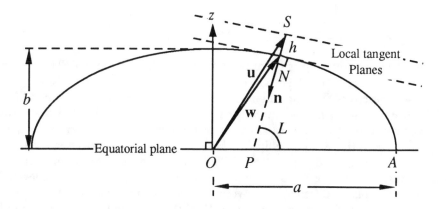

Figure 2.7 Ellipsoidal model of Earth (cross-section normal to equatorial plane).

and

$$f = 1 - \frac{b}{a}$$

Another parameter sometimes used to characterize the reference ellipsoid is the second eccentricity, e', which is defined as follows:

$$e' = \sqrt{\frac{a^2}{b^2} - 1} = \frac{a}{b} e$$

2.2.3.1 Determination of User Geodetic Coordinates: Latitude, Longitude, and Height

The ECEF coordinate system is affixed to the WGS-84 reference ellipsoid, as shown in Figure 2.7, with the point O corresponding to the center of the Earth. We can now define the parameters of latitude, longitude, and height with respect to the reference ellipsoid. When defined in this manner, these parameters are called *geodetic*. Given a user receiver's position vector of $u = (x_u, y_u, z_u)$ in the ECEF system, we can compute the geodetic longitude (λ) as the angle between the user and the x-axis, measured in the xy-plane

$$\lambda = \begin{cases} \arctan\left(\dfrac{y_u}{x_u}\right), & x_u \geq 0 \\ 180° + \arctan\left(\dfrac{y_u}{x_u}\right), & x_u < 0 \text{ and } y_u \geq 0 \\ -180° + \arctan\left(\dfrac{y_u}{x_u}\right), & x_u < 0 \text{ and } y_u < 0 \end{cases} \quad (2.1)$$

In (2.1), negative angles correspond to degrees west longitude. The geodetic parameters of latitude (ϕ) and height (h) are defined in terms of the ellipsoid normal at the user's receiver. The ellipsoid normal is depicted by the unit vector n in Figure 2.7. Notice that unless the user is on the poles or the equator, the ellipsoid normal does not point exactly toward the center of the Earth. A GPS receiver computes height relative to the WGS-84 ellipsoid. However, the height above sea level given on a map can be quite different from GPS-derived height due to the difference, in some places, between the WGS-84 ellipsoid and the geoid (local mean sea level). In the horizontal plane, differences between the local datum (e.g., North American Datum 1983 (NAD-83), European Datum 1950 (ED-50), etc.) and WGS-84 can be significant, particularly for the case of DGPS solutions.

Geodetic height is simply the minimum distance between the user (at the endpoint of the vector **u**) and the reference ellipsoid. Notice that the direction of minimum distance from the user to the surface of the reference ellipsoid will be in the direction of the vector **n**. Geodetic latitude, ϕ, is the angle between the ellipsoid normal vector **n** and the projection of **n** into the equatorial (xy) plane. Conventionally, ϕ is taken to be positive if $z_u > 0$ (i.e., if the user is in the northern hemisphere) and ϕ is taken to be negative if $z_u < 0$. With respect to Figure 2.7, geodetic latitude is the angle *NPA*, where *N* is the closest point on the reference ellipsoid to the user, *P* is the point where a line in the direction of **n** intersects the equatorial plane, and *A* is the closest point on the equator to *P*. A closed-form solution for *h* and ϕ with respect to ECEF coordinates (x_u, y_u, z_u) is described in Table 2.1 [5]. For the computations shown in Table 2.1, *a*, *b*, and *e* are the geodetic parameters described previously, and *e'* is the so-called second eccentricity with value 0.0820944379496, in accordance with WGS-84.

2.2.3.2 Conversion From Geodetic Coordinates to Cartesian Coordinates in ECEF Frame

For completeness, the equations for transforming from geodetic coordinates back to Cartesian coordinates in the ECEF system are provided below. Given the geodetic parameters λ, ϕ, and *h*, we can compute **u** = (x_u, y_u, z_u) in closed-form as follows:

$$
\mathbf{u} = \begin{bmatrix}
\dfrac{a\cos\lambda}{\sqrt{1 + (1 - e^2)\tan^2\phi}} + h \cos \lambda \cos \phi \\[4mm]
\dfrac{a\sin\lambda}{\sqrt{1 + (1 - e^2)\tan^2\phi}} + h \sin \lambda \cos \phi \\[4mm]
\dfrac{a(1 - e^2)\sin\phi}{\sqrt{1 - e^2\sin^2\phi}} + h \sin \phi
\end{bmatrix}
$$

2.3 FUNDAMENTALS OF SATELLITE ORBITS

As described in Section 2.1, a GPS user needs accurate information about the positions of the GPS satellites in order to determine his or her position. Therefore, it is important to understand how the GPS orbits are characterized. We begin by describing the forces acting on a satellite, the most significant of which is the Earth's gravity. If the Earth were perfectly spherical and of uniform density, then the Earth's gravity would behave as if the Earth were a point mass. Let an object of mass *m* be located at position vector **r** in an ECI coordinate system. If *G* is the universal gravitational

Table 2.1
Evaluation of Geodetic Height and Latitude in Terms of ECEF
Parameters (x_u, y_u, z_u)

(1) $\qquad r = \sqrt{x_u^2 + y_u^2}$

(2) $\qquad E^2 = a^2 - b^2$

(3) $\qquad F = 54b^2 z_u^2$

(4) $\qquad G = r^2 + (1 - e^2)z_u^2 - e^2 E^2$

(5) $\qquad c = \dfrac{e^4 F r^2}{G^3}$

(6) $\qquad s = \sqrt[3]{1 + c + \sqrt{c^2 + 2c}}$

(7) $\qquad P = \dfrac{F}{3\left(s + \dfrac{1}{s} + 1\right)^2 G^2}$

(8) $\qquad Q = \sqrt{1 + 2e^4 P}$

(9) $\qquad r_0 = -\dfrac{Pe^2 r}{1 + Q} + \sqrt{\dfrac{1}{2}a^2\left(1 + \dfrac{1}{Q}\right) - \dfrac{P(1 - e^2)z_u^2}{Q(1 + Q)} - \dfrac{1}{2}Pr^2}$

(10) $\qquad U = \sqrt{(r - e^2 r_0)^2 + z_u^2}$

(11) $\qquad V = \sqrt{(r - e^2 r_0)^2 + (1 - e^2)z_u^2}$

(12) $\qquad z_0 = \dfrac{b^2 z_u}{aV}$

(13) $\qquad h = U\left(1 - \dfrac{b^2}{aV}\right)$

(14) $\qquad \phi = \arctan\left(\dfrac{z_u + e'^2 z_0}{r}\right)$

(15) $\qquad \lambda = \arctan\dfrac{y_u}{x_u}$

After: [5].

constant, M is the mass of the Earth, and the Earth's gravity acts as a point mass, then, according to Newton's laws, the force, F, acting on the object would be given by

$$\mathbf{F} = m\mathbf{a} = -G\frac{mM}{r^3}\mathbf{r} \qquad (2.2)$$

where $\mathbf{a}$ is the acceleration of the object, and $r = |\mathbf{r}|$. The minus sign on the right-hand side of (2.2) results from the fact that gravitational forces are always attractive. Since acceleration is the second time derivative of position, (2.2) can be rewritten as follows:

$$\frac{d^2\mathbf{r}}{dt^2} = -\frac{\mu}{r^3}\mathbf{r} \qquad (2.3)$$

where μ is the product of the universal gravitation constant and the mass of the Earth. In WGS-84, $\mu = 3986005 \times 10^8$ m³/sec². Equation (2.3) is the expression of so-called "two-body" or Keplerian satellite motion, in which the only force acting on the satellite is the point-mass Earth.

Because the Earth is not spherical and has an uneven distribution of mass, (2.3) does not model the true acceleration due to the Earth's gravity. If the function V measures the true gravitational potential of the Earth at an arbitrary point in space, then (2.3) may be rewritten as follows:

$$\frac{d^2\mathbf{r}}{dt^2} = \nabla V \qquad (2.4)$$

where ∇ is the gradient operator, defined as follows:

$$\nabla V \underset{\text{def}}{=} \begin{bmatrix} \dfrac{\partial V}{\partial x} \\[2mm] \dfrac{\partial V}{\partial y} \\[2mm] \dfrac{\partial V}{\partial z} \end{bmatrix}$$

Notice that for two-body motion, $V = \mu/r$:

$$\nabla(\mu/r) = \mu \begin{bmatrix} \dfrac{\partial}{\partial x}(r^{-1}) \\[2ex] \dfrac{\partial}{\partial y}(r^{-1}) \\[2ex] \dfrac{\partial}{\partial z}(r^{-1}) \end{bmatrix} = -\dfrac{\mu}{r^2} \begin{bmatrix} \dfrac{\partial r}{\partial x} \\[2ex] \dfrac{\partial r}{\partial y} \\[2ex] \dfrac{\partial r}{\partial z} \end{bmatrix} = -\dfrac{\mu}{r^2} \begin{bmatrix} \dfrac{\partial}{\partial x}(x^2 + y^2 + z^2)^{\frac{1}{2}} \\[2ex] \dfrac{\partial}{\partial y}(x^2 + y^2 + z^2)^{\frac{1}{2}} \\[2ex] \dfrac{\partial}{\partial z}(x^2 + y^2 + z^2)^{\frac{1}{2}} \end{bmatrix}$$

$$= -\dfrac{\mu}{2r^2}(x^2 + y^2 + z^2)^{-\frac{1}{2}} \begin{bmatrix} 2x \\ 2y \\ 2z \end{bmatrix} = -\dfrac{\mu}{r^3} \begin{bmatrix} x \\ y \\ z \end{bmatrix} = -\dfrac{\mu}{r^3}\mathbf{r}$$

Therefore, with $V = \mu/r$, (2.4) is equivalent to (2.3) for two-body motion. In the case of true satellite motion, the Earth's gravitational potential is modeled by a spherical harmonic series. In such a representation, the gravitational potential at a point P is defined in terms of the point's spherical coordinates (r, ϕ', α) as follows:

$$V = \frac{\mu}{r}\left\{1 + \sum_{l=2}^{\infty}\sum_{m=0}^{l}\left(\frac{a}{r}\right)^l P_{lm}(\sin\phi')[C_{lm}\cos m\alpha + S_{lm}\sin m\alpha]\right\} \tag{2.5}$$

where

r	=	distance of P from the origin
ϕ'	=	geocentric latitude of P (i.e., angle between $\mathbf{r}$ and the xy-plane)
α	=	right ascension of P
a	=	mean equatorial radius of the Earth (6,378.137 km in WGS-84)
P_{lm}	=	associated Legendre function
C_{lm}	=	spherical harmonic cosine coefficient of degree l and order m
S_{lm}	=	spherical harmonic sine coefficient of degree l and order m

Notice that the first term of (2.5) is the two-body potential function. Also notice that geocentric latitude in (2.5) is different from geodetic latitude defined in Section 2.2. WGS-84 provides the spherical harmonic coefficients C_{lm} and S_{lm} through 18th degree and order.

Additional forces acting on satellites include the so-called "third-body" gravity from the Sun and Moon. Modeling third-body gravity requires knowledge of the solar and lunar positions in the ECI coordinate system as a function of time. Another force acting on satellites is solar radiation pressure, which results from momentum transfer from solar photons to a satellite. Solar radiation pressure is a function of the sun's position, the projected area of the satellite in the plane normal to the solar line-of-sight, and the mass and reflectivity of the satellite. There are additional forces acting on a satellite, including outgassing (i.e., the slow release of gases trapped in the structure of a satellite), the Earth's tidal variations, and orbital maneuvers. To model a satellite's orbit very accurately, all these perturbations to the Earth's gravitational field must be modeled. For the purposes of this text, we will collect all these perturbing accelerations in a term a_d, so that the equations of motion can be written as

$$\frac{d^2\mathbf{r}}{dt^2} = \nabla V + \mathbf{a}_d \tag{2.6}$$

There are various methods of representing the orbital parameters of a satellite. One obvious representation is to define the position vector, $\mathbf{r}_0 = \mathbf{r}(t_0)$, and the velocity vector, $\mathbf{v}_0 = \mathbf{v}(t_0)$, at some reference time, t_0. Given these initial conditions, we could solve the equations of motion (2.6) for the position vector $\mathbf{r}(t)$ and the velocity vector $\mathbf{v}(t)$ at any other time t. Only the two-body equation of motion (2.3) has an analytical solution; the computation of orbital parameters from the fully perturbed equations of motion (2.6) requires numerical integration.

Although many applications, including GPS, require the accuracy provided by the fully perturbed equations of motion, orbital parameters are often defined in terms of the solution to the two-body problem. It can be shown that there are six constants of integration, or "integrals" for the equation of two-body motion, (2.3). Given six integrals of motion and an initial time, one can find the position and velocity vectors of a satellite on a two-body orbit at any other time.

In the case of the fully perturbed equation of motion, (2.6), it is still possible to characterize the orbit in terms of six integrals of two-body motion, but those six parameters will no longer be constant. Therefore, the GPS ephemeris message includes not only six orbital parameters, but also the time of their applicability and a characterization of how they change over time. With this information, a GPS receiver can compute the "corrected" integrals of motion for a GPS satellite at the time when it is solving the navigation problem. From the corrected integrals, the position vector of the satellite can be computed, as we will show. First, we present the definitions of the six integrals of two-body motion used in the GPS system.

There are many possible formulations of the solution to the two-body problem, but GPS adopts the notation of the "classical" solution, which uses a particular set of six integrals of motion known as the Keplerian orbital elements. These Keplerian elements depend on the fact that for any initial conditions $\mathbf{r}_0$ and $\mathbf{v}_0$ at time t_0, the solution to (2.3) (i.e., the orbit), will be a conic section confined to a plane. The first three Keplerian orbital elements, illustrated in Figure 2.8, define the shape of the orbit. Figure 2.8 shows an elliptical orbit that has semimajor axis a and eccentricity e. (Hyperbolic and parabolic trajectories are possible but not relevant for Earth-orbiting satellites, such as in GPS.) In Figure 2.8, the elliptical orbit has a focus at point F, which corresponds to the center of mass of the Earth (and hence the origin of an

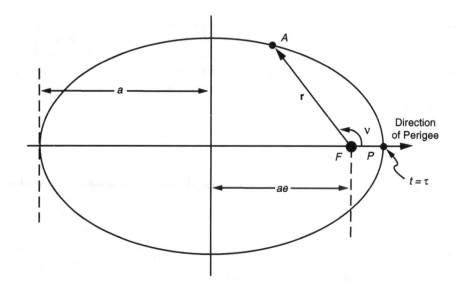

Figure 2.8 The three Keplerian orbital elements defining the shape of the satellite's orbit.

ECI or ECEF coordinate system). The time t_0 at which the satellite is at some reference point A in its orbit is known as the "epoch" and as a part of the GPS ephemeris message is called "time of ephemeris." The point P where the satellite is closest to the center of the Earth is known as perigee, and the time at which the satellite passes perigee, τ, is another Keplerian orbital parameter. In summary, the three Keplerian orbital elements that define the shape of the elliptical orbit are as follows:

a =   semimajor axis of the ellipse
e =   eccentricity of the ellipse
τ =   time of perigee passage

Although the Keplerian integrals of two-body motion use time of perigee passage as one of the constants of motion, there is an equivalent parameter used by the GPS system known as the mean anomaly at epoch. Mean anomaly is an angle that is related to the true anomaly at epoch, which is illustrated in Figure 2.8 as the angle ν. After defining true anomaly precisely, the transformation to mean anomaly and the demonstration of equivalence to time of perigee passage will be shown.

True anomaly is the angle in the orbital plane measured counterclockwise from the direction of perigee to the satellite. In Figure 2.8, the true anomaly at epoch is $\nu = \angle PFA$. From Kepler's laws of two-body motion, it is known that true anomaly does not vary linearly in time for noncircular orbits. Because it is desirable to define a parameter that does vary linearly in time, two definitions are made that transform the true anomaly to the mean anomaly, which is linear in time. The first transformation produces the eccentric anomaly, which is illustrated in Figure 2.9 with the true anomaly. Geometrically, the eccentric anomaly is constructed from the true anomaly first by circumscribing a circle around the elliptical orbit. Next, a perpendicular is dropped from the point A on the orbit to the major axis of the orbit, and this perpendicular is extended upward until it intersects the circumscribed circle at point B. The eccentric anomaly is the angle measured at the center of the circle, O, counterclockwise from the direction of perigee to the line segment OB. In other words, $E = \angle POB$. A useful analytical relationship between eccentric anomaly and true anomaly is as follows [6]:

$$E = 2 \arctan\left[\sqrt{\frac{1-e}{1+e}} \tan\left(\frac{1}{2}\nu\right)\right] \qquad (2.7)$$

Once the eccentric anomaly has been computed, the mean anomaly is given by Kepler's equation

$$M = E - e \sin E \qquad (2.8)$$

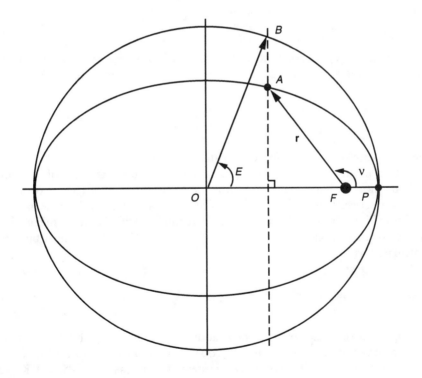

Figure 2.9 Relationship between eccentric anomaly and true anomaly.

As stated previously, the importance of transforming from the true to the mean anomaly is that time varies linearly with the mean anomaly. That linear relationship is as follows:

$$M - M_0 = \sqrt{\frac{\mu}{a^3}} \, (t - t_0) \tag{2.9}$$

where M_0 is the mean anomaly at epoch t_0, and M is the mean anomaly at time t. From Figures 2.8 and 2.9, and (2.7) and (2.8), it can be verified that $M = E = \nu = 0$ at the time of perigee passage. Therefore, if we let $t = \tau$, (2.9) provides a transformation between mean anomaly and time of perigee passage:

$$M_0 = - \sqrt{\frac{\mu}{a^3}} \, (\tau - t_0) \tag{2.10}$$

From (2.10), it is possible to characterize the two-body orbit in terms of the mean anomaly at epoch M_0 instead of the time of perigee passage τ. GPS makes use of the mean anomaly at epoch in characterizing orbits.

GPS also makes use of a parameter known as *mean motion*, which is given the symbol n and is defined to be the time derivative of the mean anomaly. Since the mean anomaly was constructed to be linear in time for two-body orbits, mean motion is a constant. From (2.9), we find the mean motion as follows:

$$n \underset{\text{def}}{=} \frac{dM}{dt} = \sqrt{\frac{\mu}{a^3}}$$

From this definition, (2.9) can be rewritten as $M - M_0 = n(t - t_0)$.

Mean motion can also be used to express the orbital period P of a satellite in two-body motion. Since mean motion is the (constant) rate of change of the mean anomaly, the orbital period is the ratio of the angle subtended by the mean anomaly over one orbital period to the mean motion. It can be verified that the mean anomaly passes through an angle of 2π radians during one orbit. Therefore, the orbital period is calculated as follows:

$$P = \frac{2\pi}{n} = 2\pi \sqrt{\frac{a^3}{\mu}} \tag{2.11}$$

Figure 2.10 illustrates the three additional Keplerian orbital elements that define the orientation of the orbit. The coordinates in Figure 2.10 could refer either to an ECI or to an ECEF coordinate system. In the case of GPS, the Keplerian parameters are defined in relation to the ECEF coordinate system described in

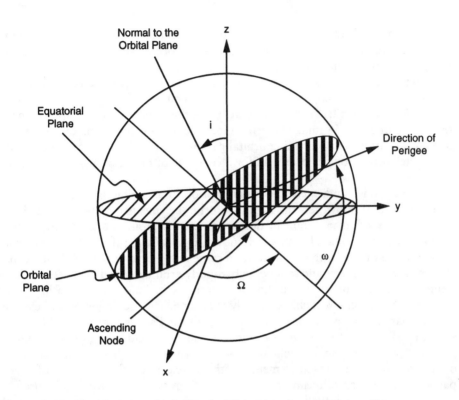

Figure 2.10 The three Keplerian orbital elements defining the orientation of the orbit.

Section 2.2. In this case, the xy-plane is always the Earth's equatorial plane. The following three Keplerian orbital elements define the orientation of the orbit in the ECEF coordinate system:

i = inclination of orbit
Ω = longitude of the ascending node
ω = argument of perigee

Inclination is the dihedral angle between the Earth's equatorial plane and the satellite's orbital plane. The other two Keplerian orbital elements in Figure 2.10 are defined in relation to the *ascending node*, which is the point in the satellite's orbit where it crosses the equatorial plane with a $+z$ component of velocity (i.e., going from the southern to the northern hemisphere). The orbital element that defines the angle between the $+x$-axis and the direction of the ascending node is called the right ascension of the ascending node. Because the $+x$-axis is fixed in the direction of the prime meridian (0° longitude) in the ECEF coordinate system, the right ascension of the ascending node is actually the *longitude* of the ascending node, Ω. The final orbital element, known as the argument of perigee, ω, measures the angle from the ascending node to the direction of perigee in the orbit. Notice that Ω is measured in the equatorial plane, whereas ω is measured in the orbital plane.

In the case of GPS satellites, the orbits are nearly (but not quite) circular, with eccentricities of no larger than 0.02 and semimajor axes of approximately 26,560 km. From (2.11), we compute the orbital period to be approximately 43,080 sec or 11 hr 58 min. The orbital inclinations are approximately 55° for the GPS constellation. The remaining orbital parameters vary between satellites, so that the constellation provides nearly uniform coverage of the entire Earth, as described in Section 7.2.

As previously indicated, the actual motion of a satellite is described by (2.6) rather than (2.3). However, the Keplerian orbital elements may be computed for a satellite at a particular instant in time from its true position and velocity vectors. In this case, the orbital elements are known as *osculating*; if all forces perturbing the point-mass force of the Earth were to cease at the time of the osculating orbital elements, the satellite would follow the two-body orbit described by those osculating elements. Because of the perturbing accelerations in (2.6), the osculating orbital elements of a satellite will change slowly over time. The osculating orbital elements do not change quickly because the first term of the Earth's gravitational harmonic series, (2.5), is still the dominant element in the force field acting on a satellite.

GPS almanac data and ephemeris data transmitted by the satellites include the osculating Keplerian orbital elements, with the exception that the time of perigee passage is converted to mean anomaly at epoch by (2.10). In order to be useful, it is necessary for the osculating elements to include the reference time, known as the time of epoch or time of ephemeris, at which the orbital elements were valid. Only at epoch are the orbital elements exactly as described by the osculating values; at all later times, the true orbital elements deviate slightly from the osculating values.

Because it is necessary for the GPS ephemeris message to contain very accurate information about the satellite's position and velocity, it is insufficient to use only the osculating Keplerian orbital elements for computing the position of a GPS satellite, except very near the epoch of those elements. One solution to this problem would be to update the GPS ephemeris messages very frequently. Another solution would be for the GPS receiver to integrate the fully perturbed equation of motion, (2.6), which would include a detailed force model, from epoch to the desired time. Because both of these solutions are computationally intensive, they are impractical for real-time operations. Therefore, the osculating Keplerian orbital elements in the GPS ephemeris message are augmented by "correction" parameters that allow the user to estimate the Keplerian elements fairly accurately during the periods of time between updates of the satellite's ephemeris message. (Particulars on ephemeris message updating are provided in Section 3.1.2.) Any time after the epoch of a particular ephemeris message, the GPS receiver uses the correction parameters to estimate the true orbital elements at the desired time.

Table 2.2 summarizes the parameters contained in the GPS ephemeris message. As can be seen, the first seven parameters of the GPS ephemeris message are time of epoch and, essentially, the osculating Keplerian orbital elements at the time of epoch, with the exceptions that the semimajor axis is reported as its square root and that mean anomaly is used instead of time of perigee passage. The next nine parameters allow for corrections to the Keplerian elements as functions of time after epoch.

Table 2.3 provides the algorithm by which a GPS receiver computes the position vector of a satellite (x_s, y_s, z_s) in the ECEF coordinate system from the orbital elements in Table 2.2. For computation (3) in Table 2.3, t represents the GPS system time at which the GPS signal was transmitted. In the notation of Table 2.3, the subscript k appearing in computation (3) and below means that the subscripted variable is measured at time t_k, the time (in seconds) from epoch to the GPS system time of signal transmission.

There are a few additional subtleties in the computations described in Table 2.3. First, computation (5), which is Kepler's equation, (2.8), is transcendental in the desired parameter, E_k. Therefore, the solution must be carried out numerically. Kepler's equation is readily solved either by iteration or Newton's method. A second subtlety is that computation (6) must produce the true anomaly in the correct quadrant. Therefore, it is necessary either to use both the sine and the cosine or to use a "smart" arcsine function. Finally, to carry out computation (14), it is also necessary to know the rotation rate of the Earth. According to WGS-84, this rotation rate is $\dot{\Omega}_e = 7.2921151467 \times 10^{-5}$ rad/sec.

Table 2.2
GPS Ephemeris Data Definitions

t_{0e}	Reference time of ephemeris
$\sqrt{a}$	Square root of semimajor axis
e	Eccentricity
i_0	Inclination angle (at time t_{0e})
Ω_0	Longitude of the ascending node (at weekly epoch)
ω	Argument of perigee (at time t_{0e})
M_0	Mean anomaly (at time t_{0e})
di/dt	Rate of change of inclination angle
$\dot{\Omega}$	Rate of change of longitude of the ascending node
Δn	Mean motion correction
C_{uc}	Amplitude of cosine correction to argument of latitude
C_{us}	Amplitude of sine correction to argument of latitude
C_{rc}	Amplitude of cosine correction to orbital radius
C_{rs}	Amplitude of sine correction to orbital radius
C_{ic}	Amplitude of cosine correction to inclination angle
C_{is}	Amplitude of sine correction to inclination angle

Table 2.3
Computation of a Satellite's ECEF Position Vector

(1)	$a = (\sqrt{a})^2$	Semimajor axis
(2)	$n = \sqrt{\dfrac{\mu}{a^3}} + \Delta n$	Corrected mean motion
(3)	$t_k = t - t_{0e}$	Time from ephemeris epoch
(4)	$M_k = M_0 + n(t_k)$	Mean anomaly
(5)	$M_k = E_k - e \sin E_k$	Eccentric anomaly (must be solved iteratively for E_k)
(6)	$\sin \nu_k = \dfrac{\sqrt{1 - e^2}\sin E_k}{1 - e \cos E_k}$ $\cos \nu_k = \dfrac{\cos E_k - e}{1 - e \cos E_k}$	True anomaly
(7)	$\phi_k = \nu_k + \omega$	Argument of latitude
(8)	$\delta\phi_k = C_{us}\sin(2\phi_k) + C_{uc}\cos(2\phi_k)$	Argument of latitude correction
(9)	$\delta r_k = C_{rs}\sin(2\phi_k) + C_{rc}\cos(2\phi_k)$	Radius correction
(10)	$\delta i_k = C_{is}\sin(2\phi_k) + C_{ic}\cos(2\phi_k)$	Inclination correction
(11)	$u_k = \phi_k + \delta\phi_k$	Corrected argument of latitude
(12)	$r_k = a(1 - e \cos E_k) + \delta r_k$	Corrected radius
(13)	$i_k = i_0 + (di/dt)t_k + \delta i_k$	Corrected inclination
(14)	$\Omega_k = \Omega_0 + (\dot{\Omega} - \dot{\Omega}_e)(t_k) - \dot{\Omega}_e t_{0e}$	Corrected longitude of node
(15)	$x_p = r_k \cos u_k$	In-plane x position
(16)	$y_p = r_k \sin u_k$	In-plane y position
(17)	$x_s = x_p \cos \Omega_k - y_p \cos i_k \sin \Omega_k$	ECEF x-coordinate
(18)	$y_s = x_p \sin \Omega_k + y_p \cos i_k \cos \Omega_k$	ECEF y-coordinate
(19)	$z_s = y_p \sin i_k$	ECEF z-coordinate

As can be seen from the computations in Table 2.3, the variations in time of the orbital parameters are modeled differently for particular parameters. For example, mean motion is given a constant correction in computation (2), which effectively corrects the mean anomaly computed in (4). On the other hand, latitude, radius, and inclination are corrected by truncated harmonic series in computations (8), (9), and (10), respectively. Eccentricity is given no correction. Finally, longitude of the node is corrected linearly in time in computation (14). It is a misnomer of GPS system terminology, as in Table 2.2, that the longitude of the node, Ω_0, is given "at weekly epoch." In reality, Ω_0 is given at the reference time of ephemeris, t_{0e}, the same as the other GPS parameters. This can be verified by inspection of computation (14) from Table 2.3. Reference [7] provides an excellent description of the tradeoffs that resulted in the use of ephemeris message parameters and computations described in Tables 2.2 and 2.3.

2.4 POSITION DETERMINATION USING PSEUDORANDOM NOISE (PRN) CODES

GPS satellite transmissions utilize direct sequence spread spectrum (DSSS) modulation. DSSS provides the structure for the transmission of ranging signals and essential navigation data such as satellite ephemerides and satellite health. The ranging signals are PRN codes that binary phase shift key (BPSK) modulate the satellite carrier frequencies. These codes look like and have spectral properties similar to random binary sequences, but are actually deterministic. A simple example of a short PRN code sequence is shown in Figure 2.11. These codes have a predictable pattern, which is periodic and can be replicated by a suitably equipped receiver.

Each GPS satellite broadcasts two types of PRN ranging codes: a "short" coarse/acquisition (C/A)-code and a "long" precision (P)-code. The C/A-code has a 1-msec period and repeats constantly, whereas the P-code satellite transmission is a 7-day sequence that repeats every midnight Saturday/Sunday. At the time of this writing, the P-code is encrypted. This encrypted code is denoted as the Y-code. The Y-code is accessible only to PPS users through cryptography. Further details regarding PRN code properties, frequency generation and associated modulation processes are contained in Chapter 4.

2.4.1 Determining Satellite-To-User Range

Earlier, we examined the theoretical aspects of using satellite ranging signals and multiple spheres to solve for user position in three dimensions. That example was predicated on the assumption that the receiver clock was perfectly synchronized to system time. In actuality, this is generally not the case. Prior to solving for three-dimensional user position, we will examine the fundamental concepts involving satellite-to-user range determination with nonsynchronized clocks and PRN codes. There are a number of error sources that affect range measurement accuracy (e.g., measurement noise, propagation delays, etc.); however, these can generally be considered negligible when compared to the errors experienced from nonsynchronized

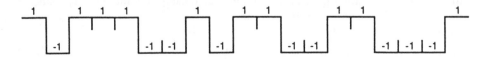

Figure 2.11 PRN ranging code.

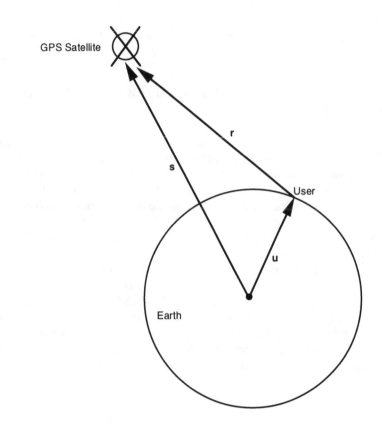

Figure 2.12 User position vector representation.

clocks. Therefore, in our development of basic concepts, errors other than clock offset are omitted. Extensive treatment of these error sources is provided in Section 7.1.2.

In Figure 2.12, we wish to determine vector **u**, which represents a user receiver's position with respect to the ECEF coordinate system origin. The user's position coordinates x_u, y_u, z_u are considered unknown. Vector **r** represents the vector offset from the user to the satellite. The satellite is located at coordinates x_s, y_s, z_s within the ECEF Cartesian coordinate system. Vector **s** represents the position of the satellite relative to the coordinate origin. Vector **s** is computed using ephemeris data broadcast by the satellite. The satellite-to-user vector **r** is

$$\mathbf{r} = \mathbf{s} - \mathbf{u} \qquad (2.12)$$

The magnitude of vector **r** is

$$\|\mathbf{r}\| = \|\mathbf{s} - \mathbf{u}\| \qquad (2.13)$$

Let r represent the magnitude of $\mathbf{r}$

$$r = \|\mathbf{s} - \mathbf{u}\| \qquad (2.14)$$

The distance r is computed by measuring the propagation time required for a satellite-generated ranging code to transit from the satellite to the user receiver antenna. The propagation time measurement process is illustrated in Figure 2.13. As an example, a specific code phase generated by the satellite at t_1 arrives at the receiver at t_2. The propagation time is represented by Δt. Within the receiver, an identical coded ranging signal is generated at t, with respect to the receiver clock. This replica code is shifted in time until it achieves correlation with the satellite-generated ranging code. If the satellite clock and the receiver clock were perfectly synchronized, the correlation process would yield the true propagation time. By multiplying this propagation time, Δt, by the speed of light, the true (i.e., geometric) satellite-to-user distance can be computed. We would then have the ideal case described in Section 2.1.2.1. However, the satellite and receiver clocks are generally not synchronized.

The receiver clock will generally have a bias error from system time. Further, satellite frequency generation and timing is based on a highly accurate free running cesium or rubidium atomic clock, which is typically offset from system time. Thus, the range determined by the correlation process is denoted as the pseudorange ρ, as it contains (1) the geometric satellite-to-user range, (2) an offset attributed to the difference between system time and the user clock, and (3) an offset between system time and the satellite clock. The timing relationships are shown in Figure 2.14, where

T_s	= System time at which the signal left the satellite
T_u	= System time at which the signal reached the user receiver
δt	= Offset of the satellite clock from system time (advance is positive; retardation (delay) is negative)
t_u	= Offset of the receiver clock from system time
$T_s + \delta t$	= Satellite clock reading at the time that the signal left the satellite
$T_u + t_u$	= User receiver clock reading at the time when the signal reached the user receiver
c	= speed of light

$$\text{Geometric range, } r = c(T_u - T_s) = c\,\Delta t$$

$$\begin{aligned} \text{Pseudorange, } \rho &= c[(T_u + t_u) - (T_s + \delta t)] \\ &= c(T_u - T_s) + c(t_u - \delta t) \\ &= r + c(t_u - \delta t) \end{aligned}$$

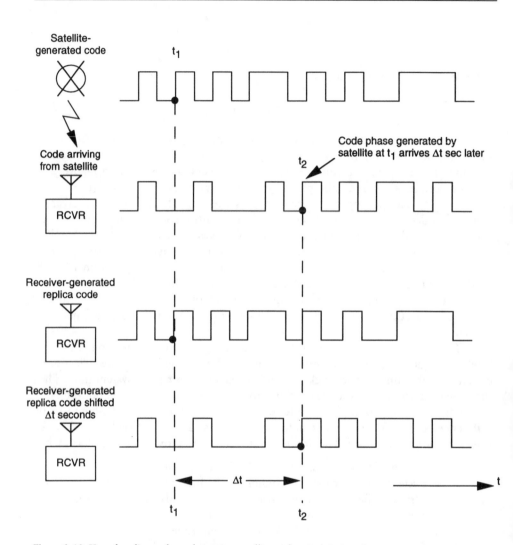

Figure 2.13 Use of replica code to determine satellite code transmission time.

Therefore, (2.14) can be rewritten as:

$$\rho - c(t_u - \delta t) = \|\mathbf{s} - \mathbf{u}\|$$

where t_u represents the advance of the receiver clock with respect to system time, δt represents the advance of the satellite clock with respect to system time, and c is the speed of light.

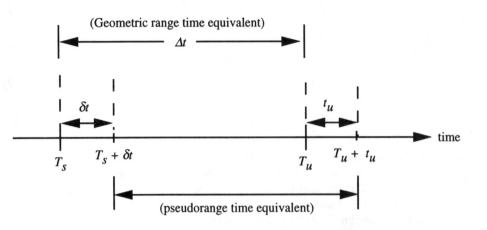

Figure 2.14 Range measurement timing relationships.

The satellite clock offset from system time, δt, is composed of bias and drift contributions. The GPS ground monitoring network determines corrections for these offset contributions and transmits the corrections to the satellites for rebroadcast to the users in the navigation message. These corrections are applied within the user receiver to synchronize the transmission of each ranging signal to system time. Therefore, we assume that this offset is compensated for and no longer consider δt an unknown. (There is some residual offset, which is treated in Section 7.1.2, but in the context of this discussion we assume that this is negligible.) Hence, the preceding equation can be expressed as

$$\rho - ct_u = \|\mathbf{s} - \mathbf{u}\| \tag{2.15}$$

2.4.2 Calculation of User Position

In order to determine user position in three dimensions (x_u, y_u, z_u) and the offset t_u, pseudorange measurements are made to four satellites resulting in the system of equations

$$\rho_j = \|\mathbf{s}_j - \mathbf{u}\| + ct_u \tag{2.16}$$

where j ranges from 1 to 4 and references the satellites. Equation (2.16) can be expanded into the following set of equations in the unknowns x_u, y_u, z_u, and t_u:

$$\rho_1 = \sqrt{(x_1 - x_u)^2 + (y_1 - y_u)^2 + (z_1 - z_u)^2} + ct_u \qquad (2.17)$$

$$\rho_2 = \sqrt{(x_2 - x_u)^2 + (y_2 - y_u)^2 + (z_2 - z_u)^2} + ct_u \qquad (2.18)$$

$$\rho_3 = \sqrt{(x_3 - x_u)^2 + (y_3 - y_u)^2 + (z_3 - z_u)^2} + ct_u \qquad (2.19)$$

$$\rho_4 = \sqrt{(x_4 - x_u)^2 + (y_4 - y_u)^2 + (z_4 - z_u)^2} + ct_u \qquad (2.20)$$

where x_j, y_j, and x_j denote the jth satellite's position in three dimensions.

These nonlinear equations can be solved for the unknowns by employing either (1) closed form solutions [8–11], (2) iterative techniques based on linearization, or (3) Kalman filtering. An overview of Kalman filtering is presented in Section 2.6 with details provided in Chapter 9. Linearization is illustrated below. (The following development regarding linearization is based on a similar development in [12].)

If we know approximately where the receiver is, then we can denote the offset of the true position (x_u, y_u, z_u) from the approximate position $(\hat{x}_u, \hat{y}_u, \hat{z}_u)$ by a displacement $(\Delta x_u, \Delta y_u, \Delta z_u)$. By expanding (2.17) to (2.20) in a Taylor series about the approximate position, we can obtain the position offset $(\Delta x_u, \Delta y_u, \Delta z_u)$ as linear functions of the known coordinates and pseudorange measurements. This process is described below.

Let a single pseudorange be represented by

$$\begin{aligned}
\rho_j &= \sqrt{(x_j - x_u)^2 + (y_j - y_u)^2 + (z_j - z_u)^2} + ct_u \\
&= f(x_u, y_u, z_u, t_u)
\end{aligned} \qquad (2.21)$$

Using the approximate position location $(\hat{x}_u, \hat{y}_u, \hat{z}_u)$ and time bias estimate $\hat{t}_u$, an approximate pseudorange can be calculated:

$$\begin{aligned}
\hat{\rho}_j &= \sqrt{(x_j - \hat{x}_u)^2 + (y_j - \hat{y}_u)^2 + (z_j - \hat{z}_u)^2} + c\hat{t}_u \\
&= f(\hat{x}_u, \hat{y}_u, \hat{z}_u, \hat{t}_u)
\end{aligned} \qquad (2.22)$$

As stated above, the unknown user position and receiver clock offset is considered to consist of an approximate component and an incremental component:

$$x_u = \hat{x}_u + \Delta x_u$$

$$y_u = \hat{y}_u + \Delta y_u \qquad (2.23)$$

$$z_u = \hat{z}_u + \Delta z_u$$

$$t_u = \hat{t}_u + \Delta t_u$$

Therefore, we can write

$$f(x_u, y_u, z_u, t_u) = f(\hat{x}_u + \Delta x_u, \hat{y}_u + \Delta y_u, \hat{z}_u + \Delta z_u, \hat{t}_u + \Delta t_u)$$

This latter function can be expanded about the approximate point and associated predicted receiver clock offset $(\hat{x}_u, \hat{y}_u, \hat{z}_u, \hat{t}_u)$ using a Taylor series:

$$f(\hat{x}_u + \Delta x_u, \hat{y}_u + \Delta y_u, \hat{z}_u + \Delta z_u, \hat{t}_u + \Delta t_u) = f(\hat{x}_u, \hat{y}_u, \hat{z}_u, \hat{t}_u) + \frac{\partial f(\hat{x}_u, \hat{y}_u, \hat{z}_u, \hat{t}_u)}{\partial \hat{x}_u} \Delta x_u +$$

$$\frac{\partial f(\hat{x}_u, \hat{y}_u, \hat{z}_u, \hat{t}_u)}{\partial \hat{y}_u} \Delta y_u + \frac{\partial f(\hat{x}_u, \hat{y}_u, \hat{z}_u, \hat{t}_u)}{\partial \hat{z}_u} \Delta z_u + \frac{\partial f(\hat{x}_u, \hat{y}_u, \hat{z}_u, \hat{t}_u)}{\partial \hat{t}_u} \Delta t_u + \ldots \tag{2.24}$$

The expansion has been truncated after the first-order partial derivatives to eliminate nonlinear terms. The partials derivatives evaluate as follows:

$$\frac{\partial f(\hat{x}_u, \hat{y}_u, \hat{z}_u, \hat{t}_u)}{\partial \hat{x}_u} = -\frac{x_j - \hat{x}_u}{\hat{r}_j}$$

$$\frac{\partial f(\hat{x}_u, \hat{y}_u, \hat{z}_u, \hat{t}_u)}{\partial \hat{y}_u} = -\frac{y_j - \hat{y}_u}{\hat{r}_j} \tag{2.25}$$

$$\frac{\partial f(\hat{x}_u, \hat{y}_u, \hat{z}_u, \hat{t}_u)}{\partial \hat{z}_u} = -\frac{z_j - \hat{z}_u}{\hat{r}_j}$$

$$\frac{\partial f(\hat{x}_u, \hat{y}_u, \hat{z}_u, \hat{t}_u)}{\partial \hat{t}_u} = c$$

where

$$\hat{r}_j = \sqrt{(x_j - \hat{x}_u)^2 + (y_j - \hat{y}_u)^2 + (z_j - \hat{z}_u)^2}$$

Substituting (2.22) and (2.25) into (2.24) yields

$$\rho_j = \hat{\rho}_j - \frac{x_j - \hat{x}_u}{\hat{r}_j} \Delta x_u - \frac{y_j - \hat{y}_u}{\hat{r}_j} \Delta y_u - \frac{z_j - \hat{z}_u}{\hat{r}_j} \Delta z_u + c \Delta t_u \tag{2.26}$$

We have now completed the linearization of (2.21) with respect to the unknowns Δx_u, Δy_u, Δz_u, and Δt_u. (It is important to remember that we are neglecting secondary error sources such as Earth rotation compensation, measurement noise, propagation delays, and relativistic effects, which are treated in detail in Section 7.1.2.)

Rearranging the above expression with the known quantities on the left and unknowns on right yields

$$\hat{\rho}_j - \rho_j = \frac{x_j - \hat{x}_u}{\hat{r}_j}\Delta x_u + \frac{y_j - \hat{y}_u}{\hat{r}_j}\Delta y_u + \frac{z_j - \hat{z}_u}{\hat{r}_j}\Delta z_u - c\Delta t_u \tag{2.27}$$

For convenience, we will simplify the above equation by introducing new variables where

$$\Delta\rho_j = \hat{\rho}_j - \rho_j$$

$$a_{xj} = \frac{x_j - \hat{x}_u}{\hat{r}_j}$$

$$a_{yj} = \frac{y_j - \hat{y}_u}{\hat{r}_j} \tag{2.28}$$

$$a_{zj} = \frac{z_j - \hat{z}_u}{\hat{r}_j}$$

The a_{xj}, a_{yj}, and a_{zj} terms in (2.28) denote the direction cosines of the unit vector pointing from the approximate user position to the jth satellite. For the jth satellite, this unit vector is defined as

$$\mathbf{a}_j = (a_{xj}, a_{yj}, a_{zj})$$

Equation (2.27) can be rewritten more simply as

$$\Delta\rho_j = a_{xj}\Delta x_u + a_{yj}\Delta y_u + a_{zj}\Delta z_u - c\Delta t_u$$

We now have four unknowns: Δx_u, Δy_u, Δz_u, and Δt_u, which can be solved for by making ranging measurements to four satellites. The unknown quantities can be determined by solving the set of linear equations below:

$$\Delta\rho_1 = a_{x1}\Delta x_u + a_{y1}\Delta y_u + a_{z1}\Delta z_u - c\Delta t_u$$
$$\Delta\rho_2 = a_{x2}\Delta x_u + a_{y2}\Delta y_u + a_{z2}\Delta z_u - c\Delta t_u$$
$$\Delta\rho_3 = a_{x3}\Delta x_u + a_{y3}\Delta y_u + a_{z3}\Delta z_u - c\Delta t_u \tag{2.29}$$
$$\Delta\rho_4 = a_{x4}\Delta x_u + a_{y4}\Delta y_u + a_{z4}\Delta z_u - c\Delta t_u$$

These equations can be put in matrix form by making the definitions

$$\Delta \mathbf{\rho} = \begin{bmatrix} \Delta\rho_1 \\ \Delta\rho_2 \\ \Delta\rho_3 \\ \Delta\rho_4 \end{bmatrix} \qquad \mathbf{H} = \begin{bmatrix} a_{x1} & a_{y1} & a_{z1} & 1 \\ a_{x2} & a_{y2} & a_{z2} & 1 \\ a_{x3} & a_{y3} & a_{z3} & 1 \\ a_{x4} & a_{y4} & a_{z4} & 1 \end{bmatrix} \qquad \Delta \mathbf{x} = \begin{bmatrix} \Delta x_u \\ \Delta y_u \\ \Delta z_u \\ -c\Delta t_u \end{bmatrix}$$

One obtains, finally,

$$\Delta\mathbf{\rho} = \mathbf{H}\Delta\mathbf{x} \tag{2.30}$$

which has the solution

$$\Delta\mathbf{x} = \mathbf{H}^{-1}\Delta\mathbf{\rho} \tag{2.31}$$

Once the unknowns are computed, the user's coordinates x_u, y_u, z_u and the receiver clock offset t_u are then calculated using (2.23). This linearization scheme will work well as long as the displacement (Δx_u, Δy_u, Δz_u) is within close proximity of the linearization point. The acceptable displacement is dictated by the user's accuracy requirements. If the displacement does exceed the acceptable value, the above process is reiterated with $\hat{\rho}$ being replaced by a new estimate of pseudorange based on the calculated point coordinates x_u, y_u, and z_u.

In actuality, the true user-to-satellite measurements are corrupted by uncommon (i.e., independent) errors such as measurement noise, deviation of the satellite path from the reported ephemeris, and multipath. These errors translate to errors in the components of vector $\Delta \mathbf{x}$, as shown below:

$$\mathbf{\epsilon}_x = \mathbf{H}^{-1}\mathbf{\epsilon}_{\mathrm{meas}} \tag{2.32}$$

where $\mathbf{\epsilon}_{\mathrm{meas}}$ is the vector containing the pseudorange measurement errors and $\mathbf{\epsilon}_x$ is the vector representing errors in the user position and receiver clock offset.

The error contribution $\mathbf{\epsilon}_x$ can be minimized by making measurements to more than four satellites, which will result in an overdetermined solution set of equations similar to (2.30). Each of these redundant measurements will generally contain independent error contributions. Redundant measurements can be processed by least squares estimation techniques that obtain improved estimates of the unknowns. Various versions of this technique exist and are usually employed in today's receivers, which generally employ more than four user-to-satellite measurements to compute user position, velocity, and time (PVT). Appendix A provides an introduction to least squares techniques.

2.5 OBTAINING USER VELOCITY

GPS provides the capability for determining three-dimensional user velocity, which is denoted $\dot{\mathbf{u}}$. Several methods can be used to determine user velocity. In some receivers, velocity is estimated by forming an approximate derivative of the user position, as shown below:

$$\dot{\mathbf{u}} = \frac{d\mathbf{u}}{dt} \approx \frac{\mathbf{u}(t_2) - \mathbf{u}(t_1)}{t_2 - t_1}$$

This approach can be satisfactory provided the user's velocity is nearly constant over the selected time interval (i.e., not subjected to acceleration or jerk) and if the errors in the positions $\mathbf{u}(t_2)$ and $\mathbf{u}(t_1)$ are small relative to difference $\mathbf{u}(t_2) - \mathbf{u}(t_1)$.

In many modern GPS receivers, velocity measurements are made by processing carrier-phase measurements, which effectively estimate the Doppler frequency of the received satellite signals. The Doppler shift is produced by the relative motion of the satellite with respect to the user. The satellite velocity vector $\mathbf{v}$ is computed using ephemeris information and an orbital model that resides within the receiver. Figure 2.15 is a curve of received Doppler frequency as a function of time measured by a user at rest on the surface of the Earth from a GPS satellite. The received frequency increases as the satellite approaches the receiver and decreases as it recedes from the user. The reversal in the curve represents the time when the Doppler shift is zero and occurs when the satellite is at its closest position relative to the user. At this point, the radial component of the velocity of the satellite relative to the user is zero. As the satellite passes through this point, the sign of Δf changes.

At the receiver antenna, the received frequency, f_R, can be approximated by the classical Doppler equation as follows:

$$f_R = f_T \left(1 - \frac{(\mathbf{v}_r \cdot \mathbf{a})}{c} \right) \qquad (2.33)$$

where f_T is the transmitted satellite signal frequency, $\mathbf{v}_r$ is the satellite-to-user relative velocity vector, $\mathbf{a}$ is the unit vector pointing along the line-of-sight from the user to the satellite, and c is the speed of propagation. The dot product $\mathbf{v}_r \cdot \mathbf{a}$ represents the radial component of the relative velocity vector along the line-of-sight to the satellite. Vector $\mathbf{v}_r$ is given as the velocity difference

$$\mathbf{v}_r = \mathbf{v} - \dot{\mathbf{u}} \qquad (2.34)$$

where $\mathbf{v}$ is the velocity of the satellite and $\dot{\mathbf{u}}$ is the velocity of the user, both referenced to a common ECEF frame. The Doppler offset due to the relative motion is obtained from these relations as

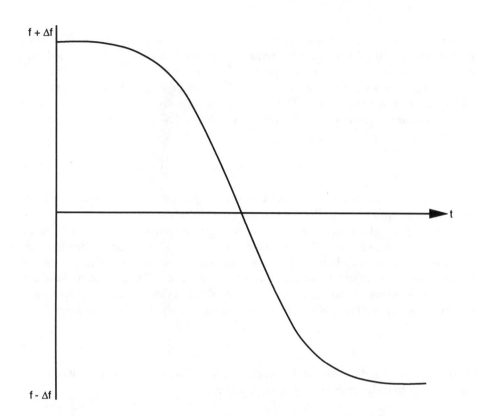

Figure 2.15 Received Doppler frequency by user at rest on Earth's surface.

$$\Delta f = f_R - f_T = -f_T \frac{(\mathbf{v} - \dot{\mathbf{u}}) \cdot \mathbf{a}}{c}$$

There are several approaches for obtaining user velocity from the received Doppler frequency. One technique is described herein. This technique assumes that the user position $\mathbf{u}$ has been determined and its displacement $(\Delta x_u, \Delta y_u, \Delta z_u)$ from the linearization point is within the user's requirements. In addition to computing the three-dimensional user velocity $\dot{\mathbf{u}} = (\dot{x}_u, \dot{y}_u, \dot{z}_u)$, this particular technique determines the receiver clock drift $\dot{t}_u$.

For the jth satellite, substituting (2.34) into (2.33) yields

$$f_{Rj} = f_{Tj} \left\{ 1 - \frac{1}{c} [(\mathbf{v}_j - \dot{\mathbf{u}}) \cdot \mathbf{a}_j] \right\} \tag{2.35}$$

The satellite transmitted frequency f_{Tj} is the actual transmitted satellite frequency. As stated in Section 2.4.1, satellite frequency generation and timing is based on a highly accurate free running atomic standard, which is typically offset from system time. Corrections are generated by the ground control/monitoring network periodically to correct for this offset. These corrections are available in the navigation message and are applied within the receiver to obtain the actual satellite transmitted frequency. Hence,

$$f_{Tj} = f_0 + \Delta f_{Tj} \tag{2.36}$$

where f_0 is the nominal transmitted satellite frequency (i.e., L1) and Δf_{Tj} is the correction determined from the navigation message update.

The measured estimate of the received signal frequency is denoted f_j for the signal from the jth satellite. These measured values are in error and differ from the f_{Rj} values by a frequency bias offset. This offset can be related to the drift rate t_u of the user clock relative to GPS system time. The value t_u has the units seconds/second and essentially gives the rate at which the user's clock is running fast or slow relative to GPS system time. The clock drift error, f_j, and f_{Rj} are related by the formula

$$f_{Rj} = f_j(1 + t_u) \tag{2.37}$$

where t_u is considered positive if the user clock is running fast. Substitution of (2.37) into (2.35), after algebraic manipulation, yields

$$\frac{c(f_j - f_{Tj})}{f_{Tj}} + \mathbf{v}_j \cdot \mathbf{a}_j = \dot{\mathbf{u}} \cdot \mathbf{a}_j - \frac{cf_jt_u}{f_{Tj}}$$

Expanding the dot products in terms of the vector components yields

$$\frac{c(f_j - f_{Tj})}{f_{Tj}} + v_{xj}a_{xj} + v_{yj}a_{yj} + v_{zj}a_{zj} = \dot{x}_u a_{xj} + \dot{y}_u a_{yj} + \dot{z}_u a_{zj} - \frac{cf_jt_u}{f_{Tj}} \tag{2.38}$$

where $\mathbf{v}_j = (v_{xj}, v_{yj}, v_{zj})$, $\mathbf{a}_j = (a_{xj}, a_{yj}, a_{zj})$, and $\dot{\mathbf{u}} = (\dot{x}_u, \dot{y}_u, \dot{z}_u)$. All of the variables on the left side of (2.38) are either calculated or derived from measured values. The components of $\mathbf{a}_j$ are obtained during the solution for the user location (which is assumed to precede the velocity computation). The components of $\mathbf{v}_j$ are determined from the ephemeris data and the satellite orbital model. The f_{Tj} can be estimated using (2.36) and the frequency corrections derived from the navigation updates. (This correction, however, is usually negligible and f_{Tj} can normally be replaced by f_0.) The f_j can be expressed in terms of receiver measurements of delta range (see Section 5.1.6 for a more detailed description of receiver processing).

To simplify the above equation, we introduce the new variable d_j, defined by

$$d_j = \frac{c(f_j - f_{Tj})}{f_{Tj}} + v_{xj}a_{xj} + v_{yj}a_{yj} + v_{zj}a_{zj} \tag{2.39}$$

The term f_j/f_{Tj} on the right side in (2.38) is numerically very close to 1, typically within several parts per million. Little error results by setting this ratio to 1. With these simplifications, (2.38) can be rewritten as

$$d_j = \dot{x}_u a_{xj} + \dot{y}_u a_{yj} + \dot{z}_u a_{zj} - c\dot{t}_u$$

We now have four unknowns: $(\dot{x}_u, \dot{y}_u, \dot{z}_u, \dot{t}_u)$, which can be solved by using measurements from four satellites. As before, we calculate the unknown quantities by solving the set of linear equations using matrix algebra. The matrix/vector scheme is

$$\mathbf{d} = \begin{bmatrix} d_1 \\ d_2 \\ d_3 \\ d_4 \end{bmatrix} \quad \mathbf{H} = \begin{bmatrix} a_{x1} & a_{y1} & a_{z1} & 1 \\ a_{x2} & a_{y2} & a_{z2} & 1 \\ a_{x3} & a_{y3} & a_{z3} & 1 \\ a_{x4} & a_{y4} & a_{z4} & 1 \end{bmatrix} \quad \mathbf{g} = \begin{bmatrix} \dot{x}_u \\ \dot{y}_u \\ \dot{z}_u \\ -c\dot{t}_u \end{bmatrix}$$

Note that $\mathbf{H}$ is identical to the matrix used in Section 2.4.2 in the formulation for the user position determination. In matrix notation,

$$\mathbf{d} = \mathbf{Hg}$$

and the solution for the velocity and time drift are obtained as

$$\mathbf{g} = \mathbf{H}^{-1}\mathbf{d}$$

The phase measurements that lead to the frequency estimates used in the velocity formulation are corrupted by errors such as measurement noise and multipath. Furthermore, the computation of user velocity is dependent on user position accuracy and correct knowledge of satellite ephemeris and satellite velocity. The relationship between the errors contributed by these parameters in the computation of user velocity is similar to (2.32). If measurements are made to more than four satellites, least squares estimation techniques can be employed to obtain improved estimates of the unknowns.

2.6 POSITION AND VELOCITY DETERMINATION USING KALMAN FILTERING

The above techniques for obtaining user PVT are derived from measurements that may be corrupted by noise and other error sources. These techniques may yield noisy navigation solutions. A method for computing a smoothed navigation solution is Kalman filtering. (An overview of the Kalman filtering process is provided herein with further elaboration supplied in Chapter 9.) The Kalman filter is a recursive algorithm that provides optimum estimates of user PVT based on noise statistics and current measurements. The filter contains a dynamical model of the GPS receiver platform motion and outputs a set of user receiver PVT state estimates as well as associated error variances. The dynamical model can be derived by a Taylor series expansion about the true position of the receiver. This approach is described below.

Let $\mathbf{u}(t)$ represent the true position of the receiver at time t. Then at time t, shortly after time t_0, the receiver will be at position

$$\mathbf{u}(t) = \mathbf{u}(t_0) + \left.\frac{d\mathbf{u}(t)}{dt}\right|_{t=t_0} (t - t_0) + \frac{1}{2!} \left.\frac{d\mathbf{u}^2(t)}{dt^2}\right|_{t=t_0} (t - t_0)^2 + \frac{1}{3!} \left.\frac{d\mathbf{u}^3(t)}{dt^3}\right|_{t=t_0} (t - t_0)^3 \ldots$$

$$(2.40)$$

where

$$\left.\frac{d\mathbf{u}(t)}{dt}\right|_{t=t_0} = \text{velocity}$$

$$\frac{1}{2!} \left.\frac{d\mathbf{u}^2(t)}{dt^2}\right|_{t=t_0} = \text{acceleration}$$

$$\frac{1}{3!} \left.\frac{d\mathbf{u}^3(t)}{dt^3}\right|_{t=t_0} = \text{jerk}$$

The terms following the third derivative expression representing jerk are usually considered negligible. The nonnegligible terms depend on the system being modeled. Some of these terms may be estimated from position measurements.

Position and velocity for most vehicles change relatively slowly over the time period of the measurements used to estimate them, so that the estimates are reasonably close. The same may not be true for acceleration or jerk in some vehicles. If these terms are nonnegligible, such as perhaps on some aircraft, they are often modeled as random quantities (i.e., white noise), in order to take their effects into account.

Filters designed for PVT determination typically estimate eight user states: position (x_u, y_u, z_u), velocity $(\dot{x}_u, \dot{y}_u, \dot{z}_u)$, receiver clock offset (t_u), and receiver clock drift $(\dot{t}_u)$. A flow diagram for PVT solution processing using a Kalman filter is shown in Figure 2.16. The filter is first initialized with approximate values for each user state. In most cases, the initialization data had been stored in receiver nonvolatile

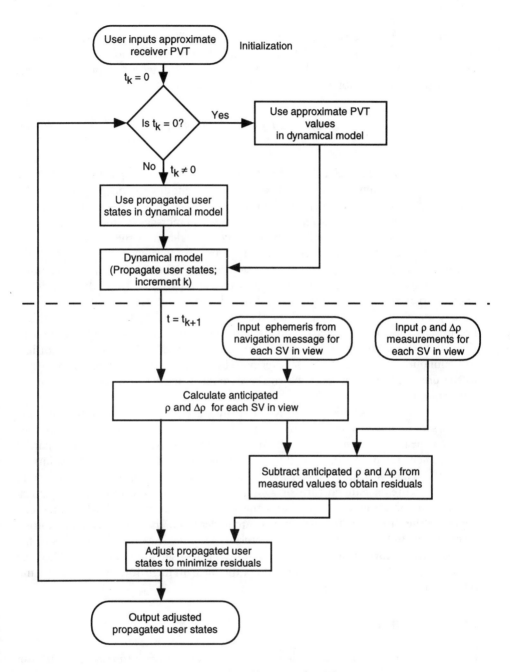

Figure 2.16 User PVT determination with Kalman filtering. (*After*: [1].)

memory when the receiver was last turned off. These initial user state estimate values are input to the dynamical model. Assume that the platform is moving with constant velocity (acceleration and jerk = 0). Therefore, (2.40) would express rectilinear motion (i.e., motion along a straight line) and is reduced to

$$\mathbf{u}(t) = \mathbf{u}(t_0) + \left.\frac{d\mathbf{u}(t)}{dt}\right|_{t=t_0} (t - t_0) \qquad (2.41)$$

As part of the recursive algorithm, the dynamical model propagates the platform position from one time point to the next. Let k represent discrete propogation epochs. After propagating the platform position to next epoch, $k + 1$, the ephemerides for each satellite in view is extracted from the navigation message. Using the propagated user position and velocity estimates, the receiver calculates the anticipated pseudorange and delta pseudorange (i.e., change in pseudorange per epoch) for each satellite. Next, pseudorange and delta pseudorange are then measured and the difference is taken between the anticipated and measured values. These differences are referred to as residuals. If the measured pseudorange and delta pseudorange values exactly match the anticipated values, the residuals would be zero; however, this is not usually the case. Nonzero residuals indicate errors in the user PVT estimates. The filter then adjusts the user state estimates to minimize the residuals according to a minimum mean squared error criterion. These adjusted state estimates are output to the user and are also fed back to the dynamical model to repeat the recursive estimation process [1].

The two key benefits of the Kalman filter are that it can operate with only partial sets of measurements and that it adjusts the state estimates to weight the effects of measurement noise. The filter provides an estimated solution using a partial measurement set until other satellites can be acquired and tracked. The ability to use measurements from less than four satellites is advantageous, such as when an aircraft executes a banked turn or a user is in a forest with an excessively thick canopy. In the latter case, satellite signals will only be received when they can penetrate the canopy or the user moves into a clearing. Also, as measurement noise increases (including SA effects for SPS users), the filter decreases the weights of the measurement information while relying more on the user state estimates. When the noise variance decreases, the filter utilizes the measurement information more and relies on the estimates less [1].

2.7 TIME AND GPS

GPS disseminates a form of UTC that provides the capability for time synchronization of users worldwide. Applications range from data "time-tagging" to communications system packet switching synchronization. Worldwide time dissemination is an especially useful feature in military frequency hopping communications systems where time synchronization permits all users to change frequencies simultaneously.

2.7.1 UTC Generation

UTC is a composite time scale. That is, UTC is comprised of inputs from a time scale derived from atomic clocks and a time scale referenced to the Earth's rotation rate. The time scale based on atomic standards is called International Atomic Time (TAI). TAI is a uniform time scale based on the atomic second, which is defined as the fundamental unit of time in the International System of Units. The atomic second is defined as "the duration of 9,192,631,770 periods of the radiation corresponding to the transition between two hyperfine levels of the ground state of the Cesium 133 atom [13]." The Bureau International des Poids et Mesures (BIPM) is the international body responsible for computing TAI. TAI is derived from an ensemble of atomic standards located at more than 50 timing laboratories in various countries. The BIPM statistically processes these inputs to calculate definitive TAI [14]. TAI is referred to as a "paper" time scale since it is not kept by a physical clock.

The other time scale used to form UTC is called Universal Time 1 (UT1) and is based on the Earth's rotation with respect to the Sun. UT1 is corrected for nonuniformities in the Earth's orbital speed and the inclination of Earth's equator with respect to its orbit plane. It is also corrected for polar motion. UT1 defines the actual orientation of the ECEF coordinate system with respect to space and celestial bodies and is the basic time scale for navigation [13]. Even with these corrections, UT1 remains a nonuniform time scale due to variations in the Earth's rotation. Also, UT1 drifts with respect to atomic time. This is on the order of several milliseconds per day and can accumulate to 1 sec in a 1-year period. The International Earth Rotation Service (IERS) is responsible for definitively determining UT1. Civil and military timekeeping applications require a time scale with UT1 characteristics but with the uniformity of an atomic time scale. UTC is a time scale with these characteristics. The IERS determines when to add or subtract leap seconds to UTC such that the difference between UTC and UT1 does not exceed 0.9 sec. Thus, UTC is synchronized with solar time [14].

The USNO maintains an ensemble of more than 20 cesium standards and using astronomical data forms its own version of UTC, denoted as UTC(USNO). UTC(USNO) is kept within 1 μsec of UTC [15].

2.7.2 GPS System Time

GPS system time (previously referred to as system time) is referenced to UTC(USNO). GPS system time is a "paper" time scale based on statistically processed readings from the atomic clocks in the satellites and at various ground control segment components. GPS system time is a continuous time scale that is not adjusted for leap seconds. GPS system time and UTC(USNO) were coincident at 0 hr January 6, 1980. As of this writing, UTC(USNO) leads GPS system time by 10 sec. The GPS control segment steers GPS system time within 1 μsec of UTC(USNO) (modulo 1 sec) [15]. An epoch in GPS system time is distinguished by the number of seconds that have elapsed since Saturday/Sunday midnight and the GPS week number. GPS weeks are numbered sequentially and originate with week 0, which began at 0 hr January 6, 1980 [14].

2.7.3 Receiver Computation of UTC(USNO)

As mentioned above, the time bias from GPS system time t_u is determined upon computation of the PVT solution. Adding this bias to the receiver clock time t_{rcv} yields GPS system time. The integer number of leap seconds t_n between GPS system time and UTC(USNO) is provided in the navigation message. Therefore, UTC(USNO) can be computed by the receiver as follows:

$$UTC(USNO) = t_{rcv} + t_u + t_n$$

The above computation will yield a value of UTC(USNO) within 200 nsec (95%) of the true UTC(USNO) for PPS users and 340 nsec (95%) for SPS users [16].

References

[1] NAVSTAR GPS Joint Program Office (JPO), *GPS NAVSTAR User's Overview*, YEE-82-009D, GPS JPO, March 1991.

[2] Langley, R., "The Mathematics of GPS," *GPS World Magazine*, Advanstar Communications, July/Aug. 1991, pp. 45–50.

[3] Long, A. C., (ed.) et al., *Goddard Trajectory Determination System (GTDS) Mathematical Theory, Revision 1*, FDD/552-89/001, Greenbelt, MD: Goddard Space Flight Center), July 1989.

[4] Defense Mapping Agency, *World Geodetic System 1984 (WGS-84)—Its Definition and Relationships with Local Geodetic Systems*, DMA TR 8350.2 Second Edition, Fairfax, VA, Defense Mapping Agency.

[5] Heikkinen, M., "Geschlossene Formeln zur Berechnung räumlicher geodätischer Koordinaten aus rechtwinkligen Koordinaten," Zeitschrift für Vermessungswesen, Vol. 5, 1982, pp. 207–211.

[6] Battin, R. H., *An Introduction to the Mathematics and Methods of Astrodynamics*, New York, NY: AIAA, 1987.

[7] Van Dierendonck, A. J., et al., "The GPS Navigation Message," *GPS Papers Published in Navigation*, Vol. I, Washington, DC: Institute of Navigation.

[8] Leva, J., "An Alternative Closed Form Solution to the GPS Pseudorange Equations," *Paper presented at Institute of Navigation (ION) National Technical Meeting*, Anaheim, CA, Jan. 1995.

[9] Bancroft, S., "An Algebraic Solution of the GPS Equations," *IEEE Trans. Aerospace and Electronic Systems*, Vol. AES-21, No. 7, Jan. 1985, pp. 56–59.

[10] Chaffee, J. W., and J. S. Abel, "Bifurcation of Pseudorange Equations," *in Proc. 1993 ION National Technical Meeting*, San Francisco, CA, Jan. 1993, pp. 203–211.

[11] Fang, B. T., "Trilateration and Extension to Global Positioning System Navigation," *Journal of Guidance, Control, and Dynamics*, Vol. 9, No. 6, Nov./Dec. 1986, pp. 715–717.

[12] Hofmann-Wellenhof, B., et al., *GPS Theory and Practice*, Second Edition, New York, NY: Springer-Verlag Wien, 1993.

[13] Seeber, G., *Satellite Geodessy: Foundations, Methods, and Applications*, New York, NY: Walter De Gruyter, 1993.

[14] Langley, R., "Time, Clocks, and GPS," *GPS World Magazine*, Advanstar Communications, Nov./Dec. 1991, pp. 38–42.

[15] Lewandowski, W., and C. Thomas, "GPS Time Transfer," *Proc. of the IEEE*, Vol. 79, No. 7, July 1991.

[16] Department of Defense/Department of Transportation, *1994 Federal Radionavigation Plan*, Springfield, VA, National Technical Information Service, May 1995.

CHAPTER 3
▼▼▼

GPS System Segments

L. F. Wiederholt
Intermetrics, Inc.

E. D. Kaplan
The MITRE Corporation

3.1 OVERVIEW OF THE GPS SYSTEM

The Global Positioning System (GPS) is comprised of three segments: satellite constellation, ground control/monitoring network, and user receiving equipment. Formal GPS Joint Program Office (JPO) programmatic terms for these components are space, operational control, and user equipment segments, respectively. The satellite constellation contains the satellites in orbit that provide the ranging signals and data messages to the user equipment. The operational control segment (OCS) tracks and maintains the satellites in space. The OCS monitors satellite health and signal integrity and maintains the orbital configuration of the satellites. Furthermore, the OCS updates the satellite clock corrections and ephemerides as well as numerous other parameters essential to determining user position, velocity, and time (PVT). Lastly, the user receiver equipment performs the navigation, timing, or other related functions (e.g., surveying). Elaboration on each of the system segments is provided next.

3.1.1 GPS Satellite Constellation

The satellite constellation consists of the nominal 24-satellite constellation. The satellites are positioned in six Earth-centered orbital planes with four satellites in

---

each plane. The nominal orbital period of a GPS satellite is one-half of a sidereal day or 11 hr 58 min [1]. The orbits are nearly circular and equally spaced about the equator at a 60° separation with an inclination relative to the equator of nominally 55°. Figure 3.1 depicts the GPS constellation. The orbital radius (i.e., nominal distance from the center of mass of the Earth to the satellite) is approximately 26,600 km. This satellite constellation provides a 24-hr global user navigation and time determination capability.

Figure 3.2 presents the satellite orbits in a planar projection referenced to the epoch time of 0000 hr July 1, 1993 UTC(USNO). Thinking of the orbits as a "ring," this figure opens each orbit and lays it flat on a plane. Similarly for the Earth's equator, it is like a ring that has been opened and laid on a flat surface. The slope of each orbit represents its inclination with respect to the Earth's equatorial plane,

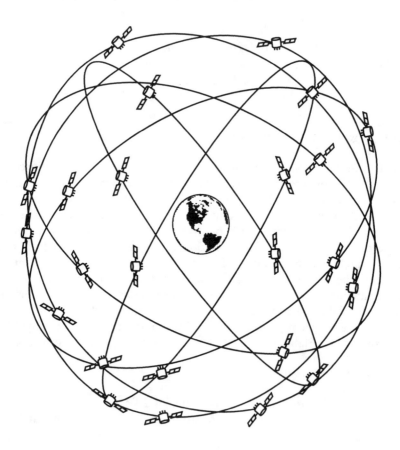

Figure 3.1 GPS satellite constellation.

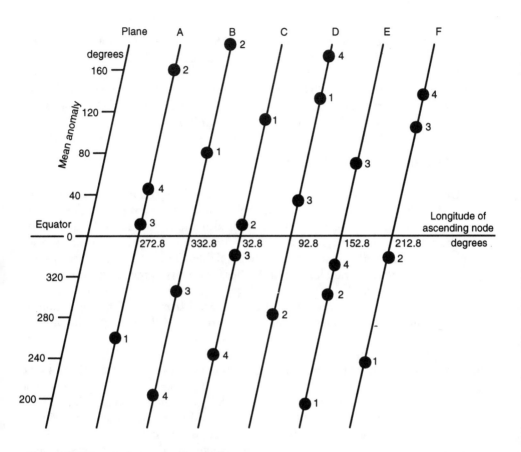

Figure 3.2 GPS constellation planar projection.

which is nominally 55°. The orbital plane locations with respect to the Earth are defined by the longitude of the ascending node while the location of the satellite within the orbital plane is defined by the mean anomaly. The longitude of the ascending node is the point of intersection of each orbital plane with the equatorial plane. The Greenwich meridian is the reference point or point where the longitude of the ascending node has the value of zero. Mean anomaly is the angular position of each satellite within the orbit with the Earth's equator being the reference or point with a zero value of mean anomaly. It can be observed that the relative phasing between most satellites in adjoining orbits is approximately 40°.

Several different notations are used to refer to the satellites in their orbits. One nomenclature assigns a letter to each orbital plane (i.e., A, B, C, D, E, and F) with each satellite within a plane assigned a number from 1 to 4. Thus, a satellite referenced as B3 refers to satellite number 3 in orbital plane B. A second notation used is a

NAVSTAR satellite number assigned by the U.S. Air Force. This notation is in the form of space vehicle number (SVN) 11 to refer to NAVSTAR satellite 11. The third notation represents the configuration of the pseudorandom (PRN) code generators onboard the satellite. These PRN code generators are configured uniquely on each satellite, thereby producing unique versions of both C/A-code and P(Y)-code. Thus, a satellite can be identified by the PRN codes that it generates.

3.1.2 Operational Control Segment (OCS)

The OCS has responsibility for maintaining the satellites and their proper functioning. This includes maintaining the satellites in their proper orbital positions (called station keeping) and monitoring satellite subsystem health and status. The OCS also monitors the satellite solar arrays, battery power levels, and propellant levels used for maneuvers and activates spare satellites (if available). The OCS updates each satellite's clock, ephemeris, and almanac and other indicators in the *navigation message* once per day or as needed. The ephemeris parameters are a precise fit to the GPS satellite orbits and are valid only for a time interval from 4 to 6 hr depending on the time from the last control segment upload based on the once-per-day normal upload schedule.

Depending on the satellite version, the navigation message data can be stored for a minimum 14 days to a maximum of 210 days duration in intervals of 4 or 6 hr. The almanac is a reduced precision subset of the ephemeris parameters. The almanac consists of 7 of the 15 ephemeris orbital parameters. Almanac data is used to predict the approximate satellite position and aid in satellite signal acquisition.

Furthermore, the OCS resolves satellite anomalies, controls SA and AS (see Sections 1.3.1 and 4.1.1), and makes pseudorange and delta range measurements at the remote monitor stations to determine satellite clock corrections, almanac, and ephemeris.

To accomplish the above functions, the control segment is comprised of three different physical components: the master control station (MCS), monitor stations, and the ground antennas. Each of these facilities is described in the following sections.

3.1.2.1 OCS Operations

An overview of control segment operations is presented in Figure 3.3. The MCS is the center of the control segment operations and is located at Falcon Air Force Base, Colorado Springs, CO. The monitor stations passively track the GPS satellites as they pass overhead by making pseudorange and delta range measurements. These measurements are made using both the L1 and L2 GPS satellite downlink frequencies. (L1 and L2 and their associated modulation formats are described in Section 4.1.1.) This raw data, in addition to the received navigation message and local weather

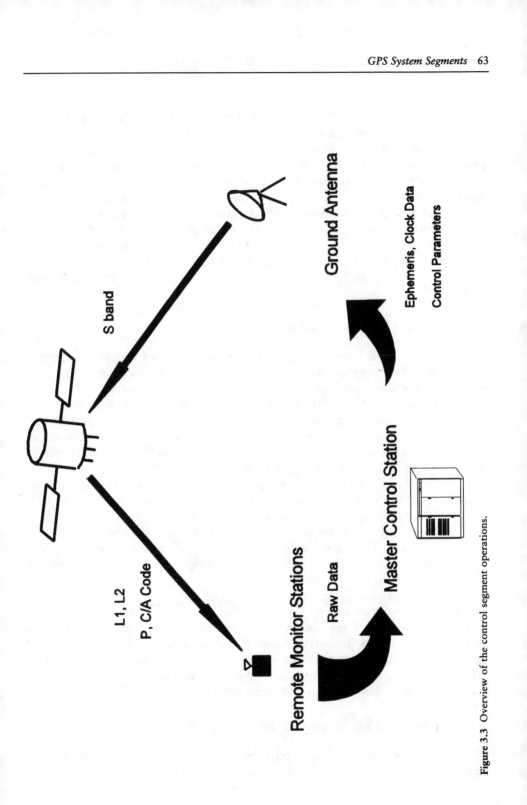

Figure 3.3 Overview of the control segment operations.

data, is transmitted to the MCS via the Defense Satellite Communications System and other ground communications systems.

The MCS processes data from the monitor stations for satellite navigation payload control. Data from all the monitor stations is used to form satellite clock corrections, ephemeris and almanac data for each satellite. This processing is described below in Section 3.1.2.4. The MCS also monitors the configuration status of satellites and ground stations. Satellite processor diagnostics can be requested and the satellite clock can be updated. The geographic distribution of the control segment facilities is depicted in Figure 3.4. A backup master control station is located at Gaithersburg, MD. This backup MCS is a temporary contractor facility. At the time of this writing, there is a DOD effort underway to move it to Vandenberg AFB, CA.

3.1.2.2 Monitor Stations Description

The monitor stations form the data collection component of the control segment. A monitor station contains a dual-frequency (L1/L2) GPS receiver that continuously makes pseudorange and delta range measurements to each satellite in view. The location of the phase center of the receiver's antenna is precisely known. The monitor station also contains two cesium clocks referenced to GPS system time. Pseudorange and delta range measurements made to each satellite in view by each monitor station receiver update the master control station's precise Kalman filter statistical estimate of each satellite's position, velocity, and timing (PVT).

The satellite transmissions are refracted and, hence, delayed by both the ionosphere and the troposphere. (Elaboration on these effects is found in Section 7.1.2.) The monitor station receiver dual-frequency measurements enable the MCS to determine the ionospheric delay for satellites within the monitor station satellite field of view. Temperature, barometric pressure, and humidity data are provided to the MCS by U.S. government weather services to aid in tropospheric delay determination within the region of each monitor station.

There are five monitor stations located at Colorado Springs, Kwajalein, Ascension Island, Hawaii, and Diego Garcia. Within the near future, a monitor station will be operational at Cape Canaveral, FL. A photograph of the monitor station and the ground uplink antenna at Diego Garcia is presented in Figure 3.5. These facilities are unmanned and provide approximately 92% tracking coverage of the GPS satellites [2]. That is, the satellites are not continuously visible to the monitor stations. As stated above, all collected data are transmitted to the MCS for processing.

3.1.2.3 Ground Uplink Antenna Facility Description

The ground uplink antenna facility provides the means of commanding and controlling the satellites and uploading the navigation messages and other data. A ground

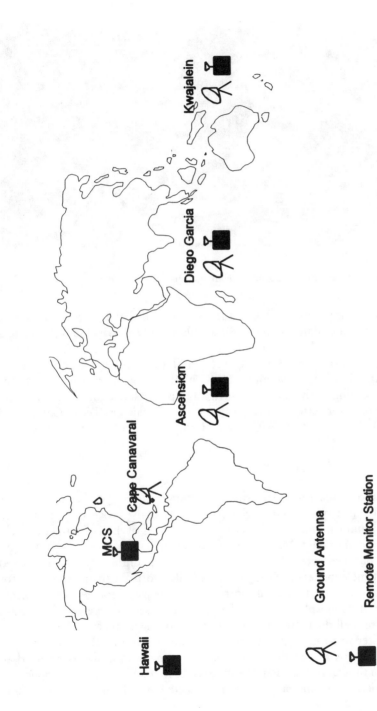

Figure 3.4 Geographic distribution of the control segment facilities.

Figure 3.5 Photo of monitor station and ground uplink antenna at Diego Garcia.

uplink antenna facility stores and uploads what is called the TT&C (telemetry, tracking, and command) data. A unique TT&C data set (which includes the navigation message) is prepared by the MCS for each satellite. This data is forwarded to the ground antenna from the MCS and stored until a particular satellite is in view. Once in view, an S-band data communication uplink is used to transmit data to the satellite for forwarding to the satellite's navigation processor. Ground antennas are collocated with monitor stations at Ascension Island, Kwajalein, Diego Garcia, and Cape Canaveral. These locations have been selected to maximize satellite coverage.

3.1.2.4 Master Control Station Processing

As mentioned above, the MCS performs a multitude of functions to support the operation of GPS as a system. One principal activity is the processing of the data collected at the remote monitor stations to form estimates of the GPS satellite clock, ephemeris, and almanac data. Many steps are involved in this processing [3, 4], with the major steps outlined here. The detailed processing is continually evolving based on control segment experience. With the data collected from the remote monitor stations, the processing starts with the correction of the pseudorange measurements for tropospheric and ionospheric delays. The corrected pseudorange and delta range measurements from all the remote monitor stations are then processed by an epoch-state Kalman filter to form a precise satellite ephemeris and clock offset solution. An epoch-state filter is a filter that maintains its estimates at a time different than the measurement times. For this filter, the state is maintained at the time of applicability of the ephemeris while measurements are collected at different times. This filter is updated every 15 min with the satellite positions computed in the ECEF Cartesian coordinate system. This process provides an accurate estimate of a satellite's ephemeris and clock offset at the time of the data collection. To be of use to a GPS user at some later time, these states must be predicted forward. The satellite position and clock corrections are predicted forward in time using precise models of the spacecraft and its environment. This model, called force integration, is a set of differential equations describing the dynamic behavior of the satellite. The force integration model includes the significant forces operating on the space vehicle over the prediction interval that have been identified as the gravity field perturbations, the sun and moon third-body mass attractions, spacecraft solar radiation pressure, and Earth UT1 and polar motion perturbations.

The prediction interval described above is subdivided into either 4- or 6-hr time intervals since the start of the prediction time. For each subdivided interval, the predicted satellite Cartesian position data is transformed to 15 orbital elements using a least squares fit algorithm. (These elements are described in Section 2.3) The ephemeris data is thus valid only over that interval. The almanac and clock data are also formed from this accurately predicted data. From this least squares fit data, the content of the navigation message in accordance with [5] is formed by scaling and truncating the ephemeris, almanac, and clock data to the described format. The fitted data set for each time interval is then uploaded to the satellites' navigation payload for storage and transmission to the user.

Another important element of the MCS processing is monitoring the reliability of the system. The control segment must take meticulous care to ensure that all clock and ephemeris data uploads and other signal transmissions are correct. This monitoring is done principally through the MCS data processing. The MCS computes the upload navigation messages, maintains an image of that satellite message for comparison, monitors the uploading of data, and verifies the correct transmission by the satellite. The OCS also monitors satellite L-band signal behavior and issues an alarm to MCS personnel within 60 sec of a detected failure.

3.1.3 User Receiving Equipment

The user receiving equipment, typically referred to as a "GPS receiver," processes the L-band signals transmitted from the satellites to determine user PVT. There has been a significant evolution, almost revolution, in the technology of GPS receiving sets, paralleling that of the electronics industry in general. The move has been from analog to digital solid state devices and surface-mount technology wherever feasible. The initial receiving sets manufactured in the mid-1970s as part of the concept validation phase were principally analog devices for military application, which were large, bulky, and heavy. With today's technology, a GPS receiver of comparable or more capability typically weighs a few pounds (or ounces) and occupies a small volume. The smallest sets today are those of "wrist watch" size while probably the largest is a naval shipboard unit with a footprint of 1,550 cm² (232.5 in²) and weight of 70 lb (mass of 31.8 kg). Selection of a GPS receiver depends on the user's application (e.g., civilian versus military, platform dynamics, etc.). Following a description of a typical receiver's components, selection criteria are addressed.

3.1.3.1 GPS Set Characteristics

A block diagram of a GPS receiving set is shown in Figure 3.6. The GPS set consists of five principal components: antenna, receiver, processor, input/output (I/O) device such as a control display unit (CDU), and a power supply.

Antenna

Satellite signals are received via the antenna, which is right-hand circularly polarized (RHCP) and provides near hemispherical coverage. Typical coverage is 160° with gain variations from about 2.5 dBic at zenith to near unity at an elevation angle of 10°. (The RHCP antenna unity gain also can be expressed as 0 dBic = 0 dB with respect to an isotropic circularly polarized antenna.) Below 10°, the gain is usually

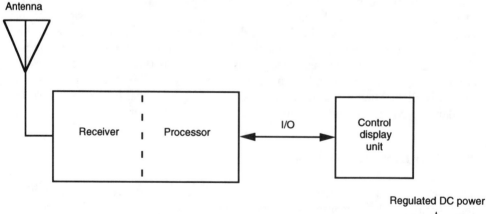

Figure 3.6 Principle GPS receiver components.

negative. Since the satellite signals are RHCP, a conical helix antenna or variation is suitable. GPS receivers that track P(Y)-code on both L1 and L2 need to accommodate 20.46-MHz bandwidths on both frequencies. If the set only tracks C/A-code on L1, the antenna (and receiver) must have a bandwidth of at least 2.046 MHz. Antenna designs vary from helical coils to thin microstrip (i.e., patch) antennas. High-dynamic aircraft prefer low profile, low air resistance patch antennas whereas land vehicles can tolerate a larger antenna. Antenna selection requires evaluation of parameters such as antenna gain pattern, available mounting area, aerodynamic performance, multipath performance, and stability of the electrical phase center of the antenna [6]. Another issue regarding antenna selection is the need for resistance to interference. (In the context of this discussion, any electronic emission whether "friendly" or hostile that interferes with the reception and processing of GPS signals is considered an interferer.) Some military aircraft employ beam steering or adaptive nulling arrays to resist interference. Beam steering techniques electronically concentrate the antenna gain in the direction of the satellites to maximize link margin. An adaptive nulling array is electronically steerable and creates nulls in the antenna pattern that are in the direction of the interferer [7] (see also Section 6.1.2.5).

Receiver

Chapter 5 provides a detailed description of receiver signal acquisition and tracking operation; however, some high-level aspects are described herein to aid our discussion.

Two basic receiver types exist today: (1) those that track both P(Y)-code and C/A-code and (2) those that only track C/A-code. PPS users generally employ sets that track P(Y)-code on both L1 and L2. These sets initiate operation with receivers tracking C/A-code on L1 tracking and then switch to tracking P(Y)-code on either L1 or L2. Y-code tracking occurs only with the aid of cryptographic equipment. (If the satellite signal is encrypted and the receiver does not have the proper cryptographic equipment, the receiver generally defaults to tracking C/A-code on L1.) On the other hand, SPS users employ sets that track the C/A-code exclusively on L1 since that is the only frequency that the C/A-code is generally broadcast on. Of these two basic receiver types, there are other variations such as codeless L2 tracking receivers, which track the C/A-code on L1 and carrier phase of both the L1 and L2 frequencies. Utilizing the carrier phase as a measurement observable enables centimeter-level (or even millimeter-level) measurement accuracy. Carrier-phase measurements are described extensively in Section 8.3.

Most receivers have multiple channels whereby each channel tracks the transmission from a single satellite. A simplified block diagram of a multichannel generic SPS receiver is shown in Figure 3.7. The received RF CDMA satellite signals are usually filtered by a passive bandpass prefilter to reduce out-of-band RF interference.

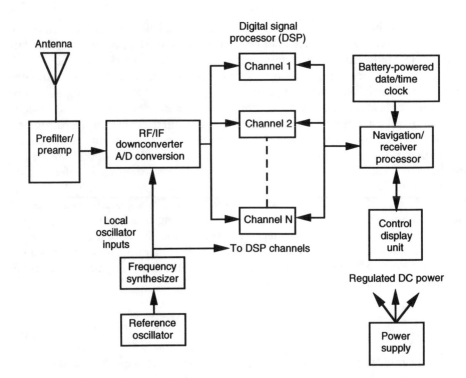

Figure 3.7 Generic SPS receiver.

This is normally followed by a preamplifier. The RF signals are then downconverted to an intermediate frequency (IF). In a typical modern GPS receiver design, the IF signals are sampled and digitized by an analog to digital (A/D) converter. The A/D sampling rate is typically eight to twelve times the PRN code chipping rate (1.023 MHz for L1 C/A-code and 10.23 MHz for L1 and L2 P(Y)-code.) The minimum sampling rate is twice the stopband bandwidth of the codes to satisfy the Nyquist criterion. For L1 C/A-code only sets, the stopband bandwidth may be slightly greater than 2 MHz. On the other hand, the stopband bandwidth is slightly more than 20 MHz for P(Y)-code sets. Oversampling reduces the receiver sensitivity to A/D quantization noise, thereby reducing the number of bits required in the A/D converter. The samples are forwarded to the digital signal processor (DSP). The DSP contains N parallel channels to simultaneously track the carriers and codes from up to N satellites. (N generally ranges from 5 to 12 in today's receivers.) Each channel contains code and carrier tracking loops to perform code and carrier-phase measurements as well as navigation message data demodulation. The channel may compute three different satellite-to-user measurement types: pseudoranges, delta ranges (sometimes referred to as delta pseudorange), and integrated Doppler, depending on the implementation. The desired measurements and demodulated navigation message data are forwarded to the processor.

Navigation/Receiver Processor

A processor is generally required to control and command the receiver through its operational sequence, starting with channel signal acquisition and followed by signal tracking and data collection. (Some GPS sets have an integral processing capability within the channel circuitry to perform these signal processing functions.) In addition, the processor may also form the PVT solution from the receiver measurements. In some applications, a separate processor may be dedicated to the computation of both PVT and associated navigation functions. Most processors provide an independent PVT solution on a 1-Hz basis. However, receivers designated for autoland aircraft precision approach and other high-dynamic applications normally require computation of independent PVT solutions at a minimum of 5 Hz. The formulated PVT solution and other navigation-related data is forwarded to the I/O device.

Input/Output Device

The I/O device is the interface between the GPS set and the user. I/O devices are of two basic types: integral or external. For many applications, the I/O device is a CDU. The CDU permits operator data entry, displays status and navigation solution parameters, and usually accesses numerous navigation functions such as waypoint entry, time-to-go, etc. Most handheld units have an integral CDU. Other installations, such as those onboard an aircraft or ship, may have the I/O device integrated with existing instruments or control panels. In addition to the user and operator interface, applications such as integration with other sensors (e.g., INS) require a digital data interface to input and output data. Common interfaces are ARINC 429, MIL-STD-1553B, RS-232, and RS-422.

Power Supply

The power supply can be either integral, external, or a combination of the two. Typically, alkaline or lithium batteries are used for integral or self-contained implementations, such as handheld portable units; whereas an existing power supply is normally used in integrated applications, such as board-mounted receivers installed inside personal computers. Airborne, automotive, and shipboard GPS set installations normally use platform power but typically have built-in power converters (ac to dc or dc to dc) and regulators. There usually is an internal battery to maintain data stored in volatile random access memory (RAM) integrated circuits (ICs) and to operate a built-in timepiece (date/time clock) in the event platform power is disconnected.

3.1.3.2 GPS Receiver Selection

At the time of this writing, there are over 50 GPS set manufacturers producing over 200 different GPS set versions [8]. GPS receiver selection is dependent on user application. The intended application strongly influences receiver design, construction, and capability. For each application, numerous environmental, operational, and performance parameters must be examined. A sampling of these parameters is provided below:

- Shock and vibration requirements, temperature and humidity extremes, as well as atmospheric salt content.
- If the receiver is to be used by government and/or military personnel, PPS operation may be required. PPS operation usually dictates that a dual-frequency set with a cryptographic capability is needed.
- The necessary independent PVT update rate must be determined. As an example, this rate is different for aircraft precision approach than for marine oil tanker guidance.
- Under what type of dynamic conditions (e.g., acceleration, velocity) will the set have to operate? GPS sets for fighter aircraft applications are designed to maintain full performance even while experiencing multiple "g's" of acceleration, whereas sets designated for surveying are not normally designed for severe dynamic environments.
- Is a differential GPS (DGPS) capability required? (DGPS is an accuracy enhancement technique covered in Chapter 8.) DGPS provides greater accuracy than standalone PPS and SPS. Most receivers are manufactured with a DGPS capability.
- Does the application require reception of a geostationary satellite-based overlay service (e.g., INMARSAT) broadcasting GPS and/or GLONASS satellite integrity, ranging, and DGPS information? (The INMARSAT overlay is described in Chapter 11.)
- Waypoint storage capability as well as the number of routes and legs need to be assessed.
- Does the GPS set have to operate in an environment that requires enhanced interference rejection capabilities? Chapter 6 describes several techniques to achieve this.
- If the receiver has to be interfaced with an external system, does the proper I/O hardware and software exist?

- In terms of data input and display features, does the receiver require an external or integral CDU capability. Some aircraft and ships use "repeater" units such that data can be entered or extracted from various physical locations. Display requirements such as sunlight-readable or night-vision-goggle-compatible must be considered.
- Are local datum conversions required, or is WGS-84 sufficient? If so, does the receiver contain the proper transformations?
- Is portability for field use required?
- Economics, physical size, and power consumption must also be considered.

As stated above, these are only a sampling of GPS set selection parameters. One must carefully review the requirements of the user application prior to selecting a receiver. In most cases, the selection will be a tradeoff that requires awareness of the impact of any GPS set deficiencies for the intended application.

3.2 SPACE SEGMENT PHASED DEVELOPMENT

The development of the control and space segments has been phased in over many years starting in the mid-1970s and is continuing. This development started with a concept validation phase and has progressed to the production phase. The satellites associated with each phase of development are called a block of satellites. Characteristics of each phase and block are presented in the following sections.

3.2.1 Characteristics Summary of Satellite Block

Three satellite blocks have been deployed and two more blocks are planned. The initial concept validation satellites were called Block (BLK) I. The last remaining prototype BLK I satellite, PRN 12, was disposed of in the fall of 1995. Block II satellites are the initial production satellites while Block IIA refers to the upgraded production satellites. Blocks I, II, and IIA have been launched and are in service. At the time of this writing, Block IIR satellites, called the replenishment satellites, are in production. Block IIF satellites, referred to as the follow-on or sustainment satellites, are in the planning stage.

Nine BLK II satellites and fifteen BLK IIA comprise the nominal constellation. Four other BLK IIA satellites have been purchased and will be used to replace failed satellites or satellites deemed unusable by MCS personnel. When all four of these extras are deployed, Block IIR satellites will then be used as replacements. BLK IIR satellites are scheduled for replenishment in the 1997–2004 timeframe. Block IIF satellite launches are planned for the post-2004 timeframe. A tabulation of the NAVSTAR satellites and their respective orbital locations is contained in Table 3.1.

Table 3.1
Satellite Constellation Configuration (as of July 1996)

Block	Satellite Number PRN	SVN	Launch Date	Orbit
II	14	14	Feb. 89	E1
II	02	13	June 89	B3
II	16	16	Aug. 89	E3
II	19	19	Oct. 89	A4
II	17	17	Dec. 89	D3
II	18	18	Jan. 90	F3
II	20	20	Mar. 90	B2
II	21	21	Aug. 90	E2
II	15	15	Oct. 90	D2
IIA	23	23	Nov. 90	E4
IIA	24	24	July 91	D1
IIA	25	25	Feb. 92	A2
IIA	28	28	April 92	C2
IIA	26	26	July 92	F2
IIA	27	27	Sept. 92	A3
IIA	01	32	Nov. 92	F1
IIA	29	29	Dec. 92	F4
IIA	22	22	Feb. 93	B1
IIA	31	31	Mar. 93	C3
IIA	07	37	May 93	C4
IIA	09	39	June 93	A1
IIA	05	35	Aug. 93	B4
IIA	04	34	Oct. 93	D4
IIA	06	36	Mar. 94	C1
IIA	03	33	Mar. 96	C2

3.2.2 Navigation Payload

The navigation payload is that part of the satellite which is responsible for reception of data from the OCS, intersatellite ranging (only on the BLK IIR and BLK IIF versions) and the transmission of ranging codes and navigation data to the user community. The navigation payload is only one part of the spacecraft with other systems being responsible for such functions as attitude control and solar panel pointing. Figure 3.8 is a generic block diagram of a navigation payload. The OCS TT&C function is responsible for uploading data and command and control information to the satellite. This data is stored in processor memory. The frequency standards subsystem contains the atomic frequency standards, of which there are currently two cesium and two rubidium standards on each production satellite. (The BLK IIR replenishment satellites contain one cesium standard and two rubidium standards.)

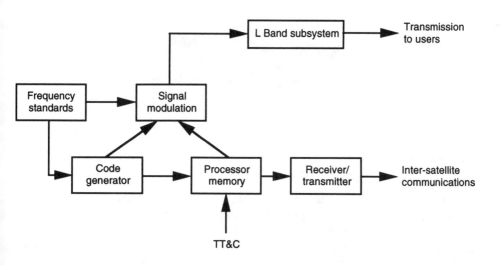

Figure 3.8 Satellite navigation payload.

Of these multiple atomic standards, one is designated as the primary and serves as the timing reference onboard the space vehicle for navigation signal generation and transmission. The other atomic standards are for redundancy. The code generator generates the C/A-code and P(Y)-codes for modulo-2 addition with the navigation message data, which are then sent to the L-band subsystem for transmission to the user. The L-band subsystem contains the L1/L2 synthesizers and associated antennas. The processor memory also interfaces to the receiver/transmitter for intersatellite ranging on BLK IIR and BLK IIF versions. This receiver/transmitter uses a separate antenna and feed system.

In addition to the GPS navigation payload, other missions have been added to the space vehicle over the course of time. These non-GPS-related missions have included a nuclear detonation detection and location payload, laser reflectors for satellite laser ranging (i.e., validation of predicted ephemeris), and free electron measurement experiments.

3.2.3 Block I-Initial Concept Validation Satellites

Block I satellites were developmental prototypes to validate the initial GPS concept, so only eleven satellites were built. The Block I satellites, built by Rockwell International, were launched between 1978 and 1985 from Vandenberg Air Force Base, California. A picture of the Block I satellite is presented in Figure 3.9. The onboard storage capability was for 14 days of navigation messages. In this satellite version, the navigation message data was only valid for a 1-hr period. Since there was no onboard

GPS Block I

Figure 3.9 BLK I satellite.

momentum management, frequent ground contact was required for momentum management. Without such management, the satellites would lose attitude determination after a short time interval. Two cesium and two rubidium atomic frequency standards were employed. These satellites were designed for a mean mission duration of 4.5 years, a design life of five years and inventory expendable (e.g. fuel, battery life, and solar panel power capacity) of seven years. Reliability improvements were made to the atomic clocks on later satellites based on failure analysis from earlier launches. Some Block I satellites operated for more than double their design life.

3.2.4 Block II-Initial Production Satellites

On-orbit operation of the Block I satellites provided valuable experience that led to several significant capability enhancements in subsystem design for the Block II satellites. These improvements included radiation hardening to prevent random memory upset from events such as cosmic rays to improve reliability and survivability. Besides these enhancements, several other refinements were incorporated to support the fully operational GPS system requirements. While most of the changes affected only the control segment/space interface, some also affected the user signal interface. The significant changes are identified as the following. To provide security, SA and AS capabilities were added. System integrity was improved by the addition of automatic error detection for certain error conditions. After detection of these error conditions, there is a changeover to the transmission of a nonstandard pseudorandom code to prevent the usage of a corrupted signal or data.

Nine Block II satellites were built by Rockwell International and the first was launched in February 1989 from Cape Canaveral Air Force Station, Florida. The onboard navigation message storage capacity is identical to the Block I version. With no autonomous onboard momentum control, frequent ground contact is required for its momentum management. With no momentum control, the satellites may start to tumble between 28 and 45 days after the last ground contact, thus their data upload is only accurate for 14 days. Again, for reliability and survivability, multiple rubidium and cesium atomic standards are onboard. These satellites were designed for a mean mission duration of 6 years, a design life of 7.5 years and inventory expendables (e.g., fuel, battery life, and solar pane power capacity) of 10 years. Figure 3.10 is a depiction of a BLK II satellite.

3.2.5 Block IIA-Upgraded Production Satellites

The Block IIA satellites are very similar to the Block II satellites, but with several system enhancements. The onboard navigation message data storage capability had been increased to 180 days of reference data. For the first 14 days on-orbit, navigation message data is valid over 4-hr intervals. Following this initial on-orbit period, the navigation message data validity interval is extended to 6 hours. With this additional onboard storage capability, the satellites can function continuously for a period of six months without ground support. The OCS is limited in its ability to forecast satellite ephemeris and clock data because orbital perturbations are nonpredictable. Therefore, the accuracy of the navigation message data will gracefully degrade over time such that the user range error (URE) will be bounded by 10,000m after 180 days. (The URE is the contribution of the pseudorange error from the OCS and space segment.) Typically, the URE is 5.5 m (1σ) based on fresh uploads of navigation message data every day. Details of pseudorange errors are extensively discussed in Section 7.1.2. With no general onboard processing capability, no updates to stored reference ephemeris data are possible. So, as a result, full system accuracy is only available when the OCS is functioning properly and navigation messages are uploaded on a daily basis; otherwise, the prediction error in the ephemeris data increases. An autonomous onboard momentum management capability has been added; therefore, less frequent ground contact is required. BLK IIA electronics are radiation hardened. Nineteen Block IIA satellites were built by Rockwell International and the first was launched in November 1990 from Cape Canaveral Air Force Station, Florida. The life expectancy of the Block IIA is the same as that of the Block II. A BLK IIA satellite is shown in Figure 3.11.

GPS Block II

Figure 3.10 BLK II satellite.

GPS Block IIA

Figure 3.11 Block IIA satellite.

3.2.6 Block IIR-Replenishment Satellites

Twenty satellites have been purchased as replenishment satellites to replace inoperative Block II/IIA satellites as they reach the end of their design life or fail catastrophically. The first Block IIR satellite is scheduled for launch in 1997. These satellites are being built by Lockheed Martin. To the user, the signal and data transmissions will be identical to the Block II/IIA satellites. While the changes are transparent to the user, the system-level operations are much different from the earlier satellites. A new capability of the satellites called autonomous navigation (AutoNav) permits the satellites to maintain their own ephemeris and clock data for 180 days by ranging off other visible satellites. To support this autonomous operation, the OCS uploads a 210-day set of predicted ephemeris and clock elements every 30 days to have data for a full 180 days of autonomous operation. With uploading of data only every 30 days, it is necessary to upload 210 days of data to ensure a full 180 days of operation with no ground contact. This can be clarified by considering the worst case scenario, which is if a failure of the OCS occurred on the last day before the 30-day upload, there would still be 180 days of uploaded data available with this approach. An upload of less than 210 days would result in a capability of less than 180 days of continued operation in this case.

AutoNav is designed to operate for the 180-day period during which the URE is bounded by 5.3m. In addition, AutoNav has the capability to monitor the integrity of the GPS system such that when AutoNav is operational, the reliability and integrity of the system are improved. The AutoNav function uses a crosslink capability for ranging and data communication between satellites. This crosslink is a radiofrequency link that receives and transmits digital data and performs precision intersatellite ranging. Two-way crosslink range measurements are used to update clock and ephemeris data relative to the stored reference data set. The crosslink uses a frequency-hopped time division multiple access (TDMA) structure. The AutoNav function can be activated or deactivated by the OCS. When AutoNav is inactive, the Block

IIR satellite operates like a Block IIA in that it transmits navigation message data from its computer memory. The crosslink data capability also permits relaying data between satellites. The Block IIR satellites have an onboard processing capability using a MIL-STD-1750A (i.e., space qualified) processor to implement the AutoNav and other functions. The onboard software was developed using the computer language Ada throughout.

One cesium and two rubidium atomic frequency standards are used for increased reliability and survivability. The BLK IIR satellites are designed for a mean mission duration of 7.5 years, a design life of 10 years and inventory expendables (e.g., fuel, battery life, and solar panel power capacity) of 10 years.

An artist's depiction of a BLK IIR satellite is shown in Figure 3.12. It can be observed that the exterior of the spacecraft is composed of an array of elements and components. The two large panels on each side extending from the main body of the spacecraft are solar panels to provide the satellite's electrical power. The bottom of the spacecraft is referred to as the Earth panel because of its orientation to the Earth. On this panel are a collection of antennas. The L-band antennae are arranged with the UHF and S-band antennae. In a small box-like compartment of the spacecraft body are located the thrusters used for maneuvering and stationkeeping. All other electronics, processors, and controllers are located inside the spacecraft body.

3.2.7 Block IIF-Follow-On "Sustainment" Satellites

As the Block IIR satellites are launched and reach their end of life, the Air Force will need a procurement to replace failing Block IIR satellites. This procurement is known as the Block IIF Sustainment Program. The DOD has defined the requirements for this program and awarded a contract to Rockwell International. The development timeframe will be such that the satellites will be available for launch in the 2004 timeframe. The potential enhancements are many. One such enhancement is a crosslink capability for all satellite commands to update status and health thus reducing the OCS workload.

3.2.8 Summary of Satellite Block Features and Error Budget

The key features of the various satellite Blocks are summarized in Table 3.2. This tabulation depicts the progression of satellite capability and functionality as GPS has matured to an operational system.

Figure 3.12 Block IIR satellite. (*Source:* Lockheed Martin, Inc. Reprinted with permission.)

Table 3.2
Summary of BLK II, IIA, and IIR Features

Block Number	AutoNav	Data Storage: Ephemeris/ Clock (Days)	Momentum Management	Period of Autonomous Operation (Days)	URE at End of Period of Autonomous Operation (m)
II	No	14	OCS	14	161.1
IIA	No	180	Onboard	180	< 10,000
IIR	Yes	210	Onboard	180	7.4

References

[1] Bates, R., et al., *Fundamentals of Astrodynamics*, New York, NY: Dover Publications, Inc., 1971.

[2] Lavrakas, J., and C. Shank, "Inside GPS: The Master Control Station," *GPS World Magazine*, Advanstar Communications, Sept. 1994, pp. 46–54.

[3] Brown, K. R., "Characterizations of OCS Kalman Filter Errors," *Proc. 4th ION Satellite Division International Technical Meeting*, Albuquerque, NM, Sept. 11–13, 1991, pp. 149–158.

[4] Scardera, M. P., "The NAVSTAR GPS Master Control Station's Kalman Filter Experience," *Flight Mechanics/Estimation Theory Symposium 1990*, NASA Conference Proceedings CP3102, 1991.

[5] ARINC Research Corporation, *NAVSTAR GPS Space Segment/Navigation User Interfaces ICD-GPS-200*, Public Release Version, April 16, 1993, Reprinted by Navtech Seminars, Arlington, VA.

[6] Seeber, G., *Satellite Geodesy: Foundations, Methods, and Applications*, New York, NY: Walter De Gruyter, 1993.

[7] Kaplan, E., "The Global Positioning System (GPS)," *Communications Quarterly*, CQ Communications, Inc., Summer 1994.

[8] "1995 GPS World Receiver Survey," *GPS World Magazine*, Advanstar Communications, Jan. 1995, pp. 46–67.

CHAPTER 4

▼▼▼

GPS SATELLITE SIGNAL CHARACTERISTICS

Phillip Ward
NAVWARD GPS Consulting

4.1 GPS SIGNAL CHARACTERISTICS

In this chapter, we examine the properties of the GPS satellite signals including frequency assignment, modulation format, and the generation of pseudorandom noise (PRN) codes. This discussion is accompanied by a description of received signal power levels as well as their associated autocorrelation characteristics. Cross-correlation characteristics are also described.

The GPS space vehicles (SVs) transmit two carrier frequencies called L1, the primary frequency, and L2, the secondary frequency. The carrier frequencies are modulated by spread spectrum codes with a unique PRN sequence associated with each SV and by the navigation data message. All SVs transmit at the same two carrier frequencies, but their signals do not interfere significantly with each other because of the PRN code modulation. Since each SV is assigned a unique PRN code and all of the PRN code sequences are nearly uncorrelated with respect to each other, the SV signals can be separated and detected by a technique called code division multiple access (CDMA). In order to track one SV in common view with several other SVs by the CDMA technique, a GPS receiver must replicate the PRN sequence for the desired SV along with the replica carrier signal, including Doppler effects. Two carrier frequencies are provided to permit the two-frequency user to measure the ionospheric delay since this delay is related by a scale factor to the difference in signal time of arrival (TOA) for the two carrier frequencies. Single frequency (L1 only) users must estimate the ionospheric delay using modeling parameters that are broadcast to the user in the navigation message. The characteristics of these signals are further explained in the following paragraphs.

4.1.1 Frequencies and Modulation Format

A block diagram that is representative of the SV signal structure for L1 (154 f_0) and L2 (120 f_0) is shown in Figure 4.1. Not shown in this figure is the signal structure for the nuclear detonation (NUDET) detection system (NDS) payload on the Block II and higher model numbered SVs. The NDS payload on GPS is beyond the scope of this book and will not be further discussed.

As shown in Figure 4.1, the L1 frequency (154 f_0) is modulated by two PRN codes (plus the navigation message data), the coarse/acquisition code (C/A-code), also called the clear/acquisition code, and the precision code (P-code). The L2 frequency (120 f_0) is modulated by only one PRN code at a time. One of the P-code modes has no data modulation. The nominal reference frequency f_0 as it appears to an observer on the ground is 10.23 MHz. To compensate for relativistic effects (see Section 7.1.2), the output of the SV's frequency standard (as it appears from the SV) is 10.23 MHz offset by a $\Delta f / f$ of -4.467×10^{-10}. This results in a Δf of -4.57×10^{-3} Hz and, excluding the effects of SA, $f_0 = 10.22999999543$ MHz [1]. To the GPS receiver on the ground, the C/A-code has a chipping rate of 1.023×10^6 chips/sec ($f_0/10 = 1.023$ MHz) and the P-code has a chipping rate of 10.23×10^6 chips/sec ($f_0 = 10.23$ MHz). (The term "chip" is used instead of "bit" to convey that no data information is in the PRN codes.) The precision code can be denied to SPS users if the control segment activates an antispoofing (AS) mode in the SV. When AS is activated, the P-code is encrypted to form what is known as the Y-code. The Y-code has the same chipping rate as the P-code. Thus, the acronym often used for the precision code is P(Y)-code. AS denies access to the P-code by SPS users. Both the C/A-code and the P(Y)-code as well as the L1 and L2 carrier frequencies are subjected to the encrypted dither frequency of SA. This SA phase modulation effect creates a pseudorandom Doppler error on both the pseudorange and delta pseudorange measurements. This SA error can be removed by the PPS user, but cannot be corrected by the SPS user. In addition, SA encrypts an offset error into the satellite's broadcast ephemeris and almanac data. This causes a position error for the SPS user. Further elaboration on SA is provided in Section 7.1.2.

Note in Figure 4.1 that the 50 bits per second (bps) data is combined with both the C/A-code and the P(Y)-code prior to modulation with the L1 carrier. This combination uses the exclusive-or process, denoted by $\oplus$. Since the C/A-code $\oplus$ data and P(Y)-code $\oplus$ data is a synchronous operation, the bit transition rate cannot exceed the chipping rate of the PRN codes. Also note that biphase shift key (BPSK)

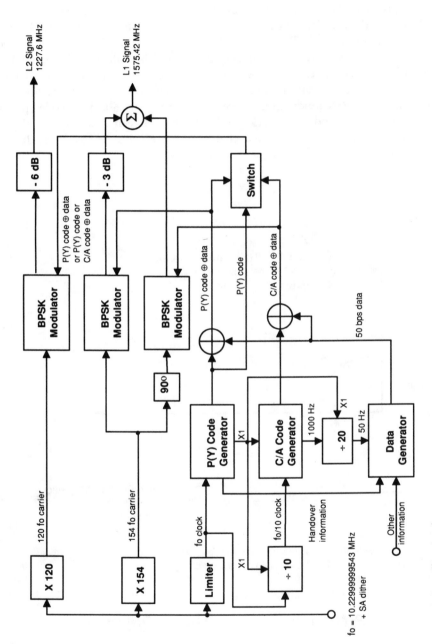

Figure 4.1 GPS satellite signal structure.

modulation is used. The P(Y)-code ⊕ data is modulated in-phase quadrature with the C/A-code ⊕ data on L1. Thus, there is a 90° phase shift between the C/A-code ⊕ data modulation and the P(Y)-code ⊕ data modulation on these two combined L1 carrier frequencies. This is illustrated by the vector phase diagram in Figure 4.2. Figure 4.3 illustrates the result of C/A ⊕ data and P-code ⊕ data. The exclusive-or process is equivalent to binary multiplication of two one-bit values. Therefore, this is equivalent to a BPSK modulation process. There are 204,600 P(Y)-code epochs between data epochs and 20,460 C/A-code epochs between data epochs, so the number of times that the phase could change in the PRN code sequences due to data modulation is relatively infrequent.

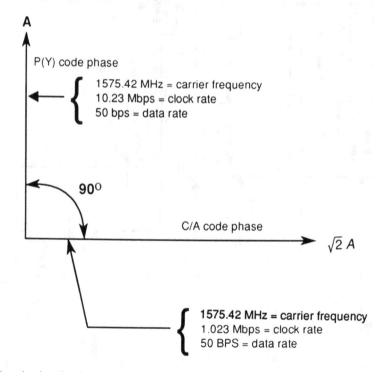

P(Y) code signal = long secure code with 50 bps data
C/A code signal = 1023 chip Gold code with 50 bps data

$$L_i(\omega_1, t) = A[P_i(t) \oplus D_i(t)]\cos(\omega_1 t) + \sqrt{2}\, A[G_i(t) \oplus D_i(t)]\sin(\omega_1 t)$$

Figure 4.2 GPS signal structure for L1.

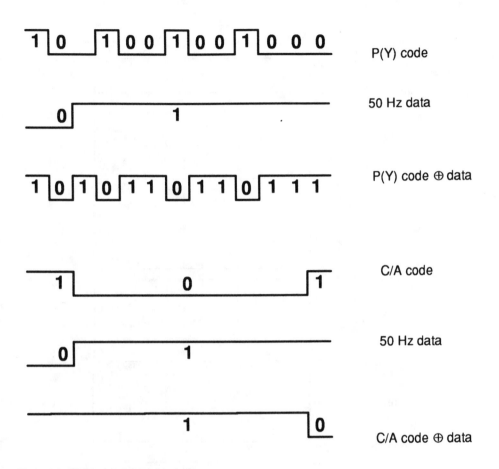

Figure 4.3 GPS code mixing with data.

Figure 4.4 illustrates how the signal waveforms would appear before and after the BPSK modulation of one P(Y)-code ⊕ data transition and one C/A-code ⊕ data transition. This is also equivalent to a BPSK modulation process. There are 154 carrier cycles per P(Y)-code chip and 1,540 carrier cycles per C/A-code chip on L1, so the phase shifts on the L1 carrier are relatively infrequent.

The L2 frequency (1,227.60 MHz) can be modulated by either the P(Y)-code ⊕ data or the C/A-code ⊕ data or with P(Y)-code alone as selected by the control segment. P(Y)-code and C/A-codes are never present simultaneously on L2, as is the case with L1. In general, P(Y)-code ⊕ data is the one selected by the control segment. There are 120 carrier cycles per P(Y)-code chip on L2, so the phase transitions on the L2 carrier are relatively infrequent. Table 4.1 summarizes the GPS signal structure on L1 and L2.

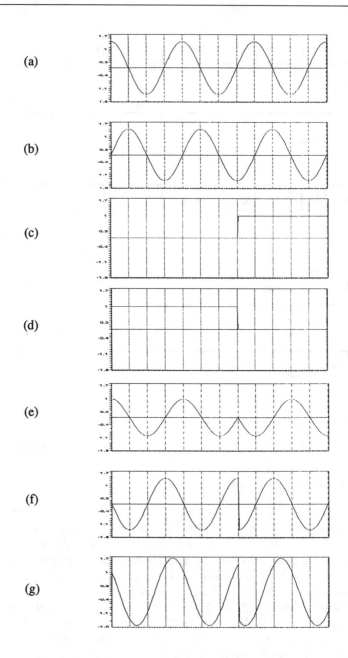

Figure 4.4 GPS L1 carrier modulation: (a) L1 carrier (0° phase), (b) L1 carrier (90° phase), (c) P(Y) code ⊕ data, (d) C/A code ⊕ data, (e) P(Y) code ⊕ data BPSK modulation on L1 carrier (0° phase) with 3dB attenuation, (f) C/A code ⊕ data BPSK modulation on L1 carrier (90° phase), and (g) composite modulated L1 carrier signal.

Table 4.1
GPS Signal Structure

Signal Priority	Primary	Secondary
Signal designation	L1	L2
Carrier frequency (Hz)	$1,575.42 \times 10^6$	$1,227.60 \times 10^6$
PRN codes (chips/sec)	P(Y) = 10.23×10^6 and	P(Y) = 10.23×10^6 or
	C/A = 1.023×10^6	C/A = $1.023 \times 10^{6*}$
Navigation message data modulation (bps)	50	50†

*The code usually selected by the control segment on L2 is P(Y)-code.
†The 50-Hz navigation data message is usually modulated on L2 P(Y)-code, but can be turned off by the control segment to improve jamming performance. There are three possibilities: P(Y)-code with data, P(Y)-code with no data, and C/A-code with data.

There is more than one atomic standard in each SV for purposes of redundancy to improve reliability, but only one at a time is selected as the reference frequency in the SV by the control segment. For example, there are two cesium and two rubidium atomic standards on the Block II and IIA SVs.

The PPS user has access to all signals on L1 and L2 and to the full accuracy of GPS. PPS users have the classified algorithms and the classified key to remove the dither and epsilon errors. However, differential GPS techniques have successfully mitigated the effects of SA on SPS users. (DGPS is discussed extensively in Chapter 8.) The PPS user has the algorithms, the special Y-code hardware per channel (called the auxiliary output chip (AOC)) and the key to gain access to the Y-code. The use of the AS Y-code denies direct (SPS GPS receiver) access to the precision code. This significantly reduces the possibility of an enemy spoofing a PPS receiver; that is, transmitting a stronger, false precise code that captures and misleads the receiver. However, AS also denies direct access to the precision code to all SPS users, friendly or otherwise.

Since there is usually no C/A-code on L2, this has the consequence of denying direct two-frequency operation to SPS users when AS is activated by the control segment. Therefore, the SPS user is limited to the L1 C/A-code. As a result, the single frequency SPS user must model the ionospheric delay instead of measuring it, which is less accurate. However, there are indirect "codeless" means of obtaining the two-frequency ionospheric measurements. The codeless designs operate at a significantly reduced signal-to-noise ratio (SNR), which requires the tracking loop bandwidths to be extremely narrow. This, in turn, reduces their ability to operate in a high-dynamic environment. As a result of AS, codeless commercial two-frequency GPS receivers have been developed. The typical codeless receiver design uses a conventional C/A-code receiver to effectively remove the line-of-sight dynamics from the L1 and L2 Y-code signals. The codeless receiver tracks the L1-L2 differential measurements by some technique that does not require a knowledge of the Y-code, such as squaring the P-code or replicating the P-code and estimating the encrypted code. The use of the conventional C/A-code receiver obtains the broadcast navigation message and identifies the SV being tracked in the codeless mode. Two SVs with the same Doppler will interfere with each other when the signal squaring codeless technique is used; therefore, the squaring scheme fails for this temporary tracking condition.

4.1.1.1 *Direct Sequence PRN Code Generation*

Figure 4.5 depicts a high-level block diagram of the direct sequence PRN code generation used in GPS to implement the CDMA technique. Each synthesized PRN code is derived from two other code generators. In each case, the second code generator output is delayed with respect to the first before their outputs are combined by an exclusive-or circuit. The amount of delay is variable. Associated with the amount of delay is the SV PRN number. In the case of P-code, the integer delay is the same as the PRN number. For C/A-code, the delay is unique to each SV. These delays are summarized in Table 4.2. The C/A-code delay can be implemented by a simple but equivalent technique that eliminates the need for a delay register. This technique is explained in the following paragraphs.

The GPS C/A-code is a Gold code [2] with a sequence length of 1,023 bits (chips). Since the chipping rate of the C/A-code is 1.023 MHz, then the repetition period of the pseudorandom sequence is $1023/1.023 \times 10^6$ or 1 millisecond. Figure 4.6 illustrates the design architecture of the GPS C/A-code generator. Not included in this diagram are the controls necessary to set or read the phase states of the registers or the counters. There are two 10-bit shift registers, G1 and G2, which generate maximum length pseudonoise (PN) codes with a length of $2^{10} - 1 = 1,023$ bits. (The one state that the shift register must not get into is the all-zero state). It is common to describe the design of linear code generators by means of polynomials of the form $1 + \Sigma x^i$, where x^i means that the output of the *i*th cell of the shift register is used as the input to the modulo-2 adder (exclusive or) and the 1 means that the output of the adder is fed to the first cell [3]. The design specification for C/A-code calls for the feedback taps of the G1 shift register to be connected to stages 3 and 10. These register states are combined with each other by an exclusive-or circuit and fed back to stage 1. The polynomial that describes this shift register architecture is: $G1 = 1 + X^3 + X^{10}$. The polynomials and initial states for both the C/A-code and P-code generator shift registers are summarized in Table 4.3. The unique C/A-code for each SV is the result of the exclusive-or of a delayed version of the G2 output sequence and the G1 direct output sequence. The delay effect in the G2 PN code is obtained by the exclusive-or of the selected positions of the two taps whose output is called G21. This is because a PN code sequence

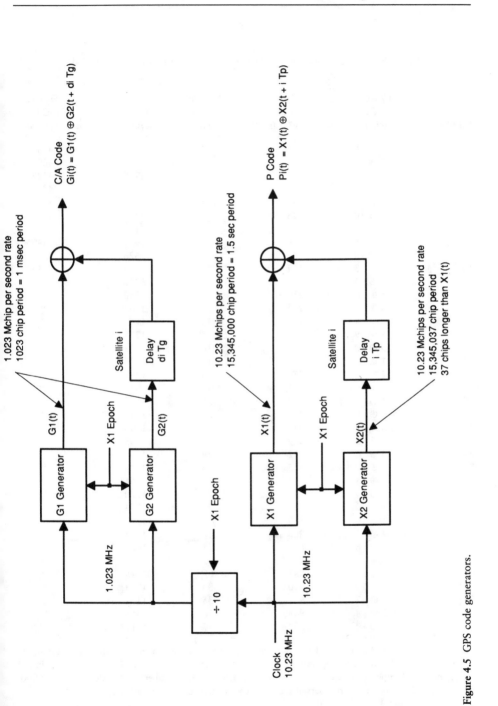

Figure 4.5 GPS code generators.

Table 4.2
Code-Phase Assignments and Initial Code Sequences for C/A-Code and P-Code

SV PRN Number	C/A-Code Tap Selection	C/A-Code Delay (Chips)	P-Code Delay (Chips)	First 10 C/A-Chips (Octal)*	First 12 P-Chips (Octal)
1	2 ⊕ 6	5	1	1440	4444
2	3 ⊕ 7	6	2	1620	4000
3	4 ⊕ 8	7	3	1710	4222
4	5 ⊕ 9	8	4	1744	4333
5	1 ⊕ 9	17	5	1133	4377
6	2 ⊕ 10	18	6	1455	4355
7	1 ⊕ 8	139	7	1131	4344
8	2 ⊕ 9	140	8	1454	4340
9	3 ⊕ 10	141	9	1626	4342
10	2 ⊕ 3	251	10	1504	4343
11	3 ⊕ 4	252	11	1642	"
12	5 ⊕ 6	254	12	1750	"
13	6 ⊕ 7	255	13	1764	"
14	7 ⊕ 8	256	14	1772	"
15	8 ⊕ 9	257	15	1775	"
16	9 ⊕ 10	258	16	1776	"
17	1 ⊕ 4	469	17	1156	"
18	2 ⊕ 5	470	18	1467	"
19	3 ⊕ 6	471	19	1633	"
20	4 ⊕ 7	472	20	1715	"
21	5 ⊕ 8	473	21	1746	"
22	6 ⊕ 9	474	22	1763	"
23	1 ⊕ 3	509	23	1063	"
24	4 ⊕ 6	512	24	1706	"
25	5 ⊕ 7	513	25	1743	"
26	6 ⊕ 8	514	26	1761	"
27	7 ⊕ 9	515	27	1770	"
28	8 ⊕ 10	516	28	1774	"
29	1 ⊕ 6	859	29	1127	"
30	2 ⊕ 7	860	30	1453	"
31	3 ⊕ 8	861	31	1625	"
32	4 ⊕ 9	862	32	1712	"
33†	5 ⊕ 10	863	33†	1745	"
34†	4 ⊕ 10	950‡	34	1713‡	"
35†	1 ⊕ 7	947	35	1134	"
36†	2 ⊕ 8	948	36	1456	"
37†	4 ⊕ 10	950‡	37	1713‡	4343

*In the octal notation for the first 10 chips of the C/A-code as shown in this column, the first digit (1) represents a "1" for the first chip and the last three digits are the conventional octal representation of the remaining 9 chips. For example, the first 10 chips of the SV PRN number 1 C/A-code are 1100100000.
†PRN codes 33 through 37 are reserved for other uses (e.g., ground transmitters).
‡C/A-codes 34 and 37 are identical.

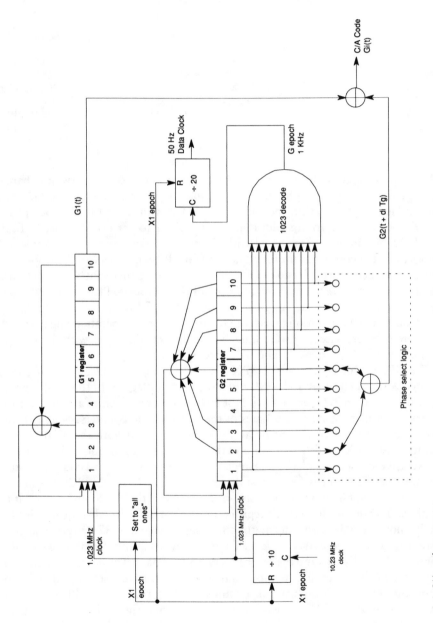

Figure 4.6 C/A-code generator.

Table 4.3
GPS Code Generator Polynomials and Initial States

Register	Polynomial	Initial State
C/A-code G1	$1 + X^3 + X^{10}$	1111111111
C/A-code G2	$1 + X^2 + X^3 + X^6 + X^8 + X^9 + X^{10}$	1111111111
P-code X1A	$1 + X^6 + X^8 + X^{11} + X^{12}$	001001001000
P-code X1B	$1 + X^1 + X^2 + X^5 + X^8 + X^9 + X^{10} + X^{11} + X^{12}$	010101010100
P-code X2A	$1 + X^1 + X^3 + X^4 + X^5 + X^7 + X^8 + X^9 + X^{10} + X^{11} + X^{12}$	100100100101
P-code X2B	$1 + X^2 + X^3 + X^4 + X^8 + X^9 + X^{12}$	010101010100

has the property that, added to a phase-shifted version of itself, it does not change but simply obtains another phase. The function of the two taps on the G2 shift register in Figure 4.6 is to shift the code phase in G2 with respect to the code phase in G1 without the need for an additional shift register to perform this delay. Each C/A-code PRN number is associated with the two tap positions on G2. Table 4.2 describes these tap combinations for all defined GPS PRN numbers and also specifies the equivalent delay in C/A-code chips. The first 32 of these PRN numbers are reserved for the space segment. Five additional PRN numbers, PRN 33 to PRN 37, are reserved for other uses such as ground transmitters (GTs). GTs were used during Phase I (concept demonstration phase) of GPS to validate the operation and accuracy of the system before satellites were launched and in combination with the earliest satellites. The GT C/A-codes 34 and 37 are identical.

The GPS P-code is generated by PN sequences using four 12-bit shift registers designated $X1A$, $X1B$, $X2A$ and $X2B$. A detailed block diagram of this shift register architecture is shown in Figure 4.7 [1]. Not included in this diagram are the controls necessary to set or read the phase states of the registers and counters. Note that the $X1A$ register output is combined by an exclusive-or circuit with the $X1B$ register output to form the $X1$ code generator and that the $X2A$ register output is combined by an exclusive-or circuit with the $X2B$ register output to form the $X2$ code generator. The composite $X2$ result is fed to a shift register delay of the SV PRN number in chips and then combined by an exclusive-or circuit with the $X1$ composite result to generate the P-code. With this shift register architecture, the P-code sequence length would be more than 38 weeks in length, but is partitioned into 37 unique sequences that are truncated at the end of 1 week. Therefore, the sequence length of each PRN code is 6.1871×10^{12} chips and the repetition period is 7 days. The design specification for the P-code calls for each of the four shift registers to have a set of feedback taps that are combined by an exclusive-or circuit with each other and fed back to their respective input stages. The polynomials that describe the architecture of these feedback shift registers are shown in Table 4.3 and the logic diagram is shown in detail in Figure 4.7.

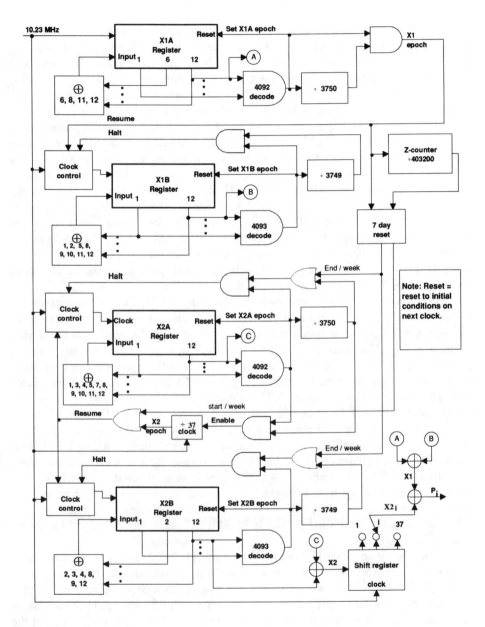

Figure 4.7 P-code generator.

Referring to Figure 4.7, the natural cycles of all four feedback shift registers are truncated as follows: X1A and X2A are reset after 4,092 chips, eliminating the last three chips of their natural 4,095 chip sequence and the registers X1B and X2B are reset after 4,093 chips, eliminating the last two chips of their natural 4,095 chip sequences. This results in the phase of the X1B sequences lagging by one chip with respect to the X1A sequences for each X1A register cycle. As a result, there is a relative phase precession between the X1A and X1B registers. A similar phase precession takes place between X2A and X2B. At the beginning of the GPS week all of the shift registers are set to their initial states simultaneously, as shown in Table 4.3. Also, at the end of each X1A epoch, the X1A shift register is reset to its initial state. At the end of each X1B epoch, the X1B shift register is reset to its initial state. At the end of each X2A epoch, the X2A shift register is reset to its initial state. At the end of each X2B epoch, the X2B shift register is reset to its initial state. The outputs (stage 12) of the A and B registers are combined by an exclusive-or circuit to form an X1 sequence derived from $X1A \oplus X1B$, and an X2 sequence derived from $X2A \oplus X2B$. The X2 sequence is delayed by i chips (corresponding to SV_i) to form $X2_i$. The P-code for SV_i is $P_i = X1 \oplus X2_i$.

There is also a phase precession between the X2A/X2B shift registers with respect to the X1A/X1B shift registers. This is manifested as a phase precession of 37 chips per X1 period between the X2 epochs (shown in Figure 4.7 as the output of the divide by 37 counter) and the X1 epochs. This is caused by adjusting the X2 period to be 37 chips longer than the X1 period. The details of this phase precession are as follows. The X1 epoch is defined as 3,750 X1A cycles. When X1A has cycled through 3,750 of these cycles or $3,750 \times 4,092 = 15,345,000$ chips, a 1.5-sec X1 epoch occurs. When X1B has cycled through 3,749 cycles of 4,093 chips per cycle, it is kept stationary for 343 chips by halting its clock control until the 1.5-sec X1 epoch resumes it. Therefore, the X1 registers have a combined period of 15,345,000 chips. X2A and X2B are controlled in the same way as X1A and X1B, respectively, but with one difference: when 15,345,000 chips have completed in exactly 1.5 sec, both X2A and X2B are kept stationary for an additional 37 chips by halting their clock controls until the X2 epoch or the start of the week resumes it. Therefore, the X2 registers have a combined period of 15,345,037 chips, which is 37 chips longer than the X1 registers.

Note that if the P-code were generated by $X1 \oplus X2$, and if it were not reset at the end of the week, it would have the potential sequence length of $15,345,000 \times 15,345,037 = 4.1547 \times 10^{14}$ chips. With a chipping rate of 10.23×10^6, this sequence has a period of 266.41 days or 38.058 weeks. However, since the sequence is truncated at the end of the week, each SV uses only one week of the sequence and 38 unique one-week PRN sequences are available. As in the case of C/A-code, the first 32 PRN sequences are reserved for the space segment and PRN 33 to 37 are reserved for other uses. The PRN 38 P-code is sometimes used as a test code in P(Y)-code GPS receivers as well as to generate a reference noise level (since, by definition, it cannot correlate with any used SV PRN signals). The unique P-code for each SV is the result of the different delay in the X2 output sequence. Table 4.2 shows this delay in P-code chips for each SV PRN number. The P-code delays (in P-code chips) are identical to their respective PRN numbers for the SVs, but the C/A-code delays (in C/A-code chips) are different from their PRN numbers. The C/A-code delays are typically much longer than their PRN numbers. The replica C/A-codes for a conventional GPS receiver are usually synthesized by programming the tap selections on the G2 shift register. Future generation C/A-code generators may require the use of the variable chip delay (or an equivalent alternative design) if more C/A-codes are added to accommodate geostationary satellites or ground transmitters, which transmit differential and integrity information.

Table 4.2 also shows the first 10 C/A-code chips and the first 12 P-code chips in octal format starting from the beginning of the week. For example, the binary sequence for the first 10 chips of PRN 5 C/A-code is 1001011011, and for the first 12 chips of PRN 5 P-code is 100011111111. Note that the first 12 P-code chips of PRN 10 to PRN 37 are identical. This number of chips is insignificant for P-code, so the differences in the sequence do not become apparent until later in the sequence.

4.1.2 Power Levels

Table 4.4 summarizes the minimum received power levels for the three GPS signals. The levels are specified in terms of decibels with respect to 1W (dBw). The specified received GPS signal power [1] is based on a linearly polarized antenna with 3-dB gain. Since the GPS SVs transmit right-hand circularly polarized (RHCP) signals, the table is adjusted for a typical RHCP antenna with unity gain. The RHCP antenna unity gain also can be expressed as: 0 dBic = 0 dB with respect to an isotropic circularly polarized antenna. The resulting RHCP antenna received signal level is slightly stronger than the minimum specified received signal.

Table 4.4
Minimum Received GPS Signal Power

Parameter	L1 C/A-Code	L1 P(Y)-Code	L2 P(Y)-Code or C/A-Code
User minimum received power at 3-dB gain linearly polarized antenna (dBw)	−160.0	−163.0	−166.0
Adjustment for unity gain antenna (dB)	−3.0	−3.0	−3.0
Adjustment for typical RHCP antenna vs. linearly polarized antenna (dB)	3.4	3.4	3.8
User minimum received power at unity gain RHCP antenna (dBw)	−159.6	−162.6	−165.2

Figure 4.8 illustrates that the minimum received power is met when the SV is at two elevation angles: 5° from the user's horizon and at the user's zenith. In between these two elevation angles, the minimum received signal power levels gradually increase up to 2-dB maximum for the L1 signals and up to 1-dB maximum for the L2 signal, and then decrease back to the specified minimums. This characteristic occurs because the shaped beam pattern on the SV transmitting antenna arrays can

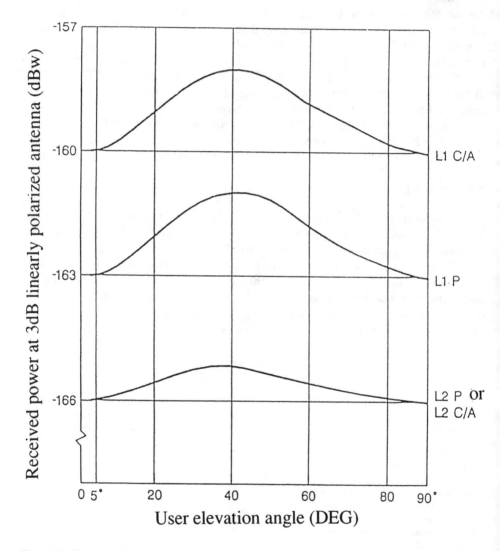

Figure 4.8 User received minimum signal power levels.

only match the required gain at the angles corresponding to the center of the Earth and to near the edge of the Earth, resulting in slightly increasing transmitting antenna array gain in between these nadir angles. The user's antenna gain pattern is typically maximum at the zenith and minimum at 5° (above the horizon) and for lower elevation angles.

The received signal levels are not expected to exceed −153.0 dBw and −155.5 dBw, respectively, for the C/A-code and P(Y)-code components on the L1 channel, nor −158.0 dBw for either signal on the L2 channel. In general, the signal powers for the SVs are at their maximum levels when the satellites are new and drop off near their end of life, although the SV orbits that result in the Earth blocking the sun can also have an effect on the available signal power. The signal power variations over the SV lifetime are therefore expected to be less than 7.0 dB, 7.5 dB, and 8.0 dB, respectively, for the L1 C/A-code, L1 P(Y)-code, and L2 P(Y)-code (or L2 C/A-code).

Table 4.5 tabulates the navigation satellite signal power budget for the BLK II GPS satellites adapted from [4] using the minimum user received power levels as the starting point. It shows the output power levels at the worst case off-axis angle of 14.3° and for the assumed worst case atmospheric loss of 2 dB. Referring to Table 4.5, the link budget for the L1 C/A-code to provide the signal power with a unity gain transmitting antenna is − 160.0 − 3.0 + 184.4 + 2.0 + 3.4 = 26.8 dBw. Since the satellite L1 antenna array has a minimum gain of 13.4 dB for C/A-code at the worst case off-axis angle of 14.3°, the minimum L1 antenna transmitter power for C/A-code is $\log^{-1}[(26.8 - 13.4)/10] = 21.88\text{W}$.

Note that a minimum of 32.60W of L1 power and 6.61W of L2 power (for a total of 39.21W) must be delivered to the satellite antenna arrays to maintain the specification. The efficiency of the high-power amplifier (HPA) subassembly determines how much actual power must be provided in the satellite.

Table 4.5
L1 and L2 Navigation Satellite Signal Power Budget

Parameter	L1 P-Code	L1 C/A-Code	L2
User minimum received power	−163.0 dBw	−160.0 dBw	−166.0 dBw
Users linear antenna gain	3.0 dB	3.0 dB	3.0 dB
Free-space propagation loss	184.4 dB	184.4 dB	182.3 dB
Total atmospheric loss	2.0 dB	2.0 dB	2.0 dB
Polarization mismatch loss	3.4 dB	3.4 dB	4.4 dB
Required satellite EIRP	+23.8 dBw	+26.8 dBw	+19.7 dBw
Satellite antenna gain @ 14.3° worst case BLK II off-axis angle	13.5 dB	13.4 dB	11.5 dB
Required minimum satellite antenna input power	+10.3 dBw 10.72W	+13.4 dBw 21.88W	+8.2 dBw 6.61W

4.1.3 Autocorrelation Functions and Power Spectral Densities

The autocorrelation characteristics of the GPS PRN codes are fundamental to the signal demodulation process. The power spectral densities of the GPS PRN codes determine the channel bandwidths required to transmit and receive the spread spectrum signals. The similarities to the GPS PRN codes will become apparent as the autocorrelation functions and the power spectrum are analyzed for the following binary signals: a rectangular pulse, a random binary code, and a maximum length PN code sequence. Figure 4.9 depicts the spectrum, the autocorrelation function and the power spectrum of a single rectangular pulse, $f_1(t)$, whose amplitude is A and whose pulse width is one chip, T_c [5]. The rectangular pulse is placed symmetrically about the time axis origin (which makes it a theoretical but not a realizable time pulse). The equation for the rectangular pulse shown in Figure 4.9(a) is given by

$$
\begin{aligned}
f_1(t) &= A \qquad |t| \le T_c/2 \\
f_1(t) &= 0 \qquad \text{elsewhere}
\end{aligned}
\tag{4.1}
$$

The Fourier transform of this function shown in Figure 4.9(b) is

$$
F_1(\omega) = AT_c \left(\frac{\sin \dfrac{\omega T_c}{2}}{\dfrac{\omega T_c}{2}} \right)
\tag{4.2}
$$

where

$\omega \quad = \ 2\pi f \ (\text{rad/sec})$
$f \quad = \ \text{frequency (Hz)}$

The autocorrelation of this function is defined as

$$
R_1(\tau) = \int_{-\infty}^{\infty} f_1(t)f_1(t + \tau)dt
\tag{4.3}
$$

where $\tau =$ the phase shift of the replica function.

It is very important to understand the mathematical process of autocorrelation, since a very similar process takes place in a GPS receiver during the code search and tracking process. The autocorrelation function involves replicating the function and then shifting its phase while multiplying it with the original function. When the phase of the replica is the same as the original function, $\tau = 0$, the maximum correlation is obtained. For the rectangular pulse, the autocorrelation function is a triangular waveform; that is, its correlation amplitude drops linearly as τ is shifted

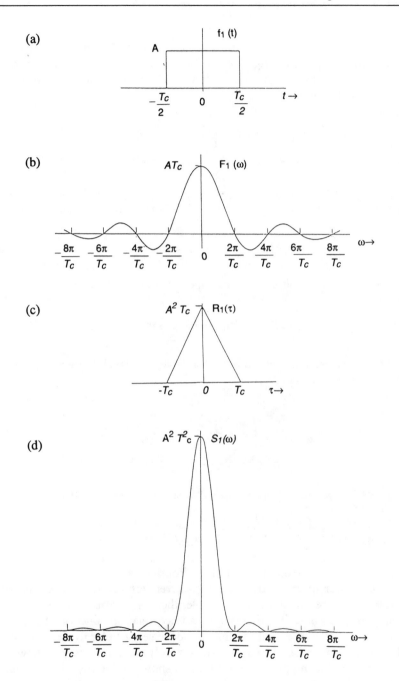

Figure 4.9 (a) A rectangular pulse showing (b) the spectrum, (c) autocorrelation function, and (d) power spectrum.

to the left or to the right of zero until the correlation amplitude becomes zero when τ is shifted to the left or to the right of the original function by $T_c/2$ or more. The resulting triangular autocorrelation function of the rectangular pulse, shown in Figure 4.9(c), is defined as

$$R_1(\tau) = A^2 T_c \left(1 - \frac{|\tau|}{T_c} \right) \qquad \text{for } |\tau| \leq T_c$$

$$R_1(\tau) = 0 \qquad\qquad\qquad \text{elsewhere} \tag{4.4}$$

Since the power spectrum is a real function, it can be determined from the following equation for the Fourier transform of the autocorrelation function of $R_1(\tau)$:

$$S_1(\omega) = \int_{-\infty}^{\infty} R_1(\tau) \cos\omega\tau \, d\tau \tag{4.5}$$

For the rectangular pulse, the power spectrum as determined by (4.5) is

$$S_1(\omega) = \int_{-T_c}^{T_c} A^2 (T_c - |\tau|) \cos\omega\tau \, d\tau \tag{4.6}$$

The power spectrum as determined from (4.6) is the well-known curve shown in Figure 4.9(d) whose equation is

$$S_1(\omega) = A^2 T_c^2 \left(\frac{\sin \dfrac{\omega T_c}{2}}{\dfrac{\omega T_c}{2}} \right)^2 \equiv A^2 T_c^2 \, \text{sinc}^2 \frac{\omega T_c}{2} \tag{4.7}$$

Note that the power spectrum in (4.7) also can be derived from the Fourier transform in (4.2) as

$$S_1(\omega) = |F_1(\omega)|^2 \tag{4.8}$$

Because many time functions do not have Fourier transforms, the usual process is to obtain the power spectrum from the autocorrelation function since this can be obtained for every time function. For example, there is no Fourier transform for a truly random binary code, but there is an autocorrelation function. In fact, the autocorrelation function of a random binary code is very similar to the autocorrelation of the rectangular pulse of (4.1). If $r(t)$ is a truly random binary code with an amplitude of $\pm A$, and a chipping period of T_c, as shown in Figure 4.10(a), then the autocorrelation function illustrated in Figure 4.10(b) is defined in equation form as [3]

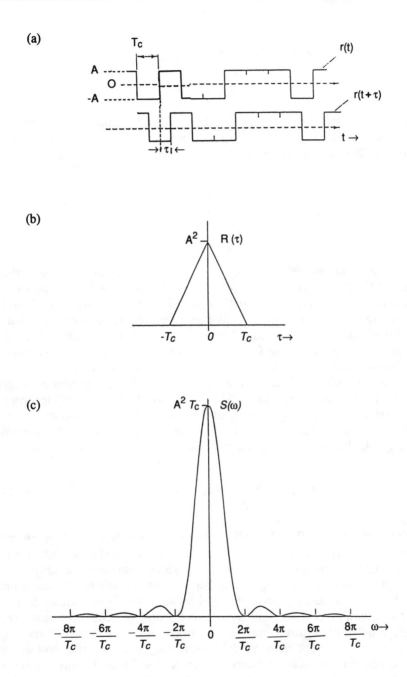

(a)

(b)

(c)

Figure 4.10 (a) A random binary code showing (b) autocorrelation function and (c) power spectrum.

$$R(\tau) = A^2\left(1 - \frac{|\tau|}{T_c}\right) \quad \text{for } |\tau| \le T_c$$

$$= 0 \qquad \text{elsewhere} \tag{4.9}$$

The power spectrum of this signal can be obtained from the Fourier transform of its autocorrelation function. Therefore, the power spectrum of a truly random binary code as illustrated in Figure 4.10(c), is defined in equation form as

$$S(\omega) = A^2 T_c\left(\frac{\sin\frac{\omega T_c}{2}}{\frac{\omega T_c}{2}}\right)^2 \equiv A^2 T_c \, \text{sinc}^2\frac{\omega T_c}{2} \tag{4.10}$$

Note that the autocorrelation function and the power spectrum of the random binary code differ from that of the singular rectangular pulse by only a scale factor, T_c. What is important about the rectangular pulse is that it correlates with itself in one and only one place. What is important about the random binary code is that it also correlates with itself in one and only one place, and it is uncorrelated with any other random binary code. The GPS satellites use codes that have very similar autocorrelation and power spectrum properties to the random binary code, but the GPS codes are periodic, predictable, and reproducible. This is why they are called "pseudo" random codes. Because the GPS PRN codes are derived from PN sequences, the autocorrelation and power spectrum of PN sequences will be described.

The formula for the autocorrelation function for a PN sequence PN(t) whose amplitude is $\pm A$, chipping period is T_c, and whose period is NT_c, is given by [6]

$$R_{PN}(\tau) = \frac{1}{NT_c}\int_0^{NT_c} PN(t)\,PN(t+\tau)dt \tag{4.11}$$

If the chip period of the PN feedback shift register is $N = 2^n - 1$, where n is the number of shift register stages used to generate the PN code, the shift register sequence is called a maximum length sequence. This is because the maximum number of usable binary states is generated in each period. This is true since the maximum number of possible states, 2^n, cannot be used because the all-zeros state, the only stable state in the PN feedback shift register, is the only one that cannot be used. Because the number of negative values (1s) is always one larger than the number of positive values (0s) in a maximum length PN sequence, the autocorrelation function of PN(t) outside of the correlation interval is $-A^2/N$. Recall that the correlation was 0 (uncorrelated) in this interval for the rectangular pulse as well as for the random binary sequence in the previous two examples. The autocorrelation function for a maximum length PN sequence is the infinite series of triangular functions with period NT_c (seconds) shown in Figure 4.11(a). The negative correlation amplitude ($-A^2/N$) is shown in Figure 4.11(a) when the phase shift τ, is greater than $\pm T_c$, or multiples of $\pm T_c(N \pm 1)$, and represents a dc term in the series. Expressing the equation for the periodic autocorrelation function mathematically [6] requires the use of the unit impulse function shifted in time by discreet (m) increments of the PN sequence period NT_c: $\delta(\tau + mNT_c)$. Simply stated, this notation (also called a Dirac delta function) represents a unit impulse with a discrete phase shift of mNT_c sec. Using this notation, the autocorrelation function can be expressed as the sum of the dc term and an

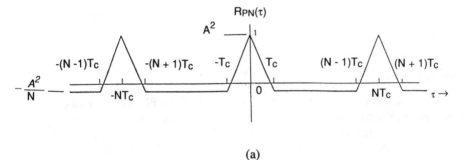

(a)

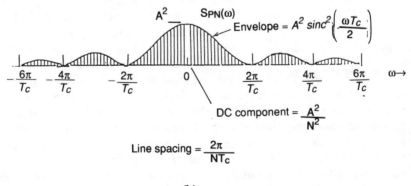

(b)

Figure 4.11 (a) The autocorrelation function of a maximum length PN code and (b) its line spectrum.

infinite series of the triangle function $R(\tau)$, defined by (4.9). The infinite series of the triangle function is obtained by the convolution (denoted by $\otimes$) of $R(\tau)$ with an infinite series of the phase-shifted unit impulse functions as follows:

$$R_{PN}(\tau) = \frac{-A^2}{N} + \frac{N+1}{N} R(\tau) \otimes \sum_{m=-\infty}^{\infty} \delta(\tau + mNT_c) \tag{4.12}$$

The power spectrum of this periodic PN sequence is derived from the Fourier transform of (4.12) and is the line spectrum shown in Figure 4.11(b). The unit impulse function is also required to express this in equation form as follows:

$$S_{PN}(\omega) = \frac{A^2}{N^2}\left(\delta(\omega) + \sum_{m=-\infty \neq 0}^{\infty} (N+1)\text{sinc}^2\left(\frac{m\pi}{N}\right)\delta\left(\omega + \frac{m2\pi}{NT_c}\right) \right) \tag{4.13}$$

where $\text{sinc}(x) = \dfrac{\sin x}{x}$ and $m = \pm 1, \pm 2, \pm 3, \ldots$

Observe in Figure 4.11(b) that the envelope of the PN sequence line spectrum is the same as the continuous power spectrum of the random binary sequence except for the small dc term of the PN sequence line spectrum and the scale factor T_c. As the period N (chips) and the chipping rate $R_c = 1/T_c$ (chips/sec) of the PN sequence increase, then the line spacing $2\pi/NT_c$ (radians) or $1/NT_c$ (Hz) of the line spectrum decreases proportionally so that the power spectrum begins to approach a continuous spectrum.

As would be expected, the GPS PRN codes have periodic correlation triangles and a line spectrum that closely resemble the characteristics of maximum length shift register PN sequences, but with several subtle differences. This is because the GPS PRN codes are *not* shift register sequences of maximum length. For example, for the C/A-code 10-bit shift register, there are only 30 usable maximum length sequences and among these available maximum length sequences the cross-correlation properties between different codes are not as good as was desired for GPS. Another problem is that the autocorrelation function of maximum length sequences has sidelobes when the integration time is one (or a few) code periods. (This can be a problem to a lesser extent with the C/A-codes as well.) In a GPS receiver, the integration and dump time associated with the correlation of its replica C/A-code with the incoming SV C/A-code (equivalent to autocorrelation) is typically 1 to 5 msec (i.e., one to five C/A-code periods). Except for a highly specialized mode of operation called data wipeoff, the integration and dump time never exceeds the 50-Hz data period of 20 msec. During search modes, these short integration and dump periods for the maximum length sequences increase the probability of high sidelobes, leading to the receiver locking onto a wrong correlation peak (a sidelobe). For these reasons, the Gold codes described earlier were selected for the C/A-codes.

Using the exclusive-or of two maximum length shift registers, G1 and G2 (with a programmable delay), there are $2^n - 1$ possible delays. Therefore, there are 1,023 possible Gold codes for the GPS C/A-code generator architecture (plus two additional maximum length sequences if the G1 and G2 sequences were used independently). However, there are only 45 Gold code combinations for the ICD-GPS-200 defined architecture of the C/A-code generator using two taps on the G2 register to form the delay. The 32 Gold codes with the best properties were selected for the GPS space segment. (There were only four more desirable two-tap combinations selected for the GTs since two GT codes are redundant.) Any future extensions of the GPS C/A-code would require a careful analysis of their properties and their effect on the space segment codes before their implementation.

The autocorrelation function of the GPS C/A-code is

$$R_G(\tau) = \frac{1}{1,023 T_{CA}} \int_{t=0}^{t=1023} G_i(t) G_i(t + \tau) dt \tag{4.14}$$

where

$G_i(t)$ = C/A-code Gold code sequence as a function of time t for SV_i
T_{CA} = C/A-code chipping period (977.5 nsec)
τ = phase of the time shift in the autocorrelation function

The C/A-code autocorrelation function is a series of correlation triangles with a period of 1,023 C/A-code chips, or 1 msec, as shown in Figure 4.12(a). As observed in Figure 4.12(a), the autocorrelation function of the GPS C/A (Gold) codes have the same period and the same shape in the correlation interval as the maximum length PN sequences. Also note that there are small correlations in the intervals between the maximum correlation intervals [7]. These small fluctuations in the autocorrelation function of the C/A-codes result in the deviation of the line spectrum from the sin x/x envelope as shown in Figure 4.12(b). However, the line spectrum spacing of 1,000 Hz is the same for both the C/A-code and the 10-bit maximum length sequence code. Figure 4.12(c) illustrates that the ratio of the power in each C/A line to the total power in the spectrum plotted in decibels can fluctuate significantly (nearly 8 dB) with respect to the −30 dB levels that would be obtained if every line contained the same power. Every C/A-code has a few "strong" lines (i.e., lines above the sin x/x envelope), which render them more vulnerable to a continuous wave (CW) RF interference at this line frequency than their maximum length PN sequence counterpart. For example, the correlation process between a CW line and a PRN code ordinarily spreads the CW line, but the mixing process at some "strong" C/A-code line results in the RF interference line being suppressed less than at other frequencies. As a result, the CW energy "leaks" through the correlation process at this strong line. This will be discussed further in Chapter 6 on RF interference effects.

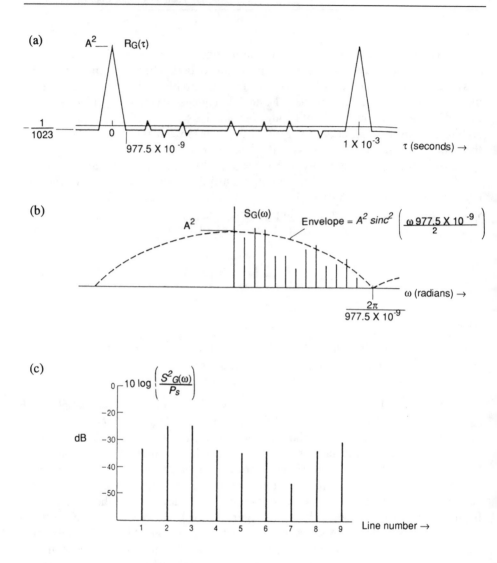

Figure 4.12 The (a) autocorrelation function, (b) spectrum, and (c) power ratio of a typical C/A-code.

Keeping in mind that the GPS C/A-codes have the above Gold code limitations, it is convenient and approximately correct to illustrate their autocorrelation functions as maximum length PN sequences, as shown in Figure 4.13. Note that there are other typical simplifications in this figure: the τ-axis is represented in C/A-code chips

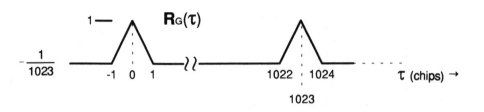

Figure 4.13 Normalized and simplified autocorrelation function of a typical C/A-code with τ in chips.

instead of seconds and the peak amplitude of the correlation function has been normalized to unity (corresponding to the PN sequence amplitude being ±1).

The autocorrelation function of the GPS P(Y)-code is

$$R_P(\tau) = \frac{1}{6.1871 \times 10^{12} T_{CP}} \int_{t=0}^{t=6.1871 \times 10^{12}} P_i(t)P_i(t + \tau)dt \qquad (4.15)$$

where

$P_i(t)$ = P(Y)-code PN sequence as a function of time t for SV_i
T_{CP} = P(Y)-code chipping period (97.8 nsec)
τ = phase of the time shift in the autocorrelation function

The P(Y)-code is also not a maximum length sequence code, but because its period is so long and its chipping rate is so fast, its autocorrelation characteristics are essentially ideal. The P(Y)-code was designed to have a one-week period made up of 403,200 periods of its 1.5-sec X1 epochs, called Z-counts. Figure 4.14 depicts a normalized autocorrelation function for P(Y)-code (amplitude $A = \pm 1$) with the phase-shift axis τ in units of P(Y)-code chips. The autocorrelation function for P(Y)-code has similar characteristics to the C/A-code, but with significant differences in values. Table 4.6 compares these characteristics. From Table 4.6, it can be observed that P(Y)-code can be considered essentially uncorrelated with itself (typically

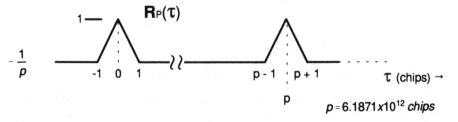

Figure 4.14 Normalized and simplified autocorrelation function of a typical P(Y)-code with τ in chips.

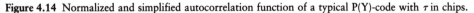

Table 4.6
Comparisons Between C/A-Code and P(Y)-Code Autocorrelation

Parameter	C/A-Code	P(Y)-Code
Maximum autocorrelation amplitude	1	1
Typical autocorrelation amplitude outside the correlation interval	$-\dfrac{1}{1023}$	$-\dfrac{1}{6.1871 \times 10^{12}}$
Typical autocorrelation (outside the correlation interval) in dB with respect to maximum correlation	-30.1	-127.9
Autocorrelation period	1 ms	1 week
Autocorrelation interval (chips)	2	2
Autocorrelation time interval (nsec)	1955.0	195.5
Autocorrelation range interval (m)	586.1	58.6
R_c = chipping rate (chips/sec)	1.023×10^6	10.23×10^6
T_c = chipping period (nsec)	977.5	97.8
Range of one chip (m)	293.0	29.3

-127.9 dB) for all intervals outside the correlation interval, whereas, the C/A-code is adequately uncorrelated with itself (typically -30.1 dB) outside its correlation interval. However, the C/A-codes can be as poorly uncorrelated with themselves as -21.3 dB outside the correlation interval (fortunately, a small percentage of the time).

When the GPS codes are combined with the 50-Hz navigation message data, there is essentially an imperceptible effect on the resulting autocorrelation functions and the power spectrum. When these are modulated onto the L-band carrier, there is a translation to L-band of the power spectrum from the baseband frequencies that have been described so far. Assuming that the PN waveform is phase shift keyed onto the carrier and that the carrier frequency and the code are not coherent, the resulting power spectrum is given by [6]

$$S_L(\omega) = \frac{1}{2}[P_c\, S_{PN}(\omega + \omega_c) + P_c\, S_{PN}(\omega - \omega_c)] \qquad (4.16)$$

where

P_c = unmodulated carrier power
ω = carrier frequency (radians)
$S_{PN}(\omega_c)$ = power spectrum of the PRN code(s) (plus data) at baseband

As can be observed from (4.16), the baseband spectra are shifted up to the carrier frequency (and down to the negative carrier frequency). In the following GPS L-band power spectrum illustrations, only the (upper) single-sided frequency is considered. The GPS signals were synthesized by a GPS signal generator and measured by a Hewlett-Packard spectrum analyzer.

Figure 4.15 is a plot of the power spectrum of the GPS P(Y)-code and C/A-code (plus 50-Hz data) PSK modulated onto the L1 carrier. The spectrum analyzer performed the plot using a 300-kHz resolution bandwidth. It is impossible to observe the line spectrum characteristics of either code. Therefore, the power spectrums appear to be continuous. The center frequency is at the L1 carrier, 1,575.42 MHz. The combined power spectra of C/A-code and P(Y)-codes are centered at the L1 carrier frequency. The first nulls of the C/A-code power spectrum are at ±1.023 MHz from the center frequency and the first nulls of the P(Y)-code power spectrum are at ±10.23 MHz from the center frequency.

Figure 4.16 is a plot of the power spectrum of the GPS P(Y)-code (plus 50-Hz data) PSK modulated onto the L2 carrier. The plot is virtually identical to Figure 4.15, except the center frequency is at the L2 carrier and the C/A-code modulation is removed. The center frequency is at the L2 carrier, 1,227.60 MHz. The power spectrum of P(Y)-code is centered at the L2 carrier frequency. The first null of the P(Y)-code is at ±10.23 MHz from the center frequency.

Figure 4.17 is a plot of the power spectrum of the GPS C/A-code (plus 50-Hz data) PSK modulated onto the L1 carrier (with the P(Y)-code turned off). The frequency scale has been adjusted to be narrower than Figure 4.15 by a factor of 10 in order to inspect the C/A-code power spectrum more closely. The resolution bandwidth of the spectrum analyzer has been reduced to 3 kHz so that the line spectrum of the C/A-code is just beginning to be visible in the plot. The "strong" lines of the C/A-code (those above the nominal sin x/x envelope) are also somewhat observable. The spectrum analyzer used to generate these plots did not have a resolution bandwidth that was narrow enough to observe the P(Y)-code line spectrum.

4.1.4 Cross-Correlation Functions and Code Division Multiple Access Performance

The GPS modulation/demodulation concept is based on the use of a different PRN code in each SV, but with the same code-chipping rates and carrier frequencies on each SV. This modulation/demodulation technique is called code division multiple access and requires the user GPS receiver to synthesize a replica of the SV-transmitted PRN code and to shift the phase of the replica PRN code so as to correlate with a unique PRN code for each SV tracked. Each SV PRN code used in the CDMA system must be minimally cross-correlated with any other SV's PRN code for any phase or Doppler shift combination within the entire code period. The autocorrelation characteristics of the GPS codes have already been discussed. The ideal cross-correlation functions of the GPS codes are defined by the following equation:

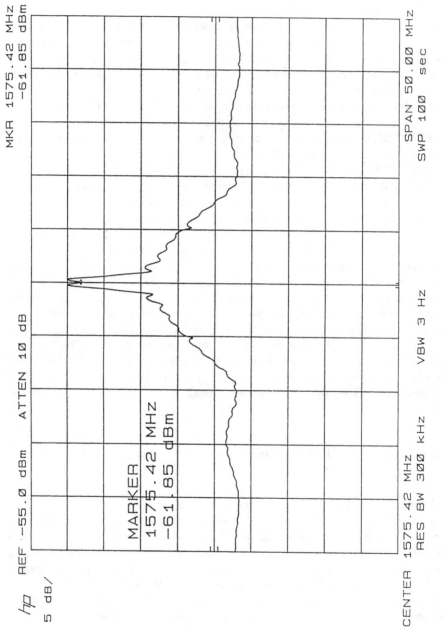

Figure 4.15 Power spectrum of L1 P(Y)-code and C/A-code from a GPS signal generator.

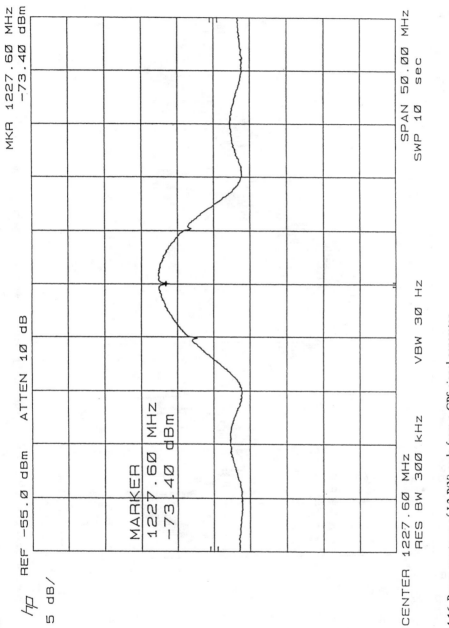

Figure 4.16 Power spectrum of L2 P(Y)-code from a GPS signal generator.

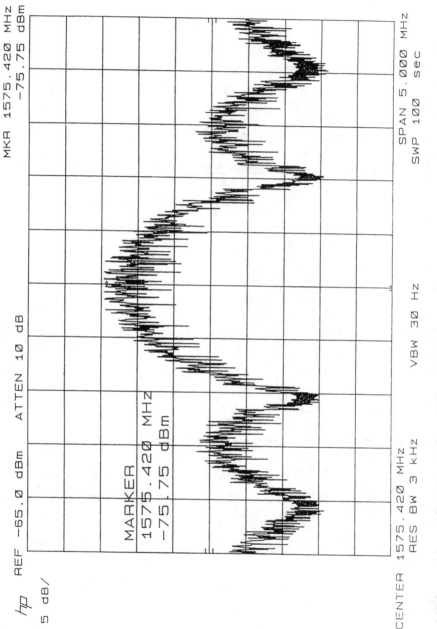

Figure 4.17 Power spectrum of L1 C/A-code from a GPS signal generator showing the line spectrum of the C/A-code.

$$R_{IJ}(\tau) = \int_{-\infty}^{\infty} PN_I(t)\, PN_J(t + \tau)\, dt = 0 \qquad (4.17)$$

where

$PN_I(t)$ = PN code sequence for satellite I

$PN_J(t)$ = PN code sequence for all other satellites J under the condition that $J \neq I$.

Equation (4.17) states that the PN code sequence of satellite does not correlate with the PN sequence of any other satellite for any phase shift. In practice, this is impossible just as it is impossible for a satellite to have the desirable characteristic of zero autocorrelation outside its correlation interval. In order for the CDMA discrimination technique to work, a certain level of cross-correlation signal rejection performance must be achieved among all the used PRN codes. Because the code length is 6.1871×10^{12} chips, the cross-correlation level of the GPS P(Y)-codes with any other GPS P(Y)-code approaches -127 dB with respect to maximum autocorrelation. Hence, the cross-correlation of the P(Y)-code of any GPS SV can be treated as uncorrelated with any other GPS SV signals for any phase shift τ. Because of this excellent P(Y)-code cross-correlation performance, no further discussion is warranted.

Because the GPS C/A-code length was a compromise at 1,023 chips, the cross-correlation properties can be poor under certain circumstances. As shown in Table 4.7, the C/A-code cross-correlation functions have peak levels that can be as poor as -24 dB with respect to its maximum autocorrelation for a zero Doppler difference between any two codes. Table 4.8 shows that for higher Doppler difference levels at the worst case intervals of 1 kHz, the cross-correlation levels can be as poor as -21 dB. This can cause false acquisitions under certain Doppler differences and antenna gain conditions. For example, an unwanted SV can have a C/A-code signal that is up to 7-dB stronger than the desired SV C/A-code signal. If the desired SV is low on the horizon, there is increased multipath loss plus reduced GPS receiver antenna gain, for a typical net loss of 4 dB. If the unwanted SV is higher in elevation,

Table 4.7
C/A-Code Maximum Cross-Correlation Power
(Zero Doppler Differences)

Cumulative Probability of Occurrence	Cross-Correlation for Any Two Codes (dB)
0.23	−23.9
0.50	−24.2
1.00	−60.2

Table 4.8
C/A-Code Maximum Cross-Correlation Power Summed for All 32 Codes
(Increments of 1-kHz Doppler Differences)

Cumulative Probability of Occurrence	Cross-Correlation @ Δ = 1 kHz (dB)	Cross-Correlation @ Δ = 2 kHz (dB)	Cross-Correlation @ Δ = 3 kHz (dB)	Cross-Correlation @ Δ = 4 kHz (dB)	Cross-Correlation @ Δ = 5 kHz (dB)
0.001	−21.1	−21.1	−21.6	−21.1	−21.9
0.02	−24.2	−24.2	−24.2	−24.2	−24.2
0.1	−26.4	−26.4	−26.4	−26.4	−26.4
0.4	−30.4	−30.4	−30.4	−30.4	−30.4

the atmospheric loss is reduced plus there is increased GPS receiver antenna gain, for a typical net gain of 3 dB. This difference in SV elevations reduces the signal separation by an additional 7 dB. The antenna SV array gain variations as a function of the differences in user elevation angles to the two SVs also contributes up to an additional 2 dB of gain to the unwanted stronger SV signal. For the signal conditions between these two SVs where there is only 21 dB of C/A-code discrimination during the cross-correlation process, the difference between the desired SV signal and the unwanted signal is only 21 − 16 = 5 dB. Discrimination against this is admittedly worst case, but possible signal strength difference can be very difficult for a C/A-code receiver, resulting in an occasional false acquisition. Fortunately, the unwanted SV signal cannot be tracked for long because both the correlation properties and the Doppler change rapidly, resulting in loss of lock and a reacquisition process for the GPS receiver. It is important that the GPS receiver design implement sophisticated C/A-code search procedures that avoid sidelobe and unwanted SV acquisitions if the receiver does not hand over to the P(Y)-code.

In the next chapter, we discuss the acquisition and tracking of the GPS satellite signals by the user's receiver. The chapter provides details on the numerous criteria that must be addressed when designing or analyzing these processes. The processes of obtaining pseudorange, delta range, and integrated Doppler measurements are also described. These parameters are the key observables in range and velocity measurements.

References

[1] ICD-GPS-200, NAVSTAR GPS Space Segment/Navigation User Interfaces (Public Release Version), ARINC Research Corporation, 11770 Warner Ave., Suite 210, Fountain Valley CA, 92708, July 3, 1991.
[2] Gold, R., "Optimal Binary Sequences for Spread Spectrum Multiplexing," IEEE Transactions Info. Theory, Vol. 33, No. 3, October 1967, pp. 619–621.

[3] Forssell, B., *Radionavigation Systems*, New York: Prentice Hall International, 1991, pp. 250–271.

[4] Czopek, F. M., "Description and Performance of the GPS Block I and II L-Band Antenna and Link Budget," *Proc. Sixth International Technical Meeting of The Satellite Division of The Institute of Navigation*, Salt Lake City, UT, Sept. 22–24, 1993, Vol. I, pp. 37–43.

[5] Lee, Y. W., *Statistical Theory of Communication*, New York: John Wiley & Sons, Inc., 1964, pp. 4–104.

[6] Holmes, J. K., *Coherent Spread Spectrum Systems*, Malabor, FL: Robert E. Krieger Publishing Company, 1990, pp. 344–394.

[7] Spilker, J. J., Jr., "GPS Signal Structure and Performance Characteristics," *Navigation, Journal of The Institute of Navigation*, Vol. 25, No. 2, 1978.

CHAPTER 5
▼▼▼

SATELLITE SIGNAL ACQUISITION AND TRACKING

Phillip Ward
NAVWARD GPS Consulting

5.1 GPS SIGNAL ACQUISITION AND TRACKING

In practice, a GPS receiver must replicate the PRN code that is transmitted by the SV that is being acquired by the receiver, then it must shift the phase of the replica code until it correlates with the SV PRN code. The same correlation properties occur when cross-correlating the transmitted PRN code with a replica code as occurs for the mathematical autocorrelation process for a given PRN code. When the phase of the GPS receiver replica code matches the phase of the incoming SV code, there is maximum correlation. When the phase of the replica code is offset by more than one chip on either side of the incoming SV code, there is minimum correlation. This is indeed the manner in which a GPS receiver detects the SV signal when acquiring or tracking the SV signal in the code-phase dimension. It is important to understand that the GPS receiver must also detect the SV in the carrier-phase dimension by replicating the carrier frequency plus Doppler (and usually eventually obtains carrier phase lock with the SV signal by this means). Thus, the GPS signal acquisition and tracking process is a two-dimensional (code and carrier) signal replication process.

In the code or range dimension, the GPS receiver accomplishes the cross-correlation process by first searching for the phase of the desired SV and then tracking the SV code state by adjusting the nominal chipping rate of its replica code generator to compensate for the Doppler-induced effect on the SV PRN code due to line-of-sight relative dynamics between the receiver and the SV. There is also an apparent Doppler effect on the code tracking loop caused by the frequency offset in the receiver's reference oscillator with respect to its specified frequency. This error effect, which is the time bias rate determined by the navigation solution, is quite small for the code tracking loop and is usually neglected. The code correlation process is implemented as a real-time multiplication of the phase-shifted replica code with the incoming SV code, followed by an integration and dump process. The objective of the GPS receiver is to keep the prompt phase of its replica code generator at maximum correlation with the desired SV code phase.

However, if the receiver has not simultaneously adjusted (tuned) its replica carrier signal so that it matches the frequency of the desired SV carrier, then the signal correlation process in the range dimension is severely attenuated by the resulting frequency response roll-off characteristic of the GPS receiver. This has the consequence that the receiver never acquires the SV. If the signal was successfully acquired because the SV code and frequency were successfully replicated during the search process, but then the receiver subsequently loses track of the SV frequency, then the receiver subsequently loses code track as well. Thus, in the carrier Doppler frequency dimension, the GPS receiver accomplishes the carrier matching (wipeoff) process by first searching for the carrier Doppler frequency of the desired SV and then tracking the SV carrier Doppler state. It does this by adjusting the nominal carrier frequency of its replica carrier generator to compensate for the Doppler-induced effect on the SV carrier signal due to line-of-sight relative dynamics between the receiver and the SV. There is also an apparent Doppler error effect on the carrier loop caused by the frequency offset in the receiver's reference oscillator with respect to its specified frequency. This error, which is common with all satellites being tracked by the receiver, is determined by the navigation filter as the time bias rate in units of seconds per second.

The two-dimensional acquisition and tracking process can best be explained and understood in progressive steps. The clearest explanation is in reverse sequence from the events that actually take place in a real-world GPS receiver. The two-dimensional search and acquisition process is easier to understand if the two-dimensional steady-state tracking process is explained first. The two-dimensional code and carrier tracking process is easier to understand if the carrier tracking process is explained first. This is the explanation sequence that will be used. The explanation will first be given in the context of a generic GPS receiver architecture with minimum use of equations. This high-level overview will then be followed by more detailed explanations of the carrier and code tracking loops, including the most useful equations.

5.1.1 GPS Receiver Code and Carrier Tracking

Most modern GPS receiver designs are digital receivers. These receiver designs have evolved rapidly toward higher and higher levels of digital component integration and this trend is expected to continue. For this reason, a high-level block diagram of a modern digital GPS receiver will be used to represent a generic GPS receiver architecture as shown in Figure 5.1. The GPS radiofrequency (RF) signals of all SVs in view are received by a right-hand circularly polarized (RHCP) antenna with nearly hemispherical gain coverage. These RF signals are amplified by a low-noise preamplifier (preamp), which effectively sets the noise figure of the receiver. There may be a passive bandpass prefilter between the antenna and preamp to minimize out-of-band RF interference. These amplified and signal-conditioned RF signals are then downconverted to an intermediate frequency (IF) using signal mixing frequencies from local oscillators (LOs). The LOs are derived from the reference oscillator by the frequency synthesizer based on the frequency plan of the receiver design. One LO per downconverter stage is required. Two-stage downconversion to IF is typical, but one-stage downconversion and even direct L-band digital sampling have also been used. The LO signal mixing process generates both upper and lower sidebands of the SV signals, so the lower sidebands are selected and the upper sidebands and leak-through signals are rejected by a postmixer bandpass filter. The signal Dopplers and the PRN codes are preserved after the mixing process. Only the carrier frequency is lowered. The analog-to-digital (A/D) conversion process and automatic gain control (AGC) functions take place at IF. Not shown in the block diagram are the baseband timing signals that are provided to the digital receiver channels by the frequency synthesizer phase-locked to the reference oscillator's stable frequency. The IF must be high enough to provide a single-sided bandwidth that will support the PRN code chipping frequency. An antialiasing IF filter must suppress the stopband noise (unwanted out-of-band signals) to levels that are acceptably low when this noise is aliased into the GPS signal passband by the A/D conversion process. The signals from all GPS satellites in view are buried in the thermal noise at IF.

At this point, the digitized IF signals are ready to be processed by each of the N digital receiver channels. No demodulation has taken place, only signal conditioning and conversion to the digital IF. These digital receiver channel functions are usually implemented in one or more application specific integrated circuits (ASICs). This is why these functions are shown as separate from the receiver processing function in the block diagram of Figure 5.1. The name "digital receiver channel" is somewhat misleading since it is not the ASIC but the receiver processing function that usually implements numerous baseband functions such as the loop discriminators and filters, data demodulation, meters, phase-lock indicators, and so forth. The receiver processing function is usually a microprocessor. The microprocessor not only performs the baseband functions, but also the decision-making functions associated with controlling the signal preprocessing functions of each digital receiver channel. It is common that a single high-speed microprocessor supports the receiver, navigation, and user interface functions.

Figure 5.2 illustrates a high-level block diagram typical of one of the digital receiver channels where the digitized IF signals are applied to the input. For simplifica-

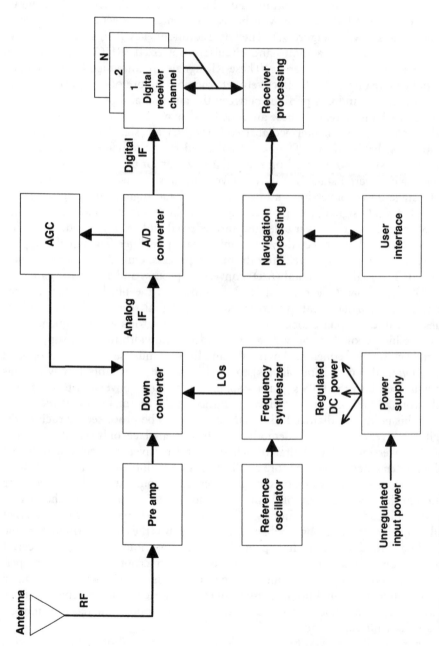

Figure 5.1 Generic digital GPS receiver block diagram.

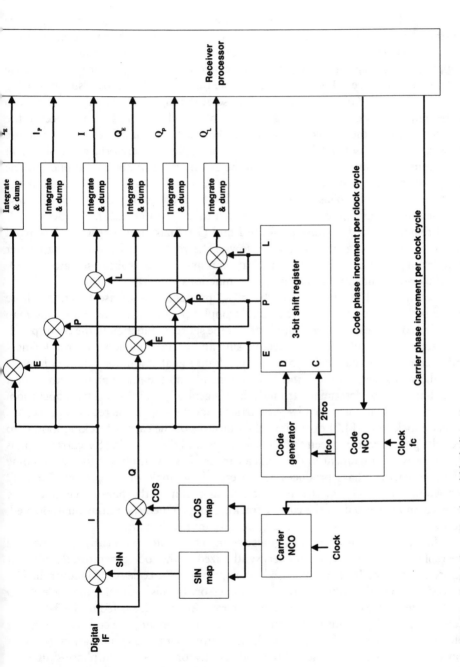

Figure 5.2 Generic digital receiver channel block diagram.

tion, only the functions associated with the code and carrier tracking loops are illustrated and the receiver channel is assumed to be tracking the SV signal in steady state. Referring to Figure 5.2, first the digital IF is stripped of the carrier (plus carrier Doppler) by the replica carrier (plus carrier Doppler) signals to produce in-phase (I) and quadra-phase (Q) sampled data. Note that the replica carrier signal is being mixed with all the GPS SV signals and noise at the digital IF. The I and Q signals at the outputs of the mixers have the desired phase relationships with respect to the detected carrier of the desired SV. However, the code stripping processes that collapse these signals to baseband have not yet been applied. Therefore, the I signal at the output of the in-phase mixers would be mostly thermal noise multiplied by the replica digital sine wave (to match the SV carrier at IF) and the Q signal at the output of the quadra-phase mixer would be the product of mostly thermal noise and the replica digital cosine wave (to match the SV carrier at IF). The desired SV signal remains buried in noise until the I and Q signals are collapsed to baseband by the code stripping process that follows. The replica carrier (including carrier Doppler) signals are synthesized by the carrier numerical controlled oscillator (NCO) and the discrete sine and cosine mapping functions.

Later, it will be shown that the NCO produces a staircase function whose period is the desired replica carrier plus Doppler period. The sine and cosine map functions convert each discreet amplitude of the staircase function to the corresponding discreet amplitude of the respective sine and cosine functions. By producing I and Q component phases 90° apart, the resultant signal amplitude can be computed from the vector sum of the I and Q components and the phase angle with respect to the I-axis can be determined from the arctangent of Q/I. In closed loop operation, the carrier NCO is controlled by the carrier tracking loop in the receiver processor. In phase lock loop (PLL) operation, the objective of the carrier tracking loop is to keep the phase error between the replica carrier and the incoming SV carrier signals at zero. Any misalignment in the replica carrier phase with respect to the incoming SV signal carrier phase produces a nonzero phase angle of the prompt I and Q vector magnitude so that the amount and direction of the phase change can be detected and corrected by the carrier tracking loop. When the PLL is phase-locked, the I signals are maximum and the Q signals are nearly zero.

In Figure 5.2, the I and Q signals are then correlated with early, prompt, and late replica codes (plus code Doppler) synthesized by the code generator, a 3-bit shift register, and the code NCO. In closed loop operation, the code NCO is controlled by the code tracking loop in the receiver processor. In this example, the code NCO produces twice the code generator clocking rate, $2f_c$, and this is fed to the 3-bit shift register. The code generator clocking rate, f_c, which contains the code chipping rate (plus code Doppler), is fed to the code generator. With this combination, the shift register produces three phases of the code generator output, each phase-shifted by 1/2 chip apart. Not shown are the controls to the code generator that permit the receiver processor to preset the initial code-tracking phase states, which are required during the code search and acquisition process.

The prompt replica code phase is aligned with the incoming SV code phase producing maximum correlation if it is tracking the incoming SV code phase. Under this circumstance, the early phase is aligned 1/2 chip early and the late phase is aligned 1/2 chip late with respect to the incoming SV code phase and these correlators produce about half the maximum correlation. Any misalignment in the replica code phase with respect to the incoming SV code phase produces a difference in the vector magnitudes of the early and late correlated outputs so that the amount and direction of the phase change can be detected and corrected by the code tracking loop.

5.1.1.1 Predetection Integration

Predetection is the signal processing after the IF signal has been converted to baseband by the carrier and code stripping processes, but prior to being passed through a signal discriminator; that is, prior to the nonlinear signal detection process. Numerous digital predetection integration and dump operations occur after the carrier and code stripping processes. This causes very large numbers to accumulate even though the IF A/D conversion process is typically with only one to three bits of quantization resolution.

Figure 5.2 shows three complex correlators required to produce three in-phase components, which are integrated and dumped to produce I_E, I_P, I_L and three quadra-phase components integrated and dumped to produce Q_E, Q_P, Q_L. The carrier wipeoff and code wipeoff processes must be performed at the digital IF sample rate, which is around 5 MHz for C/A-code and 50 MHz for P(Y)-code. The integrate and dump accumulators provide filtering and resampling at the processor baseband input rate, which is around 200 Hz (it can be higher or lower depending on the desired predetection bandwidth). The 200-Hz rate is well within the interrupt servicing rate of modern high-speed microprocessors, but the 5- or 50-MHz rates would not be manageable. This further explains why the high speed, but simple, processes are implemented in a custom digital ASIC while the low speed, but complex, processes are implemented in a microprocessor.

The hardware integrate and dump process in combination with the baseband signal processing integrate and dump process (described below) defines the predetection integration time. Later, we will learn that the predetection integration time is a compromise design. It must be as long as possible to operate under weak or RF interference signal conditions and it must be as short as possible to operate under high-dynamic stress signal conditions.

5.1.1.2 Baseband Signal Processing

Figure 5.3 illustrates typical baseband code and carrier tracking loops for one receiver channel in the closed loop mode of operation. The functions are typically performed

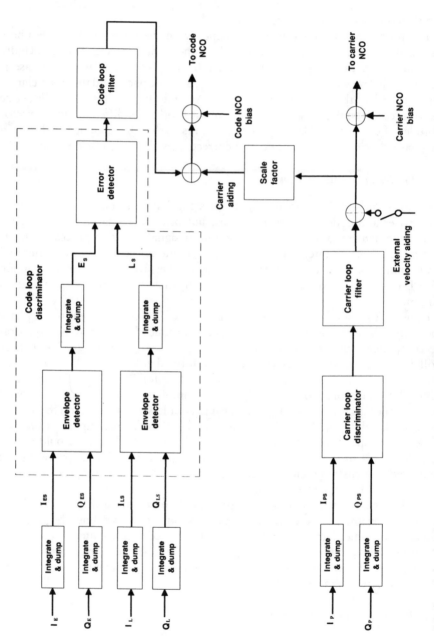

Figure 5.3 Generic baseband processor code and carrier tracking loops block diagram.

by the receiver processor shown in Figure 5.2. The combination of these carrier and code tracking baseband signal processing functions and the digital receiver channel carrier and code wipeoff and predetection integration functions form the carrier and code tracking loops of one GPS receiver channel.

The baseband functions are usually implemented in firmware. Note that the firmware need only be written once since the microprocessor runs all programs sequentially (as opposed to the simultaneous parallel processing that takes place in the digital receiver ASIC(s)). Therefore, the microprocessor program can be designed to be re-entrant with a unique variable area for each receiver channel so that only one copy of each algorithm is required to service all receiver channels. This reduces the program memory requirements and ensures that every receiver baseband processing function is identical.

The three complex pairs of baseband I and Q signals from the digital receiver may be resampled again by the integrate and dump accumulators. The total combined duration of the receiver and processor integrate and dump functions establishes the predetection integration time for the signal. Normally, this cannot exceed 20 msec, which is the 50-Hz navigation message data period. Figure 5.4 illustrates the phase alignment needed to prevent the predetection integrate and dump intervals from integrating across a SV data transition boundary. The start and stop boundaries for these integrate and dump functions should not straddle the data bit transition boundaries because each time the SV data bits change sign, the signs of the subsequent integrated I and Q data change. If the boundary is straddled, the result for that predetection integration signal for that interval will be degraded. Usually, during initial searches the receiver does not know where the SV data bit transition boundaries are located. Then, the performance degradation has to be accepted until the bit synchronization process locates them. As shown in Figure 5.4, the SV data transition boundary usually does not align with the receiver's 20-msec clock boundary, which will hereafter be called the fundamental time frame (FTF). The phase offset is shown as "bit sync phase skew," because the SV bit synchronization process initially determines this phase offset. In general, the bit sync phase skew is different for every SV being tracked. The bit sync phase skew changes as the range to the SV changes. The receiver design must accommodate these data bit phase skews.

5.1.1.3 Digital Frequency Synthesis

In this generic design example, both the carrier and code tracking loops use an NCO. One replica carrier cycle and one replica code cycle are completed each time the NCO overflows. A block diagram of the carrier loop NCO and its sine and cosine mapping functions are shown in Figure 5.5 [1].

The map functions convert the amplitude of the NCO staircase output (Figure 5.6(a)) into the appropriate trigonometric functions, as shown in Figure 5.6(b, c). Figure 5.7 illustrates the basic idea of digital frequency synthesizer design.

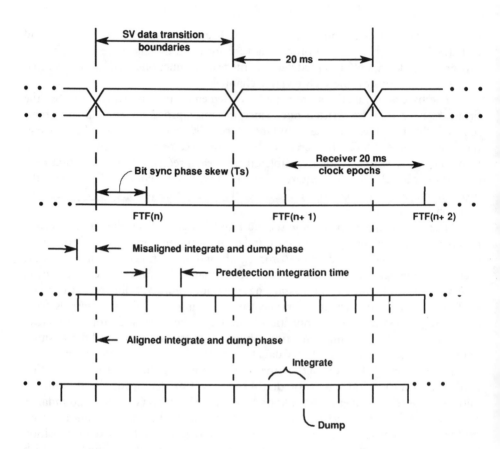

Figure 5.4 Phase alignment of predetection integrate and dump intervals with SV data transition boundaries.

5.1.1.4 Carrier Aiding of Code Loop

In Figure 5.3, the carrier loop filter output is adjusted by a scale factor and added to the code loop filter output as aiding. This is called a carrier-aided code loop. The scale factor is required because the Doppler effect on the signal is inversely proportional to the wavelength of the signal. Therefore, for the same relative velocity between the SV and the GPS receiver, the Doppler on the code chipping rate is much smaller than the Doppler on the L-band carrier. The scale factor that compensates for this difference in frequency is given by

$$\text{Scale factor} = \frac{R_c}{f_L} \quad \text{(dimensionless)} \tag{5.1}$$

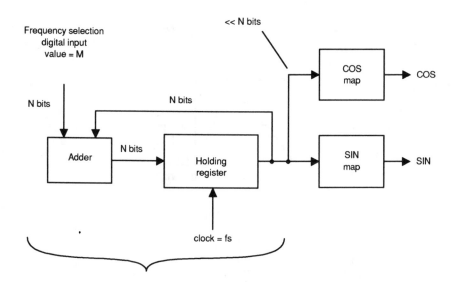

Numerical controlled oscillator (NCO)

N = Length of holding register $\dfrac{f_s M}{2^N}$ = Output frequency

2^N = Count length $\dfrac{f_s}{2^N}$ = Frequency resolution

Figure 5.5 Digital frequency synthesizer block diagram.

where

R_c = code chipping rate (Hz)
  = R_0 for P(Y)-code = 10.23×10^6 chips/sec
  = $R_0/10$ for C/A-code = 1.023×10^6 chips/sec

f_L = L-band carrier (Hz)
  = $154\, R_0$ for L1
  = $120\, R_0$ for L2

Table 5.1 shows the three practical combinations of this scale factor.

The carrier loop output should always provide aiding to the code loop because the carrier loop jitter is much less noisy than the code loop jitter and thus more accurate. The carrier loop aiding removes virtually all of the line-of-sight dynamics

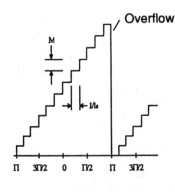

(a)

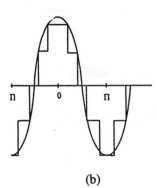

(b)

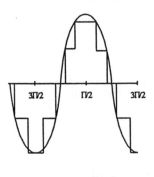

(c)

Figure 5.6 Digital frequency synthesizer output waveforms: (a) NCO output, (b) COS map output, and (c) SIN map output.

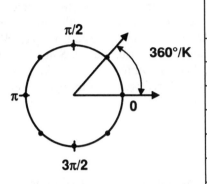

Degrees	Holding register (binary)	SIN map (2's comp)	COS map (2's comp)
0	1 0 0...	0 0 0	0 1 1
45	1 0 1...	0 1 0	0 1 0
90	1 1 0...	0 1 1	0 0 0
135	1 1 1...	0 1 0	1 1 0
180	0 0 0...	0 0 0	1 1 1
225	0 0 1...	1 1 0	1 1 0
270	0 1 0...	1 1 1	0 0 0
315	0 1 1...	1 1 0	0 1 0

Maps for $J = 3$, $K = 2^J = 8$

Notes:

1. The number of bits, J, is determined for the sin and cos outputs. The phase plane of 360° is subdivided into $2^J = K$ phase points.

2. K values are computed for each waveform, one value per phase point. Each value represents the amplitude of the waveform to be generated at that phase point. The upper J bits of the holding register are used to determine the address of the waveform amplitude.

3. Rate at which phase plane is traversed determines the frequency of the output waveform.

4. The upper bound of the amplitude error is:
   $e_{MAX} = 2\pi/K$

5. The approximate amplitude error is:
   $e \cong 2\pi/K \ [\cos \phi \ (t)]$ where $\phi \ (t)$ is the phase angle.

Figure 5.7 Digital frequency synthesizer design.

Table 5.1
Scale Factors for Carrier-Aided Code

Carrier Frequency (Hz)	Code Rate (Chips/sec)	Scale Factor
L1 = 154 R_0	C/A = R_0/10	1/1,540 = 0.00064935
L1 = 154 R_0	P(Y) = R_0	1/154 = 0.00649350
L2 = 120 R_0	P(Y) = R_0	1/120 = 0.00833333

from the code loop, so the code loop filter order can be made smaller, the predetection integration time can be made longer, and the code loop bandwidth can be made much narrower than for the unaided case, thereby increasing the code loop tracking threshold and reducing the noise in the code loop measurements. Since both the code and carrier loops must maintain track, there is nothing lost in tracking performance by using carrier aiding for an unaided GPS receiver even though the carrier loop is the weakest link.

5.1.1.5 External Aiding

As shown in Figure 5.3, external velocity aiding, say from an inertial measurement unit (IMU), can be provided to the receiver channel in closed carrier loop operation. The switch, shown in the unaided position, must be closed when external velocity aiding is applied. The external rate aiding must be converted into line-of-sight velocity aiding with respect to the GPS satellite. The lever arm effects on the aiding must be computed with respect to the GPS antenna phase center, which requires a knowledge of the vehicle attitude and the location of the antenna phase center with respect to the navigation center of the external source of velocity aiding. For closed carrier loop operation, the aiding must be very precise and have little or no latency or the tracking loop must be delay compensated for the latency. If open carrier loop aiding is implemented, less precise external velocity aiding is required, but there can be no delta range measurements available from the receiver so it is a short term, weak signal hold-on strategy. In this weak signal hold-on case, the output of the carrier loop filter must be set to zero and there is no need to process the prompt correlator signals in the carrier loop discriminator, but these signals are still used for C/N_0 computation, etc.

5.1.2 Carrier Tracking Loops

Figure 5.8 illustrates the block diagram of only the GPS receiver carrier tracking loop. The programmable designs of the carrier predetection integrators, the carrier loop discriminators, and the carrier loop filters characterize the receiver carrier tracking loop. These three functions determine the two most important performance characteristics of the receiver carrier loop design: the carrier loop thermal noise error and the maximum line-of-sight dynamic stress threshold. Since the carrier tracking loop is always the weak link in a standalone GPS receiver, its threshold characterizes the unaided GPS receiver performance.

The carrier loop discriminator defines the type of tracking loop as a PLL, a Costas PLL (which is a PLL type discriminator that tolerates the presence of data modulation on the baseband signal), or a frequency lock loop (FLL). The PLL and

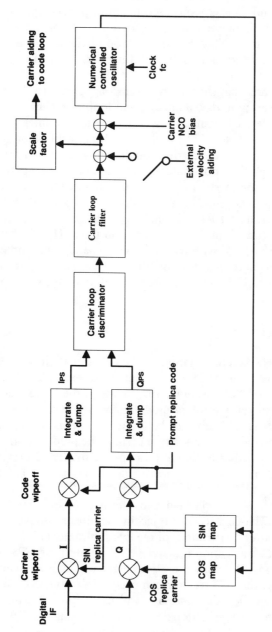

Figure 5.8 Generic GPS receiver carrier tracking loop block diagram.

the Costas loops are the most accurate but are more sensitive to dynamic stress than the FLL. The PLL and Costas loop discriminators produce phase errors at their outputs. The FLL discriminator produces a frequency error. Because of this, there is also a difference in the architecture of the loop filter, described in Section 5.1.4. There is an additional integration in the FLL filter versus the PLL filter for the same loop filter order.

There is a paradox that the GPS receiver designer must solve in the design of the predetection integration, discriminator, and loop filter functions of the carrier tracking loops. To tolerate dynamic stress, the predetection integration time should be short, the discriminator should be an FLL, and the carrier loop filter bandwidth should be wide. However, for the carrier Doppler phase measurements to be accurate (have low noise), the predetection integration time should be long, the discriminator should be a PLL, and the carrier loop filter noise bandwidth should be narrow. In practice, some compromise must be made to resolve this paradox. A well-designed GPS receiver will close its carrier tracking loops with short predetection integration times, using an FLL and a wide band carrier loop filter. Then it will systematically transition into a Costas PLL with its predetection bandwidth and carrier tracking loop bandwidth set as narrow as the anticipated dynamics permits. It will also have a provision to revert to FLL operation during high-dynamic stress periods.

5.1.2.1 Phase Lock Loops

If there were no 50-Hz data modulation on the GPS signal, the carrier tracking loop discriminator could use a pure PLL discriminator. For example, a P(Y)-code receiver could implement a pure PLL discriminator for use in the L2 carrier tracking mode if the control segment turns off data modulation. Although this mode is specified as a possibility, it is unlikely to be activated. This mode is specified in ICD-GPS-200 because pure PLL operation permits the predetection integration time to increase beyond the 20-msec limitation imposed by the 50-Hz navigation data. This reduces the squaring loss, subsequently improving the signal tracking threshold by up to 6 dB.

It is also possible to implement short-term pure PLL modes by a process called data wipeoff. The GPS receiver typically acquires a complete copy of the full navigation message after 25 iterations of the five subframes (12.5 min). The receiver then can compute the navigation message sequence until the GPS control segment uploads a new message or until the SV changes the message. Until the message changes significantly, the GPS receiver can perform data wipeoff of each bit of the incoming 50-Hz navigation data message and use a pure PLL discriminator. The receiver baseband processing function does this by reversing the sign of the integrated in-phase components (I_{ES}, I_{PS}, I_{LS}) and quadra-phase components (Q_{ES}, Q_{PS}, Q_{LS}) in accordance with a consistent algorithm. For example, if I_{PS} has a predetection integration time of 5 msec, then there are four samples of I_{PS} between each SV data bit transition that will have the same sign. This sign will be the sign of the data bit known by the receiver a priori for that data interval. Each 5-msec sample may fluctuate in sign due to noise. If the known data bit for this interval is a "0," then the data wipeoff process does nothing to all four samples. If the known data bit for this interval is a "1," then the sign is reversed on all four samples.

Table 5.2 summarizes several GPS receiver PLL discriminators, their output-phase errors, and their characteristics.

5.1.2.2 Costas Loops

Normally, only Costas carrier tracking loops are used in GPS receivers because the 50-Hz navigation message data modulation signal remains after the carrier and code signals have been wiped off the incoming SV signal. Costas loops are insensitive to 180-deg phase reversals in the I and Q signals if the predetection integration times of the I and Q signals do not straddle the data bit transitions. The distinguishing features of a Costas loop are the Costas discriminator and the phase adjusting capability with respect to the receiver's natural clock phase in the predetection integration area of the receiver. The phase adjustment features of the integrate and dump functions are required to avoid integrating across the data transition boundaries. Refer back to Figure 5.4 to review this unique feature.

Table 5.2
Common Phase Lock Loop Discriminators

Discriminator Algorithm	Output Phase Error	Characteristics
Sign $(I_{PS}) \cdot Q_{PS}$	$\sin \phi$	Near optimal at high SNR. Slope proportional to signal amplitude A. Least computational burden.
$I_{PS} \cdot Q_{PS}$	$\sin 2\phi$	Near optimal at low SNR. Slope proportional to signal amplitude squared A^2. Moderate computational burden.
Q_{PS}/I_{PS}	$\tan \phi$	Suboptimal, but good at high and low SNR. Slope not signal amplitude dependent. Higher computational burden and must check for divide by zero error near $\pm 90°$.
ATAN2 (Q_{PS}, I_{PS})	ϕ	Four-quadrant arctangent. Optimal (maximum likelihood estimator) at high and low SNR. Slope not signal amplitude dependent. Highest computational burden.

Table 5.3 summarizes several GPS receiver Costas PLL discriminators, their output phase errors and their characteristics. The first three discriminators are identical to those used in a pure PLL. The four-quadrant ATAN function (ATAN2) PLL discriminator remains linear over the full input error range of ±180°, whereas, the two-quadrant ATAN Costas discriminator remains linear over half of the input error range (±90°). Figure 5.9 compares the phase error outputs of each of these Costas PLL discriminators assuming no noise in the I and Q signals. With noise, the amplitudes of the discriminator outputs are reduced (their slopes tend to flatten) and they also tend to start rounding off in the 90° phase error region.

Referring to the carrier wipeoff process in the carrier tracking loop block diagram of Figure 5.8, and assuming that the carrier loop is in phase lock, the replica sine function is in phase with the incoming SV carrier signal (converted to IF). This results in a product at the I output, which, when averaged, produces the maximum I_{PS} amplitude. The replica cosine function is 90° out of phase with the incoming SV carrier. This results in a (cosine)(sine) product at the Q output, which, when averaged, produces the minimum Q_{PS} amplitude. For this reason, I_{PS} will be near its maximum (and will flip 180° each time the data bit changes sign) and Q_{PS} will be near its minimum (and will also flip 180° each time the data bit changes sign). These PLL

Table 5.3
Common Costas Loop Discriminators

Discriminator Algorithm	Output Phase Error	Characteristics
Sign $(I_{PS}) \cdot Q_{PS}$	$\sin \phi$	Near optimal at high SNR. Slope proportional to signal amplitude A. Least computational burden.
$I_{PS} \cdot Q_{PS}$	$\sin 2\phi$	Near optimal at low SNR. Slope proportional to signal amplitude squared A^2. Moderate computational burden.
Q_{PS}/I_{PS}	$\tan \phi$	Suboptimal, but good at high and low SNR. Slope not signal amplitude dependent. Higher computational burden and must check for divide by zero error near ±90°.
ATAN (Q_{PS}/I_{PS})	ϕ	Two-quadrant arctangent. Optimal (maximum likelihood estimator) at high and low SNR. Slope not signal amplitude dependent. Highest computational burden.

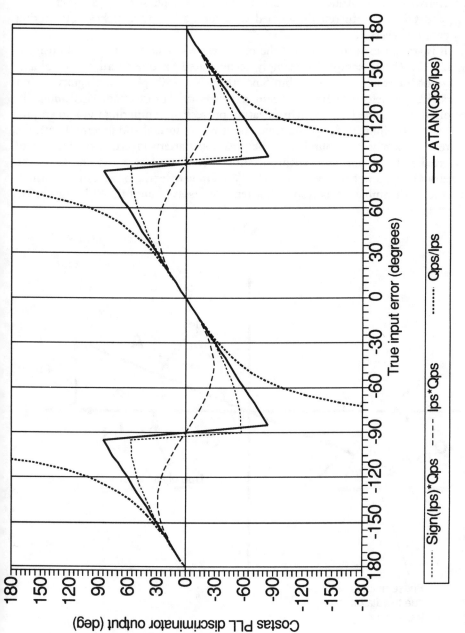

Figure 5.9 Comparison of Costas PLL discriminators.

characteristics are illustrated in Figure 5.10 where the phasor, *A*, (the vector sum of I_{PS} and Q_{PS}) tends to remain aligned with the I-axis and switches 180° during each data bit reversal.

It is straightforward to detect the bits in the SV data message stream using a Costas PLL. The I_{PS} samples are simply accumulated for one data bit interval and the sign of the result is the data bit. Since there is a 180° phase ambiguity with a Costas PLL, the detected data bit stream may be normal or inverted. This ambiguity is resolved during the frame synchronization process by comparing the known pre-amble at the beginning of each subframe both ways (normal and inverted) with the bit stream. If a match is found with the preamble pattern inverted, the bit stream is inverted and the subframe synchronization is confirmed by parity checks on the telemetry (TLM) and handover word (HOW). Otherwise, the bit stream is normal. Once the phase ambiguity is resolved, it remains resolved until the PLL loses phase

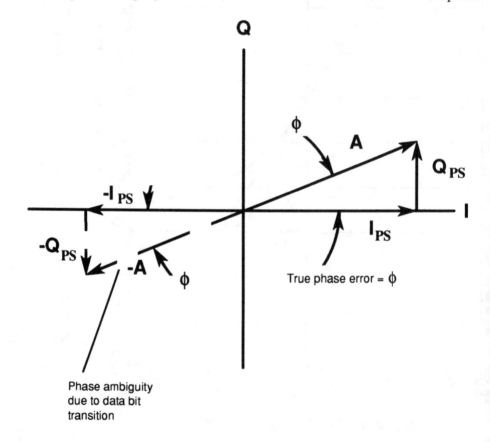

Figure 5.10 *I, Q* phasor diagram depicting true phase error between replica and incoming carrier phase.

lock or slips cycles. If this happens, the ambiguity must be resolved again. The 180° ambiguity of the Costas PLL can be resolved by referring to the phase detection result of the data bit demodulation. If the data bit phase is normal, then the carrier Doppler phase indicated by the Costas PLL is correct. If the data bit phase is inverted, then the carrier Doppler phase indicated by the Costas PLL phase can be corrected by adding 180°.

Costas PLLs as well as conventional PLLs are sensitive to dynamic stress, but produce the most accurate velocity measurements. For a given signal power level, Costas PLLs also provide the most error-free data demodulation in comparison to schemes used with FLLs. Therefore, this is the desired steady-state tracking mode of the GPS receiver carrier tracking loop. However, a well-designed GPS receiver carrier tracking loop will close the loop with a more robust FLL operated at wideband. Then, it will gradually reduce the carrier tracking loop bandwidth and transition into a wideband PLL operation. Finally, it will narrow the PLL bandwidth to the steady-state mode of operation. If dynamic stress causes the PLL to lose lock, the receiver will detect this with a sensitive phase lock detector and transition back to the FLL. The PLL closure process is then repeated.

5.1.2.3 Frequency Lock Loops

PLLs replicate the exact frequency of the incoming SV (converted to IF) to perform the carrier wipeoff function. FLLs perform the carrier wipeoff process by replicating the approximate frequency. For this reason, they are also called automatic frequency control (AFC) loops. The FLLs of GPS receivers must be insensitive to 180° reversals in the I and Q signals. Therefore, the sample times of the I and Q signals should not straddle the data bit transitions. During initial signal acquisition, when the receiver does not know where the data transition boundaries are, it is usually easier to maintain frequency lock than phase lock with the SV signal while performing bit synchronization. This is because the FLL discriminators are less sensitive to situations where some of the I and Q signals do straddle the data bit transitions, especially when the predetection integration times are small compared to the data bit transition intervals. Table 5.4 summarizes several GPS receiver FLL discriminators, their output frequency errors, and their characteristics.

Figure 5.11 compares the frequency error outputs of each of these discriminators assuming no noise in the I_{PS} and Q_{PS} samples. Figure 5.11(a) illustrates that the frequency pull-in range with a 200-Hz predetection bandwidth is twice the range of Figure 5.11(b) with 100 Hz. Adjacent pairs of samples $(t_2 - t_1)$ are taken every 5 msec and 10 msec, respectively. Note in both figures that the single-sided frequency pull-in ranges of the cross and ATAN2 (cross, dot) FLL discriminators are equal to half the predetection bandwidths. The sign(dot) · cross FLL discriminator frequency pull-in ranges are only one-fourth of the predetection bandwidths. Also note that

Table 5.4
Common Frequency Lock Loop Discriminators

Discriminator Algorithm	Output Frequency Error	Characteristics
$\dfrac{\text{sign(dot)cross}}{t_2 - t_1}$	$\dfrac{\sin[2(\phi_2 - \phi_1)]}{t_2 - t_1}$	Near optimal at high SNR. Slope proportional to signal amplitude A. Moderate computational burden.
where $\begin{aligned} \text{dot} &= I_{PS1} \cdot I_{PS2} + Q_{PS1} \cdot Q_{PS2} \\ \text{cross} &= I_{PS1} \cdot Q_{PS2} - I_{PS2} \cdot Q_{PS1} \end{aligned}$		
$\dfrac{\text{cross}}{t_2 - t_1}$	$\dfrac{\sin[(\phi_2 - \phi_1)]}{t_2 - t_1}$	Near optimal at low SNR. Slope proportional to signal amplitude squared A^2. Least computational burden.
$\dfrac{\text{ATAN2(cross,dot)}}{(t_2 - t_1)360}$	$\dfrac{\phi_2 - \phi_1}{(t_2 - t_1)360}$	Four-quadrant arctangent. Maximum likelihood estimator. Optimal at high and low SNR. Slope not signal amplitude dependent. Highest computational burden.

Note: Integrated and dumped prompt samples I_{PS1} and Q_{PS1} are the samples taken at time t_1, just prior to the samples I_{PS2} and Q_{PS2} taken at a later time t_2. These two adjacent samples should be within the same data bit interval. The next pair of samples are taken starting $(t_2 - t_1)$ sec after t_2, etc.

the sign(dot) · cross and the cross FLL discriminator outputs, whose outputs are sine functions scaled by the sample time interval $(t_2 - t_1)$ in their denominators, would more accurately approximate true frequency error if they were divided by 4. The ATAN2 (cross, dot) discriminator, whose output is a linear function scaled by $(t_2 - t_1)$ · 360 in the denominator, produces a true representation of the input frequency error within its pull-in range. The amplitudes of the discriminator outputs are reduced (their slopes tend to flatten) and they tend to start rounding off near the limits of their pull-in range as the thermal noise levels increase.

The I, Q phasor diagram in Figure 5.12 depicts the change in phase, $\phi_2 - \phi_1$, between two adjacent samples of I_{PS} and Q_{PS}, at times t_1 and t_2. This phase change over a fixed time interval is proportional to the frequency error in the carrier tracking loop. The figure also illustrates that there is no frequency ambiguity in the GPS receiver FLL discriminator because of data transitions, provided that the adjacent I and Q samples are taken within the same data bit interval. Note that the phasor A, which is the vector sum of I_{PS} and Q_{PS}, remains constant and rotates at a rate directly proportional to the frequency error when the loop is in frequency lock. It is possible

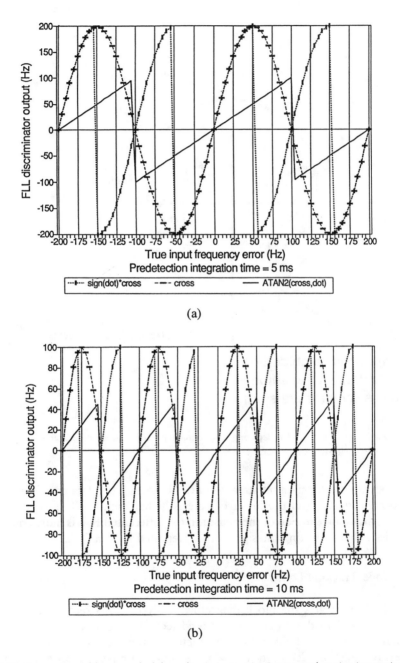

Figure 5.11 Comparison of frequency lock loop discriminators (a) 5-msec predetection integration time, (b) 10-msec predetection integration time.

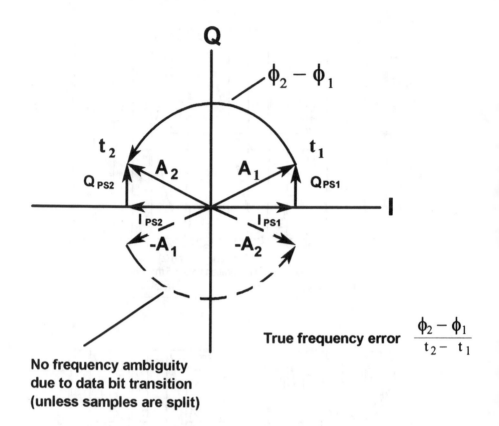

Figure 5.12 *I, Q* phasor diagram depicting true frequency error between replica and incoming carrier frequency.

to demodulate the SV data bit stream in FLL. Detecting the data transitions is more complicated in FLL and the bit error rate is higher than in PLL. This is because detecting the change in sign of the phasor in the differential FLL is more complicated and noisier than detecting the sign of the integrated I_{PS} in a PLL.

5.1.3 Code Tracking Loops

Figure 5.13 illustrates the block diagram of only the GPS receiver code tracking loop. The design of the programmable predetection integrators, the code loop discriminator and the code loop filter characterizes the receiver code tracking loop. These three functions determine the two most important performance characteristics of the receiver code loop design: the code loop thermal noise error and the maximum line-of-sight dynamic stress threshold. Even though the carrier tracking loop is the

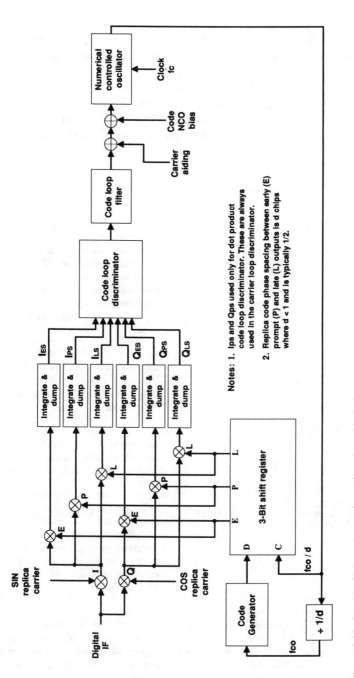

Figure 5.13 Generic GPS receiver code tracking loop block diagram.

weak link in terms of the receiver's dynamic stress threshold, it would be disastrous to attempt to aid the carrier loop with the code loop output. This is because, unaided, the code loop thermal noise is about three orders of magnitude larger than the carrier loop thermal noise.

Table 5.5 summarizes three GPS receiver noncoherent delay lock loop (DLL) discriminators and their characteristics. The fourth DLL discriminator shown is a normalized version of the third discriminator. The normalization removes the amplitude sensitivity of this DLL discriminator, which improves performance under pulse

Table 5.5
Common Delay Lock Loop Discriminators

Discriminator Algorithm	Characteristics
$\sum(I_{ES} - I_{LS})I_{PS} + \sum(Q_{ES} - Q_{LS})Q_{PS}$	Dot product power. This is the only DLL discriminator that uses all three correlators and this results in the lowest baseband computational load. For 1/2 chip correlator spacing, it produces nearly true error output within ±1/2 chip of input error.
$\sum(I_{ES}^2 + Q_{ES}^2) - \sum(I_{LS}^2 + Q_{LS}^2)$	Early minus late power. Moderate computational load. Essentially the same DLL discriminator error performance as early minus late envelope within ±1/2 chip of input error.
$\sum\sqrt{(I_{ES}^2 + Q_{ES}^2)} - \sum\sqrt{(I_{LS}^2 + Q_{LS}^2)}$	Early minus late envelope. Higher computational load. For 1/2 chip correlator spacing, produces good tracking error within ±1/2 chip of input error.
$\dfrac{\sum\sqrt{(I_{ES}^2 + Q_{ES}^2)} - \sum\sqrt{(I_{LS}^2 + Q_{LS}^2)}}{\sum\sqrt{(I_{ES}^2 + Q_{ES}^2)} + \sum\sqrt{(I_{LS}^2 + Q_{LS}^2)}}$	Early minus late envelope normalized by the early plus late envelope to remove amplitude sensitivity. Highest computational load. For 1/2 chip correlator spacing, produces good tracking error within less than ±1.5 chip of input error. Becomes unstable (divide by zero) at ±1.5 chip input error.

Note: As shown for every code loop discriminator, the power or the envelope values may be summed to reduce the iteration rate of the code loop filter as compared to that of the carrier loop filter when the code loop is aided by the carrier loop. Note that this does not increase the predetection integration time for the code loop. However, the code loop NCO must be updated every time the carrier loop NCO is updated even though the code loop filter output has not been updated. The last code loop filter output is combined with the current value of carrier aiding.

type RF interference. The other two DLL discriminators also can be normalized in a similar manner.

Figure 5.14 compares the four DLL discriminator outputs. The plots assume $1/2$-chip spacing between the early, prompt, and late correlators. This means that the 3-bit shift register is shifted at twice the clock rate of the code generator. Also assumed is an ideal correlation triangle and that there is no noise on the I and Q measurements. In reality, the correlation triangle tends to be rounded near the peak and not a perfectly linear ramp on either side of the peak owing to finite front-end bandwidth. As a result, the presence of noise tends to flatten the slopes and round the edges of the discriminators.

The normalized early minus late envelope discriminator is very popular, but the dot product power discriminator outperforms it and has the least computational burden. However, the dot product discriminator requires all three complex correlator signals. Some GPS receiver designs synthesize the early minus late replica code as a combined replica signal. The benefit is that only one complex correlator is required to generate an early minus late output. This approach is also compatible with the dot product discriminator. Since an early plus late signal is not produced, this approach is incompatible with the normalized early minus late discriminator to remove its signal amplitude sensitivity. The prompt signals can be substituted for this purpose, but with reduced performance.

To reduce the computational burden of forming the GPS signal envelopes (the magnitude of the I and Q vectors), approximations are often used. Two of the most popular approximations (named after their originators) are the JPL approximation and the Robertson approximation.

The JPL approximation to $A = \sqrt{I^2 + Q^2}$ is defined by

$$
\begin{aligned}
A_{ENV} &= \quad X + 1/8\,Y \qquad \text{if } X \geq 3Y \\
A_{ENV} &= 7/8X + 1/2\ Y \qquad \text{if } X < 3Y
\end{aligned}
\tag{5.2}
$$

where

$$
\begin{aligned}
X &= \text{MAX } (|I|, |Q|) \\
Y &= \text{MIN } (|I|, |Q|)
\end{aligned}
$$

The Robertson approximation is

$$
A_{ENV} = \text{MAX}(|I| + 1/2\ |Q|, |Q| + 1/2\ |I|)
\tag{5.3}
$$

The JPL approximation is the most accurate, but has the most computational burden.

Figure 5.15 illustrates the envelopes that result for three different replica code phases being correlated simultaneously with the same incoming SV signal. For ease

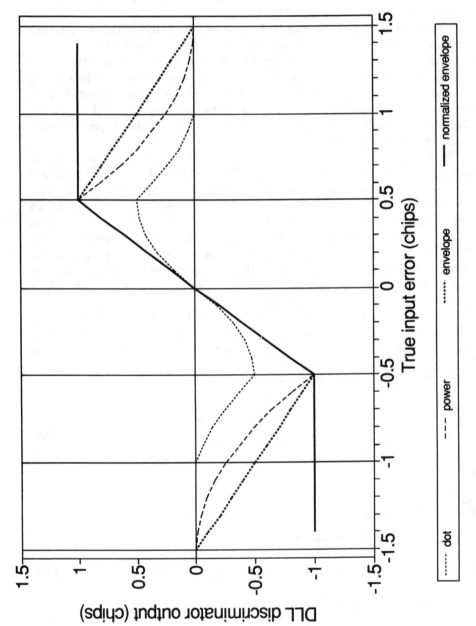

Figure 5.14 Comparison of delay lock loop discriminators.

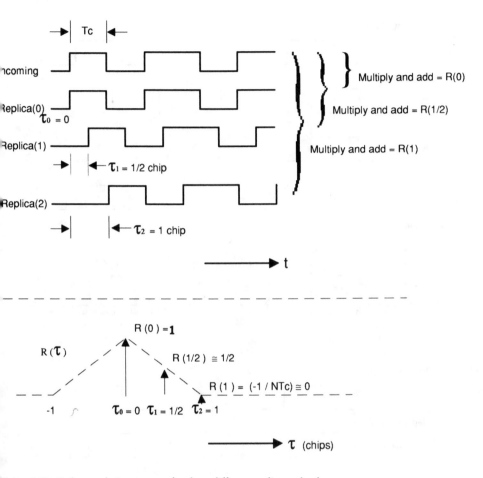

Figure 5.15 Code correlation process for three different replica code phases.

of visualization, the in-phase component of the incoming SV signal is shown without noise. The three replica phases are 1/2 chip apart and are representative of the early, prompt, and late replica codes that are synthesized in the code loop of Figure 5.13.

Figures 5.16(a–d) illustrate how the early, prompt, and late envelopes change as the phases of the replica code signals are advanced with respect to the incoming SV signal. For ease of visualization, only one chip of the continuous PN signal is shown and the incoming SV signal is shown without noise. Figure 5.17 illustrates the normalized early minus late envelope discriminator error output signals corresponding to the four replica code offsets (A), (B), (C), and (D). The closed code loop operation becomes apparent as a result of studying these replica code phase changes, the envelopes that they produce, and the resulting error output generated by the

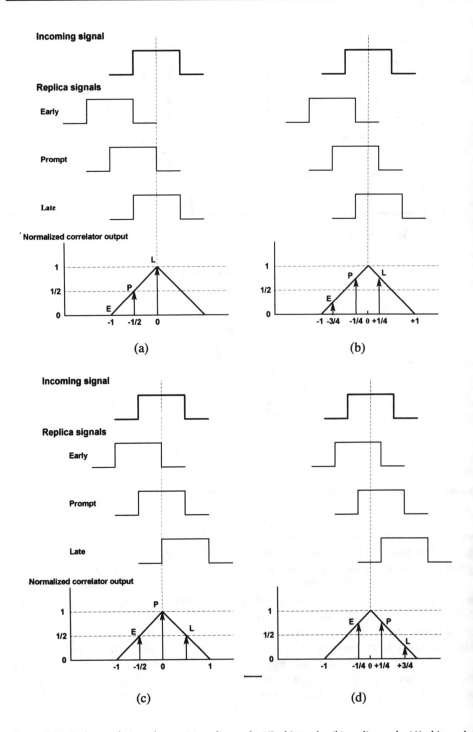

Figure 5.16 Code correlation phases: (a) replica code 1/2 chip early, (b) replica code 1/4 chip early, (c) replica code aligned, and (d) replica code 1/4 chip late.

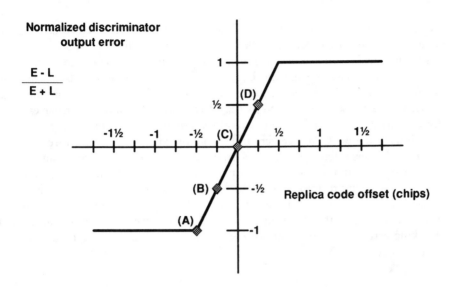

Figure 5.17 Code discriminator output versus replica code offset.

early minus late envelope code discriminator. If the replica code is aligned, then the early and late envelopes are equal in amplitude and no error is generated by the discriminator. If the replica code is misaligned, then the early and late envelopes are unequal by an amount that is proportional to the amount of error (within the limits of the correlation interval). The code discriminator senses the amount of error in the replica code and the direction (early or late) from the difference in the amplitudes of the early and late envelopes. This error is filtered and then applied to the code loop NCO where the output frequency is increased or decreased as necessary to correct the replica code generator phase with respect to the incoming SV signal code phase.

The discriminator examples given thus far have assumed that each channel of the GPS receiver contains three complex code correlators to provide early, prompt, and late correlated outputs. In early generations of GPS receiver designs, analog correlators were used instead of digital correlators. There was strong emphasis on reducing the number of expensive and power hungry analog correlators, so there were numerous code tracking loop design innovations that minimized the number of correlators. The tau-dither technique timeshares the early and late replica code with one complex (I and Q) correlator. This suffers a 3-dB loss of tracking threshold in the code loop because only half the energy is available from the early and late signals. This loss of threshold is unimportant in an unaided GPS receiver design because there is usually more than a 3-dB difference between the conventional code loop and carrier tracking loop thresholds. The extra margin in the code loop threshold only pays off for aided GPS receivers. The TI 4100 multiplex GPS receiver [2] not only used the tau-dither technique, but also timeshared only two analog correlators and the same replica code and carrier generators to simultaneously and continuously track (using 2.5-msec dwells) the L1 P-code and L2 P-code signals of four GPS satellites. It also simultaneously demodulated the 50-Hz navigation messages. Because the L2 tracking was aided by the L1 tracking, this multiplex receiver design suffered only 6-dB of tracking threshold losses instead of 12 dB.

Modern digital GPS receivers often contain many more than three complex correlators because digital correlators are relatively inexpensive; for example, only one exclusive-or circuit is required to perform the one bit multiply function. The innovations relating to improved performance through the use of more than three complex correlators include faster acquisition times [3], multipath mitigation [4], and a wider discriminator correlation interval [5]. However, there is no improvement in tracking error due to thermal noise or improvement in tracking threshold using multiple correlators.

5.1.4 Loop Filters

The objective of the loop filter is to reduce noise in order to produce an accurate estimate of the original signal at its output. The loop filter order and noise bandwidth also determine the loop filter's response to signal dynamics. As shown in the receiver block diagrams, the loop filter's output signal is effectively subtracted from the original signal to produce an error signal, which is fed back into the filter's input in a closed loop process. There are many design approaches to digital filters. The design approach described here draws on existing knowledge of analog loop filters, then adapts these into digital implementations. Figure 5.18 shows block diagrams of first-, second-, and third-order analog filters. Analog integrators are represented by $1/s$, the Laplace transform of the time domain integration function. The input signal is multiplied by the multiplier coefficients, then processed as shown in Figure 5.18. These multiplier coefficients and the number of integrators completely determine the loop filter's characteristics. Table 5.6 summarizes these filter characteristics and provides all the information required to compute the filter coefficients for first-, second-, or third-order loop filters. Only the filter order and noise bandwidth must be determined to complete the design.

Figure 5.19 depicts the block diagram representations of analog and digital integrators. The analog integrator of Figure 5.19(a) operates with a continuous time domain input, $x(t)$, and produces an integrated version of this input as a continuous time domain output, $y(t)$. Theoretically, $x(t)$ and $y(t)$ have infinite numerical resolution and the integration process is perfect. In reality, the resolution is limited by noise, which significantly reduces the dynamic range of analog integrators. There are also problems with drift.

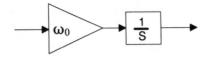

(a)

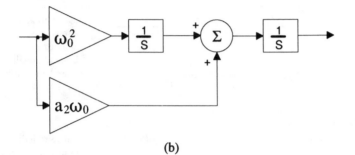

(b)

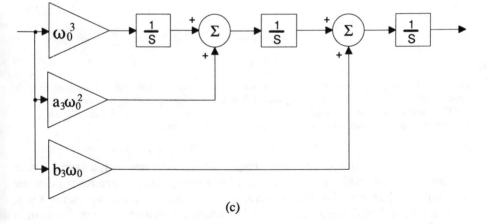

(c)

Figure 5.18 Block diagrams of (a) first-, (b) second-, and (c) third-order analog loop filters.

Table 5.6
Loop Filter Characteristics

Loop Order	Noise Bandwidth B_n (Hz)	Typical Filter Values	Steady-State Error	Characteristics
First	$\dfrac{\omega_0}{4}$ $B_n = 0.25\omega_0$	ω_0	$\dfrac{(dR/dt)}{\omega_0}$	Sensitive to velocity stress. Used in aided code loops and sometimes used in aided carrier loops. Unconditionally stable at all noise bandwidths.
Second	$\dfrac{\omega_0(1 + a_2^2)}{4a_2}$ $a_2\omega_0 = 1.414\omega_0$ $B_n = 0.53\omega_0$	ω_0^2	$\dfrac{(dR^2/dt^2)}{\omega_0^2}$	Sensitive to acceleration stress. Used in aided and unaided carrier loops. Unconditionally stable at all noise bandwidths.
Third	$\dfrac{\omega_0(a_3b_3^2 + a_3^2 - b_3)}{4(a_3b_3 - 1)}$ $a_3\omega_0^2 = 1.1\omega_0^2$ $b_3\omega_0 = 2.4\omega_0$ $B_n = 0.7845\omega_0$	ω_0^3	$\dfrac{(dR^3/dt^3)}{\omega_0^3}$	Sensitive to jerk stress. Used in unaided carrier loops. Remains stable at $B_n^- \leq 18$ Hz.

Notes: (1) The loop filter natural radian frequency ω_0 is computed from the value of the loop filter noise bandwidth B_n, selected by the designer. (2) R is the line-of-sight range to the satellite. (3) The steady-state error is inversely proportional to the tracking loop bandwidth and directly proportional to the nth derivative of range, where n is the loop filter order.

The boxcar digital integrator of Figure 5.19(b) operates with a sampled time domain input $x(n)$, which is quantized to a finite resolution, and produces a discrete integrated output $y(n)$. The time interval between each sample T represents a unit delay z^{-1} in the digital integrator. The digital integrator performs discrete integration perfectly with a dynamic range limited only by the number of bits used in the accumulator A. This provides a dynamic range capability much greater than can be achieved by its analog counterpart and the digital integrator does not drift. The boxcar integrator performs the function $y(n) = T[x(n)] + A(n - 1)$, where n is the discrete sample sequence number.

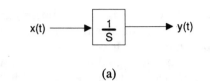

(a)

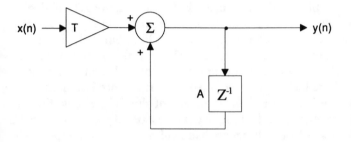

(b)

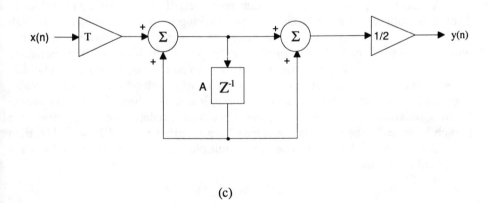

(c)

Figure 5.19 Block diagrams of (a) analog, (b) digital boxcar, and (c) digital bilinear transform integrators.

Figure 5.19(c) depicts a digital integrator that linearly interpolates between input samples and more closely approximates the ideal analog integrator. This is called the bilinear z-transform integrator. It performs the function $y(n) = T/2[x(n)] + A(n - 1) = 1/2[A(n) + A(n - 1)]$. The digital filters depicted in Figure 5.20 result when the Laplace integrators of Figure 5.18 are replaced with digital integrators as shown in Figure 5.19(c).

Figure 5.21 illustrates two FLL-assisted PLL loop filter designs. Figure 5.21(a) depicts a second-order PLL filter with a first-order FLL assist. Figure 5.21(b) depicts a third-order PLL filter with a second-order FLL assist. If the PLL error input is zeroed in either of these filters, the filter becomes a pure FLL. Similarly, if the FLL error input is zeroed, the filter becomes a pure PLL. The typical loop closure process is to close in pure FLL, then apply the error inputs from both discriminators as an FLL-assisted PLL until phase lock is achieved, then convert to pure PLL until phase lock is lost. In general, the natural radian frequency of the FLL, ω_{0f}, is different from the natural radian frequency of the PLL, ω_{0p}. These natural radian frequencies are determined from the desired loop filter noise bandwidths B_{nf} and B_{np}, respectively. The values for the second-order coefficient a_2 and third-order coefficients a_3 and b_3 can be determined from Table 5.6. These coefficients are the same for FLL, PLL, or DLL applications if the loop order and the noise bandwidth B_n are the same. Note that the FLL coefficient insertion point into the filter is one integrator back from the PLL and DLL insertion points. This is because the FLL error is in units of hertz (change in range per unit of time), whereas the PLL and DLL errors are in units of phase (range).

A loop filter parameter design example will clarify the use of the equations in Table 5.6. Suppose that the receiver carrier tracking loop will be subjected to high acceleration dynamics and will not be aided by an external navigation system, but must maintain PLL operation. A third-order loop is selected because it is insensitive to acceleration stress. To minimize its sensitivity to jerk stress, the noise bandwidth, B_n, is chosen to be the widest possible consistent with stability. Table 5.6 indicates that $B_n \leq 18$ Hz is safe. This limitation has been determined through extensive Monte Carlo simulations and is related to the maximum predetection integration time (which is typically the same as the carrier loop iteration rate). If $B_n = 18$ Hz, then $\omega_0 = B_n/0.7845 = 22.94$ rad. The three multipliers shown in Figure 5.20(c) are computed as follows:

$$\omega_0^3 = 12079.214$$

$$a_3\omega_0^2 = 1.1\omega_0^2 = 579.098$$

$$b_3\omega_0 = 2.4\omega_0 = 55.067$$

If the loop iteration rate is once each 5 msec, then $T = 0.005$ sec for use in the digital integrators. This completes the third-order filter parameter design. The

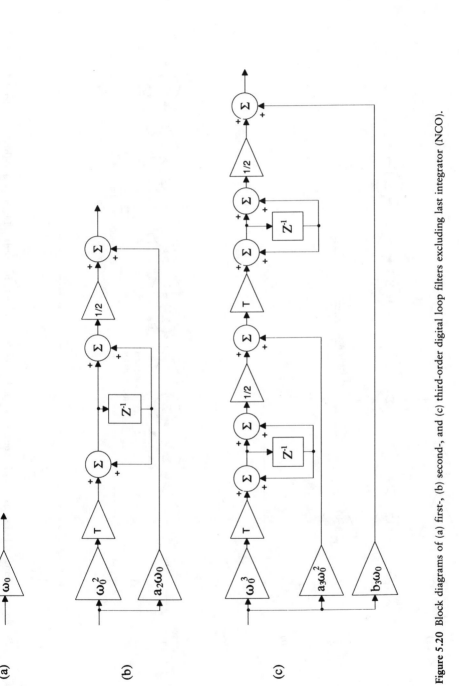

Figure 5.20 Block diagrams of (a) first-, (b) second-, and (c) third-order digital loop filters excluding last integrator (NCO).

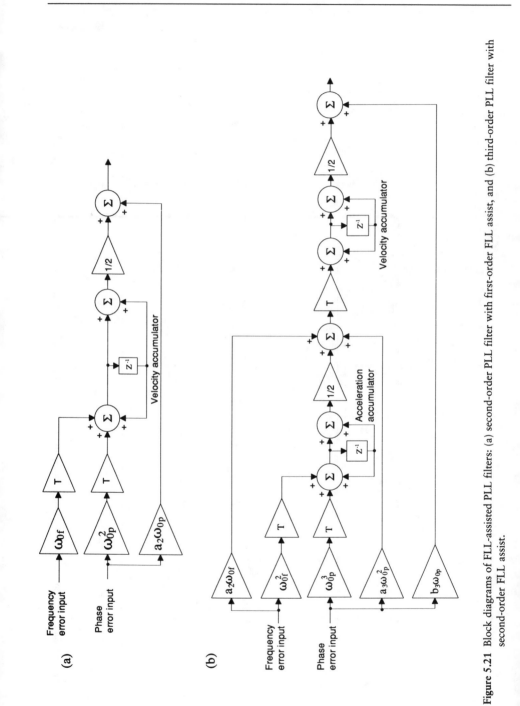

Figure 5.21 Block diagrams of FLL-assisted PLL filters: (a) second-order PLL filter with first-order FLL assist, and (b) third-order PLL filter with second-order FLL assist.

remainder of the loop filter design is the implementation of the digital integrator accumulators to ensure that they will never overflow; that is, that they have adequate dynamic range. The use of floating point arithmetic in modern microprocessors with built-in floating point hardware greatly simplifies this part of the design process.

5.1.5 Measurement Errors and Tracking Thresholds

The GPS measurement errors and tracking thresholds are closely related because the receiver loses lock when the measurement errors exceed a certain boundary. Because the code and carrier tracking loops are nonlinear, especially near the threshold regions, only Monte Carlo simulations of the GPS receiver under the combined dynamic and signal-to-noise ratio (SNR) conditions will determine the true tracking performance. However, rules of thumb can be used based on equations that predict the measurement errors of the tracking loops. Numerous sources of measurement errors are in each type of tracking loop. However, it is sufficient for rule-of-thumb tracking thresholds to analyze only the dominant error sources.

5.1.5.1 PLL Tracking Loop Measurement Errors

The dominant sources of phase error in a GPS receiver PLL are phase jitter and dynamic stress error. The 3-sigma values of this PLL error and its rule-of-thumb tracking threshold are computed as follows:

$$3\sigma_{\text{PLL}} = 3\sigma_j + \theta_e \leq 45 \text{ deg} \tag{5.4}$$

where

σ_j = 1-sigma phase jitter from all sources except dynamic stress error
θ_e = dynamic stress error in the PLL tracking loop

Equation (5.4) shows that dynamic stress error is a 3-sigma effect and is additive to the phase jitter. The phase jitter is the root sum square of every source of uncorrelated phase error, such as thermal noise and oscillator noise. Oscillator noise includes vibration induced jitter and Allan deviation-induced jitter.

As shown in (5.4), a conservative rule-of-thumb threshold for a PLL tracking loop is that the 3-sigma phase errors from all causes should not exceed 45 deg. Therefore, the 1-sigma rule-of-thumb PLL tracking threshold is 15 deg. PLL discriminator error outputs begin to flatten and round off beyond the 45-deg input phase error level when the carrier-to-noise power ratio (C/N_0) decreases toward the thermal noise threshold. The 1-sigma rule-of-thumb threshold for the PLL tracking loop is therefore

$$\sigma_{PLL} = \sqrt{\sigma_{tPLL}^2 + \sigma_v^2 + \theta_A^2} + \frac{\theta_e}{3} \leq 15 \text{ deg} \tag{5.5}$$

where

σ_{tPLL} = 1-sigma PLL thermal noise in degrees
σ_v = 1-sigma vibration induced oscillator jitter in degrees
θ_A = Allan variance-induced oscillator jitter in degrees

PLL Thermal Noise

Often, the PLL thermal noise is treated as the only source of carrier tracking error, since the other sources of PLL jitter may be either transient or negligible. The thermal noise jitter for a PLL is computed as follows:

$$\sigma_{tPLL} = \frac{360}{2\pi} \sqrt{\frac{B_n}{c/n_0}\left(1 + \frac{1}{2T\, c/n_0}\right)} \text{ (deg)} \tag{5.6}$$

$$\sigma_{tPLL} = \frac{\lambda_L}{2\pi} \sqrt{\frac{B_n}{c/n_0}\left(1 + \frac{1}{2T\, c/n_0}\right)} \text{ (m)} \tag{5.7}$$

where

B_n = carrier loop noise bandwidth (Hz)
C/N_0 = carrier to noise power expressed as a ratio
    = $10^{c/N_0/10}$ for C/N_0 expressed in dB-Hz
T = predetection integration time (sec)
λ_L = GPS propagation constant/L-band carrier frequency (m/sec)/(cycles/sec)
    = $2.99792458 \times 10^8/1.57542 \times 10^9 = 0.1903$ m/cycle for L1
    = $2.99792458 \times 10^8/1.2276 \times 10^9 = 0.2442$ m/cycle for L2

Note that (5.6) and (5.7) do not include factors relating to C/A-code or P(Y)-code or the loop filter order. Also note that (5.6) is independent of carrier frequency when the error is expressed in units of degrees. The carrier thermal noise is strictly dependent on the C/N_0, the noise bandwidth, and the predetection integration time. If the C/N_0 increases, the thermal noise decreases. Decreasing the noise bandwidth reduces the thermal noise. The part of the equation involving the predetection integration time T is called the squaring loss. Hence, increasing the predetection integration time reduces the squaring loss, which in turn decreases the thermal noise.

It is usually assumed that the GPS P(Y) (precision) codes always produce more accurate measurements than the C/A (coarse) codes, but the PLL thermal noise error is the same for either code for the same C/N_0. Since the C/A-code is 3 dB stronger than P(Y)-code, the carrier thermal noise error is smaller for C/A-code receivers than for P(Y)-code receivers, assuming no signal jamming and all other things in the receiver designs are equal. It is also usually assumed that the carrier loop measurement is a velocity measurement, when actually it is a range measurement. The PLL thermal noise error is in units of range because it is part of the carrier Doppler phase measurement. The velocity is approximated using the change in carrier Doppler phase between two carrier range measurements over a short time. Any single PLL measurement is a precise phase measurement of the carrier Doppler phase within one cycle. The differential measurement must also account for the integer number of carrier Doppler-phase cycles that occur between measurements.

Figure 5.22 illustrates the PLL thermal noise jitter plotted as a function of C/N_0 for three different noise bandwidths, assuming the maximum 20-msec predetection integration time. Even though the thermal noise jitter is not directly dependent on the loop order, there is an indirect relationship. The loop order is sensitive to the same order of dynamics (first order to velocity stress, second order to acceleration

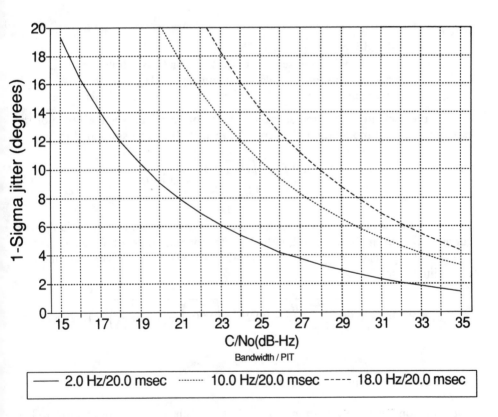

Figure 5.22 PLL thermal noise jitter.

stress and third order to jerk stress). In general, when the loop order is made higher, there is an improvement in dynamic stress performance. Thus, the thermal noise can be reduced for the same minimum C/N_0 by increasing the loop order and reducing bandwidths while also improving the dynamic performance.

Vibration-Induced Oscillator Phase Noise

Vibration-induced oscillator phase noise is a complex analysis problem. In some cases, the expected vibration environment is so severe that the reference oscillator must be mounted using vibration isolators in order for the GPS receiver to successfully operate in PLL. The equation for vibration-induced oscillator jitter is

$$\sigma_v = \frac{360 \, f_L}{2\pi} \sqrt{\int_{f_{min}}^{f_{max}} S_v^2(f_m)\frac{P(f_m)}{f_m^2}df_m} \quad \text{(deg)} \tag{5.8}$$

where
f_L = L-band input frequency in Hz
$S_v(f_m)$ = oscillator vibration sensitivity of $\Delta f/f_L$ per G as a function of f_m
f_m = random vibration modulation frequency in Hz
$P(f_m)$ = power curve of the random vibration in G^2/Hz as a function of f_m

If the oscillator vibration sensitivity S_v is not variable over the range of the random vibration modulation frequency f_m, then (5.8) can be simplified to

$$\sigma_v = \frac{360 \, f_L S_v}{2\pi} \sqrt{\int_{f_{min}}^{f_{max}} \frac{P(f_m)}{f_m^2}df_m} \quad \text{(deg)} \tag{5.9}$$

As a simple computational example, assume that the random vibration power curve is flat from 20 Hz to 2,000 Hz with an amplitude of 0.005 G^2/Hz. If $S_v = 1 \times 10^{-9}$ parts/G and $f_L = L1 = 1575.42 \times 10^6$ Hz, then the vibration-induced phase jitter using (5.9) is

$$\sigma_v = 90.265\sqrt{0.005\int_{20}^{2,000}\frac{df_m}{f_m^2}} = 90.265\sqrt{0.005\left(\frac{1}{20} - \frac{1}{2,000}\right)} = 1.42 \text{ deg}$$

Allan Deviation Oscillator Phase Noise

The equations used to determine Allan deviation phase noise are empirical. The equations are stated in terms of what the requirements are for the short-term stability of the reference oscillator as determined by the Allan variance method of stability measurement. The equation for short-term Allan deviation for a second-order PLL is [6]

$$\sigma_A(\tau) = 2.5\frac{\Delta\theta}{\omega_L\tau} \qquad \left(\frac{\Delta f}{f} \text{ dimensionless}\right) \qquad (5.10)$$

where

$\Delta\theta$ = root mean square jitter into phase discriminator due to the oscillator (rad)

ω_L = L-band input frequency = $2\pi f_L$ (rad/sec)

τ = short-term stability gate time for Allan variance measurement (sec)

The equation for a third-order PLL is similar [6]:

$$\sigma_A(\tau) = \frac{2.25\ \Delta\theta}{\omega_L\tau} \qquad \left(\frac{\Delta f}{f} \text{ dimensionless}\right) \qquad (5.11)$$

If the Allan variance, $\sigma_A^2(\tau)$, has already been determined for the oscillator for the short-term gate time, τ, then the Allan deviation-induced jitter in degrees, $\theta_A = (\Delta\theta)360/2\pi$, can be computed from the above equations. The short-term gate time used in the Allan variance measurement must be evaluated at the noise bandwidth of the carrier loop filter $\tau = 1/B_n$. Rearranging (5.10) using these assumptions, the equation for the second-order loop is

$$\theta_{A2} = 144\frac{\sigma_A(\tau)f_L}{B_n} \text{ (deg)} \qquad (5.12)$$

Rearranging (5.11) using these assumptions, the equation for the third-order loop is

$$\theta_{A3} = 160\frac{\sigma_A(\tau)f_L}{B_n} \text{ (deg)} \qquad (5.13)$$

For example, if the loop filter were third-order with a noise bandwidth, $B_n = 18$ Hz, tracking the L1 signal, and the Allan deviation for a gate time $\tau = 1/B_n = 0.056$ sec is specified to be $\sigma_A(\tau) = 1 \times 10^{-10}$ or better, then the phase jitter contribution due to this error is $\theta_{A3} = 1.40$ deg or less. Obviously, a reference oscillator with a short-term Allan deviation characteristic that is more than an order of magnitude worse than this example will cause PLL tracking problems.

Narrowband second-order loop filters are typically used for externally aided or stationary GPS receiver applications. Figure 5.23 graphically portrays the sensitiv-

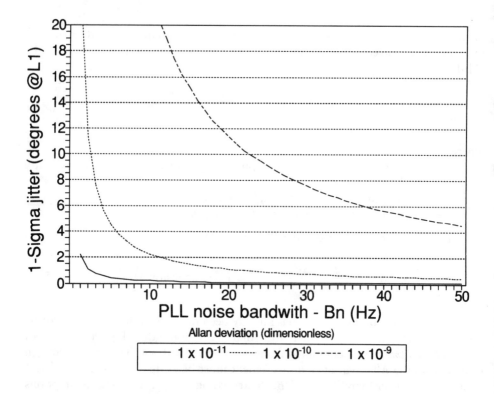

Figure 5.23 Allan deviation jitter in second-order PLL at L1.

ity of a second-order PLL to changes in short-term Allan deviation performance of the reference oscillator, especially as the noise bandwidth B_n is narrowed. The objective of narrowing the bandwidth is to reduce the thermal noise error to improve the tracking threshold. However, as Figure 5.23 illustrates, the Allan deviation effects begin to dominate at the narrower noise bandwidths. This effect is usually the primary source of aided GPS receiver narrowband PLL tracking problems assuming that the external velocity aiding accuracy is not the limiting factor. However, even for an unaided GPS receiver, a reference oscillator with a poor Allan deviation characteristic, say a $\Delta f/f$ of less than 1×10^{-9} for gate times of 1 msec to 20 msec, will prevent reliable PLL operation. Therefore, the oscillator specification for Allan deviation is important for all GPS receiver designs.

Dynamic Stress Error

The dynamic stress error is obtained from the steady-state error formulas shown in Table 5.6. This error depends on the loop bandwidth and order. The maximum dynamic stress error may be slightly larger than the steady-state error if the loop filter response to a step function has overshoot, but the steady-state error formula will suffice. There should be no more than about a 7% overshoot if the filter is designed for minimum mean square error, which is the case for the typical loop filter coefficients shown in the table. From Table 5.6, a second-order loop with minimum mean square error, the dynamic stress error is

$$\theta_{e2} = \frac{dR^2/dt^2}{\omega_0^2} = \frac{dR^2/dt^2}{\left(\dfrac{B_n}{0.53}\right)^2} = 0.2809 \frac{dR^2/dt^2}{B_n^2} \text{ (deg)} \qquad (5.14)$$

where dR^2/dt^2 = maximum line-of-sight acceleration dynamics (deg/sec²).

From Table 5.6, a third-order loop with minimum mean square error, the dynamic stress error is defined as follows:

$$\theta_{e3} = \frac{dR^3/dt^3}{\omega_0^3} = \frac{dR^3/dt^3}{\left(\dfrac{B_n}{0.7845}\right)^3} = 0.4828 \frac{dR^3/dt^3}{B_n^3} \text{ (deg)} \qquad (5.15)$$

where dR^3/dt^3 = maximum line-of-sight jerk dynamics (deg/sec³).

As an example of how this error is computed, suppose the third-order loop noise bandwidth is 18 Hz and the maximum line-of-sight jerk dynamic stress to the SV is 10G/sec = 98.0 m/sec³. To convert this to deg/sec³, multiply the jerk dynamics by the wavelength of the carrier frequency in deg/m. For L1, this wavelength is 360 deg/0.1903m = 1891.8 deg/m. For L2, this wavelength is 360 deg/0.2442m = 1474.2 deg/m. For 10 G/sec dynamic stress at L1, this results in dR^3/dt^3 = 98.0 * 1891.8 = 185,396 deg/sec³. For 10G dynamic stress at L2, dR^3/dt^3 = 144,472 deg/sec³. Using (5.15), the 3-sigma stress error for a 18-Hz third-order PLL is 15.35 deg for L1 and 11.96 deg for L2. These are well below the 45-deg rule-of-thumb levels.

Reference Oscillator Acceleration Stress Error

The PLL cannot tell the difference between the dynamic stress induced by real dynamics and the dynamic stress caused by changes in frequency in the reference oscillator due to acceleration sensitivity of the oscillator. The oscillator response to dynamic stress is

$$\theta_g = 360 \, S_g f_L \, G(t) \text{ (deg)} \qquad (5.16)$$

where

S_g = g-sensitivity of the oscillator ($\Delta f / f_L$ per G)
f_L = L-band input frequency (Hz)
      = 1575.42×10^6 Hz for L1
      = 1227.76×10^6 Hz for L2
$G(t)$ = acceleration stress in G's as a function of time

   For an unaided carrier tracking loop, the acceleration-induced oscillator error can be ignored. For example, the third-order tracking loop is sensitive to jerk dynamics, but jerk stress (G/sec) on the oscillator produces a stress error into the tracking loop in units of deg/sec^2. The third-order tracking loop is insensitive to acceleration stress. For lower order loops, the actual acceleration dynamic stress will dominate. However, for an externally aided tracking loop, this acceleration stress sensitivity must be considered.

Total PLL Tracking Loop Measurement Errors and Thresholds

Figure 5.24 illustrates the total PLL jitter as a function of C/N_0 for a third-order PLL, including all effects described in (5.5), (5.6), (5.9), (5.13), and (5.15). Equation (5.5) can be rearranged to solve for the dynamic stress error and this can be solved for the dynamic stress at threshold. Figure 5.25 illustrates the dynamic stress at threshold as a function of noise bandwidth for a third order PLL.

5.1.5.2 FLL Tracking Loop Measurement Errors

The dominant sources of frequency error in a GPS receiver FLL are thermal noise frequency jitter and dynamic stress error. The rule-of-thumb tracking threshold for the FLL is that the 3-sigma value of the jitter due to all sources of loop stress must not exceed 90° in one predetection integration time T. Therefore, the rule-of-thumb FLL tracking threshold is

$$3\sigma_{FLL} = 3\sigma_{tFLL} + f_e \leq 0.25/T \text{ (Hz)} \tag{5.17}$$

where

$3\sigma_{tFLL}$ = 1-sigma thermal noise frequency jitter
f_e = dynamic stress error in the FLL tracking loop

   Equation (5.17) shows that the dynamic stress frequency error is a 3-sigma effect and is additive to the thermal noise frequency jitter. The reference oscillator vibration and Allan deviation-induced frequency jitter are small-order effects on the FLL and are considered negligible. The 1-sigma frequency jitter threshold would be 30/(360T) = 0.0833/T Hz.

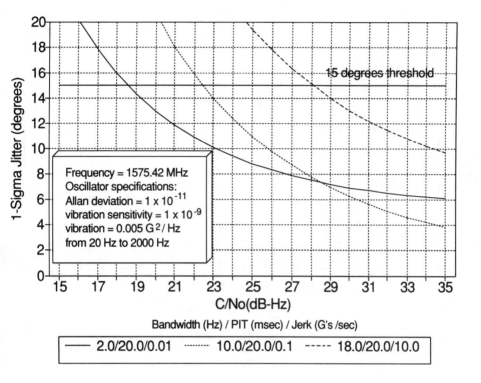

Figure 5.24 Total PLL jitter for third-order carrier loop.

The FLL tracking loop jitter due to thermal noise is

$$\sigma_{tFLL} = \frac{1}{2\pi T}\sqrt{\frac{4F\,B_n}{c/n_0}\left[1 + \frac{1}{T\,c/n_0}\right]} \quad (\text{Hz}) \qquad (5.18)$$

$$\sigma_{tFLL} = \frac{\lambda_L}{2\pi T}\sqrt{\frac{4F\,B_n}{c/n_0}\left[1 + \frac{1}{T\,c/n_0}\right]} \quad (\text{m/sec}) \qquad (5.19)$$

where

F = 1 at high C/N_0
= 2 near threshold

Note that (5.18) is independent of C/A-code or P(Y)-code and loop order. It is independent of L-band carrier frequency if the error units are expressed in hertz. Figure 5.26 illustrates the FLL thermal noise tracking jitter for typical noise bandwidths and predetection integration times.

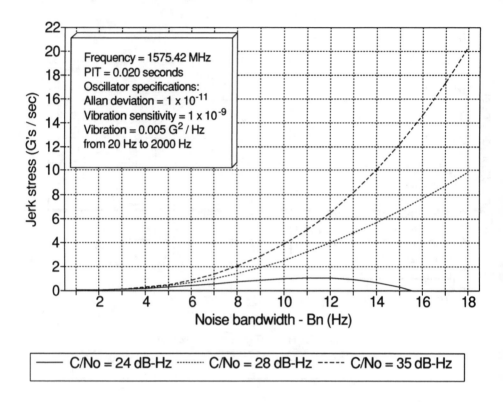

Figure 5.25 Jerk stress thresholds for third-order PLL.

Because the FLL tracking loop involves one more integrator than the PLL tracking loop of the same order, the dynamic stress error is

$$f_e = \frac{d}{dt}\left(\frac{1}{360\omega_0^n}\frac{dR^n}{dt^n}\right) = \frac{1}{360\omega_0^n}\frac{dR^{n+1}}{dt^{n+1}} \text{ (Hz)} \qquad (5.20)$$

As an example of how the dynamic stress error is computed from (5.20), assume a second-order FLL with a noise bandwidth of 2 Hz and a predetection integration time of 5 msec. From Table 5.6, for a second-order loop $B_n = 1.53\omega_0$. If the maximum line-of-sight jerk stress is 1 G/sec, then this is equivalent to $dR^3/dt^3 = 18,540$ deg/sec^3 at L1. Substituting these numbers into (5.20) results in a maximum dynamic stress error of $f_e = 30$ Hz. Since the 1-sigma threshold is $0.0833/0.005 = 16.66$ Hz, the FLL noise bandwidth should be increased.

Figure 5.27 illustrates the jerk stress thresholds for a second-order FLL as a function of noise bandwidth with C/N_0 as a running parameter. Comparing the thresholds in Figure 5.27 for an FLL with those of Figure 5.25 for a PLL, notice

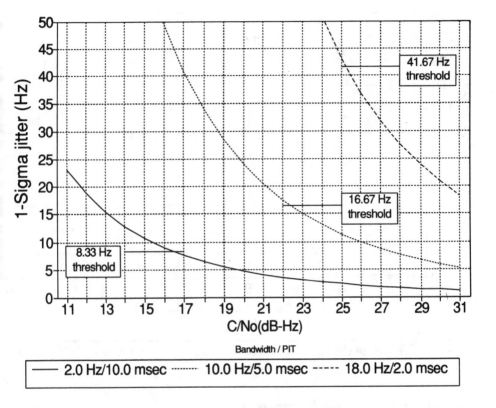

Figure 5.26 FLL thermal noise jitter.

that the second-order FLL has about an order of magnitude better dynamic stress performance than a third-order PLL at the same noise bandwidths and C/N$_0$. The PLL would have performed moderately better under dynamic stress if the predetection integration time had been reduced from 20 msec to 5 msec. This comparison reinforces the earlier statements that a robust GPS receiver design will use an FLL as a backup to the PLL during initial loop closure and during high-dynamic stress with loss of phase lock, but will revert to pure PLL for the steady-state low to moderate dynamics in order to produce the highest accuracy carrier Doppler phase measurements.

5.1.5.3 Code Tracking Loop Measurement Errors

The dominant sources of range error in a GPS receiver code tracking loop (DLL) are thermal noise range error jitter and dynamic stress error. The rule-of-thumb

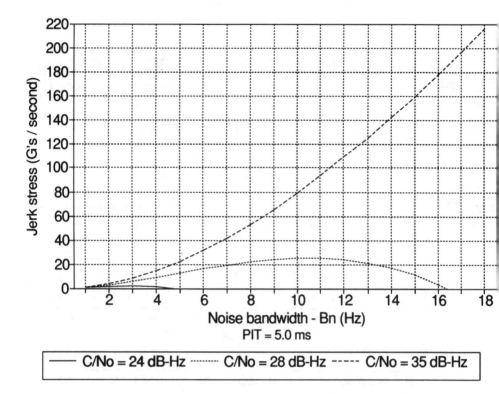

Figure 5.27 Jerk stress thresholds for second-order FLL.

tracking threshold for the DLL is that the 3-sigma value of the jitter due to all sources of loop stress must not exceed the correlator spacing d, in chips. Therefore, the rule-of-thumb tracking threshold is

$$3\sigma_{\text{DLL}} = 3\sigma_{t\text{DLL}} + R_e \leq d \quad \text{(chips)} \tag{5.21}$$

where

$\sigma_{t\text{DLL}}$ = 1-sigma thermal noise code tracking jitter
R_e = dynamic stress error in the DLL tracking loop

The DLL thermal noise code tracking jitter is

$$\sigma_{t\text{DLL}} = \sqrt{\frac{4F_1 d^2 B_n}{c/n_0}\left[2(1-d) + \frac{4F_2 d}{T\,c/n_0}\right]} \quad \text{(chips)} \tag{5.22}$$

where

F_1 = DLL discriminator correlator factor (dimensionless)
 = 1 for time shared tau-dithered early/late correlator
 = 1/2 for dedicated early and late correlators
d = correlator spacing between early, prompt, and late (dimensionless)
B_n = code loop noise bandwidth (Hz)
c/n_0 = carrier to noise power expressed as a ratio
 = $10^{C/N_0/10}$ for C/N_0 expressed in dB-Hz
T = predetection integration time (sec)
F_2 = DLL discriminator type factor (dimensionless)
 = 1 for early/late type discriminator
 = 1/2 for dot product type discriminator

As seen in (5.22), the DLL jitter is directly proportional to the square root of the filter noise bandwidth (lower B_n results in a lower jitter which, in turn, results in a lower C/N_0 threshold). Also, increasing the predetection integration time T results in a lower C/N_0 threshold, but with less effect than reducing B_n. The part of the equation involving the predetection integration time T, is called the squaring loss. Hence, increasing the predetection integration time reduces the squaring loss. Reducing the correlator spacing, d, also reduces the DLL jitter at the expense of reduced dynamic stress threshold. This is a reasonable tradeoff for carrier-aided C/A-code receivers where the correlation interval is ten times longer than the P(Y)-code and the value of N is compatible with NCO frequency limitations. Reducing the correlator spacing helps improve the C/A-code tracking loop vulnerability to multipath [4].

Note that the thermal noise is independent of tracking loop order in (5.22). Also note that the thermal noise is the same for either C/A-code or P(Y)-code when expressed in units of chips. However, all other things being equal, the thermal noise is ten times larger for the C/A-code than the P(Y)-code because the chip wavelength of the C/A-code is ten times longer than for P(Y)-code. This is readily observed if measurement is converted to meters instead of chips as follows:

$$\sigma_{tDLL} = \lambda_c \sqrt{\frac{4 F_1 d^2 B_n}{c/n_0}\left[2(1-d) + \frac{4 F_2 d}{T\, c/n_0}\right]} \quad (\text{m}) \qquad (5.23)$$

where

λ_c = GPS propagation constant/PRN code chipping rate (m/sec)/(chips/sec)
 = $2.99792458 \times 10^8/1.023 \times 10^6$ = 293.05 m/chip for C/A-code
 = $2.99792458 \times 10^8/10.23 \times 10^6$ = 29.305 m/chip for P(Y)-code

Figure 5.28(a) uses (5.22) to compare the dot product and the early/late DLL discriminator performance. At threshold, the dot product discriminator is about 1-dB better for this example. Figure 5.28(b) demonstrates the improved DLL tracking

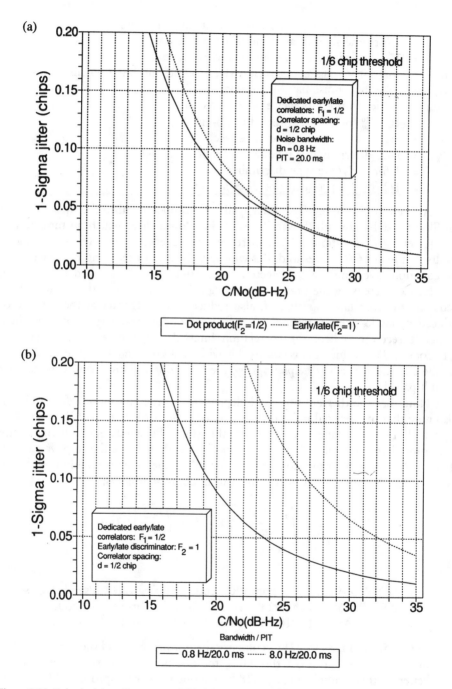

Figure 5.28 Delay lock loop jitter versus C/N_0: (a) comparison of dot product and early/late DLL discriminators, (b) effect of noise bandwidth on DLL jitter, (c) effect of predetection integration time on DLL jitter, (d) comparison of DLL jitter for different correlator spacing.

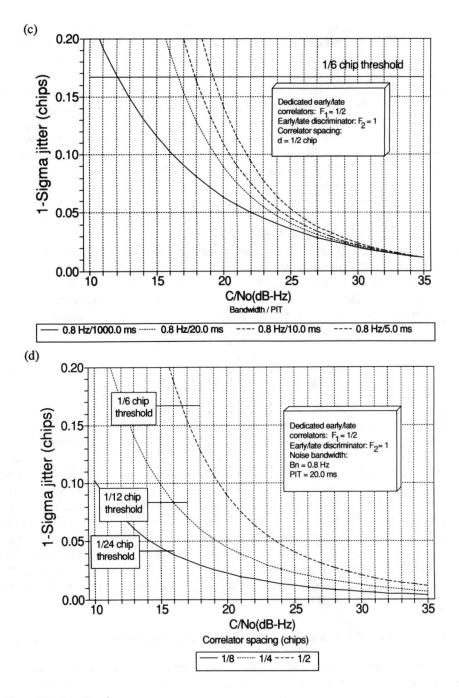

Figure 5.28 (continued)

threshold by reducing the noise bandwidth on the DLL. Figure 5.28(c) illustrates the improved DLL tracking threshold by reducing the predetection integration times. The 1-sec predetection integration time (PIT) provides the lowest code tracking threshold. To support a predetection integration time greater than 20 msec (the navigation message data bit interval), the data wipeoff process must be implemented. Recall that this technique uses the GPS receiver's a priori knowledge of the navigation message data bit stream to remove the 180° data transitions. This data wipeoff technique permits longer than 20-msec predetection integration times which, if properly implemented, can achieve nearly 6 dB of additional C/N_0 threshold improvement (see Figure 5.28(c) at threshold crossings). This is a short-term "desperation" DLL weak signal hold-on strategy for an externally aided GPS receiver when the carrier is aided open loop. Data wipeoff also improves the PLL tracking threshold when the carrier loop is closed loop aided, but not to the extent that the code loop tracking threshold is improved. Changes in any part of the SV navigation message data stream by the SV or a GPS control segment upload will cause errors in the data wipeoff, which, in turn, will cause a deterioration in the tracking threshold.

Figure 5.28(d) compares the DLL performance for different correlator spacings. Note that the thermal noise is reduced when the correlator spacing is reduced but the threshold improves. However, the dynamic stress tolerance is reduced.

The DLL tracking loop dynamic stress error is determined by

$$R_e = \frac{\dfrac{dR^n}{dt^n}}{\omega_0^n} \text{ (chips)} \qquad (5.24)$$

where dR^n/dt^n is expressed in chips/sec^n.

As an example of how the dynamic stress error is computed from (5.24), assume that the code loop is an unaided third-order DLL with a noise bandwidth of 2 Hz and $d = 1/2$ chip correlator spacing. From Table 5.6, for a third-order loop, $\omega_0 = B_n/0.7845$. If the maximum line-of-sight jerk stress is 10 G/sec, then this is equivalent to $dR^3/dt^3 = 98$ m/sec^3/293.05 m/chip $= 0.3344$ chips/sec^3 for C/A-code. Substituting these numbers into (5.24) results in a maximum dynamic stress error of $R_e = 0.02$ chip. Since the 1-sigma threshold is 1/6 chip $= 0.167$ chip, this would indicate that the DLL noise bandwidth is more than adequate for C/A-code. If the receiver was P(Y)-code, then $R_e = 0.2$ chips, which is marginally inadequate. Using carrier-aided code techniques makes the dynamic stress for the code tracking loop a small-order effect that usually can be neglected.

5.1.6 Formation of Pseudorange, Delta Pseudorange, and Integrated Doppler

Contrary to popular belief, the natural measurements of a GPS receiver are not pseudorange or delta pseudorange. This section describes these natural measurements of a GPS receiver and describes how they may be converted into pseudorange, delta pseudorange, and integrated Doppler. The natural measurements are replica code phase and replica carrier Doppler phase (if the GPS receiver is in phase lock with the satellite carrier signal) or replica carrier Doppler frequency (if the receiver is in frequency lock with the satellite carrier signal). The replica code phase can be converted into satellite transmit time, which can be used to compute the pseudorange measurement. The replica carrier Doppler phase or frequency can be converted into delta pseudorange. The replica carrier Doppler phase measurements can be converted into the so-called integrated carrier Doppler phase measurements used for ultraprecise static and kinematic surveying or positioning.

The most important concept presented in this section is the measurement relationship between the replica code phase state in the GPS receiver and the satellite transmit time. This relationship is unambiguous for P(Y)-code, but can be ambiguous for C/A-code. Every C/A-code GPS receiver is vulnerable to this ambiguity problem and, under weak signal acquisition conditions, the ambiguity will occur. When the ambiguity does occur in a C/A-code GPS receiver, it causes serious range measurement errors, which, in turn, result in severe navigation position errors.

5.1.6.1 Pseudorange

The definition of pseudorange to SV_i where i is the PRN number is as follows:

$$\rho_i(n) = c[T_R(n) - T_{Ti}(n)] \quad (\text{m}) \tag{5.25}$$

where

c = GPS propagation constant = 2.99792458×10^8 (m/sec)
$T_R(n)$ = receive time corresponding to epoch n of the GPS receiver's clock (sec)
$T_{Ti}(n)$ = transmit time based on the SV_i clock (sec)

Figure 5.29 depicts the GPS satellite SV_i transmitting its pseudorandom noise code PRN_i starting at the end of the GPS week. Corresponding to each chip of the PRN_i code is a linear SV_i clock time. When this signal reaches the GPS receiver, the transmit time $T_{Ti}(n)$ is the SV_i time corresponding to the PRN code state that is being replicated at receiver epoch n. The pseudorange derived from this measurement corresponds to a particular receive time epoch (epoch n) in the GPS receiver. Every epoch in the PRN code that is transmitted by SV_i is precisely aligned to the GPS time of week as maintained inside SV_i's timekeeping hardware. When this transmitted PRN code reaches the user GPS receiver, which is successfully correlating a replica PRN code with it, the phase offset of the replica code with respect to the beginning of the GPS week represents the transmit time of SV_i.

Typically, the GPS receiver will take a set of measurements at the same receive time epoch. This is why the receive time is not identified with any particular SV

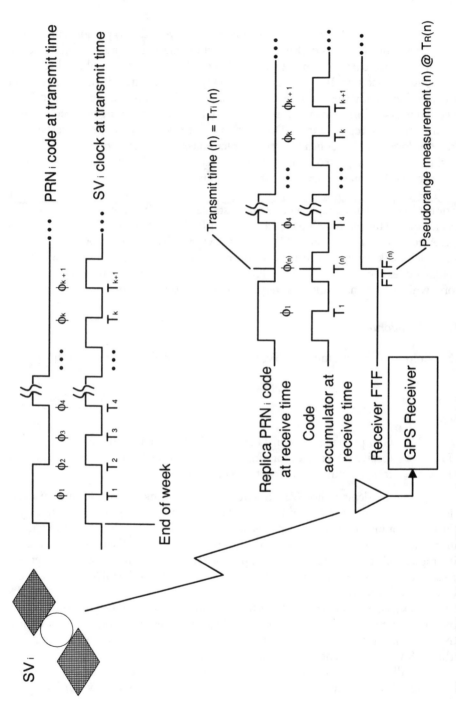

Figure 5.29 Relationship of satellite transmit time to pseudorange measurements.

PRN number in (5.25). When the GPS receiver schedules a set of measurements, it does this based on its own internal clock, which contains a bias error with respect to true GPS time (i.e., GPS system time). Eventually, the navigation process learns this bias error as a by-product of the GPS navigation solution. The SV transmit time also contains a bias error with respect to true GPS time, although the control segment ensures that this is maintained at less than 1 msec of bias error. This correction is transmitted to the receiver by SV_i as clock correction parameters via the navigation message. However, neither of these corrections is required to compute the pseudorange measurement in (5.25). These corrections are determined and applied by the navigation process.

Pseudorange Measurement

From (5.25), it can be concluded that if the receiver baseband process can extract the SV transmit time from the code tracking loop, then it can provide a pseudorange measurement. The precise transmit time measurement for SV_i is equivalent to its code phase offset with respect to the beginning of the GPS week. There is a one-to-one relationship between the SV_i replica code phase and the GPS time. Thus, for every fractional and integer chip advancement in the code phase of the PRN code generator since the initial (reset) state at the beginning of the week, there is a corresponding fractional and integer chip advancement in the GPS time. The fractional and integer chip code phase will hereafter be called the code state. The receiver baseband process timekeeper, which contains the GPS time corresponding to this code state, will hereafter be called the code accumulator.

The replica code state corresponds to the receiver's best estimate of the SV transmit time. The receiver baseband process knows the code state because it sets the initial states during the search process and keeps track of the changes in the code state thereafter. The receiver baseband code tracking loop process keeps track of the GPS transmit time corresponding to the phase state of the code NCO and the replica PRN code generator state after each code NCO update. It does this by discrete integration of every code phase increment over the interval of time since the last NCO update and adds this number to the code accumulator. The combination of the replica code generator state (integer code state) and the code NCO state (fraction code state) is the replica code state. Since the code phase states of the PRN code generator are pseudorandom, it would be impractical to read the code phase state of the PRN code generator and then attempt to convert this nonlinear code state into a linear GPS time state, say, by a table look-up.

There are too many possible code states, especially for the P-code generator. A very practical way to maintain the GPS time in a GPS receiver is to use a separate code accumulator in the GPS receiver baseband process and to synchronize this accumulator to the replica PRN code generator phase state. Figure 5.30 (derived

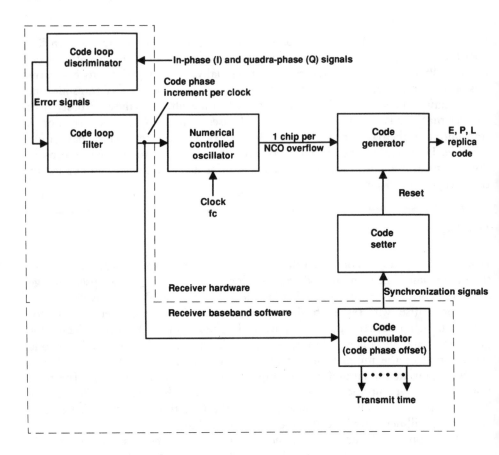

Figure 5.30 Relationship between PRN code generator and code accumulator.

from the code tracking loop of Figure 5.13) illustrates the high-level block diagram relationship between the replica PRN code generator and the code accumulator (which is not included in Figure 5.13) in the code tracking loop of one GPS receiver channel.

A typical GPS navigation measurement incorporation rate is once per second. A typical GPS receiver fundamental time frame (FTF) for scheduling measurements is 20 msec, which is the same as the 50-Hz navigation message data period. The receiver baseband process schedule for updating the code and carrier NCOs is usually some integer subset of the FTF, such as 20, 10, 5, 2, or 1 msec. Assuming that the FTF is 20 msec, the receiver measurement process maintains a monotone counter (call it the FTF counter) in 20-msec increments derived from the receiver's reference oscillator. The FTF counter is set to zero at power up, counts up, rolls over, and so forth. Assuming that the navigation measurement incorporation rate is 1 sec, the navigation process will schedule measurements to be extracted from the code and carrier tracking loops every fiftieth FTF; that is, based on the receiver's time epochs. When the receiver baseband process extracts the measurements from the code and carrier tracking loops, it time tags the measurements with the FTF count. The navigation process assigns and maintains a GPS receive time corresponding to the FTF count. The receive time initialization can be the first SV's transmit time plus a nominal propagation time of, say, 76 msec, if the navigation process does not know the GPS time accurately. This will set the initial receive time accurate to within about 20 msec.

When a pseudorange measurement is scheduled on FTF(n), the receiver baseband code tracking loop process extracts the SV_i transmit time from its code accumulator and propagates this time forward to FTF(n). The result is the SV_i transmit time with a measurement resolution of 2^{-N} of a code chip, where N is the number of bits in the code NCO adder. If the code NCO adder uses a 32-bit register, this measurement resolution is less than a quarter of a nanochip, which makes the code measurement quantization noise negligible. The receiver baseband process can compute the pseudorange measurement from the SV_i transmit time using (5.25) and time tag the measurement with FTF(n) before sending the result to the navigation process. However, the navigation process needs the (corrected) SV_i transmit time to compute the location of SV_i when it transmitted the measurement. Hence, the best measurement to send to the GPS navigation process is the (uncorrected) SV transmit time along with the FTF time tag. The navigation process applies the clock correction (including relativity correction), uses the corrected SV_i transmit time to compute the SV_i position, then computes the pseudorange plus other corrections before measurement incorporation.

Measurement Time Skew

Figure 5.4 illustrates the bit sync phase skew T_s, which exists between the SV data transition boundaries and the receiver 20-msec clock epochs (i.e., the FTFs). The control segment ensures that every SV transmits every epoch within 1 msec of true GPS time (i.e., the SV clocks are aligned to within 1 msec of true GPS time). Therefore, all of the SV data transition boundaries are approximately aligned to true GPS time at transmit time. However, at the GPS receiver the SV data transition boundaries are, in general, skewed with respect to each other and with respect to the receiver's FTF boundary. This is because the SVs are at different ranges with respect to the user GPS receiver. The user GPS receiver must adjust the phases of its integrate and dump boundaries in order to avoid integrating across the SV data bit transition boundaries. The time skew, T_s, is different for each SV being tracked and it also changes with time because the range to the SVs change with time. Therefore, the epochs from each replica code generator, such as the C/A-code 1-msec epochs, are

skewed with respect to each other and to the FTF. As a result, the integrate an
dump times and the updates to the code and carrier NCOs are performed on :
changing skewed time phase with respect to the FTF time phase, but the receive
baseband process learns and controls this time skew in discrete phase increments
The code accumulator is normally updated on the skewed time schedule that matche
the code NCO update schedule. Therefore, if all of the GPS receiver measurement
of a multiple channel GPS receiver are to be made on the same FTF, the content
of the code accumulator, when extracted for purposes of obtaining a measurement
must be propagated forward by the amount of the time skew between the cod
NCO update events and the FTF.

Maintaining the Code Accumulator

Although there are many code accumulator timekeeping conventions that woulc
work, the following convention is convenient for setting the initial code generatoi
and NCO phase states [1]. Three counters, Z, $X1$, and P, are maintained as th
code accumulator. The Z counter (19 bits) accumulates in GPS time increments o
1.5 sec, then is reset one count short of the maximum Z-count of 1 week = 403,200
Hence, the maximum Z count is 403,199. The $X1$ counter (24 bits) accumulates ir
GPS time increments of integer P chips, then is reset one count short of the maximum
$X1$ count of 1.5 sec = 15,345,000. Hence, the maximum $X1$ count is 15,344,999
The P counter accumulates in GPS time increments of fractions of a P chip, ther
rolls over one count short of one P chip. The P counter is the same length as th
code NCO adder. A typical length is 32 bits.

Note in Figure 5.13 that the code NCO synthesizes a code clock rate that i
an integer multiple, $1/d$, faster than the code generator chipping rate where d = the
code correlator spacing in chips (typically $d = 1/2$). This is required in order to
generate phase-shifted replica codes, which are necessary for error detection in the
code discriminator. The P counter tracks the fractional part of the code phase state,
which is the code NCO state multiplied by d. Using this convention and assuming
that the code NCO and code accumulator are updated every T sec, the algorithm
for maintaining the code accumulator is as follows:

$$
\begin{aligned}
P_{temp} &= P + f_c \, d \, \Delta\phi_{CO} \, T \\
P &= \text{fractional part of } P_{temp} \text{ (chips)} \\
X_{temp} &= (X1 + \text{whole part of } P_{temp})/15{,}345{,}000 \\
X1 &= \text{remainder of } X_{temp} \text{ (chips)} \\
Z &= \text{remainder of } [(Z + \text{whole part of } X_{temp})/403{,}200] \quad (1.5 \text{ sec}) \quad (5.26)
\end{aligned}
$$

where

$$
\begin{aligned}
P_{temp} &= \text{temporary } P \text{ register} \\
f_c &= \text{code NCO clock frequency (Hz)}
\end{aligned}
$$

$\Delta\phi_{CO}$ = code NCO phase increment per clock cycle

= code NCO bias + code loop filter velocity correction

d = code correlator spacing (dimensionless)

= 1/2 (typically)

T = time between code NCO updates (seconds)

The above definition of $\Delta\phi_{CO}$ contains two components: the code NCO bias and the code loop filter velocity correction. The code NCO bias (see Figure 5.13) is the phase increment per clock that accounts for the "marching of time" in the P-code replica code generator. When applied to the P replica code generator, this is 10.23×10^6 chips/sec. When applied to the C/A replica code generator, this is 1.023×10^6 chips/sec. (The code correlator spacing d requires the bias frequency to be $1/d$ higher.) The code loop filter velocity correction is the combination of carrier aiding and code loop filter output. This combined output corrects the P replica code generator for Doppler (and a small-order effect due to changes in ionospheric delay) referenced to the P-code chipping rate. Usually, the code generator provides the divide-by-ten function for the C/A-code generator if both P and C/A-codes are generated. This is the correct factor for the chipping rate and the code Doppler/ionospheric delay components.

Obtaining a Measurement From the Code Accumulator

To obtain a measurement, the code accumulator must be propagated to the nearest FTF(n). This results in the set of measurements $P_i(n)$, $X1_i(n)$, and $Z_i(n)$ for SV$_i$. When converted to time units of seconds, the result is $T_{Ti}(n)$, the transmit time of SV$_i$ at the receiver time epoch n. This is done very much like (5.26), except the time T is replaced with the skew time T_s.

$$P_{temp} = P + f_c d \, \Delta\phi_{CO} T_S$$

$P_i(n)$ = fractional part of P_{temp} (chips)

$$X_{temp} = (X_1 + \text{whole part of } P_{temp})/15{,}345{,}000$$

$X1_i(n)$ = remainder of X_{temp} (chips)

$Z_i(n)$ = remainder of $[(Z + \text{whole part of } X_{temp})/403{,}200]$ (1.5 sec)

$$(5.27)$$

Note that there is no error due to the measurement propagation process for the code accumulator measurements because the code NCO is running at a constant rate, $\Delta\phi_{CO}$ per clock, during the propagation interval. The following equation converts the code accumulator measurements to the SV$_i$ transmit time $T_{Ti}(n)$.

$$T_{Ti}(n) = [P_i(n) + X1_i(n)]/(10.23 \times 10^6) + Z_i(n) \cdot 1.5 \text{ (seconds)} \quad (5.28)$$

Synchronizing the Code Accumulator to the C/A-Code and P-Code Generators

Synchronizing the code accumulator to the C/A-code and P-code generators is the most complicated part of the pseudorange measurement process. This is because the count sequences taking place in the code generator shift registers are PN sequences while the count sequence taking place in the code accumulator is a linear sequence. Fortunately, there are predictable reset timing events in the PN shift registers that permit them to be synchronized to the code accumulator. The first thought might be to design the code generator shift registers such that they contain the linear counters, which are synchronized by the hardware and read by the receiver baseband process. However, the phase states of the code generators must be controlled by the receiver baseband process. So, it is a better design to use code setters in the hardware and maintain the code accumulator in the receiver baseband processor. By far the most simple case is the C/A-code generator setup, described first.

C/A-Code Setup

Figure 5.31 illustrates a high-level block diagram of the P and C/A-code generators, including their code setters. (Details of code generation were discussed earlier in Chapter 4.) Recall from Section 4.1.1.1 that the C/A-code generator consists of two 10-bit linear feedback shift registers, called the G1 and G2 registers [7]. The C/A-code setup requires one 10-bit code setter to initialize both the G1 and G2 registers in the C/A-code generator. The phase states of the G1 and G2 registers are the same for every SV for the same GPS time of week. It is the tap combination on the G2 register (or equivalently, the delay added to the G2 register) in combination with the G1 register that determines the PRN number. A typical C/A-code setter is capable of setting the G1 and G2 registers to their initial states and to their midpoint states. Since it requires only 1 msec for the C/A-code generator to cycle through its complete state, this code setter design example holds the maximum delay to 1/2 msec until the C/A-code generator is synchronized to the code accumulator after initialization of the code setter. This code setter design counts from 0 to 511 (1/2 C/A-code epoch) and then rolls over.

With the code setter hardware described above, the C/A-code setup process works as follows. In accordance with a future time delay equal to a fixed number of code NCO reference clock cycles later, the code accumulator value for that future time is loaded into the code setter. This value matches the desired C/A-code time after the scheduled time delay. The value for the code setter is computed just as though the 1,023-state C/A-code generator had the same linear counting properties as a 1,023-bit counter. The code setter begins counting after the scheduled time delay, starting with the loaded count value. The code setter sets the G1 and G2 registers when the count rolls over. If the value sent from the code accumulator was

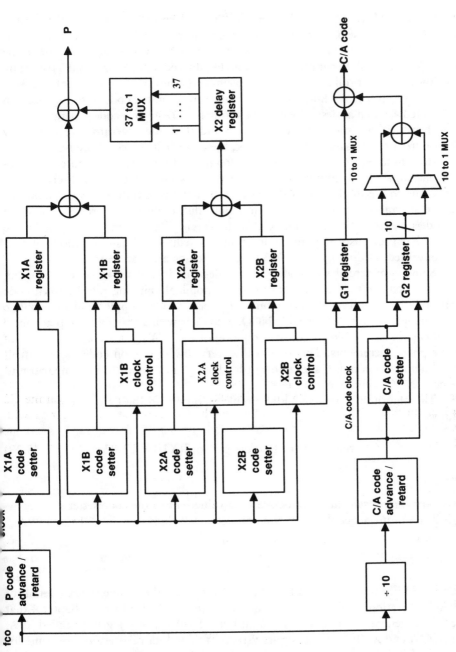

Figure 5.31 GPS code setter and code generator block diagram.

greater than 511, the C/A-code setter resets the G1 and G2 registers to their initial states. If the value sent from the code accumulator was less than or equal to 511, the code setter sets the G1 and G2 registers to their halfway points. As a result, the C/A replica code generator phase state matches the code accumulator GPS time state when the code setter rolls over and is synchronized to the code accumulator thereafter. When the receiver is tracking the SV after initialization, the code setter process can be repeated as often as desired without altering the C/A replica code generator phase state, because both the code accumulator and the code generator are ultimately synchronized by the same reference clock, the code NCO clock. If the receiver is in the search process, the C/A-code advance/retard feature shown in Figure 5.31 provides the capability to add clock cycles or swallow clock cycles in half-chip increments. The code accumulator keeps track of these changes. If the receiver can predict the satellite transmit time to within a few chips during the search process, it can use the code setter to perform a direct C/A-code search. This condition is satisfied if the receiver has previously acquired four or more satellites and its navigation solution has converged. Ordinarily, all 1,023 C/A-code chips are searched.

Some commercial C/A-code receiver designs do not use a code NCO, but instead propagate the code generator at the nominal chipping rate between code loop updates, tolerating the error build-up due to code Doppler and ionospheric delay changes. Instead of the code NCO, a counter with a fractional chip advance/retard capability is used to adjust the phase of the C/A replica code generator in coarse phase increments. This results in a very low resolution code measurement (large quantization noise) and a noisy pseudorange measurement in comparison to the code NCO technique.

The algorithm for the code accumulator output to the C/A-code setter is as follows:

$$G = \text{remainder of } [\{\text{whole part of } [(X1/10)]\}/1,023] \qquad (5.29)$$

where

G = future scheduled C/A-code time value sent to the code setter
$X1$ = future scheduled GPS time of week in P chips $(0 \le X1 \le 15,344,999)$

P-Code Setup

Figure 5.31 illustrates the high-level block diagram for the P-code setup. (Details of P-code generation were discussed earlier in Chapter 4.) Recall from Chapter 4 that the P-code generator contains four 12-bit linear feedback shift registers, called $X1A$, $X1B$, $X2A$ and $X2B$[7]. The PN phase states of these four registers are the same for every SV PRN number at the same GPS time of the week. The unique PRN code is determined by the delay of the $X2$ output. Each of the four shift registers must have a corresponding 12-bit code setter. The P-code setup is similar to the C/A-code setup, but involves a much more complex code setter process since, in general, all four shift registers must be reset at different time phases. There are two unusual code setter timing patterns that involve additional delays in the X1B, X2A, and X2B shift registers. The first occurs at the end of every X1 and X2 cycle. The second occurs at the end of the X2 cycle at the end of the GPS week.

Table 5.7 shows the count states for the first cycle of the GPS week for the four registers, starting with the 3,749th and 3,750th cycles of the X1A and X2A registers. After each cycle of X1A and X1B, the X1B epoch advances one chip ahead of X1A. The same pattern occurs between X2A and X2B. For the P-code phases shown in Table 5.7, the X1 and X2 counts match. At the beginning of the first X1 cycle of the week, the X1A and X2A registers are aligned in phase. The X1B and X2B registers are also aligned, but by the start of the last X1A cycle (3,750th) they are offset by 344 chips with respect to X1A and X2A. These last two cycles are chosen for the most representative timing illustration because the X1 period is defined as 3,750 X1A cycles, which equals 1.5 sec or 1 Z-count. When the X1B code reaches its last chip in the last X1A cycle of an X1 cycle, the X1B register is held in its final state (4,092) for 344 chips until the X1A register reaches its final state. Then X1A and X1B are reset. The Z-count is incremented by one, and the X1 cycle starts over.

The X2 period is defined by 3,750 X2A cycles plus 37 chips. In the last X2A cycle of the X2 cycle, the X2B register is held in its final state (4,092) until X2A

Table 5.7
Count States for 3,749th and 3,750th Cycles of X1A in First X1 Cycle of Week

Z	X1	X1A	X1B	D1B	X2	X2A	D2A	X2B	D2B
0	15,340,563	3,747	4,092	0	15,340,563	3,747	0	4,092	0
0	15,340,564	3,748	0	343	15,340,564	3,748	0	0	380
•	•	•	•	•	•	•	•	•	•
0	15,340,907	4,091	343	343	15,340,907	4,091	0	343	380
0	15,340,908	0	344	343	15,340,908	0	37	344	380
•	•	•	•	•	•	•	•	•	•
0	15,344,655	3,747	4,091	343	15,344,655	3,747	37	4,091	380
0	15,344,656	3,748	4,092	343	15,344,656	3,748	37	4,092	380
0	15,344,657	3,749	4,092	342	15,344,657	3,749	37	4,092	379
•	•	•	•	•	•	•	•	•	•
0	15,344,998	4,090	4,092	1	15,344,998	4,090	37	4,092	38
0	15,344,999	4,091	4,092	0	15,344,999	4,091	37	4,092	37
1	0	0	0	0	15,345,000	4,091	36	4,092	36
•	•	•	•	•	•	•	•	•	•
1	35	35	35	0	15,345,035	4,091	1	4,092	1
1	36	36	36	0	15,345,036	4,091	0	4,092	0
1	37	37	37	0	0	0	0	0	0

Note: The above count states are not the PN code states contained in the shift registers.

reaches its final state, and then the X2A register is held in its final state (4,091) and the X2B register continues to be held in its final state (4,092) for an additional 37 chips. Then X2A and X2B are reset and their cycles start over. Thus, the X2 epochs are delayed by 37 chips per Z-count with respect to the X1 epochs, until the end of the GPS week.

Note in Table 5.7 that the values for the X1A, X1B, X2A, and X2B registers are their count states, not their PN code states. The PN code states corresponding to the last two count states and the reset states are shown in Table 5.8. The only PN code states that are important to the P-code setters are the reset states, but the last two PN code states prior to reset are useful for code generator verification purposes.

The previous description for X2 is correct except for the last X1A cycle of the GPS week shown in Table 5.9. During this last cycle, the X2A register holds in its final state (4,091) and then the X2B register holds in its final state (4,092) until the end of the last X1 cycle of the week. The X1B final state holding count is the same as for the rest of the week (compare with Table 5.7).

The same future scheduling must be performed to accomplish the code setup process for the P-code generator as was used in the C/A-code setup. The X1A and X2A code setters count P-code clock cycles from 0 to 4,091 and the X1B and X2B code setters count from 0 to 4,092. This simplified code setter design example uses three countdown delay counters, D1B for X1B, D2A for X2A, and D2B for X2B, which are set by flags from the receiver baseband process at the end of an X1 or X2 cycle. It is possible to design the code setter so that the receiver baseband process does not have to set flags, but this simplified design example suffices to explain the principles involved. As observed in Tables 5.7 and 5.9, D1B is always set to a count of 343 chips. D2A is set to 37 and D2B is set to 380 unless it is at the end of the last X2 cycle of the week, in which case they are set to 1,069 and 965, respectively. The rule followed by the code setters is that if their delay counter is nonzero, they hold their final states until the delay counter counts down to zero, then they roll over to the zero (reset) states. The delay counters rule is that if their code setters

Table 5.8
PN Code States Corresponding to Final Two and Reset Count States

Code Setter States (decimal)	X1A Code (hexadecimal)	X1B Code (hexadecimal)	X2A Code (hexadecimal)	X2B Code (hexadecimal)
4,090	892	•	E49	•
4,091	124	955	C92	155
4,092	•	2AA	•	2AA
0 (reset)	248	554	925	554

Table 5.9
Count States for 3,749th and 3,750th Cycles of X1A in Last X1 Cycle of Week

Z	X1	X1A	X1B	D1B	X2	X2A	D2A	X2B	D2B
403,199	15,339,838	3,022	3,367	0	421,475	4,091	0	3,989	0
403,199	15,339,839	3,023	3,368	0	421,476	0	1,069	3,990	0
•	•	•	•	•	•	•	•	•	•
403,199	15,339,941	3,125	3,470	0	421,578	102	1,069	4,092	0
403,199	15,339,942	3,126	3,471	0	421,579	103	1,069	0	965
•	•	•	•	•	•	•	•	•	•
403,199	15,340,563	3,747	4,092	0	422,200	724	1,069	621	965
403,199	15,340,564	3,748	0	343	422,201	725	1,069	622	965
•	•	•	•	•	•	•	•	•	•
403,199	15,340,907	4,091	343	343	422,544	1,068	1,069	965	965
403,199	15,340,908	0	344	343	422,545	1,069	1,069	966	965
•	•	•	•	•	•	•	•	•	•
403,199	15,343,929	3,021	3,365	343	425,566	4,090	1,069	3,987	965
403,199	15,343,930	3,022	3,366	343	425,567	4,091	1,069	3,988	965
403,199	15,343,931	3,023	3,367	343	425,568	4,091	1,068	3,989	965
•	•	•	•	•	•	•	•	•	•
403,199	15,344,033	3,125	3,469	343	425,670	4,091	966	4,091	965
403,199	15,344,034	3,126	3,470	343	425,671	4,091	965	4,092	965
403,199	15,344,035	3,127	3,471	343	425,672	4,091	964	4,092	964
•	•	•	•	•	•	•	•	•	•
403,199	153,44,655	3,747	4,091	343	426,292	4,091	344	4,092	344
403,199	15,344,656	3,748	4,092	343	426,293	4,091	343	4,092	343
403,199	15,344,657	3,749	4,092	342	426,294	4,091	342	4,092	342
•	•	•	•	•	•	•	•	•	•
403,199	15,344,998	4,090	4,092	1	426,635	4,091	1	4,092	1
403,199	15,344,999	4,091	4,092	0	426,636	4,091	0	4,092	0
0	0	0	0	0	0	0	0	0	0

Note: The above count states are not the PN code states contained in the shift registers.

are not in the final state, they hold their delay counts until the code setter reaches its final state, then they begin counting down. The receiver baseband rule is that if the code setter counts to the reset state can be reached without using the delay counter, the receiver baseband process adjusts the code setter to the appropriate value and does not set the delay counter flag. Otherwise, it sets the appropriate delay counter flags (which instructs the code setter hardware to put the appropriate maximum delays into the counters). This rule avoids the need for the code setter hardware to set any other count state into the delay counters other than their maximum delay counts.

The code setters are loaded with the timing state valid at the first epoch that the counting process begins. As each code setter rolls over to zero, it resets its corresponding code register to that register's initial code state. In addition, the X1A divide-by-3,750 counter and the Z-counter must be set to their correct states when the X1A register is reset. Similarly, the X1B divide-by-3,749 counter, the X2A divide-by-3,750 counter, and the X2B divide-by-3,749 counter must be set to their correct states when their respective registers are reset by their code setters. Thus, when all four code setters have rolled over, the code generator is synchronized to the code accumulator. This requires approximately 500-μsec worst case.

The final step in the explanation of the P-code setter operation is the algorithm for converting the code accumulator into P-code setter states and the setting of the three flags, D1B, D2A, and D2B. The code setter timing and the rules have already been explained. Figure 5.32 depicts the logical flow diagram that covers all P-code setter timing conditions. This diagram should be compared to the count states in Tables 5.7 and 5.9. Note that if the P-code generator is already synchronized to the code accumulator, the action of the P-code setter does not alter the replica code state since the reset pulses occur at exactly the same times that they naturally occur in the code generator. However, to ensure that the receiver baseband software code accumulator always matches the P-code generator code state, it is prudent for the software to periodically repeat the code setup process.

With Y-code operation, the same P-code processes are implemented in the above manner and then encrypted by a specialized hardware design called the auxiliary output chip (AOC) before correlation with the incoming SV Y-code signals. The AOC, which is controlled but unclassified, implements a classified encryption algorithm. Only keyed PPS receivers can replicate the Y-code. This code setter design example supports direct P(Y)-code acquisition. Direct P(Y)-code acquisition is used if the receiver can accurately predict the satellite transmit time so that less time is required to acquire the P(Y)-code by direct sequence than to perform a C/A-code search and handover. The direct P(Y)-code acquisition condition is satisfied if the receiver has previously acquired four or more satellites and its navigation solution has converged. Under certain jamming conditions, it may be impossible to acquire the C/A-code, but possible to acquire P(Y)-code. Then, direct P(Y)-code acquisition is essential and can be supported if the navigation state has been transferred to the receiver with sufficient precision and the almanac or ephemeris data are present. The most sensitive navigation state parameter is precise time. Reference [3] describes a multiple correlator/search detector architecture that supports rapid direct P(Y)-code acquisition. If the receiver is engaged in the direct P(Y)-code search process, the P-code advance/retard function shown in Figure 5.31 provides the capability to add clock cycles or swallow clock cycles in 1/2 chip increments. The code accumulator keeps track of these changes.

Obtaining Transmit Time From the C/A-Code

Figure 5.33 illustrates the GPS timing relationships that enable a C/A-code receiver to determine the true GPS transmit time. The C/A-code repeats every 1 msec and is

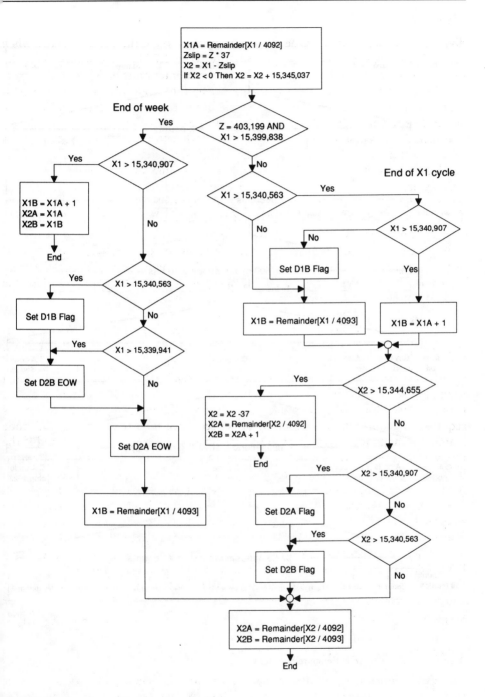

Figure 5.32 Flowchart of P-code setter algorithm.

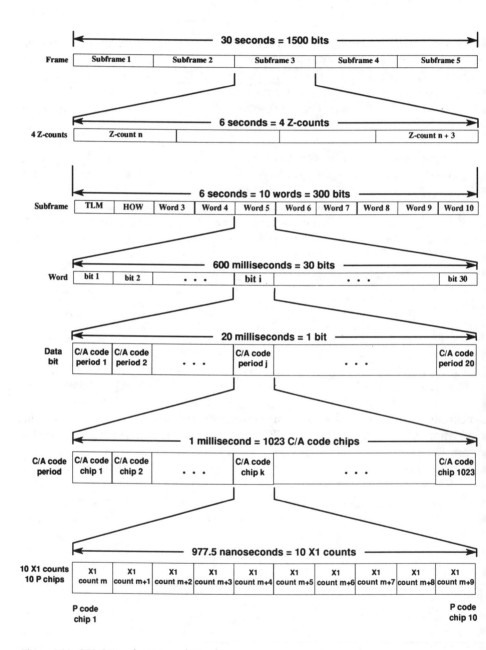

Figure 5.33 GPS C/A-code timing relationships.

herefore ambiguous every 1 msec of GPS time. There is a HOW at the beginning of every one of the five subframes of the satellite navigation message. The HOW contains the Z-count of the first data bit transition boundary at the beginning of he next subframe. This is the first data bit of the telemetry message (TLM) that precedes every HOW. The beginning of this 20-msec data bit is synchronized with the beginning of one of the satellite's C/A-code 1-msec periods, but there are 20 C/A-code periods in every data bit period. At this subframe epoch, the X1 register has just produced a carry to the Z-count, so the X1 count is zero. The C/A-code ambiguity is resolved by setting the Z-count to the HOW value and the X1 count o zero at the beginning of the next subframe.

The Z-count and X1 count will be correct if the GPS receiver has determined its bit synchronization to within 1 msec or better accuracy. This level of accuracy will perfectly align the 1-msec C/A-code epoch with the 20-msec data bit transition point of the first bit in the following TLM word. Therefore, the C/A-code transmit ime will be unambiguous and correct. If the bit synchronization process makes an error in the alignment of the 1-msec replica C/A-code epoch with the 20-msec data bit epoch, then the X1 count will be off by some integer multiple of 1 msec. If the receiver attempts a handover to P-code and fails, the typical strategy is to try the handover again with 1-msec changes in the value used for X1, then 2-msec trials, and so forth before attempting to redetermine bit synchronization. (This process can ke 6 sec or longer and prevents processing of GPS measurements until complete.)

A successful handover to P-code verifies the bit synchronization process. However, if the GPS receiver is a C/A-code receiver, the verification for correct bit synchronization is more difficult. This verification task must be performed by the navigation process. Since 1 msec of GPS time error is equivalent to about 300,000m of pseudorange error, the navigation error can be quite serious. In the unlikely case that every channel makes the identical bit sync error, the navigation position error washes out of the position solution into the time bias solution and the GPS time is n error by 1 msec. The typical bit sync error manifestations in the navigation solution are unrealistic local-level velocity and elevation computations. The latitude and longitude computations are also unrealistic, but there is usually no boundary condition for comparison. However, the velocity and elevation computations can be compared to acceptable boundary conditions.

The bit synchronization process is a statistical process that is dependent on C/N_0. It will occasionally be incorrect. It will be incorrect almost every time the C/N_0 drops below the bit synchronization design threshold. This causes serious navigation integrity problems for C/A-code receivers under conditions of signal attenuation or RF interference. This problem is compounded if there is no design provision to adapt the bit synchronization process for poor C/N_0 conditions and/or for the navigation process to check for bit synchronization errors.

5.1.6.2 Delta Pseudorange

The definition of delta pseudorange to SV_i is as follows:

$$\Delta \rho_i(n) = \rho_i(n + J) - \rho_i(n - K) \quad \text{(meters)} \qquad (5.30)$$

where

$\rho_i(n + J)$ = pseudorange at J FTF epochs later than FTF(n) (meters)
$\rho_i(n - K)$ = pseudorange at K FTF epochs earlier than FTF(n) (meters)
J = 0 or K depending on design preferences (dimensionless)

Even though (5.30) implies that delta pseudorange could be derived from the code tracking loop, the result would be a very noisy measurement. This differential measurement will be nearly a thousand times less noisy if taken from the carrier tracking loop operated as a PLL. If the carrier loop is operated as a FLL, the measurement is taken the same way, but the FLL is only about a hundred times less noisy.

The carrier Doppler phase measurements are extracted by the receiver baseband process from the carrier tracking loop using a carrier accumulator. It is more simple but similar to using the code accumulator to extract transmit time measurements from the code tracking loop. The carrier accumulator consists of the integer cycle count N_{CA} and the fractional cycle count Φ_{CA} of the carrier Doppler phase measurement.

The carrier accumulator is updated after each carrier loop output to the carrier NCO using the following algorithm:

$$\Phi_{temp} = \Phi_{CA} + f_c \, \Delta\phi_{CA} T$$
$$\Phi_{CA} = \text{fractional part of } \Phi_{temp} \text{ (cycles)}$$
$$N_{CA} = N_{CA(\text{last value})} + \text{whole part of } \Phi_{temp} \text{ (cycles)} \qquad (5.31)$$

where

Φ_{temp} = temporary Φ_{CA} register
f_c = carrier NCO clock frequency (Hz)
$\Delta\phi_{CA}$ = carrier NCO carrier Doppler phase increment per clock cycle
= carrier loop filter velocity correction + carrier loop velocity aiding (if any)
T = time between carrier NCO updates (sec)
N_{CA} = integer number of carrier Doppler phase cycles since some starting point

The fractional part of the carrier accumulator Φ_{CA} is initialized to the same state as the carrier NCO at the beginning of the search process, which is typically zero. The integer number of carrier Doppler phase cycles, N_{CA}, is ambiguous. Since only differential measurements are taken from this register, the ambiguity does not matter. The carrier integer accumulator is usually set to zero when the carrier loop is first closed following a successful search operation. Note that the "marching of time" carrier NCO bias (see Figure 5.8) is not included in the carrier accumulator because it is simply a bias term. Since only differential measurements are extracted from the carrier accumulator, this bias term, if included, would cancel out. The counter rolls over when the Doppler cycle count exceeds the count capacity or underflows if the Doppler count is in the reverse direction and drops below the zero count. The differential measurement comes out correct if the counter capacity is large enough to ensure that this happens no more than once between any set of differential measurements extracted from the carrier accumulator.

To extract a carrier Doppler phase measurement, $N_{CAi}(n)$, $\Phi_{CAi}(n)$, for SV_i corresponding to the carrier accumulator, it must be propagated forward to the nearest FTF(n) by the skew time, T_s, similar to the technique used in the code tracking loop:

$$\Phi_{temp} = \Phi_{CA} + f_c \, \Delta\phi_{CA} T_s$$
$$\Phi_{CAi}(n) = \text{fractional part of } \Phi_{temp} \text{ (cycles)}$$
$$N_{CAi}(n) = N_{CA} + \text{whole part of } \Phi_{temp} \text{ (cycles)}$$

$$(5.32)$$

Note that there is no error due to the measurement propagation process for the carrier Doppler phase measurement because the carrier NCO is running at a constant rate, $\Delta\phi_{CA}$ per clock, during the propagation interval.

The precise delta pseudorange is simply the change in phase in the carrier accumulator during a specified time. The formula for extracting the delta pseudorange from the carrier accumulator is as follows:

$$\Delta\rho_i(n) = \{[N_{CAi}(n + J) - N_{CAi}(n - K)] + [\Phi_{CAi}(n + J) - \Phi_{CAi}(n - K)]\}\lambda_L \text{ (meters)}$$
$$(5.33)$$

where

λ_L = wavelength of the L-band carrier frequency
    = 0.1903 meter/cycle for L1
    = 0.2442 meter/cycle for L2

Typically, the delta pseudorange measurement is used to formulate an average velocity over some time interval, say 120 msec, by dividing the $\Delta\rho$ measurement by this time interval. Usually, it is desirable for this average velocity term to be valid at the same time as the transmit time (pseudorange) measurement. This means that the first carrier Doppler phase measurement must be taken 60 msec before the pseudorange measurement and the second carrier Doppler phase measurement 60 msec after the pseudorange measurement. For this case, $J = K = 3$, if each FTF is 20 msec. This delta pseudorange measurement would be provided to the navigation process 60-msec latent with respect to the transmit time measurement. If no latency can be tolerated in the measurement, then for a 120-msec time interval, $J = 0$ and $K = 6$. Under this condition, the average velocity measurement corresponds to the FTF that is 60-msec earlier than the transmit time measurement.

5.1.6.3 Integrated Doppler

The definition of integrated Doppler is obtained from (5.32). The integrated Doppler measurement for SV_i at FTF(n) can be converted to units of meters as follows:

$$ID_i(n) = [N_{CAi}(n) + \Phi_{CAi}(n)]\lambda_L \text{ (meters)} \qquad (5.34)$$

This measurement, when derived from a PLL, is used for ultraprecise differential interferometric GPS applications such as static and kinematic surveying or for attitude determination. Note that when the integer cycle count ambiguity is resolved by the interferometric process, this measurement is equivalent to a pseudorange measurement with approximately one thousand times less noise than the P(Y)-code transmit time (pseudorange) measurements obtained from the code loop. The integrated Doppler noise for a high-quality GPS receiver designed for interferometric applications typically is about 1 mm (1 sigma). A P(Y)-code transmit time (pseudorange) measurement typically will have about 1m of noise. Once the integer cycle ambiguity is resolved, so long as the PLL does not slip cycles, the ambiguity remains resolved thereafter.

Two GPS receivers that are making transmit time and carrier Doppler phase measurements on their respective receiver epochs will, in general, be time skewed with respect to one another. For ultraprecise differential applications it is possible to remove virtually all of the effects of SA and other time-variable bias effects by eliminating this time skew between GPS receivers. This is accomplished by precisely aligning the measurements to GPS time epochs instead of to receiver FTF epochs. Initially, of course, the measurements must be obtained with respect to the receiver FTF epochs. After the navigation process determines the time bias between its FTF epochs and true GPS time, each request for receiver measurements can include its previous estimate of the time bias to the FTF (a very slowly changing value if the reference oscillator is stable). The receiver measurement process then propagates the measurements to the FTF plus the time bias to the true GPS time epoch. The measurements are typically taken on the GPS one second time of week epoch. SA does corrupt the navigation process time bias estimation in a standalone GPS receiver, but this bias error will seldom exceed 300 nsec. This amount of time skew error is negligible for differential GPS applications since the satellite positions change only about a millimeter in this time. However, with as little as 1 sec of time skew, the satellite positions can change by nearly 4,000m. Of course, the differential measurements can be propagated to align to the same time epoch if the GPS receiver's measurements are time skewed, but not with the accuracy that can be obtained if they are aligned to a common GPS time epoch within each GPS receiver during the original measurement process. The carrier Doppler measurement must be corrected for the frequency error in the satellite's atomic standard (i.e., reference oscillator) before measurement incorporation. This correction is broadcast in the satellite's navigation message as the a_1 term. The measurement also includes the receiver's reference oscillator frequency error. This error is determined as a time bias rate correction by the navigation solution. For some applications, it is also corrected for the differential ionospheric delay, but this is usually a negligible error.

5.1.7 Signal Acquisition

There is a large amount of literature on pseudonoise code acquisition in direct sequence receivers. For an extensive historical survey and descriptions on search detectors, [8] is recommended.

GPS signal acquisition is a search process. This search process, like the tracking process, requires replication of both the code and the carrier of the SV to acquire the SV signal (i.e., the signal match for success is two-dimensional). The range dimension is associated with the replica code. The Doppler dimension is associated with the replica carrier. The initial search process is always a C/A-code search for C/A-code receivers and usually begins with a C/A-code search for P(Y)-code receivers. The initial C/A-code search usually involves replicating all 1,023 C/A-code phase states in the range dimension. The criteria for direct C/A-code and direct P(Y)-code acquisitions were discussed in the previous section. If the range and Doppler uncertainty are known, then the search pattern should cover the 3-sigma values of the uncertainty. If the uncertainty is large in either or both dimensions, the search pattern is correspondingly large and the expected search time increases. Some criteria must be established to determine when to terminate the search process for a given SV and select another candidate SV.

The following example assumes that a C/A-code search is being performed and that all 1,023 C/A-code phases are being examined. The code phase is typically searched in $1/2$-chip increments. Each code phase search increment is a code bin. The combination of one code bin and one Doppler bin is a cell. Figure 5.34 illustrates the two-dimensional search process. If the Doppler uncertainty is unknown and the SV Doppler cannot be computed from a knowledge of the user position and time plus the SV orbit data, then the maximum user velocity plus just less than 800 m/sec maximum SV Doppler (worst case) for a stationary user must be searched in both directions about zero Doppler.

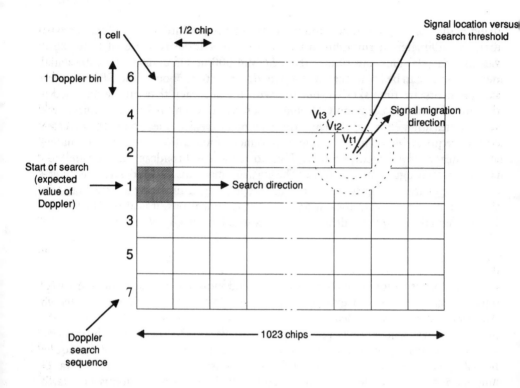

Figure 5.34 Two-dimensional C/A-code search pattern.

One Doppler bin will be defined as $2/(3T)$, where T = signal integration time per cell or dwell time per cell. Dwell times can vary from less than 1.0 msec (667-Hz Doppler bins) for strong signals up to 20.0 msec (33-Hz Doppler bins) for weak signals. The poorer the expected C/N_0, then the longer the dwell time (and overall search time) must be in order to have reasonable success of signal acquisition. Unfortunately, the actual C/N_0 is unknown until after the SV signal is acquired. If the receiver is equipped to measure the input signal noise and the RF interference and the antenna gain pattern is stored in its memory, the minimum C/N_0 can be predicted accurately, except for signal obscuration. Signal obscuration (trees, buildings, snow, or ice on the antenna, etc.), RF interference, and antenna gain roll-off significantly reduce C/N_0. The SV signal strength characteristic as a function of lifetime is a minor contributor to variations in the expected C/N_0. However, the user can depend on the control segment to ensure that the minimum signal strength for all SVs guaranteed by ICD-GPS-200 are met.

Referring to Figure 5.34, the search pattern is usually with a constant Doppler bin and in the range direction from early to late in order to avoid multipath. The direct arrival of a signal subject to multipath is always ahead in time of the reflected arrivals. In the Doppler bin direction, the search pattern is typically from the mean value of the Doppler uncertainty (zero Doppler if the actual line-of-sight velocity estimate is unknown) and then symmetrically one Doppler bin at a time on either side of this value until the 3-sigma Doppler uncertainty has been searched. Then, the search pattern is repeated, typically with a reduction in the search threshold scale factor. It is important to recognize that the C/A-code autocorrelation and cross-correlation sidelobes can cause false signal detections if these sidelobes are strong enough. The sidelobes tend to increase as the search dwell time is decreased. To counter this problem, a combination of both increased dwell time (to minimize sidelobes) and a high detector threshold setting (to reject sidelobes) can be used for the initial search pass. On subsequent search passes, the dwell time and threshold can be decreased. The penalty for this scheme is increased search time when the C/N_0 is low.

During the dwell time T in each cell, the I and Q signals are integrated and dumped and the envelope $\sqrt{I^2 + Q^2}$ is computed or estimated. Each envelope is compared to a threshold to determine the presence or absence of the SV signal. The detection of the signal is a statistical process because each cell either contains noise with the signal absent or noise with the signal present. Each case has its own probability density function (PDF). Figure 5.35 illustrates a single trial (binary) decision example where both PDFs are shown. The PDF for noise with no signal present, $p_n(z)$, has a zero mean. The PDF for noise with the signal present, $p_s(z)$, has a nonzero mean. The single trial threshold is usually based on an acceptable single trial probability of false alarm, P_{fa}. For the chosen threshold V_t, any cell envelope that is at or above the threshold is detected as the presence of the signal. Any cell envelope that is below the threshold is detected as noise. There are four outcomes of the single trial (binary) decision processes illustrated in Figure 5.35, two wrong and two right. By knowing the PDFs of the envelopes, the single trial probability can be computed by an appropriate integration with the threshold as one limit and infinity as the other. These integrations are shown as the shaded areas in Figure 5.35. The two statistics that are of most interest for the signal detection process are the single trial probability of detection, P_d, and the single trial probability of false alarm, P_{fa}. These are determined as follows:

$$P_d = \int_{V_t}^{\infty} p_s \, dz \qquad (5.35)$$

$$P_{fa} = \int_{V_t}^{\infty} p_n \, dz \qquad (5.36)$$

where

$p_s(z)$ = PDF of the envelope in the presence of the signal

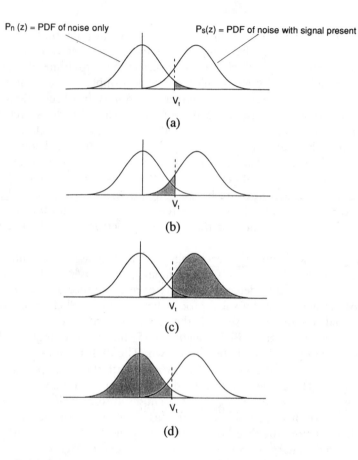

Figure 5.35 Probability density functions for a binary decision: (a) shaded area represents probability of false alarm, (b) shaded area represents probability of false dismissal, (c) shaded area represents probability of detection, and (d) shaded area represents probability of correct dismissal.

$p_n(z)$ = PDF of the envelope with the signal absent

To determine these PDFs, assume that I and Q have a Gaussian distribution. Assuming that the envelope is formed by $\sqrt{I^2 + Q^2}$, then $p_s(z)$ is a Ricean distribution [9] defined by

$$p_s(z) = \frac{z}{\sigma_n^2} e^{-\left(\frac{z^2 + A^2}{2\sigma_n^2}\right)} I_0\left(\frac{zA}{\sigma_n^2}\right) \text{ for } z \geq 0; \, p_s(z) = 0 \text{ otherwise} \qquad (5.37)$$

where

z = random variable

σ_n = root mean square (rms) noise power

A = rms signal amplitude

$I_0\left(\dfrac{zA}{\sigma_n}\right)$ = modified Bessel function of zero order

$$I_0(x) \approx \frac{e^x}{\sqrt{2\pi x}} \text{ for } x \gg 1$$

Equation 5.37 ($z \geq 0$) can be expressed in terms of the predetection signal to noise ratio as presented to the envelope detector s/n (dimensionless) as follows:

$$p_s(z) = \frac{z}{\sigma_n^2}e^{-\left(\frac{z^2}{2\sigma_n^2} + s/n\right)}I_0\left(\frac{z\sqrt{2s/n}}{\sigma_n}\right) \tag{5.38}$$

where

s/n = predetection signal to noise ratio

        = $A^2/2\sigma_n^2$ (power ratio)

s/n = $10^{S/N/10}$

S/N = predetection signal to noise ratio in dB = $C/N_0 + 10 \log T$ (dB)

C/N_0 = carrier-to-noise power density ratio in dB

T = search dwell time = predetection integration time

For the case where there is no signal present, then evaluating (5.37) for $A = 0$ yields a Rayleigh distribution for $p_n(z)$ which is defined by:

$$p_n(z) = \frac{z}{\sigma_n^2}e^{-\left(\frac{z^2}{2\sigma_n^2}\right)} \tag{5.39}$$

The result of integrating (5.36) using the PDF of (5.39) is

$$p_{fa} = e^{-\left(\frac{V_t^2}{2\sigma_n^2}\right)} \tag{5.40}$$

Rearranging (5.40) yields the threshold in terms of the desired single trial probability of false alarm and the measured 1-sigma noise power:

$$V_t = \sigma_n\sqrt{-2 \ln P_{fa}} = X\sigma_n \tag{5.41}$$

For example, if it is desired that $P_{fa} = 16\%$, then $V_t = X \sigma_n = 1.9144615\sigma_n$. Using this result, the single trial probability of detection, P_d, is computed for the expected C/N_0 and dwell time T using (5.35) and (5.38) with $\sigma_n = 1$ (normalized).

Some examples of the single trial probability of detection are shown in Table 5.10 for various signal-to-noise ratios.

Figure 5.36, taken from [10], illustrates the structure of search detectors used for signal acquisition. Referring to Figure 5.36, two types of search detectors are used in GPS receiver designs. A variable dwell time detector makes a "yes" or "no" decision in a variable interval of time if "maybe" conditions are present. A fixed dwell time detector makes a "yes" or "no" decision in a fixed interval of time. The false alarm rate and the probability of detection from single dwell time detectors (single trial decisions) are usually unsatisfactory for GPS applications. So, single dwell time search detector schemes are seldom used. All other things being equal, a properly tuned variable dwell time (sequential) multiple trial detector will search faster than a fixed dwell time multiple trial detector.

5.1.7.1 Tong Search Detector

The first example of a search algorithm is a sequential variable dwell time search detector called the Tong detector. Figure 5.37 illustrates the block diagram of the Tong detector. Search algorithms are typically implemented as a receiver baseband process. Because of its simplicity, the Tong detector can be implemented as part of the receiver correlation and preprocessing hardware, with its search parameters programmed by the baseband process. The Tong detector has a reasonable computational burden and is excellent for detecting signals with an expected C/N_0 of 25 dB-Hz or higher. If acquisition is to be performed under heavy jamming conditions where the C/N_0 will be less than this, then a hybrid maximum likelihood search detector should be used. A pure maximum likelihood search detector would require the receiver hardware to produce the results of all of the search dwells in parallel,

Table 5.10
Single Trial Probability of Detection

s/n_0 (ratio)	P_d (dimensionless)	C/N_0 (dB-Hz)			
		$T = 0.001$ sec	$T = 0.0025$ sec	$T = 0.005$ sec	$T = 0.010$ sec
1.0	0.431051970	30.00	26.02	23.01	20.00
2.0	0.638525844	33.01	29.03	26.02	23.01
3.0	0.780846119	34.77	30.79	27.78	24.77
4.0	0.871855378	36.02	32.04	29.03	26.02
5.0	0.927218854	36.99	33.01	30.00	26.99
6.0	0.959645510	37.78	33.80	30.79	27.78
7.0	0.978075147	38.45	34.47	31.46	28.45
8.0	0.988294542	39.03	35.05	32.04	29.03
9.0	0.993845105	39.54	35.56	32.55	29.54

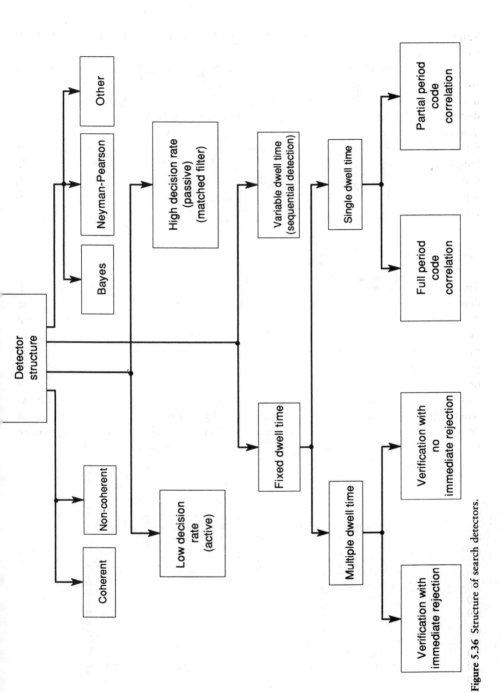

Figure 5.36 Structure of search detectors.

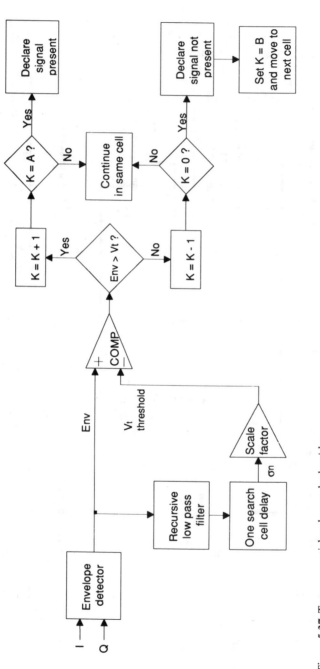

Figure 5.37 Tong sequential code search algorithm.

which is usually impractical. The Tong detector is a suboptimal search algorithm that requires an average of only 1.58 longer to make a decision than a maximum likelihood (optimum) search algorithm [11].

The operation of the Tong detector is as follows.

1. Every T sec an integrated correlation envelope is formed as $\sqrt{I^2 + Q^2}$ (or its approximation). If there are three correlators in the receiver, each correlator is typically spaced 1/2 chip apart and three Tong detectors are used. In this manner, three code bins at a time are searched and the search process speeds up by almost a factor of three. It is not quite a factor of three because all three search cells must be dismissed before the search process can proceed to the next three cells. In order to generate the I and Q signals, the receiver baseband search process has synthesized the correct Doppler (the center frequency of the respective search process Doppler bin in the search pattern) and the correct replica C/A-code phase with the corresponding code-chipping rate plus code Doppler. For example, the C/A-code phase corresponding to the first of its 1,023 states is where the C/A-code setter resets the G1 and G2 registers at the beginning of the cell integrate and dump time. The "marching of time" for the C/A-code generator plus the code Doppler keeps its phase aligned to this cell. If the cell is dismissed, then the C/A-code generator phase is advanced by 1/2 chip (times the number of correlators) and the search process is continued for that Doppler bin until the last C/A-code phase state has been reached. Then, the Doppler center frequency is shifted to the next bin in the search pattern and the process is repeated.

2. At each cell, the up/down counter (K) is initialized to $K = B = 1$. Where a higher probability of detection and lower probability of false alarm are desired at the expense of search speed, then $B = 2$. If the envelope sample exceeds the threshold V_t, then the up/down counter is incremented by 1. If the sample does not exceed the threshold, then the up/down counter is decremented by one. As shown in Figure 5.37, one technique for obtaining the rms noise σ_n, which is used to set the threshold, is to pass the correlation envelopes into a recursive low-pass filter with a delay of one search cell. A better technique is for the receiver to synthesize the rms noise by correlating the input signal with an unused PRN code; for example, the G1 register output for C/A-code search. The rms output is multiplied by a scale factor X to obtain the threshold V_t. Assuming that the envelope is formed by $\sqrt{I^2 + Q^2}$, then the scale factor is determined from (5.41), $X = \sqrt{-2 \ln(P_{fa})}$, where P_{fa} is the single trial probability of false alarm. Typically, the envelope is determined from the Robertson approximation. In this case, it has been determined [12] that a multiplier factor of 1.08677793 must be used for the scale factor, so that

$$X_R = 1.08677793\, X = \sqrt{-2.3621724 \ln (P_{fa})}$$

The determination of the most suitable single trial probability of false alarm, the overall false alarm, and the overall probability of detection is a tuning process. The final determination must be obtained by simulation. Assuming the Robertson envelope approximation, the scale factor range is typically from 1.8 (P_{fa} = 25%) for low expected C/N_0 ($\geq$ 25 dB-Hz) to 2.1 (P_{fa} = 16%) for high expected C/N_0 ($\geq$ 39 dB-Hz).

3. If the counter contents reach the maximum value, A, then the signal is declared present and the Tong search is terminated. This is typically followed by additional vernier search processes designed to find the code phase and Doppler combination that produces the peak detection of the signal before the code/carrier loop closure process is begun. If the counter reaches 0, then the signal is declared absent and the search process is advanced to the next cell. The determination of A must be by simulation. Its selection is a tradeoff between search speed and probability of detection, but a typical range is A = 12 for low expected C/N_0 to A = 8 for high expected C/N_0.

The mean number of dwell times to dismiss a cell containing noise only is determined as follows:

$$N_n = \frac{1}{1 - 2P_{fa}}$$

(5.42)

Since most of the time is spent searching cells that contain noise only, the Tong detector search speed can be estimated from

$$R_s = \frac{d}{N_n T} = \frac{d(1 - 2P_{fa})}{T} \text{ (chips/s)}$$

(5.43)

where d = chips per cell (typically 1/2 chip per cell).

For example, for P_{fa} = 16%, a dwell time of 5 msec, and 1/2 chip per cell, the code search rate is = 68 chips/sec. Note that the search speed increases when the probability of false alarm decreases.

The overall probability of false alarm for the Tong detector is [9]

$$P_{FA} = \frac{\left(\dfrac{1 - P_{fa}}{P_{fa}}\right)^B - 1}{\left(\dfrac{1 - P_{fa}}{P_{fa}}\right)^{A+B-1} - 1}$$

(5.44)

The overall probability of detection for the Tong detector is [9]

$$P_D = \frac{\dfrac{(1 - P_d)^B}{P_d}}{\dfrac{(1 - P_d)^{A+B-1}}{P_d} - 1} \qquad (5.45)$$

Figure 5.38 is a plot of (5.45) as a function of the input signal to noise ratio to the Tong detector with $B=1$, with A as a running parameter ranging from 2 to 12, and with the overall probability of false alarm set equal to 1×10^{-6} for every case [13]. It illustrates the excellent search detector performance of the Tong detector and the increased sensitivity of the detector with A being increased. The cost of increasing A is shown as a decrease in the search rate.

5.1.7.2 M of N Search Detector

The second example of a search algorithm is a fixed interval detector called the M of N search detector. The M of N search detector takes N envelopes and compares them to the threshold for each cell. If M or more of them exceeds the threshold, then the signal is declared present. If not, the signal is declared absent and the process

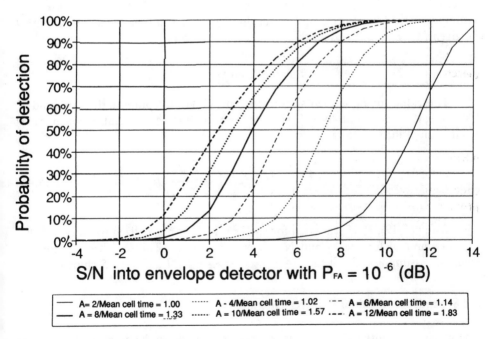

Figure 5.38 Probability of detection for Tong search detector.

is repeated for the next cell in the search pattern. These are treated as Bernoulli trials and the number of envelopes n that exceed the threshold have a binomial distribution. The same threshold setting technique is used and the same formula applies for the single trial probability of false alarm P_{fa}, as was described for the Tong detector.

The overall probability of false alarm in N trials is [14]

$$P_{FA} = \sum_{n=M}^{N} \binom{N}{n} P_{fa}^{n}(1 - P_{fa})^{N-n} = 1 - \sum_{n=0}^{M-1} \binom{N}{n} P_{fa}^{n}(1 - P_{fa})^{N-n}$$

$$= 1 - B(M - 1; N, P_{fa}) \tag{5.46}$$

where: $B(k; N, p)$ is the cumulative PDF.

The overall probability of detection in N trials is [14]

$$P_D = \sum_{n=M}^{N} \binom{N}{n} P_d^{n}(1 - P_d)^{N-n} = 1 - B(M - 1; N, P_d) \tag{5.47}$$

Figure 5.39 illustrates the M of N probability of detection versus S/N into the detector for $N = 8$ and $M = 3, 4, 5,$ and 6 when $P_{FA} = 1 \times 10^{-6}$. It is clear for these assumptions that $M = 5$ is the optimum value. The data were generated by computing P_{fa} given M, N, and P_{FA} using the following equation [14]:

$$P_{fa} = B^{-1}(M - 1; N, 1 - P_{FA}) \tag{5.48}$$

The value for P_{fa} is then substituted into (5.41) to compute the threshold V_t (assuming the signal is absent). V_t sets the lower limit of the integration when (5.38) is substituted into (5.35) as follows:

$$P_d = \int_{V_t}^{\infty} \frac{z}{\sigma_n^2} e^{-\left(\frac{z^2}{2\sigma_n^2} + s/n\right)} I_0\left(\frac{z\sqrt{2\,s/n}}{\sigma_n}\right) dz \tag{5.49}$$

Using (5.49), P_d is evaluated for each s/n with σ_n normalized to unity. Finally, PD is computed for the M and N values using (5.47). The search speed for this example, assuming a dwell time of 5 msec, is $R_S = 1/(N\,2T) = 12.5$ chips/sec.

5.1.8 Sequence of Initial Receiver Operations

The sequence of initial GPS receiver operations depends on the design of the receiver and the past history of the receiver operation. Obviously, the first operation is to

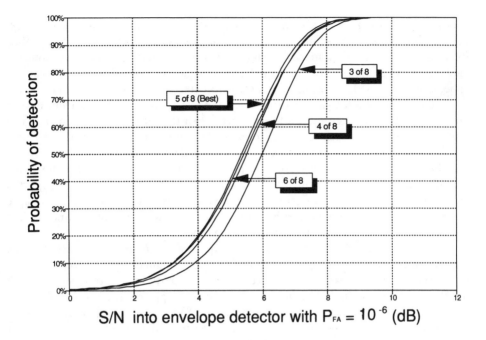

Figure 5.39 Probability of detection for *M* of *N* search detector.

select the satellites and then to conduct a search for the selected satellites. There is usually strong emphasis on how fast the receiver will acquire the selected satellites. To determine which satellites are visible and which constellation of visible satellites is the most suitable, three things are needed: (1) an up-to-date almanac, (2) rough estimates of user position and velocity, and (3) an estimate of user GPS time. If any of these parameters are missing or obsolete, the receiver has no choice but to perform what is called a "sky search," described later. If all are available, then using the user position, the GPS time estimate and the almanac, the SV positions and line-of-sight Doppler can be computed. Using the estimated user position and the SV positions, the visible SVs can be determined. From the list of visible SVs and the user position, typically the best constellation geometry for good dilution of precision is determined. The best constellation might be selected based on some criteria other than dilution of precision, depending on the application. When the constellation has been selected, the search process begins. From the user velocity and the SV line-of-sight Doppler, the total line-of-sight Doppler can be determined. This is used in the Doppler search pattern for the SV. If the approximate time and position are known and the ephemeris data has been obtained during a recent previous operation, the time to first fix can be around 30 sec for a typical five-channel GPS receiver if the signals are unobstructed. It can require up to 30 sec just to read the ephemeris data for the SV following signal acquisition. If the ephemeris is not available for the first fix, the almanac data is ordinarily used until the more precise data become available. Reading the almanac data following signal acquisition takes 12.5 min. The almanac data, used for SV selection and acquisition, is valid for several days, whereas the ephemeris data, used for navigation, begins to deteriorate rapidly after about 3 hr.

A critical piece of information is time. Most modern GPS receivers have a built-in timepiece that continues to run even when the set is powered down. They also have nonvolatile memory that stores the last user position, velocity, and time when the set is powered down, plus the ephemeris data for the last SVs tracked and the almanac. These memory features support fast initial acquisition the next time the GPS receiver is powered up, assuming that the receiver has not been transported hundreds of miles to a new location while powered down or that several days elapse between operation. The stored ephemeris can be used to compute the first fix if it has been 3 hr or less since the receiver was last powered down.

The "sky search" is actually a bootstrap mode of operation to get the GPS receiver into operation when one or more of the almanac, position/velocity, and time parameters are missing or obsolete. This mode requires the receiver to search the sky for all possible PRN codes, in all possible Doppler bins, and for all 1,023 code states of each PRN code until at least four SVs are acquired. This cold start process can require many minutes for the receiver to find visible SVs. The first four SVs found by sky search are unlikely to provide the best geometric performance, but after the almanac, position/velocity, and time information has been restored by using the first four SVs, the navigation process can then determine which SVs are visible and what is the best constellation. For "all-in-view" GPS receivers, which track eight or more SVs simultaneously, good geometry is assured if all SVs in view have been acquired and their measurements incorporated into the navigation solution. This multiple channel feature significantly improves the time to first fix for the sky search mode. Assuming that the best SVs have been selected for good geometry, there is negligible geometric performance improvement for more than 6 SVs tracked.

5.1.9 Use of Digital Processing

The use of digital processing was as important to the feasibility of the GPS navigation concept as the advancement of reliable space-qualified atomic standards. The computational burdens in the GPS space segment, control segment, and user segment are such that digital signal processing is an indispensable asset. Even the earliest GPS receivers with high analog front-end design content utilized digital processing in the receiver baseband processing, receiver control, navigation, and user interface areas. The custom component digital technology called application-specific integrated circuits (ASICs) and digital signal microprocessor technology are advancing so rapidly that all GPS receiver manufacturers currently use digital processing at higher levels of the signal processing functions. Also, the processing speed along with built-in floating point processors enables the modern GPS receiver designer to use optimum algorithms rather than approximations. Fortunately, as the feature sizes of ASICs become smaller, their power consumption is reduced and their speed is increased. These advances in technology not only reduce the component count, which reduces cost and power and increases reliability, but also can greatly improve performance. For this reason, outdated analog GPS receiver processing techniques were not discussed.

The partitioning between the microprocessor and the custom digital components depends on the digital signal processing throughput capability (bit manipulation and computational speed) of the microprocessor. It is important to keep in mind that every process performed in the microprocessor is performed in sequential steps, whereas the custom digital components perform their processing in parallel. The digital data is sampled data and there is real time between these samples in which the digital microprocessor can process the previous data. The microprocessor is interrupted every time the sampled data is updated. This is called real-time processing and the real-time processor must have completed all of the tasks within the interrupt time line and have some throughput resources left over for additional processes that are scheduled for completion on longer time lines. Fortunately, the nature of GPS digital signal processing is such that as the processing steps become more complex, there is also more real time allowed between the processes to complete the signal processing. For example, in a C/A-code digital GPS receiver, the digital samples containing the spread spectrum signals at IF of all of the visible SVs must be processed at a rate of 4 to 6 MHz. The replica C/A-code generators (one per SV tracked) must operate at 1.023 MHz. At these processing speeds, it is unlikely that the speed-power product of general-purpose digital signal microprocessors will make them the suitable choice to perform the carrier and code wipeoff functions in the very near future, perhaps never. However, after the SV signals have been despread, the processing rate per SV seldom exceeds 1 kHz and typically is of the order of 200 Hz per SV, which is well within the real-time signal processing capability of a modern digital signal microprocessor. The navigation process in a GPS receiver seldom exceeds 1 Hz, even for a high-dynamics application.

References

[1] Ward, P. W., "An Inside View of Pseudorange and Delta Pseudorange Measurements in a Digital NAVSTAR GPS Receiver," *Proc. ITC/USA/'81 International Telemetering Conference, GPS-Military and Civil Applications*, San Diego, CA, Oct. 1981.

[2] Ward, P. W., "An Advanced NAVSTAR GPS Multiplex Receiver," *Proc. of IEEE PLANS '80, Position Location and Navigation Symposium*, Atlantic City, NJ, Dec. 1980.

[3] Kohli, S., "Application of Massively Parallel Signal Processing Architectures to GPS/Inertial Sys-

tems," *Paper presented at IEEE PLANS '92 Position Location and Navigation Symposium*, Monterey, CA, April 1992.

[4] Townsend, B., D.J.R. van Nee, P. Fenton, and K. Van Dierendonck, "Performance Evaluation of the Multipath Estimating Delay Lock Loop," *Proc. ION National Technical Meeting*, Anaheim, CA, Jan. 1995, pp. 277–283.

[5] Przyjemski, J., E. Balboni, and J. Dowdle, "GPS Anti-Jam Enhancement Techniques," *Proc. ION 49th Annual Meeting*, Cambridge, MA, June 1993, pp. 41–50.

[6] Fuchser, T. D., "Oscillator Stability for Carrier Phase Lock," *Internal Memorandum G(S)-60233*, Texas Instruments Incorporated, Feb. 6, 1976.

[7] ICD-GPS-200, *NAVSTAR GPS Space Segment/Navigation User Interfaces (Public Release Version)*, ARINC Research Corporation, Fountain Valley, CA, July 3, 1991.

[8] Simon, M. K., J. K. Omura, R. A. Scholtz, and B. K. Levitt, *Spread Spectrum Communications Handbook*, Revised Edition, New York: McGraw-Hill, Inc., 1994, pp. 751–900.

[9] Scott, H. L., "PRS Acquisition and Aiding," *Internal Memorandum GPS 2924*, Texas Instruments Incorporated, Nov. 20, 1979.

[10] Polydoros, A., "On the Synchronization Aspects of Direct-Sequence Spread Spectrum Systems," Ph.D. Dissertation, Department of Electrical Engineering, University of Southern California, Aug. 1982.

[11] Tong, P. S., "A Suboptimum Synchronization Procedure for Pseudo Noise Communication Systems," *Proc. National Telecommunications Conference*, 1973, pp. 26D-1–26D-5.

[12] Scott, H. L., "Envelope Statistics," Internal Memorandum GPS-3001, Texas Instruments Incorporated, Dallas, Texas, March 31, 1980.

[13] Scott, H. L., "GPS Principles and Practices," The George Washington University Course 1081, Vol. I, March 1994.

[14] Barron, S., "M of N Search Detector," *Personal Correspondence*, Texas Instruments Incorporated, Dallas, Texas, May 25, 1995.

CHAPTER 6

▼▼▼

EFFECTS OF RF INTERFERENCE ON GPS SATELLITE SIGNAL RECEIVER TRACKING

Phillip Ward
NAVWARD GPS Consulting

6.1 EFFECTS OF RF INTERFERENCE ON TRACKING

Because GPS receivers rely on external radiofrequency (RF) signals, they are vulnerable to RF interference. RF interference can result in degraded navigation accuracy or complete loss of receiver tracking. (Some of the information presented in this chapter first appeared in [1].)

6.1.1 Types of Interference

Table 6.1 summarizes various types of RF interference. The RF interference may be friendly or intentional. There is a certain level of interference to C/A-code receivers from the C/A-codes of other GPS satellites. If pseudolites are used, operation at close range to these ground transmitters will almost certainly result in jamming of the remaining GPS satellite signals. In fact, the most efficient wideband jamming technique is the use of any one of the spread spectrum GPS codes and the GPS code-

Table 6.1
Types of RF Interference and Typical Sources

Type	Typical Sources
Wideband-Gaussian	Intentional noise jammers
Wideband phase/frequency modulation	Television transmitter's harmonics or near-band microwave link transmitters overcoming front-end filter of GPS receiver
Wideband-spread spectrum	Intentional spread spectrum jammers or near-field of pseudolites
Wideband-pulse	Radar transmitters
Narrowband phase/frequency modulation	AM stations transmitter's harmonics or CB transmitter's harmonics
Narrowband-swept continuous wave	Intentional CW jammers or FM stations transmitter's harmonics
Narrowband-continuous wave	Intentional CW jammers or near-band unmodulated transmitter's carriers

chipping rate to map the power spectrum of the jammer onto the power spectrum of the GPS signals.

Intentional jamming must be anticipated for military receivers. Hence, all classes of in-band jammers must be considered in the design. Also, GPS receivers are vulnerable to spoofing; that is, the intentional transmission of a false, but stronger version of the GPS signal so that it captures the receiver tracking loops and fools the navigation process. The encrypted antispoofing (AS) Y-code is used to replace the public P-code for military applications to minimize the potential for spoofing military GPS receivers. However, since the cost of a jammer is so much less than for a spoofer, the principal military GPS receiver threat will most likely be jamming. Y-code operation provides no advantage over P-code against enemy jamming.

RF interference is expected to originate from friendly (unintentional), out-of-band, RF interference sources for commercial GPS receivers. Unfortunately, non-linear effects may occur in high-powered transmitters causing lower power harmonics, which become in-band RF interference. An example of actual jamming of a ground mobile C/A-code receiver from the second harmonic of a commercial television transmitter is analyzed in Section 6.1.3.5.

6.1.2 Effects on Code Correlation and Loop Filtering

The effects of RF interference on code correlation and loop filtering are to reduce the C/N_0 of all of the GPS signals. If the C/N_0 is reduced below the tracking threshold of the GPS receiver, this causes the receiver to lose its ability to obtain measurements from the GPS satellite signals. Under this condition, an unaided GPS receiver loses its ability to navigate. As the line-of-sight range to the source of RF interference increases, the C/N_0 increases (improves). A good rule of thumb for the acquisition threshold C/N_0 for a GPS receiver is about 6 dB higher than the tracking threshold. If the receiver is jammed out of tracking the GPS signals, the range from the interference signal must be increased such that the effective C/N_0 increases by about 6 dB before the GPS receiver can reacquire. RF interference has the same effect on the code correlation and loop filtering functions of a GPS receiver as signal blockage, foliage attenuation, ionospheric scintillation, and multipath; that is, they all reduce the effective C/N_0 of the GPS signals.

In order to minimize the effects on the tracking loops of a GPS receiver, RF interference monitoring and mitigation features must be implemented. These features may become an important design requirement for commercial GPS receivers because RF interference is unpredictable and, when it occurs, it degrades the GPS signal integrity regardless of the health of the GPS SVs that transmit the signals. Fortunately, there is an opportunity for dual use of the antijam techniques that have been successfully developed for military GPS receivers. This section will first describe some of the most effective design techniques that have been used in military GPS receiver design and then present an analysis of the RF interference effects.

Figure 6.1 illustrates the generic digital GPS receiver block diagram that served as the basis for discussion in Chapter 5, with five numbered areas where antijam techniques are used in GPS receivers [1]. The techniques associated with each of these numbered functions will be described in the same numerical order as depicted in Figure 6.1.

6.1.2.1 Implementation of RF Interference Detector ①

The first technique is RF interference detection using a jamming-to-noise power ratio (J/N) meter. A distinguishing feature of a GPS receiver that has been enhanced to operate in the presence of RF interference is a built-in J/N meter. Detecting the presence of RF interference is given first priority because this provides an instant warning of potential loss of GPS SV signal integrity if RF interference is present. It is a very reliable indicator because it is a measure of the composite RF interference level actually being passed through the GPS receiver antenna and front end. The J/N meter is implemented at the automatic gain control (AGC) area depicted as point 1 in Figure 6.1. To implement the J/N meter, the AGC control voltage levels

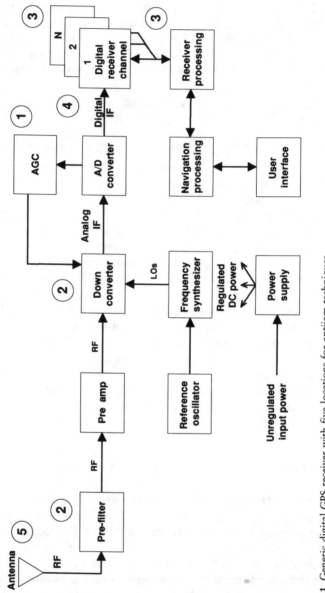

Figure 6.1 Generic digital GPS receiver with five locations for antijam techniques.

at the final IF output AGC amplifier must be digitized and provided to the receiver processing function.

The principle of operation is as follows. If the AGC control voltage level is different from the thermal noise root mean square (rms) level, then some other stronger signal is controlling the AGC. The presence of a stronger signal is RF interference because the GPS signals are all well below the thermal noise level. Precisely measuring this AGC control voltage level provides an accurate estimate of the J/N, which, in turn, can provide a good estimate of the jamming to signal power noise ratio (J/S). The J/N meter design should include a means of blanking the input signal and built-in low-power and high-power test tones, which can be injected ahead of the AGC. The signal blanking permits the IF thermal noise floor to be calibrated. Calibration is necessary because the AGC must compensate for gain and noise figure variations in the receiver front end as well as input signal variations. The two-level test tones permit the calibration of the slope of the AGC control voltage change as a function of increased signal power level. This calibration is necessary because the AGC control voltage slope is subject to variation. Because calibration is incompatible with tracking the GPS signals, it should be done each time the receiver is powered or reinitialized.

It is not necessary for the receiver to be tracking the GPS SVs to determine the presence of RF interference. The J/N measurement obtained from the AGC control voltage level does not depend on the receiver tracking SVs. Thus, the J/N meter makes it practical to adapt the GPS receiver search and tracking strategies in the presence of RF interference independent of SV tracking. A well-designed GPS receiver with antijam features will have mode transitions that optimize the receiver acquisition and tracking strategies to best cope with the detected levels of RF interference.

6.1.2.2 Front-End Filtering Techniques ②

The second technique is front-end filtering. Front-end filtering protects the GPS receiver from high-powered transmitters that are out of band with respect to the GPS L-band spectrum allocations. The passive prefilter shown in Figure 6.1 should have a sharp cutoff with deep stopband characteristics capable of suppressing high out-of-band power. Performance penalties result from placing a passive filter between the antenna and the preamp. Every 1 dB of insertion loss adds 1 dB to the receiver noise figure. This, in turn, reduces the tracking threshold by 1 dB. Cavity filters provide very low insertion loss and excellent stopband rejection characteristics, but are large and expensive. However, this could be the most cost-effective solution for out-of-band RF interference problems. For existing GPS receiver designs without the opportunity for including the other techniques described in this section, the prefilter and preamp can be combined with the antenna design.

In addition to the prefilter, the filter stages in the downconverter offer an opportunity to apply even greater filtering at increasingly narrow bandwidths. Filtering is required before and after each local oscillator (LO) mixing stage. As the downconversion process nears the final IF, it becomes practical to synthesize very narrow filter bandwidths. Theoretically, the receiver bandwidth must be infinite in order to recover all of the spread spectrum energy by the correlation process. The rule of thumb often used for a GPS receiver front-end bandwidth is two times the chipping rate; that is, two-sided bandwidths of 2.046 MHz for C/A-code and 20.46 MHz for P(Y)-code receivers. However, less than 0.1 dB of signal to (thermal) noise ratio is lost if the two-sided bandwidths are reduced from these rule-of-thumb values to passbands of 1.7 MHz for C/A-code and 17.0 MHz for P(Y)-code using a sharp cutoff filter [2]. This narrowband filtering in the downconverter not only improves the receiver performance against out-of-band RF interference, but the narrower stopband frequencies also lower the Nyquist sample criteria for the IF A/D conversion process.

Pulse Interference Suppression Techniques

Pulse interference sources are characterized by high energy levels at low duty cycles. A typical example of pulse interference is a radar transmitter. The high energy level can create interference by externally generated harmonics, which are in-band. If the transmitter is close to the GPS antenna, it can also overpower the prefilter's ability to reject out-of-band RF interference. It is good design practice to implement a limiter, typically using PIN (microwave) diodes, just ahead of the preamp to protect it from any excessive interference. The limiter looks like an open circuit to normal signals and to most RF interference signals, but it clips high-power signals. As long as the receiver front end has been designed to recover quickly from pulse interference, the clipping action of the low duty cycle interference will usually not cause a GPS receiver to fail. The limiting action of a pulse jammer captures the GPS receiver front end, preventing a successful correlation process. This is because the capturing signal dominates the signal statistics of the GPS signals plus random noise. However, this limiting action takes place only a small percentage of the time, so the pulse jammer is mitigated if the receiver front end is protected from damage and is not driven into saturation. Assuming that the baseband tracking loop discriminators are also robust during wide signal fluctuations, the loss in C/N_0 is directly proportional to the duty cycle of the pulse jammer; for example, a 3-dB loss for a 50% duty cycle due to a 6-dB signal loss and a 3-dB noise improvement.

6.1.2.3 Code/Carrier Tracking Loop Techniques ③

The third technique is enhancement of the code and carrier tracking loops. The code and carrier tracking loops are implemented in the digital receiver channels and the receiver processor depicted as point 3 in Figure 6.1. Jamming performance is improved by narrowing the predetection bandwidth of the receiver as well as the code and carrier tracking loop filter bandwidths. Reducing these bandwidths also reduces the line-of-sight dynamics that each channel can tolerate. This can be mitigated somewhat by increasing the loop filter order for an unaided receiver. Providing accurate velocity aiding from an external navigation system to the tracking loops will completely remove dynamic stress from the receiver tracking loops.

Internal Aiding Enhancements

Carrier aiding of the code loop is a common practice in GPS receivers because reducing the code loop bandwidth also reduces the thermal noise on the pseudorange measurements, which improves the navigation position accuracy. Carrier aiding of the code loop does *not* improve the jamming performance because *both* the code and carrier loops must maintain track simultaneously in order for the receiver channel to operate. Hence, the carrier loop is the weak link in a GPS receiver using a carrier-aided code loop, but with no external aiding.

External Navigation Aiding Enhancements

External aiding to a GPS receiver provides an overdetermined solution to the navigation function which adds robustness under RF interference conditions. Examples of navigation sensors that have been integrated with GPS are IMUs, Doppler radar [3], and air speed/baro altimeter/magnetic compass sensors. Since IMUs are self-contained, they are immune to RF interference. To their disadvantage, IMUs must be initialized and have a short-term (less than 0.1 of the Schuler period) drift in direct proportion to time cubed. Doppler radars provide true ground speed and altitude above true ground level. Doppler radars are subject to external RF interference, must be initialized, and they have a short-term drift in direct proportion to time. Air speed/baro altimeter/magnetic compass sensors are self-contained and therefore immune to external RF interference. They provide mean sea level altitude, air speed, and heading, but they have poor accuracy. Water speed indicators (EM logs), bottom tracking Doppler sonars, and odometer/speed sensors provide velocity aiding when combined with a heading sensor. These are immune to external RF interference. Water speed indicators have poor accuracy, but Doppler sonars and odometers can provide moderate velocity accuracy provided that a gyrocompass is used to provide accurate heading.

GPS is an absolute three-dimensional navigation system. A GPS receiver is virtually immune to drift and, with PLL operation implemented in its carrier tracking loops, can provide precise velocity of 0.02 m/sec (95%) or better for keyed PPS receivers during normal operation. Standalone SPS receivers are limited to approximately 0.6 m/sec (95%) velocity error due to SA. There is a natural synergism between GPS receivers and other external navigation sensors. Perhaps the most powerful synergism exists between tightly coupled GPS receivers and IMUs; that is, the two navigation sensors share a common navigation filter.

GPS can initialize and even calibrate the IMU in real time while preventing any navigation error buildup due to IMU drift. The IMU can aid the GPS receiver, removing most of the vehicle dynamics from its tracking loops. With reduced effective dynamics, the IMU-aided GPS tracking loops can then be operated at narrow noise bandwidths, thereby reducing their tracking thresholds to a much lower C/N_0. The lower C/N_0 tracking thresholds increase the RF interference immunity of the GPS receiver.

When the RF interference becomes so severe that the C/N_0 is reduced below the receiver's threshold C/N_0, the freshly calibrated and aligned IMU sustains the navigation function through the temporary GPS signal outages. The IMU aiding also assists the GPS receiver in rapidly reacquiring the SV signals after passing through the RF interference because the range and Doppler uncertainty growth during the GPS signal outage period is small by comparison with the unaided case. The IMU also provides other GPS integrity enhancements, which have been reported in the literature [4]. Further discussion of GPS/IMU integration as well as integration with other sensors is provided in Chapter 9.

Closed Carrier Tracking Loop Aiding

Precise external navigation aiding can provide accurate velocity aiding to the closed carrier tracking loop, (which, in turn, aids the code tracking loop), thereby removing dynamics from the carrier tracking loop. This permits the carrier tracking loop order to be reduced typically to a second-order loop. Also, the noise bandwidth can be much narrower than for the unaided case, which improves both the code and carrier tracking thresholds. The improved tracking thresholds provide accurate GPS velocity measurements under higher levels of RF interference. Therefore, the precise GPS velocity measurements permit the IMU to continue to be calibrated by the precise GPS velocity measurements for higher levels of RF interference. This is important for military weapons applications where the jamming level is expected to increase as the weapon approaches the target. The IMU will have to provide the navigation measurements during the terminal phase of the mission when the jamming level eventually overcomes the PPS GPS receiver. Since the IMU has been recently calibrated and aligned, it will accomplish the terminal navigation function more accurately. This technique could be important for commercial SPS GPS receiver Category II and III landing applications where precise carrier Doppler phase measurements from the GPS receiver could be sustained to a lower threshold C/N_0.

For the SPS technique to operate as accurately as the PPS technique, the dither error effects of SA must be removed in the SPS receiver carrier Doppler phase measurements by a differential rate correction with respect to a reference station. The SA dither correction is not supported as a rate correction by the Wide Area Augmentation System (WAAS) [5], so this must be provided by the local system for maximum accuracy.

Open Carrier Tracking Loop Aiding

An even more robust weak signal hold-on strategy under severe jamming is to open the receiver carrier tracking loop, maintain the carrier NCO with precise external velocity aiding, and continue the velocity aiding to the code tracking loop. Under this circumstance, there are no delta range measurements available from the receiver channel, so calibration of an IMU is no longer possible. The improvement against wideband (Gaussian) jammers is achieved by reducing the code loop filter bandwidth using external velocity aiding. This can be accomplished using the J/N meter to adapt the code tracking loop in a conventional receiver design with three complex (I and Q) correlators as described in Chapter 5. Another IMU-aided open carrier tracking loop technique that does not utilize the J/N meter to adapt the code loop bandwidth is called extended range adaptive tracking [6]. This technique uses a covariance algorithm based on the statistics obtained from 21 complex correlators. The algorithm optimally adjusts the code loop filter bandwidth to the instantaneous values of jamming power while correcting the code loop for residual dynamics due to errors in the external velocity aiding. Both techniques are equally effective.

6.1.2.4 Narrowband Interference Processing Techniques ④

The fourth technique is temporal filtering. Temporal filtering is implemented at the digital IF area depicted as point 4 in Figure 6.1. This design enhancement is only effective against narrowband RF interference sources. Temporal filtering uses the same principal as the J/N meter to detect the presence of RF interference, namely, that the interfering signal is expected to be above the thermal noise level, which is always above the GPS signal levels.

The temporal filtering process is accomplished by performing digital signal processing of the digitized IF signal using transversal filtering techniques. Another variant of time domain signal processing is called spectral amplitude domain processing [6]. If there is no RF interference, then the thermal noise amplitude will be fairly uniform in amplitude. If there is narrowband interference in the signal, it will be manifested by an anomaly in the amplitude. The anomaly can be adaptively filtered out by either technique. The narrowband RF interference is effectively suppressed down to the thermal noise level. If there is wideband RF interference, then, even though it can be detected by the J/N meter, it cannot be discriminated from thermal noise by temporal filtering. Only the rate-aided code/carrier tracking techniques (point 3) and antenna enhancements (point 5) are effective against wideband RF interference.

6.1.2.5 Antenna Enhancements ⑤

The fifth and last technique is implemented at the antenna area depicted as point 5 in Figure 6.1. This technique involves the use of an adaptive antenna array. One type is called a beamsteered array, which points a narrow beam of antenna gain toward each satellite tracked. This type of array contains many antenna elements and is extremely expensive. The beamsteered antenna array is not further discussed here because it is impractical for most GPS applications.

The other type is called a controlled reception pattern antenna (CRPA). A CRPA contains multiple antenna elements physically arranged into an array that can steer gain nulls toward jammers. Associated with the array is a low-noise preamplifier per element and sophisticated signal processing electronics. The CRPA electronics provides phase control for each element of the array. It adds these phase-controlled antenna element signal outputs in a manner that effectively creates a nearly uniform hemispherical gain pattern when there is no external RF interference.

The CRPA electronics detects the presence of any RF interference in the GPS L-band regions in the same manner as the J/N sensor described earlier. The objective of the adaptive antenna array is to steer a null in its hemispherical gain pattern toward each external jammer. The number of nulls it can steer is limited by the number of elements in the CRPA. In general, the CRPA can steer $N - 1$ nulls for an N-element array. The depth of the null is limited by the number of nulls that are being steered at the same time. For military avionics GPS receivers, multiple jammers must be anticipated and therefore multiple element CRPAs are required. For example, if a military CRPA contains seven elements, then it can theoretically steer six nulls toward six different jammers. Many expensive components are required in the highly specialized design of the CRPA RF and IF electronics. For this reason and because of the limited production volume, the cost of a military CRPA is typically many times more than the cost of its companion GPS receiver. However, after the code/carrier tracking techniques (point 3) have been fully exploited, the CRPA is the only way to achieve an additional 25 dB or more antijam immunity against wideband RF interference. Naturally, if the line of sight to a SV being tracked is in the region of the null being steered toward a jammer, the SV signal will be suppressed along with the jammer. But this is better than having all of the SV signals being suppressed by the jammer.

For commercial avionics GPS receivers, it is unlikely that more than one wideband RF interference will occur at a time. Two-element CRPAs, called dual-reception pattern antennas (DRPAs), can effectively steer a deep null toward one jammer [7]. Another antenna null steering technique, called a canceler, uses a reference antenna and one or more sensing antennas. The reference antenna has its gain maximized toward the region containing the SVs, and each sensing antenna has its gain maximized toward the region where the jammers are expected. As the name implies, the jamming signals in the reference antenna are canceled to the extent that they are differentiated by the same jamming signals obtained from each sensing antenna. The canceler technique is very cost effective if the region(s) containing the jammers relative to the (nearly hemispherical) region containing the GPS SVs are predictable and have very little overlap. For example, the canceler technique can be effective against horizon jammers.

6.1.3 Analyzing the Effects of RF Interference

To analyze the effect of RF interference, first determine what is the unjammed C/N_0 for the SV signals. Then determine what the tracking threshold is for the GPS receiver. This produces the effective C/N_0 that can be tolerated as a result of jamming. Using the unjammed C/N_0 and the effective C/N_0, the J/S level at the receiver input can then be calculated. From the input J/S, the range and power combinations of the RF interference can be calculated. For example, if the interference power is known, then the range to this interference source at which the effective C/N_0 threshold is reached can be computed. When a GPS receiver with reasonable J/S performance is analyzed, it is surprising how little the RF interference energy and how large the range to the source of RF interference is at threshold.

6.1.3.1 *Computing Unjammed C/N_0*

To compute the unjammed C/N_0 for each of the received signal levels, certain key design attributes of the GPS receiver must be known. The minimum GPS received signal powers are specified in ICD-GPS-200 [8]. The SV signals of the relatively new GPS satellite constellation are typically a lot "hotter" than the minimum specified signal strength. However, only the minimum is guaranteed by the GPS space segment. These minimum signal levels (from Chapter 4) are −159.6, −162.6, and −165.2 dBw for L1 C/A, L1 P(Y), and L2 P(Y)-codes, respectively.

The equation for the unjammed C/N_0 at baseband is given by

$$C/N_0 = S_r + G_a - 10 \log(kT_0) - N_f - L \text{ (dB-Hz)} \qquad (6.1)$$

where

S_r	=	received GPS signal power (dBw)
G_a	=	antenna gain toward SV (dBic)
$10 \log(kT_0)$	=	thermal noise density (dBw-Hz)

$$
\begin{aligned}
 &= -204 \text{ dBw-Hz} \\
k \quad &= \text{Boltzmann's constant (watt-sec/K)} \\
 &= 1.38 \times 10^{-23} \\
T_0 \quad &= \text{thermal noise reference temperature (K)} \\
 &= 290\text{K} \\
N_f \quad &= \text{noise figure of receiver including antenna and cable losses (dB)} \\
L \quad &= \text{implementation losses plus A/D converter loss (dB)}
\end{aligned}
$$

As a computation example, assume $S_r = -159.6$ dBw; that is, the minimum received signal power level for L1 C/A-code (see Section 4.1.2 for details). Further, assume that the antenna has unity gain toward the SV ($G_a = 0$), that the receiver noise figure is $N_f = 4$ dB, and that the implementation loss plus A/D converter loss is $L = 2$ dB for the GPS receiver (all very high quality assumptions). Substituting these values into (6.1), the unjammed carrier to noise power ratio is

$$
C/N_0 = -159.6 + 0 - (-204) - 4 - 2 = 38.4 \text{ dB-Hz}
$$

The same assumptions yield an unjammed $C/N_0 = 35.4$ dB-Hz for L1 P(Y)-code and unjammed $C/N_0 = 32.8$ dB-Hz for L2 P(Y)-code.

6.1.3.2 Computing Tracking Threshold C/N_0

The level to which the unjammed C/N_0 is reduced by RF interference is called the equivalent carrier to noise power density ratio. The equivalent carrier-to-noise power density ratio is related to the unjammed C/N_0 and the J/S as follows:

$$
[c/n_0]_{eq} = \cfrac{1}{\cfrac{1}{c/n_0} + \cfrac{j/s}{QR_c}} \quad \text{(power ratio)} \tag{6.2}
$$

where

$$
\begin{aligned}
c/n_0 \quad &= \text{unjammed carrier-to-noise power in a 1-Hz bandwidth expressed as a} \\
 &\quad\ \text{ratio} \\
j/s \quad &= \text{jammer-to-signal power expressed as a ratio} \\
R_c \quad &= \text{GPS PRN code chipping rate (chips/sec)} \\
 &= 1.023 \times 10^6 \text{ chips/sec for C/A-code} \\
 &= 10.23 \times 10^6 \text{ chips/sec for P(Y)-code} \\
Q \quad &= \text{spread spectrum processing gain adjustment factor (dimensionless)} \\
 &= 1 \text{ for narrowband jammer} \\
 &= 1.5 \text{ for wideband spread spectrum jammer} \\
 &= 2 \text{ for wideband Gaussian noise jammer}
\end{aligned}
$$

When expressed in terms of dB-Hz, this equation becomes

$$[C/N_0]_{eq} = -10 \log\left[10^{-(C/N_0)/10} + \frac{10^{(J/S)/10}}{QR_c} \right] \quad \text{(dB-Hz)} \quad (6.3)$$

where

C/N_0 = unjammed carrier-to-noise power ratio in a 1-Hz bandwidth (dB-Hz)
    = $10 \log(c/n_0)$
J/S = jammer-to-signal power ratio (dB)
    = $10 \log(j/s)$

6.1.3.3 Computing the J/S

Equation (6.3) can be rearranged to solve for the J/S as follows:

$$J/S = 10 \log\left[QR_c\left(\frac{1}{10^{[C/N_0]_{eq}/10}} - \frac{1}{10^{(C/N_0)/10}} \right) \right] \quad \text{(dB)} \quad (6.4)$$

As a computational example to determine the J/S performance of a GPS receiver at its tracking threshold, assume that the source of RF interference is a wideband jammer and that a C/A-code GPS receiver is used. Then $Q = 2$ and $R_c = 1.023 \times 10^6$ chips/sec. Further, assume that the unjammed C/N_0 is the same as for the computational example for (6.1). Then $C/N_0 = 38.4$ dB-Hz. The remaining parameter that must be determined is the $[C/N_0]_{eq}$ corresponding to the tracking threshold of the receiver. Because a GPS receiver is nonlinear, especially near its tracking threshold, a Monte Carlo simulator is required to accurately predict the signal tracking threshold for a given dynamics scenario. The rule-of-thumb techniques to predict the signal tracking threshold were described in Section 5.1.5. Since the weak link in an unaided GPS receiver is usually the carrier tracking loop threshold, this threshold is usually substituted for $[C/N_0]_{eq}$. The PLL carrier tracking loop design example taken from Section 5.1.5 will be used. This was a third-order loop with a 18-Hz noise bandwidth and a 20-msec predetection integration time. The rule-of-thumb tracking threshold was $[C/N_0]_{eq} = 28.0$ dB-Hz. Substituting these values into the above equation

$$J/S = 10 \log\left[2 \times 1.023 \times 10^6\left(\frac{1}{10^{2.8}} - \frac{1}{10^{3.84}} \right) \right] \text{ dB}$$

$$= 34.7 \text{ dB}$$

If all combinations for C/A-code and P(Y)-code and for wideband and narrowband jammers are computed for the $[C/N_0]_{eq}$ of 28.0 dB-Hz, the results are as contained in Table 6.2.

In the PLL design example, the C/N_0 threshold was reduced to $[C/N_0]_{eq}$ = 18.5 dB-Hz by reducing the carrier tracking loop bandwidth to 2 Hz. Recall that this could only be accomplished with the use of external velocity aiding to the tracking loop or by substantially reducing the maximum platform dynamics. For this improved tracking threshold, the *J/S* results are as contained in Table 6.3.

Figure 6.2 depicts the *J/S* performance as a function of the $[C/N_0]_{eq}$ thresholds for L1 C/A, L1 P(Y), and L2 P(Y) receivers for both narrowband and wideband jammers. The same assumptions were made as in the above examples to determine the unjammed C/N_0.

6.1.3.4 Computing RF Interference Signal Levels

Even though the *J/S* performance of a GPS receiver sounds impressive when the ratio is reported in decibels, it becomes less impressive when the actual jammer signal levels are considered. This is because the received GPS signal is so small. To demonstrate how little jammer power is required at the input of a GPS receiver to disable it when the *J/S* performance of the receiver is known, the following equations are required:

Table 6.2
Jammer-to-Signal Ratios (*J/S*) for 28.0-dB-Hz Tracking Threshold

J/S Environment (dB)	Signal		
	L1 C/A	L1 P(Y)	L2 P(Y)
Wideband	34.7	44.2	43.4
Spread spectrum	33.4	43.0	42.1
Narrowband	31.7	41.2	40.4

Table 6.3
Jammer-to-Signal Ratios (*J/S*) for 18.5-dB-Hz Tracking Threshold

J/S Environment (dB)	Signal		
	L1 C/A	L1 P(Y)	L2 P(Y)
Wideband	44.6	54.5	54.4
Spread spectrum	43.3	53.3	53.2
Narrowband	41.6	51.5	51.4

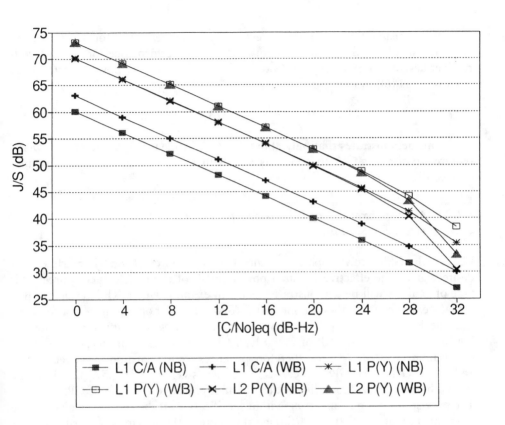

Figure 6.2 *J/S* performance as a function of receiver tracking threshold.

$$J/S = J_r - S_r \quad \text{(dB)} \tag{6.5}$$

where

J_r = received (incident) jammer power into the receiver (dBw)
S_r = received (incident) signal power into the receiver (dBw)

Rearranging (6.5),

$$J_r = J/S + S_r \quad \text{(dBw)} \tag{6.6}$$

Since $J_r = 10 \log j_r$, then

$$j_r = 10^{(J/S + S_r)/10} \quad \text{(watts)} \tag{6.7}$$

When using the minimum received signal power level for L1 C/A-code, $S_r = -159.6$ dBw and the most optimistic jamming performance for the C/A-code receiver design examples of $J/S = 44.6$ dB, the incident jammer power is determined from (6.7) as follows:

$$j_r = 10^{(44.6+(-159.6)/10)} = 3.1623 \times 10^{-12} \quad \text{watts}$$

This demonstrates that only about 3 pW of incident RF interference power is required to disable a C/A-code GPS receiver with a very substantial J/S performance of 44.6 dB.

6.1.3.5 Analysis Example of RF Interference From a Commercial Television Station

Usually, the GPS receiver operating range from the source of the RF interference is desired, given the effective radiated power (ERP) of the interference source. This type of analysis will be demonstrated using an example where RF interference was actually experienced with a commercial C/A-code receiver operating near a commercial television station [9]. The television transmitter was Channel 66 located in Hudson, MA, with an ERP of 2,000 kW. Channel 66 has a frequency allocation between 782 and 788 MHz. It therefore produces second harmonics between 1.564 and 1.576 GHz. The GPS L1 C/A-code carrier is centered at 1.57542 GHz. The second harmonics will look like wideband interference to a C/A-code GPS receiver. The television station is operating within specifications if the spurious emissions are attenuated by at least 60 dB. Although this reduces the spurious power by at least a factor of 1 million, there can remain up to 2W of second harmonic power in the GPS L1 band.

The formula for the link budget for the transmitted jammer power is given by

$$\text{ERP}_j = J_r - G_j + L_p + L_f \quad \text{(dBw)} \tag{6.8}$$

where

$$
\begin{aligned}
\text{ERP}_j &= \text{Effective radiated power of the jammer} \\
&= J_t + G_t \\
J_t &= \text{jammer transmit power into its antenna (dBw)} \\
&= 10 \log j_t \ (j_t \text{ expressed in watts}) \\
G_t &= \text{jammer transmitter antenna gain (dBic)} \\
J_r &= \text{incident (received) jammer power (dBw)} \\
&= 10 \log j_r \ (j_r \text{ expressed in watts}) \\
L_p &= \text{free-space propagation loss (dB)} \\
&= 20 \log \left(\frac{4\pi d}{\lambda_j} \right)
\end{aligned}
$$

d =   range to jammer (meters)
λ_j =   wavelength of jammer frequency (meters)
G_j =   GPS receiver antenna gain toward jammer (dBic)
L_f =   jammer power loss due to receiver front-end filtering (dB)

Assume ERP_j is 2W (3 dBw). Since the jammer frequency is in-band, the wavelength λ_j, will be assumed to be the same as L1 and L_f is therefore assumed to be 0 dB. The value G_j is assumed to be −3 dBic (0.5 gain power ratio with respect to a unity gain isotropic circularly polarized antenna toward the RF interference). Using the earlier design example of an L1 C/A-code receiver with the third-order 18-Hz noise bandwidth carrier tracking loop, the wideband J/S = 34.7 dB and the minimum guaranteed received signal S_r = −159.6 dBw. Then, from (6.6), the incident jamming power at threshold is

$$J_r = J/S + S_r = 34.7 + (-159.6) = -124.9 \quad \text{dBw}$$

The line-of-sight range to the television antenna at which the receiver reaches its loss of track threshold can now be determined from (6.8), rearranged to solve for L_p:

$$L_p = 20 \log\left(\frac{4\pi d}{\lambda_j}\right) = (J_t + G_t) - J_r + G_j - L_f = 3 + 124.9 + (-3) - 0 = 124.9 \quad \text{dB}$$

Solving for the range d, to the jammer to attenuate the 2W transmitted signal to the threshold level at the receiver input:

$$d = 26.6 \text{ km}$$

$$= 16.5 \text{ mi}$$

If the 44.6-dB J/S C/A-code receiver design (third-order PLL with a 2-Hz noise bandwidth and 20-msec predetection integration time) is used, then, J_r = −115.0 dBw. This results in a decreased range of

$$d = 8.5 \text{ km}$$

$$= 5.3 \text{ mi}$$

In the actual test, there was a 2-mile radius of interference. The shorter real-world interference radius was probably due to a lower ERP of the second harmonic interference than the 2W (maximum harmonic power) that was assumed in the analysis. There could have been a greater difference than the assumed 3 dB between the antenna gain G_a and G_j. The antenna gain is usually higher for the higher elevation SVs (G_a) than toward the television antenna on the horizon (G_j). The actual difference depends on the antenna used. It could also be due to greater signal attenuation due to foliage or terrain blockage because the television antenna was not always in the direct line of sight with respect to the GPS receiver antenna. (The test was conducted on highways that passed nearby the television antenna.) It was certainly not that the commercial GPS receiver that was used in the experiment had a better *J/S* performance than was used in the example.

It should be noted that the above test was the impetus for an extensive government field measurement program. Approximately one year after the above test was performed, both the DOT and the National Telecommunications and Information Administration (NTIA) conducted field monitoring testing at numerous television stations throughout the United States, including Channel 66 in Hudson, MA. It was found that in all cases radiated harmonic levels were below −100 dBc, which is 40-dB better than the FCC specification. The television stations are motivated to keep harmonic content low because this substantially improves the quality of the received television picture. They are also required to maintain their radiated harmonics below levels that would cause interference for users of other FCC-allocated frequency bands (such as GPS users). The interference requirement applies in addition to the basic FCC specification.

6.1.3.6 *Computing Range to RF Interference*

Using the same equations and assumptions in the previous example, Figure 6.3(a–c) are plots of the range to the jammer as a function of the ERP with *J/S* as a running parameter for L1 C/A-code, L1 P(Y)-code, and L2 P(Y)-code receivers, respectively. Using the $[C/N_0]_{eq}$ obtained from the rule-of-thumb tracking threshold analysis or by using Monte Carlo simulations, the actual *J/S* performance of a GPS receiver can be determined from Figure 6.2. Using the actual *J/S* performance, the line-of-sight range to the jammer can be determined from Figure 6.3 if the type (narrowband or wideband) and the ERP of the jammer is known. Alternatively, for a given range to the jammer, the maximum ERP can be determined.

6.1.3.7 *Factors That Reduce RF Interference Effects*

There are a number of factors that help to reduce the RF interference effects. The RF interference can only have the full effect of this analysis on the GPS receiver if it is in the line of sight of the GPS antenna and unobstructed. For commercial aviation applications, the RF interference sources will typically be at ground level while the GPS antenna will be elevated during en route navigation. This increases the line-of-sight range, but because the source of the interference will, in general, be from below the aircraft's horizon, the body of the aircraft will help to block the interference. Also, the gain pattern of the GPS antenna rolls off significantly below

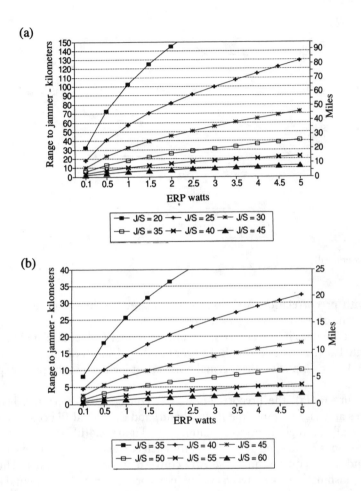

Figure 6.3 Range to jammer as a function of ERP: (a) L1 C/A-code receiver, (b) L1 P(Y)-code receiver, and (c) L2 P(Y)-code receiver.

the aircraft horizon unless GPS pseudolite ground transmitters (GTs) are being used to support local differential operation. In this case, the GPS antenna used with gain toward the ground will be vulnerable to RF interference from the ground. However, as the aircraft approaches for landing or for ground-based operation of GPS receivers in general, the RF interference signals can be attenuated due to Earth curvature, foliage, buildings, and so forth.

6.1.4 Effects of A/D Conversion

The effect of RF interference on A/D conversion depends on where this takes place in a GPS receiver. Figure 6.4(a) illustrates a high-level block diagram of a GPS

(c)

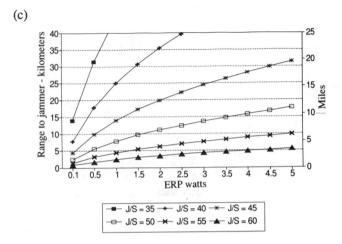

Figure 6.3 (continued)

receiver with precorrelation A/D conversion. Figure 6.4(b) illustrates a high-level block diagram of a GPS receiver with postcorrelation A/D conversion. Figure 6.5 illustrates the changes in the power spectrum for the L1 C/A-code signal plus a CW jammer signal as these pass through the four numbered stages of the receivers shown in Figure 6.4. For simplicity, the thermal noise is not included in the power spectrum illustrations.

In Figure 6.4(a), the precorrelation A/D conversion is performed at IF (at sample rates at least two times the IF stopband) and the digital IF becomes a shared function by all the digital receiver channels. In Figure 6.4(b), the postcorrelation A/D conversion is performed at baseband for each correlated output (typically early, prompt, and late) requiring multiple A/D converters for each channel. This is the main distinguishing feature between analog (postcorrelation A/D) and digital (precorrelation A/D) GPS receivers. Virtually all modern GPS receivers are digital receivers with precorrelation A/D conversion. The advantages in component count reduction are obviously in favor of the precorrelation A/D converter (digital receiver) architecture.

However, there is a serious vulnerability to continuous wave (CW) interference in a precorrelation A/D converter—it can be easily captured by the CW signal. This will disable the receiver at lower CW jamming levels than predicted in the earlier analysis examples. Note that the power spectrum at point 2 in Figure 6.5 still contains the CW signal and that this CW signal is applied to the precorrelation A/D converter in Figure 6.4(a). In particular, 1-bit A/D converters, which are so popular for commercial precorrelation GPS receivers, can be easily captured by CW interference. Since a 1-bit A/D converter design is simply a signal limiter, it usually has no AGC. As a result of CW jamming, the statistics of the zero crossings of the signal are no longer

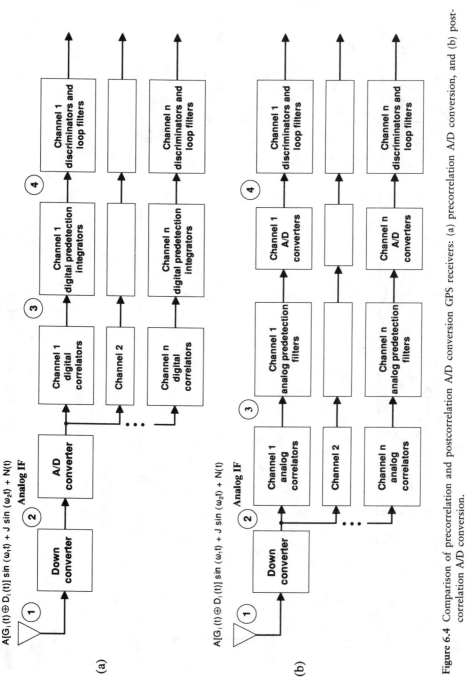

Figure 6.4 Comparison of precorrelation and postcorrelation A/D conversion GPS receivers: (a) precorrelation A/D conversion, and (b) postcorrelation A/D conversion.

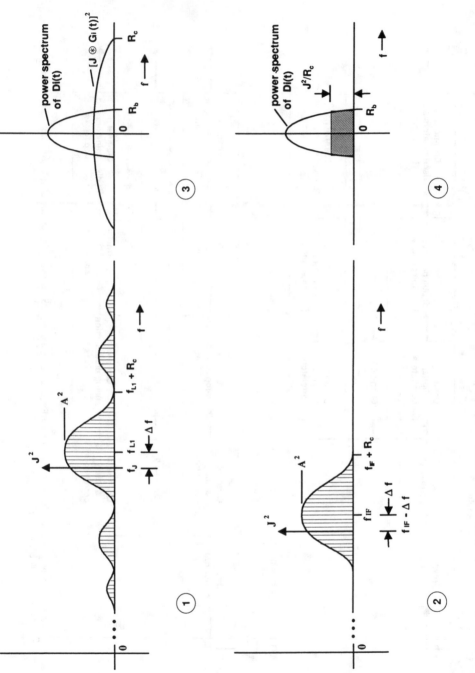

Figure 6.5 Power spectrums of C/A-code plus CW jammer at four receiver stages.

determined by a combination of random noise and the GPS signals, but become dominated by the CW signal. It is only in the regions of the CW signal zero crossings that correlation with the GPS signals can take place for 1-bit quantizations. The probability density of a CW signal is given by

$$P(x) = \frac{1}{\pi\sqrt{1 - x^2}} \tag{6.9}$$

This function is plotted in Figure 6.6. Observe in this plot that the statistics of a CW signal shows that it spends most of its time near the peak amplitudes rather than in the vicinity of the zero crossing. The result is that the combination of signal plus noise plus CW signal spends very little time near the zero crossing. Hence, there is very little correlation possible in the presence of CW jamming that captures the precorrelation A/D converter. By contrast, a postcorrelation A/D converter design prevents this problem from occurring. Referring to Figure 6.5 at point 3, the same correlation process that has despread the GPS signals has also spread the CW interference into broadband interference before it reaches the A/D converter. Therefore, in Figure 6.4(b), the power spectrum that is applied to the postcorrelation A/D converters at point 3 does not contain the CW jammer signal. Instead, the CW signal has been spread into a wideband signal by the analog correlation process. This spreading effect on the CW interference converts it to wideband noise with significantly reduced peak power. This protects the postcorrelation A/D converter from being captured by a CW jammer.

Referring to Figure 6.5, the processing gain that is achieved against CW jamming by the spread spectrum signal is defined by the ratio of the *J/S* at point 1 to the *J/S* at point 4. The *J/S* at point 1 is

$$\left(\frac{j}{s}\right)_1 = \frac{J^2}{P_s} \quad \text{(power ratio)} \tag{6.10}$$

where

J = CW jammer power at the receiver input
P_s = signal power at the receiver input

The *J/S* at point 4 is

$$\left(\frac{j}{s}\right)_4 = \frac{\left(\frac{J^2}{R_c}\right)2\,R_b}{P_s} \quad \text{(power ratio)} \tag{6.11}$$

where

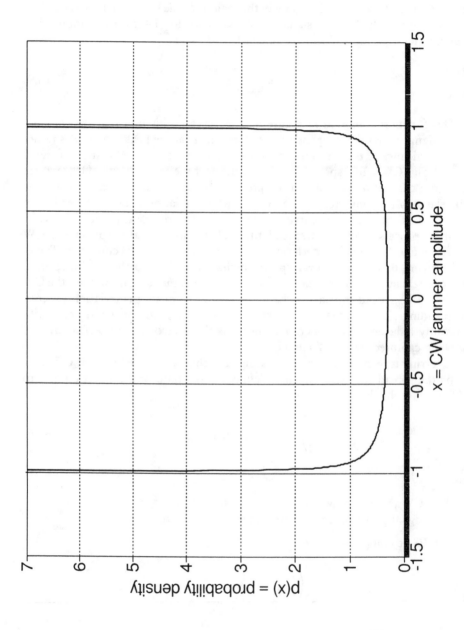

Figure 6.6 Probability density of a CW (sinusoidal) signal.

R_c = GPS PRN code chipping rate (chips/sec)
R_b = predetection bandwidth

The CW processing gain is therefore

$$P_G = \frac{\left(\frac{j}{s}\right)_1}{\left(\frac{j}{s}\right)_4} = \frac{R_c}{2\,R_b} \quad \text{(ratio)} \tag{6.12}$$

Note that the processing gain against CW is directly proportional to the code-chipping rate and inversely proportional to the predetection (data modulation) bandwidth. For C/A-code with 50-Hz data modulation, the processing gain is 1.023×10^4 or 40 dB. For the WAAS geostationary satellite C/A-code with 500-Hz data modulation, this drops to 1.023×10^3 or 30 dB. For P(Y)-code, this is 1.023×10^5 or 50 dB. (For Gaussian noise or a wideband jammer, the processing gain is 3-dB higher in each case.) The precorrelation A/D converter is not protected by this spread spectrum processing and therefore experiences the full level of CW interference. An adaptive nonlinear A/D converter technique first developed for military applications to overcome this problem is shown in Figure 6.7 [10].

This nonlinear sign/magnitude design works in concert with the AGC to move the quantization levels toward the peak of the CW signal, thereby preventing the CW signal from capturing the A/D converter.

6.1.5 Vulnerability of C/A-Code to CW

The GPS C/A-code is a Gold code with a short 1-msec period; that is, the pseudorandom sequence repeats every millisecond. Because of this, the C/A-code does not have a continuous power spectrum. Instead, it has a line spectrum that is separated by the inverse of the code period, which is 1-kHz apart. The line spectrum characteristic for the C/A-code is not ideal [11]. As a result, a CW jammer can mix with a strong C/A-code line and leak through the correlator. Although it is typical for each line in the C/A-code power spectrum to be down 24 dB or more with respect to the total power, there are usually some lines in every C/A-code that are stronger. Table 6.4 summarizes the worst line frequency and the worst line (strongest) amplitude for every C/A-code [12]. These phenomena cause more of a problem during C/A-code search and acquisition modes than in tracking modes. The lower half of Figure 6.7 shows an implementation of a CW jammer detector, which can be used as a warning flag. The P(Y)-code does not have this vulnerability.

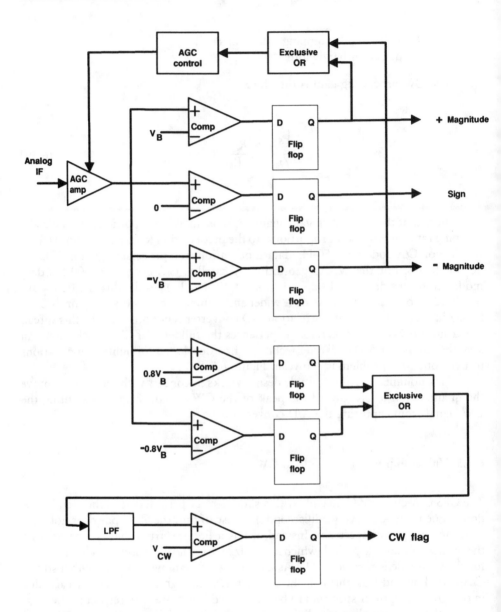

Figure 6.7 Functional block diagram of nonlinear A/D converter and CW detector.

Table 6.4
Worst C/A Line for Each of the 37 Codes

C/A-Code PRN Number	Worst Line Frequency (kHz)	Worst Line Amplitude (dB)	C/A-Code PRN Number	Worst Line Frequency (kHz)	Worst Line Amplitude (dB)
1	42	−22.71	20	30	−22.78
2	263	−23.12	21	55	−23.51
3	108	−22.04	22	12	−22.12
4	122	−22.98	23	127	−23.08
5	23	−21.53	24	123	−21.26
6	227	−21.29	25	151	−23.78
7	78	−23.27	26	102	−23.06
8	66	−21.5	27	132	−21.68
9	173	−22.09	28	203	−21.73
10	16	−22.45	29	176	−22.22
11	123	−22.64	30	63	−22.14
12	199	−22.08	31	72	−23.13
13	214	−23.52	32	74	−23.58
14	120	−22.01	33	82	−21.82
15	69	−21.9	34	55	−24.13
16	154	−22.58	35	43	−21.71
17	138	−22.5	36	23	−22.23
18	183	−21.4	37	55	−24.13
19	211	−21.77			

6.1.5.1 *Vulnerability of C/A-Code to CW at Thermal Noise Level*

Even if an adaptive antenna array or temporal filtering are used to reduce CW interference to the thermal noise level, there remains a vulnerability of C/A-code to CW interference. The approximate thermal noise floor can be determined from the following equation:

$$N_{ther} \approx 10 \log(kT_0) + 10 \log(B) + N_f \quad (dBw) \tag{6.13}$$

where

B = receiver front-end bandwidth (Hz)

If 1.7 MHz is the assumed C/A-code front-end bandwidth and 4 dB is the assumed noise figure, then, using (6.13),

$$N_{ther} \approx -204 + 62.3 + 4 = -137.7 \text{ dBw}$$

If an adaptive antenna array or temporal filter takes the CW interference down to this thermal noise floor, then $J_r = N_{ther}$. Substituting this into (6.5) and using the minimum received L1 C/A-code received power $S_r = -159.6$ dBw, gives

$$J/S = J_r - S_r = N_{ther} - S_r = -137.7 - (-159.6) = 21.9 \text{ dB}$$

This would not be a problem for most unaided C/A-code receiver designs if the source were wideband noise RF interference or even narrowband RF interference if the bandwidth were, say, 100 kHz. However, CW interference at this level could cause problems with the C/A-code receiver because of the leak-through phenomena described earlier (compare 21.9 dB J/S with the worst case leak-through levels shown in Table 6.4). The problem is worse for receivers with wider front-end bandwidths such as narrow correlator C/A-code receivers (i.e., the J/S increases).

A C/A-code (Gold code) jammer, such as the near field of a pseudolite, can also be a problem for this same situation because temporal side lobes are produced. In both cases, the problem is more serious during C/A-code search and acquisition modes than for tracking modes.

References

[1] Ward, P. W., "GPS Receiver RF Interference Monitoring, Mitigation, and Analysis Techniques," *NAVIGATION, Journal of The Institute of Navigation*, Vol. 41, No. 4, Winter, 1994–95, pp. 367–391.

[2] Ward, P. W., "Advanced GPS Receiver Systems," Navtech Seminars, Inc., Course 494, Vol. 1, Arlington, VA, February 1994.

[3] Rounds, S. F., "A Fully Integrated GPS/Doppler/Inertial Navigation System," *Proc. of the Satellite Division of the Institute of Navigation*, Colorado Springs, CO, Sept. 1987, pp. 184–187.

[4] Vieweg, S., "Aircraft Autonomous Integrity Monitoring for an Integrated Satellite/Inertial Navigation System," *Proc. of the ION GPS-93, Sixth International Technical Meeting of The Satellite Division of The Institute of Navigation*, Vol. I, Salt Lake City, UT, Sept. 1993, pp. 509–518.

[5] Van Dierendonck, A. J., and P. Enge, "The Wide Area Augmentation System (WAAS) Signal Specification," *Proc. of the ION GPS-93, Seventh International Technical Meeting of The Satellite Division of The Institute of Navigation*, Vol. II, Salt Lake City, UT, Sept. 1994, pp. 985–994.

[6] Przyjemski, J., E. Balboni, and J. Dowdle, "GPS Anti-Jam Enhancement Techniques," *Proc. ION 49th Annual Meeting*, Cambridge, MA, June 1993, pp. 41–50.

[7] Gordon, E., "Dual Reception Pattern Antenna (Patent Pending)," verbal communication, Antenna Department, Texas Instruments Incorporated, Dallas, Texas, June, 1994.

[8] ICD-GPS-200, *NAVSTAR GPS Space Segment/Navigation User Interfaces (Public Release Version)*, ARINC Research Corporation, 11770 Warner Ave., Suite 210, Fountain Valley CA, 92708, July 3, 1991.

[9] Hutchinson, A. D., and J. Weitzen, "Television Interference to GPS," Presentation to the ION GPS Test Standards Working Group Meeting, Colorado Springs, CO, June, 1994.

[10] Amoroso, F., "Adaptive A/D Converter to Suppress CW Interference in DSPN Spread-Spectrum Communications," *IEEE Transactions on Communications*, Vol. Com-31, No. 10, Oct. 1983, pp. 1117–1123.

[11] Spilker, J. J., Jr., "GPS Signal Structure and Performance Characteristics," *Navigation, Journal of The Institute of Navigation*, Vol. 25, No. 2, 1978.

[12] Scott, H. L., "GPS Principles and Practices," The George Washington University Course 1081, Vol. I, Washington, DC, March 1994.

CHAPTER 7

▼▼▼

PERFORMANCE OF STANDALONE GPS

Joseph L. Leva
The MITRE Corporation

Maarten Uijt de Haag
Ohio University

Karen Van Dyke
Volpe Center

7.1 ERROR SOURCES, MEASUREMENT ACCURACY, AND ESTIMATES OF USER POSITION AND TIME

7.1.1 Discussion

The accuracy with which a user receiver can determine its position or velocity, or synchronize to GPS system time, depends on a complicated interaction of various factors. In general, GPS accuracy performance depends on the quality of the pseudorange and delta pseudorange measurements as well as the satellite ephemeris data. In addition, the fidelity of the underlying physical model that relates these parameters is relevant. For example, the accuracy to which the satellite clock offsets relative to GPS system time are known to the user, or the accuracy to which satellite-to-user propagation errors are compensated, are important. Relevant errors are induced by the control, space, and user segments.

237

To analyze the effect of errors on accuracy, a fundamental assumption is usually made that the error sources can be allocated to individual satellite pseudoranges and can be viewed as effectively resulting in an equivalent error in the pseudorange values. The effective accuracy of the pseudorange value is termed the user-equivalent range error (UERE). The UERE for a given satellite is considered to be the (statistical) sum of the contributions from each of the error sources associated with the satellite. Usually, the error components are considered independent and the composite UERE for a satellite is approximated as a zero mean Gaussian random variable where its variance is determined as the sum of the variance of each of its components. UERE is usually assumed to be independent and identically distributed from satellite to satellite. However, for certain GPS augmentations, it is sometimes appropriate for these assumptions to be modified. (For example, if one is considering the addition of geosynchronous (GEOS) ranging satellites to the GPS constellation, the UERE associated with the GEOS might be modeled with a different variance as compared to the standard constellation satellites depending on the design characteristics of the satellites. In other situations, it might be appropriate to model certain components of UERE as correlated among the satellites.)

The accuracy of the position/time solution determined by GPS is ultimately expressed as the product of a geometry factor and a pseudorange error factor. Loosely speaking, error in the GPS solution is estimated by the formula

$$\text{(error in GPS solution)} = \text{(geometry factor)} \times \text{(pseudorange error factor)} \quad (7.1)$$

Under appropriate assumptions, the pseudorange error factor is the satellite UERE. The geometry factor expresses the composite effect of the relative satellite/user geometry on the GPS solution error. It is generically called the dilution of precision (DOP) associated with the satellite/user geometry.

Section 7.1.2 describes the major error sources in GPS and develops error budgets for the PPS and SPS pseudorange UERE. Section 7.1.3 provides a derivation of (7.1). A variety of geometry factors are defined that are used in the estimation of the various components (e.g., horizontal, vertical) of the GPS navigation solution. Section 7.1.4 discusses how these formulations can be used to relate DOP and distributions of DOP to the distribution of vertical and horizontal accuracy in GPS.

7.1.2 Pseudorange Errors

In Chapters 2 and 5, we discussed the formulation of the pseudorange measurement. To further our treatment of the pseudorange measurement and GPS error analysis, an examination of pseudorange error sources is presented within this section. The effects of satellite and receiver clock offsets and various error sources "corrupt" the satellite-to-user geometric range measurement. The satellite signal experiences delays as it propagates through the atmosphere. Further, reflections (i.e., multipath), SA, and hardware effects between the user's antenna phase center and receiver code correlation point may delay (or advance) the signal [1]. The total time offset due to all of these effects is:

$$\delta t_D = \delta t_{atm} + \delta t_{noise\&res} + \delta t_{mp} + \delta t_{hw} + \delta t_{SA}$$

where

δt_{atm}	=	delays due to the atmosphere
$\delta t_{noise\&res}$	=	receiver noise and resolution offset
δt_{mp}	=	multipath offset
δt_{hw}	=	receiver hardware offsets
δt_{SA}	=	SA degradation

The pseudorange time equivalent is the difference between the receiver clock reading when the signal (i.e., a particular code phase) was received and the satellite clock reading when the signal was sent. These timing relationships are shown in Figure 7.1, where

Δt	=	geometric range time equivalent
T_s	=	system time at which the signal left the satellite
T_u	=	system time at which the signal would have reached the user receiver without δt_D (theoretical)
T'_u	=	system time at which the signal reached the user receiver with δt_D
δt	=	offset of the satellite clock from system time (advance is positive; retardation (delay) is negative)

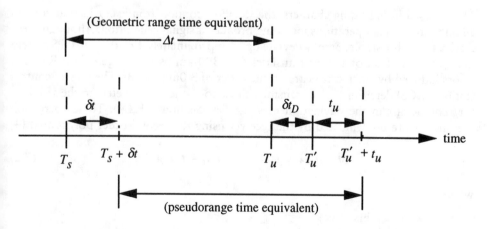

Figure 7.1 Range measurement timing relationships.

t_u =   offset of the receiver clock from system time
$T_s + \delta t$ =   satellite clock reading at time which the signal left the satellite
$T'_u + t_u$ =   user receiver clock reading at time when the signal reached the user receiver
c =   speed of light

It is observed that the pseudorange ρ is:

$$\rho = c[(T'_u + t_u) - (T_s + \delta t)]$$

$$= c(T'_u - T_s) + c(t_u - \delta t)$$

$$= c(T_u + \delta t_D - T_s) + c(t_u - \delta t)$$

$$= r + c(t_u - \delta t + \delta t_D)$$

where r is the geometric range

$$r = c(T_u - T_s) = c\,\Delta t$$

Elaboration on these pseudorange error sources including relativistic effects is provided below. Hardware delays, δt_{hw}, are also referred to as interchannel bias and will not be discussed further since they are very small in comparison to all other error sources.

7.1.2.1 Satellite Clock Error

As discussed in preceding chapters, the satellites contain atomic clocks that control all onboard timing operations including broadcast signal generation. Although these clocks are highly stable, δt may deviate up to approximately 1 msec from GPS system time [2]. (An offset of 1 msec translates to a 300-km pseudorange error.) Ranging errors induced by clock errors are on the order of 3.0m (1σ) [3]. The master control station (MCS) determines and transmits clock correction parameters to the satellites for rebroadcast in the navigation message (see Section 3.1.2.4). These correction parameters are implemented by the receiver using the second-order polynomial [4]

$$\delta t = a_{f0} + a_{f1}(t - t_{oc}) + a_{f2}(t - t_{oc})^2 + \Delta t_r \tag{7.2}$$

where

a_{f0} =   clock bias (sec)
a_{f1} =   clock drift (sec/sec)
a_{f2} =   frequency drift (i.e., aging) (sec/sec^2)

t_{oc} = clock data reference time (sec)
t = current time epoch (sec)
Δt_r = correction due to relativistic effects (sec)

Correction Δt_r compensates for one of three GPS-related relativistic effects discussed in Section 7.1.2.4.

Since the above parameters are "fitted" estimates of the actual satellite clock errors, some residual error remains.

7.1.2.2 Ephemeris Prediction Error

Optimal estimates of ephemerides for all satellites are computed and uplinked to the satellites with other navigation data message parameters for rebroadcast to the user. As in the case of the satellite clock corrections, these corrections are estimates and contain a residual error. The residual error is a vector that is depicted in Figure 7.2. The magnitude of this error is realized as an effective pseudorange error by projecting the vector onto the satellite-to-user line-of-sight vector. The effective pseudorange error is on the order of 4.2m (1σ) [3].

7.1.2.3 Selective Availability (SA)

The single largest error source for SPS users is SA. SA is intentionally induced by the DOD to degrade the user's navigation solution. SA was formally implemented on March 25, 1990. The degradation is accomplished through manipulation of the broadcast ephemeris data (orbital error component) and through dithering of the

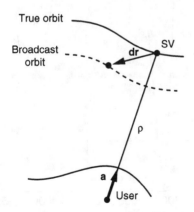

Figure 7.2 Ephemeris error. (*After*: [5].)

satellite clock (clock error component) [6]. The orbital error component is referred to as epsilon, ϵ, while the dither component is denoted as δ [7].

Accomplishment of SA through clock dithering results in a time-varying disturbance of the pseudorange that is illustrated in Figure 7.3. It is observed that the clock error shows a trend consisting of random oscillations with periods on the order of 4 to 12 minutes with variations in pseudorange error up to 70m [6]. Due to the fact that SA is generated at the transmitter side (i.e., the satellite), this error component is spatially correlated. Spatial correlation means that there is a strong relation between the error at one location and the error at a nearby location. This property of SA can be exploited to eliminate the error if DGPS is employed. DGPS removes all errors that are common to both a local GPS ground monitoring station and the user's receiver. DGPS is discussed in the following chapter.

Much effort has been expended in modeling and identifying the clock component of SA. The result is that many different models and approaches to modeling

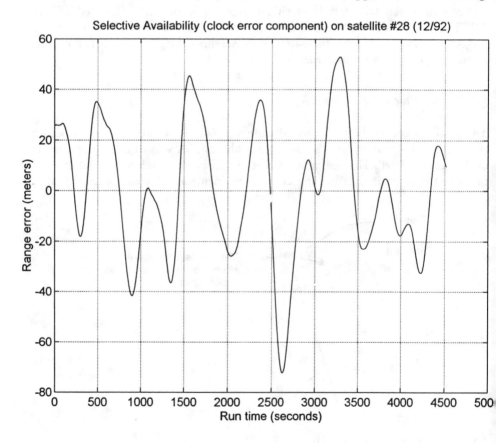

Figure 7.3 SA (clock error component), satellite #28, Dec. 1992 [6].

SA can be found in the literature. Lear [8] gives a summation of the most often used techniques to model the SA clock component. Globally, the model approaches can be divided into stochastic and deterministic models. An example of the former is the autoregressive SA model derived by Braasch [6], whereas an example of the latter is the Rater SA model contained in [8].

As stated above, another form of SA is the manipulation of the broadcast ephemerides. Introduction of intentional errors in the ephemeris parameters will result in the determination of an erroneous satellite position by the user. The broadcast ephemeris data contains 15 parameters (see Section 2.3), which means that the error could be induced in various ways. The effective pseudorange ϵ error would be the vector sum of the residual ephemeris error and the SA orbital component projected onto the satellite-to-user line-of-sight vector, as shown in Figure 7.4.

7.1.2.4 Relativistic Effects

Both Einstein's general and special theories of relativity are factors in the pseudorange measurement process. The need for special relativity (SR) relativistic corrections arises any time the signal source (in this case, GPS satellites) or the signal receiver (GPS receiver) is moving with respect to the chosen isotropic light speed frame, which in the GPS system is the ECI frame. The need for general relativity (GR) relativistic corrections arises any time the signal source and signal receiver are located at different gravitational potentials [9].

The satellite clock is affected by both special and general relativity. In order to compensate for both of these effects, the satellite clock frequency is adjusted to 10.22999999545 MHz prior to launch [2]. The frequency observed by the user at sea level will be 10.23 MHz; hence, the user does not have to correct for this effect.

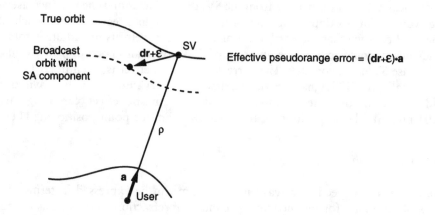

Figure 7.4 Combined effect of SA orbital error component and ephemeris prediction error.

The user does have to make a correction for another relativistic periodic effect that arises because of the slight eccentricity of the satellite orbit. Exactly half of the periodic effect is caused by the periodic change in the speed of the satellite relative to the ECI frame and half is caused by the satellite's periodic change in its gravitational potential.

When the satellite is at perigee, the satellite velocity is higher and the gravitational potential is lower—both cause the satellite clock to run slower. When the satellite is at apogee, the satellite velocity is lower and the gravitational potential is higher—both cause the satellite clock to run faster [9]. This effect can be compensated for by [4]

$$\Delta t_r = Fe\sqrt{A}\ \sin E_k \qquad (7.3)$$

where

F = $-4.442807633 \times 10^{-10}$ sec/m
e = satellite orbital eccentricity
A = semimajor axis of the satellite orbit
E_k = eccentric anomaly of the satellite orbit

Reference [5] states that this relativistic effect can reach a maximum of 70 nsec (21m in range). Correcting the satellite clock for this relativistic effect will result in a more accurate estimation of the time of transmission by the user.

Due to rotation of the Earth during the time of signal transmission, a relativistic error is introduced which is called the Sagnac effect. During the propagation time of the SV signal transmission, a clock on the surface of the Earth will experience a finite rotation with respect to the resting reference frame at the geocenter. Figure 7.5 illustrates this phenomenon known as the Sagnac effect. Clearly, if the user experiences a net rotation away from the SV, the propagation time will increase and vice versa. For example, an airborne user traveling easterly at Mach 2.5 (838.2 m/sec) such that the Earth rotation and aircraft velocity are additive, totaling 1,365 m/sec, could experience an error of 2.7m over an epoch of 100 sec under worst case SV/user geometry. The correction for this effect is given in [10].

Finally, the GPS signal experiences space-time curvature due to the gravitational field of the Earth. The magnitude of this relativistic effect can range from 0.001 ppm in relative positioning to about 18.7 mm for point positioning [11].

7.1.2.5 Atmospheric Effect

The propagation speed of a wave in a medium can be expressed in terms of the index of refraction for the medium. The index of refraction is defined as the ratio of the wave's propagation speed in free space to that in the medium by the formula

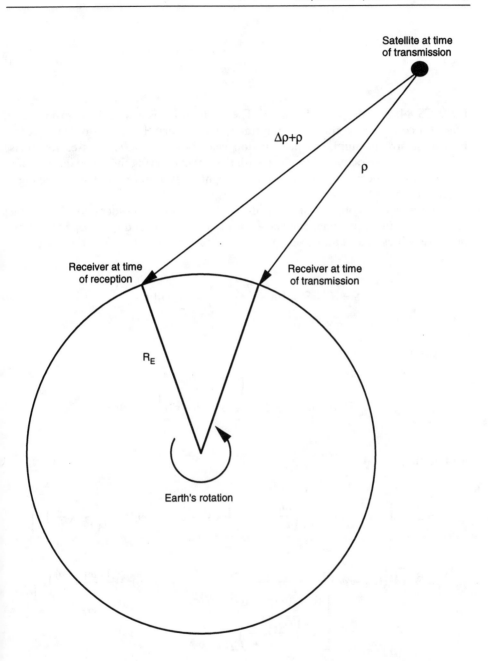

Figure 7.5 The Sagnac effect.

$$n = \frac{c}{v} \tag{7.4}$$

for WGS-84, $c = 299{,}792{,}458$ m/sec. The medium is dispersive if the propagation speed (or equivalently, the index of refraction) is a function of the wave's frequency. In a dispersive medium, the propagation velocity v_p of the signal's carrier phase differs from the velocity v_g associated with the waves carrying the signal information. The information-carrying aspect can be thought of as a group of waves traveling at slightly different frequencies.

To clarify the concepts of group and phase velocities, consider two components, S_1 and S_2, of an electromagnetic wave with frequencies f_1 and f_2 (or ω_1 and ω_2) and phase velocities v_1 and v_2, traveling in the x-direction. The sum S of these signals is

$$S = S_1 + S_2 = \sin \omega_1\left(t - \frac{x}{v_1}\right) + \sin \omega_2\left(t - \frac{x}{v_2}\right)$$

Using the trigonometric identity,

$$\sin \alpha + \sin \beta = 2 \cos\frac{1}{2}(\alpha - \beta) \cdot \sin\frac{1}{2}(\alpha + \beta)$$

we find that

$$S = 2 \cos\left[\frac{1}{2}(\omega_1 - \omega_2)t - \frac{1}{2}\left(\frac{\omega_1}{v_1} - \frac{\omega_2}{v_2}\right)x\right] \times \sin\left[\frac{1}{2}(\omega_1 + \omega_2)t - \frac{1}{2}\left(\frac{\omega_1}{v_1} + \frac{\omega_2}{v_2}\right)x\right]$$

$$= 2 \cos\frac{1}{2}(\omega_1 - \omega_2)\left[t - \frac{x}{\dfrac{\frac{1}{2}(\omega_1 - \omega_2)}{\frac{1}{2}\left(\dfrac{\omega_1}{v_1} - \dfrac{\omega_2}{v_2}\right)}}\right] \times \sin\left[\frac{1}{2}(\omega_1 + \omega_2)t - \frac{1}{2}\left(\frac{\omega_1}{v_1} + \frac{\omega_2}{v_2}\right)x\right]$$

The cosine part is a wave group (the modulation imposed on the sinusoid— that part of the wave that carries the information) that moves with velocity

$$v_g = \cfrac{\frac{1}{2}(\omega_1 - \omega_2)}{\frac{1}{2}\left(\frac{\omega_1}{v_1} - \frac{\omega_2}{v_2}\right)} = \cfrac{2\pi(f_1 - f_2)}{2\pi\left(\frac{f_1}{v_1} - \frac{f_2}{v_2}\right)} = \cfrac{f_1 - f_2}{\frac{1}{\lambda_1} - \frac{1}{\lambda_2}} = \cfrac{\left(\frac{v_1}{\lambda_1} - \frac{v_2}{\lambda_2}\right)}{\left(\frac{1}{\lambda_1} - \frac{1}{\lambda_2}\right)}$$

$$= \cfrac{\left(\frac{v_1}{\lambda_1} - \frac{v_1}{\lambda_2} + \frac{v_1}{\lambda_2} - \frac{v_2}{\lambda_2}\right)}{\left(\frac{1}{\lambda_1} - \frac{1}{\lambda_2}\right)} = v_1 - \lambda_1\frac{v_2 - v_1}{\lambda_2 - \lambda_1} \tag{7.5}$$

where λ_1 and λ_2 are the corresponding signal wavelengths.

For narrow bandwidths, such as those found in a GPS signal, we can replace $v_2 - v_1$ by the differential dv, $\lambda_2 - \lambda_1$ by the differential $d\lambda$, and λ_1 by λ, and add the subscript p to v to denote phase velocity explicitly to get

$$v_g = v_p - \lambda\frac{dv_p}{d\lambda} \tag{7.6}$$

which implies that the difference between the group velocity and phase velocity depends on both the wavelength and the rate of change of phase velocity with wavelength.

The corresponding indices of refraction are related by [11]

$$n_g = n_p + f\frac{dn_p}{df} \tag{7.7}$$

where the indices of refraction are defined by

$$n_p = \frac{c}{v_p} \qquad n_g = \frac{c}{v_g} \tag{7.8}$$

and f denotes the signal frequency. In a nondispersive medium, wave propagation is independent of frequency and the signal phase and signal information propagate at the same speed with $v_g = v_p$ and $n_g = n_p$.

Ionospheric Effects

The ionosphere is a dispersive medium located in the region of the atmosphere between about 70 km and 1000 km above the Earth's surface. Within this region, ultraviolet rays from the sun ionize a portion of gas molecules and release free electrons. These free electrons influence electromagnetic wave propagation, including the GPS satellite signal broadcasts.

The following is based on a similar development in [11]. The index of refraction for the phase propagation in the ionosphere can be approximated as

$$n_p = 1 + \frac{c_2}{f^2} + \frac{c_3}{f^3} + \frac{c_4}{f^4} \ldots \quad (7.9)$$

where the coefficients c_2, c_3, and c_4 are frequency independent but are a function of the number of electrons (i.e., electron density) along the satellite-to-user signal propagation path. The electron density is denoted as n_e. A similar expression for n_g can be obtained by differentiating (7.9) with respect to frequency and substituting the result along with (7.9) into (7.7). This results in the following:

$$n_g = 1 - \frac{c_2}{f^2} - \frac{2c_3}{f^3} - \frac{3c_4}{f^4} \ldots$$

To first-order, these approximations are

$$n_p = 1 + \frac{c_2}{f^2} \qquad n_g = 1 - \frac{c_2}{f^2} \quad (7.10)$$

The coefficient c_2 is estimated as $c_2 = -40.3\, n_e\, \mathrm{Hz}^2$. Rewriting the above yields

$$n_p = 1 - \frac{40.3\, n_e}{f^2} \qquad n_g = 1 + \frac{40.3\, n_e}{f^2} \quad (7.11)$$

Using (7.8), the phase and group velocity are estimated as

$$v_p = \frac{c}{1 - \dfrac{40.3\, n_e}{f^2}} \qquad v_g = \frac{c}{1 + \dfrac{40.3\, n_e}{f^2}} \quad (7.12)$$

It can be observed that the phase velocity will exceed that of the group velocity. The amount of retardation of the group velocity is equal to the advance of the carrier phase with respect to free-space propagation. In the case of GPS, this translates to the signal information (e.g., PRN code and navigation data) being delayed and the carrier phase experiencing an advance.

The measured range is

$$S = \int_{\mathrm{SV}}^{\mathrm{User}} n\, ds \quad (7.13)$$

Whereas, the line-of-sight (i.e., geometric) range is

$$l = \int_{SV}^{User} dl \tag{7.14}$$

The path length difference due to ionospheric refraction is

$$\Delta S_{iono} = \int_{SV}^{User} n ds - \int_{SV}^{User} dl \tag{7.15}$$

The delay attributed to the phase refractive index is

$$\Delta S_{iono,p} = \int_{SV}^{User} \left(1 - \frac{40.3 n_e}{f^2}\right) ds - \int_{SV}^{User} dl \tag{7.16}$$

Similarly, the delay induced by the group refractive index is

$$\Delta S_{iono,g} = \int_{SV}^{User} \left(1 + \frac{40.3 n_e}{f^2}\right) ds - \int_{SV}^{User} dl \tag{7.17}$$

Since the delay will be small compared to the satellite-to-user distance, we simplify (7.16) and (7.17) by integrating the first term along the line-of-sight path. Thus, ds changes to dl and we now have

$$\Delta S_{iono,p} = -\frac{40.3}{f^2} \int_{SV}^{User} n_e \, dl \qquad \Delta S_{iono,g} = \frac{40.3}{f^2} \int_{SV}^{User} n_e \, dl \tag{7.18}$$

The electron density along the path length is referred to as the total electron count (TEC) and is defined as

$$TEC = \int_{SV}^{User} n_e \, dl$$

The TEC is expressed in units of electrons/m^2. The TEC is a function of time of day, user location, satellite elevation angle, season, ionizing flux, magnetic activity, sunspot cycle, and scintillation. It nominally ranges between 10^{16} and 10^{19} with the two extremes occurring around midnight and midafternoon, respectively. We can now rewrite (7.18) in terms of the TEC:

$$\Delta S_{iono,p} = -\frac{40.3 \, TEC}{f^2} \qquad \Delta S_{iono,g} = \frac{40.3 \, TEC}{f^2} \tag{7.19}$$

Since the TEC is generally referenced to the vertical direction through the ionosphere, the above expressions reflect the path delay along the vertical direction with the satellite at an elevation angle of 90° (i.e., zenith). For other elevation angles, we multiply (7.19) with an obliquity factor. The obliquity factor accounts for the increased path length that the signal will travel within the ionosphere. The obliquity factor employed by the WAAS is (terms are defined in Figure 7.6)

$$F_{pp} = \left[1 - \left(\frac{R_e \cos \phi}{R_e + h_I} \right)^2 \right]^{-\frac{1}{2}}$$

The height of the maximum electron density, h_I, used by the WAAS is 400 km. With the addition of the obliquity factor, the path delay expressions from (7.19) become

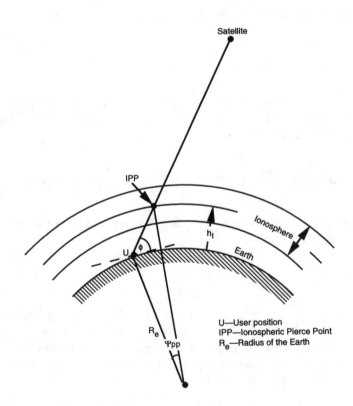

Figure 7.6 Ionospheric modeling geometry.

$$\Delta S_{\text{iono},p} = -F_{pp}\frac{40.3 \text{ TEC}}{f^2} \qquad \Delta S_{\text{iono},g} = F_{pp}\frac{40.3 \text{ TEC}}{f^2}$$

Since the ionospheric delay is frequency dependent, it can virtually be eliminated by making ranging measurements with a dual-frequency receiver. Differencing pseudorange measurements made on both L1 and L2 enables the estimation of both the L1 and L2 delays (neglecting multipath and receiver noise errors). These are first-order estimates since they are based on (7.10). The path length difference on L1 can be estimated using the following expression:

$$\Delta S_{\text{iono,corr}_{L1}} = \left(\frac{L_2^2}{L_2^2 - L_1^2}\right)(\rho_{L1} - \rho_{L2}) \tag{7.20}$$

The path length difference on L2 can be estimated by multiplying $\Delta S_{\text{iono,corr}_{L1}}$ by

$$(f_1/f_2)^2 = (77/60)^2$$

These estimated corrections are subtracted from pseudorange measurements made by each frequency; however, since these corrections are estimates, residual errors are usually present.

In case of a single-frequency receiver, it is obvious that (7.20) cannot be used. Consequently, models of the ionosphere are employed to correct for the ionospheric delay. One example is the Klobuchar model, which removes (on the average) about 50% of the ionospheric delay at midlatitudes. This model assumes that the vertical ionospheric delay can be approximated by half a cosine function of the local time during daytime and by a constant level during nighttime [12]. The original Klobuchar model was adapted by the OCS and the correction algorithm is provided in [4] and [13].

Almost three times as much delay is incurred when viewing satellites at low elevation than at the zenith. For a signal arriving at vertical incidence, the delay ranges from about 10 nsec (3m) at night to as much as 50 nsec (15m) during the day. At low satellite viewing angles (0° through 10°), the delay can range from 30 nsec (9m) at night up to 150 nsec (45m) during the day [2].

Tropospheric Delay

The troposphere is the lower part of the atmosphere that is non-dispersive for frequencies up to 15 GHz [11]. Within this medium, the phase and group velocities associated with the GPS carrier and signal information (PRN code and navigation data) on both L1 and L2 are equally delayed with respect to free-space propagation. This delay is a function of the tropospheric refractive index, which is dependent on the local temperature, pressure, and relative humidity. Left uncompensated, the range equivalent of this delay can vary from about 2.4m for a satellite at the zenith and the user at sea level to about 25m for a satellite at an elevation angle of approximately 5° [10, 11].

From (7.15), we have that the path length difference attributed to the tropospheric delay as

$$\Delta S_{\text{tropo}} = \int_{sv}^{\text{user}} (n - 1) ds$$

where the integration is along the signal path.

The path length difference can also be expressed in terms of refractivity,

$$\Delta S_{\text{tropo}} = 10^{-6} \int_{sv}^{\text{user}} N \, ds \qquad (7.21)$$

where the refractivity, N, is defined by

$$N \equiv 10^6 (n - 1)$$

The refractivity is often modeled using both a dry and wet component. The dry component, which arises from the dry air, gives rise to about 90% of the tropospheric delay and can be predicted very accurately. The wet component, which arises from the water vapor, is more difficult to predict due to uncertainties in the atmospheric distribution. Both components extend to different heights in the troposphere (see Figure 7.7); the dry layer extends to a height of about 40 km while the wet component extends to a height of about 10 km.

We define $N_{d,0}$ and $N_{w,0}$ as the dry and wet component refractivities, respectively, at standard sea level. To express both $N_{d,0}$ and $N_{w,0}$ in pressure and temperature, the formulas of [14] can be used:

$$N_{d,0} \approx a_1 \frac{p_0}{T_0}$$

with

p_0 = partial pressure of the dry component at standard sea level (mbar)
T_0 = absolute temperature at standard sea-level (K)
a_1 = empirical constant (77.624 K/mbar)

$$N_{w,0} \approx a_2 \frac{e_0}{T_0} + a_3 \frac{e_0}{T_0^2}$$

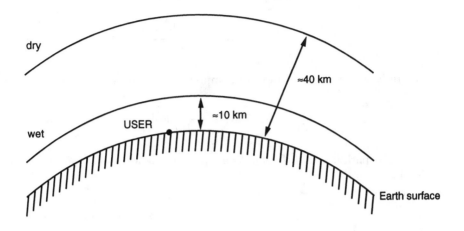

Figure 7.7 Dry and wet components of the troposphere. (*After:* [11].)

where

e_0 = partial pressure of the water vapor at standard sea level (mbar)
T_0 = absolute temperature at standard sea level (K)
a_2 and a_3 are empirical constants (–12.92 K/mbar and 371,900 K²/mbar, respectively)

Path delay also varies with the user's height, h. Thus, both the dry and wet component refractivities are dependent on the atmospheric conditions at the user's height above the reference ellipsoid. One model that takes the height into account and is successfully used by Remondi [15], combines parts of the works cited in [14, 16–18]. The dry component as a function of the height is determined by

$$N_d(h) = N_{d,0}\left[\frac{h_d - h}{h_d}\right]^{\mu} \tag{7.22}$$

and h_d, the upper extent of the dry component of the troposphere referenced to sea level, is determined from

$$h_d = 0.011385\frac{p_0}{N_{d,0} \times 10^{-6}}$$

where μ stems from the underlying use of the ideal gas law. Hopfield [17] found that setting $\mu = 4$ gives the best results for the model.

Similarly the refractivity, $N_w(h)$, of the wet component of the troposphere is determined from

$$N_w(h) = N_{w,0}\left[\frac{h_w - h}{h_w}\right]^\mu \tag{7.23}$$

where h_w is the extent of the wet component of troposphere determined by

$$h_w = 0.011385\frac{1}{N_{w,0} \times 10^{-6}}\left[\frac{1,255}{T_0} + 0.05\right]e_0$$

The path length difference when the satellite is at zenith and the user is at sea level is from (7.21):

$$\Delta S_{\text{tropo}} = 10^{-6}\int_{h=0}^{h_d}N_{d,h}dh + 10^{-6}\int_{h=0}^{h_w}N_{d,w}\,dh \tag{7.24}$$

Evaluation of (7.24) using the expressions for $N_d(h)$ and $N_w(h)$ in (7.22) and (7.23) yields

$$\Delta S_{\text{tropo}} = \frac{10^{-6}}{5}[N_{d,0}h_d + N_{w,0}h_w]$$

For elevation angles other than 90°, the model takes the form shown in Figure 7.8 where the user's height, h, is replaced by the geocentric distance r. Equation (7.24) is now expressed as [10, 11]

$$\Delta S_{\text{tropo},k} = \frac{10^{-6}N_{k,0}}{(r_k - r_0)^4}\int_{r_0}^{r_k}\frac{r(r_k - r_0)^4}{\sqrt{r^2 - r_0^2\,\sin^2E}}dr \tag{7.25}$$

with

$$r_k = \sqrt{(R_E + h_k)^2 - r_0^2\,\cos^2E} - r_0\sin E$$

where

$r_0 = R_E + h$
E is the satellite-to-user line-of-sight elevation angle
k denotes either the wet or dry component

The mapping function for arbitrary elevation angles in (7.25), found by applying the law of sines to Figure 7.8, is

$$\frac{r}{\sqrt{r^2 - r_0^2\,\sin^2 E}}$$

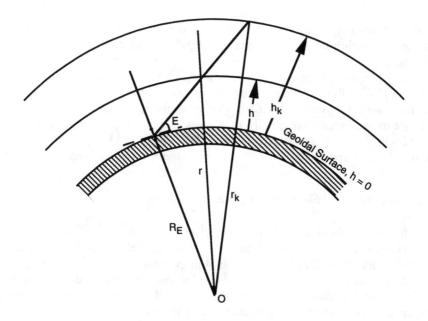

Figure 7.8 Tropospheric modeling geometry.

Equation (7.25) can be evaluated numerically using a series expansion (for details see [11]). The total path length difference is the sum of the integral evaluated separately for both the dry and wet components. This formulation also accounts for the delay attributed to the bending of the signal path due to tropospheric refraction at low elevation angles [10].

There are numerous tropospheric delay compensation models, the reason being is that the wet component is difficult to model. One method of determining this delay is to use a water vapor radiometer, which measures the sky brightness temperature via radiometric microwave observations along the signal path. However, this technique is expensive, does not provide accurate data for low elevation angles, and is impractical for most applications. Research is ongoing in this area [11].

7.1.2.6 Receiver Noise and Resolution

Measurement errors are also induced by the receiver tracking loops. In terms of the DLL, dominant sources of pseudorange measurement error are thermal noise jitter and the effects of dynamic stress error. Secondary error sources include code hardware and software resolution and oscillator stability [1]. The C/A-code composite receiver noise and resolution error contribution will be approximately an order of magnitude larger than that for P(Y)-code because the chip wavelength of the C/A-code is ten times longer than for P(Y)-code. Typical modern receiver 1σ values for the noise and resolution error are on the order of 1.5m for C/A-code and 20 cm for P(Y)-code.

Receiver noise and resolution errors affect carrier phase measurements made by either a FLL or PLL. PLL measurements errors are on the order of 1.2 mm (1σ) when tracking the C/A-code and 1.6 mm (1σ) when tracking the P(Y)-code. However, FLL phase measurements are usually an order of magnitude less accurate than those obtained with a PLL. Extensive treatment of DLL, FLL, and PLL errors is provided in Section 5.1.5. Carrier phase measurement techniques are discussed in Section 8.3.

7.1.2.7 Multipath and Shadowing Effects

One of the major errors incurred in the receiver measurement process is multipath. With multipath, a signal arrives at the receiver via multiple paths due to reflections from the Earth and nearby objects (e.g., buildings, vehicles), as shown in Figure 7.9. Multipath not only distorts the PRN code and navigation data, which is modulated onto the carrier, but also the phase of the carrier itself. Under worst-case conditions, multipath can cause the receiver tracking loops to lose lock.

The degradation of the pseudoranges is caused by the distortion of the correlation peak by the presence of the indirect signal (i.e., reflected version of the signal). Distortion of the correlation peak causes the zero crossing of the early-late curve to be shifted and thus the receiver will determine an erroneous pseudorange. The dashed correlation peak in Figure 7.10(a) is the reflection that is a scaled (expressed by the multipath-to direct ratio, (MDR)) and delayed (d) version of the direct correlation peak. (The MDR is the ratio of the reflected and direct signal.) Adding both correla-

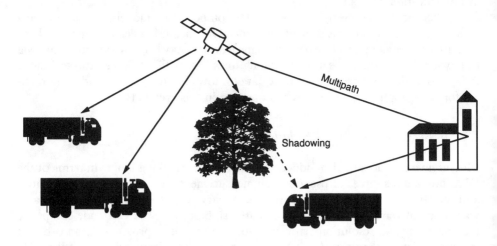

Figure 7.9 Depiction of multipath and shadowing effects.

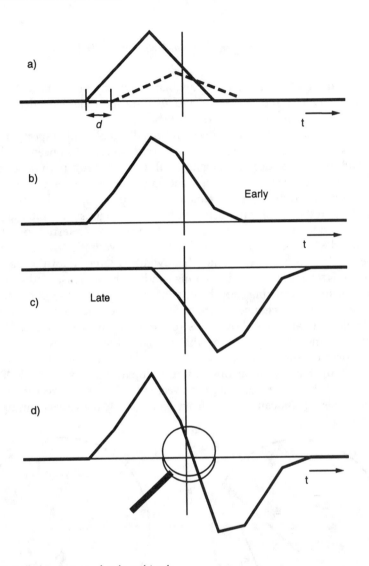

Figure 7.10 Early-late in case of code multipath.

tion peaks gives the resulting distorted early curve, shown in Figure 7.10(b)). Subtracting the late (Figure 7.10(c)) from the early gives us the so called "S-curve" (Figure 7.10(d)). An increase in the MDR results in more distortion of the S-curve and therefore larger multipath errors. Clearly, the zero crossing in Figure 7.10(d) differs from the zero crossing in the case of no multipath, resulting in a pseudorange measurement.

Considering M possible reflections, the received spread spectrum signal can be written as

$$x(t) = \sum_{i=0}^{M} a_i(t)p[t - \tau_i(t)]\cos[\omega t + \theta_i(t)]$$

where $p(t)$ is the PRN code, ω is the angular frequency of the line-of-sight signal (carrier plus Doppler) and $a_i(t)$, $\tau_i(t)$, and $\theta_i(t)$ are the time-dependent amplitude, delay, and phase of the ith signal, respectively.

An increase in the path delay of a reflected signal with respect to the direct signal causes the multipath to grow until a maximum error has been reached. After this, the multipath error decreases again until it is zero for a path delay of $1 + \tau/2$ chips where τ is the correlator spacing (ignoring error due to correlation sidelobes).

In general, all reflections are comprised of various spectral components that are dependent on the angular frequency of the line-of-sight signal and the phase rate of the ith reflection. The bandwidth of these frequencies is referred to as the fading bandwidth, which depends on the satellite/user receiver/reflector geometry as well as on the user's velocity. If the fading bandwidth is larger than the tracking loop bandwidth, it is referred to as the fast fading bandwidth; whereas, a fading bandwidth less than that of the tracking loop bandwidth is referred to as slow fading. In the case of fast fading, fast changes in the zero-crossing of the S-curve will occur that the DLL will be unable to follow. This results in an averaging effect [19]. In the case of slow fading, the DLL will be able to follow the zero crossing.

The effect on the carrier phase can be understood from the vector plots of Figure 7.11 [20]. The instantaneous carrier multipath error is the angle Ψ between the vector $\mathbf{E}_d$ of the direct signal and the vector $\mathbf{E}_m$ of the sum vector of the direct and reflected signal. As can be seen from Figure 7.11, the carrier multipath error

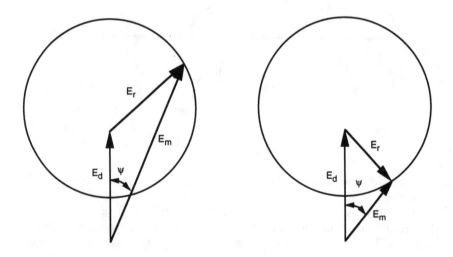

Figure 7.11 Carrier phase multipath.

increases when the phase difference of the direct and reflected signal increases, caused by the increase in path length difference. The carrier phase error Ψ reaches a maximum when the vector of the reflected signal, E_r and the sum vector are perpendicular.

As can be understood from Figures 7.10 and 7.11, the severity of the multipath is determined by the relative amplitude, the phase, the phase rate, and the delay of the indirect signals. A mathematical derivation of the magnitude of the multipath effects is provided in [19–21]. Besides being dependent on the parameters of the reflected signal, the type of receiver architecture is important for the effect.

Multipath mitigation techniques for GPS have been (and continue to be) the subject of extensive research. Multipath generally arrives along with signals from satellites at low elevation angles. Therefore, the antenna pattern gain should be designed to attenuate incoming signals at low elevation angles as well as those in the direction(s) of the reflector(s) [21]. The antenna gain "cutoff" angle (i.e., minimum desired elevation angle) is dependent on the receiver satellite selection algorithm. Some receivers normally use satellites at elevation angles $\geq 5°$; thus, attenuating the antenna gain above the minimum usable elevation angle will limit satellite availability.

To combat multipath, antenna siting is of prime importance. The antenna should be placed above the highest reflector to prevent reflected waves from arriving from and above the horizon. Certain antennas require a ground plane to increase free-space antenna gain at low elevation angles. However, the ground plane may diffract energy incident on the antenna at low elevation angles. The use of absorbent material reduces this edge diffraction effect. Research is in process to investigate the use of absorbent material to reduce these unwanted reflections in close proximity of the antenna [21]. (The optimum situation is one where we can utilize signals from satellites at low elevation angles to increase our availability, but with diminished multipath error.)

Antenna height is also a factor. In some environments, it can be easily observed that a slight variation in antenna height significantly effects receiver performance. One will note improved signal-to-noise performance by adjusting the antenna height.

Of special interest is a choke ring antenna designed specifically to reduce multipath effects, as shown in Figure 7.12. The antenna is comprised of vertical-aligned concentric rings centered about the antenna element that are connected to the ground plane. These vertical rings shape the antenna pattern such that multipath signals incident on the antenna at the horizon and negative elevation angles are attenuated.

Reference [22] provided test results that indicated that multipath-induced ranging errors varied from 50 cm to 2m for a choke ring antenna sited at a "good" location. That is, the antenna was located above all reflectors in the area. On the other hand, test data collected in an urban environment near a large building (over 30 floors) with a stationary receiver showed a worst case ranging error of approximately

Choke Ring

Figure 7.12 Choke ring antenna. (*After*: [5].)

100m. The use of a C/A-code narrow correlator receiver has shown that the peak multipath error is reduced by a factor of ten. Furthermore, the use of P(Y)-code with its smaller chip size reduces the worst case multipath to approximately 8m (1σ) for rare satellite geometries [10]. In terms of carrier phase measurements, errors up to about 5 cm can be expected using the L1 carrier [21].

A few conclusions can be drawn concerning multipath. In most cases, the multipath errors are not as pronounced as the above cited worst case values since the reflections are geometry dependent and time-variant. However, multipath errors are of concern especially in cases where high accuracy is required; thus, care must be taken with antenna siting.

7.1.2.8 Error Budgets

Based on the above discussion regarding pseudorange error constituents, we can develop error budgets to aid our understanding of standalone GPS accuracy. These budgets are intended to serve as guidelines for position error analyses. However, as indicated in (7.1), position error is a function of both the pseudorange error (UERE) and user/satellite geometry (DOP).

Let us begin with a look at the GPS JPO UERE budget for the PPS presented in Table 7.1 [3]. (This budget was developed in the early 1980s and has not been updated even though all aspects of today's space, control, and user segments have been improved. While somewhat dated, the budget does provide guidance for conducting DOD-related analyses.) It is observed that the total system UERE is comprised of components from each system segment. This budget is predicated on the use of dual-frequency measurements to determine the ionospheric delay. In the case of the predictability of satellite perturbations, it is not distinctly clear that this error component should be attributed to the space segment or the control segment; however, it still needs to be included. Satellite perturbations stem from sources such as tidal attractions, solar radiation pressure, solar winds, and gas-propellant leakage, some of which are difficult to model. The error components are root-sum-squared (rss) to form the total system UERE, which is Gaussian distributed with a 1σ value

Table 7.1
GPS JPO PPS Pseudorange Error Budget

Segment Source	Error Source	GPS 1σ Error (m)
Space	Satellite clock stability	3.0
	Predictability of satellite perturbations	1.0
	Other (thermal radiation, etc.)	0.5
Control	Ephemeris prediction error	4.2
	Other (thruster performance, etc.)	0.9
User	Ionospheric delay	2.3
	Tropospheric delay	2.0
	Receiver noise and resolution	1.5
	Multipath	1.2
	Other (interchannel bias, etc.)	0.5
System UERE	Total (rss)	6.6

Source: [3].

of 6.6m. (The system UERE value is actually 6.5m but the value reported in [3] is 6.6m, both 1σ.)

Table 7.2 is an estimate of a contemporary SPS receiver C/A-code UERE budget. The space and control segment contributions are identical to those in the P(Y)-code budget except for the inclusion of SA. As observed, SA is the dominant error source in SPS C/A-code pseudorange measurements. With respect to the PPS budgets, user segment error contributions differ for receiver noise and resolution, ionospheric delay and multipath. The value of ionospheric delay is an estimate that reflects delay compensation by an internal receiver model. The system UERE is computed with and without SA activated. Based on this estimated budget, SPS positioning accuracy would improve by a factor of approximately 4.1 times if SA were deactivated. It must be noted that even with SA off, the accuracy provided by the SPS would still be inadequate for applications such as aircraft precision landing and some forms of harbor navigation. These applications require the use of DGPS techniques, which are discussed in the next chapter.

7.1.3 Satellite Geometry and the Dilution of Precision in GPS

The defining relations for the dilution of precision parameters are developed in Section 7.1.3.1. Illustration of how these parameters vary as a function of location, time, and receiver implementation is presented in Section 7.1.3.2.

Table 7.2
Estimated SPS C/A-Code Pseudorange Error Budget

Segment Source	Error Source	GPS 1σ Error (m) With SA	GPS 1σ Error (m) Without SA
Space	Satellite clock stability	3.0	3.0
	Satellite perturbations	1.0	1.0
	Selective Availability	32.3	–
	Other (thermal radiation, etc.)	0.5	0.5
Control	Ephemeris prediction error	4.2	4.2
	Other (thruster performance, etc.)	0.9	0.9
User	Ionospheric delay	5.0	5.0
	Tropospheric delay	1.5	1.5
	Receiver noise and resolution	1.5	1.5
	Multipath	2.5	2.5
	Other (interchannel bias, etc.)	0.5	0.5
System UERE	Total (rss)	33.3	8.0

7.1.3.1 Definitions and Relationships for Dilution of Precision (DOP)

As motivation for the concept of dilution of precision as it applies to GPS, consider once again the foghorn example introduced in Section 2.1.1. In this example, a user locates his or her position from ranging measurements from two foghorns. The assumptions are that the user has a synchronized time base relative to the foghorns and has knowledge of the location of the foghorns and their transmission times. The user measures the time of arrival of each of the foghorn signals and computes a propagation time, which determines the user's range from each foghorn. The user locates his or her position from the intersection of the range rings determined from the time-of-arrival measurements.

In the presence of measurement errors, the range rings used to compute the user's location will be in error and result in error in the computed position. The concept of dilution of precision is the idea that the position error that results from measurement errors depends on the user/foghorn relative geometry. Graphically, these ideas are illustrated in Figure 7.13. Two geometries are indicated. In Figure 7.13(a), the foghorns are located approximately at right angles with respect to the user location. In Figure 7.13(b), the angle between the foghorns as viewed from the user is much smaller. In both cases, portions of the error-free range rings are indicated and intersect at the user's location. Additional ring segments are included that illustrate the variation in range ring position resulting from ranging errors to the

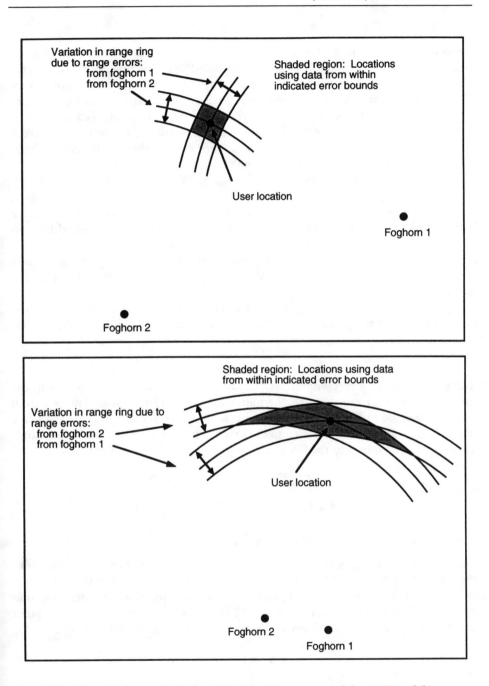

Figure 7.13 Relative geometry and dilution of precision: (a) geometry with low DOP, and (b) geometry with high DOP.

foghorns. The error range illustrated in both figures is the same. The shaded regions indicate the set of locations that can be obtained if one uses ranging measurements within the illustrated error bounds. The accuracy of the computed location is very different for the two cases. With the same measurement error variation, geometry (b) gives considerably more error in the computed user's location then in (a), as is evident from comparison of the shaded regions. Geometry (b) is said to have a larger dilution of precision then geometry (a). For comparable measurement errors, geometry (b) results in larger errors in the computed location.

A formal derivation of the DOP relations in GPS begins with the linearization of the pseudorange equations given in Section 2.4.2. The linearization is the Jacobian relating changes in the user position and time bias to changes in the pseudorange values. This relationship is inverted in accordance with the solution algorithm and is used to relate the covariance of the user position and time bias to the covariance of the pseudorange errors. The DOP parameters are defined as geometry factors that relate parameters of the user position and time bias errors to those of the pseudorange errors.

The offset Δx in the user's position and time bias relative to the linearization point is related to the offset in the error-free pseudorange values $\Delta \rho$ by the relation

$$H\Delta x = \Delta \rho \tag{7.26}$$

The vector Δx has four components. The first three are the position offset of the user from the linearization point; the fourth is the offset of the user time bias from the bias assumed in the linearization point. $\Delta \rho$ is the vector offset of the error-free pseudorange values corresponding to the user's actual position and the pseudorange values that correspond to the linearization point. H is the n by 4 matrix

$$\mathbf{H} = \begin{bmatrix} a_{x1} & a_{y1} & a_{z1} & 1 \\ a_{x2} & a_{y2} & a_{z2} & 1 \\ \vdots & \vdots & \vdots & \vdots \\ a_{xn} & a_{yn} & a_{zn} & 1 \end{bmatrix} \tag{7.27}$$

and the $\mathbf{a}_i = (a_{xi}, a_{yi}, a_{zi})$ are the unit vectors pointing from the linearization point to the location of the ith satellite. If $n = 4$ and data from just four satellites are being used, and if the linearization point is close to the user's location, the user's location and time offset are obtained by solving (7.26) for Δx (i.e., if the linearization point is close enough to the user position, iteration is not required). One obtains

$$\Delta x = H^{-1}\Delta \rho \tag{7.28}$$

and the offset of the user's position from the linearization point is expressed as a linear function of $\Delta \rho$. In the case of $n > 4$, the method of least squares can be used to solve (7.26) for Δx (see the Appendix). The least square result can be obtained formally by multiplying both sides of (7.26) on the left by the matrix transpose of H obtaining $H^T H \Delta x = H^T \Delta \rho$. The matrix combination $H^T H$ is a square 4 by 4 matrix, and one can solve for Δx by multiplying both sides by the inverse, $(H^T H)^{-1}$. (The matrix will be invertible provided the tips of the unit vectors a_i do not all lie in a plane.) One obtains

$$\Delta x = (H^T H)^{-1} H^T \Delta \rho \qquad (7.29)$$

which is the least square formulation for Δx as a function of $\Delta \rho$. We observe that if $n = 4$, $(H^T H)^{-1} = H^{-1}(H^T)^{-1}$ and (7.29) reduces to (7.28).

The pseudorange measurements are not error free and can be viewed as a linear combination of three terms,

$$\Delta \rho = \rho_T - \rho_L + d\rho \qquad (7.30)$$

where ρ_T is the vector of error-free pseudorange values, ρ_L is the vector of pseudorange values computed at the linearization point, and $d\rho$ represents the net error in the pseudorange values. Similarly, Δx can be expressed as

$$\Delta x = x_T - x_L + dx \qquad (7.31)$$

where x_T is the error-free position and time, x_L is the position and time defined as the linearization point, and dx is the error in the position and time estimate. Substituting (7.30) and (7.31) into (7.29) and using the relation $(x_T - x_L) = (H^T H)^{-1} H^T$ $(\rho_T - \rho_L)$ (this follows from the relation $H(x_T - x_L) = (\rho_T - \rho_L)$, which is a restatement of (7.26)), one obtains

$$dx = [(H^T H)^{-1} H^T] d\rho = K d\rho \qquad (7.32)$$

The matrix K is defined by the expression in brackets. Equation (7.32) gives the functional relationship between the errors in the pseudorange values and the induced errors in the computed position and time bias. It is valid provided that the linearization point is sufficiently close to the user's location and that the pseudorange errors are sufficiently small so that the error in performing the linearization can be ignored.

Equation (7.32) is the fundamental relationship between pseudorange errors and computed position and time bias errors. The matrix $(H^T H)^{-1} H^T$, which is sometimes called the least-squares solution matrix, is a $4 \times n$ matrix and depends only on the relative geometry of the user and the satellites participating in the least square solution computation. In many applications, the user/satellite geometry can be considered fixed and (7.32) yields a linear relationship between the pseudorange errors and the induced position and time bias errors.

The pseudorange errors are considered to be random variables and (7.32) expresses $d\mathbf{x}$ as a random variable functionally related to $d\mathbf{\rho}$. The error vector $d\mathbf{\rho}$ is usually assumed to have components that are jointly Gaussian and to be zero mean. With the geometry considered fixed, it follows that $d\mathbf{x}$ is also Gaussian and zero mean. The covariance of $d\mathbf{x}$ is obtained by forming the product $d\mathbf{x}\, d\mathbf{x}^t$ and computing an expected value. By definition, one obtains

$$\text{cov}(d\mathbf{x}) = E(d\mathbf{x}\, d\mathbf{x}^T) \tag{7.33}$$

where $\text{cov}(d\mathbf{x})$ denotes the covariance of $d\mathbf{x}$ and E represents the expectation operator. Substituting from (7.32) and viewing the geometry as fixed, one obtains

$$\text{cov}(d\mathbf{x}) = E(\mathbf{K}\, d\mathbf{\rho}\, d\mathbf{\rho}^T\mathbf{K}^T) = E[(\mathbf{H}^T\mathbf{H})^{-1}\mathbf{H}^T\, d\mathbf{\rho}\, d\mathbf{\rho}^T\mathbf{H}(\mathbf{H}^T\mathbf{H})^{-1}] \tag{7.34}$$
$$= (\mathbf{H}^T\mathbf{H})^{-1}\mathbf{H}^T\text{cov}(d\mathbf{\rho})\mathbf{H}(\mathbf{H}^T\mathbf{H})^{-1}$$

Note that in this computation, $(\mathbf{H}^T\mathbf{H})^{-1}$ is symmetric. (This follows from an application of the general matrix relations $(\mathbf{AB})^T = \mathbf{B}^T\mathbf{A}^T$ and $(\mathbf{A}^{-1})^T = (\mathbf{A}^T)^{-1}$, which are valid whenever the indicated operations are defined.) The usual assumption is that the components of $d\mathbf{\rho}$ are identically distributed and independent and have a variance equal to the square of the satellite UERE. With these assumptions, the covariance of $d\mathbf{\rho}$ is a scalar multiple of the identity

$$\text{cov}(d\mathbf{\rho}) = \mathbf{I}_{n\times n}\sigma^2_{\text{UERE}} \tag{7.35}$$

where $\mathbf{I}_{n\times n}$ is the $n \times n$ identity matrix. Substitution into (7.34) yields

$$\text{cov}(d\mathbf{x}) = (\mathbf{H}^T\mathbf{H})^{-1}\sigma^2_{\text{UERE}} \tag{7.36}$$

Under the stated assumptions, the covariance of the errors in the computed position and time bias is just a scalar multiple of the matrix $(\mathbf{H}^T\mathbf{H})^{-1}$. The vector $d\mathbf{x}$ has four components, which represent the error in the computed value for the vector $\mathbf{x}_T = (x_u, y_u, z_u, ct_b)$. The covariance of $d\mathbf{x}$ is a 4×4 matrix and has an expanded representation

$$\text{cov}(d\mathbf{x}) = \begin{bmatrix} \sigma^2_{x_u} & \sigma^2_{x_uy_u} & \sigma^2_{x_uz_u} & \sigma^2_{x_uct_b} \\ \sigma^2_{x_uy_u} & \sigma^2_{y_u} & \sigma^2_{y_uz_u} & \sigma^2_{y_uct_b} \\ \sigma^2_{x_uz_u} & \sigma^2_{y_uz_u} & \sigma^2_{z_u} & \sigma^2_{z_uct_b} \\ \sigma^2_{x_uct_b} & \sigma^2_{y_uct_b} & \sigma^2_{z_uct_b} & \sigma^2_{ct_b} \end{bmatrix} \tag{7.37}$$

The components of the matrix $(\mathbf{H}^T\mathbf{H})^{-1}$ quantify how pseudorange errors translate into components of the covariance of $d\mathbf{x}$.

Dilution of precision parameters in GPS are defined in terms of the ratio of combinations of the components of cov($d\mathbf{x}$) and σ_{UERE}. (It is implicitly assumed in the DOP definitions that the user/satellite geometry is considered fixed. Situations where the geometry is considered to be variable are discussed in Sections 7.1.4.2 and 7.1.4.4. It is also assumed that local user coordinates are being used in the specification of cov($d\mathbf{x}$) and $d\mathbf{x}$. The positive x-axis points east, the y-axis points north, and the z-axis points up.) The most general parameter is termed the geometric dilution of precision (GDOP) and is defined by the formula

$$\text{GDOP} = \frac{\sqrt{\sigma_{x_u}^2 + \sigma_{y_u}^2 + \sigma_{z_u}^2 + \sigma_{ct_b}^2}}{\sigma_{\text{UERE}}} \tag{7.38}$$

A relationship for GDOP is obtained in terms of the components of $(\mathbf{H}^T\mathbf{H})^{-1}$ by expressing $(\mathbf{H}^T\mathbf{H})^{-1}$ in component form

$$(\mathbf{H}^T\mathbf{H})^{-1} = \begin{bmatrix} D_{11} & D_{12} & D_{13} & D_{14} \\ D_{21} & D_{22} & D_{23} & D_{24} \\ D_{31} & D_{32} & D_{33} & D_{34} \\ D_{41} & D_{42} & D_{43} & D_{44} \end{bmatrix} \tag{7.39}$$

and then substituting (7.39) and (7.37) into (7.36). A trace operation on (7.36) followed by a square root shows that GDOP can be computed as the square root of the trace of the $(\mathbf{H}^T\mathbf{H})^{-1}$ matrix:

$$\text{GDOP} = \sqrt{D_{11} + D_{22} + D_{33} + D_{44}} \tag{7.40}$$

Equation (7.38) can be rearranged to obtain

$$\sqrt{\sigma_{x_u}^2 + \sigma_{y_u}^2 + \sigma_{z_u}^2 + \sigma_{ct_b}^2} = \text{GDOP} \times \sigma_{\text{UERE}} \tag{7.41}$$

which has the form given in (7.1) The square root term on the left side gives an overall characterization of the error in the GPS solution. GDOP is the geometry factor. It represents the amplification of the standard deviation of the measurement errors onto the solution. From (7.40), GDOP is seen to be a function solely of the satellite/user geometry. The value σ_{UERE} is the pseudorange error factor.

Several other DOP parameters are in common use that are useful to characterize the accuracy of various components of the position/time solution. These are termed position dilution of precision (PDOP), horizontal dilution of precision (HDOP), vertical dilution of precision (VDOP), and time dilution of precision (TDOP). These

DOP parameters are defined in terms of the satellite UERE and elements of the covariance matrix for the position/time solution as follows:

$$\sqrt{\sigma_{x_u}^2 + \sigma_{y_u}^2 + \sigma_{z_u}^2} = \text{PDOP} \times \sigma_{\text{UERE}} \tag{7.42}$$

$$\sqrt{\sigma_{x_u}^2 + \sigma_{y_u}^2} = \text{HDOP} \times \sigma_{\text{UERE}} \tag{7.43}$$

$$\sigma_{z_u} = \text{VDOP} \times \sigma_{\text{UERE}} \tag{7.44}$$

$$\sigma_{t_b} = \text{TDOP} \times \sigma_{\text{UERE}} \tag{7.45}$$

The DOP values can be expressed in terms of the components of $(\mathbf{H}^T\mathbf{H})^{-1}$ as follows:

$$\text{PDOP} = \sqrt{D_{11} + D_{22} + D_{33}} \tag{7.46}$$

$$\text{HDOP} = \sqrt{D_{11} + D_{22}} \tag{7.47}$$

$$\text{VDOP} = \sqrt{D_{33}} \tag{7.48}$$

$$\text{TDOP} = \sqrt{D_{44}}/c \tag{7.49}$$

(In some treatments of DOP, TDOP is defined by the formula $\sigma_{ct_b} = \text{TDOP} \times \sigma_{\text{UERE}}$. In this case, (7.49) takes the simpler form $\text{TDOP} = \sqrt{D_{44}}$. The variable ct_b represents a range equivalent of the time bias error and σ_{ct_b} is its standard deviation. In the current formulation, TDOP is defined so that when multiplied by σ_{UERE}, the standard deviation of the time bias error is obtained directly. This is the more relevant formulation if actual time accuracy is of interest. The linear relationship between t_b and ct_b yields the formula $c\sigma_{t_b} = \sigma_{ct_b}$ between their standard deviations, and one can easily convert between the formulations.)

7.1.3.2 Dilution of Precision as a Function of Position, Time, and Receiver Implementation

The DOP parameters defined in the previous subsection are expressed as combinations of components of the matrix $(\mathbf{H}^T\mathbf{H})^{-1}$. As noted earlier in (7.27), H is defined by the unit vectors pointing from the user to the satellites. Hence, $(\mathbf{H}^T\mathbf{H})^{-1}$ varies with the location of the user and the time of day since these parameters determine the user/satellite geometry. In addition, $(\mathbf{H}^T\mathbf{H})^{-1}$ is dependent on the receiver design as different receivers implement different approaches to selecting the satellites for use in the position calculation.

Several U.S. military receivers use pseudorange data from only four satellites in the position calculation. About once a minute, the receiver determines the four satellites in view that give the best GDOP, and uses these satellites in the position calculation. With this implementation, the matrix H is 4 by 4 and incorporates information from only four satellites. A number of civil receivers, on the other hand, utilize pseudorange data from all satellites in view in the position computation. The number of satellites in view from a given location depends on the receiver mask angle and varies as a function of time. (The receiver mask angle is the elevation angle relative to the horizon below which a satellite is not considered visible. Satellites very near the horizon suffer from increased atmospheric propagation errors and have a larger UERE. The receiver mask angle is generally set between 0° and 10°.) In a receiver that processes all the satellites in view, the dimension of the H matrix varies as a function of time.

As an example of how DOP varies with time, Figures 7.14(a–d) illustrate GDOP, PDOP, HDOP, and VDOP for a 24-hr period as viewed from Boston, MA. At any given time, the receiver is assumed to select the four satellites in view that give the best GDOP. The receiver mask angle was set at 5°. The plots were generated using a computer simulation of the orbiting satellites. A full constellation of 24 satellites was used with an almanac reference time of July 16, 1995, 0000 hr UTC. The calculations of the user/satellite geometry were updated at 3-min intervals. Since the GPS satellites are in 12-hr orbits, the user/satellite geometry approximately repeats every 24 hr, and a 24-hr plot characterizes the DOP at a particular location.

The discontinuities in the plots occur when satellites move in and out of view. For example, if a satellite currently in view and selected for use by the receiver moves below the mask angle, the receiver is forced to select an alternate satellite with a presumably worse GDOP. Alternatively, if a satellite initially out of view moves above the mask angle, the receiver could choose to switch to it and the DOP would change abruptly with the satellite changeover.

7.1.4 Discussion and Computation of Measurement Accuracy

The formulations in Section 7.1.3.1 define DOP in terms of components of the covariance of the position and time solution and the pseudorange measurement accuracy. The DOP parameters were shown to be functions of the user/satellite geometry. This section shows how DOP and UERE parameters can be combined to estimate distribution characteristics of the user's vertical and horizontal position estimates.

Vertical accuracy is considered first. It is the easier to analyze since it involves just one dimension; accuracy in the horizontal plane requires treatment as a two-

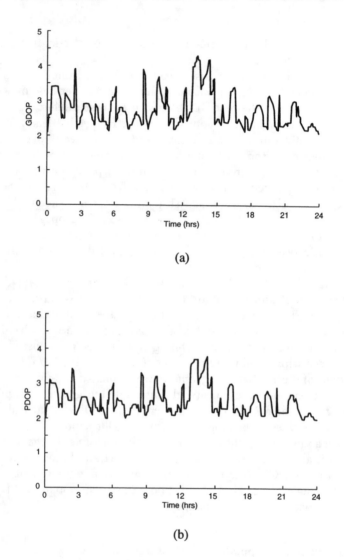

Figure 7.14 GDOP, PDOP, HDOP and VDOP for a 24-hr period from Boston, MA: (a) GDOP, (b) PDOP, (c) HDOP, (d) VDOP.

dimensional problem. In each case, two scenarios are considered. In the first, the user/satellite geometry is considered fixed. This is appropriate for estimating accuracy characteristics at a fixed location over a short time interval. The satellites used by the receiver and their relative geometry with respect to the user are assumed to be fixed. (By a fixed geometry, it is meant that the H matrix appearing in (7.32) can

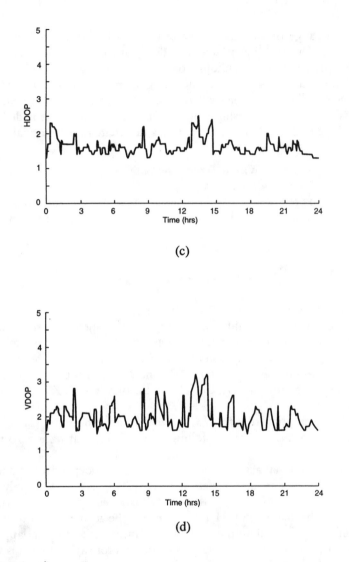

Figure 7.14 (continued)

be considered constant over the observation interval of interest. As a result of the large distance from the user to the satellites, the user/satellite geometry remains essentially fixed for a user in motion over a short time interval. For example, this assumption applies to the analysis of precision approach landing using GPS where an aircraft might be traveling at 120 knots during a 2-min approach to a runway.) In the second scenario, the user's location and/or the time of observation is considered to vary over a range of values. The accuracy distribution desired is that of the aggregate event. The question posed is to determine the accuracy of the position estimate for a user picked at random from a range of locations and from a range of times. Methods are presented for combining distributions of DOP and UERE to determine the distribution of the location accuracy that can be obtained. This type of analysis is relevant to understanding the composite accuracy provided by a GPS service over a geographical area and/or over a designated time interval.

7.1.4.1 Vertical Accuracy With a Fixed User/Satellite Geometry

Equation (7.32) expresses how pseudorange errors and geometry combine to effect the calculated position and time bias. Specializing this equation to the vertical dimension, we obtain

$$dz = \sum_{m=1}^{N} K_{3,m} d\rho_m \qquad (7.50)$$

where dz is the error in the vertical component of the computed position. The $d\rho_m$ represents the errors in the satellite pseudorange measurements where m ranges from 1 to N and N is the number of satellites being used in the position computation. The value $K_{i,j}$ represents the i, jth component of the matrix $\mathbf{K}$. For the standard least squares solution technique, $\mathbf{K} = (\mathbf{H}^T\mathbf{H})^{-1}\mathbf{H}^T$ and $\mathbf{K}$ is a function only of the user/satellite geometry. The formula (7.50) picks off the third row of $\mathbf{K}$ in the formulation for dz.

With the assumption that the $d\rho_m$ are zero mean and jointly Gaussian, and if the geometry is considered fixed, it follows from (7.50) that dz is zero mean and Gaussian.

Under the additional assumption that the $d\rho_m$ are independent and identically distributed, and have standard deviation σ_{UERE}, (7.44) and (7.48) apply, and one obtains that $\sigma_{dz} = \text{VDOP } \sigma_{\text{UERE}}$ and that VDOP is given by the square root of the third element on the diagonal of $(\mathbf{H}^T\mathbf{H})^{-1}$. Hence, if the geometry is considered fixed and the assumptions regarding the pseudorange measurement errors apply, dz has a $N(0, \text{VDOP } \sigma_{\text{UERE}})$ distribution, which is shorthand for saying that it is Gaussian, zero mean, and has standard deviation VDOP σ_{UERE}.

Statistically, one can view the vertical error as given by the formula

$$dz = \text{VDOP} \times \text{UERE} \qquad (7.51)$$

where UERE is a random variable with distribution $N(0, \sigma_{\text{UERE}})$. The multiplication of UERE and VDOP adjusts the standard deviation of the result so that

$$\sigma_{dz} = \text{VDOP } \sigma_{\text{UERE}} \qquad (7.52)$$

Equation (7.51) is a random variable formulation in the form of (7.1). VDOP is a function of the geometry, UERE represents the error in the pseudorange measurements, and dz is the induced error in the vertical component of the computed position.

With a Gaussian distribution, 68% of the measurements fall within ±1 standard deviation of the mean. Approximately 95% of the measurements fall within two standard deviations of the mean. Hence, if the geometry is considered fixed, the 95% point for the distribution of the vertical error is estimated by the formula

$$2\sigma_{dz} = 2 \text{ VDOP } \sigma_{\text{UERE}} \tag{7.53}$$

As an example, suppose that VDOP = 2.0 at a particular time and location for a user with a particular receiver implementation. The satellite UERE for unaided C/A-code (see Section 7.1.2.10) is $\sigma_{\text{UERE}} = 33.3$ m (see Table 7.2). Hence, the 2σ value for the error in the vertical direction is

$$2\sigma_{dz} = 2 \text{ VDOP } \sigma_{\text{UERE}} = 2 \times 2 \times 33.3 = 133.2 \text{ meters} \tag{7.54}$$

which gives the 95% point for the distribution of the error. The probability is 95% that the error in the vertical component of the position solution will be less than 133.2m. In a similar manner, other points on the distribution can be obtained.

7.1.4.2 Vertical Accuracy With a Variable User/Satellite Geometry

In the previous section, (7.50) expresses how the user/satellite geometry and pseudorange errors combine to effect vertical accuracy. In the present section, both the geometry and the pseudorange errors are considered random variables. Conceptually, the user's location and/or the time of observation are considered to vary over a range of values with an assumed distribution. For example, one might consider the location as being uniformly random across the continental United States and the time of observation as uniformly random over a 24-hr period. Alternatively, the location could be considered fixed and just the time element could be considered to vary. Many variants are possible. What is sought is the aggregate distribution of vertical error under the assumed distribution of allowed geometries.

In Section 7.1.4.1, it was shown that under Gaussian error assumptions and with the geometry considered fixed, the formulations in (7.50) and (7.51) are statistically equivalent. This equivalence is now extended to the more general setting where the geometry is considered to vary. Consider a random variable dz defined by the formula

$$dz = \text{VDOP} \times \text{UERE} \tag{7.55}$$

where VDOP and UERE are considered to be independent random variables. UERE is considered to have a $N(0, \sigma_{UERE})$ distribution. With the standard pseudorange error assumptions (i.e., where its covariance equals a multiple of the identity), VDOP is defined by (7.48) as the square root of the third diagonal element of the $(H^T H)^{-1}$ matrix. VDOP is a function of the user/satellite geometry and the receiver's satellite selection algorithm.

The previous section showed that for a fixed user/satellite geometry, dz as given in (7.55) and in (7.50) have identical distributions. In other words, for a given geometry, the conditional distribution of dz in these two formulations are equal. General probability considerations (see appendix to [23]) imply that it follows that the unconditional distributions of dz are identical. Hence, the formulations for dz as given in (7.50) and (7.55) are statistically equivalent where both UERE and the user/satellite geometry are considered random variables.

The mean and standard deviation for dz are easily obtained from (7.55). Since VDOP and UERE are independent and UERE is zero mean, it follows that dz is zero mean. Squaring (7.55) and taking an expected value leads to the result that the 1σ value for dz is

$$\sigma_{dz} = \text{VDOP}_{rms}\, \sigma_{UERE} \qquad (7.56)$$

where the rms subscript denotes the root mean square. A comparison of (7.56) and (7.52) indicates that when the geometry (i.e., VDOP) is considered a random variable, the rms of the VDOP distribution replaces VDOP in (7.52) to maintain a correct formulation for the standard deviation of dz.

Standard probability techniques can be applied to (7.55) to obtain the density function for dz. (One can obtain the cumulative distribution for dz by integrating the joint density function for VDOP and UERE over appropriate regions and then obtaining the density by differentiating.) Alternatively, since the conditional distribution of dz for a fixed geometry is Gaussian, the unconditional density function of dz can be expressed immediately as a linear combination of Gaussian conditional density functions.

Assume that VDOP takes on values from some discrete set and let $f_{VDOP}(x)$ denote its density function. (The distribution of VDOP is generally obtained empirically from a satellite/user simulation. The distribution can be approximated as discrete by appropriately binning the data.) For a particular value of x, $f_{VDOP}(x)$ gives the probability that the user/satellite geometry has a VDOP with VDOP $= x$. Let $f_{dz|x}(h)$ be the conditional density for dz given a particular value of VDOP. The unconditional density for dz is given by

$$f_{dz}(h) = \sum_x f_{VDOP}(x) f_{dz|x}(h) \qquad (7.57)$$

where the summation ranges over the values where the VDOP distribution is specified. The $f_{dz|x}$ are each the density for a Gaussian variable where the distribution is configured for the particular value of VDOP. The density of dz is expressed as a weighted sum of Gaussian density functions where the weights are the probability each value of VDOP will occur. The conditional distribution functions can be represented in the form

$$f_{dz|x}(h) = \frac{1}{x} f_{\text{UERE}}\left(\frac{h}{x}\right) \tag{7.58}$$

where

$$f_{\text{UERE}}(y) = \frac{1}{\sqrt{2\pi}\,\sigma_{\text{UERE}}} \exp\left(\frac{-y^2}{2\sigma_{\text{UERE}}^2}\right) \tag{7.59}$$

is the (Gaussian) density function for UERE. Putting these results together, one obtains the representation

$$f_{dz}(h) = \sum_x \frac{1}{x} f_{\text{VDOP}}(x) f_{\text{UERE}}\left(\frac{h}{x}\right) \tag{7.60}$$

for the density of dz in terms of the density for VDOP and UERE.

The cumulative distribution for dz can be obtained by integrating (7.60) term by term with respect to h. If $\text{Cum}_{dz}(h)$ denotes the probability that $dz \leq h$, one obtains

$$\text{Cum}_{dz}(h) = \sum_x f_{\text{VDOP}}(x) \text{Cum}_N\left(\frac{h}{x\sigma_{\text{UERE}}}\right) \tag{7.61}$$

The variable N denotes a $N(0, 1)$ variable and the notation Cum_N represents its cumulative distribution. Equation (7.61) represents the cumulative distribution of dz in terms of the density function of VDOP and the cumulative for a standard Gaussian random variable. A formula for Cum_N is given by

$$\text{Cum}_N(h) = \frac{1}{2}\left(\text{Erf}\left(\frac{h}{\sqrt{2}}\right) + 1\right) \tag{7.62}$$

which can readily be evaluated by computer. The Erf function represents the standard error function and is given by the formula $\text{Erf}(y) = \int_0^y (2/\sqrt{\pi})e^{-x^2}dx$.

As an example of the application of these formulations, we reproduce a portion of the study presented in [23] regarding the distribution of vertical accuracy at several locations around the world. A satellite simulation program was used to determine the VDOP distribution at Anchorage, Berlin, Boston, and Sydney. The simulation assumed a full constellation of 24 satellites and stepped in 1-min intervals through a 24-hr period. The VDOP was tabulated for the four satellites in view yielding the best GDOP (similar to the data collected to generate Figure 7.14). A 5° mask angle was used. Histograms representing the density function for VDOP are reproduced in Figure 7.15.

The distribution of vertical error was computed using (7.61) for each of the cities from the tabulated VDOP values. UERE was taken to have a value of 6.6m, which is the DOD error budget for a P(Y)-code receiver [see Section 7.1.2.8]. Figure 7.16, which is taken from [23], illustrates the resulting distributions. The cumulative distribution is given for $|dz|$ rather than for dz. (The cumulative distribution of dz and $|dz|$ are related by the formula $\text{Cum}_{|dz|}(h) = 2\,\text{Cum}_{dz}(h) - 1$ for $h \geq 0$. This results from the observation that the distribution of dz is symmetric about zero, which follows from (7.60) and the assumed symmetry for the density of UERE.)

The curves in Figure 7.16 represent the aggregate distribution of vertical error at each of the cities where the time of observation has been randomized. Although the VDOP distributions for the different cities show some variation, the cumulative distributions of vertical error are surprisingly similar, especially for probabilities below about 0.95. A formula for the 2σ value for dz is obtained by doubling each side of (7.56). The value VDOP_{rms} can be computed from the discrete density values using the formula

$$\text{VDOP}_{\text{rms}} = \left(\sum_x x^2 f_{\text{VDOP}}(x) \right)^{\frac{1}{2}} \tag{7.63}$$

Data adapted from [23] is presented in Table 7.3, which shows VDOP_{rms} and the ratio of the 95% point for dz and its 2σ value for the different cities. (The 95% point is denoted $dz_{95\%}$ and is the value of h satisfying $\text{Cum}_{|dz|}(h) = 0.95$.)

Although the VDOP distributions differ for the different cities, the VDOP_{rms} parameters are almost identical. This, in part, explains why the distribution for dz is so similar for the different cities. Furthermore, the ratio $dz_{95\%}/2\sigma_{dz}$ is nearly constant and is almost the value one would obtain for a Gaussian random variable. (If dz were Gaussian, the ratio $dz_{95\%}/(2\sigma_{dz})$ would be 0.980.) Hence, to a close approximation,

$$dz_{95\%} \approx 2\sigma_{dz} = 2\text{VDOP}_{\text{rms}}\sigma_{\text{UERE}} \tag{7.64}$$

When VDOP is considered a random variable, dz is not Gaussian. However, these results indicate that the 95% point can still be estimated as twice the standard deviation.

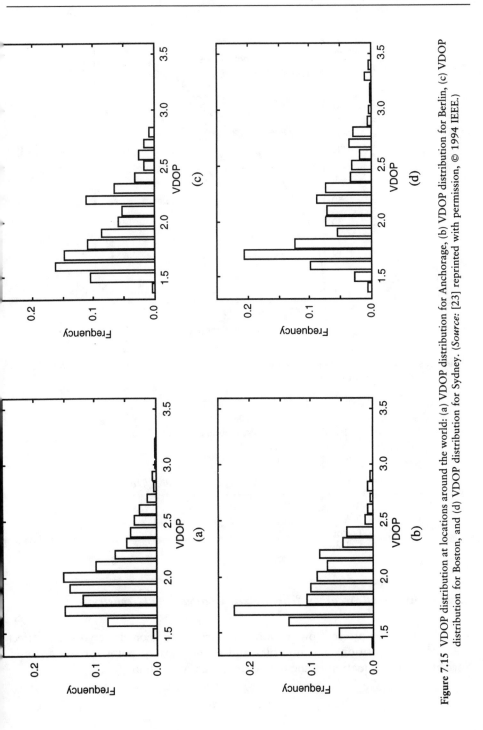

Figure 7.15 VDOP distribution at locations around the world: (a) VDOP distribution for Anchorage, (b) VDOP distribution for Berlin, (c) VDOP distribution for Boston, and (d) VDOP distribution for Sydney. (*Source:* [23] reprinted with permission, © 1994 IEEE.)

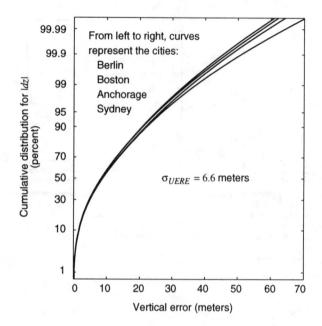

Figure 7.16 Cumulative distributions of vertical error at locations around the world. (*Source*: [23], reprinted with permission, © 1994 IEEE.)

Table 7.3
Parameters for the Distribution of Vertical Error
at Several Locations

City	VDOP$_{rms}$	$dz_{95\%}/(2\sigma_{dz})$
Anchorage	2.02	0.985
Berlin	1.92	0.99
Boston	1.93	0.99
Sydney	2.05	0.99

7.1.4.3 Horizontal Accuracy With a Fixed User/Satellite Geometry

Equation (7.32) expresses how pseudorange errors and geometry combine to effect the calculated position and time bias and is the starting point for the analysis. Specializing this equation to the horizontal plane, we obtain

$$dR = K_{2 \times n} d\rho \tag{7.65}$$

where $d\mathbf{R} = (dx, dy)^T$ is the vector component of the position error in the horizontal plane, $d\boldsymbol{\rho} = (d\rho_1, \ldots, d\rho_n)^T$ represents the pseudorange measurement errors, and n is the number of satellites being used in the position calculation. The value $\mathbf{K}_{2 \times n}$ denotes the upper $2 \times n$ submatrix of $\mathbf{K}$ and consists of its first two rows. For the standard least square solution technique, $\mathbf{K} = (\mathbf{H}^T\mathbf{H})^{-1}\mathbf{H}^T$.

If the geometry is considered fixed, (7.65) expresses the horizontal position error as a linear function of the pseudorange measurement errors. If the pseudorange errors are zero mean and jointly Gaussian, $d\mathbf{R}$ also has these properties. If the pseudorange errors are uncorrelated and identically distributed with variance σ_{UERE}^2, the covariance of the horizontal errors is given as

$$\text{cov}(d\mathbf{R}) = ((\mathbf{H}^T\mathbf{H})^{-1})_{2 \times 2} \, \sigma_{\text{UERE}}^2 \qquad (7.66)$$

where the subscript notation denotes the upper left 2×2 submatrix of $(\mathbf{H}^T\mathbf{H})^{-1}$. The density function for $d\mathbf{R}$ is

$$f_{d\mathbf{R}}(x, y) = \frac{1}{2\pi[\det(\text{cov}(d\mathbf{R}))]^{\frac{1}{2}}} \exp\left(-\frac{1}{2}\mathbf{u}^T[\text{cov}(d\mathbf{R})]^{-1}\mathbf{u}\right) \qquad (7.67)$$

where $\mathbf{u} = (x, y)^T$ and where det represents the determinant of a matrix.

The density function defines a two-dimensional bell-shaped surface. Contours of constant density are obtained by setting the exponent in parenthesis to a constant. One obtains equations of the form

$$\mathbf{u}^T[\text{cov}(d\mathbf{R})]^{-1}\mathbf{u} = m^2 \qquad (7.68)$$

where the parameter m ranges over positive values. The contour curves that result form a collection of concentric ellipses when plotted in the plane. The ellipse obtained when m equals 1 is termed the 1σ ellipse and has the equation

$$\mathbf{u}^T[\text{cov}(d\mathbf{R})]^{-1}\mathbf{u} = 1 \qquad (7.69)$$

(The 1σ ellipse is defined here as a specific cut through the probability density function and is not to be confused with 1σ containment. This latter curve is the locus of points, one point on each ray from the origin, where the points are at a distance of 1σ for the ray's direction. In general, the 1σ containment curve is a figure-eight-shaped curve that encloses the 1σ ellipse.) If the major and minor axis of the ellipse are aligned with the x and y axes, the equation for the ellipse reduces to $x^2/\sigma_x^2 + y^2/\sigma_y^2 = 1$. In general, however, the off-diagonal terms in $\text{cov}(d\mathbf{R})$ are nonzero, and the elliptical contours for the density function are rotated relative to the x and y axes. Denote the major and minor axes of the 1σ ellipse by σ_L and σ_S.

In general, the 1σ ellipse is contained in a box of width $2\sigma_x$ and height $2\sigma_y$ centered on the ellipse. Figure 7.17 illustrates graphically the relationship between the 1σ ellipse and the parameters σ_x, σ_y, σ_L, and σ_S.

The probability that the error lies within the elliptical contour defined for a specific value of m is $1 - e^{-m^2/2}$. In particular, the probability of being in the 1σ ellipse ($m = 1$) is 0.39; the probability of being in the 2σ ellipse ($m = 2$) is 0.86. (These values are in contrast to the one-dimensional Gaussian result that the probability of being within $\pm 1\sigma$ of the mean is 0.68.)

Several parameters are in common use that characterize the magnitude of the horizontal error. The distance root mean square (drms) is defined by the formula

$$\text{drms} = \sqrt{\sigma_x^2 + \sigma_y^2} \tag{7.70}$$

where σ_x and σ_y are the standard deviation of the error along the x and y axes. For a zero mean random variable such as $d\mathbf{R}$, one has drms $= \sqrt{E(|d\mathbf{R}|^2)}$ and the drms corresponds to the square root of the mean value of the squared error (hence, its name). From (7.43), one immediately has

$$\text{drms} = \text{HDOP } \sigma_{\text{UERE}} \tag{7.71}$$

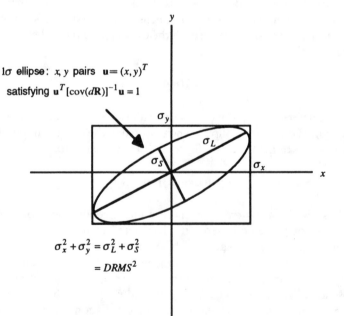

Figure 7.17 Relationship between 1σ ellipse and distribution parameters.

and the drms can be computed from the values of HDOP and σ_{UERE}. The probability that the computed location is within a circle of radius drms from the true location depends on the ratio σ_S/σ_L for the 1σ ellipse. If the two-dimensional error distribution is close to being circular ($\sigma_S/\sigma_L \approx 1$), the probability is about 0.63; for a more elongated distribution ($\sigma_S/\sigma_L \approx 0$), the probability approaches 0.69. Two times the drms is given by

$$2 \text{ drms} = 2 \text{ HDOP } \sigma_{UERE} \qquad (7.72)$$

and the probability that the horizontal error is within a circle of radius 2 drms ranges between 0.95 and 0.98 depending on the ratio σ_S/σ_L. The 2 drms value is commonly taken as the 95% limit for the magnitude of the horizontal error.

A second parameter in wide use is the error distribution circular error probable (CEP). The CEP is defined as the radius of a circle that catches 50% of the error distribution when centered at the correct (i.e., error free) location. Thus, the probability that the magnitude of the error is less than the CEP is precisely 1/2. The CEP for a two-dimensional Gaussian random variable can be approximated by the formula

$$\text{CEP} \approx 0.59(\sigma_L + \sigma_S) \qquad (7.73)$$

assuming it is zero mean. For a derivation of this and other approximations, see [24].

The CEP can also be estimated in terms of drms and, using (7.71), in terms of HDOP and σ_{UERE}. This is convenient since HDOP is widely computed in GPS applications. Figure 7.18 presents curves giving the probability that the magnitude of the error satisfies $|d\mathbf{R}| \le k$ drms as a function of k for different values of the ratio σ_S/σ_L. (The horizontal error is assumed to have a zero mean two-dimensional Gaussian distribution.) For k equal to 0.75, one obtains a probability in the range 0.43 to 0.54. Hence, one has the approximate relation

$$\text{CEP} \approx 0.75 \text{ drms} = 0.75 \text{ HDOP } \sigma_{UERE} \qquad (7.74)$$

It is interesting to note that for $k = 1.23$, the probability that $|d\mathbf{R}| \le k$ drms is roughly 0.78, almost independent of σ_S/σ_L. The probabilities associated with several other values of k are summarized in Table 7.4.

As an application of these formulations, for a geometry with HDOP = 1.5 and with σ_{UERE} = 33.3 m, estimates for the CEP, the 80% point, and the 95% point for the magnitude of the horizontal error are given as follows:

$$\text{CEP}_{50} \approx 0.75 \text{ HDOP } \sigma_{UERE} = 0.75 \times 1.5 \times 33.3 = 37.5 \text{ meters}$$
$$\text{CEP}_{80} \approx 1.28 \text{ HDOP } \sigma_{UERE} = 1.28 \times 1.5 \times 33.3 = 63.9 \text{ meters}$$
$$\text{CEP}_{95} \approx 2.0 \text{ HDOP } \sigma_{UERE} = 2.0 \times 1.5 \times 33.3 = 99.9 \text{ meters}$$
$$(7.75)$$

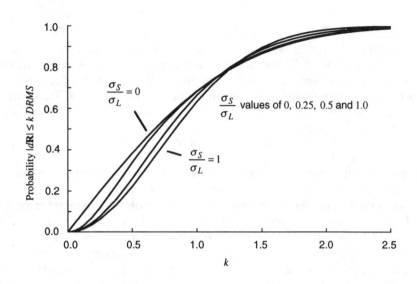

Figure 7.18 Cumulative distribution of radial error for various values of σ_S/σ_L for a two-dimensional Gaussian random variable.

Table 7.4
Approximation Formulas for the Magnitude of the
Horizontal Error

Approximation Formula*	Probability Range
$\mathrm{CEP}_{50} \approx 0.75\ \mathrm{HDOP}\ \sigma_{\mathrm{UERE}}$	0.43 to 0.54
$\mathrm{CEP}_{80} \approx 1.28\ \mathrm{HDOP}\ \sigma_{\mathrm{UERE}}$	0.80 to 0.81
$\mathrm{CEP}_{90} \approx 1.6\ \mathrm{HDOP}\ \sigma_{\mathrm{UERE}}$	0.89 to 0.92
$\mathrm{CEP}_{95} \approx 2.0\ \mathrm{HDOP}\ \sigma_{\mathrm{UERE}}$	0.95 to 0.98

*CEP_{xx} is defined as the radius of the circle that when centered at the error-free location includes xx % of the error distribution. Hence, $\mathrm{CEP}_{50} = \mathrm{CEP}$.

7.1.4.4 Horizontal Accuracy With a Variable User/Satellite Geometry

In the previous section, (7.65) expresses how the user/satellite geometry and pseudorange errors combine to effect horizontal accuracy. In the present section, both the geometry and the pseudorange errors are considered random variables. For example, one might consider the user location as being uniformly random across some region of the world and/or the time of observation as random within some interval of time. What is sought is the aggregate distribution of the horizontal error under the assumed distribution of allowed geometries. This will be formulated in terms of the distributions of UERE and the geometries. (This development parallels the development in Section 7.1.4.2 for the vertical error case.)

In Section 7.1.4.3, it is shown that under zero mean Gaussian pseudorange error assumptions and with the geometry considered fixed, the distribution of the horizontal error is zero mean Gaussian. Hence, the conditional distribution of $d\mathbf{R}$ given a fixed geometry is Gaussian. Using standard probability techniques, one can express the unconditional distribution of $d\mathbf{R}$ in terms of the conditional distribution of $d\mathbf{R}$ and the distribution of the geometry. Let $f_{d\mathbf{R}|G}(x, y)$ represent the conditional density of $d\mathbf{R}$ given a satellite/user geometry symbolized by G, and let f_G represent the density function for the geometry. The unconditional density for $d\mathbf{R}$ is obtained from the integral expression

$$f_{d\mathbf{R}}(x, y) = \int f_G f_{d\mathbf{R}|G}(x, y)dG \tag{7.76}$$

where the integration is with respect to the allowed geometries.

The density function can be evaluated using a satellite simulation program coupled with a random number generator to make random draws on the allowed geometries. In addition, knowledge of the receiver satellite selection process is required. A "draw on the geometry" means selecting a location for the user and the time of observation, and determining from the receiver characteristics the satellites that would participate in the location calculation. Denote the conditional covariance matrix for $d\mathbf{R}$ by $\mathbf{C}_i$ where i indexes the particular draw on the geometry. The value $\mathbf{C}_i$ is calculated from the satellite/user geometry using (7.66):

$$\mathbf{C}_i = ((\mathbf{H}^T\mathbf{H})^{-1})_{2\times2}\sigma_{\text{UERE}}^2 \tag{7.77}$$

The conditional density for $d\mathbf{R}$ is given by (7.67) with $\mathbf{C}_i$ substituted for cov($d\mathbf{R}$) and is denoted here as $f_{d\mathbf{R}|C_i}(x, y)$. The integral expression in (7.76) can be approximated by a summation. One is led to the formulation

$$f_{d\mathbf{R}}(x, y) = \sum_{i=1}^{N}\frac{1}{N}f_{d\mathbf{R}|C_i}(x, y) \tag{7.78}$$

for the unconditional density function where the summation ranges over the draws on the geometry and N is the number of geometries evaluated. In this expression, the unconditional density is represented as the average of the conditional density functions determined by making random draws on the geometry.

The covariance of $d\mathbf{R}$ is obtained from the density by evaluating the integral

$$\text{cov}(d\mathbf{R}) = \int\int \begin{pmatrix} x^2 & xy \\ xy & y^2 \end{pmatrix} f_{d\mathbf{R}}(x, y)dxdy \tag{7.79}$$

Substituting from (7.78) and simplifying yields

$$\text{cov}(d\mathbf{R}) = \iint \begin{pmatrix} x^2 & xy \\ xy & y^2 \end{pmatrix} \sum_{i=1}^{N} \frac{1}{N} f_{d\mathbf{R}|C_i}(x, y)dxdy$$

$$= \frac{1}{N} \sum_{i=1}^{N} \iint \begin{pmatrix} x^2 & xy \\ xy & y^2 \end{pmatrix} f_{d\mathbf{R}|C_i}(x, y)dxdy \qquad (7.80)$$

$$= \frac{1}{N} \sum_{i=1}^{N} \mathbf{C}_i$$

Thus, the covariance of $d\mathbf{R}$ is obtained as the average of the conditional covariance matrices determined from the draws on the geometry.

An expression for the unconditional drms is obtained by forming a trace operation on (7.80) followed by a square root,

$$\text{drms} = \sqrt{\sigma_x^2 + \sigma_y^2} = \left(\frac{1}{N} \sum_{i=1}^{N} (\sigma_x^2 + \sigma_y^2)_i \right)^{1/2} \qquad (7.81)$$

The expression $(\sigma_x^2 + \sigma_y^2)_i$ is the trace of the conditional covariance matrix given a specific draw on the geometry. Using (7.43), it can be expressed in terms of the conditional HDOP and σ_{UERE}. Substitution into (7.81) yields

$$\text{drms} = \left(\frac{1}{N} \sum_{i=1}^{N} \text{HDOP}_i^2 \right)^{1/2} \sigma_{\text{UERE}} \qquad (7.82)$$

The radical expression is just the rms of the HDOP values. Hence, one obtains the simplified result

$$\text{drms} = \text{HDOP}_{\text{rms}} \, \sigma_{\text{UERE}} \qquad (7.83)$$

expressing the unconditional drms as the product of the rms of the HDOP distribution and the standard deviation of UERE. This formula is analogous to (7.71) for the case of horizontal error when the geometry is considered fixed. It is analogous to (7.52) and (7.56), which apply to the analysis of vertical errors.

The question remains as to how the drms and multiples of it relate to circular probability values. In Section 7.1.4.3, it was shown that when the geometry is considered fixed and the horizontal error has a two-dimensional Gaussian distribution, the approximation formulas in Table 7.4 relate multiples of the drms to CEP values. When the geometry is considered to vary, the aggregate distribution of the horizontal error is no longer Gaussian. However, the formulas in Table 7.4 still provide useful estimates of the CEP values if the HDOP is replaced by the rms of the HDOP distribution.

As an illustration of these ideas, the distribution of horizontal error was investigated for Boston, MA, for a 24-hr period. A satellite simulation program stepped in 6-min intervals over the course of a day and tabulated the conditional covariance matrix as given in (7.77). The simulation was done for a mask angle of $5°$ and a receiver algorithm that selected the four satellites that minimized GDOP. The joint distribution of HDOP and the ratio σ_S/σ_L for the 1σ ellipse is illustrated in Figure 7.19. This distribution was converted to a distribution of radial error using an integrated version of (7.78). Figure 7.20 illustrates the resulting distribution of radial error. The probability that $|d\mathbf{R}| \le k$ drms is plotted as a function of k. The drms value is that for the aggregate distribution and is related to $HDOP_{rms}$ and σ_{UERE} by (7.83). Also illustrated are the cumulative distribution for a two-dimensional Gaussian variable for a σ_S/σ_L ratio of zero and one.

A comparison of the unconditional distribution of the radial error to that of the Gaussian cases and to the curves in Figure 7.20 show that the formulas in Table 7.4 give a good approximation for the radial error if HDOP is replaced by $HDOP_{rms}$. In the particular case in hand, $HDOP_{rms}$ evaluated to 1.5. For a σ_{UERE} of 33.3m, the 50, 80, and 95% points for the radial error are estimated as follows:

$$CEP_{50} \approx 0.75\ HDOP_{rms}\ \sigma_{UERE} = 0.75 \times 1.5 \times 33.3 = 37.5 \text{ meters}$$

$$CEP_{80} \approx 1.28\ HDOP_{rms}\ \sigma_{UERE} = 1.28 \times 1.5 \times 33.3 = 63.9 \text{ meters}$$

$$CEP_{95} \approx 2.0\ HDOP_{rms}\ \sigma_{UERE} = 2.0 \times 1.5 \times 33.3 = 99.9 \text{ meters}$$

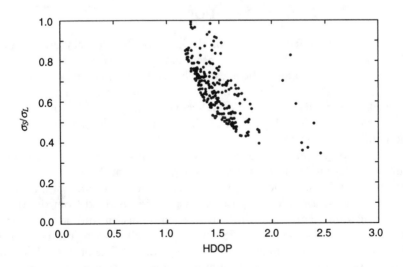

Figure 7.19 Joint distribution of HDOP and σ_S/σ_L for a 24-hr period in Boston, MA.

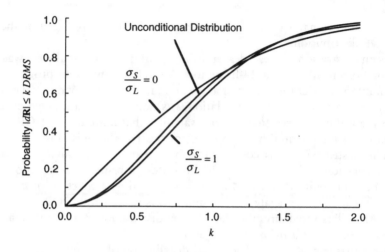

Figure 7.20 Cumulative distribution of radial error over a 24-hr period for Boston, MA.

7.2 GPS AVAILABILITY

Availability of a navigation system is the percentage of time that the services of the system are usable. Further, availability is an indication of the ability of the system to provide a usable navigation service within a specified coverage area [25].

As discussed above, GPS accuracy is generally expressed by

$$\sigma_p = \text{DOP } \sigma_{\text{UERE}}$$

where σ_p is the standard deviation of the positioning accuracy and σ_{UERE} is the standard deviation of the satellite pseudorange measurement error. For the C/A-code, σ_{UERE} is estimated to be 33.3m. The DOP factor could be HDOP, VDOP, PDOP, and so forth, depending on the dimension for which GPS accuracy is to be determined. The availability of the GPS navigation function to provide a given accuracy level is therefore dependent on the geometry of the satellites for a specific location and time of day.

In order to determine the availability of GPS for a specific location and time, the number of visible satellites, as well as the geometry of those satellites, must first be determined. GPS almanac data, which contains the positions of all satellites in the constellation at a reference epoch, can easily be obtained from the U.S. Coast Guard Navigation Center bulletin board system or as an output from some GPS receivers. Since the orbit of the GPS satellites is well known, the position of the satellites at any given point in time can then be predicted. The process of determining the satellite positions at a particular point in time is not intuitive, however, and a computer program is needed in order to perform the calculations.

7.2.1 Predicted GPS Availability Using the Full Operational Capability GPS Constellation

This section examines the availability of the GPS full operational capability (FOC) constellation. The FOC constellation is defined in Section 3.1.1. Worldwide GPS coverage is evaluated from 90° N to 90° S latitude with sample points spaced every 5° (in latitude) and for a band in longitude circling the globe spaced every 5°. This grid is sampled every 5 min in time over a 12-hr period.

Since the GPS constellation has approximately a 12-hr orbit, the satellite coverage will then repeat itself on the opposite side of the world during the next 12 hours. (The Earth rotates 180° in the 12-hr period and the satellite coverage areas will be interchanged.) A total of 386,280 space/time points are evaluated in this analysis.

GPS availability is also dependent on the mask angle used by the receiver. By lowering the mask angle, more satellites are visible; hence, a higher availability can be obtained. However, there are problems with reducing the mask angle, which are discussed later in this section. The availability obtained by applying the following mask angles is examined: 7.5°, 5°, 2.5°, and 0°.

Figure 7.21 demonstrates the GPS availability based on HDOP using an all-in-view solution. This figure provides the cumulative distribution of HDOP for each of the mask angles considered. The maximum value of HDOP is 2.55 for a mask angle less than or equal to 5°.

Figure 7.22 provides the availability of GPS based on PDOP for the same mask angles. This availability is lower than that for HDOP since unavailability in the vertical dimension is taken into consideration in the calculation of PDOP. The maximum value of PDOP for a 5° mask angle is 5.15, at 2.5° it is 4.7, and for a 0° mask angle the maximum value is 3.1.

Although these graphs demonstrate the improvement in availability that can be obtained when the mask angle is lowered, there is a danger in lowering it too far. During the mission planning process, signal blockage from buildings or other objects that extend higher than the set mask angle must be taken into consideration. Also, as stated above, there is a greater potential for atmospheric delay and multipath problems at a lower mask angle.

The threshold for the maximum acceptable DOP value is dependent on the desired accuracy level according to (4.2.1). The availability of GPS, therefore, will depend on the stringency of the accuracy requirement. For this analysis, availability of GPS is chosen to be defined as PDOP ≤ 6.

As shown in Figure 7.22, with all 24 GPS satellites operational, the value of PDOP is less than 6.0 for every location and time point analyzed at 0°, 2.5°, and 5° mask angles. Since the analysis grid is sampled every 5 min, there could be occurrences where PDOP is greater than 6.0 for a period of less than 5 min that would not be detected. Only with a 7.5° mask angle (or higher) does the GPS constellation have outages based on PDOP exceeding 6.0. At a 7.5° mask angle,

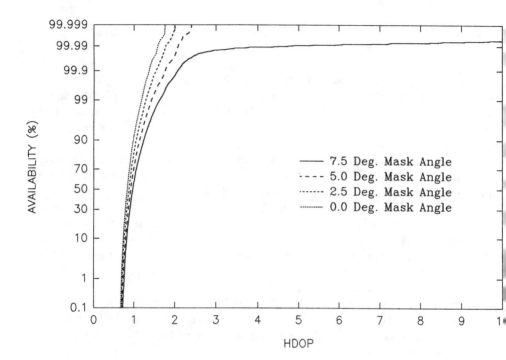

Figure 7.21 Cumulative Distribution of HDOP with 7.5°, 5°, 2.5°, and 0° mask angles.

the GPS constellation provides an availability of 99.98%. Figure 7.23 displays the locations and duration of the outages that occur. The maximum outage duration is 10 min. The GPS constellation is designed to provide optimal worldwide coverage. As a result, when outages do occur, they are concentrated in very high and very low latitudes (above 60°N and below 60°S).

7.2.2 Effects of Satellite Outages on GPS Availability

The previous figures have demonstrated the availability of GPS when all 24 satellites are operational. However, satellites need to be taken out of service for maintenance, and unscheduled outages will occur from time to time. In fact, 24 satellites may only be available 72% of the time, while 21 or more satellites are expected to be operational at least 98% of the time [26].

In order to examine the effect that a reduced constellation of satellites has on the availability of GPS, the analysis is now repeated using the same worldwide grid, but removing one, two, and three satellites from the FOC constellation. Since a 5° mask angle is most commonly used, it is the only one considered for this portion of the analysis.

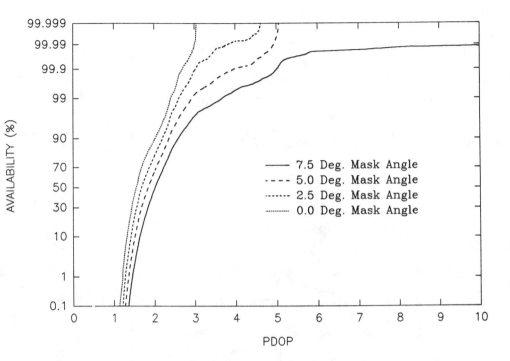

Figure 7.22 Cumulative distribution of PDOP with 7.5°, 5°, 2.5°, and 0° mask angles.

The availability of GPS when satellites are removed from the constellation is very much dependent on which satellites, or combinations of satellites, are taken out of service. The Aerospace Corporation has performed a study that determined cases of one, two, and three satellite failures that resulted in the least, average, and greatest impact on availability [27]. The choices for satellites to be removed in this analysis were based on those satellites that caused an "average" impact on GPS availability.

The orbital positions of the GPS satellites removed from the constellation are given in the following list:

- Average one satellite—SV A3;
- Average two satellites—SVs A1 and F3;
- Average three satellites—SVs A2, E3, and F2.

(Refer to Sections 3.1.1 and 3.2.1 for satellite identification and orbital location information.)

Figures 7.24 and 7.25 display the cumulative distribution of HDOP and PDOP with up to three satellites removed from the constellation and applying a 5° mask

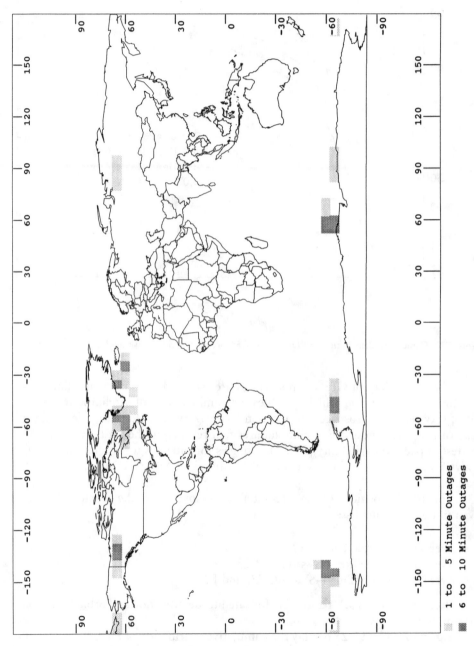

Figure 7.23 Availability of the GPS Constellation (PDOP ≤ 6) with a 7.5° mask angle.

1 to 5 Minute Outages
6 to 10 Minute Outages

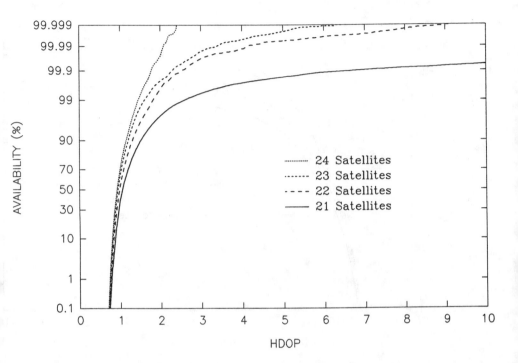

Figure 7.24 Cumulative distribution of HDOP with 5° mask angle cases of 24, 23, 22, and 21 satellites.

angle. These plots demonstrate the increasing degradation in system performance as more satellites are removed from the constellation.

The availability of GPS, based on PDOP ≤ 6 and a 5° mask angle, is 99.969% with one satellite out of service. The location and duration of the resulting outages are displayed in Figure 7.26. The maximum outage duration that occurs is 15 min. With the satellite that was selected to be removed from the constellation, the outages are concentrated in two areas and, fortunately, none of the outages occur over the Americas. This scenario could be different, however, had a different satellite been selected.

The effects of two satellites out of service are shown in Figure 7.27. Outages now last up to 25 min in several locations, but there are only a couple of occurrences of these during the day. The majority of the outages are 10 min or less. This constellation provides an availability of 99.903%.

With three satellites out of service, the overall availability of the GPS constellation drops to 99.197%. The number of outage occurrences increases dramatically and outages now last up to 65 min. The locations and corresponding duration of these outages are shown in Figure 7.28.

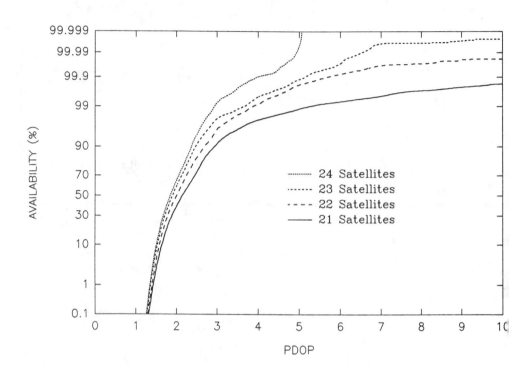

Figure 7.25 Cumulative distribution of PDOP with 5° mask angle cases of 24, 23, 22, and 21 satellites.

The scenario of having three satellites out of service at the same time should be a very rare occurrence. However, if it were to happen, the user could examine the predicted availability over the course of the day and plan the use of GPS accordingly. The following section discusses the capabilities of GPS mission planning software.

7.2.3 Off-the-Shelf Coverage Prediction Software

As mentioned previously, the determination of satellite positions and the resulting GPS availability for any location and point in time is not intuitive and requires a computer to perform the calculations. GPS prediction software is commercially available that allows a user to determine GPS coverage for a single location or for multiple locations. Some GPS receiver manufacturers also include prediction software with the purchase of a receiver. There are several GPS prediction software packages available, some with advanced capabilities such as modeling the integration of GPS with other systems (such as inertial navigation systems). This section will just cover the basic features provided by GPS mission planning software.

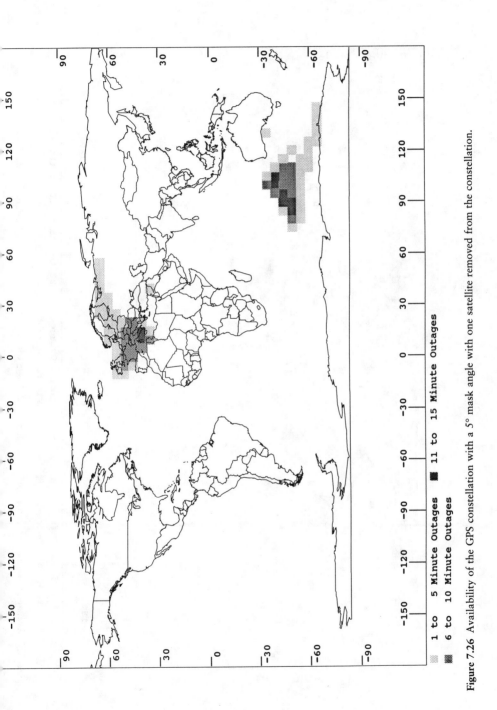

Figure 7.26 Availability of the GPS constellation with a 5° mask angle with one satellite removed from the constellation.

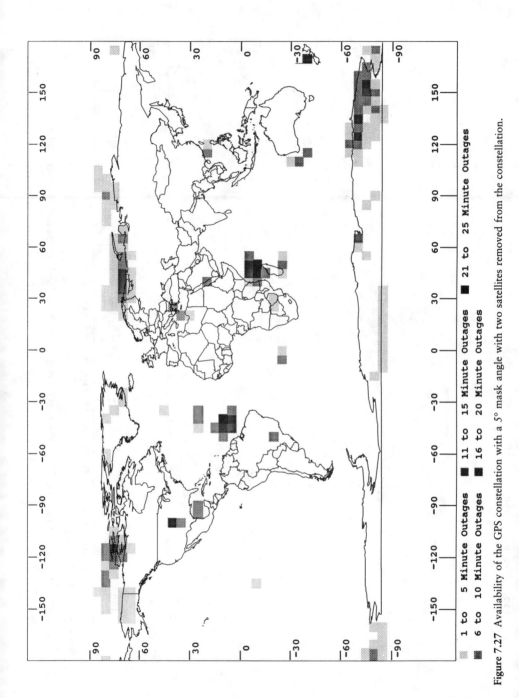

Figure 7.27 Availability of the GPS constellation with a 5° mask angle with two satellites removed from the constellation.

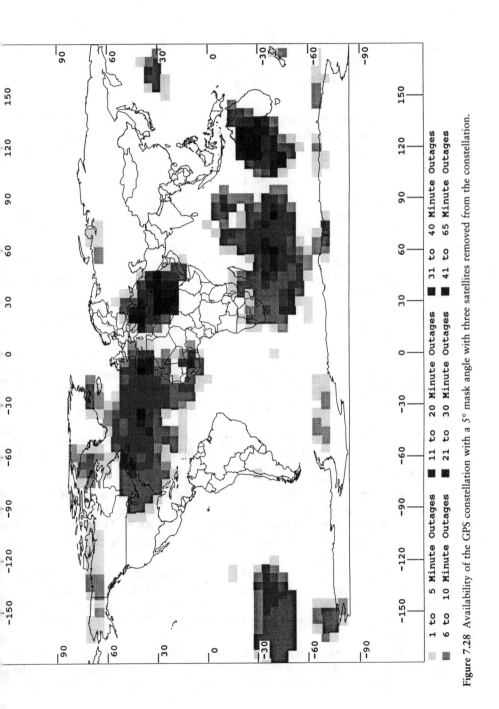

Figure 7.28 Availability of the GPS constellation with a 5° mask angle with three satellites removed from the constellation.

Although GPS has a very high availability, mission planning is important, especially if satellites have been taken out of service or if the location has terrain features which may block the visibility of satellites.

The typical input parameters used to perform GPS mission planning are as follows.

- *GPS Almanac Data:* The position of the satellites at a reference epoch may be obtained from several different sources: the U.S. Coast Guard Navigation Center BBS, a GPS receiver that outputs almanac data, or the software provider may provide its own BBS. The user needs to make sure that the almanac data is in the correct format for use with the software package.
- *Location:* Latitude, longitude, and altitude of the location for which the prediction is to be performed. Software packages may allow the user to perform predictions for multiple locations.
- *Date of Prediction:* The date for which the prediction is to be performed. The GPS almanac can be used to accurately predict up to seven days in the future.
- *Mask Angle:* The elevation angle above the horizon at which satellites are considered visible by the GPS receiver.
- *Terrain Mask:* The azimuth and elevation of terrain (buildings, mountains, etc.) that may block the satellite signal can be entered into the program to ensure an accurate prediction.
- *Satellite Failures:* If any satellites are currently out of service, their status will be reflected in the almanac data. However, if satellites are scheduled for maintenance for a prediction date in the future, the software allows the user to mark those satellites unusable. This data also can be obtained from the U.S. Coast Guard Navigation Center.
- *Maximum DOP:* As discussed previously, in order to determine availability, a maximum DOP threshold must be set (e.g., PDOP = 6). If the DOP exceeds that value, the software will declare GPS to be unusable.

Once these parameters have been input into the software, the prediction can be performed. The user then has several options for displaying GPS coverage and availability. A prediction was performed for Boston (42.35°N 71.08°W) on Dec. 23, 1994. Several of the plots available from Global Satellite Software (GSS) are presented in the following figures.

Figure 7.29 shows the location of the GPS satellites and the satellite horizon line for the selected location at a snapshot in time (12:10 UTC[USNO]). The satellites with squares next to them (17, 23, 26, and 27) are the four used to form the navigation solution. The corresponding HDOP and PDOP for that point in time also are displayed.

Figure 7.30 is an azimuth and elevation plot that gives the position of the satellites from the perspective of looking at the sky directly overhead from the selected location. The user is at the center of the concentric circles, with the outermost

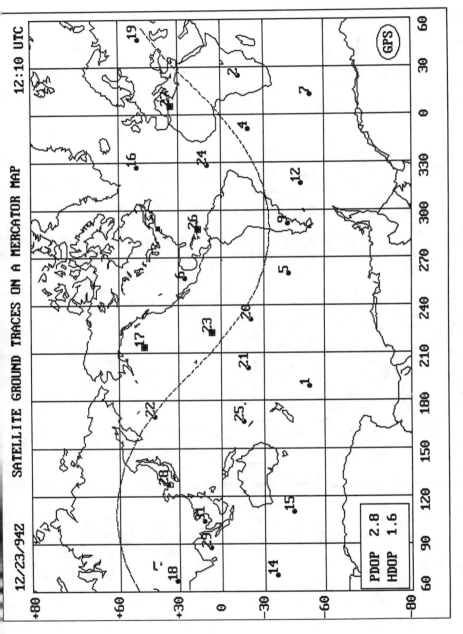

Figure 7.29 Locations of satellites worldwide.

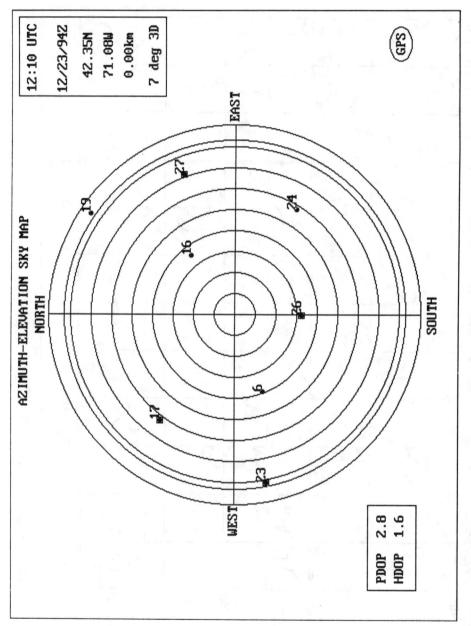

Figure 7.30 Azimuth/elevation plot.

circle representing 0° elevation, or the horizon. The second circle is at 7° elevation, which was the selected mask angle for this portion of the analysis. The third is at 10°, and each circle increases by 10°. The azimuth is 0° at North and increases in the clockwise direction.

Figure 7.31 displays the rise and set time for the 25 GPS satellites at the selected location over a 24-hr period. (The reason that there are 25 satellites in the constellation is that one of the Block I prototype satellites was still operational at the time of this evaluation, adding to the 24 Block II/IIA satellites). This graph can be very useful for a researcher who wants to plan an experiment with a particular set of satellites and doesn't want the satellite geometry to change significantly due to a rising or setting satellite.

The solid line at the bottom of the graph indicates that GPS is available for the entire day (PDOP ≤ 6). Gaps in this line would indicate that GPS is unavailable. This unavailability is demonstrated in Figure 7.32 when satellites 16, 25, and 26 are removed (by the author) from the constellation. As shown in this figure, removing three satellites from the GPS constellation results in two outage periods during the day for Boston.

Another feature of mission planning software involves determining the number of satellites that will be visible at a location over the course of a day. This information is useful for applications that may require the maximum number of visible satellites. Figure 7.33 displays the number of visible satellites over a 24-hr period with all of the satellites operational. As shown in this figure, the minimum number of satellites available is 6 and the maximum is 10 for this location. At lower latitudes (near the equator), it is possible to have as many as 12 GPS satellites visible at a time.

A profile of PDOP over 24 hr is given in Figure 7.34. On the right-hand side of the figure, plots of GDOP, HDOP, and VDOP are shown. The software allows the user to toggle between these graphs and display the one of primary interest.

Figure 7.35 displays PDOP after three satellites have been removed from the constellation. Notice that the spikes in the PDOP correspond to the outages shown in Figure 7.32. Mission planning software such as GSS is very useful, especially if the user has flexibility to schedule data collection or GPS operations around periods of poor satellite geometry.

7.3 GPS INTEGRITY

In addition to providing a navigation function, a navigation system must have the ability to provide timely warnings to users when the system should not be used. This capability is known as the integrity of the system.

7.3.1 Discussion of Criticality

Anomalies can occur, caused by either the satellite or the MCS, which result in unpredictable range errors above the operational tolerance. These errors are different

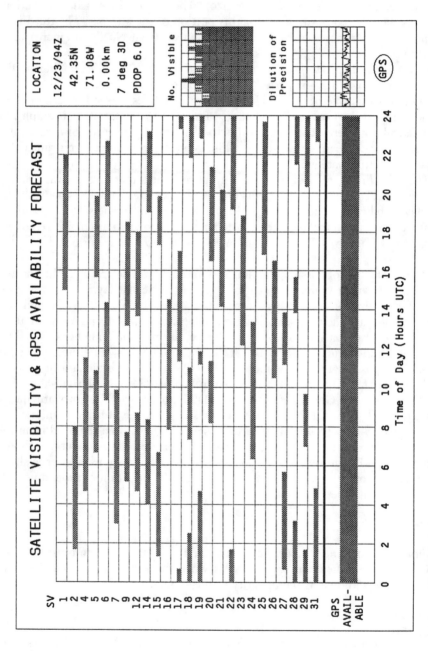

Figure 7.31 Satellite visibility/availability over a 24-hr period.

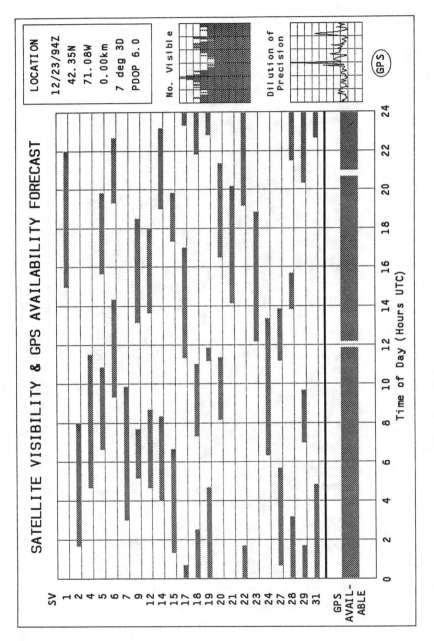

Figure 7.32 Satellite visibility/availability over a 24-hr period with satellites 16, 25, and 26 removed from the constellation.

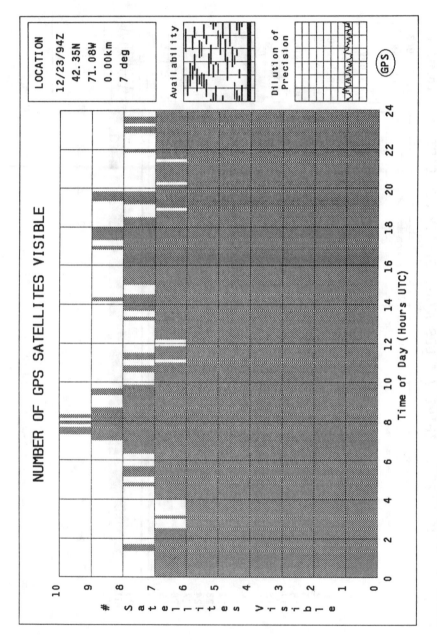

Figure 7.33 Number of visible GPS satellites over a 24-hr period.

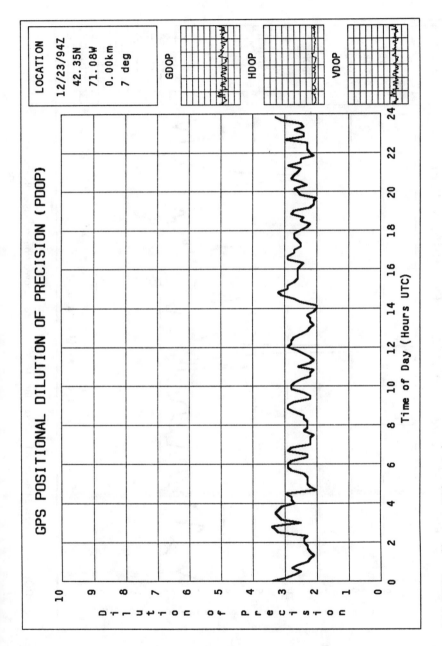

Figure 7.34 PDOP profile over a 24-hr period.

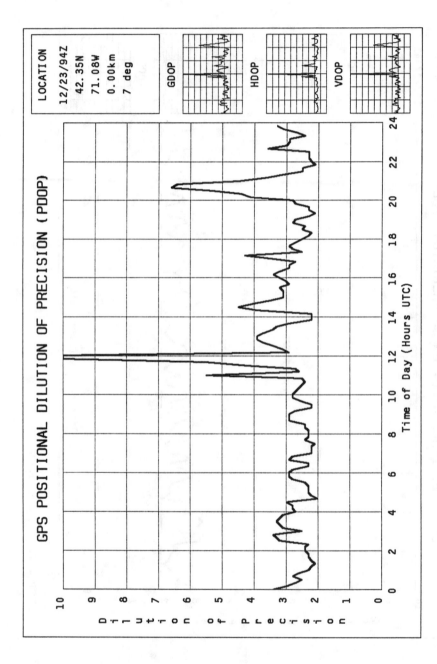

Figure 7.35 PDOP profile over a 24-hr period with satellites 16, 25, and 26 removed from the constellation.

from the predictable degraded accuracy resulting from poor satellite geometry, which was discussed in the previous section. Integrity anomalies should be rare, occurring only a few times per year [28], but can be critical, especially for air navigation.

7.3.2 Sources of Integrity Anomalies

There are four main sources that can cause integrity problems: the satellite clock, the satellite ephemeris, problems specific to the Block I satellites, and the MCS [28]. Satellite clock anomalies are due to frequency standard problems such as random run-off, a large jump, or a combination of both. The MCS has reported clock jumps when the beam current or temperature of the frequency standard vary greatly.

Block I satellites are subject to ephemeris anomalies that occur when the satellite exits the Earth's shadow after eclipse season and the solar panels attempt to reacquire sun tracking. (During the eclipse period, the satellite is blocked from the sun and must rely on internal power for operation. As the satellites age, however, they can no longer sustain operation without additional power from the sun collected by the solar panels.) The satellites will fire thrusters to adjust the attitude, which can result in large ranging errors. This capability has been disabled on succeeding satellite versions. Also, Block I satellites did not have the radiation hardening against the space environment that has been built into the Block II/IIA/IIR satellites. Consequently, Block I satellites are subject to "bit hits," which affect the navigation message, as well as C-field tuning "word hits." The C-field tuning register that aligns the cesium beam is affected by solar radiation. Changing the bits that account for the alignment/direction of the cesium beam results in ranging errors of thousands of meters in only a few minutes. Block I satellites also are subject to P-code slips that cause loss of the P-code tracking, resulting in errors in the order of thousands of meters. At the time of this writing, there is only one Block I satellite left in orbit, thus, these problems should be minimal.

Most MCS problems are due to hardware, software, or human error. One past problem involved an error in the covariance estimate of the MCS's Kalman filter. As a result of these anomalies, errors of several thousands of meters can occur before the problem is detected. The GPS ground monitoring network currently does not provide coverage for all satellites 24 hours a day [28]. Therefore, if an integrity problem were to occur, it may not be detected immediately.

The MCS is continuously working to minimize integrity anomalies as much as possible by installing redundant hardware, robust software, and providing training to prevent human error. The best response time, however, may still be several minutes, which is insufficient for aviation applications. There are methods, however, by which the user is independently able to detect a satellite anomaly if it does occur.

7.3.3 Integrity Enhancement Techniques

The integrity problem is crucial for aviation since the user is traveling at high speeds and can quickly deviate from the flight path. The integrity function becomes especially critical if GPS is to be used as a primary navigation system. RTCA Special Committee 159 (SC-159), a Federal advisory committee to the Federal Aviation Administration, has devoted much effort to developing techniques to provide integrity for airborne use of GPS. The two methods used for GPS integrity monitoring are receiver autonomous integrity monitoring (RAIM) and the wide area augmentation system (WAAS).

7.3.3.1 RAIM

RAIM is a technique that uses an overdetermined solution to perform a consistency check. The RAIM algorithm is contained within the receiver and hence the term "autonomous" monitoring. Five satellites are used in the navigation solution to detect a satellite anomaly. This function is sufficient for supplemental airborne use of GPS. If a problem is detected, the pilot switches over to the primary onboard navigation system. For GPS to be used as a primary means of navigation, however, the system must not only be able to detect the presence of an anomaly, but it also must be able to remove the faulty satellite from the navigation solution. This can be done by identifying which satellite is causing the problem (referred to as isolation) or, alternatively, selecting another set of satellites that does include the anomalous satellite (denoted as exclusion). This capability is known as fault detection and isolation (FDI) or fault detection and exclusion (FDE).

For use of GPS as a primary navigation system, the RAIM algorithm works with six or more visible satellites. If an integrity problem is detected, the algorithm then forms n solutions of $n - 1$ satellites each, in order to isolate which satellite contains the anomaly and remove it from the navigation solution. As stated above, an alternative process is that the algorithm may work with a set of six satellites, even if more are visible. If a detection occurs, the algorithm searches for another set of six satellites with an HPL below the alert limit, thereby excluding the faulty satellite from the navigation solution, but not isolating which satellite caused the detection. This section discusses the basics of a "snapshot" RAIM algorithm that has been developed in support of RTCA SC-159 [29].

The linearized GPS measurement equation is given as

$$y = Hx + \epsilon \tag{7.84}$$

where

x is the 4×1 vector whose elements are incremental deviations from the nominal state about which the linearization takes place. The first three elements are the east, north, and up aircraft position components, and the fourth element is the aircraft receiver clock bias.

y is the $n \times 1$ vector whose elements are the differences between the noisy measured pseudoranges and the predicted ones based on the nominal position and clock bias (i.e., the linearization point). The value n is the number of visible satellites (number of measurements).

H is the $n \times 4$ linear connection matrix between x and y. It consists of three columns of direction cosines and a fourth column containing the value 1, which corresponds to the receiver clock state.

ϵ is the $n \times 1$ measurement error vector. It may contain both random and deterministic (bias) terms.

GPS RAIM is based on the self-consistency of measurements, where the number of measurements, n, is greater than or equal to 5. One measure of consistency is to work out the least squares estimate for x, substitute it into the right-hand side of (7.84), and then compare the result with the empirical measurements in y. The difference between them is called the range residual vector, w. In mathematical terms,

$$\hat{x}_{LS} = (H^T H)^{-1} H^T y \text{ (least squares estimate)}$$

$$\hat{y}_{LS} = H\hat{x}_{LS}$$

$$w = y - \hat{y}_{LS} = y - H(H^T H)^{-1} H^T y = [I_n - H(H^T H)^{-1} H^T]y$$
$$= [I_n - H(H^T H)^{-1} H^T](Hx + \epsilon) = [I_n - H(H^T H)^{-1} H^T]\epsilon \qquad (7.85)$$

Since ϵ is not known to the user aircraft, (7.85) is only used in simulations. Let

$$S \equiv I_n - H(H^T H)^{-1} H^T \qquad (7.86)$$

where I_n is the $n \times n$ unit matrix. Then, the $n \times 1$ range residual vector, w, is given as

$$w = Sy, \text{ (used by aircraft)}$$

or

$$w = S\epsilon, \text{ (used in the simulations)}$$

The range residual vector, w, could be used as a measure of consistency. This is not ideal, however, because there are four constraints (associated with the four unknown components of the vector x) among the n elements of w, which obscure some of the aspects of the inconsistency that are of interest. Therefore, it is useful to perform a transformation that eliminates the constraints and transforms the information contained in w into another vector known as the parity vector, p. Performing a transformation on y,

$$p = Py$$

where the parity transformation matrix P is defined as an $(n - 4) \times n$ matrix, which can be obtained by QR factorization of the H matrix [30]. The rows of P are: mutually orthogonal, unity in magnitude, and mutually orthogonal to the columns of H. Due to these defining properties, the resultant p has special properties, especially with respect to the noise [29]. If ϵ has independent random elements that are all $N(0, \sigma^2)$, then

$$p = Pw \qquad (7.87(a))$$

$$p = P\epsilon \qquad (7.87(b))$$

$$p^T p = w^T w \qquad (7.87(c))$$

These equations state that the same transformation matrix P that takes y into the parity vector, p, also takes either w or ϵ into p. The sum of the squared residuals is the same in both range space and parity space. In performing failure detection, it is much easier to work with p than with w.

Using a case of six visible satellites as an example, the following analysis demonstrates how the parity transformation affects a deterministic error in one of the range measurements. Suppose there is a range bias error, b, in satellite 3. From (7.87(b)),

$$p = \begin{bmatrix} P_{11} & P_{12} & P_{13} & \cdots & P_{16} \\ P_{21} & P_{22} & P_{23} & \cdots & P_{26} \end{bmatrix} \begin{bmatrix} 0 \\ 0 \\ b \\ 0 \\ 0 \\ 0 \end{bmatrix} \text{ or }$$

$$p = b \times (\text{3rd column of P})$$

The third column of P defines a line in parity space called the characteristic bias line associated with satellite 3. Each satellite has its own characteristic bias line. The magnitude of the parity bias vector induced by the range bias b, is given by

|parity bias vector| = $b \cdot |(\mathbf{P}_{13}\ \mathbf{P}_{23})^T|$, (bias on satellite 3, assuming $b > 0$)

where $|(\mathbf{P}_{13}\ \mathbf{P}_{23})^T| = \sqrt{\mathbf{P}_{13}^2 + \mathbf{P}_{23}^2}$. In general,

(range bias, b, on ith satellite) =
$$\text{(norm of parity bias vector)/(norm of } i\text{th column of } \mathbf{P})$$

The position error vector $\mathbf{e}$ is defined as: $\mathbf{e} = \hat{\mathbf{x}}_{LS} - \mathbf{x}$

$$\mathbf{e} = (\mathbf{H}^T\mathbf{H})^{-1}\mathbf{H}^T\mathbf{y} - \mathbf{x}$$
$$= (\mathbf{H}^T\mathbf{H})^{-1}\mathbf{H}^T(\mathbf{H}\mathbf{x} + \boldsymbol{\epsilon}) - \mathbf{x}$$
$$= (\mathbf{H}^T\mathbf{H})^{-1}\mathbf{H}^T\boldsymbol{\epsilon} \text{ (Vector position error)}$$

$$\text{(position error vector)} = (\mathbf{H}^T\mathbf{H})^{-1}\mathbf{H}^T \begin{bmatrix} 0 \\ 0 \\ b \\ 0 \\ 0 \\ 0 \end{bmatrix}$$

These equations provide a means of getting back and forth from a bias in parity space to the corresponding bias in range space, and finally to the corresponding position error. The norm of the first two components of the position error vector provide the horizontal radial position error.

The objective is to protect against excessive horizontal position error. The RAIM algorithm must detect if the horizontal error goes beyond a certain threshold within a specified level of confidence. Since the position error cannot be observed directly, something must be inferred from the quantity that can be observed, which in this case is the parity vector.

The magnitude of the parity vector is used as the test statistic (mathematical indicator) for detection of a satellite failure. The inputs to the parity space algorithm are the standard deviation of the measurement noise, the measurement geometry, as well as the maximum allowable probabilities for a false alarm and a missed detection. The output of the algorithm is the horizontal protection level (HPL), which defines the smallest horizontal radial position error that can be detected for the specified false alarm and missed detection probabilities.

The parity space method is based on modeling the test statistic using a chi distribution with $n - 4$ degrees of freedom for six or more visible satellites. The sum of the squared measurement residuals has a chi-square distribution. A Gaussian distribution is used for the case where five satellites are in view. The general formulas for the chi-square density functions are provided below.

For a central chi-square,

$$f_{cent}(x) = \frac{x^{k/2-1}e^{-x/2}}{2^{k/2}\Gamma(k/2)} \text{ defined for } x > 0$$
$$= 0 \qquad\qquad x \leq 0$$

where Γ is the gamma function.

For a noncentral chi-square,

$$f_{n.c.}(x) = \frac{e^{-(x+\lambda)/2}}{2^{k/2}} \sum_{j=0}^{\infty} \frac{\lambda^j x^{k/2+j-1}}{\Gamma(k/2 + j)2^{2j}j!} \text{ defined for } x > 0$$
$$= 0 \qquad\qquad\qquad x \leq 0$$

where λ is the noncentrality parameter. It is defined in terms of the normalized mean m and the number of degrees of freedom k, as $\lambda = km^2$.

The chi-square density functions for a case of six visible satellites (2 degrees of freedom) are shown in Figure 7.36. These density functions are used to define the detection threshold to satisfy the false alarm and missed detection probabilities.

For supplemental navigation, the maximum allowable false alarm rate is one alarm per 15,000 samples or 0.002/hr. One sample is considered to be a 2-min interval based on the correlation time of SA. The maximum false alarm rate for GPS primary means navigation is 0.333×10^{-6} per sample. The minimum detection

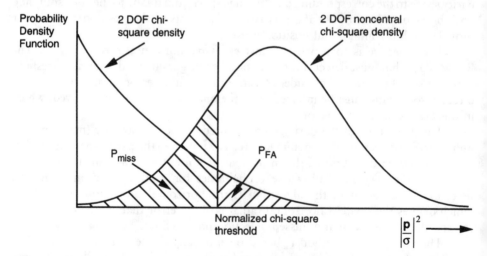

Figure 7.36 Chi-square density functions for 2 degrees of freedom.

probability for both supplemental and primary means of navigation is 0.999, or a missed detection rate of 10^{-3} [31].

Figure 7.37 displays a linear no-noise model of the estimated horizontal position error versus the test statistic, forming a characteristic slope line for each visible satellite. These slopes are a function of the linear connection, or geometry matrix, $\mathbf{H}$, and vary slowly with time as the satellites move about their orbits. The slope associated with each satellite is given by

$$\text{SLOPE}(i) = \frac{\sqrt{A_{1i}^2 + A_{2i}^2}}{\sqrt{S_{ii}}} \text{ for } i = 1, 2, 3, \ldots, n$$

where

$$A \equiv (\mathbf{H}^T\mathbf{H})^{-1}\mathbf{H}^T$$

and $\mathbf{S}$ was defined previously in (7.86), but also can be computed directly from $\mathbf{P}$ as

$$\mathbf{S} = \mathbf{P}^T\mathbf{P}$$

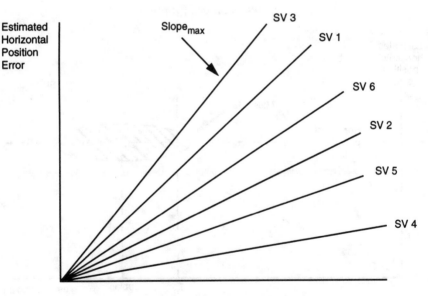

Figure 7.37 Characteristic slopes for six visible satellites.

For a given position error, the satellite with the largest slope has the smallest test statistic and will be the most difficult to detect. Therefore, there is a poor coupling between the position error to be protected and the magnitude of the parity vector that can be observed when a bias actually occurs in the satellite with the maximum slope.

The oval-shaped "cloud of data" shown in Figure 7.38 is a depiction of the scatter that would occur if there were a bias on the satellite with the maximum slope. This bias is such that the fraction of data to the left of the detection threshold is equal to the missed detection rate. Any bias smaller than this value will move the data cloud to the left, increasing the missed detection rate beyond the allowable limit. This critical bias value in parity space is denoted as pbias. The pbias term is completely deterministic, but it is dependent on the number of visible satellites [29]:

$$\text{pbias} = \sigma_{\text{UERE}}\sqrt{\lambda}$$

where λ is the noncentrality parameter of the noncentral chi-square density function and σ_{UERE} is the standard deviation of the satellite pseudorange measurement error.

The HPL is determined by

$$\text{HPL} = \text{Slope}_{\text{max}} \times \text{pbias}$$

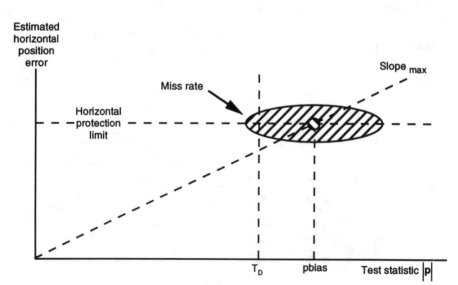

Figure 7.38 Scatter plot with critical bias on Slope$_{\text{max}}$ satellite.

The HPL is then compared to the maximum alert limit for the appropriate phase of flight (see Table 7.5).

If the HPL is below the alert limit, RAIM is said to be available for that phase of flight. Since the HPL is dependent on the satellite geometry, it must computed for each location and point in time. The RAIM algorithm works with a minimum of five visible satellites to calculate the HPL. If the HPL exceeds the alert limit when GPS is being used as a supplemental airborne NAVAID, the pilot switches over to the primary navigation system.

Availability of RAIM

Since RAIM requires a minimum of five visible satellites in order to perform fault detection and a minimum of six for fault detection and isolation/exclusion, it will have a lower availability than the navigation function. An analysis of the 24 satellites has been performed to evaluate the availability of RAIM over the Conterminous U.S. (CONUS) [32–35].

At a 7.5° mask angle, the availability of RAIM fault detection is well above 99% for the en route and terminal phases of flight and 94.4% for nonprecision approaches. In order to improve availability, the barometric altimeter can be included as an additional measurement in the RAIM solution. With baro aiding, availability improves to nearly 100% for en route navigation and 99.9% for the terminal phase of flight. The maximum outage durations are decreased by a factor of two, to 5 min for en route and 10 min during terminal navigation. Availability also increases to greater than 99% for nonprecision approaches as well, with a maximum outage duration of 40 min.

The availability of fault detection and isolation with baro aiding ranges from 68.3% during nonprecision approaches to 98.16% for en route navigation (FDI without baro aiding isn't considered in this analysis due to its low availability). For a nonprecision approach, FDI outages can last almost 2 hours at a location. These results are summarized in Tables 7.6 and 7.7.

Worldwide RAIM fault detection availability for a nonprecision approach at a 7.5° mask angle is displayed in Figure 7.39. This availability includes augmentation

Table 7.5
GPS Integrity Performance Requirements

Phase of Flight	Horizontal Alert Limit
En route	2 nmi
Terminal	1 nmi
NPA	0.3 nmi

Source: [31].

Table 7.6
RAIM Availability Over CONUS With a 7.5° Mask Angle

RAIM Function	En Route	Terminal	Nonprecision Approach
Fault detection	99.83%	99.65%	94.40%
Fault detection with baro aiding	99.993%	99.90%	99.20%
Fault detection and isolation with baro aiding	98.16%	91.70%	68.30%

Table 7.7
Maximum Duration of RAIM Outages Over CONUS With 7.5° Mask Angle

RAIM Function	En Route	Terminal	Nonprecision Approach
Fault detection	10 min	20 min	55 min
Fault detection with baro aiding	5 min	10 min	40 min
Fault detection and isolation with baro aiding	40 min	70 min	115 min

with the barometric altimeter. As shown in this figure, outages can last up to 50 min in several locations, but there is virtually 100% coverage near the equator. This high availability of RAIM near the equator is due to the increased number of visible satellites.

As discussed in Section 7.2, availability can be improved by lowering the mask angle. Tables 7.8 and 7.9 demonstrate the significant improvement in availability and reduction of outage duration when the mask angle is lowered to 5°.

Wide Area Augmentation System (WAAS)

As the results in the previous section demonstrate, GPS alone will not be able to provide the integrity of a primary means navigation system for most phases of flight. GPS must be augmented in order to improve the availability of integrity. The primary augmentation to GPS that the FAA is developing is the wide area augmentation system (WAAS). WAAS will provide additional ranging capability, integrity information, and differential corrections at the L1 frequency, which is broadcast from geostationary satellites. RAIM will provide system integrity when the aircraft is outside the WAAS coverage region or a catastrophic failure occurs. Elaboration on WAAS is provided in Chapter 11.

The initial four INMARSAT satellites that will broadcast the WAAS signal as an augmentation to GPS can be included in a similar analysis to that performed in Section 7.2 to determine the distribution of HDOP and PDOP. The same analysis

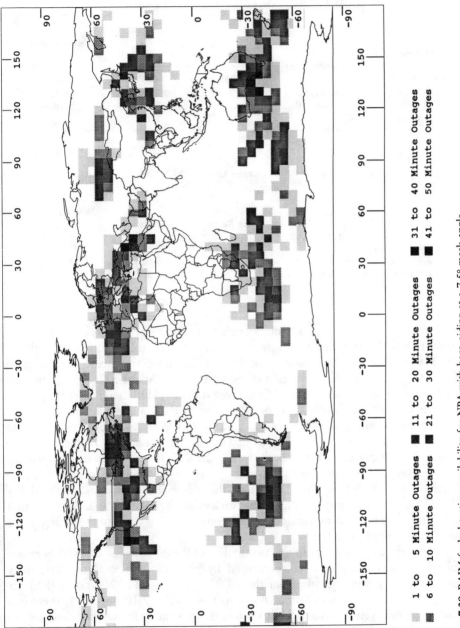

Figure 7.39 RAIM fault detection availability for NPA with baro aiding at a 7.5° mask angle.

Table 7.8
RAIM Availability Over CONUS With a 5° Mask Angle

RAIM Function	En Route	Terminal	Nonprecision Approach
Fault detection	99.98%	99.94%	97.26%
Fault detection with baro aiding	100%	99.991%	99.92%
Fault detection and isolation with baro aiding	99.73%	97.11%	81.40%

Table 7.9
Maximum Duration of RAIM Outages Over CONUS With 5° Mask Angle

RAIM Function	En Route	Terminal	Nonprecision Approach
Fault detection	5 min	10 min	35 min
Fault detection with baro aiding	0 min	5 min	15 min
Fault detection and isolation with baro aiding	25 min	55 min	100 min

was performed as before with a 5° mask angle and up to three satellites removed from the constellation in order to investigate the overall improvement in the availability of GPS. The locations of the ranging geostationary satellites are Pacific Ocean region (POR) at 180°, Indian Ocean region (IOR) at 64.5° E, Atlantic Ocean region west (AORW) at 55.5° W, and Atlantic Ocean region east (AORE) at 15.5° W.

The cumulative distributions of HDOP and PDOP augmented with the four geostationary satellites are displayed in Figures 7.40 and 7.41, respectively. Again applying a PDOP threshold of 6.0 to determine the availability of these satellite constellations, it can be seen that both the 24- and 23-satellite constellations provide coverage 100% of the time. With two satellites removed from the constellation, the availability is 99.97%, and with 21 satellites the constellation provides an availability of 99.65%. This is an improvement from an availability of 99.9% and 99.2% that the 22 and 21 satellite constellations respectively provided without the aiding of the geostationary satellites.

Next, the improvement in the availability of RAIM over the CONUS is examined when the constellation is augmented by geostationary satellites. The three geostationary satellites visible from the CONUS (POR, AORW, and AORE) are used to augment the constellation. As shown in Tables 7.10 and 7.11, there is a significant improvement in availability when the geostationary satellites are used to augment the constellation. There is 100% availability of fault detection if baro aiding also is included. The availability of FDI increases from 68.3% to 94.6% for

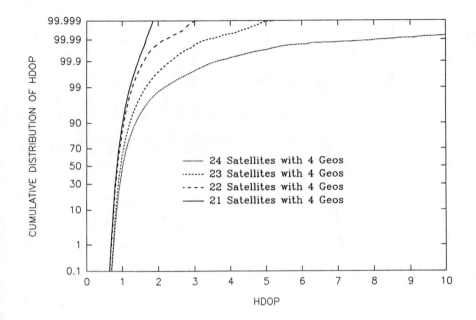

Figure 7.40 Cumulative distribution of HDOP with four geostationary satellites.

nonprecision approach when the geostationary satellites are added. Outage durations also are significantly reduced for all phases of flight.

When the mask angle is reduced to 5°, there is 100% availability of fault detection for the en route and terminal phases of flight. The availability for a nonprecision approach increases to 99.88% with a maximum outage duration of 15 min. There also is 100% availability of FDI for en route navigation when baro aiding is applied in conjunction with the geostationary satellites. The effect of reducing the mask angle is illustrated in Tables 7.12 and 7.13.

Table 7.10
RAIM Availability Over CONUS With a 7.5° Mask Angle
and Three Geostationary Satellites

RAIM Function	En Route	Terminal	Nonprecision Approach
Fault detection	99.997%	99.98%	99.32%
Fault detection and isolation	99.43%	98.12%	77.20%
Fault detection and isolation with baro aiding	99.98%	99.47%	94.60%

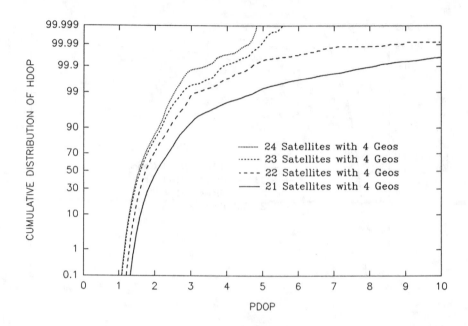

Figure 7.41 Cumulative distribution of PDOP with four geostationary satellites.

Table 7.11
Maximum Duration of RAIM Outages Over CONUS With a 7.5° Mask Angle and
Three Geostationary Satellites

RAIM Function	En Route	Terminal	Nonprecision Approach
Fault detection	5 min	15 min	30 min
Fault detection and isolation	25 min	60 min	190 min
Fault detection and isolation with baro aiding	15 min	40 min	85 min

Table 7.12
RAIM Availability Over CONUS With a 5° Mask Angle and Three Geostationary
Satellites

RAIM Function	En Route	Terminal	Nonprecision Approach
Fault detection	100%	100%	99.88%
Fault detection and isolation	99.90%	99.52%	89.37%
Fault detection and isolation with baro aiding	100%	99.91%	98.13%

Table 7.13
Maximum Duration of RAIM Outages Over CONUS With a 5° Mask Angle and
Three Geostationary Satellites

RAIM Function	En Route	Terminal	Nonprecision Approach
Fault detection	0 min	0 min	15 min
Fault detection and isolation	10 min	30 min	120 min
Fault detection and isolation with baro aiding	0 min	15 min	45 min

References

[1] Ward, P., "An Inside View of Pseudorange and Delta Pseudorange Measurements in a Digital NAVSTAR GPS Receiver," *International Telemetering Conference, GPS-Military and Civil Applications*, San Diego, CA, Oct. 14, 1981, pp. 63–69.

[2] Spilker, J. Jr., *GPS Signal Structure and Performance Characteristics*, GPS Papers in Navigation, Vol. 1, Institute of Navigation, 1980.

[3] DOD, *NAVSTAR GPS User Equipment Introduction (Public Release Version)*, GPS Joint Program Office, Feb. 1991.

[4] ARINC Research Corporation, *NAVSTAR GPS Space Segment/Navigation User Interfaces, Interface Control Document (ICD), NAVSTAR GPS, ICD-GPS-200, Rev. B-PR (Public Release Version)*, ARINC Research Corporation, Fountain Valley, California, 1991.

[5] Seeber, G., *Satellite Geodesy*, Berlin, Germany: Walter de Gruyter, 1993.

[6] Braasch, M. S., et al., "Improved Modeling Of GPS Selective Availability," *Proc. of the 1993 ION National Technical Meeting*, San Francisco, CA, Jan. 20–22, 1993, pp. 121–130.

[7] Doucet, K., and Y. Georgiadou, "The Issue of Selective Availability," *GPS World Magazine*, Advanstar Communications, Sept./Oct. 1990, pp. 53–56.

[8] Lear, W., M. Montez, L.Rater, and L. Zyla, "The Effect Of Selective Availability On Orbit Space Vehicles With SPS GPS Receivers," *ION GPS-92*, Albuquerque, NM, Sept. 16–18, 1992. pp. 825–840.

[9] Hatch, R., "Relativity and GPS-I," *Galilean Electrodynamics*, Vol. 6, No. 3, May/June 1995, pp. 52–57.

[10] Diggle, D., "An Investigation Into the Use of Satellite-Based Positioning Systems for Flight Reference/ Autoland Operations," Ph.D. Dissertation, Department of Electrical and Computer Engineering, Ohio University, Athens, Ohio, 1994.

[11] Hofmann-Wellenhof, B., H. Lichtenegger, and J. Collins, *GPS Theory and Practice*, New York, NY: Springer-Verlag, 1993.

[12] Jorgensen, P. S., "An Assessment of Ionospheric Effects on the User," *NAVIGATION: Journal of the Institute of Navigation*, Vol. 36, No. 2, Summer 1989.

[13] Uijt de Haag, M., and M. S. Braasch, *DGPS Signal Model, Vol. I, Reference: DGPS And Its Error Sources*, Athens, OH, Ohio University/Delft University of Technology, 1994.

[14] Smith, E. Jr., and S. Weintraub, "The Constants in the Equation for Atmospheric refractive Index at Radio Frequencies," *Proc. of the Institute of Radio Engineers*, No. 41, 1953.

[15] Remondi, B., "Using the Global Positioning System (GPS) Phase Observable for Relative Geodesy: Modeling, Processing, and Results," Ph.D. Dissertation, Center for Space Research, University of Austin, Austin, Texas, (1984).

[16] Goad, C., and L. Goodman, "A Modified Hopfield Tropospheric Refraction Correction Model," Paper presented at the Fall Annual Meeting of the American Geophysical Union, San Fransisco, California, 1974.

[17] Hopfield, H., "Two-quartic Tropospheric Refractivity Profile for Correcting Satellite Data," *Journal of Geophysical Research*, Vol. 74, No. 18, 1969.

[18] Saastomoinen, J., "Atmospheric Correction for the Troposphere and Stratosphere in Radio Ranging of Satellites," Use of Artificial Satellites for Geodesy, Geophysical Monograph 15, American Geophysical Union, Washington, DC, 1972.

[19] van Nee, R.D.J., "Spread-Spectrum Code and Carrier Synchronization Errors Caused by Multipath and Interference," *IEEE Transactions On Aerospace And Electronic Systems*, Vol. 29, No. 4, Oct. 1993.

[20] Breeuwer, E. J., "Modeling and Measuring GPS Multipath Effects," M.Sc. Thesis, Faculty of Electrical Engineering, Telecommunications and traffic Control Systems Group, Delft University of Technology, Delft, The Netherlands, 1991.

[21] Braasch, M. S., "On The Characterization Of Multipath Errors In Satellite-Based Precision Approach And Landing Systems," Ph.D. Dissertation, Department of Electrical and Computer Engineering, Ohio University, Athens, OH, 1992.

[22] Braasch, M. S., "Optimum Antenna Design for DGPS Ground Reference Stations," *Proc. of ION GPS-94, Seventh International Meeting of the Satellite Division of the Institute of Navigation*, Sept. 20–23, 1994, pp. 1291–1297.

[23] Leva, J. L., "Relationship between Navigation Vertical Error, VDOP, and Pseudo-range Error in GPS," *IEEE Transactions On Aerospace And Electronic Systems*, Vol. 30, No. 4, Oct. 1994, pp. 1138–1142.

[24] Nelson, W., "Use of Circular Error Probability in Target Detection," United States Air Force Hanscom Air Force Base, ESD-TR-88-109, May 1988.

[25] DOD/DOT, 1994 *Federal Radionavigation Plan*, DOT-VNTSC-RSPA-95-1 DOD-4650.5, May 1994.

[26] Ananda, M., J. Leung, P. Munjal, and B. Siegel, "RAIM Detection and Isolation Integrity Availability With and Without CAG," *Proc. of ION GPS-94, Seventh International Meeting of the Satellite Division of the Institute of Navigation*, Salt Lake City, UT, Sept. 20–23, 1994, pp. 619–630.

[27] Sotolongo, G. L., "Proposed Analysis Requirements for the Statistical Characterization of the Performance of the GPSSU RAIM Algorithm for Appendix A of the MOPS," RTCA 308-94/SC159-544, July 20, 1994.

[28] Shank, C., and J. Lavrakas, "GPS Integrity: An MCS Perspective," *Proc. of ION GPS-93, Sixth International Technical Meeting of the Satellite Division of the Institute of Navigation*, Salt Lake City, UT, Sept. 22–24, 1993, pp. 465–474.

[29] Brown, R. G., "GPS RAIM: Calculation of Thresholds and Protection Radius Using Chi-Square Methods-A Geometric Approach," RTCA 491-94/SC159-584, Dec. 1994.

[30] van Graas, F., P. A. Kline, "Hybrid GPS/LORAN-C," OU/AEC92-3TM00006/46+46A-1, July 1992.

[31] RTCA, "Minimum Operational Performance Standards for Airborne Supplemental Navigation Equipment Using Global Positioning System (GPS)," Document No. RTCA/DO-208, Prepared by: SC-159, July 1991.

[32] Van Dyke, K. L., "Analysis of Worldwide RAIM Availability for Supplemental GPS Navigation," DOT-VNTSC-FA360-PM-93-4, May 1993.

[33] Brown, R. G., G. Y. Chin, J. H. Kraemer, G. C. Nim, and K. L. Van Dyke, "ARP Fault Detection and Isolation: Method and Results," DOT-VNTSC-FA460-PM-93-21, Dec. 1993.

[34] Van Dyke, K. L., "RAIM Availability for Supplemental GPS Navigation," *NAVIGATION, Journal of the Institute of Navigation*, Vol. 39 No. 4, Winter 1992–93, pp. 429–443.

[35] Van Dyke, K. L., "Fault Detection and Exclusion Performance Using GPS and GLONASS," *Proc. of the ION National Technical Meeting*, Anaheim, CA, Jan. 18–20, 1995, pp. 241–250.

CHAPTER 8
▼▼▼

DIFFERENTIAL GPS

R. J. Cosentino
The MITRE Corporation

D. W. Diggle
Ohio University

8.1 INTRODUCTION

The GPS SPS provides accuracy of approximately 100m (2 drms, 95%) horizontally and 156m (95%) vertically [1]. Many civil applications require greater accuracy. For instance, the U.S. Coast Guard is requiring that GPS guidance error be limited to 8m to 20m for marine navigation in some harbors and restricted waterways [2], and to make this possible the Coast Guard is installing 50 DGPS onshore stations along the coastline—to be completed by January 1996—that will provide accuracies of under 5m up to a distance of 400-km offshore. Wide area DGPS (WADGPS) services are also available. In addition to the FAA WAAS scheduled for initial operation in 1997, there are private WADGPS services. Some private WADGPS services provide nearly global coverage [3, 4]. The offshore oil exploration and seismic survey industries aided the development of these private WADGPS systems and remain principle users. Further, the land surveying community is a prime DGPS user. Both the offshore industry and the land survey community pioneered and perfected many high-accuracy measurement techniques. In addition, geographical information systems (GIS) utilize DGPS and a data logger to establish a database of items and their corresponding locations. GIS is in use throughout industry and sectors such as forestry for inventory control. The FAA, with industry cooperation, is developing augmentations to standalone GPS that provide aircraft precision approach vertical guidance within 1m. Some automotive ITS applications require sufficient accuracy to determine the particular side of a street where a vehicle is located.

It is important to note that even with selective availability (SA) off, the standard positioning service (SPS) could not provide sufficient accuracy for these applications. Without SA, SPS accuracy would be on the order of 25m (2 drms, 95%) in the horizontal plane and 43m (95%) in the vertical plane.

The use of DGPS enhances standalone GPS accuracy and removes common (i.e., correlated) errors from two or more receivers viewing the same satellites. In the basic form of DGPS, one of these receivers is called the monitoring or reference receiver and is surveyed in; that is, its precise position is known. The other receivers are denoted as "rovers" or users and are in line of sight of the reference station. The reference station makes code-based GPS pseudorange measurements, just as any standard GPS receiver, but because the monitoring station knows its precise position, it can determine the "biases" in the measurements. For each satellite in view of the monitoring station, these biases are computed by differencing the pseudorange measurement and the satellite-to-reference station geometric range. These biases contain errors incurred in the pseudorange measurement process (e.g., ionospheric and tropospheric delay, receiver noise, etc.) and the receiver clock offset from GPS system time, t_m. For real-time applications, the reference station transmits these biases, which are called differential corrections, to all users in the coverage area. The users incorporate these corrections to improve the accuracy of their position solution, which is obtained in ECEF coordinates. DGPS achieves enhanced accuracy since the reference and user receivers experience common errors that can be removed by the user. Position errors less than 10m are typically realized.

Some pseudorange measurement errors are spatially correlated, so that with the basic *local area* DGPS (LADGPS) technique described above, the position solutions of users further away from the station will be less accurate than those closer to the monitoring station. This loss of accuracy due to spatial decorrelation can be improved with more sophisticated techniques that fall under the heading of WADGPS. Both LADGPS and WADGPS are discussed in Section 8.2.

To provide even greater, submeter accuracy, DGPS techniques that utilize phase information of the GPS satellite signal carrier frequencies have been developed and are being refined. These techniques are based on interferometric measurements of the satellite carrier frequencies and are occasionally referred to as "carrier phase tracking." Extremely high accuracies (≈ 20 cm in dynamic applications and millimeter level for static applications) can routinely be achieved by processing the received satellite signal Doppler frequencies. This frequency information is integrated to form phase measurements that are processed to achieve the aforementioned accuracies. These techniques are commonly used for offshore and land surveying as well as seismic studies. Interferometry can also provide the accuracy for aircraft Category III precision approach ("blind landing"). These measurement techniques can also be used to monitor the deflections in dams as a result of hydrostatic and thermal stress changes. Further, the high accuracy obtained from carrier phase measurements could be utilized by tectonic plate movement detection systems [2]. Interferometric techniques are discussed in Section 8.3.

8.2 CODE-BASED TECHNIQUES

Several code-based techniques have been proposed to increase standalone GPS accuracy. These techniques vary in sophistication and complexity from a single reference station that calculates the errors at its position for use with nearby GPS receivers to worldwide networks that provide data for estimating errors from detailed error models at any position near the Earth's surface. They are usually sorted into two categories, LADGPS and WADGPS, but there is no general agreement as to the precise meaning of these terms. For the purposes of this chapter, in LADGPS, each reference station shown in Figure 8.1 determines the pseudorange measurement errors at its location and passes this information to the users; in WADGPS, a network of monitoring stations determines and continually updates the time-varying and spatially varying components of the total error over the entire region of coverage and makes the correction values available to users within the coverage region.

8.2.1 Local Area DGPS

A LADGPS station typically serves receivers within close proximity. For aircraft using very high frequency (VHF) datalinks, the range is limited by the distance that the station can communicate with the receivers through direct line-of-sight data links. For the maritime services, which use medium frequency (MF), LADGPS is extended up to 400 km or more. As stated above, LADGPS accuracy depends on the fact that some of the pseudorange error components are common to all receivers within the local geographical area. If the receiver is close to the reference station, the error components attributed to the space and control segments may be entirely removed while the overall error contributed by the user segment may be reduced significantly. It is for this reason, the offshore industry utilizes wide area DGPS services; LADGPS is limited by spatial decorrelation of the errors.

Table 8.1 gives estimates of the pseudorange error components from various sources in the space, control, and user segments for the SPS. The total root-mean-square (rms) nondifferential pseudorange error is estimated to be 33.3m. Some of the error sources produce the same errors in any two receivers viewing the same satellites—timing errors arising from uncorrected satellite clock drift and SA dither. (The SA error component value used in Table 8.1 is estimated.) Other error sources are spatially correlated if the reference station and user receiver are collocated. As the two receivers move farther apart, the spatially correlated errors—uncorrected satellite perturbations (from such sources as tidal attractions, solar radiation pressure,

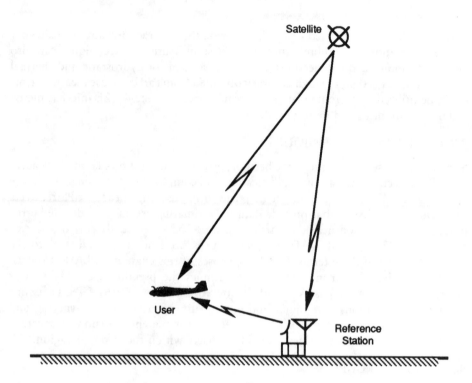

Figure 8.1 Local DGPS concept.

solar winds, and gas-propellant leakage, some of which are difficult to model), SA ephemeris error, ephemeris prediction error, and atmospheric errors—increasingly differ in the two receivers until they are essentially no longer correlated.

The last column in Table 8.1 shows the reduction in pseudorange error magnitude that is possible with DGPS when the user receiver is located close enough to the reference station such that the signal paths from the satellites to the user and reference station receiver are essentially identical. Errors from all sources, except multipath and those internal to the receiver (e.g., hardware propagation delays, called interchannel bias and noise), are completely correlated. Later in the chapter, we determine how the spatially correlated errors increase with increasing separation of the user from the reference station.

8.2.1.1   *Error-Reduction Techniques of LADGPS*

Conceptually, the simplest way to implement LADGPS is to place the GPS reference receiver at a surveyed location, compute the coordinate differences (in latitude,

Table 8.1
Estimated GPS C/A-Code Pseudorange Error Budget

Segment Source	Error Source	GPS 1σ Error (m)	LADGPS 1σ Error (m)
	Satellite clock stability	3.0	0
Space	Satellite perturbations	1.0	0
	Selective Availability	32.3	0
	Other (thermal radiation, etc.)	0.5	0
Control	Ephemeris prediction error	4.2	0
	Other (thruster performance, etc.)	0.9	0
User	Ionospheric delay	5.0	0
	Tropospheric delay	1.5	0
	Receiver noise and resolution	1.5	2.1
	Multipath	2.5	2.5
	Other (interchannel bias, etc.)	0.5	0.5
System UERE	Total (rms)	33.3	3.3

After: [1].

longitude, and geodetic height) between the GPS-derived position and the surveyed location, and transmit these differences to the users. The user receivers employ these coordinate differences to correct their own GPS position solutions. For the most part, the coordinate differences represent the common errors in the reference and user receiver GPS position solutions at the measurement time. This technique requires that all receivers make pseudorange measurements to the same set of satellites to ensure that common errors are experienced. Therefore, the user receivers must coordinate their choice of satellites with the reference station, or the reference station must determine and transmit position corrections for all combinations of visible satellites. When eight or more satellites are visible, the number of combinations becomes impractically large (80 or more combinations of 4 satellites), impelling the use of techniques that are simpler to implement.

Instead of determining position coordinate errors, the reference station can determine and disseminate pseudorange corrections. While this method was discussed above, the following provides associated mathematical treatment.

In order for the user receiver to accurately determine its position with respect to the Earth (e.g., for map-matching applications), the reference station must have accurate knowledge of its own position in Earth-centered Earth-fixed (ECEF) coordinates. Given that the reported position of the ith satellite is (x_i, y_i, z_i) and the reference station m is surveyed in at position (x_m, y_m, z_m), the geometric distance R_m^i, from the reference station to the satellite is

$$R_m^i = \sqrt{(x_i - x_m)^2 + (y_i - y_m)^2 + (z_i - z_m)^2}$$

The reference station then makes a pseudorange measurement ρ_m^i, to the ith satellite. This measurement consists of

$$\rho_m^i = R_m^i + \epsilon_{m,\text{space}} + \epsilon_{m,\text{control}} + \epsilon_{m,\text{user}} + c\delta t_m \qquad (8.1)$$

where $\epsilon_{m,\text{space}}$, $\epsilon_{m,\text{control}}$, $\epsilon_{m,\text{user}}$ are the space, control, and user segment pseudorange errors, respectively, tabulated in Table 8.1 and δt_m represents the reference station clock offset from GPS system time.

The reference station differences the pseudorange measurement with the geometric range, R_m^i, to form the differential correction

$$\Delta\rho_m^i = \rho_m^i - R_m^i = \epsilon_{m,\text{space}} + \epsilon_{m,\text{control}} + \epsilon_{m,\text{user}} + c\delta t_m$$

This correction is uplinked to the user receiver, where it is differenced with the user receiver's pseudorange measurement to the same satellite:

$$\rho_u^i - \Delta\rho_m^i = R_u^i + \epsilon_{u,\text{space}} + \epsilon_{u,\text{control}} + \epsilon_{u,\text{user}} + c\delta t_u$$
$$- (\epsilon_{u,\text{space}} + \epsilon_{u,\text{control}} + \epsilon_{u,\text{user}} + c\delta t_m)$$

For the most part, the user receiver's pseudorange error components will be identical to those experienced by the reference station with the exception of multipath and receiver noise. The corrected pseudorange can be expressed as

$$\rho_{u,\text{cor}}^i = R_u^i + \epsilon_u' + c\delta t_{\text{combined}} \qquad (8.2)$$

where ϵ_u' represents residual user segment errors and $\delta t_{\text{combined}}$ is the combined clock offset.

Rewriting (8.2) in Cartesian coordinates yields

$$\rho_{u,\text{cor}}^i = \sqrt{(x_i - x_u)^2 + (y_i - y_u)^2 + (z_i - z_u)^2} + \epsilon_u' + c\delta t_{\text{combined}} \qquad (8.3)$$

By making pseudorange measurements to four or more satellites, the user receiver position can be computed by using one of the position determination techniques discussed in Chapter 2.

Because pseudorange corrections are transmitted at discrete times by the reference station and the satellite motion causes changes in the pseudorange error that changes significantly between transmissions, the transmitted error correction

$$\Delta\rho_m^i(t_m) = -[\rho_m^i(t_m) - R_m^i(t_m)]$$

the negative of its pseudorange error, is accurate only at the instant of time t_m for which the correction was calculated. To enable the user receiver to compensate for this motion, the station also transmits a pseudorange rate correction, $\Delta\dot{\rho}_m^i(t_m)$. The user receiver then adjusts the pseudorange correction to correspond to the time of its own pseudorange measurement, t, as follows:

$$\Delta\rho_m^i(t) = \Delta\rho_m^i(t_m) + \Delta\dot{\rho}_m^i(t_m) \cdot (t - t_m)$$

The corrected user receiver pseudorange is then calculated:

$$\rho_{cor}^i(t) = \rho^i(t) + \Delta\rho_m^i(t)$$

(Note that the pseudorange subscript u is dropped since the corrected pseudorange pertains only to the user receiver.) Even with the pseudorange rate correction, the receiver pseudorange will be in error as time interval $t - t_m$ increases, owing to the radial acceleration of the satellite. Figure 8.2 shows the case for a satellite in an overhead orbit. At the maximum acceleration of 0.2 m/sec/sec, the uncorrected error

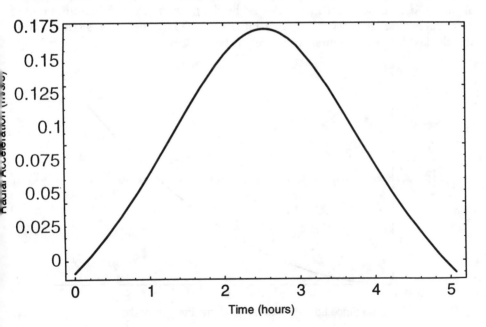

Figure 8.2 Radial acceleration of a satellite whose orbit passes overhead.

due to radial acceleration as a function of time is shown in Figure 8.3. A 1m error can accumulate in only 3 sec at that acceleration if the pseudorange corrections are not applied. However, because this acceleration is predictable and slowly changing, it can be readily estimated from the changes in the pseudorange rate correction. More problematic is the changing SA error, which from the user's perspective is less predictable. Suppose for an example, there is a change of 4 mm/sec/sec in the second derivative of dither in SA. This will cause a pseudorange error of 20 cm in 10 sec or an error of 0.8m in 20 sec. Updating the pseudorange and pseudorange rate corrections at 2-sec intervals will keep the errors due to SA below a centimeter.

8.2.1.2 *Message Format*

Protocols have been defined for communications between reference stations and users so that users can interpret the data transmitted by the stations. Several protocols have been developed throughout industry, but the one defined by the Radio Technical Commission for Maritime Services (RTCM) Study Committee 104 (SC-104) has been accepted by the international community and is in widespread use [5]. As shown in Figure 8.4, the RTCM-104 basic frame format consists of a variable number of 30-bit words, the first two of which form the header information. The first word of the header, shown in Figure 8.5, contains an 8-bit preamble, consisting of the fixed sequence 0110110, followed by the *frame ID*, which identifies one of 64 possible message types. Next, a 12-bit *station ID* identifies the reference station and the last 8 bits of the first word are parity check bits.

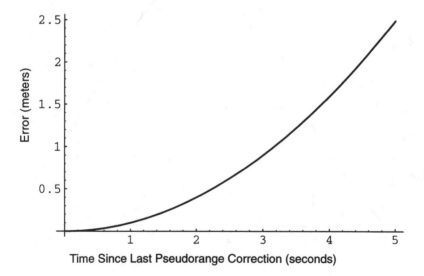

Figure 8.3 Uncorrected pseudorange error due to maximum satellite acceleration.

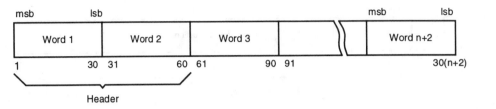

Figure 8.4 RTCM SC-104 DGPS message frame.

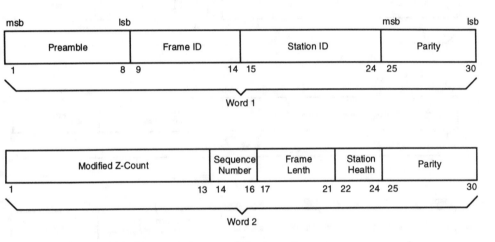

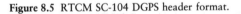

Figure 8.5 RTCM SC-104 DGPS header format.

The first 13 bits of the second word, the *modified Z-count*, comprise the time reference for the message. The following three bits form the *sequence number*, which increments on each frame and is used to verify frame synchronization. The frame length is needed to identify the beginning of the next frame, since the length of the frame is variable depending on the message type and the number of satellite reports. The 3-bit *station health* provides an estimate of the differential error, and the last 8 bits provide an error check.

Message Format 1 (Differential Correction Data)

Following the standard two-word header, the first bit of this message format, shown in Figure 8.6, is used as a scale factor for the data set. (Scale factor particulars are described in the following paragraph.) This is succeeded by the user differential range error (UDRE), also described below, and then by 5 bits that identify which satellite the data set belongs to are given as well as parity bits. This message structure

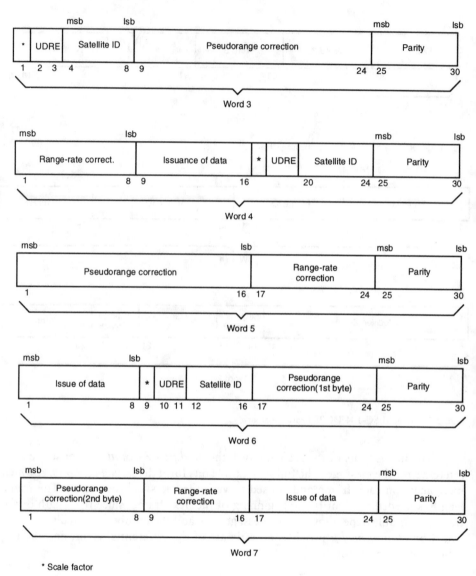

Figure 8.6 Message Type 1 format.

also provides the pseudorange correction $\Delta\rho_m^i(t_m)$, range-rate correction $\Delta\dot{\rho}_m^i(t_m)$, and the time (the *modified Z-count*) t_m. Words 3 through 7 are repeatedly broadcast with data for all satellites in view of the reference station.

The first bit of Word 3 is a scale factor, either 0.02m for the pseudorange correction and 0.002m/sec for the range rate correction or 0.32m for the pseudorange correction and 0.032m/sec for the range rate correction. The 2-bit UDRE (Table 8.2) gives an estimate of the uncertainty in the pseudorange correction determined by the reference station. The satellite ID identifies the satellite to which the subsequent pseudorange and range rate corrections pertain. The issuance of data identifies the set of orbital and clock parameters that the reference station used to calculate the corrections. If the user receiver is using older orbital and clock parameters than the reference station, it can use the data available in the Type 2 message (described below) to correct for the difference in orbital and clock parameters.

Message Type 2 Format (Delta Differential Correction Data)

Periodically, the satellite updates the orbital and clock parameters transmitted to the receivers. If the reference station transmits pseudorange corrections based on this new data before a user receiver has updated its data base with these new parameters, then the user receiver uses Message Type 2, which contains corrections to be applied to the pseudorange and range rate corrections to provide the proper adjustments when using the older orbital and clock parameters.

Particulars on the Type 1 and Type 2 message formats as well as those described below are contained in [5]. Further, Table 8.3 summarizes all 63 message types.

- Type 3 is a fixed six-word format that transmits the position of the reference station in ECEF coordinates with the least significant bit representing one centimeter.
- Type 4 was developed with surveying applications in mind and provided instantaneous phase measurements; however, it has been superseded by Message Types 18 to 21 and is now retired.

Table 8.2
Ranges of Estimated Standard Deviation in UDRE

Code	Range of Expected Standard Deviation
11	$8\text{m} < \sigma$
10	$4\text{m} < \sigma \leq 8\text{ m}$
01	$1\text{m} < \sigma \leq 4\text{ m}$
00	$\sigma \leq 1\text{ m}$

Table 8.3
Summary of RTCM SC-104 Message Types

Message Type	Status	Use
1	Fixed	C/A-code pseudorange (PR) corrections
2	Fixed	PR correction difference data for use with old orbital and clock parameters
3	Fixed	Reference station coordinates
4	Retired	No longer used; superseded by Types 18 to 21
5	Fixed	Satellite constellation health information
6	Fixed	Filler message (Alternating 1's and 0's in body of message)
7	Fixed	Radio beacon network description
8	Tentative	Pseudolite almanac information
9	Fixed	C/A-code PR corrections for subsets of satellites (3 or less)
10	Reserved	P-code differential corrections
11	Reserved	C/A-code L2 corrections
12	Reserved	Pseudolite station parameters
13	Tentative	Ground transmitter parameters
14	Reserved	Auxiliary message for surveying
15	Reserved	Ionosphere and troposphere correction measurements
16	Fixed	ASCII-coded messages for display
17	Tentative	Ephemeris almanac
18	Tentative	Uncorrelated carrier phase measurements
19	Tentative	Uncorrected PR measurements (for surveying)
20	Tentative	Corrections to the carrier phase measurements
21	Tentative	Corrections to the PR measurements
22 to 58	—	Undefined
59	Tentative	Proprietary message
60 to 63	Reserved	Multipurpose messages

After: [5].

- Type 5 messages are concerned with satellite health. Type 6 messages serve as filler, if needed; they consist of simply the two-word header or the two-word header plus a third word consisting of 24 alternating 1s and 0s, followed by the 6-bit parity check.
- Type 7 messages provide information on a network of maritime radio beacons that serve as reference stations, including identification, location, service range, and health. This message type was developed to provide the information needed to allow maritime user receivers to switch automatically from reference station to reference station as they move along the coast. Beacon position information is coarse, but accurate enough to determine the next nearest station.
- Type 8 messages provide almanac information on pseudolites, and are transmitted by the pseudolites.

- Type 9 messages provide the same information as Type 1 messages, but each message contains correction data on only a subset of all the satellites visible— three or fewer. This message type allows a faster update of fast-changing corrections, especially those due to SA. Because the corrections have different time references, they require a more stable clock than Type 1 messages.
- Type 10 messages are reserved for differential corrections of P(Y)-code users.
- Type 11 messages are reserved for differential corrections of C/A-code users, in the event that C/A-code is ever transmitted on the L2 frequency.
- Type 12 messages are reserved for pseudolites to transmit clock offset parameters and the location of the antenna phase center.
- Type 13 messages give the position of the transmitter sending the differential corrections. They also contain a status bit that indicates an unusual occurrence, the details of which may be found in Type 16 messages.
- Type 14 messages are reserved for surveying applications.
- Type 15 messages are reserved for ionospheric and tropospheric data. This message would carry measurement data for more accurate modeling of the atmospheric delays than receiver models can provide without the data.
- Type 16 messages are special messages containing ASCII characters that can be displayed on a screen or printed out.
- Type 17 messages contain satellite ephemeris information. This would allow the use of DGPS for a satellite transmitting incorrect ephemeris data. The DGPS transmitter would continue to send the old valid ephemeris until the satellite error is corrected or the satellite is no longer in view.
- Types 18 to 21 contain pseudorange and carrier phase data and corrections that support real-time kinematic applications and relative DGPS positioning.

8.2.1.3 Spatial Limits to the Accuracy of LADGPS

Table 8.1 estimates the errors in DGPS when the user is collocated with the reference station. As the user receiver moves away from the reference station, those common errors that are spatially correlated become increasingly decorrelated. In this section, we develop expressions that allow a rough estimate of the errors introduced by spatial decorrelation. For tropospheric and ionospheric delays, models are used to determine delays that depend on variable parameters that change over space and time. For example, in the ionospheric model, the delay depends directly on the total electronic content (TEC), which varies more than two orders of magnitude, so that we have to calculate either bounds on the delays or typical delays. Nevertheless, these expressions give us an idea of the magnitudes of the various error components that we may expect as the user moves away from the reference station.

Errors Arising From the Viewing Angle and Satellite Position Estimation Error

The corrections needed for satellite perturbations, ephemeris prediction error, and the satellite position errors due to the SA ephemeris offset components all change with the viewing angle of the receiver. To determine the amount of change, let the separation between the user U and reference station M be denoted as p (Figure 8.7). We will refer to the actual orbital satellite position as the true position. The error in the estimated satellite position (i.e., broadcast ephemeris) is represented as ϵ_s. Let d_m and d'_m be the true and estimated distances, respectively, of the reference station to the satellite, and let d_u and d'_u be the corresponding distances of the user to the satellite. Let ϕ_m be the angle formed by the directions of the reference station to the user and to the actual satellite position. Let α be the angle formed by the directions of the reference station to the actual and estimated positions of the satellites, S and S', respectively. The Law of Cosines gives us the following two relationships:

$$d''^2_u = d'^2_m + p^2 - 2pd'_m\cos(\phi_m - \alpha')$$

$$d^2_u = d^2_m + p^2 - 2pd_m\cos\phi_m$$

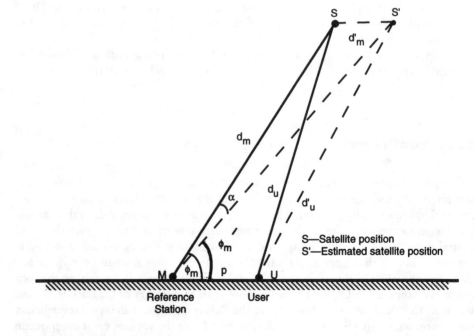

S—Satellite position
S'—Estimated satellite position

Figure 8.7 Variation of pseudorange correction with viewing angle.

where α' is the difference $\phi_m - \phi'_m$ in elevation angles between the actual and estimated satellite positions from the monitor station. (The absolute value of α' is less than or equal to the absolute value of α and the two are equal when the two triangles lie in the same plane.)

Solving the first equation for $d'_m - d'_u$ and the second for $d_u - d_m$, and neglecting the higher order terms in the binomial expansion of the square root in each of these equations, we obtain

$$d'_m - d'_u \approx -\frac{1}{2} \cdot \left(\frac{p}{d'_m}\right) \cdot p + p \cdot \cos\phi_m + \alpha'p \cdot \sin\phi_m + \frac{1}{2} \cdot \alpha'^2 p$$

$$d_u - d_m \approx +\frac{1}{2} \cdot \left(\frac{p}{d'_m}\right) \cdot p - p \cdot \cos\phi_m$$

Adding these two equations, we find that the difference between the errors, $\epsilon_u = d'_u - d_u$ and $\epsilon_m = d'_m - d_m$, is

$$\epsilon_m - \epsilon_u = (d'_u - d'_m) + (d_m - d_u) = \alpha'p \cdot \sin\phi_m + \frac{1}{2} \cdot \alpha'^2 p$$

or

$$|\epsilon_m - \epsilon_u| = |(d'_u - d'_m) + (d_m - d_u)| \leq \alpha \cdot p \cdot \sin\phi_m + \frac{1}{2} \cdot \alpha^2 p$$

where the equality holds if the estimated satellite position lies in the plane defined by the user position, reference station position, and true satellite position.

The difference $\epsilon_m - \epsilon_u$ is the error introduced by the pseudorange correction at the user.

To simplify the expression, assume that the angle ϕ_m is greater than $10°$, that the separation between the user and reference station is less than 1,000 km, and that the direction $\overline{SS'}$ is parallel to the direction $\overline{MU}$. Then,

$$\epsilon_m - \epsilon_u \leq \alpha \cdot p \cdot \sin\phi_m \approx \left(\frac{\epsilon_s \cdot \sin\phi_m}{d_m}\right) \cdot p \cdot \sin\phi_m = \left(\frac{\epsilon_s}{d_m}\right) \cdot p \cdot \sin^2\phi_m \quad (8.4)$$

Equation (8.4) implies that the error increases directly with the separation between the reference station measuring the error and the user receiver employing the correction. Suppose, for example, that the error in the satellite's estimated position is 10m and suppose the user is 100 km from the reference station. Then the error in the correction due to that separation is less than

$$\left(\frac{10\text{m}}{2 \times 10^4\text{km}}\right) \times 100\text{km} = 0.05\text{m} \tag{8.5}$$

for elevation angles $>10°$.

Errors From Tropospheric Delay

As discussed in Section 7.1.2.5, the speed of electromagnetic radiation varies, depending on temperature, pressure, and relative humidity, as it passes through the troposphere. Because these factors, in turn, depend on local conditions, such as cloudiness and precipitation, the correlation in the delays at two receivers due to the troposphere usually decreases more rapidly than for delays caused by the ionosphere. At a receiver separation of 100 km, the surface refractivities are uncorrelated and, thus, the difference in tropospheric delays are uncorrelated. Considerations of the physics behind tropospheric delay are provided in Section 7.1.2.5. In this section, we simply obtain an estimate of the kind of delay difference we can expect from the signal traveling through the troposphere and choose a model developed by Altshuler [6], which expresses the tropospheric delay of a signal from a GPS satellite to a user at the Earth's surface, as follows:

$$\epsilon_u^{\text{Tropo}} = \csc\phi(1.4588 + 0.0029611 \cdot N_s)$$
$$-0.3048[0.00586(N_s - 360)^2 + 294] \cdot \phi^{-2.30}$$

where

$\epsilon_u^{\text{Tropo}}$	=	tropospheric delay experienced by the user in meters
ϕ	=	elevation angle from the user to the satellite in degrees
N_s	=	surface refractivity

If we denote the elevation angle of the satellite from the reference station by ϕ_m, then from Figure 8.8 we can determine the difference $\csc\phi - \csc\phi_m$ in terms of the horizontal distance p between the user and reference station and the height d_s of the satellite, as follows:

$$\csc\phi - \csc\phi_m = \frac{d_u}{d_s} - \frac{d_m}{d_s} = \frac{d_u - d_m}{d_s} \approx p \cdot \frac{\cos\phi_m}{d_s}$$

where d_m is the distance from the monitoring station to the satellite and d_u is the distance from the user receiver to the satellite. This yields the following equation for the delay difference where, for the moment, N_s is assumed constant (less than 1.5 mm):

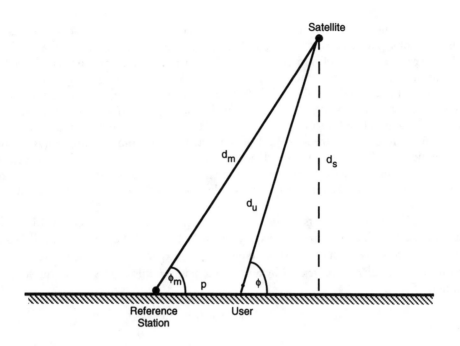

Figure 8.8 Horizontal tropospheric delay difference.

$$\epsilon_u^{\text{Tropo}} - \epsilon_m^{\text{Tropo}} \approx p \cdot \frac{\cos\phi_m}{d_s} \cdot (1.4588 + 0.0029611 \cdot N_s)$$

$$-0.3048 \cdot [0.00586 \cdot (N_s - 360)^2 + 294] \cdot (\phi^{-2.30} - \phi_m^{-2.30}) \quad (8.6)$$

The second term of the right member in (8.6) was added to fit data at low elevation angles—about 10° or less—and is negligible for useful GPS elevation angles (i.e., greater than 10°). Thus, the error in the correction is proportional to the separation between the user and reference station.

Suppose, for example, that the elevation angle is 45° and $p = 100$ km. Then, if we use a midrange value for N_s of 360, we find from the model that the deviation of the tropospheric correction at the user position differs from that at the reference station position by an amount

$$\epsilon_u^{\text{Tropo}} - \epsilon_m^{\text{Tropo}} = p \cdot \frac{\cos\phi_m}{d_s} \cdot (1.4588 + 0.0029611 \cdot N_s)$$

$$= 100\text{km} \cdot \frac{\cos 45°}{2 \times 10^4 \text{ km}} \cdot (1.4588 + 0.0029611 \times 360)$$

$$\approx 0.01\text{m}$$

Thus, the error is in the order of 1 cm. The variation of the deviation as a function of separation, refractivity, and elevation angle is shown in Figure 8.9. Note that over the entire 100-km separation, the variation of delay difference due to variation in the surface refractivity is less than 1.5 mm for this tropospheric model, an order of magnitude smaller than that due to a variation in elevation angle from 10° to 90°. Thus, allowing N_s to vary in the derivation of (8.6) would have produced a small, negligible additional term in (8.6). However, the total delay difference is also small. Even for extreme values of refractivity (400) and low angles (10°), the differences in delays are not much more than 1 cm. These small differences are expected to be exceeded in reality, due to the deviation of the actual troposphere from the model. However, we can conclude that the differences in delays will be small.

A difference in heights between the user receiver and the reference station has a greater effect than a horizontal displacement. Reference [6] develops the following relationship between the tropospheric delay ϵ_m^{Tropo}, experienced by the reference station and delay ϵ_h^{Tropo} experienced by a user at a height h kilometers above the station (Figure 8.10):

$$\epsilon_h^{Tropo} = \epsilon_m^{Tropo} \cdot e^{-\left[(0.0002N_s + 0.07)h + \left(\frac{0.83}{N_s} - 0.0017\right)h^2\right]}$$

At an altitude of 1 km above the reference station, the user experiences a delay of

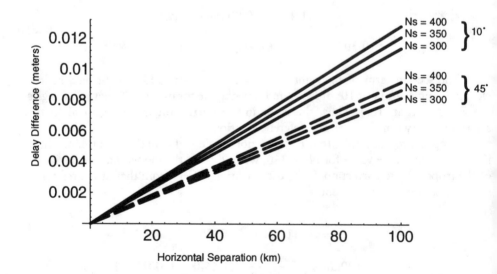

Figure 8.9 Variation in delay difference with refractivity and elevation angle.

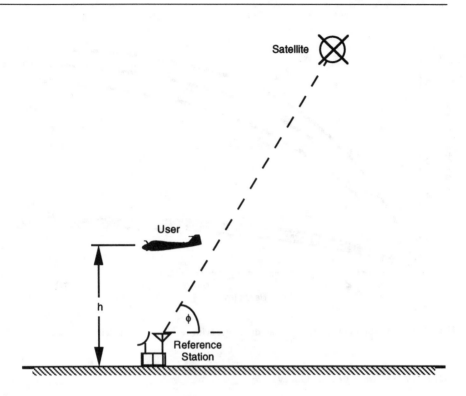

Figure 8.10 Vertical tropospheric delay difference.

$$\epsilon_h^{\text{Tropo}} = \epsilon_m^{\text{Tropo}} \cdot e^{-\left[(0.0002 \times 360 + 0.07) \times 1 + \left(\frac{0.83}{360} - 0.0017\right) \times 1^2\right]}$$

$$= 0.45 \times \epsilon_m^{\text{Tropo}} = 0.45 \times 3.6\text{m} = 1.6\text{m}$$

and the difference in delays is

$$\epsilon_m^{\text{Tropo}} - \epsilon_h^{\text{Tropo}} = 3.6 - 1.6 = 2\text{m}$$

That is, assuming $N_s = 360$ and that the elevation angle is 45°, the delay at a height of 1 km is only 45% of the 3.6m delay at the reference station, or 1.6m. The difference is 2m.

The variation in the difference in tropospheric delays between a signal reaching the ground having a refractivity of N_s and the signal at an altitude h above the ground is shown in Figure 8.11 for two difference elevation angles of the satellite.

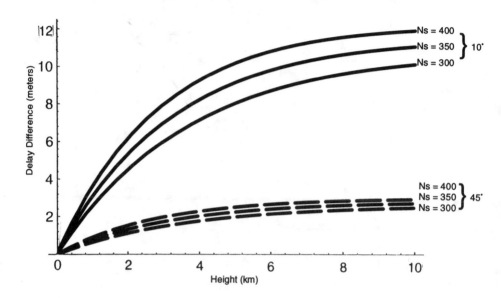

Figure 8.11 Variation in the vertical delay difference with refractivity and elevation angle.

Errors From Ionospheric Delay

As given in Section 7.1.2.5, we have the following relationship between the delay ϵ^{Iono}, expressed in units of length, due to the ionosphere; the frequency f of the signal; the elevation angle ϕ' at the ionospheric pierce point; and the total electron content (TEC) along the path of the signal:

$$\epsilon^{\text{Iono}} = \frac{1}{\sin \phi'} \cdot \frac{40.3}{f^2} \cdot \text{TEC}$$

The $\sin \phi'$ term account for the direction of the satellite from the vertical. The *ionospheric pierce point* is that point on the displacement vector from the user position to the satellite position midway through the ionosphere, typically taken to be 300 km to 400 km in altitude [7] (see Figure 8.12). Angle ϕ' differs from angle ϕ because of ionospheric refraction.

The difference in delay due to a horizontal separation of user and reference station is

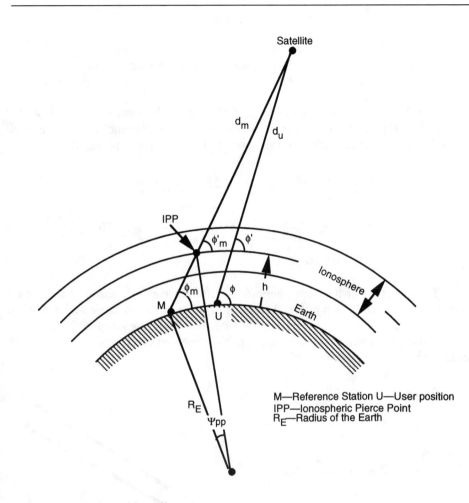

Figure 8.12 Ionospheric delay difference.

$$\epsilon_u^{\text{Iono}} - \epsilon_m^{\text{Iono}} = \frac{1}{\sin\phi'} \cdot \frac{40.3}{f^2} \cdot \text{TEC} - \frac{1}{\sin\phi'_m} \cdot \frac{40.3}{f^2} \cdot \text{TEC}$$

$$= \left(\frac{1}{\sin\phi'} - \frac{1}{\sin\phi'_m}\right) \cdot \frac{40.3}{f^2} \cdot \text{TEC}$$

$$= \frac{p}{d_m} \cdot \left(\frac{p}{d_m} - \cos\phi'_m\right) \cdot \frac{40.3}{f^2} \cdot \text{TEC} \tag{8.7}$$

where

p = distance between the user and the reference station
ϕ_m = elevation angle of the satellite from the reference station
ϕ_m' = elevation angle at the reference station's ionospheric pierce point

The TEC usually lies in the range 10^{16} to 10^{18} electrons/m^2, with 50×10^{16} electrons/m^2 typical in the temperate zones, so that the difference in delays experienced by the reference station and the user 100 km away is typically [8]

$$|\epsilon_u^{\text{Iono}} - \epsilon_m^{\text{Iono}}| = \left|\frac{p}{d_m} \cdot \left(\frac{p}{d_m} - \cos\phi_m'\right) \cdot \frac{40.3}{f^2} \cdot \text{TEC}\right|$$

$$\approx \left|-\frac{100 \text{ km}}{2 \times 10^4 \text{km}} \cdot \cos 45° \cdot \frac{40.3}{(1.575 \times 10^9)^2} \cdot 50 \times 10^{16}\right|$$

$$= 0.03\text{m}$$

The variation of the ionospheric delay difference as a function of separation is shown in Figure 8.13 for three values of satellite elevation angle and a TEC of 50×10^{16} electrons/m^2. At some point beyond the 100-km separation shown in the graphs, the curves will cease to be linear as the effects of variations in the TEC with distance become apparent.

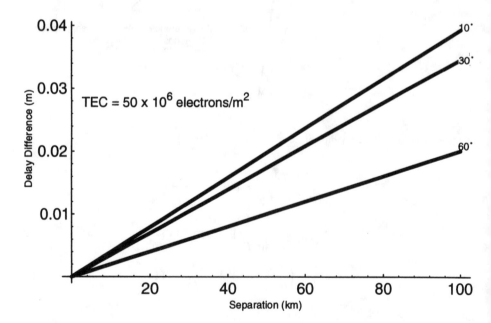

Figure 8.13 Variation of ionospheric delay difference with receiver separation.

From (8.4), (8.6), and (8.7), we have that the difference in delays experienced by the user and reference stations owing to different viewing angles and to tropospheric and ionospheric phenomena varies directly with the horizontal distance between them. The rate at which the differences increase with distance depends on factors that vary with time. Typical differences for separations of 100 km are found to be about 1m, except for the effect of the troposphere on altitude differences. These differences in the delays translate to differences in pseudorange measurement errors with the effect on the position solution also being a function of the dilutions of precision.

8.2.1.4 *Extending the Range of Accurate DGPS*

To extend the region over which DGPS corrections can be made without the decorrelation that accompanies the separation of the user from the station, three or more reference stations may be distributed along the perimeter of the region of coverage. The user receiver then obtains a more accurate correction estimate by a weighted average of the corrections from the stations. Because the error in the estimated corrections varies with distance from the station, the weights may be determined by geometric considerations alone to give the largest weight to the closest station, such as by choosing those weights that describe the user position as the weighted sum of the station positions [9]. For example, with three stations at locations denoted by latitude ϕ and longitude λ, the three weights w_1, w_2, and w_3 of stations $M_1(\phi_1, \lambda_1)$, $M_2(\phi_2, \lambda_2)$ and $M_3(\phi_3, \lambda_3)$ for user $U(\phi, \lambda)$ may be determined by the following set of three equations (Figure 8.14):

$$\phi = (w_1 \cdot \phi_1 + w_2 \cdot \phi_2 + w_3 \cdot \phi_3)$$
$$\lambda = (w_1 \cdot \lambda_1 + w_2 \cdot \lambda_2 + w_3 \cdot \lambda_3)$$
$$(w_1 + w_2 + w_3) = 1$$

Lapucha [3] describes a two-step approach to using multiple monitoring stations to improve the accuracy of the user's position estimate. In the first step, the pseudorange corrections from each monitor are used to determine the position of the user individually. The second step entails computing a weighted average of the individual position estimates to provide a more accurate estimate. Each weight is formed from the inverse of the product of the distance of the monitor from the user and the standard deviation from the average of the estimates from that station, normalized by the sum of the weights. The error introduced by each monitor receiver is thus diluted by its weight, so that if, for example, the weights were all equal, then each monitor receiver error would be diluted by a factor of $1/n$. But since the errors are uncorrelated, the standard deviation of their sum is $1/\sqrt{n}$; thus, the standard deviation of the total error due to the monitors is decreased by a factor of $\sqrt{n}$ from that of one monitor.

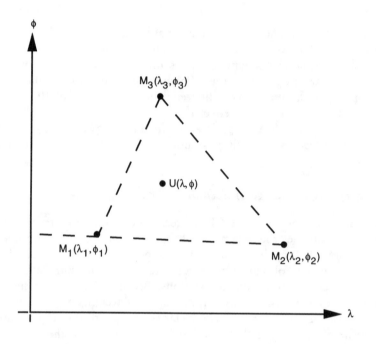

Figure 8.14 Calculating the correction weights.

In addition, the approach that Lapucha describes has a feature usually found only in WADGPS: the components of the total pseudorange error due to tropospheric and ionospheric delays are calculated using tropospheric and ionospheric delay models. These delays are then removed from the range residuals and the variance of the range residuals are compared to a threshold to check for excessive magnitude. If the variance for any station is too large, its measurements are not used in forming the weighted average of the position estimate. This test provides a means of testing and isolating a faulty monitoring station.

In the next section, we consider the WAAS system that calculates a weighted average of four corrections to compensate for ionospheric delays.

8.2.2 Wide Area DGPS

WADGPS attempts to attain meter-level accuracy over a large region by using a fraction of the number of reference stations required by LADGPS to attain the same accuracy within the same coverage region. The general approach—in contrast to that of LADGPS—is to break out the total pseudorange error into its components and to estimate each component for the entire region, rather than just at the station positions.[1] The accuracy, then, does not depend on the closeness of the user to a single reference station.

The WADGPS concept includes a network of reference stations that aid in the accurate determination of satellite ephemerides, atmospheric delay, and discrepancies between GPS system time and satellite time tags (i.e., Z-count). Thoughts vary on the architecture of the intercommunications among these networks. The simplest concept perhaps is a system having a master control station that accepts the measurements from all the reference stations distributed throughout the region of coverage (which could include a continent or even the entire world) and updates the satellite ephemeris predictions, estimates the uncorrected satellite clock drift and SA dither, and keeps track of the temporally and spatially varying atmospheric delays (Figure 8.15). For large or far-ranging systems, this architecture places a severe burden on one master control station and on the communications system to produce updates and distribute them to the reference stations reliably and in a timely manner. Regional control stations (RCS) (Figure 8.16) being closer to the reference stations and less burdened with processing, can more readily provide timely correction updates and provide active or standby redundancy to take over the functions of a neighboring regional control station, if necessary. These RCSs work in conjunction with one master control station. In this case, the master control station synchronizes the RCS clocks and performs various duties such as coordinating measurements on the satellite

Figure 8.15 Single MCS serving all RSs.

[1]See, Brown, A., "Extended Differential GPS," *Navigation: Journal of the Institute of Navigation*, Vol. 36, No. 3, Fall 1989, and Leick, A., *GPS Satellite Surveying*, New York, NY: John Wiley & Sons, 1990, for parallel discussions of the pseudorange components.

Figure 8.16 RCSs serving local RSs.

by different regional stations and monitoring the health of the RCS. This less central-ized architecture does have the problem of synchronizing the clocks in all RCSs and the master control station to one system time. Time synchronization amongst ele-ments of the ground control network is essential (just as with GPS itself) to ensure correction and measurement time-tagging. For example, the smooth switching to a redistribution of communications due to scheduled maintenance or unscheduled failure of a regional station is dependent on network time synchronization.

There are three basic types of errors that must be dealt with: errors in the satellite ephemeris estimates, errors in the reported satellite clock times (i.e., error between time reported by the satellite and GPS system time), and errors due to atmospheric delay (both tropospheric and ionospheric).

8.2.2.1 Satellite Ephemeris

Three sources of errors in the satellite ephemerides (satellite perturbations, satellite ephemeris prediction errors, and SA epsilon) are included in the SPS error budget of Table 8.1. These errors may be avoided by having a network of reference stations predict and transmit their own more accurate determinations of the satellite ephemer-ides, based on their own measurements. The reference stations then transmit the three-dimensional error in the reported ephemeris, or the ephemeris itself, so that the user receiver can accurately calculate the resulting pseudorange error at its own position.

One proposed approach to measuring satellite positions is to reverse the basic GPS algorithm. Here, four or more ground stations whose positions are accurately known each calculate the pseudorange to a given satellite after estimating and removing the atmospheric delays. If the ground stations have their clocks closely synchronized, they can accurately determine both the range to the satellite and the difference between the satellite time reports and their own system time. However, this technique encounters some of the same error sources as standalone GPS. Refinements have been sought that mitigate errors in the ground station measurement process.

One such technique, *double differencing*, removes errors arising in both the satellite and reference station to enhance the accuracy of satellite position estimates [8]. Measurements are made in sets, with each requiring two satellites and two reference stations. By differencing the pseudorange measurements made by each reference station to the same satellite, common satellite errors in the pseudoranges are eliminated.

Let:

1. $\rho^i_{m_1}$, $\rho^i_{m_2}$ = measured pseudoranges from monitor stations M_1 and M_2, respectively, to satellite S_i
2. $R^i_{m_1}$, $R^i_{m_2}$ = geometric ranges from monitor stations M_1 and M_2, respectively, to satellite S_i
3. $\Delta R^i_{m_1}$, $\Delta R^i_{m_2}$ = errors in the reported ephemerides
4. t^i = time of signal transmission from satellite S_i
5. δ^i = error in the reported satellite clock time
6. t_{m_1} and t_{m_2} be the time of signal reception at M_1 and M_2, respectively
7. δ_{m_1} and δ_{m_2} be the clock offsets from monitors M_1 and M_2, respectively

If the monitor station positions are accurately known, and if atmospheric delays are removed, then the pseudoranges can be expressed as

$$\rho^i_{m_1} = c(t_{m_1} - t^i) - c \cdot \delta^i + c \cdot \delta_{m_1}$$

$$\rho^i_{m_1} = R^i_{m_1} - c \cdot \delta^i + c \cdot \delta_{m_1}$$

Similarly,

$$\rho^i_{m_2} = R^i_{m_2} - c \cdot \delta^i + c \cdot \delta_{m_2}$$

Differencing the pseudoranges yields

$$\rho^i_{m_{12}} = \rho^i_{m_1} - \rho^i_{m_2} = R^i_{m_1} - R^i_{m_2} + c \cdot \delta_{m_1} - c \cdot \delta_{m_2} \tag{8.8}$$

It can be observed that the satellite errors common to both pseudorange measurements have canceled in (8.8). This term is denoted as the *single difference*.

A second single difference is computed by the same two stations using a second satellite S_j, yielding the following equation:

$$\rho^j_{m_{12}} = \rho^j_{m_1} - \rho^j_{m_2} = R^j_{m_1} - R^j_{m_2} + c \cdot \delta_{m_1} - c \cdot \delta_{m_2} \qquad (8.9)$$

Since the same reference stations are used in both sets of measurements, taking the difference of (8.8) and (8.9) gives us the second difference or *double difference* (DD) free of station clock biases:

$$\rho^{ij}_{m_{12}} = \rho^i_{m_{12}} - \rho^j_{m_{12}} = R^i_{m_1} - R^i_{m_2} - R^j_{m_1} + R^j_{m_2} \qquad (8.10)$$

All of the monitor-related errors now cancel and we are left with only the true range terms in (8.10). The left side of (8.10) is known from measurements; whereas, the right side contains the ranges from each station to each of the satellites. An expression for these distances contains six unknowns—the three position coordinates for each of the two satellites. The term $\rho^{ij}_{m_{12}}$ now becomes the basic measurement term, and (8.10) replaces the basic equation (8.1).

We now have one equation with six unknowns. By pairing up a third station with the first, we obtain a second, independent equation without introducing any additional unknowns since the position of the station is known. Again, by pairing up a fourth station with the first, we obtain a third, independent equation. We can continue to pair up three additional stations with the first to obtain the final three independent equations that we need. In this description, each pairing includes the first station. This is not necessary; it is simply one way of ensuring that each station pair we choose produces an independent equation. The set of stations in each pairing can also be entirely different from those in every other pairing to form a network of *unconnected baselines* over the region of coverage.

To obtain greater accuracy with the differencing technique, carrier phase tracking is used instead of code tracking [7]. The mathematical concept is identical; the pseudoranges are simply replaced by their equivalent number of cycles of carrier signal. Carrier phase tracking is described later in this chapter.

As with the standard use of GPS, satellites may be tracked with more than the minimum necessary for increased accuracy.

8.2.2.2 Atmospheric Propagation Delays

Tropospheric and ionospheric propagation delays affect both the satellite position measurements made by the ground monitoring network and the user pseudorange measurements. Compensating for them is necessary if the greatest accuracy possible in the user position estimate is to be attained. The dependency of tropospheric delay on the pressure, temperature, and water vapor pressure is reflected in the various tropospheric delay models; thus, for the most accurate estimates of tropospheric delay, estimates of these quantities need to be made at the user positions. These measurements decorrelate quickly and are essentially uncorrelated at 100 km, posing a dilemma for WADGPS, the essence of which is to use widely scattered stations. Three ways of handling tropospheric delay corrections are discussed below. Similarly, ionospheric delay depends on the electron density, which may vary significantly over space and time. Here, too, measurements are needed to complete the model, which must take into account both the spatial and temporal variations of delay. Ionospheric delays are much larger than tropospheric delays, so that in virtually all WADGPS systems a large effort is put into obtaining accurate ionospheric delay corrections.

Ionospheric Propagation Delay

As an example of an ionospheric delay model, the ionospheric corrections in the FAA's WAAS are made from data that gives the vertical delays at a subset of a predefined set of 929 grid points, distributed somewhat evenly in latitude and longitude [10]. The delays at some subset of the grid points are transmitted to the users. Each user receiver calculates the latitude and longitude of an ionospheric pierce point (IPP) for each satellite and calculates its delay by interpolating the delays from the four nearest grid points. Using the law of sines, the user first calculates the angle Ψ_{pp} (Figure 8.12):

$$\Psi_{pp} = \frac{\pi}{2} - \phi_m - \sin^{-1}\left(\frac{R_E}{R_E + h} \cdot \cos\phi_m\right)$$

where R_E is the radius of the Earth.

This equation is an application of the law of sines to Figure 8.12. The user then calculates the latitude, ϕ_{pp}, and longitude, λ_{pp}, of the IPP:

$$\phi_{pp} = \sin^{-1}(\sin\phi \cdot \cos\psi_{pp} + \cos\phi \cdot \sin\psi_{pp} \cdot \cos\theta)$$

$$\lambda_{pp} = \lambda + \sin^{-1}\left(\frac{\sin\psi_{pp} \cdot \sin\theta}{\cos\phi_{pp}}\right)$$

where the angle θ is the azimuth angle of the satellite from the user's position. Next, the receiver determines the IPP position relative to the four surrounding grid points (Figure 8.17):

$$x_{pp} = \frac{\lambda_{pp} - \lambda_1}{\lambda_2 - \lambda_1} \qquad y_{pp} = \frac{\phi_{pp} - \phi_1}{\phi_2 - \phi_1}$$

The interpolation is weighted, giving greater weights to the nearer grid points. The weights are given by

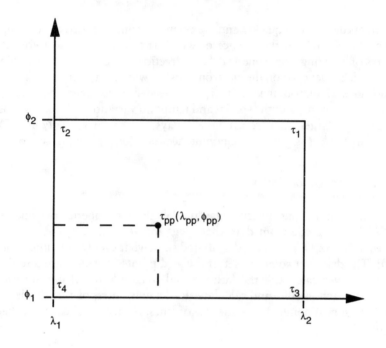

Figure 8.17 Finding the relative IPP position.

$$W_1 = x_{pp}^2 \cdot y_{pp}^2 \cdot [9 - 6x_{pp} - 6y_{pp} + 4x_{pp}y_{pp}]$$
$$W_2 = (1 - x_{pp})^2 \cdot y_{pp}^2 \cdot [9 - 6(1 - x_{pp}) - 6y_{pp} + 4(1 - x_{pp})y_{pp}]$$
$$W_3 = x_{pp}^2 \cdot (1 - y_{pp})^2 \cdot [9 - 6x_{pp} - 6(1 - y_{pp}) + 4x_{pp}(1 - y_{pp})]$$
$$W_4 = (1 - x_{pp})^2 \cdot (1 - y_{pp})^2 \cdot [9 - 6(1 - x_{pp}) - 6(1 - y_{pp}) + 4(1 - x_{pp})(1 - y_{pp})]$$

Finally, the vertical delay at the IPP is determined by

$$\tau_{pp}(\lambda_{pp},\ \phi_{pp}) = \sum_{i=1}^{4} W_i \cdot \tau_i$$

where the τ_i are the vertical delays at the four grid points. The only calculation left accounts for a difference in delay due to the slant range to the satellite. The delay $\tau_{pp}(\lambda_{pp},\ \phi_{pp})$ is multiplied by the obliquity factor F where

$$F = \frac{1}{\sqrt{1 - \left(\dfrac{R_E \cos \phi}{R_E + h}\right)^2}}$$

Tropospheric Propagation Delay

The tropospheric propagation delay is a function of temperature, pressure, and relative humidity. Measurements of these quantities at widely spaced monitoring stations would be ineffective owing to the short spatial correlation of these quantities. Instead, the WAAS user receiver determines an average signal delay as a function of the season (day of the year) that is valid at its position for elevation angles greater than 5°. (The positions of satellites with elevation angles of less than 5° are not determined in the WAAS.) The tropospheric delays for elevation angles greater than 5° are calculated from the following equation:

$$\tau(h, \phi_u, d, E) = \begin{cases} \dfrac{\tau_{0v}(\delta N_s)}{\sin(E + 0.35°)} \cdot (1 - a_0 \cdot h); & 0 \le h \le 1{,}500\text{m} \\[2ex] \dfrac{\tau_{1.5v}(\delta N_s, h)}{\sin(E + 0.35°)} \cdot e^{-a_{1.5} \cdot h}; & h \ge 1{,}500\text{m} \end{cases}$$

where h is the user's altitude above sea level in meters,

$$a_0 = 1.264 \times 10^{-4} \text{ per meter}$$

$$\tau_{0v}(\delta N_s) = 2.506 \times (1 + 0.00125 \cdot \delta N_s) \text{ meters}$$

$$a_{1.5} = 1.509 \times 10^{-4} \text{ per meter}$$

$$\tau_{1.5v}(\delta N_s, h) = 2.484 \cdot (1 + 0.0015363 e^{-a_N \cdot h} \cdot \delta N_s)$$

$$a_N = 2.133 \times 10^{-4} \text{ per meter}$$

and δN_s is a function of height, d is the day of the year, and ϕ_u is the latitude in degrees in the following equation:

$$\delta N_s = \delta N_s(h, d, \phi_u) = \delta N_h(d) + \delta N_{\phi_u}(d)$$

$$\delta N_h(d) = 3.61 \times 10^{-3} \cdot h \cdot \cos\left[\frac{2\pi(d - d_\phi)}{365}\right]$$

$$\delta N_{\phi_u}(d) = \left\{-0.8225 + 0.1 \times \cos\left[\frac{2\pi(d - d_\phi)}{365}\right]\right\} \cdot |\phi_u|$$

$$d_h = \begin{cases} 152 & \text{in the northern hemisphere} \\ 335 & \text{in the southern hemisphere} \end{cases}$$

$$d_\phi = \begin{cases} 213 & \text{in the northern hemisphere} \\ 30 & \text{in the southern hemisphere} \end{cases}$$

The difference in the values of the parameters d_h and d_ϕ in the northern and southern hemispheres accounts for the difference (183 days) in seasons in these hemispheres.

The WAAS model is a compromise between the accuracy available with measurements of temperature, pressure, and relative humidity that become decorrelated within 100 km of the measuring station and the accuracy obtained by using a worldwide average of the Earth's refractivity. Delay estimates based on the average worldwide refractivity of the Earth's surface result in errors with a standard deviation of about 8% of the true delay. By taking into account the user's latitude, height above sea level, season, and elevation angle, this standard deviation can be reduced to 6% for an improvement of 25% in the estimate of the tropospheric delay. In Section 8.2.2.4, we discuss two other approaches to handling tropospheric delay.

8.2.2.3 Satellite Clock Time Reports

With accurate satellite ephemerides and an accurate atmospheric delay model, the reference stations can accurately calculate GPS system time or an internal monitoring network system time. The pseudorange measurement ρ_m^i contains errors ϵ_t^i, ϵ_{t_m}, $\epsilon_m^{\text{Tropo}}$, ϵ_m^{Iono}, in the satellite clock time, reference station clock time, tropospheric delay, and ionospheric delay, respectively, as shown below:

$$\rho_m^i = c \cdot [(t^i + \epsilon_t^i) - (t_m + \epsilon_{t_m})] + \epsilon_m^{\text{Tropo}} + \epsilon_m^{\text{Iono}}$$

$$= c \cdot (t^i - t_m) + c \cdot \epsilon_t^i - c \cdot \epsilon_{t_m} + \epsilon_m^{\text{Tropo}} + \epsilon_m^{\text{Iono}}$$

$$= \rho_m^i + c \cdot \epsilon_t^i - c \cdot \epsilon_{t_m} + \epsilon_m^{\text{Tropo}} + \epsilon_m^{\text{Iono}}$$

If the atmospheric delays are accurately modeled and the reference station clock carefully monitored, the errors they introduce into the pseudorange measurements can removed. And if the satellite ephemeris is accurate, the true range is also known accurately. Then, the discrepancy ϵ_t^i, between the time reported by satellite S_i and the GPS system time can be determined and reported by the reference station to the user.

Typically, the determination of errors in a satellite clock, ephemeris prediction, or atmospheric delay depends on an accurate determination of the errors due to the other two error sources. This implies that at the start, the error determinations have transient components in which the accuracy in the estimation of each error improves with each iteration of the correction algorithms until, finally, the attainable accuracies of the chosen techniques are reached.

8.2.2.4 *Alternative Atmospheric Models*

A number of studies have been performed to estimate the accuracy to be expected from WADGPS. Besides Brown and [9] mentioned earlier, Kee, Parkinson, and Axelrad [11] and Ashkenazi, Hill, and Nagel [12] have investigated the accuracy achievable by WADGPS. Kee, Parkinson, and Axelrad investigated a hypothetical WADGPS that covered the United States, including Alaska and Hawaii, with 15 monitoring stations, situated principally around its borders, and one master control station. Each station has a dual-frequency receiver for ionospheric correction measurements (see Section 7.1.2.5). The local ionospheric errors (tropospheric delays are modeled as receiver noise in this paper) are transmitted along with the raw pseudorange measurements, made using a rubidium clock, to the master control station (MCS) for processing. The MCS calculates a three-dimensional pseudorange correction factor for each satellite, a satellite clock correction factor, and eight coefficients for an ionospheric delay correction model, and estimates of the monitor station clock offsets. The satellite ephemeris correction vector and the ionospheric correction coefficients are transmitted to the user to correct the raw user-measured pseudoranges.

The accuracy of the system was determined by simulating a 12-hr period with 81 users uniformly distributed across the United States. The overall rms errors achieved in the continental United States were 1.1m horizontally and 1.5m vertically. These errors varied slightly with position: better results were achieved on average in the central region of the country than along the borders, and areas with a greater concentration of monitor stations provided greater accuracy in position estimates.

Ashkenazi, Hill, and Nagel proposed a DGPS system of regions that cover more than three continents. It separates the differential correction into three separate components: an ephemeris correction, an atmospheric delay correction, and satellite clock error corrections. The ephemeris correction is given as a three-dimensional vector to account for the change in the error component of ephemeris with change in position. The satellite ephemerides are determined independently of the GPS-broadcasted position estimates to avoid the SA errors. In measuring satellite positions, the double differencing technique is used to help provide the accuracy needed in the satellite position estimates.

The tropospheric and ionospheric delays are treated together. The troposphere and ionosphere are assumed to produce delays that are equal in magnitude. The estimated delays at each station are used to produce a three-dimensional atmospheric delay model for each region that is updated hourly. The satellite clock corrections include corrections for SA and must therefore be transmitted at 5-sec intervals or more often.

A simulation using 18 monitoring stations (working in pairs to implement the double-differencing technique) shows that the WADGPS system investigated provided position estimates with errors of two or three meters horizontally that were not dependent on the distance of the user from the monitoring station. This accuracy was estimated to be equivalent to that obtainable by filling the coverage region with a grid of LADGPS stations 200 km apart. The simulation was followed up with field data tests, which suggest that WADGPS provides the same accuracy as LADGPS with stations placed 400 km apart. The horizontal mean error of 0.5m and standard deviation of 2.6m suggests that the satellite ephemeris errors and clock biases have been well estimated, but the mean height error of 4.5m suggests that atmospheric modeling could be improved.

8.3 CARRIER-BASED TECHNIQUES

The constant motion of the GPS satellite constellation demands that the receiver, in general, be capable of accounting for the changing Doppler frequency shift on L1. Where dual-frequency receivers are used, both the L1 and L2 are tracked. The shift in frequency arises due to the relative motion between the satellites and the receiver(s). Typical satellite motion with respect to an Earth-fixed observer can result in Doppler frequencies between ±5,000 Hz with respect to the L1 and L2 carriers. Integration of the Doppler frequency offset results in an extremely accurate measurement of the advance in signal carrier phase between time epochs (see Section 5.1.6). Interferometric techniques can take advantage of these precise phase measurements and, assuming sources of error can be mitigated, real-time positional accuracies of approximately $\lambda/10$ (i.e., in the centimeter range for L1 and L2) are achievable. Using DD processing techniques on the C/A- or P(Y)-code carrier phase observables removes most of the error sources [13]. One major exception remains, however, and that is multipath—it can be mitigated, but not eliminated. (Receiver noise is still present, but its contribution is generally much less than that of multipath.)

While changes in signal phase from epoch to epoch can be measured with extreme accuracy, the number of whole carrier cycles along the propagation path from satellite to receiver remains ambiguous. This obstacle can be overcome by forming DD pseudorange (code) observables and then "centering" a corresponding carrier phase DD observable at the mean value of the code DD. The result is a "smoothed-code" DD observable that is unambiguous. This technique has been successfully applied to C/A-code and phase observables by using a complementary Kalman filter [14]. Code DD accuracies to within $\pm 5\lambda$, or about 1m at L1, have been demonstrated in low multipath environments.

Further refinement of the propagation path length measurement is required to achieve the desired centimeter-level accuracies. This is done through computational-intensive techniques that search the smoothed-code DD in integer multiples of λ. This is known as "carrier-cycle integer-ambiguity resolution" and is an active area of investigation in the field of kinematic DGPS research. Remondi [13] has made extensive use of the "ambiguity function" for resolving these unknown integer wavelength multiples; but, the pioneering work in this area arose from the efforts of Counselman and Gourevitch [15] and Greenspan et al. [16]. As a rule, the ambiguity function approach is successful for postprocessing applications arising in land surveying where one has the luxury of time. For applications where the user is moving with respect to the fixed reference station and real-time accuracy is required (i.e., kinematic environment), rapid resolution of carrier-cycle integer ambiguities is highly desirable and an absolute must if centimeter-level accuracies are to be achieved.

Advantage can be taken by combining the L1 and L2 frequencies to speed the ambiguity resolution process, and this approach has been the subject of a number of articles in the literature (e.g., Hatch [17]). Although the P-code has been encrypted (now called the Y-code) by the DOD, several receiver manufacturers have been successful in recovering the full carrier phase and pseudorange P-code observables. This has allowed the continued use of the dual-frequency nature of the GPS signal structure. This dual-frequency structure is exploited to produce the sum and difference of the L1 and L2 frequencies. The result is sum and difference wavelengths of 10.7 cm and 86.25 cm, respectively. Using the difference wavelength (known as the wide lane) makes the integer ambiguity search more efficient. A change of one wide-lane wavelength results in virtually a fourfold increase in distance over that of one wavelength at either the L1 and L2 frequencies alone. Obviously, the search for the proper combination of integer ambiguities progresses more quickly using wide-lane observables, but the requirements on the receiver for simultaneous dual-frequency tracking—here, the P(Y) code is generally used—are more stringent. In particular, the noise factor for the wide-lane processing goes up by a factor of nearly six [18]. These matters aside, wide-lane techniques hold great promise for obtaining rapid "on-the-fly," integer ambiguity resolution, and the methodology will be presented later in this chapter.

8.3.1 Precise Baseline Determination in Real Time

Determination of the carrier-cycle ambiguities on-the-fly is key to any application where precise positioning at the centimeter level, in real time, is required. Such techniques have been successfully applied to aircraft precision approach and automatic landing for approach baselines extending to 50 km in some instances [19–22]. They are equally applicable, however, to land-based or land-sea applications (e.g., precise desert navigation, off-shore oil exploration, etc.). In contrast, land-surveying applications and the like, often involving long baselines, have had the luxury of the postprocessing environment and as a result, accuracies at the millimeter level are today commonplace. Techniques applied in such instances involve resolution of carrier cycle ambiguities on the data sets collected over long periods of time (generally an hour or more). In addition, postprocessing of the data lends itself to recognition and repair of cycle slips. Precision can be further enhanced by use of precise satellite ephemerides. These topics, while of interest, are beyond the scope of this presentation. Texts such as *GPS Satellite Surveying* by Leick [8] ably cover these applications.

The following discussion focuses on an integer ambiguity resolution technique first proposed by van Graas and Braasch [14], which capitalizes on the efforts of Potter and Suman [23] to resolve the inconsistencies between redundant measurements. The latter work maintains that "all information about the 'inconsistencies' resides in a set of linear relationships known as *parity equations*." While these techniques were originally applied to inertial systems and their associated instruments (e.g., accelerometers and gyros), there is similar applicability to GPS measurement inconsistencies that, in this instance, manifest themselves in the integer wavelength ambiguities inherent in the carrier-phase observables. Walsh [24] has shown that a similar approach using a technique that minimizes least square residuals has application to the rapid resolution of the ambiguities albeit in a static, nonkinematic, environment. He, too, suggests the use of the wide-lane measurements to reduce computational overhead, thus speeding up the ambiguity-resolution process.

8.3.1.1 Carrier Phase Measurement

Once the receiver locks on to a particular satellite, it not only makes C/A- and/or P(Y)-code pseudorange measurements on L1 and L2 (if L2-capable), it also keeps a running cycle count based upon the Doppler frequency shift present on the L1 and L2 carrier frequencies (one cycle represents an advance of 2π radians of carrier phase or one wavelength). Each epoch, this running cycle count (the value from the previous epoch plus the advance in phase during the present epoch) is available from the receiver. More specifically, the advance in carrier phase during an epoch is determined by integrating the carrier Doppler frequency offset (f_D) over the interval of the epoch. Frequency f_D is the time rate of change of the carrier phase; hence, integration over an epoch yields the carrier phase advance (or recession) during the epoch. Then, at the conclusion of each epoch, a fractional phase measurement is made by the receiver. This measurement is derived from the carrier phase tracking loop of the receiver. Mathematically, the relationship is as follows:

$$\phi_{L1_n} = \phi_{L1_{n-1}} + \int_{t_{n-1}}^{t_n} f_{DL1}(\tau)d\tau + \phi_{r_{L1_n}} \text{ where } \phi_{L1_0} = 0$$

$$\phi_{L2_n} = \phi_{L2_{n-1}} + \int_{t_{n-1}}^{t_n} f_{DL2}(\tau)d\tau + \phi_{r_{L2_n}} \text{ where } \phi_{L2_0} = 0$$

where

ϕ is the accumulated phase at the epoch shown
n and $n-1$ are the current and immediately past epochs

f_D is the Doppler frequency as a function of time

ϕ_r is the fractional phase measured at the epoch shown

Even though the receiver carrier-phase measurement can be made with some precision (0.01 cycle for receivers in the marketplace) and any advance in carrier cycles since satellite acquisition by the receiver can be accurately counted, the overall phase measurement contains an unknown number of carrier-cycles. This is called the carrier-cycle integer ambiguity (N). This ambiguity exists because the receiver merely begins counting carrier cycles from the time a satellite is placed in active track. Were it possible to relate N to the problem geometry, the length of the path between the satellite and the user receiver, in terms of carrier cycles or wavelengths, could be determined with the extreme accuracies mentioned above.

Figure 8.18 depicts such a situation and also illustrates the effect of the calculated carrier-phase advance as a function of time (e.g., ϕ_1, ϕ_2). Clearly, determining N for each satellite used to generate the user position is of paramount concern when interferometric techniques are used. As the term interferometry implies, phase measurements taken at two or more locations are combined. Normally, the baseline(s) between the antennas are known and the problem becomes one of reducing the combined phase differences to determine the precise location of the source of the signal. In the case of relative DGPS, the baseline is unknown, but the location of the signal sources (the GPS satellites sometimes referred to as space vehicles (SVs)) can be precisely determined using ephemerides available from the navigation data in the satellite transmission.

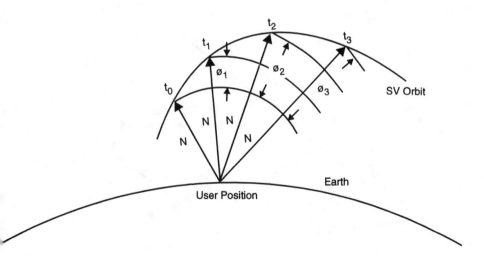

Figure 8.18 Carrier-phase geometric relationships.

8.3.1.2 Double-Difference Formation

Generation of both carrier-phase and pseudorange (code) DDs is key to determining the baseline vector between the ground and airborne platform antennas. In so doing, satellite ephemerides must be properly manipulated to ensure that the carrier-phase and code measurements made at the two receiver locations are adjusted to a common measurement time base with respect to GPS system time. Formation of the DD offers tremendous advantage because of the ultimate cancellation of receiver and satellite clock biases as well as most of the ionospheric propagation delay. If the two antennas are located at the same altitude, the tropospheric propagation delay will largely cancel as well. This is not the case if one of the antennae is on an airborne platform, and thus the path delay due to the troposphere experienced at the two antenna locations differs based upon their altitude differential.

Carrier Phase Double Difference

Figure 8.19 schematically depicts a simple GPS interferometer interacting with a single satellite. The phase centers of two antennas are located at k and m, and $\mathbf{b}$ represent the unknown baseline between them. SV p is at a mean distance of 20,200 km and we assume the paths of propagation between the satellite and the two antennas are parallel. The lengths of the propagation path between SV p and k (Φ_k^p) or SV p and m (Φ_m^p), in terms of fractional and integer carrier cycles, are as follows:

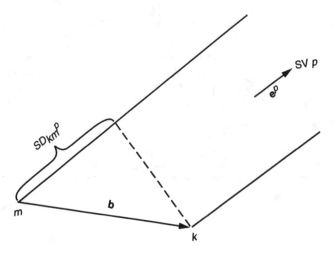

Figure 8.19 GPS interferometer—one satellite.

$$\Phi_k^p(t) = \phi_k^p(t) - \phi^p(t) + N_k^p + S_k + f\tau_p + f\tau_k - \beta_{\text{iono}} + \delta_{\text{tropo}}$$
$$\Phi_m^p(t) = \phi_m^p(t) - \phi^p(t) + N_m^p + S_m + f\tau_p + f\tau_m - \beta_{\text{iono}} + \delta_{\text{tropo}} \tag{8.11}$$

where

k and m refer to the receiver/receiver antennas phase centers
p is the satellite signal source
ϕ^p is the transmitted satellite signal phase as a function of time
$\phi_k^p(t)$ and $\phi_m^p(t)$ are the receiver measured satellite signal phases as a function of time
N is the unknown integer number of carrier cycles from p to k or p to m
S is phase noise due to all sources (e.g., receiver, multipath)
f is the carrier frequency
τ is the associated satellite or receiver clock bias
β_{iono} is the advance of the carrier (cycles) due to the ionosphere
δ_{tropo} is the delay of the carrier (cycles) due to the troposphere

The minus sign associated with the ionospheric effects will be discussed in Section 8.3.1.2 on pseudorange DDs.

The interferometric variable, the single difference (SD), is now created by differencing the carrier-cycle propagation path lengths (SV p to k and m):

$$SD_{km}^p = \phi_{km}^p + N_{km}^p + S_{km}^p + f\tau_{km} \tag{8.12}$$

The nomenclature remains the same as in (8.11) but certain advantages accrue in forming the SD metric. Prime among these are the cancellation of the transmitted satellite signal phase and clock biases, and the formation of a combined integer-ambiguity term that represents the integer number of carrier cycles along the path from m to the projection of k onto the mp line of sight. A combined phase-noise value has been created as well as a combined receiver clock-bias term. With regard to the ionosphere, these effects cancel, too, if the receivers are closely spaced (baselines less than 50 km). This condition will be assumed to exist for purposes of the discussion. Errors in satellite ephemerides have not been considered, but are usually very small (ranging from 5m to 10m). Since they are a common term like the satellite clock bias, they cancel when the single difference is formed.

Figure 8.20 extends the GPS interferometer to two satellites. For q, the additional SV, a second SD metric can be formed:

$$SD_{km}^q = \phi_{km}^q + N_{km}^q + S_{km}^q + f\tau_{km} \tag{8.13}$$

As with (8.12), the expected cancellation of satellite-transmitted signal phase and clock bias occurs, and a short baseline will be assumed such that ionospheric and tropospheric propagation delays cancel as well.

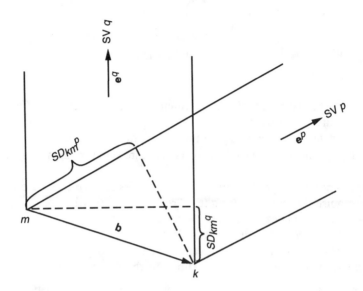

Figure 8.20 GPS interferometer—two satellites.

The interferometric DD is now formed using the two SDs. Involved in this metric are two separate satellites and the two receivers, one at either end of the baseline, **b**. Differencing (8.12) and (8.13) yields the following:

$$DD_{km}^{pq} = \phi_{km}^{pq} + N_{km}^{pq} + S_{km}^{pq}$$

where the superscripts p and q refer to the individual satellites, and k and m are the individual antennas. With the formation of the DD, the receiver clock-bias terms now cancel. Remaining is a phase term representing the combined carrier-phase measurements made at k and m by the receivers using SVs p and q, an integer term made up of the combined unknown integer ambiguities and a system phase-noise term consisting primarily of combined multipath and receiver effects [23]. It now remains to relate the DD to the unknown baseline **b**, which exists between the two receiver antennas.

Referring again to Figure 8.20, it is evident that the projection of **b** onto the line of sight between p and m can be written as the inner (dot) product of **b** with a unit vector e^p in the direction of satellite p. This projection of **b** (if converted to wavelengths) is SD_{km}^p. Similarly, the dot product of **b** with a unit vector e^q in the direction of satellite q would relate to SD_{km}^q. Rewriting SD equations (8.12) and (8.13) with this substitution yields

$$SD_{km}^p = (\mathbf{b} \cdot \mathbf{e}^p)\lambda^{-1} = \phi_{km}^{pq} + N_{km}^{pq} + S_{km}^p + f\tau_{km}$$

$$SD_{km}^q = (\mathbf{b} \cdot \mathbf{e}^q)\lambda^{-1} = \phi_{km}^q + N_{km}^q + S_{km}^q + f\tau_{km}$$

Clearly, we can incorporate this result into the double difference as well:

$$DD_{km}^{pq} = (\mathbf{b} \cdot \mathbf{e}^{pq})\lambda^{-1} = \phi_{km}^{pq} + N_{km}^{pq} + S_{km}^{pq} \qquad (8.14)$$

where $\mathbf{b} \cdot \mathbf{e}^{pq}$ is the inner product between the unknown baseline vector and the difference of the unit vectors to satellites p and q. Since determining the unknown baseline between the antennae is at the heart of the matter, it is this second formulation for the DDs, (8.14), that will serve as the basis for further derivation.

Of the variables shown in (8.14), there is only one that can be precisely measured by the receiver and that is the carrier phase. In actuality, then, it is the carrier-phase measurements of the receivers that are combined to produce the DDs. The term DD_{cp} is adopted to represent this and implicit in its formulation is conversion to meters. The noise term will be dropped to simplify the expression. In the end, as the carrier-cycle ambiguity search progresses, the noise sources tend to cancel. There remains to be determined the baseline vector ($\mathbf{b}$), which has three components (b_x, b_y, b_z), plus an unknown integer carrier-cycle ambiguity (N) associated with each of the DD_{cp} terms. Toward this end, four independent DDs will be used; the reasoning behind this will be explained shortly. In terms of satellites, two satellites are required to form each DD. Thus, in order to form four independent DD equations, a minimum of five satellites is necessary. The transfiguration and extension of (8.14) to four DDs appears as follows:

$$\begin{bmatrix} DD_{cp1} \\ DD_{cp2} \\ DD_{cp3} \\ DD_{cp4} \end{bmatrix} = \begin{bmatrix} e_{12_x}, e_{12_y}, e_{12_z} \\ e_{13_x}, e_{13_y}, e_{13_z} \\ e_{14_x}, e_{14_y}, e_{14_z} \\ e_{15_x}, e_{15_y}, e_{15_z} \end{bmatrix} \begin{bmatrix} b_x \\ b_y \\ b_z \end{bmatrix} + \begin{bmatrix} N_1 \\ N_2 \\ N_3 \\ N_4 \end{bmatrix} \lambda \qquad (8.15)$$

where DD_{cp1}, for example, is the first of four independent DDs, $\mathbf{e}_{12}$ represents the differenced unit vector between the two satellites under consideration, $\mathbf{b}$ is the baseline vector, N_1 is the associated integer carrier-cycle ambiguity, and λ is the applicable wavelength. The wavelength is introduced at this point to provide consistency with DD_{cp} and $\mathbf{b}$, which are now in meters. During this and subsequent discussion, all DD formulations will be in units of length. Using matrix notation, (8.15) takes the following form:

$$\mathbf{DD}_{cp} = \mathbf{H}\,\mathbf{b} + \mathbf{N}\lambda \qquad (8.16)$$

where: DD_{cp} is the a 4 by 1 column matrix of carrier phase DDs, H is a 4 by 3 data matrix containing the differenced unit vectors between the two satellites represented in the corresponding DD, b is a 3 by 1 column matrix of the baseline coordinates, and N is a 4 by 1 column matrix of integer ambiguities. Once the carrier-phase DDs are formed, a similar set of DDs is determined using the pseudoranges between each antenna and the same set of satellites.

Pseudorange (Code) Double Difference

As in the case of the carrier phase measurement, the receiver makes a pseudorange measurement each epoch for all satellites being actively tracked. The pseudorange suffers from similar propagation and timing effects as is the case for the carrier phase. The only basic difference is that where the ionosphere advances the carrier phase, the pseudorange information experiences a group delay. In considering the propagation of electromagnetic waves through a plasma, of which the ionosphere is an example, the propagation velocity (v_g) of the modulation on a carrier is retarded, while the phase velocity (v_p) of the carrier itself is advanced [25]. The following relationship holds:

$$v_g v_p = c^2$$

where c is the speed of light. Thus, when the code DD is formed, the effects of the ionospheric delay are additive. Formulation of the code DD begins with the pseudorange equation, as follows:

$$P_k^p(t) = t_k^p(t) - t^p(t) + Q_k + \tau_p + \tau_k + \gamma_{iono} + \delta_{tropo}$$
$$P_m^p(t) = t_m^p(t) - t^p(t) + Q_m + \tau_p + \tau_m + \gamma_{iono} + \delta_{tropo}$$

where

P is the receiver measured pseudorange time equivalent in seconds
k, m refer to receiver/receiver antennas phase centers
p is the satellite signal source
t_k^p or t_m^p is signal reception time as measured by the receiver clocks
t_p is signal transmission time as determined from the SV clock
Q is noise (timing jitter) due to all sources (e.g., receiver, multipath)
τ is the associated satellite or receiver clock bias
γ_{iono} represents group delay (sec) of the modulation due to the ionosphere
δ_{tropo} represents the delay (sec) of the modulation due to the troposphere

Note the absence of the integer carrier-cycle ambiguity N—the pseudorange measurement is unambiguous. In other words, code DD observables formed from the pseudoranges measured by the receivers are precise and contain no carrier-cycle ambiguities. Unfortunately, pseudorange cannot be measured as accurately as the carrier phase, so it is noisier. Also of note is the change in the sign for the ionospheric effects from that in (8.11) due to the group delay. The precise nature of the code DD will serve as the basis for code/carrier smoothing to be described in the next section.

Pseudorange SDs are now formed:

$$SD^p_{km_{pr}} = t^p_{km} + Q^p_{km} + \tau_{km}$$

$$SD^q_{km_{pr}} = \rho^q_{km} + Q^q_{km} + \tau_{km}$$

Finally, the pseudorange DD, in meters, is formed:

$$DD^{pq}_{km_{pr}} = t^{pq}_{km} + Q^{pq}_{km}$$

Paralleling the development of the carrier phase DDs, the same five satellites are used to form four independent code DDs. Figure 8.21 is similar to Figure 8.19 with the exception that it has been labeled in terms of pseudoranges. It is evident that the inner product of the baseline **b** and the unit vector to satellite p can be expressed as the difference of two pseudoranges to the satellite, one measured at receiver antenna k, the other at m. Recasting the baseline vector **b** in terms of the code SDs and DDs is virtually identical to that previously done with the carrier

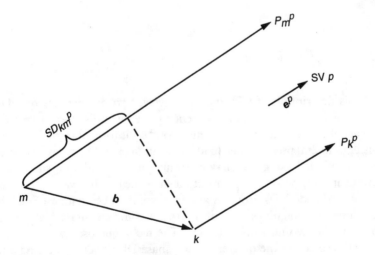

Figure 8.21 Code-equivalent GPS interferometer.

phase SD and DD formulations. There is one very important difference, however, and it is that there are no ambiguities when code measurements are used. Further, the DDs are converted to units of length by multiplying by the speed of light and, for simplicity, the noise term is dropped. The pseudorange-based equivalent of (8.15) is depicted below:

$$
\begin{bmatrix} DD_{pr_1} \\ DD_{pr_2} \\ DD_{pr_3} \\ DD_{pr_4} \end{bmatrix} = \begin{bmatrix} e_{12_x} & e_{12_y} & e_{12_z} \\ e_{13_x} & e_{13_y} & e_{13_z} \\ e_{14_x} & e_{14_y} & e_{14_z} \\ e_{15_x} & e_{15_y} & e_{15_z} \end{bmatrix} \begin{bmatrix} b_x \\ b_y \\ b_z \end{bmatrix} \tag{8.17}
$$

Once again, the integer ambiguities N, as appear in (8.15), are absent because the pseudorange is unambiguous. Using matrix notation to express (8.17) yields the following, which is the code DD counterpart of (8.16):

$$
\mathbf{DD}_{pr} = \mathbf{H}\,\mathbf{b} \tag{8.18}
$$

where: $\mathbf{DD}_{pr}$ is the 4 by 1 column matrix of pseudorange (code) DDs, $\mathbf{H}$ is a 4 by 3 data matrix containing the differenced unit vectors between the two satellites represented in the corresponding DD, and $\mathbf{b}$ is a 3 by 1 column matrix of the baseline coordinates.

8.3.1.3 Pseudorange (Code) Smoothing

Thus far in this description of GPS interferometry, two distinct sets of DDs have been created. The first is based upon differencing the low noise (less than 1 cm) but ambiguous carrier phase measurements; the second set is formed from the unambiguous but noisier (1 to 2m) pseudorange (code) measurements. The two sets of measurements can be combined using a variety of techniques to produce a smoothed-code DD measurement. This is extremely important since the baseline vector $\mathbf{b}$ determined from the smoothed-code DDs provides an initial solution estimate for resolving the carrier-cycle integer ambiguities. Based on [14], a complementary Kalman filter is used to combine the two measurement sets. The technique uses the average of the noisier code DDs to center the quieter carrier phase DDs, thereby placing a known limit on the size of the integer ambiguity. The filter equations are as follows:

$$DD_{s_n}^- = DD_{s_{n-1}}^+ + (DD_{cp_n} - DD_{cp_{n-1}})$$

$$p_n^- = p_{n-1}^+ + q$$

$$k_n = p_n^-(p_n^- + r)^{-1}$$

$$DD_{s_n}^+ = DD_{s_n}^- + k_n(DD_{pr_n} - DD_{s_n}^-)$$

$$p_n^+ = (1 - k_n)p_n^-$$

$$(8.19)$$

The first line of (8.19) propagates the smoothed-code DD to the current time epoch (n) using the estimate of the smoothed-code DD from the previous epoch ($n - 1$) and the difference of the carrier phase DD across the current and past epochs. The estimate (DD_s^+), which is based upon averaging the DD_{pr} (code) difference, centers the calculation; the DD_{cp} (carrier phase) difference adds the latest low-noise information. Note that differencing two carrier-phase DDs across an epoch removes the integer ambiguity; hence, the propagated smoothed-code double difference (DD_s^-) remains unambiguous. The estimation-error variance (p_n^-) is brought forward (line two) using its previously estimated value plus the variance of the carrier phase DD measurement (q). The Kalman gain, (k_n), is next calculated in preparation for weighting the effect of the current code DD measurement. Line three shows that as the variance on the code DD (r) approaches zero, the Kalman gain tends to unity. This is not surprising since the higher the accuracy of a measurement (smaller the variance), the greater is its effect on the outcome of the process. Lines four and five of (8.19) propagate the estimate of the smoothed-code double difference (DD_s^+) and estimation-error variance to the current epoch (n) in preparation for repeating the process in the next epoch ($n + 1$). The value DD_s^+ (to be used in the next epoch) involves the sum of the current value of the smoothed-code DD (just predicted) and its difference from the current code DD (just measured) weighted by the Kalman gain. Intuitively, if the prediction is accurate, then there is little need to update it with the current measurement. Finally, the estimation-error variance (p) is updated. The update maintains a careful balance between the "goodness" of the code and that of the carrier-phase DDs based upon whether the Kalman gain approaches unity or zero or lies somewhere in between.

Equation (8.19) represents a set of scalar complementary Kalman filter equations that can operate on each of the requisite DD measurement pairs (code and carrier phase) in turn. Alternatively, these equations can be set up in matrix form and accomplish the same end once all DD measurements for a given epoch are calculated and collected together in respective arrays. Either approach is satisfactory, but for ease of programming the scalar formulation is used here.

Figure 8.22 shows actual carrier phase (top) and code (bottom) DD measurements collected over a period of 20 min during a flight test [14]. The offset between the two plots is arbitrary, but can be thought of in terms of some unknown integer

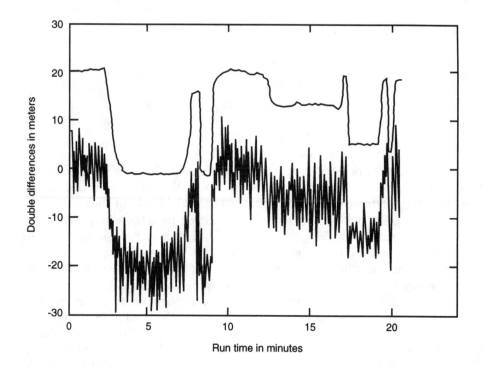

Figure 8.22 Carrier-phase and raw-code DDs.

ambiguity included in the carrier-phase DD measurements. It is apparent that the two sets of data are quite similar with the exception of apparent noise on the code DDs.

Figure 8.23 shows the output of the complementary Kalman filter (i.e., the smoothed-code DDs (bottom) and the original carrier phase DDs (top) over the same 20-min interval). With the exception of the first few epochs (nominally about 10), the smoothed-code DD virtually mirrors the carrier phase DD. It has the added advantage that it is centered about the original code DD measurements and is thus unambiguous.

Depending upon the multipath in the local environment, the smoothed-code DD, once the complementary Kalman filter is initialized, is generally within ±1–2m. In terms of carrier wavelengths, this represents approximately ±5 to 10λ at L1.

Figure 8.24 shows the difference between the carrier phase and smooth-code DDs of Figure 8.23 with the nominal offset removed from the former. For this particular set of data, the difference is well within ±1m and is indicative of low multipath at both the ground and at an airborne antennae. Again, the behavior prior to completing the initialization of the complementary Kalman filter is clearly evident during the first few epochs; but, once initialized, the difference is very well behaved.

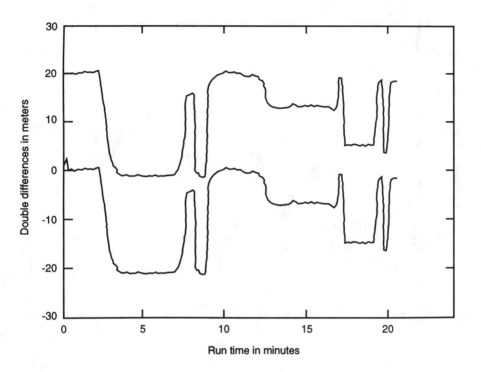

Figure 8.23 Carrier-phase and smoothed-code DDs.

8.3.1.4 Initial Baseline Determination (Floating Solution)

The smoothed-code DD from the complementary Kalman filter, once the filter is initialized, is key to determining the floating solution. The floating baseline-solution is a least squares fit yielding an estimate of the baseline vector **b**, accurate to within a few integer wavelengths depending upon the effects of satellite geometry and the severity of the multipath environment surrounding the antennas at either end of the baseline.

Using the vector notation introduced with (8.18), the DD baseline equation for the smoothed-code DDs is as follows:

$$\mathbf{DD}_s = \mathbf{H}\,\mathbf{b}_{\text{float}} \tag{8.20}$$

In a general least squares sense, $\mathbf{DD}_s$ is an m by 1 column matrix of DDs for $m + 1$ satellites, **H** is an m by 3 data matrix containing the differenced unit vectors between the two satellites represented in the corresponding DD, and **b** is a 3 by 1 column matrix of the estimated floating baseline solution coordinates. Were the

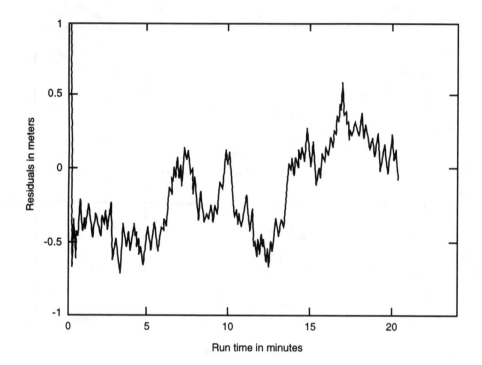

Figure 8.24 Carrier-phase minus smoothed-code DDs.

least-squares solution for **b** the only desired result, the generalized inverse approach using H^TH could be applied immediately. In this situation, however, the floating baseline solution represents an intermediate step along the way to the desired final result, which is an integer-ambiguity resolved or the fixed baseline solution. With this end in mind, some matrix conditioning is performed on the elements of (8.20) prior to determining the floating baseline solution. The **H** matrix is decomposed using "**QR**" factorization where **Q** is a real, orthonormal matrix (thus $Q^TQ = I$) and **R** is an upper triangular matrix [26]. "**QR**" factorization allows the least squares residual vector to be obtained by projecting the DDs onto a measurement space that is orthogonal to the least-squares solution space spanned by the columns of **H**. Hence, the least-squares residual vector is projected onto the left null space of **H** and is called parity space, while the least-squares solution is mapped onto the column space of **H**, known as the estimation space [23]. Since the parity space and the estimation space are orthogonal, the residuals therein are independent of the estimate. This will be used to an advantage to isolate the carrier-cycle integer ambiguities and subsequently adjust the smoothed-code DDs. Incorporating the properties of the "**QR**" factorization into (8.20) yields

$$DD_s = QRb_{float}$$

Capitalizing on the property of the orthonormal matrix where the inverse and transpose are equivalent and then rearranging gives

$$R\ b_{float} = Q^T DD_s$$

Expanding the matrices for clarity yields

$$
\begin{bmatrix}
R_{11} & R_{12} & R_{13} \\
0 & R_{22} & R_{23} \\
0 & 0 & R_{33} \\
0 & 0 & 0
\end{bmatrix}
\begin{bmatrix}
b_x \\
b_y \\
b_z
\end{bmatrix}
=
\begin{bmatrix}
Q_{11}^T & Q_{12}^T & Q_{13}^T & Q_{14}^T \\
Q_{21}^T & Q_{22}^T & Q_{23}^T & Q_{24}^T \\
Q_{31}^T & Q_{32}^T & Q_{33}^T & Q_{34}^T \\
q_1 & q_2 & q_3 & q_4
\end{bmatrix}
\begin{bmatrix}
DD_{s_1} \\
DD_{s_2} \\
DD_{s_3} \\
DD_{s_4}
\end{bmatrix}
\tag{8.21}
$$

Equation (8.21) lends itself readily to horizontal partitioning, and elements of the Q^T matrix have been labeled with capital Q to show the portion that corresponds to the least-squares solution (estimation space) and with small q to indicate the elements making up the least-squares residual vector (parity space). Subscript u denotes an upper triangular matrix. The partitioning of (8.21) is

$$R_u b_{float} = Q_u^T DD_s \tag{8.22}$$

$$0 = q\ DD_s \tag{8.23}$$

Solving (8.22) gives the floating baseline solution shown below:

$$b_{float} = R_u^{-1} Q_u^T DD_s \tag{8.24}$$

Equation (8.23), while ideally equal to zero, is the least-squares residual vector and can be exploited to provide the means for resolving the carrier-cycle integer ambiguities, a discussion of which follows in the next section. The floating baseline solution is freshly calculated for each epoch and serves as a temporal benchmark during the ambiguity resolution phase while the fixed baseline solution is being pursued. Once the fixed baseline solution is in hand, the floating solution subsequently serves as a cross-check to ensure the continued integrity of the former. Recall that this is a dynamic process—one end of the baseline is usually airborne—thus both the fixed and floating baseline solutions will vary from epoch to epoch and must be constantly monitored. On the other hand, the carrier-cycle integer ambiguities, once resolved, remain fixed in the solution since the receivers dynamically track the growth or contraction of the number of carrier cycles between the baseline antennae and the respective satellites used in the solution for the baseline. This holds true as long as all satellites remain in constant track by the receivers with no cycle slips occurring.

8.3.1.5 Carrier-Cycle Ambiguity Resolution

Using the complementary Kalman filter to produce the smoothed-code DDs ensures that each of the DD measurements contributes to a solution whose accuracy is within 1 to 2m, as previously stated. In terms of integer wavelengths at L1, for example, the DDs values are each within about ± 5 to 10λ. Intuitively, it would seem possible to iterate each DD through this range of carrier wavelengths, recalculate the least-squares solution for each iteration, and then examine the residuals. Residuals "near" to zero, since there is noise in the process, would be identified, and the number of integer wavelengths added to each of the DDs would be kept as a candidate integer ambiguity set for the particular trial. This could be done on an epoch-by-epoch basis and those sets of integer ambiguities that continued to remain valid would be marked and tallied. The list would diminish over time and eventually one set of integer ambiguities would emerge victorious. The approach just described would take place in "parity space" since we would be adjusting the DDs measurements (iteratively) and subsequently examining the new set of least-squares residuals that resulted. To search the uncertainty volume about the floating baseline solution would be computational inefficiency at its extreme. For example, an uncertainty of $\pm 11\lambda$ would require initially that 23^4 least-square solutions be generated each epoch and the residuals for each examined. Even though the number would diminish over time, the technique would in general remain computationally inefficient.

A far better approach is to screen candidate integer ambiguity sets/test points using predetermined criteria, and then test only those sets which meet that criteria. Examples of the most prominent techniques currently in use are summarized in Erickson [27]. These include the fast ambiguity resolution approach (FARA) of Frei and Beutler [28], the least squares ambiguity search technique (LSAST) by Hatch [29], and the ambiguity function method (AFM) by Counselman and Gourevitch [15] (later refined by Remondi [13]). The applications cited by Erickson for these techniques are directed more toward the static surveying environment vice the kinematic DGPS regime, but the Erickson article provides insight into these methods, all of which could find application in more dynamic situations where real-time applications are involved.

To generalize the foregoing, an initial solution is obtained, a search domain about the solution is established, and some methodology is used to preselect candidate test points/ambiguity sets within the domain, which are subsequently used to generate candidate fixed solutions. Finally, using a given selection criteria, the candidate fixed solutions are accepted or rejected until ultimately only one remains. AFM and LSAST can potentially accomplish this in a single epoch of several minutes; FARA generally requires two to three such epochs.

Thus far in the development of the methodology used for resolving the carrier-cycle integer ambiguities, the steps necessary to develop the initial solution have been covered in detail. These include the formation of both carrier-phase and pseudorange (code) DDs, the creation of the smoothed-code DDs, the formulation of the DD baseline equations, and the separation of these equations into a least-squares (floating) baseline solution and a least-squares residual vector. A search volume has been established based upon the accuracy inherent in the smoothed-code DDs—nominally ±1 to 2m. It remains to formulate the DDs in a manner such that they can be selectively examined over the search volume as a function of integer carrier-cycle ambiguities. Once this is accomplished, candidate ambiguity sets can be isolated, thresholded, and eventually retained or eliminated. From those few remaining sets, fixed baseline solutions are determined. These solutions are then subjected to additional checks (e.g., comparison with the floating solution, among others), until the ultimate fixed baseline solution emerges.

The "QR" factorization is a powerful technique that allows the least-squares residuals to be isolated from the least-squares solution space without the necessity of performing the least-squares solution itself. Application of the residuals to the process of sorting out the integer ambiguities is the next area of interest. To do so requires that the carrier phase DD measurement be examined in light of its constituent parts. The following equation so illustrates:

$$DD_{cp} = (\phi_{DD} + \hat{n} + R_b + S)\lambda \tag{8.25}$$

where ϕ_{DD} is the DD fractional phase from the receiver measurements, n is the unknown DD ambiguity, R_b is the inherent receiver channel bias plus residual propagation delays, S is the noise due to all sources (e.g., receiver, multipath), and the use of λ converts the DD to units of length. Strictly speaking, multipath is not noise. It does, however, add a noise-like uncertainty to the DD measurement which, unfortunately, cannot be uniquely separated at a given instant in time from other noise sources. To solve this dilemma, multipath is simply included with the noise.

Equation (8.25) can be re-expressed using the smoothed-code DDs and with the knowledge that the uncertainty in the sources on the right-hand side of the equation is bounded. The terms ϕ_{DD} and $\hat{n}$ are replaced with ρ_{DD} and $\bar{n}$. This follows from the knowledge that the smoothed-code DDs are precise to within ±1 to 2m, their inherent noise level. This noise level is equivalent to ±11 wavelengths at L1 and allows the integer ambiguity to be bounded; hence, $-11 \leq \bar{n} \leq +11$. The term ρ_{DD}, then, represents the geometric distance (in carrier cycles) of the smoothed-code DD within the noise bound. The equation now appears as follows:

$$DD_s = (\rho_{DD} + \bar{n} + R_b + S)\lambda$$

The resolution of $\tilde{n}$ can now be attacked using the residuals from the least squares solution developed as (8.22). This equation is expanded and shown below:

$$
\mathbf{q} \, \mathbf{DD}_s = [q_1(\rho_{DD_1} + \tilde{n}_1 + R_{b_1} + S_1) + q_2(\rho_{DD_2} + \tilde{n}_2 + R_{b_2} + S_2)
$$
$$
+ q_3(\rho_{DD_3} + \tilde{n}_3 + R_{b_3} + S_3) + q_4(\rho_{DD_4} + \tilde{n}_4 + R_{b_4} + S_4)]\lambda = \eta \tag{8.26}
$$

where the q_r are the elements of the least squares residual vector and $\tilde{n}_r$ represents a wavelength ambiguity number associated with the applicable DD. Ideally, the value of η, the measurement inconsistency, would be zero, but this could only be true in the presence of noiseless measurements and resolved carrier-cycle integer ambiguities.

In any particular epoch, the values for q remain constant—the residual of the least squares solution does not change until another set of measurements is taken, the DDs computed and smoothed, and the "QR" factorization completed. In modern receivers, great effort is expended to minimize interchannel biases; the same holds true for receiver noise. This leaves multipath as the major component of "noise." Fortunately, multipath, over time, behaves in a noise-like fashion, although not necessarily tending to a zero mean [30]. It is worthwhile, then, to consider (8.26) with emphasis on the component that is constant from epoch to epoch, knowing that the other sources of error will be mostly random or small over an extended period of time. This component is the unknown carrier-cycle integer ambiguity in each of the smoothed-code DDs. If the ambiguity can be removed from the DD, then the only remaining error sources are noise-like and will approach zero or, in the case of multipath, some mean value. Equation (8.26) is rewritten below in light of these ideas:

$$
q_1[DD_{s_1} - \tilde{n}_1\lambda] + q_2[DD_{s_2} - \tilde{n}_2\lambda]
$$
$$
+ q_3[DD_{s_3} - \tilde{n}_3\lambda] + q_4[DD_{s_4} - \tilde{n}_4\lambda] = \gamma \tag{8.27}
$$

Once again it is noted that the smoothed-code DDs are bounded within ±1 to 2m depending upon the multipath environment. With this in mind, the values for $\tilde{n}$ in (8.27) can be adjusted such that the result is "near" to zero—at least within some predetermined threshold (γ). Assuming that the receiver noise and interchannel biases can be kept to below $\lambda/2$ (which is generally the case), it becomes possible to use (8.27) to resolve the carrier-cycle ambiguities. Putting (8.27) into matrix form:

$$
\mathbf{q}[DD_s - N\lambda] = \gamma \tag{8.28}
$$

where $N = [\tilde{n}_1 \ \tilde{n}_2 \ \tilde{n}_3 \ \tilde{n}_4]$ and represents a set of integer values which, when substituted into the equation, satisfy the threshold constraint. The question now becomes one of how to find the N vectors that produce such a result.

Since there are only four multiplication operations and three additions required to examine each case, one answer to such a question is to use an exhaustive search. With a ±1 to 2m bound on the accuracy using the smoothed-code DDs, such a search requires that components of N contain iterations covering ±11λ at L1 where the wavelength is 19.03 cm. There are 2^{34}, slightly less than 300,000, possible candidates for the first epoch, which is not an unreasonable number. Were it necessary, more efficient search strategies could be implemented; however, when the wide-lane wavelength is examined at the end of this chapter, the number of candidates will drop to less than 3,000, which then makes the exhaustive search almost trivial. In any event, as the integer values are cycled from [−11 −11 −11 −11] to [+11 +11 +11 +11], those integer sets that are within the threshold are retained and become candidates for the fixed baseline solution.

8.3.1.6 *Final Baseline Determination (Fixed Solution)*

Each epoch, the various N sets that meet the γ threshold constraint of (8.28) are stored or, if stored previously, a counter (j) is incremented to indicate persistence of the particular ambiguity set. For those sets that persist, a sample mean (η_{avg}) is calculated based upon the first 10 values of the residual. The variance (η_{σ^2}) about the sample mean is determined as well. These calculations are as follows:

$$\eta_{avg_j} = \frac{[\eta_{avg_{j-1}}(j-1) + \eta_j]}{j} \quad j \leq 10 \text{ and } \eta_{avg_0} = 0$$

$$\eta_{\sigma_j}^2 = \eta_{\sigma_{j-1}}^2 + (\eta_{avg_j} - \eta_j)^2 \quad j = 1, 2$$

$$\eta_{\sigma_j}^2 = \frac{[(j-2)\eta_{\sigma_{j-1}}^2 + (\eta_{avg_j} - \eta_j)]^2}{(j-1)} \quad j > 2$$

Those ambiguity sets with the smallest variance (usually about 10 in number) are then ranked in ascending order. Persistence is defined as a minimum of 10 epochs (seconds for the research of which this discussion is based upon) and has been determined experimentally. For a particular ambiguity set to be selected for the fixed solution, one additional requirement must now be met. The ratio of the residual calculated for the ambiguity set with the smallest and next smallest variances must exceed a minimum value. This value has also been determined experimentally and set to 0.5 cm.

Upon selection of an ambiguity set, the $\tilde{n} \cdot \lambda$ values of the N vector become literally the amount of path length used to adjust the current smoothed-code DD to create the exact (resolved) DD path length. To complete the process, the smoothed-code DDs are recomputed using the ambiguity set(s) that were generated during the search/selection process. The following relationship is used:

$$DD_r = DD_s - N\lambda \tag{8.29}$$

The resolved smoothed-code DDs (DD_r) are then used to calculate the fixed baseline solution using (8.24) as modified below:

$$b_{fixed} = R_u^{-1}Q_u^T DD_r \tag{8.30}$$

The rms of the difference between the floating and fixed baseline solution is calculated for the current and subsequent epochs and monitored for consistency. Should the difference begin to diverge, the fixed baseline solution is discarded and a new search for integer ambiguities begun. Recall that the receivers, once acquisition of a given satellite is established, keep track of advances or retreats in the receiver-to-satellite path length. Hence, a valid integer-ambiguity set in one epoch remains equally valid in the next and subsequent epochs. This being the case, the fixed baseline solution can be recalculated each epoch by adjusting the current set of smoothed-code DDs with the resolved ambiguity set (N), followed by an updated least squares solution (i.e., successive application of (8.29) and (8.30)). Particularly noteworthy is that during the entire carrier-cycle ambiguity resolution process, it is unnecessary to generate the least-squares solution. All calculations remain in the measurement (parity) space using the least-squares residual vector obtained during the "**QR**" factorization. It is only after the proper consistency among the measurements (DDs) emerges (i.e., the emergence of a final resolved integer-ambiguity set) that the fixed baseline solution is calculated. True, the floating baseline solution is calculated each epoch, but this is more for monitoring than mathematical necessity. Remaining in the measurement space minimizes computational overhead and speeds the process as a result.

Two separate phenomena work to accelerate the process, which nominally takes three to four minutes before the carrier-cycle integer ambiguities are determined with sufficient confidence. First, the GPS constellation is dynamic. Its movement in relationship to the ground and user receiver antennas provides an overall change in geometry that has a very positive influence when interferometric techniques are used. Second, under most conditions, the user platform is also in motion. This movement provides additional changes in geometry. Additionally, if the user is airborne there is a substantial averaging effect on the multipath seen by the airborne antenna. In point of fact, with kinematic GPS implementations, multipath from the ground site is the single biggest contributor to error in the overall airborne system.

As a further aid to resolving the ambiguities, satellites in track by the receiver, beyond the minimum five required, can be used for cross checking, thereby accelerating the ambiguity-resolution process. With six satellites, for example, two sets of four independent DDs can be generated. This provides a second floating baseline solution and a corresponding least-squares residual vector that can be "searched." Double-difference measurements that are common between the two floating baseline-solutions will produce associated integer ambiguities, which can be compared for consistency. Such redundancy usually leads to faster isolation of the proper ambiguity set.

8.3.1.7 Wide-Lane Considerations

With some receivers, it is possible to track satellites in the GPS constellation on both L1 and L2 simultaneously. With dual-frequency tracking, the P(Y)-code must be used, because the C/A-code is not modulated on both L1 and L2 carrier frequencies. Use of dual-frequency techniques permits the ionospheric path delay to be precisely determined and, in some cases, eliminated. Additionally, there are advantages to using the P(Y)-code owing to its higher chipping rate—10 times that of the C/A-code. The advantages include increased pseudorange accuracies (since receiver correlation of the signal with added precision is possible) and reduced multipath errors. These positive aspects aside, great utility in isolating the carrier-cycle integer ambiguities can be obtained by combining the two frequencies to produce a wide-lane metric, the wavelength of which is roughly 86 cm. This is almost five times greater than the L1 wavelength. The wide-lane wavelength results from the beat frequency of the L1 and L2 carriers:

$$f_{wl} = 1575.42 - 1227.6 = 347.82 \text{ MHz}$$

$$\lambda_{wl} = 86.25 \text{ centimeters}$$

When applied to searching the uncertainties of smoothed-code DD measurements, the bound of ±1 to 2m on the search volume can be spanned with $\pm 3\lambda_{wl}$ instead of $\pm 11\lambda$ at L1. This results in a hundredfold decrease in the number of integer-ambiguity set residuals that must be computed and examined during a given epoch. The penalty for using the wide-lane wavelength is an increased noise level (S_{wl}) as shown below:

$$S_{wl} = \lambda_{wl}\sqrt{\left(\frac{S_{L1}}{\lambda_1}\right)^2 + \left(\frac{S_{L2}}{\lambda_2}\right)^2}$$

Current receiver technology, however, can readily cope with this increase in noise and, assuming the magnitude of the noise level on each carrier is approximately equal, the equation reduces to 5.7 times either S_{L1} or S_{L2}, the L1 or L2 noise levels, respectively.

The creation of the wide-lane carrier phase (ϕ_{wl}) as shown below is straightforward:

$$\phi_{wl} = \phi_{L1} - \phi_{L2}$$

Just as there exists a combination (the difference) of L1 and L2 that yields a wide-lane metric, there exists an alternative combination (the sum) that yields a narrow lane. It can be shown that frequency-independent errors (e.g., clock, troposphere and ephemeris errors) are unchanged in either the wide-lane or narrow-lane observations from their L1 and L2 values [18]. Such is not the case with frequency-dependent effects (e.g., ionospheric, multipath, and noise effects), so wide-lane carrier phase observables must be paired with narrow-lane pseudorange observables to realize the same frequency-dependent effects. A detailed explanation can be found in a 1989 paper by G. Wuebbena [31]. The narrow-lane pseudorange relationship (P_{nl}) is presented without further elaboration:

$$P_{nl} = \frac{f_{L1}P_{L1} + f_{L2}P_{L2}}{f_{L1} + f_{L2}}$$

There is no change in the formation of either the carrier-phase or the pseudorange (code) DDs once the wide-lane carrier phase and narrow-lane pseudorange observables are formed, and the methodology previously described in terms of the L1 carrier and code measurements is directly applicable. The prime advantage accrues from the fact that the search volume can be canvassed far more efficiently since fewer wide-lane wavelengths need to be searched. As mentioned earlier, to search the same $\pm 11\lambda$ at L1 could be done with $\pm 3\lambda_{wl}$. In terms of N, the iterations would range from [−3 −3 −3 −3] to [+3 +3 +3 +3]. The integers in the ambiguity sets that result from the search represent a greater physical span, but other than that, the procedure for isolating the proper set of carrier-cycle integer ambiguity values is unchanged.

Once the proper wide-lane integer ambiguity set is determined, it is most advantageous to revert to single-frequency tracking: the signal strength of L1(C/A-code) is 6-dB greater than that of the P(Y)-code on L2 and there is an almost sixfold reduction in noise when using single-frequency observables over their dual-frequency counterparts. In essence, such a move significantly improves system robustness. While the transformation is quite straightforward, it is not without pitfalls. A close look at the formation of the wide-lane carrier phase DD shows the following:

$$DD_{cP_{wl}} = DD_{cP_{L1}} - DD_{cP_{L2}} \tag{8.31}$$

This being the case, the integer ambiguity set for L1 can be determined by expanding and rearranging (8.16) as shown below:

$$DD_{cP_{L1}} - N_{L1}\lambda_{L1} = Hb = DD_{cP_{wl}} - N_{wl}\lambda_{wl} \tag{8.32}$$

Combining (8.31) and (8.32) allows the recovery of the L1 integer ambiguity set

$$N_{L1} = \frac{N_{wl}\lambda_{wl} - DD_{cp_{L2}}}{\lambda_{L1}} \qquad (8.33)$$

Care must be taken at this point since the calculation of the L1 ambiguity set will occasionally be incorrect. Referring to (8.14), it is shown that the carrier phase DD also contains an amount of noise; ultimately, this noise is swept into the resolved ambiguities. An intuitive glance at (8.33) leads to the conclusion that conversion to the L1 ambiguity set seldom if ever produces integer values. Generally speaking, the results are very close to integers, and the proper set can usually be realized by picking the nearest integer values. Occasionally, however, there is enough noise on one or more of the wide-lane measurements to cause the next higher or lower integer-ambiguity value to emerge from the conversion process. Paielli [19], who has also used wide-lane techniques with subsequent conversion to the L1 wavelength for ambiguity resolution, points out that a phase error as small as 1.2 cm can produce a conversion error of 9.72 cm ($\lambda/2$ at L1), which results in the selection of the wrong ambiguity if the nearest integer is chosen. The conclusion is, that while reversion to single-frequency tracking adds robustness, the conversion process must be done with care. The L1 integer-ambiguity values that are generated by rounding the results from (8.33) must be near integer values to begin with or the operation potentially becomes suspect. One approach to solving this problem would be to follow (8.33) with a limited search around the L1 ambiguities.

8.3.2 Static Application

While land surveying is probably the most common of static applications, there are many other near-static applications that are taking advantage of interferometric techniques. Among these could be counted precise dredging requirements for harbors and inland waterways, accurate leveling of land for highway construction and agricultural needs (especially land under irrigation), trackage surveys done to exacting standards for high-speed rail service, and a whole host of others. Generally, the driving factor in near-static or low-dynamic applications is the necessity for centimeter-level accuracy in the vertical dimension. For land surveying, requirements for accuracies in the millimeter regime in three dimensions are not uncommon.

The classical approach, used initially by Counselman and Gourevitch [15], demanded occupation times of up to several hours with simultaneous collection of GPS pseudorange and phase data at both ends of a prescribed baseline. Their classic paper reported "analyses of data from different observation periods yielded baseline determinations consistent within less than 1 cm in all vector components." That was in December 1980, the baseline was 92.07m, and the occupation time was a minimum of 1 hr. The survey data was processed after the fact, as remains typical today. The requirement for the occupation time of at least 1 hr was driven by the need to have sufficient movement in the GPS satellite constellation to allow the carrier-cycle integer ambiguities to be resolved. Another key consideration was the overall lack of GPS satellites, which eliminated the use of redundant measurements for resolving the carrier-cycle ambiguities. In this pioneering work, the ambiguity function method was used for determining the integer-cycle ambiguities.

Once the level of accuracy using GPS interferometric techniques was established, it became a natural desire to improve the efficiency of their application. The technique of kinematic surveying came into being as a result. Here, through use of a known survey point and an existing baseline, the carrier-cycle ambiguities are first determined. One technique that can be used to do this quickly is an antenna swap wherein GPS data is collected for several minutes at each end of the baseline, the receivers/antennas are then exchanged without losing satellite lock, and another period of GPS data is collected. Several minutes of GPS data, with epoch times on the order of 10 sec, are required during each occupation period to collect sufficient data to resolve the ambiguities. Four (and preferably more) satellites yielding improved satellite geometry are required to accomplish this. Subsequent to the antenna swap, one receiver/antenna is moved to each of the points making up the survey. Generally, the receiver/antenna at the known survey point becomes the control point (base station) for the survey and the other becomes the rover. Following a 1- to 2-min occupation of each survey point, the rover is returned to its initial starting location to provide data for closure of the overall survey. In all instances, it remains necessary to have continuous track on a minimum of the same four (but preferably more) GPS satellites. The GPS data is postprocessed and the survey results calculated. For baselines of up to 10 km, the effects of the ionosphere are minimal and centimeter-level accuracies can be expected. There are variations on the static and kinematic surveying methods, but generally the resulting accuracies are at the decimeter level, not the centimeter level. Further, it is the kinematic method that allows for the extension of GPS interferometric techniques to the near-static or low-dynamic environment mentioned previously.

Nowadays, with a complete GPS constellation of 24 satellites and the availability of low-noise receivers that can track both the L1 and L2 P(Y)-codes, it has become possible to resolve the carrier-cycle ambiguities without the need of either the presurveyed baseline or an initial period of GPS data collection (e.g., the antenna swap procedure). The term applied to this technique is "on-the-fly" or OTF. Implicit in this approach is differential, carrier phase integer-cycle ambiguity resolution. As a rule, the base station broadcasts either differential corrections or raw measurement data over a datalink and the rover computes its position relative to the base station by combining its own measurements with the information received over the datalink. Such an implementation reduces the dependence on postprocessing and permits the user to know immediately whether the survey is progressing in a successful manner. In most instances, the base station is located at a precisely known surveyed point; thus, the rover can determine its absolute position (i.e., latitude, longitude, and elevation), since it has calculated the baseline vector between it and the base station. Accuracies on the order of 10 cm ($\lambda/2$ at L1) are achievable in near-real time with the rover in motion. With longer occupation times, the accuracy will increase as multipath tends to average out.

8.3.3 Airborne Application

Flight reference systems (FRSs) using carrier phase or interferometric GPS (IGPS) techniques have been implemented and flight tested on transport-category aircraft. The underlying principle of operation is similar to that used for kinematic surveying and is also referred to as differential carrier-phase tracking. Figure 8.25 depicts such a system where differential techniques are employed. In this case, raw observables from all satellites in view are transmitted from a ground subsystem via datalink. The carrier-cycle ambiguity resolution is done OTF aboard the aircraft. Onboard the aircraft, position relative to the runway touchdown point is calculated in near-real time and provided to the aircraft autoland system [20]. The objectives of this IGPS FRS included such things as 0.1m accuracy rms (each axis), one or more updates per second, UTC(USNO) time synchronization better than 0.1 msec real time, all-weather operation, and repeatable flight paths. The latter requirement calls for full aircraft integration and coupled flight. Specific applications for such systems

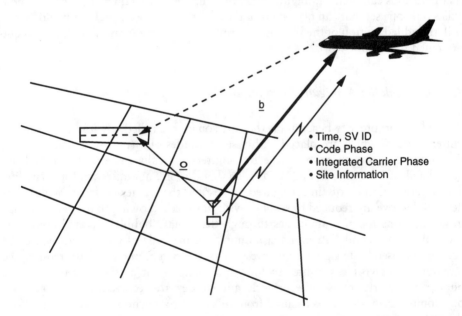

Figure 8.25 Interferometric GPS flight reference system.

include evaluation of approach/landing systems (e.g., ILS and MLS), and test range instrumentation calibration (e.g., all manner of tracking systems: laser, infrared, optical and radar). Precision instrumentation of test ranges themselves can be accomplished with special GPS receiver/datalink equipment aboard aircraft using the range. Such a system would perform the ambiguity resolution at an appropriate ground site for each vehicle using the range and provide position data to designated range tracking facilities. In addition, feasibility studies in the areas of precision landing/autoland, low-visibility surface operations (taxiing, docking), high-speed turn-off, parallel runway operations, input to electronic charts, and four-dimensional navigation can also be supported.

8.3.3.1 *Standalone Ambiguity Resolution*

Using the approach outlined in Section 8.3.1, approximately 2 to 5 min are required to resolve the carrier-phase integer-cycle ambiguities. The time required depends upon a sufficiency of satellites, six or more are generally needed. Good satellite geometry is also beneficial, as is motion of the airborne platform (though not necessarily required). The latter supplements the normal motion of the GPS constellation. Motion of the constellation is vital to the resolution of the carrier-cycle ambiguities. As the various candidate ambiguity sets are identified and evaluated over time, there exists only one set that can persist given the dynamics of the constellation and, better still, the added motion of the platform. Simply stated, without motion, the technique presented would not work.

8.3.3.2 *Pseudolite Ambiguity Resolution*

Pseudolites, or integrity beacons, as they are sometimes called, are low-power transmitters, two of which are placed within several miles of a runway threshold along the nominal approach path. These transmitters typically operate at L1 and are modulated with an unused PRN code such that they are not mistaken for a satellite. The several minutes of time required to resolve the carrier-cycle ambiguities as described above are reduced to seconds with this method owing to the rapid change in geometry as the aircraft passes through the signal "bubble" created above the pseudolites. A second GPS antenna mounted on the belly of the aircraft is used to acquire the pseudolite signals. The presence of the two pseudolites also reduces the requirement of visible satellites to four and ensures that as the aircraft exits the bubble, the carrier-phase integer-cycle ambiguities are resolved. Centimeter-level positioning accuracy is thus ensured from this point to touchdown and rollout. Both the real-time cycle ambiguity resolution and the centimeter-level positioning accuracy have been demonstrated in flight testing with transport category aircraft [21, 22].

8.3.3.3 Accuracy

Once the carrier phase ambiguities are resolved, the accuracy of the DD measurement is determined by the carrier phase measurement. In this case, multipath is the dominant error source. If the reflected signal is weaker than the direct signal, the phase measurement can be in error by up to 0.25 wavelength. If the reflected signal is stronger than the direct signal, cycle slips are likely to occur. Typical wide-lane DD measurement errors are on the order of 2 to 10 cm (2σ). Due to geometry, vertical positioning errors are between 1.5 to 2 times the DD measurement error, resulting in up to 20 cm (2σ) vertical positioning errors. Horizontal positioning errors are generally less than 20 cm (2σ). If both the ground and the airborne antennas are placed in a rich multipath environment, vertical positioning error further degrades to approximately 40 cm. However, as soon as the aircraft is in motion, airborne multipath is mitigated due to the rapid changing path length difference between the direct and reflected signals, which tends to average the multipath error.

The use of dual-frequency measurements can be very important for an IGPS FRS in some applications. It allows for the mitigation of ionospheric errors for longer baselines, but it also reduces the effect of tropospheric modeling residuals. Once the ambiguities are resolved, the system could revert back to a single-frequency system. Because of the shorter wavelength of the L1 signal, multipath error would be reduced by approximately a factor of 4.5.

The effect of SA is negligible for most differential systems due to the fact that the ground and airborne GPS receiver measurements are usually synchronized with GPS time, some to within 2 msec. A constant SA velocity error is removed through a simple linear extrapolation. SA acceleration error growth is limited due to the 2-msec synchronization. Typically, SA acceleration is on the order of a few mm/sec^2. After 1 sec, the unknown SA acceleration can not introduce more than 1 cm of error ($\frac{1}{2}at^2$). Even in the worst imaginable case of an SA acceleration of 100 m/sec^2 (10.2 g), the SA error growth during the 2-ms interval would only amount to 0.2 mm. Tracking loop error would likely be a much larger concern under these circumstances. It is noted, however, that the airborne position can only be calculated to the centimeter-level accuracy after the measurements from the reference receiver are received. This can introduce data latencies of 1 to 2 sec. During this time, the aircraft position must be propagated to maintain the desired flight path. During periods of time with normal SA levels, the airborne integrated carrier phase measurements, corrected for SA velocity error, can be used to propagate the aircraft position with centimeter-level accuracy. During times of exceptionally large SA accelerations, the aircraft inertial velocities could be used to propagate the aircraft position.

8.3.3.4 Carrier Cycle Slips

The carrier-phase observable must be tracked continuously by the receiver, or the agreement between the fixed and floating baseline solution will diverge rapidly. Loss of signal can occur due to the rising or setting of a satellite, excessive maneuvering of the user (a large bank angle in the case of an airborne user during approach or takeoff), or an obstructed view of the sky in the direction of the satellite. In any event, a loss of signal continuity, no matter how brief, results in an unknown signal loss or gain of carrier cycles when the signal is reacquired by the receiver. In a kinematic environment, detection of cycle slips is vital, since allowing corrupted carrier phase measurements to propagate forward usually causes immediate loss of the fixed solution. As such, identification of the cycle slip becomes paramount and, rather than attempt repair, the offending satellite is "ignored" for a predetermined number of epochs with the assumption that the signal will quickly return to normal. At the conclusion of this time-out period, the data from the offending satellite is once again accepted, and the carrier-cycle integer ambiguity resolution process restarted for the satellite. In the interim, if a minimum of four satellites (not including the offending satellite) had their ambiguities resolved at the time of cycle-slip detection, the fixed baseline solution is maintained. Otherwise, at best only a floating baseline solution can be provided.

References

[1] NAVSTAR-GPS Joint Program Office, *NAVSTAR-GPS User Equipment: Introduction, Public Release Version*, Feb. 1991.

[2] Department of Defense/Department of Transportation, *1994 Federal Radionavigation Plan*, Springfield, VA, National Technical Information Service, May 1995.

[3] Lapucha, D., and M. Huff, "Multi-Site Real-Time DGPS System Using Starfix Link: Operational Results," *ION GPS-92*, Albuquerque, NM, Sept. 16–18, 1992, pp. 581–588.

[4] Mack, G., G. Johnston, and M. Barnes, "Skyfix—The Worldwide Differential GPS System," *Proc. DSNS-93*, Amsterdam, The Netherlands, March 29–April 2, 1993.

[5] RTCM Special Committee No. 104, "RTCM Recommended Standards for Differential NAVSTAR GPS Service," Version 2.1, Radio Technical Commission for Maritime Services, Washington DC, Jan. 3, 1994.

[6] Altshuler, E. E., "Corrections for Tropospheric Range Error," Report AFCRL-71-0419, Air Force Cambridge Research Laboratory, Hanscom Field, Bedford, MA, July 27, 1971.

[7] Hofmann-Wellenhof, B., H. Lichtenegger, and J. Collins, *GPS Theory and Practice*, Vienna: Springer-Verlag, 1992.

[8] Leick, A., *GPS Satellite Surveying*, New York NY: John Wiley & Sons, 1990.

[9] Loomis, P., L. Sheynblatt, and T. Mueller, "Differential GPS Network Design," *Proc. ION GPS-91*, Albuquerque, NM, Sept. 11–13, 1991 pp. 511–530.

[10] Federal Aviation Administration, "Wide Area Augmentation System Specification," FAA-E-2892, Washington DC, May 1994.

[11] Kee, C., B. W. Parkinson, and P. Axelrad, "Wide Area Differential GPS," *Navigation: Journal of the Institute of Navigation*, Vol. 38, No. 2, Summer 1991, pp. 123–145.

[12] Ashkenazi, V., C. J. Hill, and J. Nagel, "Wide Area Differential GPS: A Performance Study," *Proc. of the Fifth International Technical Meeting of the Satellite Division of the Institute of Navigation (ION GPS-92)*, Albuquerque NM, Sept. 16–18, 1992, pp. 589–598.

[13] Remondi, B., "Using the Global Positioning System (GPS) Phase Observable for Relative Geodesy:

Modeling, Processing, and Results," Ph.D. Dissertation, Center for Space Research, University of Austin, Austin, Texas, 1984.

[14] van Graas, F., and M. Braasch, "GPS Interferometric Attitude and Heading Determination: Initial Flight Test Results," *NAVIGATION: Journal of the Institute of Navigation*, Vol. 38, No. 4, Winter, 1991–1992, pp. 297–316.

[15] Counselman, C., and S. Gourevitch, "Miniature Interferometer Terminals for Earth Surveying: Ambiguity and Multipath with Global Positioning System," *IEEE Transactions on Geoscience and Remote Sensing*, Vol. GE-19, No. 4, Oct. 1981.

[16] Greenspan, R. L., A. Y. Ng, J. M. Przyjemski, and J. D. Veale, "Accuracy of Relative Positioning by Interferometry with Reconstructed Carrier, GPS Experimental Results," *Proc. of the 3rd International Geodetic Symposium on Satellite Doppler Positioning*, Las Cruces, NM, Feb. 1982.

[17] Hatch, R., "The Synergism of GPS Code and Carrier Measurements," *Proc. of the Third International Symposium on Satellite Doppler Positioning*, New Mexico State University, Vol. 2, Feb. 1982.

[18] Abidin, H., "Extrawidelaning for 'On the Fly' Ambiguity Resolution: Simulation of Multipath Effects," *Proc. of the ION Satellite Division's 3th International Meeting*, ION GPS-90, Colorado Springs, CO, Sept. 1990.

[19] Paielli, R. A., B. D. McNally, R. E. Bach, Jr., and D. N. Warner, Jr., "Carrier Phase Differential GPS for Approach and Landing: Algorithms and Preliminary Results," *Proc. of the Sixth International Technical Meeting*, ION GPS-93, Salt Lake City, UT, Sept. 1993, pp. 831–840.

[20] van Graas, F., D. W. Diggle, and R. M. Hueschen, "Interferometric GPS Flight Reference/Autoland System: Flight Test Results," *NAVIGATION: Journal of the Institute of Navigation*, Vol. 41, No. 1, Spring 1994, pp. 57–81.

[21] Cohen, C. E., B. Pervan, D. G. Lawrence, H. S. Cobb, J. D. Powell, and B. W. Parkinson, "Real-Time Flight Testing Using Integrity Beacons For GPS Category III Precision Landing," *NAVIGATION: Journal of the Institute of Navigation*, Vol. 41, No. 2, Summer 1994.

[22] Cohen, C. E., et al., "Flight Test Results of Autocoupled Approaches Using GPS and Integrity Beacons," *Proc. of the ION Satellite Division's 7th International Technical Meeting*, Salt Lake City, UT, Sept. 1994, pp. 1145–1153.

[23] Potter, J., and M. Suman, "Thresholdless Redundancy Management with Arrays of Skewed Instruments," *AGARD Monograph*, No. 224, NATO, Neuilly sur Seine, France, 1979.

[24] Walsh, D., "Real-Time Ambiguity Resolution While on the Move," *Proc. of the ION Satellite Division's 5th International Meeting*, ION GPS-92, Albuquerque, NM, Sept. 1992, pp. 473–481.

[25] Chen, H. C., *Theory of Electromagnetic Waves, A Coordinate-Free Approach*, New York NY: McGraw-Hill Book Company, 1983.

[26] Golub, G. H., and C. F. Van Loan, *Matrix Computations*, 2nd Edition, Baltimore, MD: The Johns Hopkins University Press, 1989.

[27] Erickson, C., "An Analysis of Ambiguity Resolution Techniques for Rapid Static GPS Surveys using Single Frequency Data," *Proc. of the ION Satellite Division's 5th International Meeting*, Albuquerque, NM, Sept. 1992, pp. 453–462.

[28] Frei, E., and G. Beutler, "Rapid Static Positioning Based on the Fast Ambiguity Resolution Approach 'FARA': Theory and First Results," *manuscript geodaetica*, Vol. 15, 1990.

[29] Hatch, R., "Instantaneous Ambiguity Resolution," *Proc. of the IAG International Symposium 107 on Kinematic Systems in Geodesy, Surveying and Sensing*, Springer-Verlag, New York, Sept. 10–13, 1990.

[30] Braasch, M. S., "On the Characterization of Multipath Errors in Satellite-Based Precision Approach and Landing Systems," Ph.D. Dissertation, Department of Electrical and Computer Engineering (Avionics Engineering Center), Ohio University, Athens, Ohio, 1992.

[31] Wuebbena, G., "The GPS Adjustment Software Package GEONAP—Concepts and Models," *Proc. of the Fifth International Geodetic Symposium on Satellite Positioning*, Las Cruces, NM, March 1989.

CHAPTER 9
▼▼▼

INTEGRATION OF GPS WITH OTHER SENSORS

Michael Foss
Vehicle Guidance

G. Jeffrey Geier
Motorola

9.1 GPS/INERTIAL NAVIGATION

In the previous chapters, we have observed that GPS receivers can be thought of as discrete-time position/velocity sensors with sampling intervals of approximately 1 sec. The need to provide continuous navigation between the update periods of the GPS receiver, during periods of shading of the GPS receiver's antenna, and through periods of interference, is the impetus for integrating GPS with various additional sensors. The most popular are inertial sensors, but the list also includes dopplometers (Doppler velocity/altimeters), altimeters, speedometers, and odometers to name a few. The method most widely used for this integration is the Kalman filter. The Kalman filter is an estimator. It estimates the instantaneous state of a linear system perturbed by Gaussian white noise. One of the key attributes of the Kalman filter is that it provides a means of inferring information by the use of indirect measurements. It does not have to read control variable(s) directly, but it can read an indirect measurement (including associated noise) and estimate the control variable(s). In the use of GPS, the control variables as we will see later on in this chapter are position, velocity, and possible attitude errors. The indirect measurements are GPS measurements.

This chapter consists of two major sections. In Section 9.1, we discuss the reasons behind the need for the integration of GPS and the use of inertial sensors. The Kalman filter is described, as well as an example of an elementary Kalman filter implementation. In Section 9.2, the implementation issues related to a GPS/inertial integration as a vehicle navigator for ITS applications are presented. A description of the sensors, their integration with the Kalman filter, and test data taken during field testing of this practical multisensor system is presented.

Navigation employing GPS and inertial sensors is a synergistic relationship. The integration of these two types of sensors not only overcomes performance issues found in each individual sensor, but produces a system whose performance exceeds that of the individual sensors. GPS provides bounded accuracy, while inertial system accuracy degrades with time. Not only does the GPS sensor bound the navigation errors, but the GPS sensor calibrates the inertial sensor. In navigation systems, GPS receiver performance issues include susceptibility to interference from external sources, time to first fix (i.e., first position solution), interruption of the satellite signal due to blockage, integrity, and signal reacquisition capability. The performance issues related to inertial sensors are their associated quality and cost.

9.1.1 GPS Receiver Performance Issues

One primary concern with using GPS as a standalone source for navigation is signal interruption. Signal interruption can be caused by shading of the GPS antenna by terrain or manmade structures (e.g., buildings, vehicle structure, and tunnels) or by interference from an external source. An example of signal interruption is shown in Figure 9.1. Each vertical line in this figure indicates a period of shading while driving in an urban environment. The periods of shading (i.e., less than three-satellites availability) actually caused by buildings, are denoted by the black lines in the lower portion of Figure 9.1. (This experiment was conducted when five to six satellites above a 5° mask angle were available for ranging.) When only three usable satellite signals are available, most receivers revert to a two-dimensional navigation mode by utilizing either the last known height or a height obtained from an external source. If the number of usable satellites is less than three, some receivers have the option of not producing a solution or extrapolating the last position and velocity solution forward in what is called "dead-reckoning" (DR) navigation. Inertial measurements can be used as a flywheel to provide navigation during shading outages. In addition, position aiding from the inertial system can be used to help the GPS receiver reacquire the satellite signal. By sending vehicle position to the receiver, the receiver can accurately estimate the range from the given position to the satellites, and thus initialize its internal code loops.

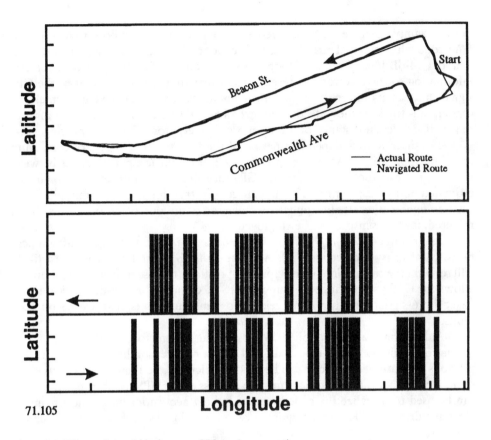

Figure 9.1 Effects of signal blockage on GPS receiver operation.

In the case of interference, it was shown in Chapter 6 that a well-designed receiver without any additional antijam enhancements can track the C/A-code in the presence of wideband jamming up to approximately 35-dB jammer to signal (J/S). This increases to approximately 44-dB J/S for P(Y) code tracking on both L1 and L2. Thus, a 2W L1 in-band jamming source will deny C/A-code signal tracking out to about 27 km from the GPS receiver antenna assuming line of sight from the jammer to the victim receiver, a GPS receiver antenna gain of −3 dBic towards the jammer, and a received satellite signal power of −160 dBw. This denial radius reduces to 14 km for the P(Y)-code signal on L1 assuming a received signal level of −163 dBw. In military systems, in which a target is collocated with a jamming source, an alternate method of navigation is required during the terminal phase of a mission. When inertial components are incorporated with a GPS receiving system, velocity aiding from the inertial system to the GPS receiver can be used to increase the antijam capability of the receiver up to an additional 14 dB (approximately). The receiver in our example incurred an improvement of about 10 dB for both C/A-code and P(Y)-code when aided. Thus, during P(Y)-code tracking, the carrier loops lose lock at about 44-dB J/S and the code loops lose lock at about 54 dB. By sending velocity information to the receiver, the receiver can calculate the Doppler shift of the GPS signals and set its internal circuitry to maintain lock without having to track the carrier, thus tracking the code loops in up to a 54-dB J/S environment. This translates to a reduced denial distance of 4 km (approximately) for P(Y)-code tracking.

The discrete-time-dependent nature of the GPS solution is also of concern in real-time applications. As shown in Figure 9.2, if a vehicle's path changes between updates, the extrapolation of the last GPS measurement produces an error in the estimated and true position. This is particularly true for high-dynamic platforms such as fighter aircraft. In applications where continuous precision navigation is required, inertial sensors can be employed.

An area of concern in the use of GPS, especially in commercial aircraft applications, is integrity (see Section 7.3). An anomalous GPS satellite signal most likely will result in the calculation of an erroneous position. The use of inertial components allows the GPS pseudorange measurement to be compared against statistical limits (typically 6-sigma deviation) and reject those measurements that are beyond the limits.

Aiding that can be supplied by an inertial system to the GPS receiver can be platform position and velocity as well as their corresponding uncertainties. As previously mentioned, velocity can be used to calculate the Doppler of the received signal. In the acquisition and reacquisition process of the GPS receiver, position data can be used to initialize the code loops and allow acquisition in a timely manner. Since acquiring the GPS signal requires a two-dimensional search, missing the signal,

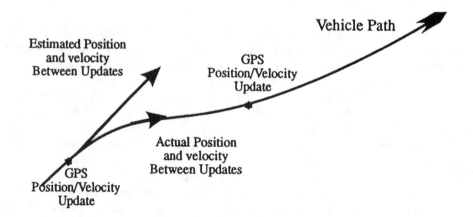

Figure 9.2 Extrapolation of GPS navigation solution in a dynamic environment.

especially on P(Y)-code, can be catastrophic. By utilizing the position and velocity uncertainties from the navigation processor, the limits for the code/carrier search can be set, allowing a much reduced range, as shown in Figure 9.3, to be searched and a more rapid recovery if the search limits are exceeded.

9.1.2 Inertial Sensor Performance Issues

The inertial sensors we are referring to are of two types, gyroscopes and accelerometers. The output of a gyroscope is a signal proportional to angular movement about its input axis ($\Delta\theta$) and the output of an accelerometer is a signal proportional to the change in velocity sensed along its input axis ($\Delta\nu$). A three-axis inertial measurement unit (IMU) would then require three gyroscopes and three accelerometers to inertially determine its position and velocity in free space.

One of the significant factors related to the quality of an inertial system is the drift of the gyroscopes, measured in degrees/hour. The drift of a gyro is a false output signal caused by deficiencies during the manufacturing of the sensor. In inertial sensors, these are caused by mass unbalances in a gyroscope's rotating mass and by nonlinearities in the pickoff circuits as is seen in fiber-optic gyroscopes (FOGs). This false signal is in effect telling the navigation system that the vehicle is moving when it is actually stationary. The manufacturing of gyros with low drift is very costly. A gyroscope with drifts of greater than 100 deg/hr would cost less than $1,000. (All costs are in 1995 U.S. dollars.) An inertial unit with a drift from 1 to 100 deg/hr are currently priced from $1,000 to $10,000. Accuracies of less than 1 deg/hr are available at prices ranging from $10,000 to a $100,000. As you can see, the quality of the inertial sensors has a large role in the cost effectiveness of a

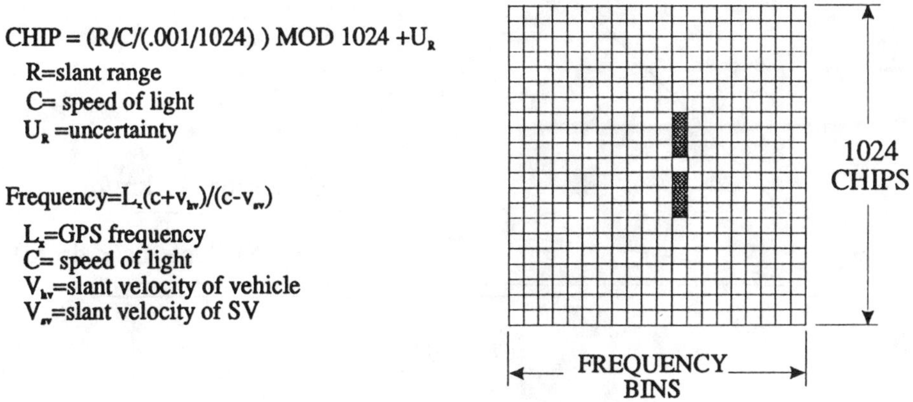

CHIP = (R/C/(.001/1024)) MOD 1024 +U_R

   R=slant range
   C= speed of light
   U_R =uncertainty

Frequency=L_x(c+v_{hv})/(c-v_{sv})

   L_x=GPS frequency
   C= speed of light
   V_{hv}=slant velocity of vehicle
   V_{sv}=slant velocity of SV

1024
CHIPS

FREQUENCY
BINS

Figure 9.3 Aiding supports the acquisition/reacquisition process.

navigation system. If 0.0001-deg/hr gyroscopes were to cost less than $100, GPS may not be needed today. But in actuality, inertial sensors are expensive, and a significant result of the integration of GPS with inertial sensors is the ability to use lower performing, more cost-effective sensors. This is shown in Figure 9.4, where the upper curves show the performance of three classes of inertial sensors. When these systems are integrated with GPS, the lower curve dictates the performance of the integrated GPS/inertial (GPSI) system. Therefore, during operation of a navigation system when both GPS and inertial components are operational, the inertial navigation errors are bounded by the accuracy of the GPS solution.

One significant contribution the GPS receiver makes to the operation of the inertial subsystem is the calibration of the inertial sensors (see Figure 9.5). Inertial instruments are specified to meet a turn-on to turn-on drift requirement. (Each time a gyro is powered up, its initial drift rate differs.) The major errors are the gyro bias and accelerometer bias, which are typically six of the states within an inertial or GPSI Kalman filter. During the operation of a GPSI system, the Kalman filter will produce an estimate of these biases as derived from the velocity data received from the GPS receiver. GPS receiver velocity accuracy is nominally 0.2 m/sec, 95% (P(Y) code), and approximately 0.4 to 0.6 m/sec, 95% (C/A-code). (The C/A-code velocity accuracy range is due to SA and low-cost clock drift.)

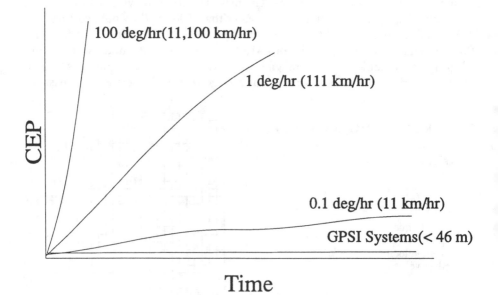

Figure 9.4 Comparison of navigation accuracies.

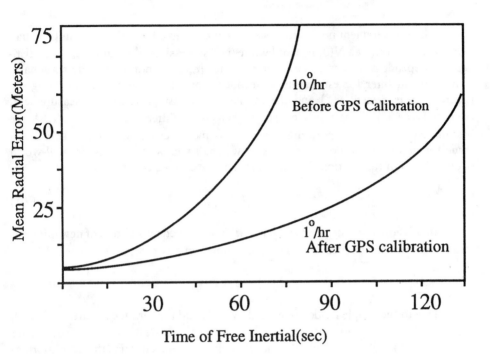

Figure 9.5 Inertial navigation before and after GPS calibration.

9.1.3 The Kalman Filter

The integration of GPS and inertial sensors is typically accomplished through use of a Kalman filter [1]. Kalman filtering, introduced in 1960 by Dr. R. E. Kalman [2], is a statistical technique that combines a knowledge of the statistical nature of system errors with a knowledge of system dynamics, as represented as a state space model, to arrive at an estimate of the state of a system. This state can include any number of unknowns. In a navigation system, we are usually concerned with position and velocity, as a minimum, but its not unusual to see filters for system models with state vector dimensions ranging from 6 to 60. The state estimate utilizes a weighing function, called the Kalman gain, which is optimized to produce a minimum error variance. For this reason, the Kalman filter is called an optimal filter. For linear system models, the Kalman filter is structured to produce an unbiased estimate.

Let us first look at a simplified filter for estimating a constant but unknown scalar quantity x. Assume a measurement model in which at each measurement time t_n, noise is added to x, producing an observation $y(t_n)$ of the form

$$y(t_n) = x + \epsilon_m(t_n)$$

The measurement noise sequence $\{\epsilon_m(t_n)\}$ is assumed to be zero mean Gaussian with variance σ_m^2, i.e., $N(0, \sigma_m^2)$ and white (i.e., successive values of $\epsilon_m(t_n)$ are statistically independent of each other). The sequence $\{\epsilon_m(t_n)\}$ is not necessarily stationary. The Kalman filter for estimating x produces an estimate of x, incorporating the current measurement $y(t_n)$ and the estimate of x just prior to the measurement, denoted as $\hat{x}(t_n^-)$. Since x is a constant, there is no difference between $\hat{x}(t_{n-1}^+)$, the estimate just after incorporating the previous measurement, and $\hat{x}(t_n^-)$. This is not true for more general system models as we shall see. When we discuss real-world applications in this section. The measurement update equation is given by:

$$\hat{x}(t_n^+) = \hat{x}(t_n^-) + k(t_n)[y(t_n) - \hat{x}(t_n^-)] \tag{9.1}$$

In this equation, the prior estimate $\hat{x}(t_n^-)$ is corrected by addition of new information contained in the measurement. The estimation error $\tilde{x}(t_n^+)$ is given by

$$\tilde{x}(t_n^+) = x - \hat{x}(t_n^+)$$

Due to the simple model expressed by (9.1) and the zero mean nature of $\epsilon_m(t_n)$, $\hat{x}(t_n^-)$ is effectively an estimate of measurement $y(t_n)$ (i.e., $\hat{x}(t_n^-) = \hat{y}(t_n)$). The difference sequence $y(t_n) - \hat{y}(t_n)$ is called the innovation process and contains the new information obtained by the measurements. The parameter $k(t_n)$ in (9.1) is the Kalman gain and contains the statistical parameters required to form the combination of the prior estimate and new data resulting in a minimum error variance estimate. The quality of the estimate is characterized by the error variance, but since the estimate is unbiased, the error variance equals the estimate variance $\sigma_{\hat{x}}^2(t_n)$, and its value is different before and after updating the estimate by incorporating the measurement. The Kalman gain is computed as follows:

$$k(t_n) = \frac{\sigma_{\hat{x}}^2(t_n^-)}{\sigma_{\hat{x}}^2(t_n^-) + \sigma_m^2} \tag{9.2}$$

Note that if the measurement is less accurate (i.e., σ_m^2 is large), the weighting given to the new data is reduced because σ_m^2 appears in the denominator. After the measurement update, the error covariance is reduced according to

$$\sigma_{\hat{x}}^2(t_n^+) = [1 - k(t_n)]\sigma_{\hat{x}}^2(t_n^-) \tag{9.3}$$

If we further assume that the measurement noise variance is constant, then it is easy to show that the error variance is given by $\sigma_{\hat{x}}^2(t_n^+) = \sigma_m^2/n$ and thus asymptotically approaches zero as more data is obtained. This property makes the estimate a consistent estimate. Thus, (9.1) to (9.3) provide a data processing scheme that recursively combines our previous state estimate with new measurement data in a way that is statistically optimal. A block diagram of the basic filter structure is shown in Figure 9.6.

In real-world applications, the state vector contains several components that are not constant but evolve dynamically, such as position and velocity. Also, the system state model includes plant noise, which expresses modeling errors as well as actual noise and system disturbances. Since, in general, the system state varies dynamically between measurements, the estimate just after the measurement update $\hat{x}(t_n^+)$ must be extrapolated to the next measurement time according to the system state model to compute $\hat{x}(t_{n+1}^-)$. Also, in the more general vector case, the performance of the Kalman filter estimate is characterized by an error covariance matrix denoted as $\mathbf{P}(t_n)$ and defined by

$$\mathbf{P}(t_n) = E\left[(\mathbf{x}(t_n) - \hat{\mathbf{x}}(t_n))(\mathbf{x}(t_n) - \hat{\mathbf{x}}(t_n))^T\right]$$

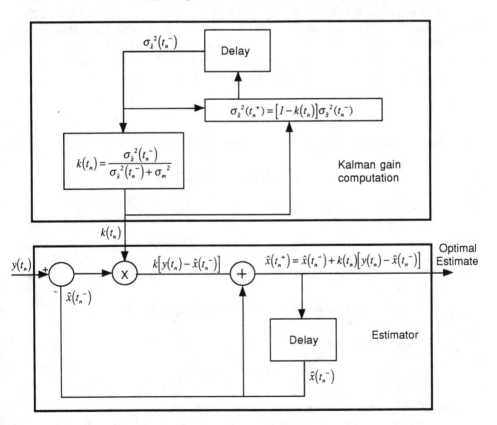

Figure 9.6 Basic Kalman filter.

Here we summarize the Kalman filter equations for the general case. The state system model is given by

$$\mathbf{x}(t_n) = \Phi(t_n, t_{n-1})\mathbf{x}(t_{n-1}) + \mathbf{u}(t_n)$$

where $\Phi(t_n, t_{n-1})$ denotes the system one-step transition matrix and $\mathbf{u}(t_n)$ is the plant or process noise vector that is assumed to be white, zero mean and distributed normally. This is represented by the function $N(0, \mathbf{Q}(t_n))$ with covariance matrix $\mathbf{Q}(t_n)$. The measurement model is

$$\mathbf{y}(t_n) = \mathbf{H}(t_n)\mathbf{x}(t_n) + \epsilon_m(t_n)$$

where $\mathbf{y}(t_n)$ is a vector and the measurement matrix $\mathbf{H}(t_n)$ characterizes the sensitivity of the measurements to each of the state components. Vector $\epsilon_m(t_n)$ is the measurement noise and is a white random process distributed normally as $N(0, \mathbf{R}(t_n))$ with covariance matrix $\mathbf{R}(t_n)$. The Kalman filter, once processing is initiated, alternates between two sets of equations describing (1) the extrapolation of estimate and error covariance between measurements, and (2) the incorporation of the new measurements into the estimate. The state estimate extrapolation is given by

$$\hat{\mathbf{x}}(t_n^-) = \Phi(t_n, t_{n-1})\hat{\mathbf{x}}(t_{n-1}^+)$$

and the error covariance extrapolation is given by

$$\mathbf{P}(t_n^-) = \Phi(t_n, t_{n-1})\mathbf{P}(t_{n-1}^+)\Phi^T(t_n, t_{n-1}) + \mathbf{Q}(t_{n-1})$$

The state estimate measurement update is given by

$$\hat{\mathbf{x}}(t_n^+) = \hat{\mathbf{x}}(t_n^-) + \mathbf{K}(t_n)[\mathbf{y}(t_n) - \mathbf{H}(t_n)\hat{\mathbf{x}}(t_n^-)]$$

where $\mathbf{K}(t_n)$ is the Kalman gain matrix and is computed by

$$\mathbf{K}(t_n) = \mathbf{P}(t_n^-)\mathbf{H}^T(t_n)[\mathbf{H}(t_n)\mathbf{P}(t_n^-)\mathbf{H}^T(t_n) + \mathbf{R}(t_n)]^{-1}$$

The error covariance update is

$$\mathbf{P}(t_n^+) = [\mathbf{I} - \mathbf{K}(t_n)\mathbf{H}(t_n)]\mathbf{P}(t_n^-)$$

Figure 9.7 shows the Kalman filter processing scheme.

In practice, one is concerned with the computational issues arising from the use of finite precision in computers. If care is not taken, the filter can become unstable

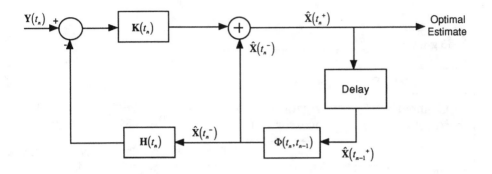

Figure 9.7 Kalman filter processing scheme.

and the solution diverges from the correct values. In inertial navigation systems, where a full model may require up to 60 states, much analysis is placed on proper selection of the critical states to produce what is called a suboptimal Kalman filter, which is computationally well-behaved. Also of concern are wraparound error (i.e., in 16-bit systems $32,767 + 1 = -32,768$) that may cause a complete reversal on signs and roundoff errors [3, 4]. One modification seen in filters used with inertial systems is the use of the filter to determine the error in the state. By setting the initial estimate of the state to zero and inputting the observed error in the state for $y(t_n)$ in place of the observed state, our state vector has become the estimated error of the state, more commonly known as the error state vector, instead of the estimated state. One can then periodically (usually every filter cycle) apply the estimated correction to the output data and reset the filter error states to zero. By doing this, the magnitude of the variables used in the filter are small, minimizing roundoff and nonlinearity errors, and it minimizes some of the computation errors by setting many of the elements in our matrices operation to zero. This method also allows the measurement processing and Kalman filtering to execute at different frequencies. For example, one can process measurements at 100 Hz and run the filter at 1 Hz. Before outputting the data, the latest correction from the filter is applied to the data.

9.1.4 GPSI Integration Methods

Integration of GPS and inertial navigation systems was initiated in the early 1980s [1, 5] with a configuration that later came to be known as a loosely integrated or loosely coupled configuration. This configuration included a GPS receiver with an 8-state Kalman filter, an IMU, a navigation processor that contains a 15- to 18-state Kalman filter, navigation equations to convert the $\Delta\theta$'s and $\Delta\nu$'s from the IMU to platform attitude, position and velocity, as well as other functions that we will discuss later in this chapter. The configuration, as shown in Figure 9.8, accepted

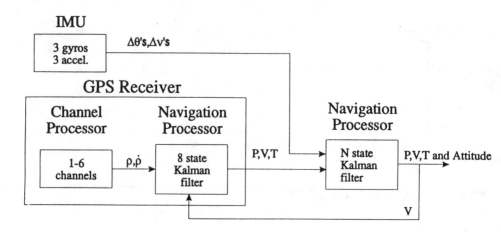

Figure 9.8 Loosely integrated GPSI system.

GPS position from the GPS receiver, and $\Delta\theta$'s and $\Delta\nu$'s from the inertial unit. Although used in many initial applications, this system has a feed forward loop from the navigation processor and two separate filters that open the possibility of instability caused by mutual feedback. Mission scenarios for this configuration must be thoroughly simulated to ensure the stability of the filter. In situations where instability occurs, the gains in the filter are reduced, which may result in sluggish system operation. Today, most integrations are tightly integrated, as shown in Figure 9.9. This configuration is also referred to as tightly coupled. In tightly integrated systems, the Kalman filter in the GPS receiver is eliminated and pseudorange and pseudorange-rate data from the GPS channel processor is sent directly to the naviga-

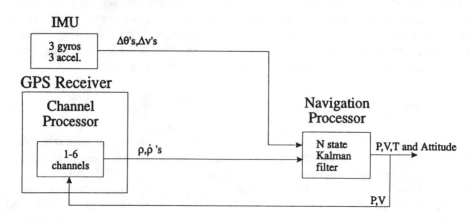

Figure 9.9 Tight integration of a GPSI system.

tion processor. In this configuration, unmodeled errors resulting from the GPS receiver's Kalman filter are eliminated and the system designer is allowed to set gains as tight as possible.

In the tight integration of a GPSI system, as in most inertial systems, we utilize the Kalman filter to estimate the error in our state—not the state itself—and use the estimated error state vector $\hat{x}$ to correct the output of the navigation equations, as shown in Figure 9.10.

To demonstrate what we have described, we will implement a simplified GPSI system with a single gyro and a single-channel GPS receiver whose antenna is collocated with the IMU, eliminating the need for lever-arm compensation. (Lever-arm compensation is required when the GPS receiver antenna and IMU do not share the same origin in a 3-axis right-handed coordinate system.) The inertial components that have been purchased for this system have an uncompensated drift uncertainty of 10 deg/hr. A single channel receiver refers to a GPS receiver with the capability to measure pseudorange and pseudorange rate from only one satellite at a time. In addition to providing pseudorange and pseudorange rate, the receiver also forwards the position of the current satellite, the velocity of the current satellite, the time of the GPS measurement, and the deviations σ_ρ and $\sigma_{\dot{\rho}}$ of both the pseudorange and pseudorange-rate. Ionospheric, relativistic, satellite clock, and tropospheric corrections are applied to the pseudorange data within the receiver prior to its forwarding to the navigation processor. We will denote corrected pseudorange and pseudorange rate as ρ_{cor} and $\dot{\rho}_{cor}$, respectively. In order to implement this system, we must first formulate the states, the observation models, and the noise model statistics, and initialize our error covariance matrix P_0 and the estimated error state vector $\hat{x}_0$.

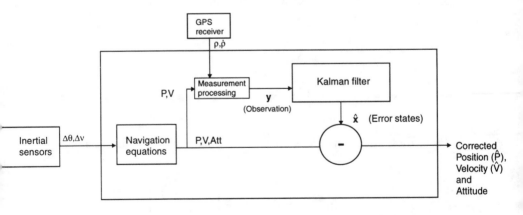

Figure 9.10 GPSI functional block diagram.

9.1.4.1 States

The states selected are position error (x direction, δx), velocity error (x direction, $\delta \dot{x}$), GPS receiver clock bias (t_u), and clock drift ($\dot{t}_u$). This minimum set has been selected to minimize the number of mathematical calculations that have to be performed. Receiver clock bias and drift are required because they will eventually be subtracted from the corrected pseudorange and pseudorange rate measurements, respectively, to form the measurement-based satellite-to-user range r_m and range rate $\dot{r}_m$. In this example, we have chosen position and velocity along our x-axis as our system outputs. Therefore, the error state vector is

$$\mathbf{x} = \begin{bmatrix} \delta x \\ \delta \dot{x} \\ \delta t \\ \delta \dot{t} \end{bmatrix}$$

Units for the states consists of kilometers (km) for position, meters/second (m/sec) for velocity, meters (m) for clock bias, and m/sec for clock drift. All data is referenced to an Earth-centered Earth fix (ECEF) reference frame.

9.1.4.2 Transition Matrix

To formulate the state transition matrix, one can write down the transition equations for position, velocity, clock bias, and clock drift as follows:

$$\delta x_n = \delta x_{n-1} + \delta \dot{x}_{n-1} \Delta t$$

$$\delta \dot{x}_n = \delta \dot{x}_{n-1}$$

$$\delta t_{u_n} = \delta t_{u_{n-1}} + \delta \dot{t}_{u_{n-1}} \Delta t$$

$$\delta \dot{t}_{u_n} = \delta \dot{t}_{u_{n-1}}$$

From these equations, the state transition matrix can be formulated as

$$\boldsymbol{\Phi}(t_n, t_{n-1}) = \boldsymbol{\Phi}(t_1, t_0) = \begin{bmatrix} 1 & \Delta t & 0 & 0 \\ 0 & 1 & 0 & 0 \\ 0 & 0 & 1 & \Delta t \\ 0 & 0 & 0 & 1 \end{bmatrix}$$

For this example, we will denote $\boldsymbol{\Phi}(t_1, t_0)$ as $\boldsymbol{\Phi}$.

9.1.4.3 Measurement Matrix

The elements in the measurement matrix $H(t_1)$ relate observations—in this case, range error and range rate error—to the state vector. To accomplish this, as each measurement is received, we create a line-of-sight unit vector from the user's inertial-based position to the satellite's position. This unit vector is then placed in the measurement matrix to decompose the range error and range rate error into its x-dimension component. The navigation processor computes the unit vector from the user to the satellite by subtracting the user's inertial position (x_{ui}, y_{ui}, z_{ui}) from the satellite position (x_j, y_j, z_j) (where j denotes the jth satellite), generating an estimated range vector to the satellite. This is then normalized to a unit vector by dividing the range vector by its scalar range. Normally each element of the unit vector is placed in the measurement matrix to convert the range error and range rate error, but in our case we only need to incorporate the x-axis component of its xyz components as shown below. The errors in the clock bias and drift states are simply set to 1, since the line-of-sight pseudorange and pseudorange rate errors directly map into the clock bias and clock drift states.

Let

$$\tilde{r}_x = x_j - x_{ui}$$
$$\tilde{r}_y = y_j - y_{ui}$$
$$\tilde{r}_z = z_j - z_{ui}$$
$$\tilde{r} = \sqrt{(\tilde{r}_x)^2 + (\tilde{r}_y)^2 + (\tilde{r}_z)^2} \tag{9.4}$$

$$H(t_1) = \begin{bmatrix} \dfrac{\tilde{r}_x}{\tilde{r}} & 0 & 1 & 0 \\ 0 & \dfrac{\tilde{r}_x}{\tilde{r}} & 0 & 1 \end{bmatrix}$$

9.1.4.4 Initialization

Both P_0 and $\hat{x}_0$ are initialized from known data. This data is obtained from specifications on the GPS receiver for clock bias and drift, and the inertial specification for gyro bias. The initial position and velocity are obtained from the mission scenario. For example, an aircraft may be parked (velocity = 0.0) at a specific location at the time the navigation processor is initialized. In our example, we will assume the parameter values in Table 9.1.

From this data, we can formulate

Table 9.1
Initial Assumptions

Parameter	One Sigma Value	Variance	Comment
Position	20 km	400 km²	Accuracy of external source
Velocity	10 m/sec	100 m/sec²	Accuracy of external source
Clock bias	10⁵ m	10¹⁰ m²	Accuracy of C/A-code
Clock drift	100 m/sec	10⁴ m/sec²	Characteristic of user clock

$$\mathbf{P}_0 = \begin{bmatrix} 400 & 0 & 0 & 0 \\ 0 & 100 & 0 & 0 \\ 0 & 0 & 10^{10} & 0 \\ 0 & 0 & 0 & 10^4 \end{bmatrix}$$

$$\hat{\mathbf{x}}_0 = \begin{bmatrix} 0 \\ 0 \\ 0 \\ 0 \end{bmatrix}$$

We must also set our process noise covariance matrix $\mathbf{Q}(t_0)$ and our measurement noise covariance matrix $\mathbf{R}(t_1)$. The $\mathbf{Q}(t_0)$ matrix is a 4 by 4 matrix whose entries above and below the principle diagonal are zero. The diagonal elements of $\mathbf{Q}(t_0)$ represent the noise variances in the GPS receiver in the measurement of pseudorange and pseudorange rate. The measurement noise covariance matrix is a 2 by 2 diagonal matrix whose elements represent the noise variances in the pseudorange and pseudorange rate measurements. This is easily computed by the GPS receiver, which integrates 1-msec samples to form 1-sec GPS measurements. In our example, the noise for the GPS receiver we are using is 1m for pseudorange measurements and 0.1 m/sec for pseudorange rate measurements. We place the variance, the square of the deviation, into the $\mathbf{Q}(t_0)$ matrix as shown:

$$\mathbf{Q}(t_0) = \begin{bmatrix} 1 & 0 & 0 & 0 \\ 0 & 0.01 & 0 & 0 \\ 0 & 0 & 0 & 0 \\ 0 & 0 & 0 & 0 \end{bmatrix}$$

The measurement noise is received with the pseudorange and pseudorange rate measurement. When we process the measurement and form the observation, we will set the $\mathbf{R}(t_1)$ matrix, where

$$\mathbf{R}(t_1) = \begin{bmatrix} \sigma_\rho^2 & 0 \\ 0 & \sigma_\rho^2 \end{bmatrix}$$

9.1.4.5 Data Synchronization

One issue that we must deal with is that of data synchronization. The Kalman filter, being a sampled state system, assumes the time of the GPS measurement and the inertial measurement are identical. Failure to synchronize the measurement data results in unmodeled errors and requires the user to increase the process noise variances to compensate for this error. To accomplish this, two issues must be addressed. The first is the timing of inertial data with the GPS receiver time. The second is the buffering of inertial data to allow synchronization of the inertial data with the GPS data.

Timing of the inertial data is accomplished by having the GPS receiver transmit a 1-sec timing pulse to the navigation processor. This signal, tied to a high-level interrupt, forces the inertial clock to the next second. The inertial clock is a software clock that is incremented by each inertial measurement received by the navigation processor (typically at a rate of 100 Hz to 800 Hz). The inertial clock is thus resynchronized to GPS receiver clock time once per second. To initialize the inertial clock, the GPS receiver must implement a specific message that will inform the navigation processor of the GPS receiver time at the next interrupt. This must be accomplished well before the receipt of the interrupt to give the navigation processor time to respond to the interrupt and the message and prepare to set the inertial clock before the next interrupt is received.

Since the GPS receiver and the inertial are asynchronous, a circular queue—called a history queue—contains 1 or 2 sec of inertial position data. By examining the time of the GPS measurement, the latest inertial position whose time tag is less than that of the GPS measurement can be extracted from the queue. Using the next queue entry, the data is then interpolated to the time of the GPS measurement.

With "pencil in hand" and raw data taken from a GPS satellites given in Table 9.2, we can start to see how our system will respond. In our system, the user inputs the estimated initial position as 42.1° latitude, −71.2° longitude and zero altitude. This, in ECEF coordinates, is: (1527397, −4486699, 4253850). When the GPS measurement data is received by the navigation processor, the measurement matrix (9.4) is formulated.

To do this, we utilize the position of the satellite x_{sv}, y_{sv}, z_{sv} and subtract the user's inertial-based position at the time of the GPS measurement x_{ui}, y_{ui}, z_{ui}. To obtain the user's inertial-derived position at the time of the GPS measurement, we utilize the previously mentioned history buffer. By obtaining this inertial position in ECEF coordinates just before the time of the GPS measurement and using the next history buffer entry, the data is interpolated to give an accurate inertial user

Table 9.2
Data Received From a GPS Measurement

Parameter		Value
Time		250,812.171875 sec
Satellite position (ECEF)		
	x	−11,095,241m
	y	−3,414,814m
	z	23,488,864 m
Satellite velocity (ECEF)		
	$\dot{x}$	91.63 m/sec
	$\dot{y}$	−294.00 m/sec
	$\dot{z}$	3.700 m/sec
Pseudorange measurement		23,049,952m
Pseudorange-rate measurement		16.952 m/sec
Pseudorange deviation		7m
Pseudorange-rate deviation		0.05 m/sec

position at the time of the GPS measurement. In our example, the history buffer contains the value (1527397, −4486699, 4253850) for the position before and after the GPS measurement time because the vehicle was parked during the initialization. Thus, the interpolated value will be (1527397, −4486699, 4253850). Using (9.4), the measurement matrix is formulated as shown below:

$$\tilde{r}_x = x_{sv} - x_{ui} = -11,095,241 - 1,527,397 = -12,622,638$$

$$\tilde{r}_y = y_{sv} - y_{ui} = -3,414,814 - (-4,486,699) = 1,071,885$$

$$\tilde{r}_z = z_{sv} - z_{ui} = 23,488,864 - 4,253,850 = 19,235,014$$

$$\tilde{r} = \sqrt{(\tilde{r}_x)^2 + (\tilde{r}_y)^2 + (\tilde{r}_z)^2} = 23,031,841$$

$$\mathbf{H}(t_1) = \begin{bmatrix} \dfrac{\tilde{r}_x}{\tilde{r}} & 0 & 1 & 0 \\ 0 & \dfrac{\tilde{r}_x}{\tilde{r}} & 0 & 1 \end{bmatrix}$$

$$= \begin{bmatrix} -\dfrac{12,622,638}{23,031,841} & 0 & 1 & 0 \\ 0 & -\dfrac{12,622,638}{23,031,841} & 0 & 1 \end{bmatrix}$$

$$= \begin{bmatrix} -0.548 & 0 & 1 & 0 \\ 0 & -0.548 & 0 & 1 \end{bmatrix}$$

Extrapolate the Error Covariance Matrix and Add in the Process Noise

It can be shown that with a $\Delta t = 1$ second and using the 1-step state transition matrix Φ, the first extrapolated covariance $P(t_1^-)$ can be calculated as follows:

$$\Phi P_0 = \begin{bmatrix} 1 & 1 & 0 & 0 \\ 0 & 1 & 0 & 0 \\ 0 & 0 & 1 & 1 \\ 0 & 0 & 0 & 1 \end{bmatrix} \begin{bmatrix} 400 & 0 & 0 & 0 \\ 0 & 100 & 0 & 0 \\ 0 & 0 & 10^{10} & 0 \\ 0 & 0 & 0 & 10^4 \end{bmatrix}$$

$$= \begin{bmatrix} 400 & 100 & 0 & 0 \\ 0 & 100 & 0 & 0 \\ 0 & 0 & 1.1E10 & 1.0E4 \\ 0 & 0 & 0 & 1.0E4 \end{bmatrix}$$

$\Phi P_0 \Phi^T$ computes to

$$\Phi P_0 \Phi^T = \begin{bmatrix} 500 & 100 & 0 & 0 \\ 100 & 100 & 0 & 0 \\ 0 & 0 & 1.1E10 & 1.0E4 \\ 0 & 0 & 1.0E4 & 1.0E4 \end{bmatrix}$$

The extrapolated covariance, $P(t_1^-) = \Phi P_0 \Phi^T + Q(t_0)$ computes to

$$\Phi P_0 \Phi^T + Q(t_0) = \begin{bmatrix} 501 & 100 & 0 & 0 \\ 100 & 100 & 0 & 0 \\ 0 & 0 & 1.1E10 & 1.0E4 \\ 0 & 0 & 1.0E4 & 1.0E4 \end{bmatrix}$$

Compute the Kalman Gain Matrix **K**

The Kalman gain matrix **K** is computed where

$$K(t_1^-) = P(t_1^-)H^T(t_1)[H(t_1)P(t_1^-)H^T(t_1) + R(t_1)]^{-1}$$

First compute $P(t_1^-)H^T(t_1)$:

$$\mathbf{P}(t_1^-)\mathbf{H}^T(t_1) = \begin{bmatrix} 501 & 100 & 0 & 0 \\ 100 & 100 & 0 & 0 \\ 0 & 0 & 1.1E10 & 1.0E4 \\ 0 & 0 & 1.0E4 & 1.0E4 \end{bmatrix} \begin{bmatrix} -.548 & 0 \\ 0 & -.548 \\ 1 & 0 \\ 0 & 1 \end{bmatrix}$$

$$= \begin{bmatrix} -274.6 & -54.8 \\ -54.8 & -54.8 \\ 1.1E10 & 1.0E4 \\ 1.0E4 & 1.0E4 \end{bmatrix}$$

$\mathbf{H}(t_1)\mathbf{P}(t_1^-)\mathbf{H}^T(t_1)$ can then be computed, resulting in a 2 by 2 matrix as shown:

$$\mathbf{H}(t_1)\mathbf{P}(t_1^{-1})\mathbf{H}^T(t_1) = \begin{bmatrix} 1.1E10 & 1.0E4 \\ 1.0E4 & 1.0E4 \end{bmatrix}$$

Measurement noise $\mathbf{R}(t_1)$ is added:

$$\mathbf{H}(t_1)\mathbf{P}(t_1^-)\mathbf{H}^T(t_1) + \mathbf{R}(t_1) = \begin{bmatrix} 1.1E10 & 10436 \\ 10436 & 10436 \end{bmatrix} + \begin{bmatrix} 1 & 0 \\ 0 & 0.01 \end{bmatrix} = \begin{bmatrix} 1.1E10 & 10436 \\ 10436 & 10436 \end{bmatrix}$$

and $[\mathbf{H}(t_1)\mathbf{P}(t_1^-)\mathbf{H}^{T}(t_1) + \mathbf{R}(t_1)]^{-1}$ equals

$$[\mathbf{H}(t_1)\mathbf{P}(t_n^-)\mathbf{H}^T(t_1) + \mathbf{R}(t_1)]^{-1} = \begin{bmatrix} 9.05E-11 & -9.05E-11 \\ -9.05E-11 & 9.58E-5 \end{bmatrix}$$

As required above, the gain matrix $\mathbf{K}(t_1)$ is computed as follows:

$$\mathbf{K}(t_1) = \mathbf{P}(t_1^-)\mathbf{H}^T(t_1)[\mathbf{H}(t_1)\mathbf{P}(t_1^-)\mathbf{H}^T(t_1) + \mathbf{R}(t_1)]^{-1}$$

$$= \begin{bmatrix} -1.990E-8 & -5.251E-3 \\ 4.900E-13 & -5.252E-3 \\ 9.999E-1 & -2.878E-3 \\ 1.174E-12 & 9.971E-1 \end{bmatrix}$$

Extrapolate the Current State $\mathbf{\Phi}\hat{\mathbf{x}}_0$

To extrapolate the error state $\hat{\mathbf{x}}(t_1^-)$ as required in for this step, 3, $\hat{\mathbf{x}}(t_1^-) = \mathbf{\Phi}\hat{\mathbf{x}}_0$ results in the following:

$$\hat{\mathbf{x}}(t_1^-) = \mathbf{\Phi}\hat{\mathbf{x}}_0 = \begin{bmatrix} 1 & 1 & 0 & 0 \\ 0 & 1 & 0 & 0 \\ 0 & 0 & 1 & 1 \\ 0 & 0 & 0 & 1 \end{bmatrix} \begin{bmatrix} 0 \\ 0 \\ 0 \\ 0 \end{bmatrix} = \begin{bmatrix} 0 \\ 0 \\ 0 \\ 0 \end{bmatrix}$$

Compute the Observation Vector y(t₁) and the Predicted
Observation $H(t_1)\hat{x}(t_1^-)$

The range observation is the difference between the estimated satellite-to-user range $\tilde{r}$, and the measurement-based range r_m. To compute the observation, range $\tilde{r}$ must first be computed. To do this, we utilize the ECEF position of the satellite forwarded from the GPS receiver with the measurement data and subtract the user's inertial-based position at the time of the GPS measurement. The user's position at the time of the GPS measurement is extracted from the history buffer and interpolated to give an accurate user position. The estimated satellite-to-user range is then be calculated as follows:

$$[\tilde{r} = (x_{sv} - x_{ui})^2 + (y_{sv} - y_{ui})^2 + (z_{sv} - z_{ui})^2]^{\frac{1}{2}}$$

$$= [(-11,095,241 - 1,527,397)^2$$

$$+ (-3,414,814 - (-4,486,699))^2 + (23,488,864 - 4,253,850)^2]^{\frac{1}{2}}$$

$$= 23,031,841$$

The current clock bias (t_u) can be calculate by using the initial clock bias of 0 and adding the clock drift for 1 sec. Assuming an equivalent drift rate $c\dot{t}_u$, of 10 m/sec, the clock bias at this first iteration is $ct_u + c\dot{t}_u \Delta t = 0 + 10 = 10$. Thus, the range observation is

$$OBS(r) = \tilde{r} - r_m$$

$$= \tilde{r} - \rho_{cor} + ct_u$$

$$= 23,031,841 - 23,049,952 + 10$$

$$= -18,101$$

Next, we compute the observed range rate, which is the line-of-sight component of the satellite's range rate minus the user's range-rate. To determine the line of sight component, a line-of-site vector is formulated as follows:

$$LOS_x = \frac{x_{sv} - x_{ui}}{\tilde{r}} = \frac{-11,095,241 - 1,527,397}{23,031,841} = -0.548$$

$$LOS_y = \frac{y_{sv} - y_{ui}}{\tilde{r}} = \frac{-3,414,814 - (-4,486,699)}{23,031,841} = -0.0465$$

$$LOS_z = \frac{z_{sv} - z_{ui}}{\tilde{r}} = \frac{23,488,864 - 4,253,850}{23,031,841} = 0.835$$

The estimated range-rate, $\dot{\tilde{r}}$, is

$$\dot{r} = \text{LOS}_x(\dot{x}_{sv} - \dot{x}_{ui}) + \text{LOS}_y(\dot{y}_{sv} - \dot{y}_{ui}) + \text{LOS}_z(\dot{z}_{sv} - \dot{z}_{ui})$$
$$= -0.548(91.63 - 0.0) + 0.0465(-294.01 - 0.0) - 0.835(3.70 - 0.0)$$
$$= -60.81 \text{ meters/sec}$$

The observed error of range-rate is

$$\text{OBS}(\dot{r}) = \dot{r} - \dot{r}_m$$
$$= \dot{r} - (\dot{\rho}_{cor} - c\dot{t}_u)$$
$$= -60.8 - (-552 - 10)$$
$$= 501.2$$

The observation vector is thus

$$y(t_1) = \begin{bmatrix} -18101 \\ 501.2 \end{bmatrix}$$

The predicted observation $H(t_1)\hat{x}(t_1^-)$, is calculated to be zero since the current estimate of the error state is zero.

$$H(t_{12})\hat{x}(t_1^-) = \begin{bmatrix} 0.0 \\ 0.0 \end{bmatrix}$$

Compute the Error State Estimate

The error state vector is $\hat{x}(t_1^-)$
$$\hat{x}(t_1^+) = \hat{x}(t_1^-) + K(t_1)[y(t_1) - H(t_1)\hat{x}(t_1^-)] \cdot y(t_1) - H(t_1)\hat{x}(t_1^-)$$
computes to

$$y(t_1) - H(t_1)\hat{x}(t_1^-) = \begin{bmatrix} -18101 \\ 501.2 \end{bmatrix} - \begin{bmatrix} 0 \\ 0 \end{bmatrix} = \begin{bmatrix} -18101 \\ 501.2 \end{bmatrix}$$

Multiplying by the gain matrix and adding in the previous error state vector yields

$$\hat{x}(t_1^+) = \hat{x}(t_1^-) + K(t_1)[y(t_1) - H(t_1)\hat{x}(t_1^-)]$$

$$= \begin{bmatrix} 0 \\ 0 \\ 0 \\ 0 \end{bmatrix} + \begin{bmatrix} -1.990E-8 & -5.251E-3 \\ -4.900E-13 & -5.252E-3 \\ 9.999E-1 & -2.878E-3 \\ 1.174E-12 & 9.971E-1 \end{bmatrix} \begin{bmatrix} -18101 \\ 501.2 \end{bmatrix}$$

$$= \begin{bmatrix} -2.632 \\ -2.632 \\ -18,102.6 \\ 499.7 \end{bmatrix}$$

Adjust the Covariance for the Current Estimate ($\sigma_{\hat{x}}$)

The covariance of the new estimate is computed using the equation

$$P(t_1^+) = [I - K(t_1)H(t_1)]P(t_1^-)$$

$$P(t_1^+) = [I - K(t_1)H(t_1)]P(t_1^-) = \begin{bmatrix} 500.70 & 99.71 & 274.40 & 54.64 \\ 99.71 & 99.72 & 54.65 & 54.65 \\ 274.40 & 54.64 & 151.40 & 29.95 \\ 54.64 & 54.64 & 29.96 & 29.96 \end{bmatrix}$$

Apply the Corrections and Reset the Error State Vector

$$\delta x = 1,527,397 + (-2.63) = 1,527,394 \text{ m}$$

$$\delta \dot{x} = 0 + (-2.63) = -2.6 \text{ m/sec}$$

$$ct_u = 0 + (-18103) = -18,103 \text{ m}$$

$$c\dot{t}_u = 0 + 499.7 = 499.7 \text{ m/sec}$$

$$\hat{x}(t_1^+) = \begin{bmatrix} 0 \\ 0 \\ 0 \\ 0 \end{bmatrix}$$

After the first iteration, we can see that almost all of the correction from the GPS receiver has been placed into the clock bias and clock drift. As we proceed with further iterations, the error will be placed in the clock, position, and velocity error.

After a few hundred iterations, the filter should stabilize (if the noise parameters have been properly set and truncation/roundoff errors have been minimized). The errors in the position and velocity will not exceed the errors in the pseudorange and pseudorange rate measurements.

9.1.5 Reliability and Integrity

It is difficult for a GPS receiver to determine the precise point at which it loses lock. A capability that prevents erroneous measurements from entering the filter is thus required. With filter processing, a check can be made using the observed error in the GPS signal compared to the predicted covariance to see if the measurement being processed is within reasonable limits. The extrapolated covariance at the time of the measurement is calculated in a similar manner to the formulation used in our filter, $P(t_1^-) = \Phi P_0 \Phi^T + Q(t_0)$. Since we are dealing with a single measurement, the equation of the range and range rate can be separated from the matrix calculation and reduced as follows:

$$\Phi P_0 \Phi^T + q_{33} = [0\ 0\ 1\ \phi_{23}] \begin{bmatrix} p_{00} & p_{01} & p_{02} & p_{03} \\ p_{10} & p_{11} & p_{12} & p_{13} \\ p_{20} & p_{21} & p_{22} & p_{23} \\ p_{30} & p_{31} & p_{32} & p_{33} \end{bmatrix} \begin{bmatrix} 0 \\ 0 \\ 1 \\ \phi_{23} \end{bmatrix} + q_{33}$$

$$= [(p_{20} + \phi_{23}p_{30})(p_{21} + \phi_{23}p_{31})(p_{22} + \phi_{23}p_{32})(p_{23} + \phi_{23}p_{33})] \begin{bmatrix} 0 \\ 0 \\ 1 \\ \phi_{23} \end{bmatrix} + q_{33}$$

$$= p_{22} + \phi_{23}p_{32} + \phi_{23}(p_{23} + \phi_{23}p_{33}) + q_{33}$$

Since $p_{ij} = p_{ji}$, let

$$\alpha_\rho = p_{22} + 2\ \phi_{23}p_{23} + (\phi_{23})^2 p_{33} + q_{33}$$

One can do the same thing for GPS velocity measurement and get

$$\alpha_\rho = p_{33}q_{33} + q_{44}$$

The error in the observation that we earlier called the innovations process we will denote as gamma (Γ), which can be calculated by subtracting the predicted observation $H(t_1)\hat{x}(t_1^-)$ from the observation. The value Γ^2 is compared to $m^2\alpha$, where m is the $m\sigma$ limit (typically $3 \leq m \leq 6$). If Γ^2 exceeds the $m^2\alpha$ limit, the measurement is declared bad and not processed by the filter.

Another technique that is used is a function of the GPS receiver. Most bad measurements are caused by disruptions in the GPS signal. These disruptions result in changes in the power levels of the GPS signal being received. By calculating the received power level during each GPS sub dwell (1 ms) and comparing them to set thresholds, the receiver can recognize significant fluctuations. When thresholds are exceeded, the measurement is declared bad and not utilized by the filter.

9.2 INTELLIGENT TRANSPORTATION SYSTEMS (ITS)

In this section, the role of integrated navigation systems in ITS is discussed. Candidate sensors that can be used to augment the GPS solution are reviewed, as are several current navigation systems.

9.2.1 ITS Overview

The U.S. ITS program consists of the following six application areas [6]:

1. Advanced traffic management systems;
2. Advanced traveler information systems;
3. Advanced public transportation systems;
4. Advanced vehicle control systems;
5. Advanced rural transportation systems;
6. Commercial vehicle operations.

The ITS program is aimed at applying advanced concepts and technologies in communications, navigation, and information systems to reduce traffic congestion and improve transportation efficiency as well as highway safety. Furthermore, the program seeks to reduce the environmental damage caused by automobiles. In the advanced traffic management systems (ATMS) application area, information on traffic movement is integrated to measure congestion and detect accidents. This information can then be used to manage traffic flow through the control of traffic lights, ramp metering signals, highway advisory radio, and variable message signs. Advanced traveler information systems (ATIS) provide assistance to travelers in planning or making trips. They support pretrip planning using computers and include address finding, tourist information retrieval, and route planning functions. The advanced public transportation systems (APTS) area makes use of ATIS technologies to improve the safety and efficiency of buses, trains, subways, taxis, and demand-responsive services. Automatic vehicle location systems, combined with digital map displays, are useful in real-time passenger information systems used to support APTS. Advanced vehicle control systems (AVCS) include smart cruise controls, collision avoidance systems, and vehicle platooning. In the advanced rural transportation systems (ARTS) application area, problems specific to rural areas are addressed, including collisions with livestock, running off roads, and weather-induced accidents. Finally, commercial vehicle operations (CVO) include fleet management, automatic toll taking, and stolen vehicle recovery for public transportation and safety vehicles.

Potential products that may emerge in each area are reviewed in [6]. This section will focus on the in-vehicle navigation system, which could be used to support ATIS, APTS, and CVO applications. Applications are considered herein that could be used to aid travelers in finding their hotel or a recommended restaurant, increase the efficiency of public transportation and safety systems, and increase driver safety.

Three distinct ITS applications have led to in-vehicle product developments: vehicle navigation and route guidance, vehicle tracking, and vehicle emergency messaging. Examples of product developments in each area are provided in the following paragraphs. A generic vehicle navigation and route guidance system architecture is depicted in Figure 9.11, illustrating the major components of the system. Included in the figure is a GPS receiver—the primary source of absolute positioning information, a possible set of auxiliary navigation sensors to augment the GPS positions, a computer for generating a map-matched position and performing route guidance, and two possible displays. The map display is required in the system if the driver selects the route (based on the displayed position of the vehicle on the map and a selected desired future location). As a possible addition or alternative to the map display, a directions display may be included. This can take the form of a set of displayed instructions, (e.g., turn right at the next intersection, then continue for three blocks...) or verbal and/or visual (i.e., turn signal) driver commands. The digital map is an essential element for the navigation and guidance function: digital maps

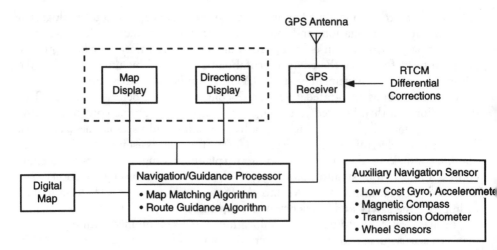

Figure 9.11 Generic vehicle navigation/route guidance system architecture.

are currently available for major cities [7, 8] within the continental U.S. In generating a correct map-matched position from the GPS solution augmented by the auxiliary navigation sensors, the map-matching algorithm may make use of the (recent) history of vehicle positions in addition to the current position estimate. A robust approach to map matching must consider both the sources of error contributing to the integrated GPS/auxiliary sensor solution as well as errors inherent in the digital maps [9, 10]. Route guidance algorithms attempt to generate "optimal" trajectories based upon minimizing travel time to the selected destination; thus, information about one-way streets and speed limits, in addition to possible road construction, must be stored in the map data base to ensure maximum effectiveness of the route guidance.

The Zexel system [11] is an example of a vehicle navigation and route guidance system that utilizes most of the features illustrated in Figure 9.11. The Zexel system includes a GPS receiver integrated with a low-cost gyro and an interface to the transmission odometer of the vehicle. A magnetic compass is also included in the navigation sensor suite. Once the integrated position is matched to a street location, an optimal route to a selected destination can be found and a sequence of directional commands can be generated to assist the driver in following the computed route. The system has been successfully demonstrated and is currently for sale; experience with the system has generally been favorable, with drivers finding it useful in locating points of interest (e.g., restaurants and hotels) when traveling.

In vehicle tracking applications, knowledge of the vehicle's position is maintained at a centralized fleet management facility; real-time navigation information is generally not available to or of primary interest to the driver of the vehicle. A typical system architecture is illustrated in Figure 9.12. Note the components that are shared in common with the vehicle navigation system of Figure 9.11: the GPS

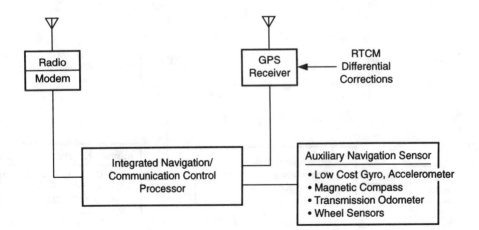

Figure 9.12 Generic vehicle tracking system architecture.

receiver and (optional) RTCM differential link, the auxiliary navigation sensors, and the navigation computer. For the tracking system, no map matching or route guidance is performed in the vehicle; thus, the navigation computer's sole function is to provide an "optimal" estimate of the vehicle's position for communication to the fleet management center. At the base station, map matching may be performed in attempting to place the vehicle on the correct street location. The communication system serves a critical role in any tracking system: central station polling of each participant can be used to manage the data flow. Alternatively, time division multiple access (TDMA) using GPS time as a standard can be used. A thorough review of communication alternatives for fleet management is provided in [12]. Trimble Navigation's Placer™/DR navigation system provides a cost-effective solution to the integrated navigation system requirement for vehicle tracking [13]. It integrates Trimble's six-channel GPS receiver with a low-cost gyro and an interface to the vehicle's transmission odometer to provide a continuous and accurate position solution. This system is reviewed as a case study in the concluding section of this chapter.

In emergency messaging applications, the communication to the central facility is dictated by the vehicle, either through driver initiation or automatically. Figure 9.13 illustrates a typical architecture. The unique elements for this system are the interfaces to the cellular phone for broadcast of current position and alarm status and to the crash detection sensor (typically a low-cost accelerometer). Upon exceeding some acceleration threshold, or driver activation, the phone automatically places a "911" call for dispatch to the vehicle's location, as determined by the complement of navigation sensors. An example of this system is Motorola's Cellular Positioning and Emergency Messaging Unit [14], which integrates Motorola's VP ONCORE eight-channel GPS receiver with a Motorola cellular transceiver. Provision is also

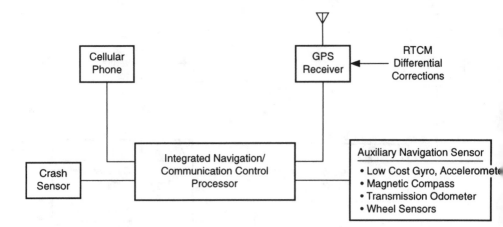

Figure 9.13 Generic emergency messaging system architecture.

made for inclusion of a hands-free microphone, for driver communications in disabling emergency situations.

In all three applications, the GPS receiver utilized should be a multichannel receiver (at least six channels, but preferably eight), capable of rapid signal reacquisition to ensure maximum coverage under conditions of rapid visibility changes induced by signal obscuration, typical of operations in the "urban canyon." In addition, it should be capable of applying real-time differential corrections, as could be generated by a reference station using the RTCM standard [15], to permit improved accuracies and, so, reduced potential for errors in the navigation system. For the vehicle tracking and emergency messaging applications, an alternative to the use of real-time differential corrections exists: uncorrected positions can be transmitted to the base station where the differential corrections can be computed and applied. This alternative will be referred to as "inverse differential," and will be discussed in more detail in the next section. (Differential GPS techniques are discussed in Chapter 8.) Integration of one or more of the auxiliary sensors listed in Figure 9.11 should ensure complete position coverage, but also improve navigation accuracy and reduce susceptibility to gross positioning errors—these issues are discussed further in the following sections.

9.2.2 Review of Automotive Sensors and Subsystems

9.2.2.1 Low-Cost Inertial Sensors

In this section, the sensors referenced in the ITS applications descriptions are described in greater detail. As shown in the generic vehicle navigator (Figure 9.11), a variety of auxiliary sensors may be used in the system. In particular, for the navigation sensors, the essential features of each device are reviewed. Two types of accelerometers could be used. High g (typically 50 g's) accelerometers, with their sensitive axes orthogonal, along the longitudinal and lateral axes of the vehicle are used to detect a crash condition, and low g accelerometers (typically $\leq$ 5 g's) could be used to determine vehicle velocity (in place of a transmission odometer). Each of the ITS applications could also make use of one to three low-cost gyros mounted in the vehicle. A single gyro (called a heading gyro), mounted in the vehicle such that its input axis senses heading change, a magnetic compass (used to determine initial heading), and some method of determining the speed of the vehicle (e.g., an interface to the transmission odometer, inertial accelerometers, or wheel sensors) are often used to provide on-street navigation (called "dead reckoning") during periods of partial or complete obscuration of the GPS satellite signals.

Two gyros/accelerometers can be used to determine two-dimensional direction, and three gyros/accelerometers can be used to determine three-dimensional solution position and velocity as well as roll, pitch, and heading. The three-gyro/accelerometer approach compensates for vertical movement of the vehicle and roll/pitch errors. Low-cost accelerometer technology attributes are contained in Table 9.3. At the time of this writing, several manufacturers are developing low-cost, micromachined, highly sensitive (≤0.01g) accelerometers as well as integrated accelerometer/gyroscope assemblies.

Table 9.4, an update from Table 1 of [13], summarizes the current state of low-cost gyro technology. Of the alternatives listed, the vibrational gyro is the most widely used, owing to its early availability, low cost, and acceptable performance. Current research and development activities are focused on silicon micromachined gyros [16], which could prove to be the lowest cost solution, and FOGs, which are the best performers. Unlike the precision gyros used for high-performance navigation systems in highly dynamic environments, the low-cost vibrational and solid state gyros exhibit poor bias and scale factor stability with temperature, and so require nearly continuous calibration to remain useful. (Gyro errors are discussed in Sections 9.2.3 and 9.2.4.)

9.2.2.2 GPS Receiver

The GPS receiver is the single source of absolute positioning information in each of the ITS applications and provides PVT information. The accuracy of nondifferentially

Table 9.3
Low-Cost Accelerometer Alternatives

Accelerometer Type	Sensitivity	Cost*/Availability	Reliability
Mechanical	0.1 mg	$400/now	Fair
Vibrational	0.1 mg	$300/now	Excellent
Micromachined	0.5 mg	$20/now	Excellent

*The indicated costs reflect automotive quantity purchases.

Table 9.4
Low-Cost Gyro Alternatives

Gyro Type	Drift (deg/hr)	Cost*/Availability	Reliability
Mechanical	100	$100/1996	Fair
FOG	10	$150/1997	Excellent
Vibrational	3600	$30/1997	Good
Better vibrational	100	$300/1997	Very good
Solid state	100	$30/1997	Excellent

*The indicated costs reflect automotive quantity purchases.

corrected GPS-based position and velocity fixes is limited by SA. This generally implies that GPS-based horizontal position errors are, at best, limited to about 100m, 95% of the time. In the urban canyon, however, signal obscuration conditions can produce poor fix geometries (i.e., large HDOP values), resulting in several hundred meters of error. In addition to the potential for poor geometry, GPS receivers may track reflected signals, which contributes additional range and range rate error. Although reverse polarization (i.e., left-hand versus right-hand circular polarization) isolation in the GPS antenna should attenuate single reflections, there is no isolation against double (or even-number) bounced reflections, and the reflected signal will generally be a combination of circularly and linearly polarized components, for which the isolation is reduced.

Use of differential corrections in either a real-time or inverse mode will remove the error induced by SA and other correlated errors, as previously discussed in Chapter 8, and generally produce positioning accuracies of a few meters. However, DGPS does not reduce the errors induced by reflected signal tracking. Currently, the infrastructure is being put in place to support global access to differential corrections. Corrections are being broadcast over FM radio subcarriers as well as via satellite.

An alternative to applying corrections directly to the vehicle (e.g., for tracking or emergency response systems) is to apply them to the GPS positions as they are received at the base station. However, several issues must be considered for this type of operation, including the commonality of satellite tracking and solution methods between the vehicle and the base station. As long as the vehicle receiver is tracking a subset of the satellites tracked by the base station receiver, a position domain correction can be constructed for each broadcast position from an appropriate collection of pseudorange corrections for the common satellites. The process can break down, however, when the vehicle receiver is tracking a satellite that is not tracked by the base station. This case requires that the uncommon satellite (or satellites) be removed from the real-time solution, which implies that individual pseudorange measurements are broadcast; this generally places an intolerable burden on the communication link for tracking systems, but could perhaps be utilized with emergency messaging.

Solution method commonality refers to the fact that differences between the vehicle receiver's real-time solution approach and that utilized at the base station should be identical, or the differential performance will degrade. Algorithm features of the vehicle receiver that can produce performance degradation include:

- The application of model-based ionospheric and tropospheric corrections;
- The use of a two-dimensional fix algorithm;
- Filtering of the GPS positions.

Application of model-based ionospheric and/or tropospheric corrections by the vehicle receiver will remove a portion of the position error contribution from these error sources. When the base station applies its position domain correction, expecting the position error to contain the full error contributions from ionospheric and tropospheric delays, these contributions are nearly corrected twice, resulting in degraded differential accuracy. This potential problem can be solved by turning off these corrections in the vehicle receiver or subtracting these corrections from the pseudorange corrections at the base station (using the same model equations applied by the vehicle receiver) before a position correction is derived. This latter method is generally preferred, since application of the ionospheric and tropospheric models at the base station will automatically compensate for the spatial decorrelation of these error sources.

Vehicle receiver solutions that are calculated using a fixed altitude (i.e., two-dimensional solutions) will include an error component induced by the error in the assumed altitude; this error component will not be removed by the application of a position domain differential correction. To remove this error component, the base station must be able to determine, at least approximately, the error in the vehicle receiver's fixed altitude. This can be done by either assuming the vehicle's true altitude is the same as the (surveyed) altitude of the base station or by using a terrain map at the base station.

Finally, if the vehicle's real-time navigation solution is the result of filtering the GPS position solutions using one or more dead-reckoning sensors, the differential performance will again suffer since the auxiliary sensors can remove some of the correlated errors in the GPS positions, which the position domain correction is also attempting to remove. This problem can be circumvented by sending unfiltered solutions to the base station for correction.

9.2.2.3 GPS and Dead Reckoning (DR)

As referenced above, integration of nondifferential GPS positions with a dead-reckoning system can improve the accuracy of the real-time solution. To gain insight into the magnitude of the potential performance improvement, a Kalman filter operating in steady state will be utilized. The following assumptions will be made in characterizing the integrated navigation system performance:

- The DR system error can be modeled by a fixed percent of distance traveled.
- The DR system error is uncorrelated across GPS updates.
- The vehicle is traveling at a fixed speed.
- GPS position fixes with a specified HDOP are available every 100 sec.

Note that the GPS fix frequency allows us to assume that successive fixes are uncorrelated (i.e., the correlation time associated with SA is about 100 sec). The following error variance equations describe a conventional (one-dimensional) Kalman filter operating under these conditions (the single state could correspond to either the north or east position error component):

Covariance propagation:

$$\sigma_{int}^2(t_n^-) = \sigma_{int}^2(t_{n-1}^+) + (dF)^2$$

where

σ_{int}^2 = integrated GPS/DR system position error variance
d = the distance traveled in one propagation interval
F = the fraction of distance traveled error associated with the DR system

Kalman gain computation:

$$k(t_n) = \frac{\sigma_{int}^2(t_n^-)}{\sigma_{int}^2(t_n^-) + \sigma_m^2}$$

where

σ_m^2 = HDOP^2 σ_p^2 (i.e., computed position fix error variance)
σ_p^2 = the pseudorange error variance

Covariance update:

$$\sigma_{int}^2(t_n^+) = [1 - k(t_n)]\sigma_{int}^2(t_n^-)$$

The steady-state conditions of the Kalman filter are determined by setting $\sigma_{int}^2(t_n^+)$ equal to $\sigma_{int}^2(t_{n-1}^+)$. Table 9.5 summarizes the one sigma positioning accuracies

Table 9.5
Steady-State GPS/DR Integrated Performance

Vehicle Speed (m/sec)	DR System Accuracy	Integrated System Position Error (1-sigma)
5	2	24.7
10	2	33.7
20	2	44.3
5	5	37.0
10	5	47.7
20	5	57.3

which can be achieved for an integrated GPS/DR system with an HDOP of 2 (in steady state).

Note from Table 9.5 that the accuracy improvements are greater at lower speeds since the DR error accumulation is a smaller fraction of the expected GPS fix error, which permits the filter to do a better job of averaging the measurement error. At the highest speed and worse DR system performance, the 1-sigma integrated performance is only 10% better than the 1-sigma unaugmented GPS position accuracy (66m), while, on the other hand, at the lowest speed and better DR performance, more than a factor of two improvement in accuracy is realized.

9.2.2.4 Transmission and Wheel Sensors

Vehicle transmission and wheel sensors can be used to determine the speed and heading changes of the vehicle. A transmission odometer is used in each of the previous applications to sense vehicle speed. Depending upon the type of sensor utilized, the speed determination by a transmission odometer can become unreliable at low speed; if variable reluctance sensing [17] is used, the sensor output becomes zero as the magnetic flux change becomes small. Depending on the specific sensor utilized and the signal processing circuitry, speeds of 0.5 to 1 m/sec may be undetectable. On the other hand, use of Hall-effect sensors [17], whose output is position rather than rate sensitive, can detect vehicle speed reliably down to stationary conditions. For this reason, Hall-effect sensors are preferred, but are generally more expensive to install.

Independent of the type of sensor utilized, transmission odometer-based speed determination can be totally unreliable under three distinct conditions:

- Wheel slipping;
- Wheel skidding;
- Vehicle motion when the tires are stationary.

The first problem can be solved by installing sensors so they detect the motion of the nondriven wheels (e.g., the nondriven wheels of a front wheel drive vehicle are the rear wheels and vice versa). Otherwise, tire slippage can lead to gross positioning errors in the DR system, since the sensed speed will generally greatly exceed the true speed of the vehicle. Typically, 24 to 48 pulses are generated for each wheel revolution. The second problem, wheel skidding, is much more difficult to solve; however, the potential for it can be reduced but not eliminated by use of antilock braking systems (ABS). Detection of and recovery from skidding conditions should be an important consideration in the design of the sensor integration algorithm. (This concern is addressed in the next section.) Finally, motion of the vehicle when the tires are stationary (e.g., as could occur when the vehicle is transported onboard a ferry), can also lead to excessive positioning error, and is a second recovery mode for the sensor integration algorithm.

Excepting these anomalies, speed determination is affected by the ability to measure distance traveled using the circumference of the wheel. The scale factor that converts wheel revolution to distance traveled can be accurately calibrated at installation by driving a known distance. However, slow variations in tire pressure can degrade the initial calibration and, over time, affect the accuracy of the scale factor.

Wheel sensors suffer from the same problems described for the transmission sensors; however, with potentially more serious error conditions. Individual wheel sensors can be used to determine heading changes of the vehicle as well as speed. This is done by measuring the difference in the distance traveled by each nondriven wheel, a technique known as differential odometry. If the vehicle is making a right turn, the left wheel has to travel farther than the right wheel to complete the turn and vice versa. Assuming that the sensors are installed on nondriven rear wheels, the following equation can be used to compute heading change, h:

$$h = (L_c - R_c)/B \qquad (9.5)$$

where:

L_c = left-wheel pulse count increment (scaled to distance by scale factor)
R_c = right-wheel pulse count increment (scaled to distance by scale factor)
B = the wheelbase length

For wheel sensors installed on the front wheels, (9.5) must be replaced by an equation that reflects the variation of wheel track with heading change (i.e., the effective wheelbase changes) [18]. Heading determination via differential odometry is susceptible to gross errors when the pulse count difference is induced by either tire slipping or skidding, as discussed for the transmission odometer, but also due to significant differential tire pressure. This effect is generally calibrated by driving in a straight line; alternatively, real-time calibration approaches are possible [19]. The effects of wheel sensor pulse count quantization cannot be neglected in the sensor integration algorithm, since even small quantization error levels can produce significant heading error, over time, as illustrated by the equation below:

$$\sigma_{\Delta h} = (\sigma_q)\sqrt{t} \qquad (9.6)$$

where:

$\sigma_{\Delta h}$ = heading error (rad)
σ_q = quantization error (rad)

Note that (9.6) assumes that quantization errors are independent from propagation step to propagation step.

9.2.2.5 Magnetic Compass

Magnetic compasses provide an inexpensive means of determining vehicle heading, and have been used to augment several DR systems (e.g., the Zexel system [11]). The major problem associated with the use of a magnetic compass as a primary or sole heading reference is its sensitivity to magnetic anomalies. Although compass designs can be self-calibrating, this calibration serves only to remove the "static" disturbance of the Earth's magnetic field (e.g., as could be induced by the vehicle itself). Dynamic sources of disturbance, which could be generated by other passing cars or the steel trusses of a bridge, can induce very significant errors in the compass' heading indication. Thus, the compass is usually relegated to a backup role, or as a complement to another system. When used in a Kalman filter design with differential odometry, as illustrated in Figure 9.14, the gross errors associated with the compass can usually be filtered or eliminated using the heading changes sensed by the differential wheel count. As illustrated in Figure 9.14, the Kalman residual test, which compares the current magnetic compass reading with the current best estimate of heading (propagated forward in time using the heading change sensed by differential odometry), can be used to screen gross errors induced by magnetic disturbances. The success of this test will depend upon the integrity of the differential odometry-based heading trajectory (e.g., the test can fail if the vehicle is skidding when significant magnetic interference is present).

9.2.2.6 Digital Map

Digital maps are, of course, essential for route guidance and navigation applications. Maps are available for major cities [7], with various resolutions ranging from a few

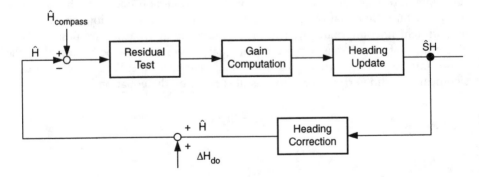

Figure 9.14 Kalman filter blending of magnetic compass heading with differential odometry.

meters to ten to twenty meters, depending upon the quality of the data used to generate the map. In attempting to place a GPS-derived position on a map, the map-matching process, as previously mentioned, can make use of the vehicle's recent history, in addition to its current estimated position and velocity; further discussion of map matching is beyond the scope of this introduction. Consult [9, 10] for detailed information. In addition to the position estimates, solution-quality information (e.g., HDOP value) can assist the map-matching process in resolving ambiguities. Map matching based on reliable digital maps can improve real-time navigation in addition to supporting the route guidance function. Given successful placement of the vehicle's position on a road, the map-matched position and velocity (i.e., heading) can be used to reset or adjust the current estimates of vehicle position and velocity.

9.2.3 Sensor Integration Principles

Each of the auxiliary navigation sensors and subsystems discussed in the previous section can be integrated with GPS to provide a system with improved navigation performance and robustness. A single, optimal selection of sensors to complement GPS cannot generally be made, since the sensor selection will be driven by many factors other than performance, including the cost of the sensor relative to the cost limits for the entire system and the availability of sensors in the vehicle. For example, a navigation system that is developed for a vehicle already equipped with differential odometry for ABS may not require that any other navigation sensors be added to complement the GPS receiver. On the other hand, a vehicle that is not so equipped will require a low-cost gyro and/or magnetic compass for complete position coverage.

9.2.3.1 Kalman Filter Model Limitations

Given that no single sensor is the optimal complement to GPS, this section will concentrate on the general principles of sensor integration for the class of sensors that could be used to complement GPS. The Kalman filter, introduced earlier in this chapter and referenced in the sensor description, would seem to be the ideal tool for the integration. While this is generally true, caution must be exercised. Blind application of Kalman filtering can lead to unacceptable results, since the filter is based on two fundamental assumptions that may not be not valid in this application. These assumptions are:

- Unmodeled measurement errors are white (i.e., uncorrelated).
- Unmodeled error dynamics are white (i.e., uncorrelated).

The first assumption is certainly violated when operating nondifferentially, owing to the correlated pseudorange and Doppler errors dominated by SA. For example, a vehicle that is known to be stationary (through Hall-effect sensing of the odometer pulses) can average the GPS position fixes received from the receiver and reduce navigation error. Ignoring the correlations inherent in SA would produce a $1/\sqrt{n}$ standard deviation reduction for the position error, where n is the number of measurement samples (i.e., processing 10 positions with a standard deviation of 60m would produce a predicted position error of approximately 19m, 1-sigma). In actuality, the error would still be close to 60m, due to the bias-like nature of the SA error component over just 10 sec. Several approaches exist for circumventing this correlated measurement error problem, including the following:

- State augmentation;
- Use of consider states [20];
- Reduction of processing rate;
- Alternative gain computation (e.g., gain scheduling or covariance lower limiting).

Both state augmentation and the use of consider states (i.e., modeling the error as nonwhite, but not attempting to estimate it) increase the computational burden associated with the Kalman filter, and so may not be acceptable approaches. By reducing the processing rate, successive measurements can become uncorrelated, so the fundamental assumption can become valid. However, it may be difficult in real time, in a dynamic environment, to decide which measurements to ignore. Therefore, several measurements may have to be saved in order to ensure that the correct measurements are selected for updating the filter, thus complicating the filter implementation. Finally, use of non-Kalman gain adaptation may prove effective. This adaptation can take the form of gains that are preprogrammed as a function of possible measurement scenarios and/or covariance lower limiting to prevent measurement averaging within the expected correlation time of SA.

The second assumption is often violated when representing unmodeled error effects as white noise in the process model. As an example, let's consider the effect of gyro scale factor error upon heading error in turning a corner. Assume a 1% scale factor error (a typical value for a low-cost gyro), and further assume that the scale factor error is not included as a state in the filter, but represented as uncorrelated noise over each second. If the turn is completed in 3 sec with a constant turn rate of 30 deg/sec, the scale factor error will result in 0.9 deg of error when the turn is completed. The 1-sigma heading error σ_h, predicted by the Kalman filter (using an uncorrelated noise model with a variance equal to the error variance associated with the scale factor error) is given by

$$\sigma_h^2 = 3\sigma_{SF}^2 \Delta h^2 \tag{9.7}$$

where

σ_{SF} = 1-sigma scale factor error (1% in this example)
Δh = heading change each second

For this example,

$$\sigma_h^2 = 3(0.01)^2(30)^2$$

The resultant σ_h is 0.52 deg, which is optimistic by a factor of $\sqrt{3}$. If an assumption can be made about the average duration of the turn, a scale factor can be introduced in (9.7) that results in a match of the actual error behavior; that is,

$$\sigma_h^2 = \sigma_h^2 + 3 \ \sigma_{SF}^2 \Delta h^2 \tag{9.8}$$

Use of (9.8) will produce a correct result when completing the 90° turn in three seconds. In general, a scaling must be introduced for the uncorrelated error propagation to match bias-like error propagation.

9.2.3.2 Measurement Selection and Modeling

Two distinct options exist in blending GPS information with the DR trajectory: (1) processing GPS position and velocity solutions or (2) processing individual pseudorange and Doppler measurements from each satellite. There is not a single, preferred selection for all applications. Each approach has certain advantages in specific environments. Use of GPS position and velocity solutions may be the only option available if the integration is performed external to the GPS receiver itself and raw measurement information is not output; furthermore, even if raw measurement information is available, information that permits computation of the LOS vectors to each satellite (i.e., receiver-computed satellite positions or ephemeris) is also required, which may not be readily available from the receiver. On the other hand, access to individual satellite measurements permits maximum use of all available data (e.g., a single satellite with its LOS along the current vehicle's track could help in reducing the along track error accumulation of the DR system). Another issue that affects the selection of measurement or solution processing is the solution method utilized within the GPS receiver (i.e., what level of filtering may be performed on the data prior to its integration with the DR system). The following paragraphs review these issues in detail.

In processing GPS positions and velocities, it cannot generally be assumed that individual measurements (e.g., latitude and longitude) are independent, since they are correlated through the GPS satellite geometry. Assuming that the GPS receiver makes use of a least squares algorithm in updating its position (and velocity), the position error covariance matrix is given by the (previously discussed) expression

$$P = \sigma_\rho^2 (H^T H)^{-1}$$

The matrix product of H transposed with itself will produce a matrix with off-diagonal elements, which result in significant error correlations between, for example, GPS latitude and longitude error. These effects can be handled by setting the measurement error covariance of the integration filter equal to the position error covariance, ensuring that the correlations will be accounted for by the filter. A more difficult issue, however, is the time error correlation that can exist in the measurements. This correlation can arise from filtering that is performed within the GPS receiver or the time-correlation of the measurement error sources.

There are three sources of filtering within the GPS receiver:

- The tracking loops themselves (affecting both pseudorange and Doppler measurements);
- Carrier smoothing of the pseudoranges [21];
- Any additional filtering performed in the position domain.

As long as the tracking loop bandwidths are sufficiently high (e.g., 10 Hz or higher), there should not be a significant correlation problem. This is almost always true for the carrier tracking loop (affecting the Doppler measurements), but may not be true for the code loop (affecting the pseudorange measurements), especially if it is carrier-aided. The carrier-smoothing filter will produce time correlations up to 100 sec [21], which does present a modeling issue to the filter designer. While it seems judicious to request unfiltered pseudoranges from the receiver, this can degrade performance since the carrier smoothing will do a much better job in attenuating noise and multipath in the measured pseudoranges than the DR trajectory will [21]. The time correlation associated with the GPS error sources has been discussed previously; SA, the dominant error source when operating nondifferentially has a correlation time of roughly 100 sec, which cannot be ignored in designing the filter. Even when operating differentially, time correlations may still exist since SA dither will "leak" through, with a magnitude dependent upon the correction latency, and multipath will not be removed by the differential corrections (in fact, it can be made worse by multipath at the reference station). Thus, even in processing "raw" measurements from the GPS receiver, there are time correlation problems that need to be addressed. Finally, the GPS receiver manufacturer may implement a Kalman filter within the receiver, which introduces additional time correlation into the position and velocity solutions.

9.2.3.3 *State Selection and Modeling*

The selection of states for real-time implementation of a Kalman filter represents a tradeoff between model fidelity and microprocessor-imposed throughput burden. The throughput constraint is particularly acute when the filter is embedded within the GPS receiver microprocessor and must share the central processing unit (CPU) with other, higher priority tasks (e.g., signal acquisition and tracking). The following states represent the minimum state vector size believed to be acceptable:

- East position error;
- North position error;
- Altitude error (pseudorange measurement processing option);
- Receiver clock offset (pseudorange measurement processing option);
- Heading error;
- Transmission odometer scale factor error;
- Vertical velocity error (Doppler measurement processing option);
- Receiver clock drift (Doppler measurement processing option).

Thus, a total of eight states are required for the pseudorange and Doppler measurement processing option, and four for processing position and velocity solutions. Further savings can be realized by decoupling the states; however, such discussions are beyond the scope of this treatment. Note that it is assumed that at least the transmission odometer of the vehicle is used in formulating this state vector. Possible additional states that could be included are a function of the source of the heading information and are listed below:

- Gyro scale factor error;
- Gyro bias;
- Wheel base associated with differential odometry;
- Average scale factor error (for differential odometry);
- Differential scale factor error (for differential odometry).

The decision to include these states should be made on the basis of their observability (i.e., given the magnitude of the error source and its stability, how well could the filter be expected to estimate it). For example, the vehicle's wheelbase should be sufficiently stable to permit its estimation, yet may be known to better than 1% across the expected set of vehicles and so may not produce sufficient heading error to enable its accurate estimation.

9.2.4 Vehicle Tracking System Example

In this section, [13], presented at the Institute of Navigation's Forty Ninth Annual Meeting, which reviews the design of a low-cost navigation system for vehicle tracking applications, will be used in a case study. First, the positioning requirements for vehicle tracking are reviewed, followed by a discussion of the sensor selection process that leads to a suitable navigation system. Experiences with the system in the urban canyons of the world are then provided.

9.2.4.1 Vehicle Tracking Requirements

The following factors are generally considered in designing a navigation system to support vehicle tracking:

- Required reporting frequency;
- Accuracy/integrity of the solution;
- Reliability of the system;
- Cost of the system.

The required reporting frequency for vehicle tracking is a function of the intended application; the achievable reporting rate is determined from the capabilities of the communication system that sends the position information to a centralized base station, and the number of vehicles that are tracked. The reporting can be done on the basis of polling from the base station, fixed time intervals, or fixed distances traveled by each vehicle. In each of these cases, typical navigation solution rates (e.g., 1 Hz) are generally an overkill; thus, the reporting frequency will not drive the navigation system design. A more important, related issue is the latency of the reported solution, and 1 sec is generally satisfactory.

Required navigation solution accuracy is specified as either block-width or street-width. Block-width accuracy can generally be met using standalone GPS, with an expected 100m 2-drms error specification, while use of GPS in a differential mode is necessary to meet street-width accuracy requirements. DR system accuracies are expressed as a percent of distance traveled; low-cost systems will achieve accuracies in the 2% to 5% range. Complete loss of GPS for extended time periods can therefore compromise the accuracy budget, since a 5% system can accumulate 100m of error after 2 km of travel. Assuming an average outage of 1 city block (i.e., with GPS fixes derived at each intersection), an average error accumulation of 5m can be expected for a 5% system, which should not compromise the error budget. Perhaps more important than accuracy is the integrity of the solution. For GPS, tracking of reflected rather than direct signals, jamming, and even spoofing (see Section 1.3.1) can produce solution errors outside of the expected accuracy bounds. DR systems that make use of sensed wheel motion can suffer significant error accumulation under wheel slippage; in addition, gross initial heading errors will result in error accumulation that is excessive. Reliability numbers for the navigation system are typically expressed as a mean time between failures (MTBF) of five years.

Cost considerations dictate that the in-vehicle navigation system be at lowest possible cost; practically speaking, $1,000 seems acceptable for many applications.

Integration of GPS with a DR system helps meet several of the navigation system requirements that a GPS-only system would find difficult to meet. The solution latency can be guaranteed to be less than 1 sec with a GPS/DR system, whereas obscuration of GPS signals can result in latencies of up to several minutes in the urban canyon environment. Depending upon the accuracy of the DR system and/or its frequency of calibration, the dead-reckoned trajectory can, in principle, be used to filter the effects of SA, and so potentially improve the accuracy of GPS when operating nondifferentially. Of greater importance than this, however, is the use of the inherent redundancy in the integrated system to improve the integrity of the navigation solution (i.e., to afford protection from gross errors in either subsystem). In the next section, the possible sensors that could be used for DR are reviewed; this motivates the selected sensors that comprise the GPS/DR system used for this case study. The integration algorithms are reviewed at a conceptual level, and, finally, experiences with the system in major urban areas are summarized.

9.2.4.2 DR Sensor Selection

In simplest terms, dead reckoning requires a continuous source of speed and heading information. For most vehicle tracking applications, an accuracy of 5% of distance traveled is adequate; however, accuracy improvements beyond this will extend the duration of the maximum tolerable GPS outage. In addition, the selected DR system must be relatively easy to install and, following an initial calibration, should operate autonomously in the absence of hard failures of the navigation equipment. The sensors that comprise the DR subsystem can be classified as either sources of velocity information or sources of heading information. Possible sources of velocity information include the vehicle's odometer, longitudinally mounted accelerometers, and Doppler radars. Use of information from the vehicle's odometer is a very attractive option, since it comes nearly free; installation requirements are relatively straightforward (in the worst case, it may be necessary to install a transmission transducer). The odometer, once calibrated, provides good long-term stability; changes due to tire pressure variation and vehicle velocity are not expected to be significant, and are calibrated in real time using GPS. The only potential problem in using the odometer is the sensitivity to wheel slippage and skidding, which requires special action. This condition can be detected as an excessive divergence from GPS resulting in a reinitialization to the GPS-only position. Low-cost accelerometers represent an attractive alternative to the use of the odometer, since their accuracy does not degrade under wheel slippage conditions and when skidding; however, the accelerometer bias must be removed initially and periodically recalibrated. Calibration of the accelerometer bias presents a problem, due to the difficulty in separating linear and gravitational accelerations; for example, calibration on a 1% grade can introduce a bias acceleration error that produces 500m of error in only 100 sec. Unless the accelerometer bias levels are sufficiently stable such that only infrequent recalibration (using GPS) is required, their use is not generally acceptable. However, augmentation of the accelerometer with low-cost attitude sensing provides for an acceptable solution, albeit at increased cost. The use of a Doppler radar is not given serious consideration, due to its relatively high cost.

Potential sources of heading information include magnetic compasses, accelerometers, differential odometry, and gyros. Magnetic compasses are an attractive low-cost source of heading information, but require calibration to remove the effects of local magnetic disturbances. Some units perform this calibration autonomously, but are still sensitive to transient effects as could be induced by passing under a steel structure. Because of these transient errors, the raw magnetic compass heading must be filtered utilizing heading rate information; this requirement limits the utility of the magnetic compass to heading initialization. The laterally mounted accelerometer suffers from the same drawbacks as the longitudinally mounted accelerometer previously described for speed determination, and so is not given serious consideration. Differential odometry is an attractive alternative, if such a capability is already built in to the vehicle. As an add-on, however, it represents a significant installation requirement, and so is not a general solution. Low-cost gyros are available that can output heading rate information, but their stability and reliability are marginal. The possible gyro alternatives have been listed in Table 9.4. Mechanical gyros, which use spinning rotors, do not meet the MTBF requirement. There are alternative approaches based upon vibrating elements, which are more robust. The bias stability is still bothersome, but approaches have been developed to perform adequate calibration; one approach is described in the next section. Since the gyros provide only heading rate information, a reliable method for heading initialization is required. Based upon the preceding discussion, the DR sensor combination that was selected for integration with GPS was the lower cost vibrational heading rate gyro combined with the velocity information from the odometer interface. At the time of this experiment, the chosen gyro was the only option that met the cost, reliability, availability, and performance criteria. In the next section, the methods used to integrate the DR information with GPS positions, and the approaches used to calibrate the DR sensors are discussed. This discussion should further motivate the sensor selection.

9.2.4.3 GPS/DR Integration

The GPS/DR system is composed of a GPS receiver board, an antenna, a dead-reckoning processor board, a gyro, and an interface cable. The system is shown in Figure 9.15. All of the GPS-related functions (tracking, data retrieval, channel

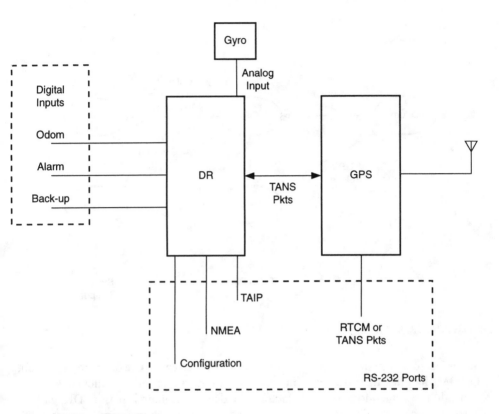

Figure 9.15 Placer GPS/DR™ system.

management, GPS position solutions, etc.) are performed on the GPS board. The DR board is the hub of the GPS/DR system. The DR board includes a second processor, the A/D for the gyro, pulse counter for the odometer signal and interfaces to the GPS board and the user. The user interface to the Placer GPS/DR takes place via four RS-232 ports. The Trimble ASCII interface protocol (TAIP) port provides for the output of position and status information and input of differential corrections, as well as control of port characteristics, frequency of data output, checksum, and so forth. Another port outputs National Marine Electronics Association (NMEA) formatted messages. A third port is used to configure operational parameters for the unit and provide the interface for initial calibration. The last port can be used for the input of differential corrections or to monitor the GPS portion of the GPS/DR unit. The RTCM SC-104 recommended formats for differential corrections are supported. The GPS data is available in Trimble advanced navigation sensor (TANS) packet format. Communication between the DR and GPS boards is accomplished via TANS packets. The data flow diagram in Figure 9.16 highlights the

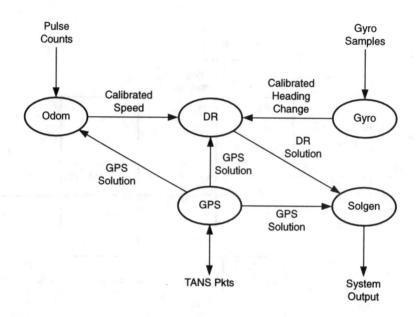

Figure 9.16 DR data flow.

major DR functions and the primary data flow between each. The odometer function, ODOM, handles the odometer interface. It monitors the pulses, calculates speed, and calibrates the odometer scale factor. The dead-reckoning function, DR, gathers current gyro and odometer data to propagate a DR solution and accepts GPS-derived position data to filter the DR solution. The gyro function reads the gyro rate information, estimates the current gyro bias, and determines the change in heading, which is used by the DR function to filter GPS-derived heading and maintain an accurate heading estimate. The GPS function provides the interface to the GPS position and velocity data. It decodes packets and sends commands to the receiver as requested. The solution generator function, Solgen, monitors the dead-reckoning position and the GPS position to provide a system position.

The following DR algorithms will be discussed: position filter, heading filter, odometer scale factor calibration, gyro scale factor calibration, and gyro bias estimation. A filtered position solution will provide the user with a level of multipath rejection. The filter will also smooth satellite constellation switch-induced jumps while in autonomous GPS. The position filter blends the GPS solution with the dead-reckoning solution using mode-dependent fixed gains. The processing that allows the use of a low-cost gyro in this application is a Kalman-like heading filter that accounts for correlated measurement noise. Special care was used in the heading filter design, since prolonged driving in the dead-reckoning mode with an initial heading error will be a dominant error source. The filter monitors the gyro bias estimator for stability of the bias and will reject headings that are deemed too erroneous. Reinitialization logic, however, assures that the filter will not stay with a bad heading, ignoring GPS. A digital odometer signal can be derived from an existing digital pulse if the vehicle has one, by the addition of a signal conditioner if an analog pulse is available or by inserting a transducer into the transmission line if no suitable pulse is available.

Odometer scale factor calibration is performed by comparing odometer-derived speed with GPS speed whenever the vehicle is moving fast enough while tracking GPS and the estimated acceleration is minimal. The gyro scale factor is determined at installation. The vehicle is turned through a prescribed number of clockwise and counterclockwise revolutions. The algorithm compares the difference between the measured angle and the expected angle and assigns the difference to the error in the gyro scale factor. Two filters, stationary and moving, continually update the system estimate of the gyro bias. The stationary filter has a short time constant and operates whenever the vehicle is stopped, as indicated by the absence of odometer pulses during the previous interval. A second, inherently less reliable, filter with a correspondingly longer time constant estimates the gyro bias while moving in straight lines. The ability of these filters to operate without the aid of GPS helps reduce the effects of bias errors while propagating a DR solution. The configuration of the GPS receiver is an important factor in the system performance. For a GPS-only system, operational parameters are chosen to get the best combination of quality of fixes versus quantity such that gaps in position reports are minimized. The same is true for GPS in the integrated system. The error characteristics of the dead-reckoning solution and GPS are complementary. From point to point, DR can provide very smooth, continuous updates. Over time, however, the small errors in each update add together to be unacceptable. GPS's instantaneous errors are bounded, but are susceptible to outages, reflections and SA effects. The GPS receiver in the integrated system can be configured to minimize errors by reducing the number of fixes. With respect to a nominal "off the shelf" receiver, the Placer/DR is designed such that (1) higher signal strength is required to guard against reflected signals and multipath, and (2) better geometries are selected so any SA induced error won't be amplified unnecessarily. The combined GPS/DR solution is robust.

9.2.4.4 GPS/DR Test Experience

The Placer GPS/DR system has been tested in many major urban areas such as New York, Tokyo, Chicago, Boston, San Francisco, Toronto, and Buenos Aires. While GPS coverage has improved dramatically over the last few years, the problems posed to GPS in urban areas still include signal reflection, limited coverage, and relatively poor satellite geometries when getting fixes. Even in areas that wouldn't be characterized as urban canyons, GPS coverage may be affected. The following cities pose problems for GPS, not only because of skyscrapers, but because of their own obscurations:

- Buenos Aires: narrow streets with long blocks (GPS signals not received at intersections);
- Chicago: underground streets, elevated trains;
- Pittsburgh: tunnels, bridges;
- San Francisco: tall buildings and hills;
- Tokyo: narrow streets.

San Francisco is a very stressful city for GPS due to tall buildings and steep hills. Figures 9.17 and 9.18 show raw GPS only and GPS/DR position output, respectively, in San Francisco; in both cases, the GPS solution is autonomous (i.e., nondifferential), so it is dominated by SA. Because of the obscuration problems, many of the GPS fixes in San Francisco are two-dimensional fixes. When a GPS receiver has insufficient data to form a complete three-dimensional position solution, it can assume an altitude and solve for the horizontal coordinates. The hills make these two-dimensional fixes less accurate due to inevitable errors in the altitude. The sawtooth behavior of the GPS only data comes from the 2D fixes on steep hills. The corresponding combined position report removes the excursions because the filter accounts for the fact that two-dimensional solutions are inherently less accurate.

Tokyo has a great deal of obscurations for GPS as well. Figures 9.19 and 9.20 show the route in Tokyo of GPS-only and GPS/DR positions. (These tests were also conducted without a DGPS capability.) The GPS data in Figure 9.19 is not raw data; it is the filtered data for which GPS contributed to the solution. Although much of the trip had good GPS coverage, there are gaps of over 400m and over 30 sec. During these gaps, a position uncertainty goes well beyond the normally quoted 100m 2-drms value. Propagating a GPS-derived position using the last known GPS velocity to fill these gaps for more than a few seconds is risky. Error growth during this propagation can be large due to heading and speed changes. The error grows to over 400m at one point. The presented data is nondifferential. Differential GPS provides better calibration for the DR sensors, so the system solution improves while GPS signals are being tracked and the quality of the DR alone solution improves as well.

9.2.4.5 Summary and Conclusions

Urban areas provide unique problems for GPS-only vehicle location systems. Reflected signals and relatively poor geometries make GPS-derived position fixes less accurate than those made in a more benign environment. Obscuration of signals occurs frequently. GPS-only propagation can only be used over short time intervals.

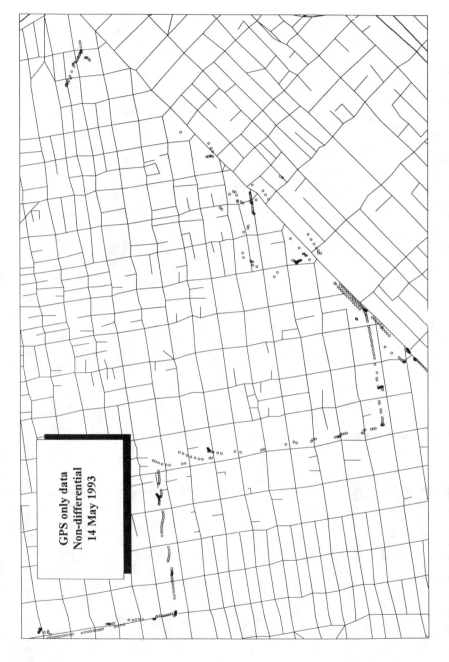

GPS only data
Non-differential
14 May 1993

Figure 9.17 San Francisco "raw" GPS positions.

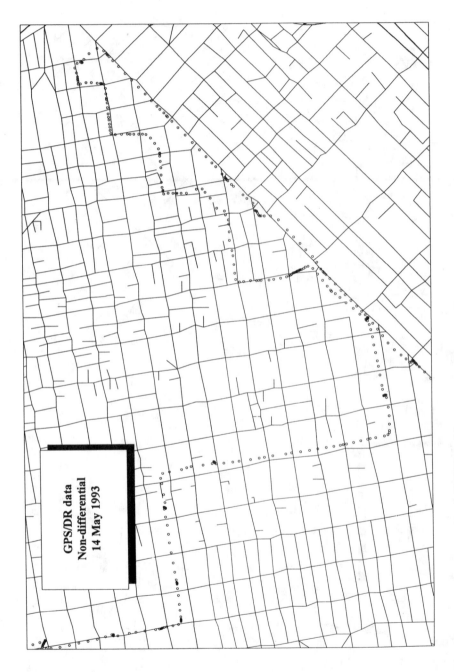

Figure 9.18 San Francisco combined GPS/DR positions.

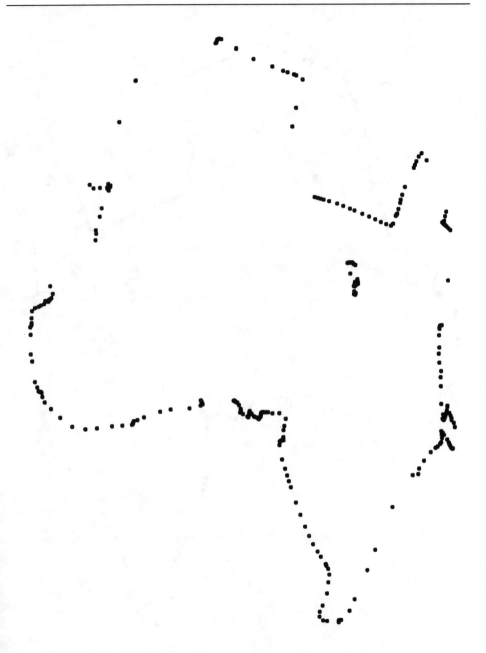

Figure 9.19 Tokyo filtered GPS-only positions.

Figure 9.20 Tokyo combined GPS/DR positions.

To combat these problems, a DR capability was added to a GPS sensor. The system used a low-cost vibrational gyro and the vehicle's odometer output combined with GPS to provide an accurate, robust navigation system for urban environments. The system has performed well in harsh urban environments. The accumulated DR error is generally under 2% of distance traveled. Additionally, GPS errors from reflected signals are suppressed due to the filtering.

References

[1] Gelb, A., et al., *Applied Optimal Estimation*, Cambridge, MA: MIT Press, 1992.

[2] Kalman, R. E, "A New Approach to Linear Filtering and Prediction Problems," *Journal of Basic Engineering (ASME)*, Vol. 82D, March 1960, pp. 35–37.

[3] Frazer, D. E., E. Mickle, J. Nielson, and K. Rigg, "T-33 Aircraft Demonstration of GPS Aided Inertial Navigation," *Proc. Institute of Navigation Satellite Division Technical Meeting*, Sept. 1987.

[4] Thornton, C. L., and G. J. Bierman, *UDUT Covariance Factorization for Kalman Filtering*, New York, NY: Academic Press, 1980.

[5] Nielson, J. T., "GPS Aided Inertial Navigation," *NAECON*, IEEE 1986, p. 20.

[6] Sweeney, L. E., Jr., "An Overview of Intelligent Vehicle Highway Systems (IVHS)," *Proc. Wescon/ 93*, 1993, Moscone Convention Center, San Francisco, CA, Sept. 28–30, pp. 258–262.

[7] Sweeney, L. E., Jr., "Digital Road Maps: The Route to an Information Revolution," a presentation at the ASME Annual Banquet, San Jose State University, San Jose, CA, Nov. 12, 1992.

[8] Sweeney, L. E., Jr., and W. B. Zavoli, "Trends in Digital Road Map Databases for Microcomputer Applications in Transportation," *4th International Conference on Microcomputers in Public Transportation (TRB)*, 1992, San Francisco, CA, Aug. 16–19, p. 74.

[9] ETAK U.S. Patent 4,796,191: *Vehicle Navigation System and Method*, Jan. 3, 1989.

[10] ETAK U.S. Patent 5,311,195: *Combined Relative and Absolute Positioning Method and Apparatus*, May 10, 1994.

[11] "An Automobile Option for Self-Navigating Car," *New York Times*, Jan. 5, 1995.

[12] Sushko, M., "Automatic Vehicle Location (AVL) Communication Methods for DGPS Based Systems," *Proc. Institute of Navigation 1993 National Technical Meeting*, San Francisco, CA, Jan. 1993, pp. 179–194.

[13] Geier, G. J., A. Heshmati, P. McLain, K. Johnson, and M. Murphy, "Integration of GPS with Dead Reckoning for Vehicle Tracking Applications," *Proc. 49th Annual Meeting of the Institute of Navigation*, Cambridge, MA, June 21–23, 1993, pp. 75–82.

[14] "Motorola Cellular Positioning and Emergency Messaging Unit Data Sheet," Motorola, 4000 Commercial Avenue, Northbrook, IL, 60062.

[15] RTCM Paper 194-93/SC104-STD, "RTCM Recommended Standards for Differential NAVSTAR GPS Service," Version 2.1, developed by RTCM Special Committee No. 104, Jan. 3, 1994.

[16] Blanco, J., and J. Geen, "Micromachined Inertial Sensor Development at Northrop," *Proc. 49th Annual Meeting of the Institute of Navigation*, Cambridge, MA, June 21–23, 1993, pp. 577–586.

[17] Ribbens, W. B., "Understanding Automotive Electronics," *SAMS*, 1992, pp. 138–143.

[18] Bastow, D., *Car Suspension and Handling*, London: Pentech Press, 1988.

[19] Motorola U.S. Patent 5,058,023: *Vehicle Position Determining Apparatus*, October 15, 1991.

[20] Brown, R. G., and P.Y.C. Hwang, *Introduction to Random Signals and Applied Kalman Filtering*, New York: John Wiley and Sons, Inc., 1992.

[21] Brown, R. G., and P.Y.C. Hwang, "GPS Navigation, Combining Pseudorange with Continuous Carrier Phase Using a Kalman Filter," *Journal of the Institute of Navigation*, Vol. 37, No. 2, Summer 1990, pp. 181–196.

CHAPTER 10
▼▼▼

THE RUSSIAN GLONASS SYSTEM

Scott Feairheller, Jay Purvis, and Richard Clark
United States Air Force

10.1 FUNCTIONAL DESCRIPTION

The Global Navigation Satellite System (GLONASS) is a Russian space-based radio-navigation system that provides position, velocity, and time (PVT) information to suitably equipped users. Like the U.S. GPS, GLONASS provides both civil and military navigation services.

Functionally, GLONASS is similar to GPS. The space segment, which is due to be completed in 1995, will consist of a 21 satellite constellation plus 3 active spares. (The GPS constellation is comprised of 24 active satellites.) The ground support segment consists of a number of sites scattered throughout Russia that control, track and upload ephemeris, timing information, and other data to the satellites. Each satellite transmits two L-band navigation signals. A variety of user equipment for both civil and military applications has been developed by the Russians. Civil user equipment is also being developed by other parties outside of Russia.

10.2 PROGRAM OVERVIEW

GLONASS is overseen and operated by Russia's Ministry of Defense. The program was started in the mid-1970s at the Scientific Production Association of Applied

Mechanics (NPO PM), a long-time developer of military satellites. Originally, GLONASS was to support naval demands for navigation and time dissemination. Early system testing convincingly demonstrated that GLONASS could support civilian use while concurrently meeting Russian defense needs. Thus, the mission was broadened to include civilian users [1].

The first satellite launch in the program occurred on October 12, 1982. An initial test constellation of four satellites was deployed by January 1984. Normally, 3 satellites are launched simultaneously on an SL-12 Proton launch vehicle from Kazakhstan. As of March 1995, there have been 23 launches in the program, placing a total of 59 GLONASS satellites in orbit, along with 2 Etalon passive geodetic satellites, and 8 ballast payloads. (Ballast payloads are used to balance the payload if less than 3 satellites are launched.)

At a meeting of the Special Committee on Future Air Navigation Systems (FANS) of the International Civil Aviation Organization (ICAO) in 1988, the USSR offered the world community free use of GLONASS navigation signals. A similar offer was made at the 35th Session of the International Maritime Organization (IMO) Subcommittee of Navigation Safety in the same year. These offers were later affirmed by the Government of Russia [1].

In 1990–91, the Russians established a test constellation of 10 to 12 satellites. This was followed by extensive testing of the system. As a result, in September 1993, Russian President Boris Yeltsin officially proclaimed GLONASS to be an operational system, part of the Russian Armoury, and the basis for the Russian Radionavigation Plan [2].

In April 1994, the Russians initiated the first of seven launches planned for 1994 and 1995 to complete the constellation. Full operational capability should be declared by Russians when the 24-satellite constellation is completed.

10.3 ORGANIZATIONAL STRUCTURE

The Russian Ministry of Defense is both the principle user and owner of GLONASS. Within the Ministry of Defense, responsibility for GLONASS policy and operation falls under the Military Space Forces (VKS). GLONASS responsibility is further delegated within the VKS to the State Department of Space Means (GUKOS). GUKOS must approve all GLONASS-related policies. GUKOS has management responsibility for the following GLONASS areas: (1) system control center, (2) master system time clock, (3) command and tracking stations, (4) laser tracking stations, and (5) GLONASS Coordinating Scientific Information Center (CSIC) [1].

While the military retains ultimate control of GLONASS, use of GLONASS for civilian applications is the responsibility of the Russian Space Agency (RSA). Within the RSA, GLONASS issues and policy are the responsibility of the Department of Space Apparatus for Communications, Navigation, and Geodesy [1].

Under GUKOS oversight, overall program direction as well as technical and design support services are provided by a large number of Russian space and electronics enterprises. The GLONASS systems integrator is the Scientific Production Association of Applied Mechanics (NPO PM), located in the formerly secret city of Krasnoyarsk-26 in Siberia. This enterprise is also charged with GLONASS spacecraft design and is responsible for all space segment research and development. Ground segment research and development is the responsibility of NPO Space Device Engineering (NPO KP). NPO KP also designs and builds some subsystems, the command and tracking stations, and the time synchronization equipment [1].

The Russian Institute of Radio Navigation and Time (RIRV) in St. Petersburg, formerly NPO Rus, designed and supports the time synchronization or master clock system, supplies the satellite clocks, and develops user equipment. Research and development to support user equipment is performed at both RIRV and NPO KP. The Central Scientific Research Institute of Machine Building (TsNIIMash) and the Moscow Aviation Institute (MAI) also conduct research and development for various system elements as consultants to the primary enterprises involved [1].

Despite the leading role of Space Forces, other organizations represented GLONASS in international negotiations until 1993. The Russian Aviation experts represented GLONASS in negotiations with the West. Additionally, the Internavigation Commission became involved in representing GLONASS after 1990. Originally, the Internavigation Commission was set up in 1985 to negotiate and enforce civilian navigation agreements. As GLONASS was never originally intended to be used for civilian purposes, the commission was not expected to play a major role in determining system requirements. As civilian interest grew, the commission involvement in the GLONASS program also grew. The commission has attempted to play a more substantive role in negotiating and coordinating international policy and agreements and in 1994 set up a GLONASS Information Center [1, 3].

10.4 CONSTELLATION AND ORBIT

The GLONASS constellation will consist of 21 active satellites plus 3 active on-orbit spares. A depiction of the constellation is provided in Figure 10.1. The 24 satellites will be uniformly located in three orbital planes 120° apart in right ascension. A 21-satellite constellation provides continuous 4-satellite visibility over 97% of the Earth's surface, whereas a 24-satellite constellation provides continuous observation of no fewer than 5 satellites simultaneously from more than 99% of the Earth's surface. The 21-satellite constellation is deemed adequate for most navigation purposes by the Russians. The constellation will be populated by filling predefined orbital "slots" similar to those used in GPS. Thus, while the GLONASS system is being completed and when older satellites reach their end of life, gaps or "holes" in this symmetrical arrangement will exist [1]. Figure 10.2 shows the satellite orbits

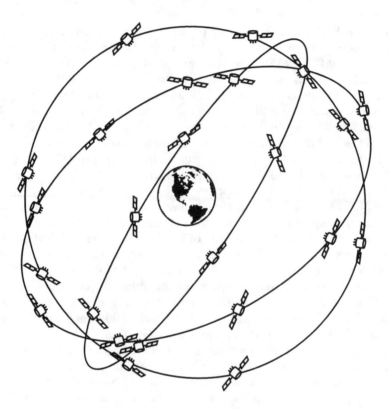

Figure 10.1 GLONASS satellite constellation.

in a planar projection referenced to epoch 0117 hours UTC(Soviet Union [SU])
August 21, 1995. This projection is based on the planned full constellation.

Under the 21-satellite concept, the performance of all 24 satellites will be
determined by GLONASS controllers and the "best" 21 will be activated. The
remaining 3 will be held for back-up or in reserve. Periodically, the "mix" will be
evaluated and, if necessary, a new best set of 21 will be defined. A number of
proposals within the Russia Government have discussed increasing the constellation
size to 27 satellites. Under the 27-satellite concept, 24 satellites will be active and
3 inactive satellites will remain in reserve. At the time of this writing, official Russian
documentation on GLONASS continues to indicate that the constellation will be 21
satellites plus 3 active spares [1, 2, 4, 5].

When necessary to maintain system accuracy, 3 new satellites will be launched
and used either to replace malfunctioning satellites or held in reserve for future use.
Once the permanent system of 21 operational and 3 spare satellites is established,
a single satellite failure would not lower the system design probability of successful

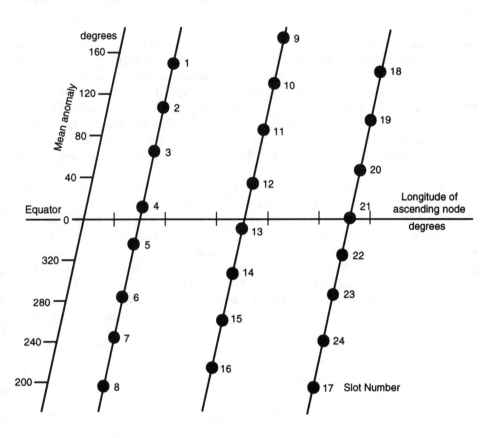

Figure 10.2 GLONASS constellation planar projection.

fix determination below 94.7%. (Available reference material did not specify if the term "successful fix determination" is referring to a horizontal and/or vertical fix.) There are provisions to activate either a backup satellite from available on-orbit satellite reserves, or to prepare 3 new satellites for launch (1 replacement satellite and 2 others for future orbital reserves) [1].

Each GLONASS satellite is in a 19,100-km circular orbit referenced to the Earth's surface with an inclination of 64.8°. The orbital period is 11 hours and 15 minutes. The current orbital configuration and overall system design (including satellite nominal L-band antenna beamwidths of 35° to 40°) provide navigation service to users up to 2,000 km above the Earth's surface [1].

10.5 SPACECRAFT DESCRIPTION

From 1982 to the present, the GLONASS constellation has been populated by various versions of GLONASS spacecraft. Within the GLONASS series, there have been two major block changes (referred to as Types I and II) and three variants (referred to as a, b, and c) within the second block. The main difference between the spacecraft blocks is the design lifetime. Early satellites had design lifetimes of one to two years. Currently, the Russians are launching GLONASS Type IIc spacecraft with a three-year design lifetime. The constellation will be replenished with GLONASS-M spacecraft, where "M" stands for "Modified" in the 1996–1998 timeframe [1]. A tabulation of the GLONASS satellites, their respective orbital locations, and frequency assignments is contained in Table 10.1. Satellite frequency channel assignments are discussed in Section 10.9.

A GLONASS spacecraft consists of a pressurized, hermetically sealed cylinder that is three-axis stabilized (i.e., oriented in all three axes of motion, usually measured as in-track, cross-track, and radial from the satellite's point of view). This assembly consists of the horizon sensor, laser retroreflectors, a 12-element navigation signal antenna, and various command and control antennas. Attached to the sides of the pressurized cylinder are the solar panels, orbital correction engines, a portion of the attitude control system, and the thermal control louvers [1].

Each spacecraft bus is supported by six subsystems denoted as (1) the onboard navigation complex, (2) the control complex, (3) the attitude control subsystem,

Table 10.1
Satellite Constellation Configuration (as of April 1995)

Block	COSMOS	Orbital Plane/Slot	Frequency Channel K	Launch Date
IIc	2111	1/5	23	Dec. 90
IIc	2178	1/8	2	Jan. 92
IIc	2179	1/1	23	Jan. 92
IIc	2204	3/21	24	July 92
IIc	2206	3/24	1	July 92
IIc	2235	1/7	21	Feb. 93
IIc	2236	1/2	5	Feb. 93
IIc	2275	3/18	10	Apr. 94
IIc	2276	3/17	24	Apr. 94
IIc	2277	3/23	3	Apr. 94
IIc	2287	2/12	22	Aug. 94
IIc	2288	2/14	9	Aug. 94
IIc	2289	2/16	22	Aug. 94
IIc	2294	1/4	12	Nov. 94
IIc	2295	1/3	21	Nov. 94
IIc	2296	1/6	13	Nov. 94
IIc	2307	3/20	1	Mar. 95
IIc	2307	3/22	10	Mar. 95
IIc	2307	3/19	3	Mar. 95

(4) the orbital maneuver subsystem, (5) the thermal control subsystem, and (6) the power supply subsystem. Each subsystem is discussed below [1].

10.5.1 Onboard Navigation Complex

The onboard navigation complex (OBNC) is the nucleus of the satellite. The OBNC is composed of an information logical complex (ILC) unit, a set of three spacecraft atomic clocks, a memory unit, a TT&C link receiver, and navigation transmitters. The complex operates in one of two modes: recording mode or the transmission mode. In recording mode, navigational information is uplinked to the satellite and then stored in onboard memory. Under normal conditions, new navigational data is uplinked to the satellite every orbit. In transmission mode, the OBNC generates navigational signals on two carrier frequencies; one frequency from each band: 1,246 to 1,257 MHz and 1,602 to 1,616 MHz. As in GPS, these navigational signals supply the users with information such as satellite ephemeris data, atomic clock corrections, and almanac data, and provide a satellite-to-user ranging capability [1].

The ILC performs three primary functions: (1) recording of satellite ephemeris and system almanac data uplinked from the ground stations; (2) controlling of navigation signal formulation including the navigation frames, which are analogous to the GPS navigation message; and (3) performing of regular diagnosis of OBNC performance [1].

The onboard clock is the most critical element of the GLONASS satellite. It is the long-term stability and predictability of modern atomic clocks that makes the concept of navigation satellite systems possible [1].

The current Block IIc spacecraft carry three "Gem" Cesium-beam frequency standards, which are produced by RIRV. The standards have dimensions of 370 by 450 by 500 mm, weigh 39.6 kg, and have an operational lifetime of 17,500 hr. Each standard has the following frequency stability (i.e., Allan variance) characteristics for the following averaging times: 5×10^{-11} at 1 sec, 1×10^{-11} at 100 sec, 2.5×10^{-12} at 1 hr, and 5×10^{-13} at 1 day [1, 6].

10.5.2 Onboard Control Complex

The onboard control complex manages the operational mode of each GLONASS satellite. It controls the OBNC, transmits TT&C data, and controls as well as regulates satellite power distribution. The complex is composed of the ranging subsystem, an onboard equipment control unit, and a TT&C processing and control system. The ranging subsystem provides satellite range measurement information directly to the ground control segment via TT&C link when queried [1].

10.5.3 Attitude Control System

The attitude control system performs initial orientation of the satellite and maintains proper orientation throughout the life of the satellite. This process begins immediately after satellite separation from the launch vehicle. Using the satellite's onboard propulsion system, the attitude control system stabilizes the satellite and dampens any gross oscillations. Upon reaching the desired orbital position, the attitude control system points the solar array toward the sun and points the antenna subassembly toward Earth. The margin of error involved in Earth and Sun orientations is no greater than 3° and 5°, respectively [1].

10.5.4 Maneuvering System

The maneuvering system initially places the spacecraft in its assigned orbital plane position. It also maintains the satellite's latitude argument and controls the satellite's thruster system. Each GLONASS satellite has 24 orientation thrusters of 10g thrust each and two position correction thrusters of 500g thrust each [1].

10.5.5 Thermal Control System

The thermal control system regulates the satellite's internal temperature. The spacecraft's design, especially its orientation and heat discharge value, allows use of a louvered gas thermal control system that utilizes the external surface of the pressurized container as a radiator. Heat dissipation regulation is carried out by a series of louvers, opening or closing the outlet to the radiator, depending on the internal gas temperature. An internal fan circulating the gas dissipates the heat from individual devices [1].

10.5.6 Power Supply System

The power supply system, composed of a solar cell, storage battery, control relays, and a voltage regulator, provides electrical power to onboard spacecraft equipment. The initial power output of the solar cell is 1600W, with an area of 17.5m². When illuminated by the Sun, the solar array charges the storage battery, which in turn provides power to the satellite and equipment when the satellite is in the sun's shadow. The storage battery has a discharge capacity of 70 amp-hours. In 1982, GLONASS became the first Russian satellite to be built with nickel-hydrogen batteries. Experience and testing on GLONASS have provided extended battery life, which is the primary factor that will allow satellite lifetimes to be extended to a minimum of five years as planned on the first generation of GLONASS-M satellites [1].

10.6 GROUND SUPPORT

The ground-based control complex (GBCC) is responsible for the following functions: (1) measurement and prediction of individual satellite ephemeris; (2) uploading of predicted ephemeris, clock corrections, and almanac information into each GLONASS satellite for later incorporation into the navigation message; (3) synchronization of the satellite clocks with GLONASS system time; (4) calculation of the offset between GLONASS system time and UTC(SU); and (5) spacecraft command, control, housekeeping, and tracking [1].

The functions of the ground control segment had been performed by a number of sites located within the former Soviet Union. With the demise of the USSR, the ground support segment has been reduced to sites within Russia, with the exception of one laser tracking site as indicated in Table 10.2. Further changes may also occur in the future, including the additional of other control sites within the VKS control network [1–4].

10.6.1 System Control Center

The System Control Center (SCC) is a military complex run by the Russian Space Forces and is located in Golitsyno-2, about 70 km southwest of Moscow. The SCC schedules and coordinates all system functions for GLONASS [1].

10.6.2 Central Synchronizer

The central synchronizer forms GLONASS system time. Signals from the central synchronizer are relayed to the phase control system (PCS), which monitors satellite

Table 10.2
GLONASS Ground Control Support Network

Site Function	Former USSR Network	Current Russian Network
System control center	Golitsyno-2	Golitsyno-2
Central synchronizer	Moscow	Moscow
Phase control system	Moscow	Moscow
Command and tracking stations	St. Petersburg, Yeniseisk, Komsomolsk, Balkhash and Ternopol	St. Petersburg, Yeniseisk and Komsomolsk
Laser tracking stations	Komsomolsk, Balkhash, Kitab, Evpatoria and Ternopol	Komsomolsk and Kitab
Navigational field control equipment	Moscow, Komsomolsk and Ternopol	Moscow and Komsomolsk

clock time/phase as transmitted by the navigation signals. The PCS performs two types of measurements in order to determine the satellite time/phase offsets. The PCS directly measures the range to the satellites by use of radar techniques. The PCS also simultaneously compares the satellite transmitted navigation signals to a reference time/phase generated by a highly stable frequency standard (relative error approximately 10^{-13}) at the ground site. These two measurements are then differenced to determine the satellite clock time/phase offsets. The range to the satellite can only be measured with an accuracy of 3m to 4m, which limits the accuracy of the time/phase measurements. Measurements from the PCS are used to predict the satellite clock time/phase corrections, which are uploaded by the ground station into the satellite. This comparison of each satellite's time/phases errors is carried out at least on a daily basis [1, 7].

10.6.3 Command and Tracking Stations

The command and tracking stations (CTS) measure individual satellite trajectories and uplink required control and payload information to the satellite's onboard processor. Trajectory tracking is carried out every 10 to 14 orbits. Tracking involves between three and five measurement sessions, each lasting 10 to 15 min. Range to the satellite is measured by radar techniques with a maximum error of between 2m and 3m. These radiofrequency ranges are periodically calibrated using a laser ranging device at the laser tracking stations. Each satellite carries laser retroreflectors specifically for this purpose. Ephemeris is predicted 24 hr in advance and uploaded once per day. The spacecraft clock correction parameters are renewed twice a day. Therefore, timing errors of the satellites' ranging signals can lead to a pseudorange measurement error of at most 5m to 6m. Any interruption in the normal operation of the ground segment interrupts the accuracy of GLONASS signals. Tests have shown that the spacecraft clock can maintain acceptable accuracy (one part in 5×10^{13}) for no more than two to three days of autonomous operations. Although the satellite's central processor is capable of 30 days of autonomous operations, this variability in the time standard is the limiting component for autonomous GLONASS operations [1].

10.6.4 Laser Tracking Stations

GLONASS is supported by the Etalon (Komsomolsk) and Maidanak (Kitab) laser stations. These stations calibrate radiofrequency tracking measurements. These systems use second-generation-class laser systems and are currently being upgraded to third-generation-class laser systems [1, 2].

Second-generation Etalon stations are able to measure the position of satellites visible in reflected solar light down to stellar magnitudes of less than 13. Range errors based on a 15-sec averaging interval are about 1.5 to 2 cm and between 2 and 3 arc-sec in angular position. Detailed specifications of these third-generation military systems remain classified [1].

GLONASS is supported by an experimental multifunctional optical and laser complex located near Kitab in southern Uzbekistan on Mt. Maidanak. Cameras located on Mt. Maidanak are capable of measuring ranges to an object up to an altitude of 40,000 km and down to a visible stellar magnitude of 16. Maximum error of satellite angular coordinate determination does not exceed 1 to 2 arc-sec under normal operating conditions and 0.5 arc-sec under special experimental conditions. Maximum ranging error is not more than 1.5 to 1.8 cm, and the error of the fix to the UTC(SU) scale is not more than ± 1 μsec. GLONASS measurements are relayed via secure radio link to the system control center once per hour. Mt. Maidanak provides unique climatic characteristics with more than 220 clear days annually, thus making it a reliable source of correction data to the system control center [1, 2].

10.6.5 Navigation Field Control Equipment

The navigation field control equipment stations monitor the GLONASS navigation signals. If anomalies are observed, they are reported back to the SCC [1].

10.7 USER EQUIPMENT

GLONASS is designed to support both Russian military and civilian applications. Originally, the Soviet Navy requested development of the system. Currently, GLONASS is employed in the Russian Air Force, Army, and Navy. In particular, the Russian Navy uses the GLONASS system for submarine navigation, ship navigation, and weapon guidance; whereas, the air force uses GLONASS for aircraft and helicopter navigation. GLONASS is used by the army primarily for troop location. Civil use of GLONASS is planned for applications similar to those that employ GPS in the West. Additionally, the current plans of the Ministry of Transport for upgrading the Russian air traffic control system are centered around the use of GLONASS for navigation, especially for the underdeveloped regions east of the Urals [1].

The Russian GLONASS user segment is still very small compared to usage of GPS outside Russia. The Russians project that the number of future GLONASS civil users will be less than those using GPS. At the time of this writing, estimates on the total number of GLONASS users (both civil and military) range from 1,500 to 2,500. Until the breakup of the USSR, the primary customer for GLONASS was the Russian Navy, followed by the Ministry of Transport (particularly its departments of air transportation), and the state-controlled fishing fleets. The breakup of the Soviet Union, which fractured the historical customer-designer-manufacturer relationship, and the lag in electronics have been cited as reasons why the user segment remains small. Despite this, there is no evidence of widespread use of GPS as a substitute. Present available estimates of the number of GPS users in Russia are on the order of only 500 [1, 8, 9].

As of 1995, the Russians have developed two generations of user equipment (UE). The first-generation receivers typically work only with GLONASS and tend to be larger and heavier than comparable GPS receivers found in the West. There are three basic designs: one-, two-, and four-channel receivers. In addition, many of the first-generation receivers are composed of several modules. In contrast, the second-generation receivers are five-, six-, and twelve-channel designs, and, for civil applications, work with both GPS and GLONASS. Development of second-generation equipment began in the early 1990s and therefore incorporates large-scale integrated circuits and digital processing [10].

Many different types of GLONASS user equipment have been manufactured in Russia. Table 10.3 illustrates the characteristics of some typical Russian user equipment. In addition, several European and U.S. companies are offering GLONASS user equipment [1].

In the former Soviet Union, UE was created following a "customer-designer-manufacturer" scheme. Despite the transition to a market-based economy, to a significant extent this scheme continues today in Russia and the C.I.S. Usually, government agencies act as the "customer" paying for creation of UE from their part of the state budget. A single department representing ground users is absent in Russia. Large Russian enterprises act as the "designers." They develop UE according to customer requirements and specifications. The ultimate design documents become

Table 10.3
Russian GLONASS and GPS/GLONASS Receivers

Receiver Trade Name	Shkiper	SNS-85	Gorn-M	Daman-M	Period	Reper	Shkiper-M	Gnom
Developer	NPO KP	RIRV	RIRV	RIRV	RIRV	NPO KP	NPO KP	NPO KP
Mass, kg	21.5	15	29.8	32.5	15.5	5	4.5	3
Channels	1	1	1	1	1	6	6	6
Frequency bands	1	1	2	2	1	1	1	1
Position (3σ), m	100	100–150	30–50	100	300	0.02	45	75
Velocity (3σ), cm/sec	10	20–30	N/A	N/A	N/A	3–5	7.5	10
Time to first fix, sec	174	240	240	180	300	60–180	60–180	60–180
User type	Naval	Airborne	Airborne	Land	Land	Survey	Naval	Airborne

the property of the customer. The main designers of UE in Russia are the Russian Institute of Radio Navigation and Time of St. Petersburg, the Kompas Design Bureau, and the Russian Scientific and Research Institute of Space Instrumentation, all in Moscow. "Manufacturers" get documents and money for production directly from the customers. Some large enterprises are designers and manufacturers simultaneously. The largest producers of GLONASS UE in the CIS are: (1) Moscow Radio Plant, Moscow; (2) NPO Space Devices Engineering (NPO KP), Moscow; (3) Neva Plant, Khmelnitski, Ukraine; (4) Radioizmeritel Plant, Kiev, Ukraine; (5) Volna Plant, Grodno, Belarus; and (6) Navigator Plant, St. Petersburg [1].

10.8 REFERENCE SYSTEMS

GLONASS provides position and time in Russian reference systems.

10.8.1 Geodetic References

Since August 1993, GLONASS has transmitted ephemeris data in the Earth Parameter System 1990 (PZ-90). Prior to that time, GLONASS provided data in the Soviet Geodetic System 1985 (SGS-85). PZ-90 is similar in quality to the Earth model employed in WGS-84 used by GPS [3]. The basic characteristics of PZ-90 are provided in Table 10.4 [3, 11, 12].

Details on the SGS-90 are provided in the Russian document "Parameters of the General Earth Ellipsoid and Earth Gravity Field SGS-90" by the Military Topographic Department of the General Staff, *Editorial Department*, Moscow 1991. To date, the Russians have not made this document publicly available, but are expected to in the near future [13].

Although GLONASS transmits ephemeris and almanac data using PZ-90, the output of most Russian-built receivers is in the Soviet Krasovskiy-1942 (SK-42) reference coordinate system. SK-42 is used as the reference for Russian and former Soviet Bloc maps in Eastern Europe and Asia [12].

The Russians have performed a limited number of measurements within western Russia and determined a preliminary rotation matrix between PZ-90 and WGS-84. Details of this rotation matrix are contained in [12]. The Russians believe that this matrix is good to within 5m to 10m, but caution that measurements should be made in a number of locations throughout the world in order to verify the rotation matrix and the magnitude of its error [12].

10.8.2 Time References

GLONASS provides time in both GLONASS system time, which is kept in Moscow, and in UTC(SU), which is kept at the All Union Institute for Physical,

Table 10.4
PZ-90 Characteristics

Name and Designation of the Constant	Unit of Measurement	Value
Fundamental Geodetic Constants		
Angular rate of rotation of Earth (ω)	rad/sec	$7.292\ 115 \times 10^{-5}$
Geocentric gravitational constant, including atmosphere (GM)	m^3/sec^2	$398,600.44 \times 10^9$
Geocentric gravitational constant of atmosphere (GM$_A$)	m^3/sec^2	0.35×10^9
Speed of light (c)	m/sec	299,792,458
Parameters of the Common Terrestrial Ellipsoid		
Semimajor axis (a_e)	m	6,378,136
Denominator of compression ($1/\alpha$)	unit of denominator	298.25784
Acceleration of gravity at the equator (γ_e)	mgal	978,032.8
Correction in the acceleration of gravity, γ, due to the attraction of atmosphere at sea level ($\delta\gamma_a$)	mgal	-0.9
Other Constants		
Second harmonic coefficient (J^0_2)	—	$1,082,625.7 \times 10^{-9}$
Fourth harmonic coefficient (J^0_4)	—	$-2,370.9 \times 10^{-9}$
Normal potential on the surface of the common terrestrial ellipsoid (U_0)	m^2/sec^2	62,636,861

Technical, and Radio-Technical Measurements (VNIIFTRI) in Mendeleevo near Moscow [1, 7].

10.9 GLONASS SIGNAL CHARACTERISTICS

Unlike GPS, where each satellite transmits a unique PRN code pair (C/A and P(Y)) on the same frequency in a CDMA format, each GLONASS transmits the same PRN code pair. However, each GLONASS satellite transmits on a different frequency. This process is denoted as frequency division multiple access (FDMA). FDMA is the same method used by commercial radio and television stations. Each station is analogous to a GLONASS satellite, and the radio receivers are analogous to GLO-NASS receivers. A GLONASS receiver "tunes" in a particular GLONASS satellite in the same manner one would tune in their favorite radio station; by tuning in the frequency allocated to the desired satellite.

The choice of FDMA over CDMA is one of the design tradeoffs. FDMA typically results in larger, more expensive receivers because of the extra front-end components required to process multiple frequencies. In contrast, CDMA signals can be processed with the same set of front-end components. FDMA does have some redeeming qualities in terms of interference rejection. A narrowband interference source that disrupts only one FDMA signal would disrupt all CDMA signals simultaneously. Furthermore, FDMA eliminates the need to consider the interference effect between multiple signal codes (cross-correlation). Thus, GLONASS offers more frequency-based interference rejection options than GPS and also has a more simplified code selection criteria.

GLONASS satellites transmit signals centered on two discrete L-band carrier frequencies. Each carrier frequency is modulated by the modulo-2 summation of either a 511-kHz or 5.11-MHz PRN ranging code sequence and a 50-bps data signal. This 50-bps data signal contains the navigation frames and is denoted as the navigation message. Figure 10.3 shows a simplified block diagram of the signal generator. Details of the frequencies, modulation, PRN code properties, and navigation message are covered below [1, 14, 15].

10.9.1 GLONASS Frequencies

Each GLONASS satellite is allocated a pair of carrier frequencies, referred to as L1 and L2, according to the following equation:

$$ f = \left(178.0 + \frac{K}{16} \right) \cdot Z \quad (\text{MHz}) $$

where

K = an integer value between −7 and +12
Z = 9 for L1, 7 for L2

The spacing between adjacent frequencies on L1 is 0.5625 MHz, and 0.4375 MHz for L2. Originally, K was a unique integer for each satellite and varied from 0 to 24. But, due primarily to interference with radio astronomy measurements, the Russians have proposed the following modifications to their frequency assignments [16]:

- From present until 1998: K = 0 to 12;
- 1998 to 2005: K = −7 to 12;
- After 2005: K −7 to 4.

The end result is to move the frequencies away from the radio astronomy band. Additionally, the final configuration will only use 12 values of K (K = −7 to

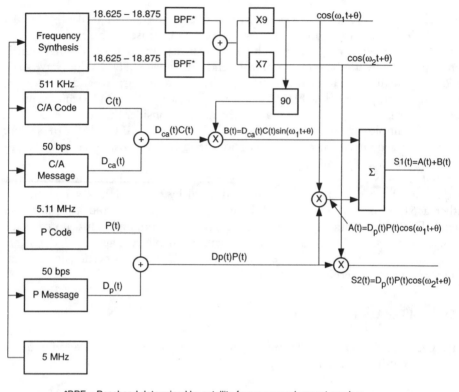

*BPF = Passband determined by satellite frequency assignment number.
Frequency synthesis is for k=0 to 24; this will change for new satellites.

Figure 10.3 Satellite signal generator.

4), but there are 24 satellites. The plan is to have satellites on opposite sides of the Earth (antipodal) share the same K number (i.e., broadcast on the same frequency). This center frequency modification will have little effect on terrestrial users who cannot see antipodal satellites simultaneously. Space-based receivers may require special discriminating functions such as Doppler checks in order to track the proper satellite. This ability to discriminate antipodal satellites is important since the antenna beamwidths on the GLONASS-M satellites are specifically designed to accommodate space-based users [1, 16].

The values of K listed above are the proposed values for satellites operating under normal conditions. Other values of K may be assigned for certain command and control processing or under "exceptional circumstances" according to the Russians [1].

10.9.2 Modulation

In a similar manner as GPS, each satellite modulates its L1 carrier frequency with two PRN ranging sequences. (As shown in Figure 10.3, both sequences are modulo-2 added with navigation data before modulating the carrier.) One sequence, called the P-code, is reserved for military purposes. The other sequence, called the C/A-code, is for civil use and aids acquisition of the P-code. Each satellite modulates its L2 carrier frequency solely with the modulo-2 summation of P-code and navigation data. The P-code and C/A-code sequences are the same for all satellites [1, 14, 15].

10.9.3 Code Properties

Both GLONASS and GPS use pseudorandom codes that facilitate satellite-to-user ranging and have inherent interference rejection. GLONASS C/A-code and P-code sequences are described below [1, 14, 15].

10.9.3.1 GLONASS C/A-Code

The GLONASS C/A-code has the following characteristics:

- Code type: Maximal length 9-bit shift register;
- Code rate: 0.511 Mchips/sec;
- Code length: 511 chips;
- Repeat rate: 1 msec.

A maximal length code sequence exhibits predictable and desirable autocorrelation properties (see Section 4.1). The 511-bit C/A-code is clocked at 0.511 Mchips/sec, thus the code repeats every millisecond. This use of a relatively short code clocked at a high rate produces undesirable frequency components at 1-kHz intervals that can result in cross-correlation between interference sources, reducing the interference rejection benefit of the spread frequency spectrum. On the plus side, the FDMA nature of the GLONASS signal significantly reduces any cross-correlation between satellite signals because of the frequency separation. The reason for the short code is to allow quick acquisition, requiring a receiver to search a maximum of 511 code phase shifts. The fast code rate is necessary for range discrimination with each code phase representing approximately 587m.

10.9.3.2 GLONASS P-Code

The Russians have emphatically stated numerous times that the P-code is strictly a military signal. As such, there is very little Russian information available on the

GLONASS P-code. Most P-code information is derived from analysis of the code performed by various independent individuals or organizations such as that provided in [15]. Based on [15], P-code characteristics are:

- Code type: Maximal length 25-bit shift register;
- Code rate: 5.11 Mchips/sec;
- Code length: 33,554,432 chips;
- Repeat rate: 1 sec (repeat rate is actually at 6.57-sec intervals, but chipped sequence is truncated such that it repeats every 1 sec).

As with the C/A-code, the maximal length code has exceptional, predictable, autocorrelation properties. The significant difference between the P-code and the C/A-code is that the P-code is much longer compared to its clock rate, thus repeating only once every second. Although this produces undesirable frequency components at 1-Hz intervals, the cross-correlation problem is not as severe as with the C/A-code. As with the C/A-code, FDMA virtually eliminates any problems involving cross-correlation between satellite signals. While the P-code gains in terms of correlation properties, it sacrifices in terms of acquisition. The P-code contains 511 million code phase shift possibilities. Thus, a receiver typically acquires C/A-code first, and then uses the C/A-code to help narrow the number of P-code phase shifts to search. Each P-code phase, clocked at 10 times the C/A-code, represents 58.7m in range. A handover word (HOW) like the one used in GPS to facilitate handover to P(Y)-code is not necessarily needed. The GLONASS P-code repeats once every second, making it possible to use the timing of the C/A-code sequence to assist in the handover process. This is an example of one more design tradeoff between the desired security and correlation properties of a long sequence and the desire for a faster acquisition scheme. GPS employs the former implementation while GLONASS employs the latter [15].

10.9.3.3 Comparison of GLONASS Codes to GPS Codes

Because of the CDMA nature of GPS, the GPS design could not ignore the effect of cross-correlation between satellite signals. The Gold codes used by GPS were specifically chosen because of the ability to mathematically bound the autocorrelation and cross-correlation properties of the C/A-codes. Nonetheless, in most respects, the GLONASS and GPS C/A-codes are comparable in terms of correlation properties. On the other hand, the longer GPS P-code means GPS has better correlation properties than GLONASS P-code. However, under certain configurations, the shorter GLONASS P-code may make it easier to directly acquire than the GPS P(Y)-code.

10.9.4 Navigation Message

Unlike GPS, GLONASS has two types of navigation messages. The C/A-code navigation message is modulo-2 added to the C/A-code at the satellite, whereas, a

P-code unique navigation message is modulo-2 added to the P-code. Both navigation messages are 50 bps data streams. The primary purpose of these messages is to provide information on satellite ephemeris and channel allocations.

The ephemeris information allows the GLONASS receiver to accurately compute where each GLONASS satellite is located at any point in time. Although ephemeris is the predominant navigation information, there is an assortment of other items provided such as:

- Epoch timing;
- Synchronization bits;
- Error correction bits;
- Satellite health;
- Age of data;
- Spare bits.

In addition, the Russians plan on providing data that will facilitate the combined use of GPS and GLONASS, particularly differences between GLONASS system time and GPS system time as well as differences between WGS-84 and PZ-90.

An overview of the C/A-code and P-code navigation messages is provided next [14, 15].

10.9.4.1 C/A Navigation Message

Each GLONASS satellite broadcasts a C/A-code navigation message that contains a superframe consisting of 5 frames. Each frame contains 15 lines with each line containing 100 bits of information. Each frame takes 30 sec to broadcast, so the entire superframe is broadcast once every 2.5 min [14].

The first 3 lines of each frame contain the detailed ephemeris for the satellite being tracked. Since each frame repeats every 30 sec, a receiver will receive a satellite's ephemeris within 30 sec once data reception begins [14].

The other lines of each frame consist primarily of approximate ephemeris (i.e., almanac) information for all the other satellites in the constellation. Each frame can hold the ephemeris for 5 satellites. Since the constellation will have 24 satellites, all 5 frames must be read in order to get the approximate ephemeris for all the satellites. This takes approximately 2.5 min [1, 14].

The approximate ephemeris information is not as accurate as the detailed ephemeris, and is not used for the actual ranging measurement. Nonetheless, the approximate ephemeris is sufficient to allow the receiver to quickly align its code phase and acquire the desired satellite. Once acquired, the satellite's detailed ephemeris is used for the ranging measurement.

As with GPS, the ephemeris information is often valid for hours. Therefore, a receiver does not need to continually read the data message in order to compute accurate position.

10.9.4.2 P-Code Navigation Message

The Russians have not publicly published any specifics on their P-code. Nonetheless, a number of independent organizations and individuals have investigated the P-code waveform and published their results [14]. The following information is extracted from the published information. The important thing to remember is the Russians publicly provided the detailed information on their C/A-code data message and have given certain guarantees regarding its continuity. No such information or guarantees exist regarding the P-code data. Thus, the P-code data structure described below may change at any time without notice.

Each GLONASS satellite broadcasts a P-code navigation message consisting of a superframe, consisting of 72 frames. Each frame contains 5 lines with each line containing 100 bits of information. Each frame takes 10 sec to broadcast, so the entire superframe is broadcast once every 12 min [14].

The first 3 lines of each frame contain the detailed ephemeris for the satellite being tracked. Since each frame repeats every 10 sec, a receiver will receive a satellite's ephemeris within 10 sec once data reception occurs.

The other lines of each frame consist primarily of approximate ephemeris information for the other satellites in the constellation. All 72 frames must be read to get all the ephemeris, taking 12 min [14].

10.9.4.3 Comparing C/A-Code and P-Code Navigation Message

The two most distinguishing differences between the data messages deal with the length of time required to obtain ephemeris information.

The time to obtain detailed ephemeris is:

P-code: 10 sec
C/A-code: 30 sec

The time to obtain almanac (approximate ephemeris) for all satellites is:

P-code: 12 min
C/A-code: 2.5 min

10.10 SYSTEM ACCURACY

GLONASS provides two levels of accuracy similar to GPS. The high-accuracy service is exclusively for Russian military use while the lesser accuracy service is for civil use. The high-accuracy service has an antispoofing capability that is under the control of the Russian Ministry of Defense. Based on Western observations, this feature is typically not activated and the service is available for navigation. Observations by the University of Leeds and 3S Corporation report that the accuracy provided by the military service is similar to the specification for the GPS PPS, approximately 20m (2 drms, 95% probability) in the horizontal plane and 34m (2-sigma), in the vertical dimension. However, according to the Russians, the military accuracies for GLONASS remain classified [1, 14].

The specification for GLONASS civil accuracy is 100m (2 drms, 95% probability) in the horizontal, 150m (2-sigma) in the vertical, and 15 cm/sec (2-sigma) in velocity. A full GLONASS constellation (21 satellites plus 3 active spares) is designed to have a 94.7% probability of providing civilian navigational information to the above-mentioned design accuracy. The specification for derived time is within 1 msec of GLONASS system time and within 5 msec of UTC(SU) [1].

In practice, GLONASS accuracy is much better than the specified values cited above. Tests of the operational system have demonstrated civil accuracies of 26m (2 drms, 95% probability) in the horizontal plane and 45m (95% probability) in the vertical plane [17]. Velocity measurement accuracy is between 3 and 5 cm/sec in velocity [1, 18].

10.11 FUTURE GLONASS DEVELOPMENT

The Russians plan a number of changes to the GLONASS program in the future. These changes include improvements to the ground support segment, augmentation of the system with differential services, and improvements to the space segment [1].

10.11.1 Ground Segment Improvements

The Russians are planning several upgrades to the ground support segment. Improvement of the time/phase control system is planned to achieve a time accuracy to within 100 nsec of GLONASS system time and within 1 μs of UTC(SU). In addition, corrections with respect to UTC(SU) and the offset between GPS and GLONASS system time should be inserted in the GLONASS navigation message in the near future. Further, the GLONASS control center will be upgraded with an automatic measuring/computing system that will relieve the workload on controllers. By the year 2000, the control segment will add mobile command and tracking equipment to augment the current network of support sites [1].

10.11.2 Differential GLONASS Improvements

At the time of this writing, the Russians are considering four distinct implementations to augment GLONASS with differential services. Russian research indicates that differential techniques can improve accuracy 1.3 to 1.7 times for baselines of about

1,500 to 2,000 km, 2 to 3 times for baselines of about 400 to 600 km, and 4 to 6 times for baselines of about 200 to 300 km [1].

One scheme proposes to use the network of the existing Russian Military Space Force's Command and Control sites to double as differential reference sites. One advantage of this plan from the Russian perspective is that it would use preexisting accurately surveyed sites as reference points. The plan would also use the CSIC as a hub for computing differential corrections and extending the coverage over Asia, Europe, and Northern Africa. The differential radio communications links to transmit the differential corrections currently have not been selected or installed [5].

A second scheme is similar to the US Coast Guard's plans to use existing maritime radio beacons to transmit differential corrections. The Russians have a similar proposal and are currently testing the Zver-M radiobeacon, which is capable of transmitting GLONASS differential signals in the Baltic Sea. If successful, this equipment could be installed throughout the Russian territory. The Russians have actively participated in RTCM Special Committee SC-104 to develop a series of standards that will permit the seamless use of DGPS, differential GLONASS and differential GPS/GLONASS services [1].

A third scheme is comparable to the US FAA plans for local-area differential GPS for Category II and III landing approaches. The Russians plan to use differential GLONASS and differential GPS/GLONASS for Categories I, II, and III, all categories of landing approach. In addition, they are actively researching the use of pseudolites for transmission of these corrections [3].

A fourth scheme proposes the use of the existing ground-based radionavigation aid, Chaika, to transmit differential GLONASS corrections in addition to its navigation service. Chaika is the Russian counterpart of Loran-C. The status of the program is unclear, but is discussed extensively in the 1994 CIS Federal Radionavigation Plan [10].

10.11.3 Space Segment Enhancements

The Russians plan to introduce two new generations of spacecraft to the GLONASS constellation beginning in 1996. Both generations are commonly referred to as GLONASS-M. The first series of GLONASS-M is basically an improved spacecraft with a longer lifetime. The second series is a new spacecraft design and is expected to provide greater satellite autonomy by using radio and laser crosslinks to assist in determining satellite ephemeris and onboard time. In addition, the Russian Space Agency has a proposal for improvements beyond GLONASS-M under a program called "Metrika." Currently, Metrika remains unfunded [1, 19].

Ground testing of the first series of GLONASS-M satellites was initiated in 1994 and is expected to be completed in 1995. Originally, on-orbit testing was scheduled for 1995, but has been postponed until 1996 [20]. The GLONASS-M is basically an improved spacecraft with longer lifetime, enhanced clock features, and changes to the navigation radio frequencies. The spacecraft mass will be increased from the current satellite mass of approximately 1,300 kg to approximately 1,480 kg, mostly due to an increase in fuel loading. Minor modifications to the GLONASS Proton launch system will be required to launch these heavier satellites. The additional fuel, improved batteries, and improved spacecraft electronics will allow the spacecraft design lifetime to be increased to 5 yr. Along with the lengthened lifetime, the satellite will have a better attitude control system, thus improving the accuracy of the ephemeris calculation. In addition, the satellite will carry a more stable cesium standard. The Russians also plan to transmit the navigation signals on radiofrequency channels 0 to 12 (1,602 to 1,610) on the GLONASS-M satellites. The Russians plan to replenish the GLONASS constellation with GLONASS-M spacecraft in the 1996–1998 time frame, after the current stock of replacement GLONASS spacecraft is depleted. The Russians are obligated to upgrade to this new design to meet international obligations to the United Nation's (UN) International Frequency Registration Board (IFRB). Russia has committed to vacating the radio band above 1,613 MHz by 1998, which would require them to deploy nearly a full constellation of GLONASS-M satellites by that time. Complete replenishment of the constellation is expected by 2000 [1, 16].

Beyond this, the Russians plan a second series of GLONASS-M satellites. The program includes the following published goals [1]:

- Continuous, efficient, and accurate navigational support of an unlimited number of mobile users in any region of the world and any part of air and space at altitudes of up to 40,000 km, including air traffic control;
- Support of geodetic surveying in any region of the world, particularly in inaccessible and poorly equipped regions;
- Continuous efficient frequency-time support;
- Information relay support on the observed object's location;
- Support of heading determination;
- Fix accuracies within: 10 to 15m, 0.01 m/sec, and 15 arc-sec in heading (the reference material did not indicate if "fix accuracies" refers to either horizontal or vertical positioning performance. Further, the available reference material did not indicate the statistical boundaries of the accuracy descriptions);
- Relay to users of the difference between the GLONASS-M time scale and the UTC(SU) with an error limit of 20 to 30 nsec (3-rms error) [1].

The second series of GLONASS-M should begin to be launched after the 2000. The Russians have committed to the IFRB to eliminate interference in the 1,610 to 1,613 band by 2005. This commitment will require near completion of the GLONASS constellation with this second series of the GLONASS-M satellite by that time. The spacecraft in this series will be a total redesign and included new features like a nonpressured bus, intersatellite crosslink and seven-year design lifetime. The specified characteristics of the design are as follows [1, 16].

The orbit will be 20,000-km circular (above the Earth's surface) with inclination of somewhere between 55° and 65° [1].

The spacecraft will use an unpressurized modular design with a mass in final orbit of 2,000 kg and a lifetime of seven years. The possibility of using a new launch vehicle and deployment bus is also under consideration. The solar panels will be 28m² with an available power of 1,400W. The current GLONASS solar arrays are rated at only five years. Therefore, the increase in design lifetime will require improvements in production technology of solar panels. Russian experience with solar panels for satellite in other orbits indicates that is possible to achieve the seven-year goal [1].

The navigation payload will have an improved ensemble of clocks providing daily frequency stabilities on the order of 1×10^{-14}. This will likely require upgrade to a hydrogen maser standard. Currently, testing of a hydrogen master clock is planned on a Russian Meteor-3M satellite under project "H-Maser" being conducted with the Germans and Swiss. The current scheme also calls for navigation support to increase up to 40,000 km in altitude. This will require widening the satellite transmitted beam width from 38° to 60°. This beam widening is planned only for the upper L-band frequencies (1,600-MHz region) and will require an increase in transmitter power to 120W (a growth of 2.5 times) [1].

The satellite will be augmented with a capability for long-term autonomous operation using intersatellite measurements to solve the ephemeris-time support problem. The design will include onboard avionics for intersatellite measurements in the laser and radio ranges. Onboard laser measurements would significantly reduce the problem of satellite self-positioning, but they would require that satellites have an inertial navigation system integrated with their onboard avionics. The inertial navigation system would be updated through stellar observations. Laser signals could either be reflected by a corner reflector (passive scheme) or would switch on a laser transmitter through a receiving device (active scheme). There will also be a dedicated communication line for navigational data exchange between satellites. Avionics for intersatellite measurements will be used to determine ephemeris and time synchronization for each satellite's navigational signals and amend the navigation message without ground support. The parameters measured by avionics are: pseudorange with an accuracy of 1m (3-rms error), optical range with an accuracy of 0.1m (3-rms error), and angular coordinates in respect to the stars with an accuracy of 1 arc-sec. This should allow autonomous operation for up to 60 days without degradation of the accuracy characteristics. Autonomous operation appears to be limited to about 60 days by deviations in the errors in extrapolation of the Earth's rotation irregularity (which are 30 to 40 m/sec [1-rms deviation] in 60 days). When converted to ephemeris, these errors lead to satellite position errors between 45 and 70m [1].

The next planned space segment upgrade after the second GLONASS-M series is the Metrika program. To date, little information has been published on Metrika. The available literature appears to indicate that the program will integrate a new generation of satellites with three passive Etalon-class laser-retroreflecting satellites and highly accurate laser tracking sites to solve both basic geophysical and geodynamic problems and determine satellite time and ephemeris. Like GLONASS-M, the satellites will perform laser intersatellite measurements. However, Metrika satellites will also perform intersatellite measurements to the Etalon-class satellites. Literature indicates that the program is sponsored by the Russian Space Agency and is not supported by the Russian Space Forces; therefore, the future is unclear [1, 19].

10.12 GLONASS INFORMATION CENTERS

The Russians have formed two information centers that provide information on GLONASS. Both were operational as of 1995. The Russian Military Space Forces operates the CSIC and the Intergovernmental Navigation Research Center operates the Intergovernmental Navigation Information Center (INIC) [5].

The CSIC is set up to render assistance on both GLONASS and integration of GPS and GLONASS to both domestic and international users of the systems. The CSIC is the main interface between the military operators of GLONASS and the Russian Department of Air Traffic and the Ministry of Transport. The CSIC advertises that it can provide assistance in the following areas [5]:

1. Provide consultations, information, and expertise to increase the effective use of the GLONASS system.
2. Provide official representation of the GLONASS system and its users at conferences, symposiums, and negotiations.
3. Facilitate dialogue with domestic and foreign users of the GLONASS.
4. Issue licenses for the use of the navigational services provide by the GLONASS.
5. Certify GLONASS and GPS/GLONASS user equipment.
6. Provide official research on the utility of the GLONASS system.
7. Promote combined use of the GLONASS and GPS systems.

The center can be reached by contacting Mr. V. Gorev at:

Scientific Information Coordination Centre of the Military Space Forces
Kazakova ul., 23
Moscow, Russia 103064
Russian Federation
Fax: 7095 333-8133
e-mail: sfcsic@iki3.bitnet; sfcsic@mx.iki.rssi.ru; and sfcsic@iki3.rssi.ru

The second information center has been set up at the INIC. The mission of the INIC is to establish and manage navigation data exchange between the departmental navigation centers in Russia and foreign countries. The INIC address is [1]:

22 Academician Pilyugin Ulitsa
117393 Moscow, Russia
Tel: 7095 132-7506
Fax: 7095 132-0822 or 7095 132-7421
Telex: 621050 MNET SU
e-mail: postmaster@internavi.msk.su

10.13 ACKNOWLEDGMENTS

The primary source for this section was the report entitled "Russia's Global Navigation Satellite System," which was produced under U.S. Air Force Contract Number F33657-90-D-0096. The contract was performed by ANSER (Washington, DC) with some assistance from the Russian Space Agency. ANSER assembled a team of Russian GLONASS experts in Russia to compile and author the report. The Russian authors included: V. F. Cheremisin, V. A. Bartenev, and M. F. Reshetnov of the NPO Prikladnoy Mekhaniki (Applied Mechanics), Y. G. Gouzhva and V. V. Korniyenko of the Russian Institute of Radio Navigation and Time, N. E. Ivanov and V. A. Salishchev of the Scientific Research Institute of Space Device Engineering, Y. V. Medvedkov of the Russian Space Agency, V. N. Pochukaev of the Central Scientific Research Institute of Machine Building, M. N. Krasilshikov and V. V. Malyshev of the Moscow Aviation Institute, V. I. Durnev, V. L. Ivanov, and Lebedev, of the Russian Space Forces, and V. P. Pavlov of the Flight Control Center. The team from ANSER included E. N. O'Rear and R. Turner from the Arlington office and S. Hopkins, R. Dalby, and D. Van Hulle from the Moscow office. In addition, the authors would like to thank the following navigation experts who reviewed the initial draft of the ANSER report and provide many valuable comments: P. Misra of Lincoln Laboratory; L. Chesto, Chairman of RTCA Special Committee 159; J. Danaher; 3-S; and R. Braff, Editor for *NAVIGATION, the Journal of the Institute of Navigation* [4].

References

[1] ANSER, "Russia's Global Navigation Satellite System," Arlington, VA, ANSER, US Air Force Contract Number F33657-90-D-0096, May 1994.
[2] Kazantsev, V. N., M. F. Reshetnev, A. G. Kozlov, and V. F. Cheremisin, "Overview and Design of the GLONASS System," *Proc. Int. Conference on Satellite Communications*, Volume II, Moscow, Russia, Oct. 18–21, 1994, pp. 207–216.
[3] Observations by the Scott Feairheller from his Moscow Trip under the US-Russia GPS-GLONASS Agreement, July 24–28, 1994.

[4] Feairheller, S., "The Russian GLONASS System: A US Air Force/Russian Study," *Proc. 7th Int. Technical Meeting of Satellite Division of US Institute of Navigation*, Salt Lake City, UT, Sept. 20–23, 1994, pp. 293–304.

[5] Lebedev, Colonel M., "Space Navigation System "GLONASS"-Application Prospective," Scientific Information Coordination Center for Military Space Forces, *Proc. RTCA 1994 Symposium*, Reston, VA, Nov. 30, Dec. 1, 1994, pp. 199–210.

[6] Gouzhva, Y. G., A. G. Gevorkyan, and V. V. Korniyenko, "Atomic Frequency Standards for Satellite Radionavigation Systems," *Proc. 45th Annual Symposium on Frequency Control*, Los Angeles, CA, May 29–31, 1991, pp. 591–593.

[7] Koshelyaevsky, N. B., and S. B. Pushkin, "National Time Unit Keeping Over Long Interval Using An Ensemble of H-Maser," *Proc. 22nd Annual Precise Time and Time Interval Applications and Timing Meeting*, Vienna, VA, Dec. 14–6, 1990, pp. 97–116.

[8] Denisov, V. I., "The Conception of Radionavigation Systems Development in the C.I.S. and International Cooperation of Safe Navigation of Marine, Air, and Land Users," *Proc. of the Seventeenth Annual Meeting International Omega Association*, Amsterdam, The Netherlands, Aug. 3–7, 1992, pp. 6-1–6-8.

[9] Gouzhva, Y. G., V. V. Korniyenko, and I. Pushkina, "GLONASS Status and Development: Assessment of System Potential For Civil Users," Paper presented at the Nordik Radionavigation Conference, Stockholm, Sweden—Helsinki, Finland, Oct. 18–22, 1993.

[10] Radionavigation Intergovernmental Advisory Council's "Intergovernmental Radio-navigation Programme of the Member States of the Commonwealth of Independent States," published by the Internavigation Research & Technical Centre, Moscow. Validated by Resolution of the Council Heads of the CIS on the Internavigational Radionavigation Programme, April 15, 1994.

[11] Boykov, V. V., V. F. Galazin, and Ye. V. Korablev, "Geodesy: Application of Geodetic Satellites for Solving the Fundamental and Applied Problems," *Geodeziya i Katografiya*, No. 11, Nov. 1993, pp. 8–11.

[12] Boykov, V. V., V. F. Galazin, B. L. Kaplan, V. G. Maximov, and Yu. A. Bazlov, "Experimental of Compiling the Geocentric System of Coordinates PZ-90," *Geodeziya i Katografiya*, No. 11, Nov. 1993, pp. 18–21.

[13] "GLONASS Receiver Equipment for Ships, Performance Standards, Methods of Testing and Required Testing Results," International Electrotechnical Commission Technical Committee No. 80: Navigational Instruments, Paper Number 80 (SWG-4a)5(A), 1993.

[14] Beser, J., and J. Danaher, "The 3S Navigation R-100 Family of Integrated GPS/GLONASS Receivers: Description and Performance Results," *Proc. of the US Institute of Navigation National Technical Meeting*, San Francisco, CA., Jan. 20–22, 1993, pp. 25–45.

[15] Stein, B. and W. Tsang, "PRN Codes for GPS/GLONASS: A Comparison," *Proc. of the US Institute of Navigation National Technical Meeting*, San Diego, CA, Jan. 23–25, 1990, pp. 31–35.

[16] Technical Description and Characteristics of Global Space Navigation System GLONASS-M - Information Document, International Telecommunications Union, Document 8D/46-E and 8D/46(Add.1)-E, Nov. 22, 1994 and Dec. 6, 1994, respectively.

[17] Misra, P., "Integrated Use of GPS and GLONASS in Civil Aviation," *MIT Lincoln Laboratory Journal*, Vol. 6, No. 2, Summer/Fall 1993.

[18] Misra, P., M. Pratt, and R. Muchnik, "GLONASS Performance in 1994: A Review," *Massachusetts Institute of Technology Lincoln Laboratory Report: ATC Project*, Memorandum No. 42PM-SATN-AV-0100, Feb. 8, 1995.

[19] Malyshev, V. V., M. N. Krsilshikov, S. V. Kudryashov, and K. I. Sypaio, "Development of Algorithms and Software for the GPS of the Third Generation," *Proc. of International Astronautical Federation (IAF)*, IAF-94-A.4.043, Jerusalem, Israel, Oct. 9–14, 1994.

[20] Kuranov, V., Telephone conversation with Working Group B, International Civil Aviation Organization (ICAO) Global Navigation Satellite System Panel (GNSSP), Feb. 14, 1995.

CHAPTER 11
▼▼▼

INMARSAT CIVIL NAVIGATION SATELLITE OVERLAY

James Nagle
INMARSAT

Ronald J. Cosentino
The MITRE Corporation

11.1 FUNCTIONAL DESCRIPTION

The function of the INMARSAT Civil Navigation Geostationary satellite overlay is to extend and compliment the GPS and GLONASS satellite systems. The overlay navigation signals are generated at ground-based facilities and uplinked to INMARSAT-3 satellites. These satellites contain special satellite repeater channels for rebroadcasting the navigation signals to users. The use of satellite repeater channels differs from the navigation signal broadcast technique employed by GLONASS and GPS. GLONASS and GPS satellites carry their own navigation payloads that generate their respective navigation signals.

INMARSAT has carried out extensive studies and trials leading to the development of a civil geostationary satellite overlay to GLONASS and GPS to provide data that would allow satellite navigation systems to meet the stringent requirements of reliability and integrity of information required by aviation and maritime authorities. INMARSAT is a space segment provider; whereas, service providers such as transport ministries (e.g., U.S. Federal Aviation Administration, Transport Canada) are responsible for implementing and operating the informational aspects. The overlay is intended to provide the following services:

1. The transmission of integrity and health information on each GLONASS and GPS satellite in real time to ensure users do not use "faulty" satellites for navigation. This feature has been called the GNSS Integrity Channel (GIC).
2. The transmission of additional ranging signals, in addition to the GIC service, to supplement GPS, thereby increasing GPS signal availability. Increased signal availability also translates to an increase in RAIM availability. This feature has been called Ranging GIC (RGIC).
3. The transmission of GPS and GLONASS wide-area differential corrections, in addition to the GIC and RGIC services, to increase the accuracy of the civil GPS and GLONASS signals. This service is called Wide Area Differential GNSS (WADGNSS).

The combination of the overlay services is referred to as the Wide Area Augmentation System (WAAS). The overlay system concept is shown in Figure 11.1.

As observed in Figure 11.1, users ② receive navigation signals ① transmitted from GPS and GLONASS satellites. These signals are also received by wide-area reference station/integrity monitoring networks ③ operated by governmental agencies. The monitored data are sent to a regional integrity network central processing facility ④. At the central processing facility, the data is processed to form the integrity and WADGNSS correction messages, which are then forwarded to the navigation Earth stations (NES) ⑤. At the NES, the spread spectrum navigation signal is precisely synchronized to a reference time and modulated with the GIC message data and WADGNSS corrections. This composite signal is transmitted to a satellite on a C-band uplink ⑥. Onboard the INMARSAT satellite ⑦, this navigation signal is frequency-translated within the navigation payload and transmitted to the user on L1 ⑧ and to the NES at C-band ⑨. This C-band signal is used for maintaining the navigation signal timing loop. The timing of the signal is done in a very precise manner in order that the signal appears as though it was generated onboard the satellite as a GPS ranging signal. One NES and the central processing facility could be collocated. The shadowing NES ⑩ functions as a "hot standby." It receives identical data from the central processing facility and maintains a timing loop so that it may assume operational status in the event of a failure at the primary NES. It is expected that these functions would alternate on a regular basis.

11.2 THE INMARSAT ORGANIZATION

Headquartered in London, England, INMARSAT is an internationally owned cooperative that provides mobile communications worldwide. INMARSAT was estab-

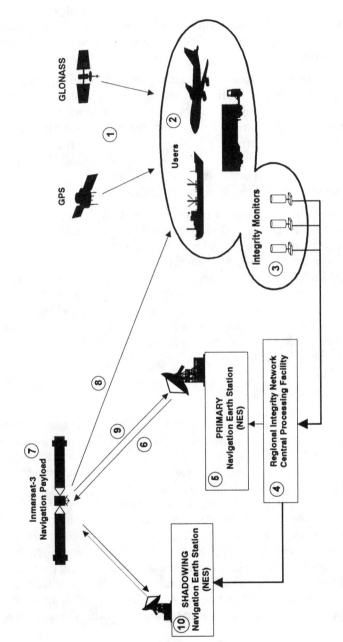

Figure 11.1 Wide Area Augmentation System (WAAS).

lished in July 1979 as a result of a 1973 conference convened by the International Maritime Organization (IMO). Twenty-eight countries joined INMARSAT at the start; as of January 1995, it had 76 member countries. As stated in Article 3 of the INMARSAT convention,

> The purpose of INMARSAT is to make provision for the space segment necessary for improving maritime communications and, as practicable, aeronautical and land mobile communications and communications on waters not part of the marine environment, thereby assisting in improving communications for distress and safety of life, communications for air traffic services, the efficiency and management of transportation by sea, air and on land, maritime, aeronautical and other mobile public correspondence services and radiodetermination capabilities.

As defined by the International Telecommunication Union, radiodetermination includes both radionavigation and radiolocation. The development of the overlay to GPS and GLONASS is part of INMARSAT's effort to advance the radiodetermination capabilities of the INMARSAT Charter.

The INMARSAT-3 satellites are a constellation of geostationary satellites scheduled for launch in 1996. Their main purpose is the provision of mobile communications services; however, the inclusion of a navigation payload represents the first initiative to provide radionavigation services via a geostationary satellite from a payload designed specifically for the application. INMARSAT currently plans to launch a total of five INMARSAT-3 satellites.

11.3 PROGRAM HISTORY

Many civil users propose to use GPS and/or GLONASS as their primary navigation aid in lieu of ground-based navigation aids, which have limited coverage. However, before GPS/GLONASS can be used as a primary means of navigation for aviation or shipping purposes, certain stringent safety and operational standards, such as availability and integrity, need to be considered.

One of the advantages of using satellite navigation systems like GPS and GLONASS is that, when approved for civil aviation use, they will support most phases of flight including some of the less demanding categories of precision approaches. The implementation of nonprecision approaches will be possible virtually anywhere in the world. This will aid those airports, particularly in developing parts of the world, where approaches are based on visual flying rules. Also, the higher accuracy expected from satellite navigation will allow reductions in aircraft spacing during the en route phases of flight, thus allowing for the expansion in air traffic expected over the next 20 years.

Neither the GPS or GLONASS systems by themselves provide sufficient notice to users of satellite health or data problems. The basic problem is that the design of GPS and GLONASS does not allow the users to be given timely (real time) notice of a satellite failure or excessive error. There is also some concern that both systems individually may not provide adequate global coverage. In addition, if GPS and GLONASS are to be used together, there are problems of compatibility between the time standards and the coordinate reference systems used by the U.S. and C.I.S in their systems. A geostationary augmentation service is capable of broadcasting the time offset between the two time standards and the user receiver can accommodate the differences in the coordinate reference systems. Hence, the two shortfalls can be overcome.

During the mid-1980s, the European Space Agency, the French National Center for Space Studies, and INMARSAT were conducting studies of techniques for using geostationary satellites to complement GPS and GLONASS. In 1989, INMARSAT began test transmissions of GPS-like spread spectrum signals through an Atlantic Ocean–region satellite to prove the feasibility of using a navigation repeater to transmit PRN-coded spread spectrum ranging signals. The test results indicated that transmitting these signals through geostationary satellites is possible.

INMARSAT then placed several technical feasibility contracts with various experts in the West and the former Soviet Union to investigate the needs of such a system and determine the appropriate signal structure and message format. The initial concept was that INMARSAT-3 satellites would carry a dedicated repeater channel that would transmit integrity and warning information. This was followed shortly afterwards with a proposal to improve this further by also transmitting PRN-coded spread spectrum ranging signals that would augment the GPS and GLONASS systems. At about the same time, the RTCA Special Committee 159 (SC-159) in the U.S. was established with the aim of developing the Minimum Aviation System Performance Standards (MASPS) for the operation and use of GPS for air navigation [1]. Its report on this subject included an appendix devoted to the topic of providing a GPS integrity channel through geostationary satellites.

As a result of growing international acceptance of the geostationary overlay concept, INMARSAT included the navigation repeater package option as a mandatory bid item in a 1989 procurement of INMARSAT-3 satellites to be delivered and launched in the mid-90s. In 1991, INMARSAT signed a contract with Martin Marietta Astro Space, formally GE Astro Space, for four INMARSAT-3 satellites. INMARSAT placed an order for a fifth satellite in 1994. The five satellites, whose delivery began in 1995, will include the navigation repeater packages. A depiction of the INMARSAT-3 satellite is shown in Figure 11.2.

11.4 INMARSAT-3

This section deals with the INMARSAT-3 satellite and the planned constellation. A physical description of the satellite is provided, along with a detailed overview of

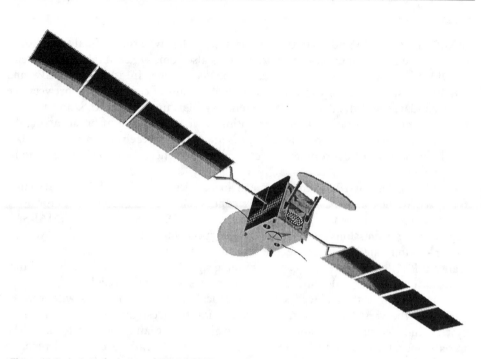

Figure 11.2 Artist's depiction of INMARSAT-3 satellite.

the navigation transponder. The orbital assignments for the forthcoming constellation are given, and the anticipated coverage is depicted.

11.4.1 Satellite Description

The INMARSAT-3 satellites are based on the GE Astro Space boxed-shape 4,000 bus, which is 2.5m high and has a 3.2m radial envelope centered on a thrust cone. Payloads and solar arrays are mounted on north- and south-facing panels. L-band receive and transmit reflectors, mounted on east and west panels, are fed by an array of "cup-shaped" radiating elements. The dedicated navigation transponder antenna is located on the Earth-facing panel.

The INMARSAT-3 satellite will weigh about 1,100 kg at the beginning of its on-orbit life. INMARSAT-3 is 3-axis stabilized with the attitude maintained by hydrazine thrusters and reaction wheels aligned for pitch control. The solar panels generate 2,400W of power and backup power is provided by two nickel hydrogen batteries. The INMARSAT-3 satellite has a design lifetime of 13 years.

The main mission payload of INMARSAT-3 are the communication transponders. An INMARSAT-3 satellite will carry up/down L-band global and spot beams and four (two as backup) up/down C-band global beams for communications applications. That is, communications information is uplinked to the satellite on both C-band and L-band and is frequency-translated by the transponders for downlink within the same band. The uplink signal is rebroadcast to users within a large coverage area as well as in some smaller areas.

As a secondary payload, INMARSAT-3 will carry the navigation transponders that provide the WAAS capability. Two frequencies (L1, 1,575.42 MHz and C-band, 3,600.00 MHz) are used to allow correction of ionospheric delay. The WAAS signal will be broadcast to the users at L1. For additional integrity purposes and for checking the data received by the satellite, the information being broadcast to users is also downlinked back to the control site in C-band. The L-band repeater is power-limited to ensure that the navigation signal can never interfere with the GPS and GLONASS signals.

11.4.2 INMARSAT-3 Navigation Transponder

The navigation transponder (Figure 11.3) is implemented in two parts, a C-band to C-band link (referred to as the C-C link) and a C-band to L-band link (referred to as the C-L link). The transponder receives the uplinked navigation signal on 6,455.42 MHz via the main payload C-band receiver. The uplink signal is RHCP. This signal is split and frequency-translated for simultaneous transmission to users on L1 (L-band) and to fixed Earth stations on 3,630.42 MHz (C-band). Within the transponder, these two links share common hardware until they are filtered at the intermediate frequency (IF) 180.92 MHz.

The interface to the navigation module is at the redundant RHCP input splitters in the IF processor. These redundant signals are downconverted to IF and channelized via 2.2-MHz bandwidth surface acoustic wave (SAW) filters.

For the C-C link, separate dual-redundant chains provide an initial upconversion, amplification and telecommandable gain adjustment (i.e., the link gain is adjusted by the ground control segment). The cross-strapped redundancy outputs interface with the main payload, at the left hand circularly polarized (LHCP) output combiners at the output of the main and redundant IF processors. The signals are then further upconverted and amplified in the main payload C-band high-power amplifier (HPA) prior to transmission via the C-band output multiplexer and transmit antenna. The C-band downlink polarization is LHCP.

For the C-L band link, the IF signals are upconverted to L1 and amplified by the L-band HPA, which is dual-redundant. This HPA consists of two nonredundant amplifiers of the same design as used in the main communications payload. However, unlike the communications transponder, the navigation transponder operates with a constant modulation envelope and therefore the amplifier may be operated close to saturation giving an overall dc-RF efficiency of 40%. The amplifier operates at an RF output power of 17W with a consequent dc power consumption of 42.5W.

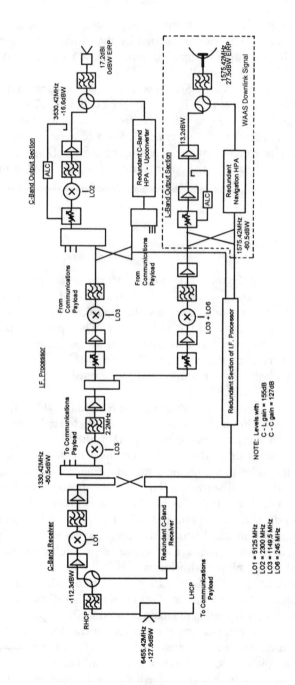

Figure 11.3 INMARSAT-3 navigation transponder.

The amplifier also contains the necessary L-band transmit output filtering. The filtered output is then forwarded to the navigation transmit antenna, which is a parabolic reflector of 0.7m diameter giving an unshaped global beam with an edge of cover gain of 15.8 dBi.

11.4.3 Constellation

The INMARSAT-3 constellation will initially consist of four satellites located at the following longitudes in a geostationary orbit: 180° for the Pacific Ocean Region (POR), 64.5°E for the Indian Ocean Region (IOR), 55.5°W for the Atlantic Ocean Region West (AORW), and 15.5°W for the Atlantic Ocean Region East (AORE). The location of the fifth INMARSAT-3 satellite will be determined at a later date. Coverage of the Earth from the four INMARSAT-3 satellite locations based on a minimum elevation angle of 5 degrees is shown in Figure 11.4. The satellite control center for the INMARSAT satellites is located at INMARSAT headquarters, London England.

11.5 WAAS SIGNAL SPECIFICATION

The WAAS signal is compatible with a new generation of user receiving equipment designed to provide navigation in conjunction with GPS-derived position, velocity,

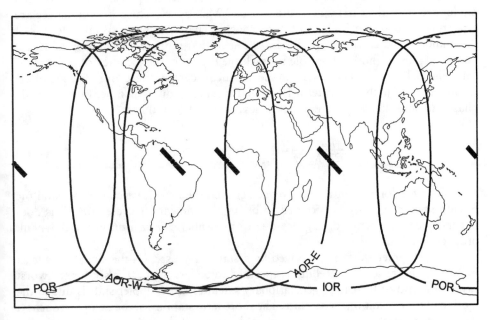

Figure 11.4 Planned INMARSAT-3 coverage.

and time. The data rate and the format of the data modulation superimposed on the spread spectrum carrier are different than those used in the GPS signal. Contained within this data stream are a variety of "messages." These messages are generated by the navigation service provider and are intended to provide users with information about the integrity and performance of the GPS and GLONASS satellite constellations. The messages also provide information such as ionospheric delay corrections that may be used to improve user positioning and time reference accuracy. This section provides an overview of the signal specification defined for the WAAS as developed by INMARSAT in cooperation with RTCA Inc. This signal specification is contained within [2].

11.5.1 WAAS Signal Characteristics

The signal broadcast via the WAAS geostationary satellite to the WAAS users is designed to minimize standard GPS receiver hardware modifications. The GPS frequency and GPS-type of modulation including a coarse/acquisition (C/A) PRN code are used. In addition, the code phase timing is synchronized to GPS system time to emulate a GPS satellite and provide a ranging capability. The WAAS broadcast uses a single carrier frequency on L1. Message symbols at a rate of 500 symbols/sec are modulo-2 added to a 1,023-bit PRN code, which is binary phase shift key (BPSK) modulated onto the carrier at a rate of 1.023 Mchips/sec. The 500 symbols/sec are synchronized with the 1-kHz C/A-code epochs. The phase noise spectral density of the unmodulated carrier is specified to be such that a phase locked loop of 10-Hz one-sided noise bandwidth is able to track the carrier to an accuracy of 0.1 radians rms. The lack of coherence between the broadcast carrier phase and the code phase is limited so that the short-term fractional frequency difference between the code phase rate and the carrier frequency is less than $5(10^{-11})$; that is,

$$\left| \frac{f_{code}}{1.023 \text{ MHz}} - \frac{f_{carrier}}{1,575.42 \text{ MHz}} \right| < 5(10^{-11}) \qquad (11.1)$$

Over the long term, the difference between the broadcast code phase and the broadcast carrier phase is specified to be within one carrier cycle (1σ). This does not include code/carrier divergence due to ionospheric refraction in the downlink propagation path.

The Doppler shift, as perceived by a stationary user, on the signal broadcast by WAAS geostationary satellites is specified to be less than 20 m/sec for the worst case at the end of life of the geostationary satellite. The Doppler shift is due to the motion of the geostationary satellite. The short-term stability of the carrier frequency, the square root of the Allan Variance, at the input of the user's receiver antenna is specified to be better than $5(10^{-11})$ over 1 to 10 sec, excluding the effects of the ionosphere and Doppler. As stated above, the broadcast signal is RHCP. Broadcast signal polarization ellipticity is specified to be no worse than 2 dB for the angular range of ±9.1° from boresight.

The received radiated power level into a 0-dBi RHCP antenna from a WAAS geostationary satellite on or near the surface of the Earth is specified to be greater than −161 dBw at elevation angles higher than 5°. The maximum received signal strength is specified to be −155 dBw into such an antenna. The expected typical received power versus elevation angle is shown in Figure 11.5.

The correlation loss resulting from modulation imperfections and filtering inside the WAAS satellite payload is specified to be less than 1 dB. The maximum uncorrected code phase of the broadcast signal is specified not to deviate from the equivalent WAAS network time by more than can be accommodated by the geostationary time correction provided in the geostationary data message ($±2^{-20}$ sec). The maximum corrected code phase deviation is limited in accordance with the overall signal-in-space performance requirements.

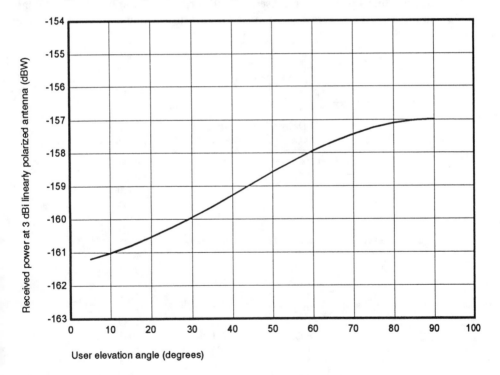

Figure 11.5 INMARSAT-3 typical received power levels.

11.5.2 WAAS C/A-Codes

The C/A-codes used by WAAS geostationary satellites broadcasting a GPS look-alike signal belong to the same family of 1,023-bit Gold codes as the 37 C/A-codes reserved by the GPS system and specified in [3]. The WAAS C/A-codes were specifically selected to not adversely interfere with GPS signals. The 19 selected WAAS C/A codes are shown in Table 11.1.

The WAAS C/A-codes are identified by the PRN number, the G2 delay in chips and the initial G2 state. The definition of either the G2 delay or initial G2 setting is required for implementation of the generation of the WAAS C/A-codes.

Like the GPS C/A-codes, the PRN number is arbitrary, but starting with 120 instead of 1. The actual codes are defined by either the G2 delay or the initial G2 register setting. The codes are ranked by the average number of cross-correlation peaks when correlating these codes with the 36 GPS codes with zero Doppler difference. In the octal notation for the first 10 chips of the WAAS code as shown in the table, the first digit on the left represents a "0" or "1" for the first chip. The last three digits are the octal representation of the remaining nine chips. For example,

Table 11.1
WAAS Ranging C/A-Codes

PRN	G2 Delay (Chips)	Initial G2 Setting (Octal)*	First 10 WAAS Chips (Octal)*
120	145	1106	0671
121	175	1241	0536
122	52	0267	1510
123	21	0232	1545
124	237	1617	0160
125	235	1076	0701
126	886	1764	0013
127	657	0717	1060
128	634	1532	0245
129	762	1250	0527
130	355	0341	1436
131	1012	0551	1226
132	176	0520	1257
133	603	1731	0046
134	130	0706	1071
135	359	1216	0561
136	595	0740	1037
137	68	1007	0770
138	386	0450	1327

the initial G2 setting for PRN 120 is 1001000110. Note that the first ten WAAS chips are simply the octal inverse of the initial G2 setting.

11.5.3 WAAS Signal Data Contents and Formats

A given WAAS geostationary satellite may broadcast only integrity data or both integrity data and WAAS data. The integrity data provides "use/don't use" information on all satellites in view of the applicable region, including the WAAS geostationary satellites. The corrections provided for satellites in view of the applicable region also include an estimate of the accuracy of those corrections. Information common to both the integrity and corrections data are not repeated in order to minimize the required data rate. The delivered level of accuracy can be controlled by adjusting the accuracy of the corrections, but integrity is always provided.

11.5.3.1 Data Rate

The baseline data rate is 250 bps. The data is rate 1/2 encoded with a forward error correction (FEC) code. Therefore, the symbol rate that the GPS receiver must process is 500 symbols/sec. The FEC coding uses constraint length $K = 7$ convolutional as standard for Viterbi decoding, with an encoder logic arrangement as illustrated in Figure 11.6. The G1 symbol is selected on the output as the first half of a 4 msec data bit period. Soft decision decoding is assumed in the receiver. The coding gain of this combination of FEC and decoding is 5 dB over uncoded operation.

11.5.3.2 Network Timing

WAAS network time is maintained and corrected to GPS system time. WAAS data blocks are synchronized with the GPS data blocks. When using WADGNSS corrections, the user's solution for time will be with respect to the WAAS network time, and not with respect to GPS system time. If corrections are not used, WAAS network time will be within the error budget required for nonprecision approach operations. Estimates of the time difference between WAAS network time and UTC (USNO) are provided in a WAAS data message.

In order to maintain data block synchronism with the GPS data frames, the data input to the convolution encoder (Figure 11.6) is applied 7-bits (14 symbols or 28 msec) early. In this way, the data blocks, although then encoded, are still coherent with 1-sec epochs of GPS time as transmitted from the WAAS geostationary satellite. The user's decoders will also introduce a fixed delay that depends on their respective algorithms (usually 5 constraint lengths, or 35 bits) for which they must compensate to determine GPS system time from the received signal.

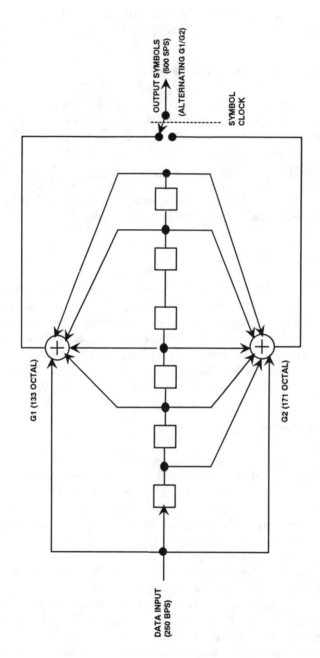

Figure 11.6 WAAS convolutional encoder for $K = 7$, rate 1/2 code.

11.5.3.3 Satellite Clock Error Correction

The WAAS transmits fast and slow WADGNSS clock correction data. The fast corrections are intended to correct for rapidly changing errors such as GPS SA clock dither errors, while the slow corrections are for slower changing errors due to long-term satellite clock and ephemeris errors. The rapidly changing errors are common to all users and are broadcast as such. Fast corrections messages are broadcast at least once every 6 sec. All other messages shall be broadcast in between.

The slower corrections provide users with ephemeris and clock error estimates for each satellite in view. Although long-term satellite clock errors are common to all regions, they are slow-varying and issue of data dependent. Therefore, they are best accommodated as part of the slower corrections.

The error corrections are formatted to have a maximum resolution of 0.125m to satisfy accuracy requirements for the WAAS.

11.5.3.4 Tropospheric Models

Because tropospheric refraction is a local phenomenon, the geostationary broadcast messages do not include any explicit tropospheric corrections. A tropospheric delay compensation model must reside in the user receiver. Tropospheric model particulars are described in Section 8.2.2.2.

11.5.3.5 Ionospheric Models

Each INMARSAT-3 coverage region is partitioned into geographical regions or bands, as shown in Figure 11.7.

These bands are divided into ionospheric grid points (IGPs). An IGP defines the locations of the ionospheric compensation delay estimates to be applied. The service provider's ground segment determines the ionospheric delay at each IGP within the coverage area. Since the spacing between the IGPs is large, the user computes the weighted average of the ionospheric compensation delay estimates for the four IGPs nearest to the point where each GPS and INMARSAT satellite signal penetrate the ionosphere. This point is denoted as the "pierce point" and relies upon the concept of a shell model of the ionosphere. Following these calculations, these delay estimates are adjusted for obliquity. Details of the computation are contained in Section 8.2.2.2.

11.5.3.6 PRN Masks

Masks are used to designate which PRN belongs to which correction slot. GPS is favored and are the first 37 PRNs of the mask. These masks improve the efficiency

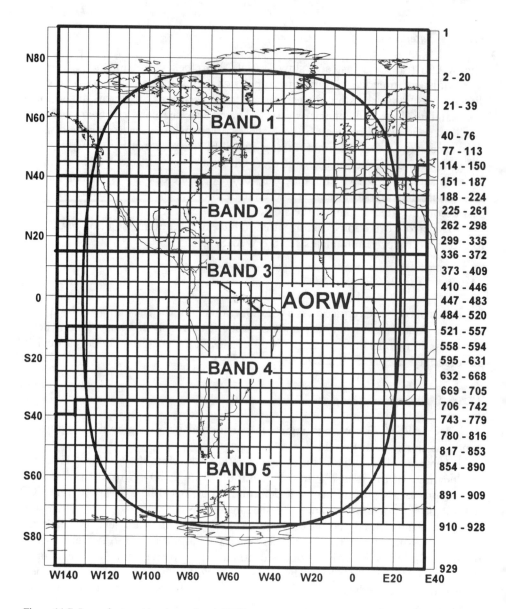

Figure 11.7 Ionospheric grid points using AORW as an example.

of the broadcast by preventing the continual inclusion of PRNs for fast corrections. The WAAS can provide data for a maximum of 52 satellites.

11.5.3.7 Issue of Data

The long-term satellite correction data for each satellite supported is accompanied by the GPS information to prevent erroneous application of correction data. The WAAS issue of data (IOD) is identical to the GPS IOD ephemeris defined in [3]. Various other WAAS IODs are also applied to prevent erroneous use of the PRN and IGP masks.

11.5.3.8 Format Summary-Block Format

The block format for the 250 bps data rate consisting of an 8-bit part of a distributed preamble, a 6-bit message type, a 212-bit data field, and 24-bits of cyclic redundancy check (CRC) parity is shown in Figure 11.8.

The distributed preamble is a 24-bit unique word, distributed over three successive blocks. These three 8-bit words are made up of the sequence of bits 01010011 10011010 11000110. The start of every other 24-bit preamble is synchronous with a 6-sec GPS subframe epoch. The preambles and timing information provided in the messages facilitate data acquisition. They also aid the user receiver to perform time synchronization during initial acquisition before GPS satellites are acquired, thus aiding the receiver in subsequent GPS satellite acquisitions. The message type field is 6 bits long, which allows for 64 different message types. Twenty-four bits of CRC parity provide protection against burst as well as random errors.

11.5.4 Message Types

The WAAS data block format allows for 64 different message types. Table 11.2 lists the message types that have been defined by INMARSAT in cooperation with

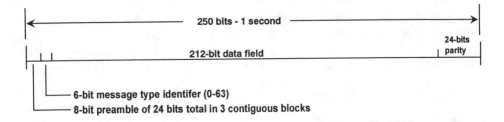

Figure 11.8 Data block format.

Table 11.2
WAAS Message Types

Type	Contents
0	Don't use this GEO for anything (for WAAS testing)
1	PRN Mask assignments, set up to 52 of 210 bits
2	Fast corrections
3–8	Reserved for future messages
9	GEO navigation message (X, Y, Z, time, etc.)
10–11	Reserved for future messages
12	WAAS network/UTC(USNO) offset parameters
13–16	Reserved for future messages
17	GEO satellite almanacs
18	Ionospheric grid point mask #1
19	Ionospheric grid point mask #2
20	Ionospheric grid point mask #3
21	Ionospheric grid point mask #4
22	Ionospheric grid point mask #5
23	Reserved for future messages
24	Mixed fast corrections/long-term satellite error corrections
25	Long-term satellite error corrections
26	Ionospheric delay corrections
27	WAAS service message
28–62	Reserved for future messages
63	Null message

RTCA SC-159. The reader is referred to [2] for a complete description of the messages and their application.

11.6 UTILIZATION BY LAND AND MARITIME USERS

Although the signal format described above has been developed to support aeronautical requirements, the signal may also be used by land and maritime users with a suitable receiver. Once the WAAS service has been declared operational, it is expected that many additional applications will be developed to take into account the enhanced accuracy that will be available. It is envisioned that there will be a multitude of receivers available with an INMARSAT overlay signal reception capability in mid-1996. At the time of this writing, the receiver specifications are being developed.

11.7 PROPOSED EVOLUTION TO A CIVIL SYSTEM

Within the near future, satellite navigation services will be rapidly embraced. However, there are some users (or potential users) of these services who are concerned that reliance on single-nation-controlled systems (i.e., GPS and GLONASS) may eventually lead to denial of service for brief or extended periods of time. These concerns are being addressed by both INMARSAT and the European Community and are discussed in the following sections.

11.7.1 INMARSAT Proposal

INMARSAT has proposed several evolutionary steps toward the goal of an independent civil constellation. The INMARSAT-3 overlay is the first of four steps towards this goal. In phases two and three, it is envisioned that around the year 2000 a newly designed Navigation LightSat (NLS) payload will be installed as a secondary payload on geostationary and intermediate circular orbit (ICO) communications satellites. Unlike the navigation transponder payload on INMARSAT-3, the NLS payload would contain the necessary electronics to provide an internally generated ranging signal. It is proposed that the WAAS-type ground infrastructure expected to be in place for GNSS integrity monitoring could also support the NLS payload satellites. Capabilities may include a broadcast on L2 or another frequency to provide real-time ionospheric delay compensation [4].

After phases two and three, if the civil community desired a totally independent satellite navigation system, the NLS payload could be installed as the sole payload on 15 spacecraft. These would be in ICO or higher GLONASS/GPS-type orbits functioning as autonomous "GPS-like" satellites. INMARSAT states that the technical considerations surrounding the deployment of the civil constellation are straightforward; however, the major issues are financial and institutional. How the constellation will be paid for and what agency will be responsible for its operation would need to be determined [4].

11.7.2 European Efforts

The WAAS, mentioned in preceding sections of this chapter, describes the approach of the FAA in the United States in augmenting the GPS for use in civil aviation. This augmented system provides the accuracy, availability, integrity, and continuity of function required to maintain the level of safety provided by present navigation and landing aids when used for those services for which it is designated. Concurrent with this effort in the United States, Europe has formed a tripartite group, comprising EUROCONTROL, the European Space Agency, and the European Commission, to develop a program that would be Europe's contribution to a civil global navigation satellite system [5, 6].

The ultimate goal of the program is to act in concert with other developers to produce a GNSS that meets the safety-critical requirements for users on land and at sea, and can be used as the sole means of navigating and landing by aircraft. The program is concerned with first- and second-generation GNSS systems. The first generation, GNSS1, will consist essentially of augmentations to the GPS and GLONASS systems. Europe's contribution, the European Geostationary Navigation Overlay Service (EGNOS), is similar to the WAAS and will initially consist of one master control station, thirteen ranging and integrity monitoring stations, two navigation land Earth stations with at least one hot standby for redundancy, two geostationary navigation transponders, and four geostationary ranging stations, to provide ranging, integrity, and WADGPS over a core area of Europe by 1999. This IOC will be gradually expanded to include a wider area and increased redundancy, designed to fit seamlessly with similar systems being developed in neighboring regions. FOC of EGNOS is planned to be reached in the year 2002 and will include an additional master control station, an additional geostationary navigation transponder, seven additional ranging and integrity monitoring stations, two additional geostationary ranging stations, and full redundancy in the navigation land Earth stations [5, 6].

When fully operational, EGNOS will be technically capable of achieving sole means certification, but because GNSS1 uses GPS and GLONASS, which are not under international civil control, some states may be unwilling to accept GNSS1 as the sole means of navigation in their airspace. For this reason, there is some thought to making the second generation of a global navigation satellite system, *GNSS2*, entirely independent of the GPS or GLONASS so that it can be put entirely under international civil control. However, as of this writing, the system architecture of GNSS2 has not been defined [5, 6].

References

[1] RTCA, "Report on Special Committee 159 on Minimum Aviation System Performance Standards (MASPS) for Global Positioning System (GPS)," DO-202, 1988.

[2] RTCA, "Minimum Operational Performance Standards for Sensors Using Global Positioning System/ Wide Area Augmentation System," RTCA Paper No. 396-95/SC159-6661, Final (6th) Draft, July 24, 1995.

[3] Department of Defense, "Global Positioning System (GPS) Standard Positioning System (SPS) Signal Specification," Washington DC, Nov. 5, 1993.

[4] Lundberg, O., "Waypoints for Radionavigation in the 21st Century," *Proc. Institute of Navigation GPS-94*, Keynote Address, Salt Lake City, UT, Sept. 20–23, 1994, pp. 3–15.

[5] Watt, A., and J. Storey, "The Technical Implementation of a Common European Programme for Satellite Navigation," *ION National Conference*, Anaheim CA, Jan. 18–20, 1995, pp. 63–70.

[6] Solari, G., and P. Pablos, "Constellation Options for Future Civil GNSS," *ION National Conference*, Anaheim, CA, Jan. 18–20, 1995, pp. 71–78.

CHAPTER 12

▼▼▼

GPS MARKETS AND APPLICATIONS

Scott Lewis
Northstar Technologies

12.1 GPS: AN ENABLING TECHNOLOGY

It has been said that GPS is to position what the clock was to time. Consider the plight of market forecasters shortly after the invention of the clock. They could neither have quantified the existing uses for such a device, nor could they have even begun to imagine the impact that accurate timekeeping would have on the world, on the way we live and the other products and services that would be enabled by the new technology. This is the situation we are in with GPS. We can only guess at some of the eventual uses that this enabling technology will bring about.

The analogy with the invention of the clock can be further extended by considering that the chronometer was originally intended as a navigation device, as was GPS. The initial conception of GPS was as a military positioning, weapons aiming, and navigation system. It was to replace the TACAN, Transit, and Omega navigation systems, and to provide worldwide weather-independent guidance for military use. Political factors, including the downing of Korean Airlines Flight 007 by Soviet interceptors and the public outcry that ensued, prompted President Reagan to announce in 1984 that a portion of the navigational capabilities provided by GPS would be made available to the civil community. This was done so that the sort of navigational errors that put the Korean airliner in jeopardy would not be made again. Thus, there is a commitment on the part of the U.S. government to provide a stipulated level of service from GPS, without fee, "for the foreseeable future." This assurance has allowed considerable investment to be made by industry in the development of hardware, software, and systems that, to be viable, depend upon the long-term availability of GPS signals. Acceptance by several other countries of this assurance from the U.S. government has been less vigorous. Nevertheless, the availability of GPS signals and inexpensive receiving equipment will certainly allow users all over the world to avail themselves of the technology regardless of their country's official position. A key assumption in the consideration of market dimension for GPS is that, VHF omnidirectional range (VOR), TACAN, Omega, Transit, and much of Loran-C usage in North America will be replaced by GPS starting in 1998 [1].

It is true that there are currently significant activities in the establishment of Loran-C and it's Russian equivalent, Chayka, outside of North America, and these systems will undoubtedly see a degree of use for the next 10 or 15 years. At the time of this writing, the GLONASS constellation is in the process of being deployed, even though the program has been plagued by launch and on-orbit equipment failure and has suffered from confusion since the dissolution of the USSR. The fate of these other positioning systems will have a bearing on the speed and degree of distribution of GPS user equipment outside of North America. Some allowances have been made in an attempt to account for the effect that international Loran-C, Chayka, and GLONASS services will have on GPS acceptance, but it is expected that the user equipment market will be dominated by GPS-based products by the end of the century.

An econometric model has been developed that extrapolates current GPS-related business volumes over the next decade. Experience from similar technologies such as cellular telephony and personal computing can be used to establish acceptance rates and equipment cost curves, but a major weakness in this method is evident from consideration of the remarks at the beginning of this chapter. It is difficult to forecast the impact of an enabling technology like GPS.

Much of the data presented here was derived from a study performed by KV Research, to which the author contributed. The 1992 study was entitled "Differential GPS Markets in the 1990's, A Cross Industry Study." This study is conservative in comparison to other market surveys that have been performed. Through the time of this writing (August 1995), it has accurately predicted trends and expenditures in the GPS marketplace.

12.2 USES OF GPS FOR MARINE, AIR, AND LAND NAVIGATION

Marine and air navigation are perhaps the two most obvious applications of a globally available positioning technology using satellite signals. Lack of visual navigation references and a corresponding lack of things that might block the line-of-sight

GPS signals make the marine and airborne uses ideal for GPS. In fact, these are the environments that the system's designers had in mind at its conception. The inherent accuracy of unaided, single channel C/A-code GPS, as set by SA, of 100m 2 drms is adequate for nearly all airborne or seaborne en route requirements.

Approaches to airports or harbors are another matter however, and for these situations, DGPS techniques have been developed. This brings another factor into the market dimension, as there is a demand for equipment to generate and transmit differential corrections, for equipment to receive and apply them, and for services that generate and broadcast correction signals.

Integrity is another issue to consider when dealing with marine harbor and aircraft navigation, particularly in approach mode. Various enhancements for integrity monitoring and reporting are being studied and implemented. These too have an impact on the rate of acceptance of the technology as well as on the ultimate size of these markets.

12.2.1 Marine Navigation

There are about 17 million boats in North America, 46 million worldwide. Of these, almost 98% are pleasure craft. This is certainly not a market to be ignored, and there are at least a dozen manufacturers competing for a share of the recreational marine navigation business at this writing. Commercial coastal and inland vessels comprise about 970,000 potential platforms for GPS, and there are more than 80,000 registered merchant vessels worldwide, most of which are involved in fishing.

The International Loran Association estimates that there are currently over a million Loran-C receivers installed in North America alone. Most of these are in ships and boats, and all, shipborne or not, are candidates for replacement with GPS.

Acceptance of the U.S. Coast Guard's system of differential correction broadcasts discussed in Section 12.6 has proven to be high, and other countries are implementing similar systems, particularly in the North Sea and Scandinavian waters. These systems provide accuracy in the 5 to 8m range within about 150 miles of the correction beacon, and also yield speed over ground (SOG) accuracy of about a tenth of a knot. This can be a benefit to commercial fishermen in providing the ability to monitor small changes in speed caused by a dragged net's snagging, allowing rapid response to prevent serious damage. There is also obvious application in sailboat and yacht racing for this kind of speed accuracy. Combination of SOG with wind speed and speed through the water gives information about set and drift and apparent wind speed and direction. Accurate speed of advance (SOA) is also available, aiding the yachting tactician in finding the fastest route to the mark.

Figure 12.1 shows a marine navigator with database management capability and graphical display of position and speed information. In this market, ease of use and the ability to manage a large database of waypoints and sophisticated cartography are key requirements.

Figure 12.1 Northstar 941X Marine Navigator (*courtesy of* Northstar Technologies).

Most of the 33 major North American ports as well as those around the world require the boarding of a local pilot, to guide a commercial vessel into harbor. There are at least 1,700 registered pilots in North America, all of whom could make good use of accurate, portable, and familiar navigation equipment.

Ferries and cruise lines, with their precious human cargo are also prime targets for accurate navigation systems. There are about 954 ferries operating in North America, and about 100 major cruise ships.

Since the grounding of the oil tanker Exxon Valdez in March of 1989, and the resulting oil-spill damage, there has been a timetabled mandate to provide ADS capabilities to all oil carriers using the Port of Valdez in Alaska. Similar requirements for other world harbors are not far behind. These systems derive a ship's position from GPS and transmit it via radio link to a control station on the shore. The ship's position can then be monitored by the Coast Guard, or other agency, and dangerous situations can be alarmed and rectified. Because of the heavy dependence on the communications link, and the development of new long-range communications technologies, communications carriers such as Inmarsat are heavily involved in these systems and will be the primary market for this positioning technology. Most of the world's 6,153 oil tankers will be equipped with ADS equipment by the end of the century.

Fisheries management is a worldwide mandate, requiring swift action by governments. Dwindling fish stocks are prompting the establishment of strict guidelines for fishermen and the closure of entire grounds. The situation is also making countries that share sea boundaries more and more sensitive to foreign fishing in their waters. These tensions engender the need for accurate position determination and recording, to prove or disprove a boundary violation. Many of the 38,000 North American–registered fishing vessels, and those in most other countries, could be subject to mandatory automatic dependent surveillance by the end of the century. Even if not mandated, the 42,000 vessels that fish near international boundaries may find it prudent to carry such gear for their own protection against false accusations.

GPS can aid in the berthing and docking of large vessels, by means of position, attitude, and heading reference systems (PAHRS). These installations use multiple antennas aboard the vessel to determine an accurate representation of the ship's situation. Combined with appropriate reference cartography, this can be an immense aid in the handling of large vessels in close quarters. The over 80,000 seagoing merchant vessels worldwide are candidates for this sort of system.

There is a market for extremely accurate positioning for seismic survey and oil exploration activities as well as in dredging, buoy laying, and maintenance. There are about 2,400 dredges and 300 buoy tenders in operation around the world. Dredge operators are paid based on the amount of material they remove from a harbor or shipping channel, so accurate measurement of position can optimize the operation, reducing cost and wasted effort.

In the late 1970s and the 1980s, tremendous changes took place in the oil and gas production industries. In 1985, six of every seven wells drilled were dry, at an average cost of $5.4 million per well, and in 1990, the 22 major oil companies spent a total of almost $35 billion in exploration and production. Declining oil prices and the fact that new oil and gas resources tended to be smaller, in less hospitable environments, and harder to find, led exploration teams to look for ways of reducing the risk of drilling dry wells, and for ways to reduce the overall cost of exploration. Accurate positioning became key in this endeavor, enabling the development of precise seismic maps and location of drill sites with respect to identified geologic structure. The availability of GPS and accurate DGPS has proven a boon to these activities, especially in the offshore case, where exploration teams have paid upwards of $900 per day for accurate satellite, or land-based positioning services.

The availability of such accurate systems for navigation will require much resurveying of published marine chart information. A good portion of the data currently represented on marine charts is over 50 years old and hydrographic services are involved in the production of digital databases to an agreed-upon international format (DX90). Some agencies have announced that they will not release data in this format until the area in question has been resurveyed, as the implied accuracy of the format is much greater than the accuracy of the information contained therein. This information is being used in a new generation of navigational aids known as

ECDIS. There is a less sophisticated family of electronic charting systems (ECS) in wide use today by merchant, recreational, and fishing fleets. These systems work by displaying electronic versions of paper charts, with ship's position overlaid and constantly updated by GPS or other positioning systems. A typical ECDIS as pictured in Figure 12.2 can cost near $100,000 per installation and provide almost autono-

Figure 12.2 Sperry Marine voyage management station (*courtesy of* Sperry Marine, Inc.).

mous operation of the vessel. Simpler ECS installations as pictured in Figure 12.3 cost from $4,000 to $10,000 and are used primarily as aids to situational awareness in conjunction with radar and visual references. A third class of marine charting device is becoming very popular due to very low unit cost. Navigators with simple built-in or cartridge-updatable databases allow a vector map of a selected area to be drawn on a screen. These systems are excellent for providing a degree of situational awareness to a recreational boater, but will probably not be certified for use on commercial vessels.

Marine use of GPS has been widely accepted, and differential services are beginning to be well established as of this writing. Recreational vessels make good use of basic GPS for navigation, and the early acceptance of differential GPS bodes well for the health of that sector. The huge number of vessels and the value of GPS in marine navigation, fishing, and waterway maintenance, coupled with strong economic activity, will allow steady growth to a level of near $400 million annually by 2001.

12.2.2 Air Navigation

There are essentially two kinds of markets and two regimes of operation to consider in the airborne area. There are 224,000 general aviation (GA) aircraft registered in

Figure 12.3 Laser plot ECS (*courtesy of* LaserPlot, Inc.).

the United States and Canada. The U.S.-based Aircraft Owners and Pilots Association asserts that this represents 77% of the world GA aircraft population, so there would be an additional 67,000 in the rest of the world. These aircraft are privately owned by individuals or companies for personal or corporate transportation, or recreational flying.

The second category is the air carrier industry, which employs just over 5,000 aircraft in North America and a similar number worldwide.

Both of these markets will have a high demand for GPS as a long-range area navigation system, since phase-out of current VHF omnidirectional range (VOR) and nondirectional beacon (NDB) is slated to begin in 2005 and 2000, respectively [1]. Loran-C provides effective coverage over most of North America, and coverage is growing in Northern Europe, the Middle East, and parts of Asia. Of course, none of these land-based systems can provide contiguous coverage over uninhabited or oceanic areas, as does GPS. For this regime of navigation, most transoceanic airliners currently rely on inertial navigation systems (INS) and Omega, a ground-based very low frequency (VLF) radionavigation system. Support of the Omega transmitters will be withdrawn in late 1997 [1]. Further, the accuracy characteristics of INS and GPS make them excellent partners in the delivery of accurate and reliable navigation information, and it can be expected that almost universal acceptance of GPS/INS-combined systems in commercial and longer range aircraft will be inevitable by the end of the 20th century.

In the GA aircraft market, Loran-C navigators are found on nearly 70% of all active aircraft. This represents some 120,000 units, sold in the years between 1980 and 1993. Penetration of GPS in the same market has been about 7% to mid-1994, and it is anticipated that the availability of GPS approach capability will be a significant factor in the decision to replace existing Loran-C navigators in GA aircraft. Figure 12.4 shows a typical airborne GPS navigator for GA use.

Through mid-1995, development activity is focusing on providing commercial and GA airborne systems with sufficient integrity to perform nonprecision approaches (NPA). These are the most common types of instrument approaches performed by GA pilots. The Federal Aviation Administration has instituted a program to implement NPA. This so-called "overlay" program allows the use of a specially certified GPS navigator in place of a VOR or nondirected beacon (NDB) receiver to fly the conventional VOR or NDB approach. New NPA that define waypoints independent of ground-based facilities, and that simplify the procedures required to be flown, are being put into service at the rate of about 500 to 1,000 approaches per year, and so will take 6 to 10 years to implement at the 5,000 public use airports in the United States. Other countries have less ambitious plans to implement such procedures, but it is expected that there will be almost universal acceptance of some sort of GPS approach capability at most of the world's airports by the turn of the century.

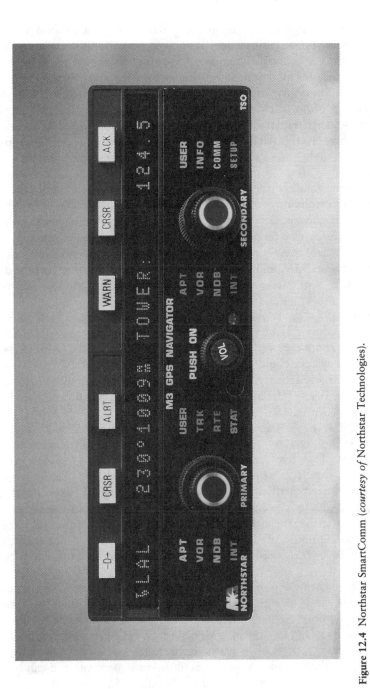

Figure 12.4 Northstar SmartComm (*courtesy* of Northstar Technologies).

In the execution of a nonprecision approach, the pilot or autopilot is given direction to enable the aircraft to be maneuvered into the appropriate position for a descent toward the runway. The descent is made with reference to an approach "plate," which dictates minimum safe altitudes for each phase of the approach. No altitude information is given by the navigation system. Since unaided GPS yields an altitude accuracy of no better than about 500 ft, it is not capable of fulfilling this role in any case. Differential GPS is required to provide appropriate accuracies for altitude guidance on approach. The resulting Category I, II, and III approaches involve guidance to the runway threshold in all three dimensions. Local area differential corrections, broadcast from an airport-based reference station, can provide the required accuracy to allow the most demanding Category III landings. The use of "kinematic" GPS techniques is also being investigated by various researchers (see Section 8.3). One concept developed by Stanford University involves the placement of artificial satellites, or "pseudolites," near the approach end of the runway. An aircraft would receive these pseudolite signals and use them to resolve carrier-phase ambiguities. The aircraft could then have centimeter-level accuracy for the duration of the approach. Without precision approach capabilities, commercial air travel would be unreliable and dangerous.

Since mid-1994, the FAA has been funding the development of WAAS. WAAS will broadcast on the GPS L1 frequency so that signals might be accessible to modified GPS receivers without the need for a dedicated corrections radio. Altitude accuracy attained by this system could be on the order of a few meters, which would be sufficient for Category I, the type of approach most often required. Further accuracy would be obtained using reference stations at the airport in question and broadcasting on a dedicated frequency.

In mid-1994, the FAA announced the cancellation of major microwave landing systems (MLS) contracts in favor of development of potentially less expensive GPS landing systems. This reinforces the impetus toward a seamless navigation and guidance system for aircraft in U.S. airspace.

There is a huge potential for ground- and satellite-based support systems that use or augment GPS. Market projections in this chapter do not take this potential into account, but rather the airborne GPS segment of activity only. Consulting firm Booz-Allen and Hamilton predicted in 1994 that the worldwide air traffic control and management market could be as large as $200 billion over the ten years ending 2004.

Another area being exploited by GPS technology is airborne ADS, where ground control facilities can receive position transmissions of aircraft in an operating area and plot them without the use of expensive radar and without the requirement of line-of-sight contact. In fact, any aircraft can receive the same information in flight and display its own version of its traffic environment. These systems can augment or replace ground-based radar in positive control environments and can be used as part of collision avoidance systems on the ground or in the aircraft.

GPS also allows the simplification of many cockpit tasks by use of position and speed data in combination with the extensive databases that most airborne navigators have. The equipment can be used to decide which communications frequencies are most appropriate for a given location and regime of flight. Units such as the Northstar "SmartComm" pictured in Figure 12.4 do just this, providing the name, frequency, and radio call of the appropriate facilities. Other similar functions, such as landing gear warnings, can be realized in the same manner.

Much activity in the GA market as of 1995 involves the use of handheld GPS to augment the installed base of Loran-C receivers. These GPS devices needn't be certified, and are useful as a backup to other navigation systems. Handheld receivers with aviation databases, moving map displays, and sophisticated navigation capabilities are available for less than $1,000. The GA market will see a surge of activity after publication of GPS nonprecision approaches is complete for a good portion of the busiest airports, in the 1995–96 time frame. There will be another active period after the development of precision approach capabilities, discussed in Section 12.6.1, by about 1999. It is likely that this market, due to the limited number of aircraft and slow rate of airframe replacement, will saturate and begin to decline in the first years of the next century.

The use of GPS by commercial air carriers has been limited up to 1994, but will flourish as the ability to capitalize on improved traffic separation and precision approach capabilities will allow economic benefit to them. GPS to date, has been used as a backup to certified Omega and inertial navigation systems. Since early 1993, some operators have been setting up their own local area differential systems to allow for the execution of precision approaches in areas where other methods are not practical. These systems have proven very successful and should pave the way for more privately owned services where the need arises.

12.2.3 Land Navigation

By far, the most promising market for GPS navigation in terms of sheer size is for land navigation products. There are more than 420 million cars and 130 million trucks in the world, with 150 million and 40 million the North American portions. Initial adaptation of the technology is taking place in fleet tracking applications. The value of current fleet information is evident for delivery, emergency vehicle, and scheduled service fleet dispatch and control. Automatic vehicle location systems (AVLS) are being developed or installed in many of North America's 10.3 million trucking and emergency fleets, currently involving about a million vehicles in North America.

Urban transit busses are finding application of GPS for schedule maintenance and safety enhancement. There are about 750,000 urban transit busses in North America and as of early 1992, at least 30 North American transit authorities were working on AVLS or had them installed, involving over 18,000 vehicles.

The drive toward increasing the capacity of existing transportation infrastructure has spawned a field of endeavor known as intelligent transportation systems (ITS). These systems are meant to modify traffic flow according to demand and other factors. One way to do this involves the monitoring of the progress of vehicles that are transmitting their position to a central location. Traffic signals or rerouting signs can then be used to respond to situations where a particular "probe" vehicle is not progressing as it should do under optimum conditions.

Another aspect of ITS involves the automatic collection of highway and other tolls and tariffs. This eliminates the need for vehicles to stop at state lines or at toll booths on toll roads and bridges if their position is being reported and appropriate accounting arrangements are made between the tariff-collecting authority and the vehicle's operator. This is of course most appropriate for commercial operations, but it is not inconceivable that private automobiles could be subject to the same kind of system. It would be possible in early implementation to provide a through lane at toll booths for appropriately equipped vehicles. GPS is not central to this kind of technology, since the location of the required toll payment is always known, and the vehicle could pass a local code reader that would initiate toll billing, but then there are other potential tariff systems that could be envisaged where total road usage could be tracked and taxed rather than just on given roadways, as is done now.

In the United States, The Americans with Disabilities Act requires that municipal transport facilities announce and display location information to passengers with sight and hearing disabilities. This requires that both audible and visual presentations be provided. Most transit systems do not fully comply with this requirement. Systems to provide this information automatically are attractive, and low-cost GPS enables them.

Land navigation opportunities for GPS are enormous. The incorporation of moving maps and databases into private passenger vehicles will generate more demand for GPS products than all other markets combined. Early land-based adapters of the technology, of course, are the fleet operators, who can gain significant benefits from more efficient tracking and dispatch operations with integrated navigation and communications facilities.

Demonstration systems are proving the viability of in-vehicle navigation systems in trials in Florida, California, and Japan. Economic activity related to this market segment is difficult to quantify, but a growth rate of $2 billion per year toward the latter half of the decade would generate a bit over 4% penetration of the automotive market by 2001. This estimate could well be too conservative, given the acceptance of early trials.

Results from a 1992–93 trial program called TravTek in Florida indicate that consumers would be willing to spend on the order of $900 for the in-vehicle moving map navigation system. A 1991 study conducted by Sonneville Associates projected a 50% automotive market penetration could be achieved if the unit cost per vehicle was $1,200, and 30% at a cost of $1,850. These estimates are much more optimistic than those contained in this chapter.

The University of Michigan's Delphi study claims that 5% of new vehicles would be equipped with onboard navigation systems in 1996, 10% in 1997, and up to 50% by 2011.

12.3 GPS IN SURVEYING, MAPPING, AND GEOGRAPHICAL INFORMATION SYSTEMS

For several reasons, GPS receiver technology owes much to its early application in the business of land surveying. The production of maps and charts, and the georeferencing of data using GPS are natural outgrowths of the accurate and reliable techniques developed for the land-survey market.

12.3.1 Surveying

The development of the GPS took several years. Beginning in the late 1970s, some level of signal coverage was available. Far from the 24-hr coverage we have today, however, there were few times when three satellites were visible to a particular location, and even fewer when satellite geometries were sufficient to provide a reasonable degree of accuracy. This situation is of course unacceptable for any navigation function; with proper planning, however, static determination of position could be achieved. The huge economic advantage of using GPS in surveying applications drove the development of very sophisticated GPS equipment and tools to predict GPS coverage and derive position with centimeter accuracy. Delays in the launch of GPS satellites caused by the Challenger disaster in 1986 further strengthened the head start that surveying applications got over navigational uses of the system, and significant refinements in the use of carrier-phase, dual-frequency postprocessed differential positions were made. Extreme accuracy is possible by applying information on satellite position available after the fact to the data obtained in the field. The major GPS equipment manufacturers survived this period by providing products to this sector, and many business initiatives to provide equipment to the navigation community failed during the delayed system deployment.

The value of the technology in the surveying business stems from the fact that absolute positions with respect to a universal coordinate system (WGS-84) are available, and can be determined with a much smaller survey crew. A single surveyor can collect data in the field, where it would take a two- or three-person crew to achieve the same results using conventional methods. Collected data can be processed to the required accuracy using inexpensive computing facilities, and the GPS equipment in the field can be used by the surveyor for rough surveys or the location of benchmarks or other features. Real-time differential and kinematic techniques can provide accurate real-time information in the field and obviate the need for postprocessing the data, further reducing the cost of surveying operations.

As has been discussed earlier, the survey market was first to develop the use of GPS. A great deal of sophistication has been brought to products in this area, and to a large extent the market is mature, with a handful of suppliers well entrenched. The survey market as we know it now may well become saturated by 1997 or so, but the use of GPS as an aid for position-based data collection for geographical information systems (GIS) will continue to fuel growth in the market.

12.3.2 Mapping

A major early implementation of GPS was in the provision of ground truthing, or orientation of aerial photogrammetry. Aircraft or spacecraft are used to photograph large areas of the Earth's surface. Index marks are often surveyed on the ground to provide reference locations on these photographs, which can be used in determining their scale and orientation. GPS can be used to survey these references. Further, the use of these references can be eliminated altogether if the position of the camera can be known accurately enough at the precise moment it took the picture. This technology has been developed using GPS augmented by accurate inertial navigation systems (INS). Inertial systems have excellent short-term stability, but tend to drift over time and require reinitialization. GPS on the other hand, has its inherent absolute referencing capabilities and can provide excellent augmentation for an INS. The two can be used together in this kind of application, INS to help resolve cycle ambiguities inherent in the kinematic method of GPS use, and to carry positioning duties over short periods of GPS outage that may occur.

The generation of road maps, or any other kind of feature map, is now extremely easy, achieved simply by recording a series of positions as a receiver is moved over the area to be mapped. Any degree of postprocessing necessary to achieve desired accuracy is available. Specific locations recorded may be annotated with location-specific information, such as street address, elevation, or vegetation type. This type of data collection is particularly useful for the building of data for GIS.

12.3.3 Geographical Information Systems

Anyone charged with the responsibility of managing a distributed inventory, such as might be the case with a utility, municipality, or steelyard, might appreciate the ability to locate and identify this inventory quickly and accurately. This is the role played by GPS in conjunction with GIS. The last ten years has seen a proliferation of GIS software packages and programs. Government agencies and utilities have been eager to adopt this technology, but find that the initial input of data and timely updating thereof is a huge task using conventional means of data collection. With

GPS, it is possible to capture position-referenced data in the field with a simple handheld computer.

The situation is best illustrated by the example of the management of a municipality's streetlights. There may be a mix of fluorescent, sodium, mercury, and incandescent lights, with several varieties of each. The maintenance engineer capable of recognizing the types can be dispatched with a GPS-based data collector to log the location of each type of installation. This information can be loaded into a central database, so that when maintenance is necessary, the appropriate replacements can be ordered, stocked, and dispatched.

Steel mills store large quantities of product in huge yards, stacked in such a way as to prevent warping. The stacks must be rotated periodically, on a set schedule. Further, there are different types of product that are indistinguishable from one another, except for the record of where each was put. The layout of these yards does not lend itself to physical marking, so accurate GPS can be used to locate each stack and reference its contents to a central database. The management of other yard inventory items such as shipping containers or lumber is similar, and GPS applications have been investigated here also.

A rapidly growing and highly visible endeavor is the management of natural resources. Environmental impact studies involve the collection of large amounts of position-related data, and geographical information systems are prevalent here, too. GPS is instrumental in collecting data to provide input to animal population studies and the like.

Finally, a whole new discipline, referred to as precision farming, or farming by the foot, is emerging. The application of pesticides, herbicides, and fertilizers is becoming an increasingly exacting science. Many farm implement manufacturers are producing variable-rate application equipment that is controlled by sophisticated electronics coupled to a sort of GIS. It has been shown that material input costs can be reduced by 40%, and yield enhancements of a similar magnitude can be expected. Furthermore, the harmful effects of the runoff of unneeded fertilizers can be mitigated. It is possible that the variable application of fertilizers might be legislated for this reason. GPS of course is central to the soil mapping to determine requirements and to the control of application vehicles.

At least two firms are offering products to guide airborne applicators of pesticides. These systems involve customized mapping routines to direct the pilot of the crop duster swath by swath over a particular field. This allows the replacement of the flagperson, who would direct the pilot from the ground (a job with a very hazardous environment), with more accurate electronic guidance. This reduces the amount of overspray and can significantly decrease the amount of time and material used.

12.4 RECREATIONAL MARKETS FOR GPS-BASED PRODUCTS

There are some obvious recreational applications of global positioning technology, such as in hiking and orienteering. Search and rescue teams can also make good use of the technology. There are also some applications that are not so obvious, and it is here that our belief in the assertion that there are more uses for GPS than we can imagine is put to the test. There are several organizations developing positioning systems for golfing application. Differential corrections are required, as accuracy of a few feet is needed. Course managers are attracted to the idea as a method to speed up play and improve the utilization of an existing resource. Receivers have been put on golf carts to display from a database the distance to the green, to the pin, and to any hazards that may be of interest from a given location.

Another recreational use is in self-guided tours. Currently offered in Yellowstone Park and other similar locales, the self-guided tour relies upon the CD-ROM-based talking book technology to play a short vignette on a video screen, complete with sound and pictures. Currently, the tourist is prompted to enter a code at a given location by an intrusive sign or by reference to a printed map. GPS will allow the conduction of such tours without this kind of reference and can trigger the vignettes automatically. The unit could also direct the tourist based on his or her present position and knowledge of where he or she has been previously.

12.5 GPS TIME TRANSFER

The fact that GPS is based on accurate time references implies that the signals can be used for the synchronization of very accurate clocks and time standards. Each satellite has multiple atomic clocks on board, and each is frequently updated to system time. A prime application of this accurate timing capability is in the control of data communications networks, where data packets time share the same communications bandwidth. Receivers and transmitters can be synchronized, reducing the data overhead required of the system. There are a few manufacturers of equipment dedicated solely to the extraction of accurate time from the GPS signal.

12.6 DIFFERENTIAL APPLICATIONS AND SERVICES

Perhaps the largest submarket involves the provision and use of differential corrections. One can derive one's own differential corrections and transmit them to specific locations using almost any means of communications, from HF radio to satellite link. It makes better sense, however, to share such a system with other users, and there are market opportunities in providing such signals. The U.S. Coast Guard provides correction signals, broadcast over an existing network of nondirectional beacon transmitters around the coast of the United States and in the Great Lakes. The U.S. Army Corps of Engineers, in conjunction with the Coast Guard, is providing similar coverage for the Mississippi and Ohio River valleys, and other countries' authorities are implementing similar systems.

Coverage of the U.S. Coast Guard beacons, expected by late 1996, is shown in Figure 12.5. These broadcasts are provided free of charge, but require the purchase of specialized receivers and demodulators to decode the signals, sent at 283 to 325 kHz. The figure excludes the coverage in the Mississippi and Ohio River basins, which is nearly complete at the time of this writing.

Several companies, such as Accupoint, have begun to develop differential correction networks using their leased broadcast FM subcarrier resources; and others, like Differential Corrections Inc. (DCI) are setting about to do the same thing with broadcast FM radio networks. Most of the populated areas of North America are covered by broadcast FM signals, so the use of subcarrier modulation is a relatively

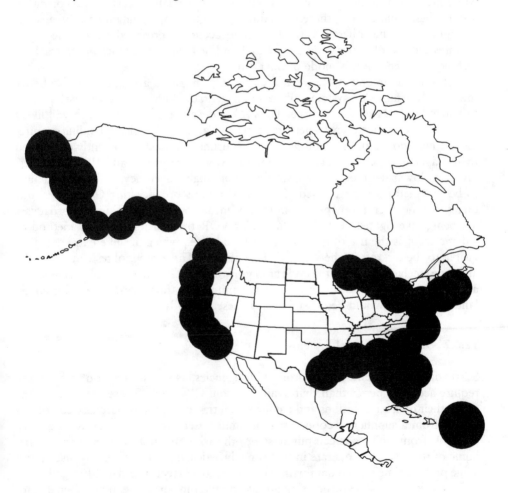

Figure 12.5 U.S. Coast Guard DGPS network.

inexpensive way of reaching a large segment of the differential correction market. These companies hope to sell their signals to the public at rates that range from a few dollars per month to several hundred, according to the accuracy and integrity required. Receiver technology for this sort of system is much less expensive than in the NDB case, but the recurring cost of buying access to signals makes the two systems equally attractive.

12.6.1 Precision Approach Aircraft Landing Systems

Most instrument approaches carried out by commercial air carriers are precision approaches. Unlike NPA, these procedures give glideslope guidance to the aircraft on approach. The inherently poor altitude accuracy provided by unaided GPS requires the use of either code differential and/or kinematic carrier-phase tracking techniques to enable this mode of operation.

Precision landing systems require not only enhanced accuracy but also better integrity (warnings of system failure or inaccuracy within 6 sec or less) than is provided by the basic GPS service. The FAA is developing WAAS, which will likely provide sufficient accuracy to perform close to Category I precision landing requirements. This would allow about 90% of the airline approaches currently performed to use a GPS approach augmented in this way. Category II and III approaches, involving lower weather minima, would require higher accuracy, which would have to be provided by airport-based differential stations broadcasting GPS corrections directly to the aircraft on approach. Various means of providing this data broadcast are being investigated, including the use of VOR frequencies. Another method of enhancement is the use of ground-based pseudolites, which act like extra satellites visible to the aircraft in the vicinity of an airport. These pseudolites can allow the airborne receiver to resolve the cycle ambiguity inherent in kinematic GPS techniques, allowing an altitude accuracy of a few centimeters. Category IIIb, or automatic landing systems, would be possible using these methods.

12.6.2 Other Differential Systems

Surveyors, cartographic and hydrographic agencies, as well as a host of other users require accuracy better than that available from GPS's SPS. These users can either set up their own base stations and datalink facilities, or they may purchase correction signals from a supplier or cooperative of similar users. Many services are presently available from which one can purchase or otherwise obtain differential corrections. Some of these services operate in real time, broadcasting their signals to users, and some provide time-tagged data with which one can correct field data after gathering it. This is known as postprocessing and is common in surveying applications. State survey and geodetic organizations are using GPS to form "active control networks," that rely on GPS to tie together positions rather than referencing them back to fixed monuments by conventional surveying means.

12.7 MILITARY AND SPACE APPLICATIONS

GPS was conceived and constructed by the U.S. military, and although the application of the technology by the commercial sector has far surpassed any military potential, no discussion of the market would be complete without reference to this important segment.

In the planning of GPS, the military held several nondevelopmental item (NDI) competitions. These competitions solicited major electronics suppliers, detailing minimum performance standards for handheld, vehicle-mounted, airborne, and embedded GPS receivers. The results were the precision lightweight GPS receiver (PLGR), the miniature airborne GPS receiver (MAGR), and the embedded GPS/inertial (EGI) receiver, which are standard items for use by troops on tactical vehicles, aircraft and missiles. The conflict in the Persian Gulf occurred before much of this technology could be implemented, however, and the military called on industry to provide currently available products for their use. It is interesting to note that during the conflict, SA was turned off, giving the highest possible accuracy without the use of the P(Y)-code. Such use highly popularized the technology, having a strong effect on the public perception of the utility of GPS. Television coverage of the success of precision targeting, although not usually attributable to GPS, added to this perception.

The military market has been estimated on the basis of projecting out the current level of contracting activity through the decade. Military and political priorities may well change, however, and could slow the rate of equipage from that projected. A few military market benchmarks by the year 2000 are

1. A total of 93,999 of the handheld PLGRs should be delivered at a projected cost of $112.8 million.
2. A total of 10,000 U.S. DOD airborne units will be delivered at a cost of $12 million.
3. There will be 6,000 receivers required for precision guided munitions at a total cost of at least $89 million.

The use of GPS in spacecraft has been widespread. DOD and NASA have application for navigation, relative positioning, and attitude determination. GPS has flown on several shuttle missions, and has been useful in providing better orbital positioning in much shorter time than had been previously possible. Incorporation of GPS attitude determination in the space station design is currently mandated. These spaceborne systems have unique problems with respect to environment, dynamics, and satellite visibility. Applications for use of GPS at orbits higher than 11,000 miles are being studied as well.

Not to be forgotten is the actual space segment of the GPS itself. Replenishment of the existing space vehicles through the Block IIF program over the next 10 years will cost as much as $2 billion. WAAS is expected to cost at least $500 million through 1998.

12.8 EQUIPMENT MANUFACTURERS AND SEGMENTATION

Due to the nature of the development of the GPS constellation, and the delays encountered, many companies hoping to capitalize on the early market for GPS equipment were unsuccessful. Those that were successful tended to focus on the surveying market, where continuous satellite coverage was not necessary to derive huge benefits from the use of the technology. Trimble Navigation, and the spin-off Ashtech, are the primary examples of this, and are dominant suppliers of GPS technology today. Magnavox entered the market early, and did much to advance the state of receiver technology. Rockwell also was an early entrant, using elements of its military receiver success to bolster commercial receiver technology. Texas Instruments was a casualty of system delay and high-cost approach, while Motorola's efforts resulted in good receiver technology with disappointing market acceptance. NovAtel in Calgary, Alberta, embarked on a program to develop GPS technology to incorporate into cellular telephones, but ended up with a highly accurate technology more applicable to more precise requirements. This has resulted in a license to Litton for incorporation into commercial avionics products. Magellan and Pro-Nav (later renamed Garmin) developed success in the low-cost handheld markets, Garmin with a proprietary multiplexing technology. On the Japanese front, Japan Radio Corporation (JRC) and Furuno have developed receivers and Pioneer has licensed Trimble technology. Efforts of these manufacturers are predictably aimed at the huge automotive market, focusing on low cost and high volume. Korea's Koden has entered the market with proprietary technology. Dominant in Europe are Philips and Sercel. Philips jointly developed technology with their subsidiary Magnavox in the United States. Through a series of sales, much of that GPS technology is now the property of the Swiss firm Leica. In the United Kingdom, Navstar was an early entry, concentrating at first on Royal Navy requirements; and Plessey has completed development of a GPS chip set available to volume manufacturers wishing to incorporate GPS into their products. Plessey's sister company, Canadian Marconi, offers this 12-channel technology to both automotive and avionics markets, partly though its Northstar division in the United States. II Morrow, owned by United Parcel Service, produces navigation equipment for land and avionics use. A list of GPS receiver manufacturers is contained in Table 12.1.

Table 12.1
GPS Manufacturers

Company	Address	City	State	Country	Type	Markets
3S Navigation	23141 Plaza Pointe Drive	Laguna Hills	CA	USA	GPS/ GLONASS receiver	Land, marine, military, surveying, timing
Allen Osborne Associates, Inc.	756 Lakefield Road, Building J	Westlake Village	CA	USA	Equipment and receiver	Timing, survey, military, land
Allied Signal	400 N. Rogers Rd.	Olathe	KS	USA	Receiver and equipment	Avionics
Arnav Systems, Inc.	Box 73730	Puyallup	WA	USA	GPS equipment	Avionics
Ashtech, Inc.	1170 Kifer Road	Sunnyvale	CA	USA	GPS equipment and receiver	Survey, land, military, aviation, OEM
Austron, Inc.	Box 14766	Austin	TX	USA	GPS receiver	Timing
Canadian Marconi Co.	600 Dr. Frederic Phillips Blvd.	St. Laurent	QC	Can	GPS equipment and receiver	Military, avionics, OEM, land
Carl Zeiss, Inc.	Geschaftsbere-ich Vermessung	7082 Ober-kochen		Ger	GPS geodetic equipment supplier	Survey
Del Norte Technology, Inc.	1100 Pamela Dr. Box 696	Euless	TX	USA	DGPS & GPS receiver	Aviation, surveying
Northstar Div. of CMC	30 Sudbury Road	Acton	MA	USA	GPS equipment	Marine, aviation, land
GARMIN Corp.	11206 Thomp-son Avenue	Lenexa	KS	USA	GPS receiver and equipment	Marine, aviation, land, OEM

Table 12.1 (continued)

Company	Address	City	State	Country	Type	Markets
GEC-Plessey Avionics Ltd.	Martin Road, West Leigh	Havant, Hampshire		UK	GPS receiver	Avionics
II Morrow Incorporated	Box 13549	Salem	OR	USA	GPS module and receiver	Land, marine, aviation
ITT Avionics	100 Kingston Road	Clifton	NJ	USA	GPS module and receiver	Military aviation
Interstate Electronics Corp.	1001 East Ball Road Box 3117	Anaheim	CA	USA	GPS equipment and receiver	Aviation, military, land, OEM
Japan Radio Co.	1-1 Shymoren-jaku 5-chome Mitaka	Tokyo		Japan	GPS modules	Land, OEM
Kinemetrics/ Truetime	3243 Santa Rosa Avenue	Santa Rosa	CA	USA	GPS receiver	Timing
Koden International, Inc.	77 Accord Park Drive	Norwell	MA	USA	GPS receiver	Land, marine
Leica Heerbrugg AG	9435 Heerbrugg	Heerbrugg		Switz	GPS equipment	Survey, OEM
Litton Systems, Inc.	Guidance & Control Systems Div	Woodland Hills	CA	USA	GPS equipment	Avionics
Lowrance Electronics	12000 E. Skelly Drive	Tulsa	OK	USA	GPS equipment	Marine, land
Magellan Systems Corp	960 Overland Ct.	San Dimas	CA	USA	GPS module and receiver	Marine, avionics, land, OEM
Leica	23868 Haw-thorne Blvd.	Torrance	CA	USA	GPS module and receiver	Marine, military, surveying, OEM

Table 12.1 (continued)

Company	Address	City	State	Country	Type	Markets
Micrologic, Inc.	9610 DeSoto Avenue	Chats-worth	CA	USA	GPS equipment and receiver	Aviation, land, marine
Motorola, Inc.	1301 E Algon-quin Road	Schaum-berg	IL	USA	GPS module	OEM
Navsys Corp.	14960 Wood-carver Rd.	Colorado Springs	CO	USA	GPS receiver design	Military
NovAtel Com-munication Ltd	1020 64th Ave-nue NE	Calgary	AB	Can	GPS module	OEM
Odetics, Inc.	1515 South Man-chester Avenue	Anaheim	CA	USA	GPS module	Timing
Pioneer Electronic Corp.	25-1 AZA-Nishi-machi Yamada	Kawagoe		Jap	GPS equipment	Land
Rauff & Soren-sen Shipmate	Ostre Alle 69530	Storing		Den	GPS equipment	Marine
Raytheon Co.	528 Boston Post Road, M/S 3203	Sudbury	MA	USA	GPS equipment	Marine
Rockwell International	N Douglas St.	El Segundo	CA	USA	GPS equipment and receiver	Military, avionics, land
SEL	Lorenzstrasse 10	D-7000 Stuttgart 40		Ger	GPS equip-ment	Land
STC Compo-nents, Inc.	636 Remington Road	Schaum-burg	IL	USA	GPS receiver	Military, avionics
STC Navigation Systems	Brixham Rd. Paignton	Devon		UK	GPS receiver	
Sagem	27 rue Le Blanc	Paris, Cedex 15		Fr	GPS equipment	Avionics
Sercel	46 Rue de Bel Air BP 439	Carquefou Cedex		Fr	GPS equipment and receiver	Timing, survey

Table 12.1 (continued)

Company	Address	City	State	Country	Type	Markets
Sagem	27 rue Le Blanc	Paris, Cedex 15		Fr	GPS equipment	Avionics
Sextant Avionique	25 Rue Jules Vedrines	Valence Cedex		Fr	GPS receiver	Avionics
Shipmate Marine Electronics	5 Elm Court / Crystal Drive	Smithwick, W. Midlands		UK	GPS equipment	Marine
Sitex Marine Electronics	14000 Roosevelt Blvd.	Clearwater	FL	USA	GPS equipment	Marine
Sokkia	9111 Barton Street	Overland Park	KS	USA	GPS equipment	Survey
Sony Corp. of America	1 Sony Drive	Park Ridge	NJ	USA	GPS receiver and equipment	Aviation, marine, military, land
Techsonic Industries, Inc.	Five Hummingbird Lane	Eufala	AL	USA	GPS equipment and receiver	Marine, land
Trimble Navigation	645 Mary Ave.	Sunnyvale	CA	USA	GPS receiver and equipment	Survey, avionics, marine, military, land
TrueTime, Inc.	3243 Santa Rosa Avenue	Santa Rosa	CA	USA	GPS equipment	Timing
Zexel Technologies	70 Southside Dr.	Decatur	IL	USA	GPS equipment	Land

12.9 USER EQUIPMENT NEEDS FOR SPECIFIC MARKETS

Each market has its own specific set of requirements that define elements of design for GPS receivers and associated processing hardware and software. For instance, the tracking loop of a receiver may be optimized to give the best accuracy possible through the use of time averaging. This would be desirable in a survey receiver where it is the accuracy of the position that is of utmost importance, and the time required to obtain a position may be of secondary concern. On the other hand, such a feature would be unacceptable in an airborne application, as it would fail to register a change in velocity for some time after the fact. Thus, optimization of the tracking loop software for the intended purpose is important. Certain other tradeoffs between power consumption, accuracy, reliability, and cost can also be expected to be necessary. Table 12.2 describes some of these characteristics. Additional receiver selection criteria are discussed in Section 3.1.3.

12.10 FINANCIAL PROJECTIONS FOR THE GPS INDUSTRY

As is usual with most electronic devices, GPS receivers first hit the market at very high unit costs. The situation here was exacerbated by the complex nature of the processing required to correlate GPS signals. The large amounts of processing required many processors running in parallel. As application-specific integrated circuits (ASICs) were developed, production costs began to fall dramatically. Stiff competition for a market yet to develop prompted a rapid fall in the prices of GPS modules offered to system integrators.

The rapid fall of GPS module costs continued from several thousand dollars per unit to $1,000 in 1991 and, as illustrated in Figure 12.6, has dropped to about $200 in 1994. It is projected to stabilize at something just under $100 per unit by the year 2000. These modules are the core of any GPS-based positioning device and include the radiofrequency front end, correlators, and processing sufficient to compute a navigation solution. All have the ability to process differential corrections. Further cost savings in end products can be obtained by combining the application's processing requirements into the GPS processor. Display driving, waypoint management, or data logging are examples of integrated functions that will allow the effective cost of GPS-based products to fall further. Examples are the 5-channel Rockwell GPS Microtracker™ (Figure 12.7) and the 12-channel Canadian Marconi Company AllStar (Figure 12.8). The Microtracker module has the following dimensions:

- Width: 5.1 cm (2 in);
- Length: 7.1 cm (2.8 in);
- Height: 1.0 cm (0.4 in).

The AllStar has the following dimensions:

- Width: 6.7 cm (2.7 in);
- Length: 10.2 cm (4.0 in);
- Height: 1.9 cm (0.8 in).

In quantifying the market for GPS products over the next decade, there are of course some large assumptions to be made. One is a projection of average unit cost in each market. Another is the rate of acceptance of the products in each, and

Table 12.2
Equipment Requirements by Type of Use

Market	Mission	Requirements
Aviation	Airborne navigation, approach, collision avoidance, automatic dependent surveillance	Reliability, signal integrity check, high dynamics, database accuracy, differential upgradability
Marine	Marine navigation, waterway maintenance	Rugged, waterproof, effective user interface, low power consumption Low-med. dynamics Differential capability
Survey	Precise positioning	Accuracy, dual frequency, carrier phase output, data handling capability, low dynamics
Land	Land vehicle navigation	Small size, inexpensive, medium dynamics, fast reacquisition, low to medium power, differential capable
Military	Targeting, guidance, navigation, survey, range simulation, civil works	Possibly P-code capable, rugged, reliable
Recreational (handheld)	Hunting, hiking	Very low power, low cost low accuracy, fast reacquisition, small size, low dynamics

another is that the markets one can now envisage are the ones that will develop. For this exercise, these factors were estimated for five market segments. Table 12.3 shows estimates of overall size for the market areas in question. The table also shows the major assumptions used in generating the volume of business to be expected over the decade 1992–2001. Figures are in U.S. dollars and represent the retail level of cumulative sales of user hardware in each area. As in any projection of the future,

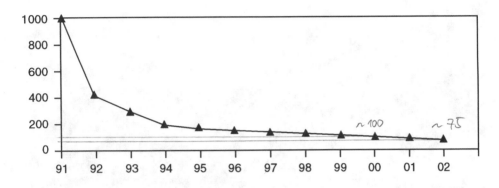

Figure 12.6 GPS receiver cost trends 1991–2002 (US dollars).

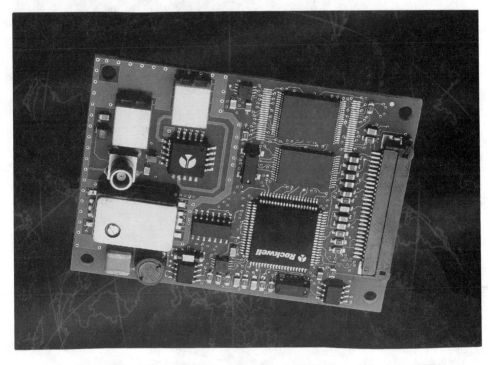

Figure 12.7 Rockwell GPS Microtracker™ (*courtesy of* Rockwell Telecommunications, 1995).

no claim can be made regarding accuracy of the figures presented, but the presentation of the assumptions used in calculating them allows the reader to inject his or her own perceptions into the derivation of market size.

Some facets of the GPS business are nonspecific with regard to activity area. Handheld GPS receivers, for instance, could be used in any one of the market areas

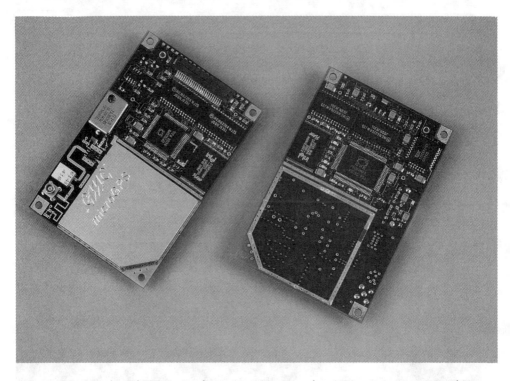

Figure 12.8 A 12-channel GPS receiver for use in positioning and navigation systems (*courtesy of* Canadian Marconi Company).

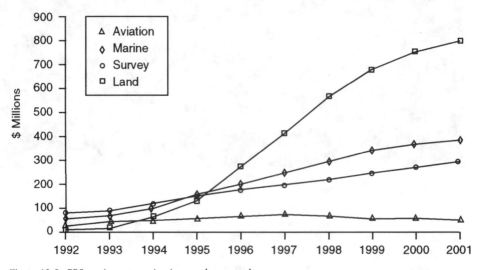

Figure 12.9 GPS equipment navigation market growth.

Table 12.3
Overview of GPS Markets

Market	Benchmark	Assumptions	Market Size
Aviation	29K general aviation aircraft	70% of 120K Lorans replaced, 40% penetration of balance of 170K, 70% of 20K new aircraft @ avg cost of $2,335/unit installed	$388M
	4,500 air carrier aircraft*	80% penetration existing, 100% of 500 new aircraft @$25,000/unit installed	$103M
Marine	48M vessels worldwide		$2,120M
	500K recreational boats over 45 feet	70% penetration @ $3K/unit	
	1,200K recreational boats 24–44 feet	50% penetration @ 1.2K/unit	
	80K seagoing ships	90% penetration @ $8K/unit	
	80K fishing boats	40% penetration @ $3K/unit	
	5K workboats	80% penetration @ $3K/unit	
Survey/GIS	17K registered surveyors*	40% of 40K worldwide surveyors, units replaced every 5 yrs @$30K/unit	$1,948M
	20K agencies using GIS*	50% penetration, 10 data collectors/ agency, 30K agencies worldwide, units replaced every 5 yrs @ $3.3K/unit	
Land Nav	424M cars, 128M trucks, 4M busses, $214B to be spent on ITS/ITS 1992–2001	4.3% of 556M vehicles @ $400/unit	$9,690M

*U.S. data.

Table 12.3 (continued)

Market	Benchmark	Assumptions	Market Size
Military*	PLGR program: 94K units at $5K	All aircraft, ships, troops to be GPS equipped by 2000	$470M
	3A/3S/3H program	714K units	$3,570M
	MAGR	F/A18, AV8B, F117A, F15E, B2	
	EGI(GEM)	T-45 GPS/ INS	

*U.S data.

discussed. The conclusions that can be drawn from these figures however, is that there is huge growth, and the relative sizes of each of the markets will shape the kind of developmental effort that will be expended.

Further analysis of these markets can give some estimate of the amount of economic activity GPS will engender over the next few years. That is to say that the economic impact that this technology can have, including peripheral activity involving databases, displays, and tracking systems, could far outweigh the amount of retail sales totaled up for each market. For example, the total air traffic control system market might be as big as $200 billion between 1994 and 2004, and the ITS market as big as $600 billion over the same period. Figure 12.9 estimates growth rates for four major market segments.

Reference

[1] Department of Defense/Department of Transportation, "1994 Federal Radionavigation Plan," Springfield, VA, National Technical Information Service, May 1995.

Bibliography

Beukers, John M., Developing a Commercial Market for GPS Receiving Equipment, Beukers Technology Inc., 03/01/1991.

Dyment, M., et al., Differential GPS Markets in the 1990's: A North American Cross-Industry Study, KV Research Inc., 09/01/1992.

Harris, Richard P., The Role of GPS in Implementing GIS-Based Resource Management Systems, Sealaska Corporation, GPS World, 3(3) 03/01/1992, p. 59.

Intelligent Vehicle Highway Society of America, Strategic Plan for Intelligent Vehicle Highway Systems in the United States, 02/14/1992.

International Civil Aviation Organization, Special Committee on Future Air Navigation Systems Report, ICAO Doc. 9524, FANS/4, 01/01/1988.

King, Glenn M., et al., Statistical Abstract of the United States 1991—The National Data Book, Economics and Statistical Administration and Bureau of the Census, U.S. Department of Commerce, 01/01/1991.

Krakiwski, E. J., Assessment of Emerging Technology for Future Navigation Systems in the Canadian Transportation Sector, University of Calgary, TP-1055E, 04/01/1990.

Langley, Richard B., The Federal Radionavigation Plan, University of New Brunswick, GPS World, (3) 03/01/1992, p. 50.

Lechner, Wolfgang, The Potential for Global Satellite Systems for Precision Aircraft Navigation, Avionic Center Braunschweig, GPS World, 3(6) 06/01/1992, p. 40.

Lee, Young C., Receiver Autonomous Integrity Monitoring (RAIM) Capability for Sole-Means GPS Navigation in the Oceanic Phase of Flight, The MITRE Corporation, IEEE 1992 Position Location and Navigation Symposium, 03/01/1992, p. 464.

Lewandowski, W., et al., "GPS Time Transfer," IEEE Special Issue on Time, 08/01/1991.

Loh, Robert, Analysis of GPS for Precision Approaches, Federal Aviation Administration, DGPS '91, 09/16/1991, p. 107.

Loh, Robert, et al., Development and Test Results of Wide Area Differential GPS for Precision Approaches, Federal Aviation Administration, IEEE 1992 Position Location and Navigation Symposium, 03/01/ 1992, p. 548.

Mack, Giles A. H., SKYFIX—A Professional DGPS Service Using Geostationary Communications Satellite, Racal Survey Ltd, Proceedings of ION GPS-91, 09/11/1991, p. 1071.

Mammano, F., et al., PATHFINDER System Design, US Fed. Highway Adm., Conference Record of Papers Presented at the First Vehicle Navigation & Information Systems Conference (VNIS '89); New York, IEEE, 564, 01/01/1989, p. 484–488.

McDonald, Keith D., Application and Technology Projections for GPS Civil User Equipment, Sat Tech Systems, IEEE 1992 Position Location and Navigation Symposium, 03/01/1992, p. 554.

McDonald, Keith D., Navigation Satellite Systems—A Perspective, Sat Tech Systems Inc., DGPS'91, 09/16/1991.

McDonald, Keith D., "GPS in Civil Aviation," GPS World, 09/01/1991, p. 52.

McDonald, Keith D., "GPS Progress and Issues," GPS World, 01/01/1990, p. 16.

McDonald, Keith D., et al., "An Assessment of GPS Receivers for Navigation and a Survey of Their Applications," Sat Tech Systems Inc., VHP Associates, IEEE 1992 Position Location and Navigation Symposium, 03/01/1992, p. 557.

McDonald, Keith D., et al., GPS Receivers—Survey of Equipment Characteristics and Performance, Navtech Seminars, Incorporated, 10/10/1990.

Pekilis, B., et al., Automatic Vehicle Location and Control System for Small and Medium Ontario Transit Properties: Phase I, Ministry of Transportation of Ontario, 09/01/1991.

Radio Technical Commission for Avionics, Minimum Operational Performance Standards for Airborne Supplemental Navigation Equipment Using Global Postioning System (GPS), 07/12/1991.

Rostenne, J., et al., "Radionavigation/Location Requirements for Surface Users in Canada: Present and Future," Thompson-Hickling Aviation Incorporated, Transport Canada, 11/01/1989.

RTCM, Recommended Standards for Differential NAVSTAR GPS Service Version 2.0, RTCM Special Committee No. 104, 01/01/1990.

U.S. Coast Guard, Statement of Work/GPS Tracking System Specification, 03/31/1992.

U.S. Coast Guard and U.S. Department of Transportation, Summary Record of the Civil GPS Service Interface Committee, 01/30/1992.

U.S. Department of Commerce, U.S. Industrial Outlook, 01/01/94.

U.S. Department of Transport/Department of Defense, Federal Radionavigation Plan, DOT-VNTSC-RSPA-92-2/DOD-4650.5, 01/01/1993.

▼▼▼

APPENDIX:
LEAST SQUARES

Joseph L. Leva
The MITRE Corporation

The linearized pseudorange equations as developed in Section 2.4.2 have the matrix form

$$H\Delta x = \Delta\rho \tag{A.1}$$

The value Δx is the vector offset of the user's position and time bias from the values at the linearization point. It has four components: the first three define the position offset of the user, and the fourth gives the offset in time of the user time bias from the bias assumed at the linearization point. The value $\Delta\rho$ is the vector difference between the pseudorange values associated with the user's position and those associated with the linearization point. The value $\Delta\rho$ has N components where N is the number of satellites in view under consideration. The value H is the $N \times 4$ matrix

$$H = \begin{bmatrix} a_{x1} & a_{y1} & a_{z1} & 1 \\ a_{x2} & a_{y2} & a_{z2} & 1 \\ \vdots & \vdots & \vdots & \vdots \\ a_{xn} & a_{yn} & a_{zn} & 1 \end{bmatrix} \tag{A.2}$$

where the $a_i = (a_{xi}, a_{yi}, a_{zi})$ are the unit vectors pointing from the linearization point to the location of the ith satellite.

If $N = 4$ and if the linearization point is close to the user's location, the GPS single-point solution for the user's location and time offset is obtained by forming the vector $\Delta\rho$ from the pseudorange measurements and solving (A.1) for Δx. In this case, (A.1) represents four equations in four unknowns (i.e., in the components of Δx). Provided $\mathbf{H}$ is nonsingular, one obtains the solution

$$\Delta x = \mathbf{H}^{-1}\Delta\rho \qquad (A.3)$$

If $N > 4$, (A.1) represents a system with more equations than unknowns. Generally, the system will be inconsistent in that errors in the value of $\Delta\rho$ will preclude any value of Δx from exactly solving the system. The method of least squares can be used to obtain an estimate for the user's position and time offset.

Ordinary Least Squares

Assume that $N \geq 4$ and that a set of pseudorange measurements have been made. Assume also that the linear connection matrix $\mathbf{H}$ and the vector $\Delta\rho$ are available and fixed for the discussion. We seek a value for Δx so that $\mathbf{H}\Delta x$ is close to $\Delta\rho$.

For any particular value of Δx, the vector quantity $\mathbf{r} = \mathbf{H}\Delta x - \Delta\rho$ is called the residual. With this terminology, we seek a Δx so that the residual is small. The ordinary least square solution is defined as the value of Δx that minimizes the square of the residual. This is equivalent to minimizing the sum of the squares of the components in the residual vector. (The square of a vector is defined as the inner product of the vector with itself. Hence, the square of the residual is just the sum of the squares of its components.) The square of the residual is denoted as R_{SE} and is viewed as a function of Δx,

$$R_{SE}(\Delta x) = (\mathbf{H}\Delta x - \Delta\rho)^2 \qquad (A.4)$$

Given $\mathbf{H}$ and $\Delta\rho$, the least square problem is to find the value of Δx that minimizes R_{SE}.

The solution to the least square problem is obtained in a straightforward way using calculus. The basic idea is to differentiate (A.4) with respect to Δx to obtain the gradient of R_{SE}. The minimum for R_{SE} must occur at a value of Δx that gives a zero for the gradient. (To see this, recall that the gradient vector points in the direction of maximal increase for the function. Hence, if the gradient is not zero at some value of Δx, a perturbation in Δx in the direction opposite to the gradient will decrease the value of R_{SE}. Thus, Δx could not represent a minimum and a necessary requirement at the minimum is for the gradient to be zero.) Hence, the gradient is set to zero and solved for Δx to seek a value that will minimize R_{SE}. In general, the condition on the gradient is not sufficient to guarantee that the obtained value is a minimum (the gradient is zero at a local maximum as well). However, it is shown later that for the least square problem, the obtained value does give the minimum. Proceeding now in more detail, we expand (A.4) to obtain the matrix relation

$$R_{SE}(\Delta x) = (H\Delta x - \Delta \rho)^2 = (\Delta x)^T H^T H \Delta x - 2(\Delta x)^T H^T \Delta \rho + (\Delta \rho)^2 \qquad (A.5)$$

(A bit of matrix/linear algebra is involved here. The square term is represented as a matrix product: $(H\Delta x - \Delta \rho)^2 = (H\Delta x - \Delta \rho)^T (H\Delta x - \Delta \rho)$ and standard matrix manipulations are applied.) Differentiating, the gradient of R_{SE} is obtained as a row vector as

$$\nabla R_{SE} = 2(\Delta x)^T H^T H - 2(\Delta \rho)^T H \qquad (A.6)$$

We take the transpose of this equation and set it to zero, obtaining

$$2H^T H \Delta x - 2H^T \Delta \rho = 0 \qquad (A.7)$$

Provided that $H^T H$ is nonsingular, we solve for Δx and obtain

$$\Delta x = (H^T H)^{-1} H^T \Delta \rho \qquad (A.8)$$

Denote the value for Δx given in (A.8) as Δx_{LS}. We will now show that this value indeed gives a minimum in the residual R_{SE}. To this end, we evaluate the squared residual at an arbitrary offset dx from Δx_{LS}. Working from (A.4), we obtain

$$\begin{aligned} R_{SE}(\Delta x_{LS} + dx) &= (H\Delta x_{LS} - \Delta \rho + Hdx)^T (H\Delta x_{LS} - \Delta \rho + Hdx) \\ &= (H\Delta x_{LS} - \Delta \rho)^T (H\Delta x_{LS} - \Delta \rho) + 2A + dx^T H^T Hdx \end{aligned} \qquad (A.9)$$

where $A = dx^T H^T (H\Delta x_{LS} - \Delta \rho)$. A substitution for Δx_{LS} from (A.8) into this expression for A shows that it evaluates to zero. The first term in the final expression in (A.9) is just $R_{SE}(\Delta x_{LS})$. Hence, (A.9) simplifies to

$$R_{SE}(\Delta x_{LS} + dx) = R_{SE}(\Delta x_{LS}) + dx^T H^T Hdx \qquad (A.10)$$

The final term in this expression cannot be negative: $dx^T H^T Hdx = \|Hdx\|^2 \geq 0$ for any value of dx. Hence the squared residual is never smaller than its value at Δx_{LS}.

A linear algebra argument can be made to show that if $H^T H$ is nonsingular, $dx^T H^T Hdx > 0$ for any dx with $dx \neq 0$. In this case, R_{SE}, attains its minimum value at Δx_{LS}, and is strictly larger than this minimum at any other value of Δx. (The linear algebra argument can proceed as follows: if $dx^T H^T Hdx = 0$, then $\|Hdx\|^2 = 0$, which implies $Hdx = 0$ and, finally, that $H^T Hdx = 0$. If $H^T H$ is nonsingular, $H^T Hdx = 0$

implies that $d\mathbf{x} = 0$. One concludes that if $\mathbf{H}^T\mathbf{H}$ is nonsingular, the only value of $d\mathbf{x}$ with $d\mathbf{x}^T\mathbf{H}^T\mathbf{H}d\mathbf{x} = 0$ is with $d\mathbf{x} = 0$. Since one always has $d\mathbf{x}^T\mathbf{H}^T\mathbf{H}d\mathbf{x} \geq 0$, if $\mathbf{H}^T\mathbf{H}$ is nonsingular, one concludes that $d\mathbf{x}^T\mathbf{H}^T\mathbf{H}d\mathbf{x} > 0$ if $d\mathbf{x} \neq 0$.) Hence, if $\mathbf{H}^T\mathbf{H}$ is nonsingular, the least square problem has a unique solution. The solution is given by (A.8).

The condition that $\mathbf{H}^T\mathbf{H}$ is nonsingular is equivalent with the condition that the columns of $\mathbf{H}$ are independent (rank $\mathbf{H} = 4$). These statements are also equivalent with the condition that the tips of the unit vectors from the linearization point to the satellites do not all lie in a common plane. If these conditions are violated, the least squares problem does not have a unique solution. In this event, R_{SE} is minimized for any value of $\Delta\mathbf{x}$ that solves (A.7).

As a final note, we observe that if $N = 4$ and if $\mathbf{H}$ is nonsingular, the least square solution in (A.8) reduces to the solution given in (A.3).

KEY ACRONYMS

2-D	two-dimensional
3-D	three-dimensional
ABS	antilock braking systems
A/D	analog-to-digital
AC	alternating current
ADS	automatic dependent surveillance
AFB	Air Force base
AFC	automatic frequency control
AFM	ambiguity function method
AGC	automatic gain control
AOC	auxiliary output chip
AORE	Atlantic Ocean Region East
AORW	Atlantic Ocean Region West
APTS	advanced public transportation systems
AS	Antispoofing
ASIC	application specific integrated circuit
ATC	air traffic control

ATIS	advanced traveler information systems
AutoNav	autonomous navigation
AVLS	automatic vehicle location systems
baro	barometric
BBS	bulletin board service
BIPM	Bureau International des Poids et Mesures
BLK	satellite block
bps	bits per second
BPSK	binary phase shift key
CIS	Commonwealth of Independent States
C/A-code	coarse/acquisiton or clear/acquisition code
C/N$_0$	carrier-to-noise density ratio
CAA	Civil Aviation Administration
CAT	category
CDMA	code division multiple access
CDU	control display unit
CEP	circular error probable
cm	centimeters
COMSAT	Communications Satellite Organization
CPU	central processing unit
CRC	cyclic redundancy check
CRPA	controlled reception pattern antenna
CSIC	Coordinating Scientific Information Center
CVO	commercial vehicle operations
CW	continuous wave
dB	decibel
DC	direct current
DD	double difference
DFT	discrete Fourier transform
DLL	delay lock loop
DME	distance measuring equipment
DNSS	Defense Navigation Satellite System
DOD	Department of Defense
DOP	dilution of precision
DOT	Department of Transportation

DR	dead reckoning
DRMS	distance root mean square
DRPA	dual reception pattern antenna
DSP	digital signal processor
DSSS	direct sequence spread spectrum
ECDIS	electronic chart display information system
ECEF	Earth-centered Earth fixed
ECI	Earth-centered inertial
ECS	electronic charting system
ED-50	European Datum 1950
EGI	embedded GPS/inertial receiver
ERP	effective radiated power
FAA	Federal Aviation Administration
FARA	fast ambiguity resolution approach
FCC	Federal Communications Commission
FDE	fault detection and exclusion
FDI	fault detection and isolation
FDMA	frequency division multiple access
FLL	frequency lock loop
FOC	full operational capability
FOGs	fiber optic gyroscopes
FRS	flight reference system
Ft.	Fort
FTF	fundamental time frame
GA	general aviation
GDOP	geometric dilution of precision
GEO	geosynchronous ranging satellite
GIC	GNSS integrity channel
GIS	geographical information system
GLONASS	Global Navigation Satellite System (Russian definition)
GNSS	Global Navigation Satellite System (ICAO definition)
GPS	Global Positioning System
GPSI	integrated GPS/inertial system
GR	general relativity
GSS	Global Satellite Software

GT	ground transmitter
HDOP	horizontal dilution of precision
HOW	handover word
HPA	high-power amplifier
HPL	horizontal protection level
Hz	hertz
I/O	input/output
ICAO	International Civil Aviation Organization
IERS	International Earth Rotation Service
IF	intermediate frequency
IGP	ionospheric grid point
IGPS	interferometric GPS
ILS	instrument landing system
IMU	inertial measurement unit
INMARSAT	International Maritime Satellite Organization
INS	inertial navigation system
IOC	initial operational capability
IOD	issue of data
IOR	Indian Ocean Region
IPP	ionospheric pierce point
ISS	international space station
ITS	intelligent transportation systems
J/N	jammer-to-noise
J/S	jammer-to-signal
JPO	Joint Program Office
kg	kilogram
kHz	kilohertz
km	kilometer
lbs	pounds
LADGPS	local area DGPS
LHCP	left hand circularly polarized
LO	local oscillator
LOS	line-of-sight
LSAST	least squares ambiguity search technique
m	meter

MAGR	Miniature Airborne GPS Receiver
MASPS	Minimum Aviation System Performance Standards
mbar	millibar
MCS	master control station
MF	medium frequency
MHz	megahertz
MLS	microwave landing system
msec	millisec
MTBF	mean time between failures
NAD-83	North American Datum 1983
NASA	National Aeronautics and Space Administration
NAV	navigation
NAVAID	navigation aid
NCO	numerical controlled oscillator
NDB	nondirectional beacon
NES	navigation Earth stations
NMEA	National Marine Electronics Association
nmi	nautical miles
NPA	nonprecision approch
NRL	Naval Research Laboratory
nsec	nanosecond
NTIA	National Telecommunications and Information Administration
OCS	operational control segment
OSD	Office of the Secretary of Defense
OTF	"on the fly"
P-code	precision code
PDF	probability density function
PDOP	position dilution of precision
PLGR	Precision Lightweight GPS Receiver
PLL	phase lock loop
PLS	precision landing systems
PN	pseudonoise
POR	Pacific Ocean Region
ppm	parts per million
PPS	Precise Positioning Service

preamp	preamplifier
PRN	pseudorandom noise
PSK	phase shift key
PVT	position, velocity and time
PZ-90	Earth Parameter System 1990
RAIM	receiver autonomous integrity monitoring
RCS	regional control station
RF	radio frequency
RGIC	Ranging GIC
RHCP	right hand circularly polarized
RIRV	Russian Institute of Radio Navigation and Time
rms	root mean square
RS	reference stations
RTCA	RTCA, Inc. (formerly Radio Technical Commission for Aeronautics)
RTCM	Radio Technical Commission for Maritime Services
SA	Selective Availability
SC-159	Special Committee 159
SD	single difference
sec	second
SGS-85	Soviet Geodetic System 1985
SNR	signal-to-noise ratio
SPS	Standard Positioning Service
SR	special relativity
SU	Soviet Union
SV	space vehicles
SVN	space vehicle number
TACAN	tactical air navigation
TAI	International Atomic Time
TAIP	Trimble ASCII interface protocol
TDMA	time division multiple access
TDOA	time difference of arrival
TDOP	time dilution of precision
TEC	total electron count
TLM	telemetry message

TOA	time of arrival
TT&C	telemetry, tracking, and command
U.S.	United States
UDRE	user differential range error
UE	user equipment
UERE	user equivalent range error
URE	user range error
USNO	United States Naval Observatory
UT1	Universal Time 1
UTC	Coordinated Universal Time
VDOP	vertical dilution of precision
VHF	very high frequency
VOR	VHF omnidirectional ranging
VTS	vessel traffic services
WAAS	Wide Area Augmentation System
WADGPS	wide area differential GPS
WADGNSS	wide area differential GNSS
WGS-84	World Geodetic System 1984

▼▼▼

ABOUT THE AUTHORS

Richard Clark received his Bachelor's degree in Physics from the University of Illinois and his Master's degree in Physics from Northern Illinois University. After teaching physics and mathematics at the secondary level in the United States and Europe in 1977, Mr. Clark joined the U.S. Air Force, developing technology assessments on electronics and spacecraft.

Ronald Cosentino received his B.S.E.E. at the Polytechnic Institute of Brooklyn and his M.A. in Mathematics at Fordham University. He has spent the last 17 years at MITRE, working first in the areas of communication systems and of signal processing and architectures for VLSI, and now in the areas of precision landing systems and air traffic management.

David W. Diggle graduated from Ohio University in Athens with a B.S. in Electrical Engineering in the Spring of 1968. Following brief employment with the General Electric Co. in Cleveland, he entered the U.S. Air Force. Early on in his military career, he received an M.S. in Electrical Engineering from the Air Force Institute of Technology. His work involved the application of computers to inertial guidance system repair; analysis of foreign air-to-air and surface-to-air missiles, as well as radar and air defense systems; a stint as a field engineer; later, as a Headquarters Air Force (Pentagon) staff officer; and lastly as a senior lecturer at the U.S. Naval Academy, Annapolis, Maryland. Upon retirement from the Air Force, Dave returned to Ohio University, beginning a doctoral program in the Fall of 1990 and working as a research associate for the O.U. Avionics Engineering Center. His area of expertise became real-time precise positioning using the GPS. He received his Ph.D. in Electrical and Computer Engineering in March 1994 and subsequently joined the staff of the Avionics Engineering Center on a full-time basis as research scientist. Based upon the research performed for his doctoral dissertation, the RTCA honored him with their Jackson Award in November 1994. The award is given annually for the outstanding contribution to the field of avionics. Dave's work continues to center on the application of GPS positioning to aircraft precision approach and landing systems. Dave is a member of the Institute of Navigation, Sigma Xi, and the Eta Kappa Nu and Tau Beta Pi engineering honoraria. In addition, he holds a private pilot certificate, completed through the O.U. Aviation Department.

Scott Feairheller has over 12 years of experience in international satellite navigation systems. Since 1989, he has served as the DOD technical representative to the GPS-GLONASS portion of the 1988 US-USSR Transportation Agreement and the 1994 US-Russia Transportation Agreement. He currently works for the U.S. Air Force as an aerospace engineer. Scott received his B.S. from the University of Dayton in 1982 and is currently working toward his M.S. with a thesis on international satellite navigation policy. Mr. Feairheller has been a member of the U.S. Institute of Navigation since 1987 and has served as Chairman of the GLONASS Session for ION GPS-95.

Michael Foss holds a B.S.E.E. and an M.S.E.E. from Northeastern University. He has been working in the field of real-time systems for the last 20 years and in the field of integrating GPS and inertial sensors for the last decade, developing various GPS/inertial navigation systems. His work has included the design, development, and evaluation of aided GPS receivers. This effort extends to problems associated with integrating various receivers with low-cost inertial components. He is currently president of Vehicle Guidance, Inc., a manufacturer of GPS/inertial systems for use in land applications.

G. Jeffrey Geier is a member of the technical staff with Motorola's Position and Navigation Systems business in Scottsdale, Arizona. Mr. Geier has more than 26 years of experience with integrated navigation systems, Kalman filtering, GPS navigation and signal processing, and integrity monitoring. He is currently integrating Motorola's ONCORE eight-channel GPS receiver with automotive sensors for use in emergency messaging applications, making use of Motorola cellular phones. Mr. Geier is also an instructor for NavTech Seminars, and teaches a two-day course in GPS integration with inertial systems nationwide; he recently taught a two-week graduate course in integration of low-cost sensors with GPS as a distinguished lecturer at the University of Calgary, Canada. He is a member of the Institute of Navigation and the Institute of Electrical and Electronics Engineers. Mr. Geier holds two GPS-related patents, and received his B.S. and M.S. degrees in Aeronautics and Astronautics from MIT.

Elliott D. Kaplan is a member of the MITRE Corporation technical staff. He received a B.S.E.E. from Polytechnic Institute of New York and an M.S.E.E. from Northeastern University. Elliott has been involved with civil and military GPS programs since 1988. His professional activities extend to various GPS-related disciplines. He is a member of the MITRE Institute adjunct facility and also serves as a guest lecturer to Worcester Polytechnic Institute. Elliott is currently involved with assessing the effects of intentional and nonintentional interference on GPS receiver operation. He is also charged with examining the applicability of GPS in precision approach applications. Elliott is a member of the American Institute of Aeronautics and Astronautics, IEEE, and ION.

Joseph L. Leva holds a B.S. in Engineering Physics from the University of Michigan and an M.S. in Mathematics from Carnegie Mellon University. He has worked the past 18 years at The MITRE Corporation on a number of defense-related projects. His professional interests include mathematical analysis, digital signal processing, and algorithm development. He has worked on radar and position location system projects and has over 14 years experience in TOA and TDOA processing. Joe has published a number of papers in the GPS field dealing with the probabilistic treatment of DOP and closed form solution to the pseudorange equations. He is a member of the Institute of Navigation.

Scott C. Lewis is general manager of the Northstar Technologies Division of Canadian Marconi, located in Acton, MA. He was a founder, president, and CEO of Anatek, Microcircuits, Inc., a successful high-technology engineering and manufacturing company based in Vancouver, BC. As principal of Lewis Associates, Inc., Scott has led seminars on product development and marketing, and has prepared marketing and business plans for a variety of companies involved in GPS, geographic information systems, and vehicle location technologies. In 1992, he coauthored the market analysis entitled "Differential GPS Markets in the 1990's: A Cross Industry Study." Mr. Lewis holds a B.A.Sc. in Electrical Engineering from the University of Waterloo.

James Nagle is the Navigation Services group leader with the Spectrum, Standards, and Special Projects Division of INMARSAT. He joined INMARSAT in 1989 after completing 23 years with the U.S. Coast Guard, from which he retired at the rank of Commander. His last assignment with the Coast Guard was as Chief, Radionavigation Applications and Developments branch where he was instrumental in the establishment of the USCG differential GPS program and the U.S. Civil GPS Service. During his career he was active in the design, operation, and maintenance of various radionavigation systems worldwide in addition to command at sea and specialized staff assignments. Since joining INMARSAT, he has been responsible for developmental efforts in the radiodetermination and navigation program.

Mike Pavloff received his Bachelor's Degree in Physics at Harvard and his Master's degree in Aeronautics and Astronautics at MIT. Mike joined the MITRE Corporation in 1988, where he was a member of the Space Systems Analysis Specialty Group. Mike's professional interests include mobile satellite communications, satellite orbit determination, spacecraft design, and space systems acquisition. Since 1988, Mike has also been on the faculty at Harvard, where he has taught calculus and linear algebra and helped design and write a new calculus curriculum as well as a textbook under a National Science Foundation grant. Mike is now a space systems engineer with Hughes Space and Communications Company of El Segundo, California.

Jay Purvis received his B.S.E.E. from Christian Brothers University in Memphis, TN and his M.S.E.E. from the Air Force Institute of Technology in Dayton, OH. Jay joined the U.S. Air Force in 1985, specializing in space electronic warfare (EW) technologies. Jay's professional interests encompass satellite navigation and communications, EW analyses, and modeling. He has performed several analyses related to U.S. military satellite communications systems, and developed modeling tools to assess EW effects on such systems. Over the past few years, Jay broadened his analyses to include other emerging satellite navigation systems and augmentations. Jay recently separated from the Air Force to form the consulting company, Purvis Technologies, specializing in satellite navigation applications and countermeasures.

Maarten Uijt de Haag received his M.S.E.E. from Delft University of Technology in 1994. In July 1994, he joined the Avionics Engineering Center of Ohio University as a visiting scholar until October 1994. In January 1995, he returned to Ohio University's Avionics Engineering Center as a research engineer and he is currently involved in a variety of GPS-related projects. Maarten's professional interests include communications, software engineering, system applications for GPS, integrated navigation systems, and digital signal processing.

Karen L. Van Dyke received her B.S. and M.S. degrees in Electrical Engineering from the University of Massachusetts at Lowell. Since 1988, she has been with the Center for Navigation at the DOT/Volpe Center. Karen is currently conducting GPS availability and integrity studies for the FAA. She also has worked on the design and implementation of a GPS outage reporting system for the USAF and FAA, which is used to brief pilots during preflight planning. Ms. Van Dyke has been actively involved with the civil GPS service Interface Committee and she currently serves on the Institute of Navigation Council and the Boston Section Executive Committee of IEEE.

Phillip W. Ward is president of NAVWARD GPS Consulting, which he founded in 1991 in Dallas, Texas. From 1960 to 1991, he was senior member of the technical staff at Texas Instruments Incorporated in the Defense Systems & Electronics Group. During a 1967–1970 educational leave of absence from TI, he was a member of the technical staff at the Massachusetts Institute of Technology Instrumentation Lab (now the Stark Draper Lab). Phil earned his B.S.E.E. degree from the University of Texas at El Paso, and his M.S.E.E. from Southern Methodist University in 1965. He has also taken postgraduate courses in computer science at MIT. Phil has been involved in the field of navigation since 1958 and with GPS receiver design since 1976. He served as the lead systems engineer on several of TI's advanced GPS receiver development programs. He developed five generations of GPS receivers for TI, including the TI 4100 NAVSTAR Navigator Multiplex Receiver, the first commercial GPS receiver. For his pioneering work in the development of TI 4100, Phil received the Colonel Thomas L. Thurlow Navigation Award in 1989, the highest award given by the Institute of Navigation. At the MIT Instrumentation Lab, he worked with the Apollo Guidance Computer Design Team. He is past president of the ION and has served in other capacities, including chair of the Satellite Division. He is also a senior member of the IEEE.

Lawrence F. Wiederholt has been employed for the last 19 years at Intermetrics in Cambridge, MA. During that time he has worked on a variety of navigation systems, with the principal focus being GPS. Most of that time, he worked with GPS receivers and user navigation solution formation using Kalman filtering and least squares estimation techniques. Integration of GPS with other sensors such as inertial navigation systems, baro-altimeter, and Doppler radars was a part of this experience. The work entailed analysis, simulation, real-time software development, field test, and evaluation. For the last five years, he has worked on the AutoNav function for the GPS Block IIR satellites. Larry has also performed assignments for the Calspan Corporation in Buffalo, NY, and the Aerospace Corporation in El Segundo, CA. While at the Calspan Corporation, he developed and used filtering algorithms for the postflight evaluation of ballistic missile tracking radar to identify ballistic missile parameters and tracking radar error sources. While at the Aerospace Corporation, he worked on filtering algorithms for satellite attitude determination. Dr. Wiederholt has Ph.D., M.S., and B.S. degrees in Electrical Engineering from the University of Wisconsin-Madison and a B.A. degree from Loras College. He is a member of the Institute of Navigation and the Institute of Electrical and Electronic Engineers.

The Artech House Mobile Communications Series

John Walker, Series Editor

Personal Communications Networks, Alan David Hadden

RF and Microwave Circuit Design for Wireless Communications, Lawrence E. Larson, editor

Smart Highways, Smart Cars, Richard Whelan

Spread Spectrum CDMA Systems for Wireless Communications, Savo G. Glisic, Branka Vucetic

Transport in Europe, Christian Gerondeau

Understanding GPS: Principles and Applications, Elliott D. Kaplan, editor

Universal Wireless Personal Communications, Ramjee Prasad

Vehicle Location and Navigation Systems, Yilin Zhao

Wireless Communications for Intelligent Transportation Systems, Scott D. Elliott and Daniel J. Dailey

Wireless Communications in Developing Countries: Cellular and Satellite Systems, Rachael E. Schwartz

Wireless Data Networking, Nathan J. Muller

Wireless: The Revolution in Personal Telecommunications, Ira Brodsky

For further information on these and other Artech House titles, including previously considered out-of-print books now available through our In-Print-Forever™ (IPF™) program, contact:

Artech House
685 Canton Street
Norwood, MA 02062
781-769-9750
Fax: 781-769-6334
Telex: 951-659
e-mail: artech@artech-house.com

Artech House
Portland House, Stag Place
London SW1E 5XA England
+44 (0) 171-973-8077
Fax: +44 (0) 171-630-0166
Telex: 951-659
e-mail: artech-uk@artech-house.com

Find us on the World Wide Web at: www.artech-house.com